Communications
in Computer and Information Science **1178**

Commenced Publication in 2007
Founding and Former Series Editors:
Phoebe Chen, Alfredo Cuzzocrea, Xiaoyong Du, Orhun Kara, Ting Liu,
Krishna M. Sivalingam, Dominik Ślęzak, Takashi Washio, Xiaokang Yang,
and Junsong Yuan

Editorial Board Members

Simone Diniz Junqueira Barbosa ⓘ
  Pontifical Catholic University of Rio de Janeiro (PUC-Rio),
  Rio de Janeiro, Brazil
Joaquim Filipe ⓘ
  Polytechnic Institute of Setúbal, Setúbal, Portugal
Ashish Ghosh
  Indian Statistical Institute, Kolkata, India
Igor Kotenko ⓘ
  St. Petersburg Institute for Informatics and Automation of the Russian
  Academy of Sciences, St. Petersburg, Russia
Lizhu Zhou
  Tsinghua University, Beijing, China

More information about this series at http://www.springer.com/series/7899

Paweł Sitek · Marcin Pietranik ·
Marek Krótkiewicz · Chutimet Srinilta (Eds.)

Intelligent Information and Database Systems

12th Asian Conference, ACIIDS 2020
Phuket, Thailand, March 23–26, 2020
Proceedings

 Springer

Editors
Paweł Sitek (iD)
Kielce University of Technology
Kielce, Poland

Marek Krótkiewicz (iD)
Wrocław University of Science
and Technology
Wrocław, Poland

Marcin Pietranik (iD)
Wrocław University of Science
and Technology
Wrocław, Poland

Chutimet Srinilta (iD)
King Mongkut's Institute
of Technology Ladkrabang
Bangkok, Thailand

ISSN 1865-0929　　　　　　ISSN 1865-0937　(electronic)
Communications in Computer and Information Science
ISBN 978-981-15-3379-2　　　ISBN 978-981-15-3380-8　(eBook)
https://doi.org/10.1007/978-981-15-3380-8

This Springer imprint is published by the registered company Springer Nature Singapore Pte Ltd.
The registered company address is: 152 Beach Road, #21-01/04 Gateway East, Singapore 189721, Singapore

Preface

ACIIDS 2020 was the 12th event in a series of international scientific conferences on research and applications in the field of intelligent information and database systems. The aim of ACIIDS 2020 was to provide an international forum of research workers with scientific backgrounds on the technology of intelligent information and database systems and its various applications. The ACIIDS 2020 conference was co-organized by King Mongkut's Institute of Technology Ladkrabang (Thailand) and Wrocław University of Science and Technology (Poland) in cooperation with the IEEE SMC Technical Committee on Computational Collective Intelligence, European Research Center for Information Systems (ERCIS), The University of Newcastle (Australia), Yeungnam University (South Korea), Leiden University (The Netherlands), Universiti Teknologi Malaysia (Malaysia), BINUS University (Indonesia), Quang Binh University (Vietnam), and Nguyen Tat Thanh University (Vietnam). It took place in Phuket, Thailand during March 23–26, 2020.

The ACIIDS conference series is already well established. The first two events, ACIIDS 2009 and ACIIDS 2010, took place in Dong Hoi City and Hue City in Vietnam, respectively. The third event, ACIIDS 2011, took place in Daegu (South Korea), followed by the fourth event, ACIIDS 2012, in Kaohsiung (Taiwan). The fifth event, ACIIDS 2013, was held in Kuala Lumpur (Malaysia) while the sixth event, ACIIDS 2014, was held in Bangkok (Thailand). The seventh event, ACIIDS 2015, took place in Bali (Indonesia), followed by the eighth event, ACIIDS 2016, in Da Nang (Vietnam). The ninth event, ACIIDS 2017, was organized in Kanazawa (Japan). The 10th jubilee conference, ACIIDS 2018, was held in Dong Hoi City (Vietnam), followed by the 11th event, ACIIDS 2019, in Yogyakarta (Indonesia).

This volume contains 50 peer-reviewed papers, selected for oral and poster presentation from among 180 submissions from all over the world. Papers included in this volume cover the following topics: advanced big data, machine learning, and data mining methods and applications; industry applications of intelligent methods and systems; artificial intelligence, optimization, and databases in practical applications; intelligent applications of the Internet of Things (IoT); and recommendation and user centric applications of intelligent systems.

The accepted and presented papers focus on new trends and challenges facing the intelligent information and database systems community. The presenters showed how research work could stimulate novel and innovative applications. We hope that you found these results useful and inspiring for your future research work.

We would like to express our sincere thanks to the honorary chairs for their support: Prof. Suchatvee Suwansawat (President of King Mongkut's Institute of Technology, Ladkrabang, Thailand), Cezary Madryas (Rector of Wrocław University of Science and Technology, Poland), Prof. Moonis Ali (President of the International Society of Applied Intelligence, USA), and Prof. Komsan Maleesee (Dean of Engineering, King Mongkut's Institute of Technology, Ladkrabang, Thailand).

Our special thanks go to the program chairs, special session chairs, organizing chairs, publicity chairs, liaison chairs, and local Organizing Committee for their work towards the conference. We sincerely thank all the members of the international Program Committee for their valuable efforts in the review process, which helped us to guarantee the highest quality of the selected papers for the conference. We cordially thank the organizers and chairs of special sessions who contributed to the success of the conference.

We would like to express our thanks to the keynote speakers for their world-class plenary speeches: Prof. Włodzisław Duch from the Nicolaus Copernicus University (Poland), Prof. Nikola Kasabov from Auckland University of Technology (New Zealand), Prof. Dusit Niyato from Nanyang Technological University (Singapore) and Prof. Geoff Webb from the Monash University Centre for Data Science (Australia).

We cordially thank our main sponsors: King Mongkut's Institute of Technology Ladkrabang (Thailand), Wrocław University of Science and Technology (Poland), IEEE SMC Technical Committee on Computational Collective Intelligence, European Research Center for Information Systems (ERCIS), The University of Newcastle (Australia), Yeungnam University (South Korea), Leiden University (The Netherlands), Universiti Teknologi Malaysia (Malaysia), BINUS University (Indonesia), Quang Binh University (Vietnam), and Nguyen Tat Thanh University (Vietnam). Our special thanks are also due to Springer for publishing the proceedings and sponsoring awards, and to all the other sponsors for their kind support.

We wish to thank the members of the Organizing Committee for their excellent work and the members of the local Organizing Committee for their considerable effort. We cordially thank all the authors, for their valuable contributions, and the other participants of this conference. The conference would not have been possible without their support. Thanks are also due to many experts who contributed to making the event a success.

March 2020

Paweł Sitek
Marcin Pietranik
Marek Krótkiewicz
Chutimet Srinilta

Organization

Honorary Chairs

Suchatvee Suwansawat — President of King Mongkut's Institute of Technology Ladkrabang, Thailand

Cezary Madryas — Rector of Wrocław University of Science and Technology, Poland

Moonis Ali — President of International Society of Applied Intelligence, USA

Komsan Maleesee — Dean of Engineering, King Mongkut's Institute of Technology Ladkrabang, Thailand

General Chairs

Ngoc Thanh Nguyen — Wrocław University of Science and Technology, Poland

Suphamit Chittayasothorn — King Mongkut's Institute of Technology Ladkrabang, Thailand

Program Chairs

Kietikul Jearanaitanakij — King Mongkut's Institute of Technology Ladkrabang, Thailand

Tzung-Pei Hong — National University of Kaohsiung, Taiwan

Ali Selamat — Universiti Teknologi Malaysia, Malaysia

Edward Szczerbicki — The University of Newcastle, Australia

Bogdan Trawiński — Wrocław University of Science and Technology, Poland

Steering Committee

Ngoc Thanh Nguyen (Chair) — Wrocław University of Science and Technology, Poland

Longbing Cao — University of Technology Sydney, Australia

Suphamit Chittayasothorn — King Mongkut's Institute of Technology Ladkrabang, Thailand

Ford Lumban Gaol — Bina Nusantara University, Indonesia

Tu Bao Ho — Japan Advanced Institute of Science and Technology, Japan

Tzung-Pei Hong — National University of Kaohsiung, Taiwan

Dosam Hwang — Yeungnam University, South Korea

Bela Stantic — Griffith University, Australia

Geun-Sik Jo	Inha University, South Korea
Hoai An Le-Thi	University of Lorraine, France
Zygmunt Mazur	Wrocław University of Science and Technology, Poland
Toyoaki Nishida	Kyoto University, Japan
Leszek Rutkowski	Częstochowa University of Technology, Poland
Ali Selamat	Universiti Teknologi Malaysia, Malyasia

Special Session Chairs

Marcin Pietranik	Wroclaw University of Science and Technology, Poland
Chutimet Srinilta	King Mongkut's Institute of Technology Ladkrabang, Thailand
Paweł Sitek	Kielce University of Technology, Poland

Liaison Chairs

Ford Lumban Gaol	Bina Nusantara University, Indonesia
Quang-Thuy Ha	VNU University of Engineering and Technology, Vietnam
Mong-Fong Horng	National Kaohsiung University of Applied Sciences, Taiwan
Dosam Hwang	Yeungnam University, South Korea
Le Minh Nguyen	Japan Advanced Institute of Science and Technology, Japan
Ali Selamat	Universiti Teknologi Malaysia, Malyasia

Organizing Chairs

Wiboon Prompanich	King Mongkut's Institute of Technology Ladkrabang, Thailand
Adrianna Kozierkiewicz	Wrocław University of Science and Technology, Poland
Krystian Wojtkiewicz	Wrocław University of Science and Technology, Poland

Publicity Chairs

Rathachai Chawuthai	King Mongkut's Institute of Technology Ladkrabang, Thailand
Marek Kopel	Wrocław University of Science and Technology, Poland
Marek Krótkiewicz	Wrocław University of Science and Technology, Poland

Webmaster

Marek Kopel   Wroclaw University of Science and Technology,
                               Poland

Local Organizing Committee

Pakorn Watanachaturaporn   King Mongkut's Institute of Technology Ladkrabang,
                               Thailand
Sorayut Glomglome   King Mongkut's Institute of Technology Ladkrabang,
                               Thailand
Watchara Chatwiriya   King Mongkut's Institute of Technology Ladkrabang,
                               Thailand
Sathaporn Promwong   King Mongkut's Institute of Technology Ladkrabang,
                               Thailand
Putsadee Pornphol   Phuket Rajabhat University, Thailand
Maciej Huk   Wrocław University of Science and Technology,
                               Poland
Marcin Jodłowiec   Wrocław University of Science and Technology,
                               Poland

Keynote Speakers

Włodzisław Duch   Nicolaus Copernicus University, Poland
Nikola Kasabov   Auckland University of Technology, New Zealand
Dusit Niyato   Nanyang Technological University, Singapore
Geoff Webb   Monash University Centre for Data Science, Australia

Special Sessions Organizers

*1. CSHAC 2020: Special Session on Cyber-Physical Systems in Healthcare:
Applications and Challenges*

Michael Mayo   University of Waikato, New Zealand
Abigail Koay   University of Waikato, New Zealand
Panos Patros   University of Waikato, New Zealand

*2. ADMTA 2020: Special Session on Advanced Data Mining Techniques
and Applications*

Chun-Hao Chen   Tamkang University, Taiwan
Bay Vo   Ho Chi Minh City University of Technology, Vietnam
Tzung-Pei Hong   National University of Kaohsiung, Taiwan

3. CVIS 2020: Special Session on Computer Vision and Intelligent Systems

Van-Dung Hoang   Quang Binh University, Vietnam
Kang-Hyun Jo   University of Ulsan, South Korea

| My-Ha Le | Ho Chi Minh city University of Technology and Education, Vietnam |
| Van-Huy Pham | Ton Duc Thang University, Vietnam |

4. MMAML 2020: Special Session on Multiple Model Approach to Machine Learning

Tomasz Kajdanowicz	Wrocław University of Science and Technology, Poland
Edwin Lughofer	Johannes Kepler University Linz, Austria
Bogdan Trawiński	Wrocław University of Science and Technology, Poland

5. CIV 2020: Special Session on Computational Imaging and Vision

Manish Khare	Dhirubhai Ambani Institute of Information and Communication Technology, India
Prashant Srivastava	NIIT University, India
Om Prakash	Inferigence Quotient, India
Jeonghwan Gwak	Korea National University of Transportation, South Korea

6. ISAIS 2020: Special Session on Intelligent Systems and Algorithms in Information Sciences

Martin Kotyrba	University of Ostrava, Czech Republic
Eva Volna	University of Ostrava, Czech Republic
Ivan Zelinka	VŠB – Technical University of Ostrava, Czech Republic
Pavel Petr	University of Pardubice, Czech Republic

7. IOTAI 2020: Special Session on Internet of Things and Artificial Intelligence for Energy Efficiency-Recent Advances and Future Trends

| Mohamed Elhoseny | Mansoura University, Egypt |
| Mohamed Abdel-Basset | Zagazig University, Egypt |

8. DMPI-4.0 2020: Special Session on Data Modelling and Processing for Industry 4.0

Du Haizhou	Shanghai University of Electric Power, China
Wojciech Hunek	Opole University of Technology, Poland
Marek Krótkiewicz	Wrocław University of Science and Technology, Poland
Krystian Wojtkiewicz	Wrocław University of Science and Technology, Poland

9. ICxS 2020: Special Session on Intelligent and Contextual Systems

Maciej Huk	Wroclaw University of Science and Technology, Poland
Keun Ho Ryu	Ton Duc Thang University, Vietnam
Goutam Chakraborty	Iwate Prefectural University, Japan
Qiangfu Zhao	University of Aizu, Japan
Chao-Chun Chen	National Cheng Kung University, Taiwan
Rashmi Dutta Baruah	Indian Institute of Technology Guwahati, India

10. ARAIS 2020: Special Session on Automated Reasoning with Applications in Intelligent Systems

Jingde Cheng	Saitama University, Japan

11. ISCEC 2020: Special Session on Intelligent Supply Chains and e-Commerce

Arkadiusz Kawa	Łukasiewicz Research Network – The Institute of Logistics and Warehousing, Poland
Justyna Światowiec-Szczepańska	Poznań University of Economics and Business, Poland
Bartłomiej Pierański	Poznań University of Economics and Business, Poland

12. IAIOTDAT 2020: Special Session on Intelligent Applications of Internet of Things and Data Analysis Technologies

Rung Ching Chen	Chaoyang University of Technology, Taiwan
Yung-Fa Huang	Chaoyang University of Technology, Taiwan
Yu-Huei Cheng	Chaoyang University of Technology, Taiwan

13. CTAIOLDMBB 2020: Special Session on Current Trends in Artificial Intelligence, Optimization, Learning, and Decision-Making in Bioinformatics and Bioengineering

Dominik Vilimek	VŠB – Technical University of Ostrava, Czech Republic
Jan Kubicek	VŠB – Technical University of Ostrava, Czech Republic
Marek Penhaker	VŠB – Technical University of Ostrava, Czech Republic
Muhammad Usman Akram	National University of Sciences and Technology Pakistan, Pakistan
Vladimir Juras	Medical University of Vienna, Austria
Bhabani Shankar Prasad Mishra	KIIT University, India
Ondrej Krejcar	University of Hradec Kralove, Czech Republic

14. SAILS 2020: Special Session on Interactive Analysis of Image, Video and Motion Data in Life Sciences

Konrad Wojciechowski	Polish-Japanese Academy of Information Technology, Poland
Marek Kulbacki	Polish-Japanese Academy of Information Technology, Poland
Jakub Segen	Polish-Japanese Academy of Information Technology, Poland
Zenon Chaczko	University of Technology Sydney, Australia
Andrzej Przybyszewski	UMass Medical School, USA
Jerzy Nowacki	Polish-Japanese Academy of Information Technology, Poland

15. AIMCP 2020: Special Session on Application of Intelligent Methods to Constrained Problems

Jarosław Wikarek	Kielce University of Technology, Poland
Mukund Janardhanan	University of Leicester, UK

16. PSTrustAI 2020: Special Session on Privacy, Security and Trust in Artificial Intelligence

Pascal Bouvry	University of Luxembourg, Luxembourg
Matthias R. Brust	University of Luxembourg, Luxembourg
Grégoire Danoy	University of Luxembourg, Luxembourg
El-ghazali Talbi	University of Lille, France

17. IMSAGRWS 2020: Intelligent Modeling and Simulation Approaches for Games and Real World Systems

Doina Logofătu	Frankfurt University of Applied Sciences, Germany
Costin Bădică	University of Craiova, Romania
Florin Leon	Gheorghe Asachi Technical University, Romania

International Program Committee

Muhammad Abulaish	South Asian University, India
Waseem Ahmad	Waiariki Institute of Technology, New Zealand
R. S. Ajin	Idukki District Disaster Management Authority, India
Jesus Alcala-Fdez	University of Granada, Spain
Bashar Al-Shboul	University of Jordan, Jordan
Lionel Amodeo	University of Technology of Troyes, France
Toni Anwar	Universiti Teknologi Petronas, Malaysia
Taha Arbaoui	University of Technology of Troyes, France
Mehmet Emin Aydin	University of the West of England, UK
Ahmad Taher Azar	Prince Sultan University, Saudi Arabia
Thomas Bäck	Leiden University, The Netherlands

Amelia Badica	University of Craiova, Romania
Costin Badica	University of Craiova, Romania
Kambiz Badie	ICT Research Institute, Iran
Hassan Badir	École Nationale des Sciences Appliquées de Tanger, Morocco
Zbigniew Banaszak	Warsaw University of Technology, Poland
Dariusz Barbucha	Gdynia Maritime University, Poland
Ramazan Bayindir	Gazi University, Turkey
Maumita Bhattacharya	Charles Sturt University, Australia
Leon Bobrowski	Białystok University of Technology, Poland
Bülent Bolat	Yildiz Technical University, Turkey
Mariusz Boryczka	University of Silesia, Poland
Urszula Boryczka	University of Silesia, Poland
Zouhaier Brahmia	University of Sfax, Tunisia
Stephane Bressan	National University of Singapore, Singapore
Peter Brida	University of Žilina, Slovakia
Andrej Brodnik	University of Ljubljana, Slovenia
Piotr Bródka	Wroclaw University of Science and Technology, Poland
Grażyna Brzykcy	Poznan University of Technology, Poland
Robert Burduk	Wrocław University of Science and Technology, Poland
Aleksander Byrski	AGH University of Science and Technology, Poland
Tru Cao	Ho Chi Minh City University of Technology, Vietnam
Leopoldo Eduardo Cardenas-Barron	Tecnologico de Monterrey, Mexico
Oscar Castillo	Tijuana Institute of Technology, Mexico
Dariusz Ceglarek	WSB University in Poznań, Poland
Stefano A. Cerri	University of Montpellier, France
Zenon Chaczko	University of Technology Sydney, Australia
Altangerel Chagnaa	National University of Mongolia, Mongolia
Somchai Chatvichienchai	University of Nagasaki, Japan
Chun-Hao Chen	Tamkang University, Taiwan
Rung-Ching Chen	Chaoyang University of Technology, Taiwan
Shyi-Ming Chen	National Taiwan University of Science and Technology, Taiwan
Leszek J. Chmielewski	Warsaw University of Life Sciences, Poland
Sung-Bae Cho	Yonsei University, South Korea
Kazimierz Choroś	Wrocław University of Science and Technology, Poland
Kun-Ta Chuang	National Cheng Kung University, Taiwan
Piotr Chynał	Wrocław University of Science and Technology, Poland
Dorian Cojocaru	University of Craiova, Romania
Jose Alfredo Ferreira Costa	Federal University of Rio Grande do Norte (UFRN), Brazil

Ireneusz Czarnowski	Gdynia Maritime University, Poland
Piotr Czekalski	Silesian University of Technology, Poland
Theophile Dagba	University of Abomey-Calavi, Benin
Tien V. Do	Budapest University of Technology and Economics, Hungary
Grzegorz Dobrowolski	AGH University of Science and Technology, Poland
Rafał Doroz	University of Silesia, Poland
Habiba Drias	University of Science and Technology Houari Boumediene, Algeria
Maciej Drwal	Wrocław University of Science and Technology, Poland
Ewa Dudek-Dyduch	AGH University of Science and Technology, Poland
El-Sayed M. El-Alfy	King Fahd University of Petroleum and Minerals, Saudi Arabia
Keiichi Endo	Ehime University, Japan
Sebastian Ernst	AGH University of Science and Technology, Poland
Nadia Essoussi	University of Carthage, Tunisia
Rim Faiz	University of Carthage, Tunisia
Victor Felea	Universitatea Alexandru Ioan Cuza din Iaşi, Romania
Simon Fong	University of Macau, Macau SAR
Dariusz Frejlichowski	West Pomeranian University of Technology, Poland
Blanka Frydrychova Klimova	University of Hradec Králové, Czech Republic
Mohamed Gaber	Birmingham City University, UK
Marina L. Gavrilova	University of Calgary, Canada
Janusz Getta	University of Wollongong, Australia
Daniela Gifu	Universitatea Alexandru Ioan Cuza din Iaşi, Romania
Fethullah Göçer	Galatasaray University, Turkey
Daniela Godoy	ISISTAN Research Institute, Argentina
Gergo Gombos	Eötvös Loránd University, Hungary
Fernando Gomide	University of Campinas, Brazil
Antonio Gonzalez-Pardo	Universidad Autónoma de Madrid, Spain
Janis Grundspenkis	Riga Technical University, Latvia
Claudio Gutierrez	Universidad de Chile, Chile
Quang-Thuy Ha	VNU University of Engineering and Technology, Vietnam
Dawit Haile	Addis Ababa University, Ethiopia
Pei-Yi Hao	National Kaohsiung University of Applied Sciences, Taiwan
Spits Warnars Harco Leslie Hendric	BINUS University, Indonesia
Marcin Hernes	Wrocław University of Economics and Business, Poland
Francisco Herrera	University of Granada, Spain
Koichi Hirata	Kyushu Institute of Technology, Japan

Bogumiła Hnatkowska	Wrocław University of Science and Technology, Poland
Huu Hanh Hoang	Posts and Telecommunications Institute of Technology, Vietnam
Quang Hoang	Hue University of Sciences, Vietnam
Van-Dung Hoang	Quang Binh University, Vietnam
Jaakko Hollmen	Aalto University, Finland
Tzung-Pei Hong	National University of Kaohsiung, Taiwan
Mong-Fong Horng	National Kaohsiung University of Applied Sciences, Taiwan
Yung-Fa Huang	Chaoyang University of Technology, Taiwan
Maciej Huk	Wrocław University of Science and Technology, Poland
Dosam Hwang	Yeungnam University, South Korea
Roliana Ibrahim	Universiti Teknologi Malaysia, Malaysia
Mirjana Ivanovic	University of Novi Sad, Serbia
Sanjay Jain	National University of Singapore, Singapore
Jarosław Jankowski	West Pomeranian University of Technology, Poland
Kietikul Jearanaitanakij	King Mongkut's Institute of Technology Ladkrabang, Thailand
Khalid Jebari	LCS Rabat, Morocco
Janusz Jeżewski	Institute of Medical Technology and Equipment ITAM, Poland
Joanna Jędrzejowicz	University of Gdańsk, Poland
Piotr Jędrzejowicz	Gdynia Maritime University, Poland
Przemysław Juszczuk	University of Economics in Katowice, Poland
Dariusz Kania	Silesian University of Technology, Poland
Nikola Kasabov	Auckland University of Technology, New Zealand
Arkadiusz Kawa	Poznań University of Economics and Business, Poland
Zaheer Khan	University of the West of England, UK
Muhammad Khurram Khan	King Saud University, Saudi Arabia
Marek Kisiel-Dorohinicki	AGH University of Science and Technology, Poland
Attila Kiss	Eötvös Loránd University, Hungary
Jerzy Klamka	Silesian University of Technology, Poland
Frank Klawonn	Ostfalia University of Applied Sciences, Germany
Shinya Kobayashi	Ehime University, Japan
Joanna Kolodziej	Cracow University of Technology, Poland
Grzegorz Kołaczek	Wrocław University of Science and Technology, Poland
Marek Kopel	Wrocław University of Science and Technology, Poland
Józef Korbicz	University of Zielona Gora, Poland
Raymondus Kosala	BINUS University, Indonesia
Leszek Koszałka	Wroclaw University of Science and Technology, Poland
Leszek Kotulski	AGH University of Science and Technology, Poland

Jan Kozak	University of Economics in Katowice, Poland
Adrianna Kozierkiewicz	Wrocław University of Science and Technology, Poland
Ondrej Krejcar	University of Hradec Králové, Czech Republic
Dariusz Król	Wrocław University of Science and Technology, Poland
Marek Krótkiewicz	Wrocław University of Science and Technology, Poland
Marzena Kryszkiewicz	Warsaw University of Technology, Poland
Adam Krzyzak	Concordia University, Canada
Jan Kubicek	VSB – Technical University of Ostrava, Czech Republic
Tetsuji Kuboyama	Gakushuin University, Japan
Elżbieta Kukla	Wrocław University of Science and Technology, Poland
Julita Kulbacka	Wrocław Medical University, Poland
Marek Kulbacki	Polish-Japanese Academy of Information Technology, Poland
Kazuhiro Kuwabara	Ritsumeikan University, Japan
Halina Kwaśnicka	Wrocław University of Science and Technology, Poland
Annabel Latham	Manchester Metropolitan University, UK
Bac Le	VNU University of Science, Vietnam
Kun Chang Lee	Sungkyunkwan University, South Korea
Yue-Shi Lee	Ming Chuan University, Taiwan
Florin Leon	Gheorghe Asachi Technical University of Iasi, Romania
Horst Lichter	RWTH Aachen University, Germany
Igor Litvinchev	Nuevo Leon State University, Mexico
Rey-Long Liu	Tzu Chi University, Taiwan
Doina Logofatu	Frankfurt University of Applied Sciences, Germany
Edwin Lughofer	Johannes Kepler University Linz, Austria
Lech Madeyski	Wrocław University of Science and Technology, Poland
Nezam Mahdavi-Amiri	Sharif University of Technology, Iran
Bernadetta Maleszka	Wrocław University of Science and Technology, Poland
Marcin Maleszka	Wrocław University of Science and Technology, Poland
Yannis Manolopoulos	Open University of Cyprus, Cyprus
Konstantinos Margaritis	University of Macedonia, Greece
Vukosi Marivate	Council for Scientific and Industrial Research, South Africa
Urszula Markowska-Kaczmar	Wrocław University of Science and Technology, Poland
Takashi Matsuhisa	Karelia Research Centre, Russian Academy of Science, Russia

Tamás Matuszka	Eötvös Loránd University, Hungary
Vladimir Mazalov	Karelia Research Centre, Russian Academy of Sciences, Russia
Héctor Menéndez	University College London, UK
Mercedes Merayo	Universidad Complutense de Madrid, Spain
Jacek Mercik	WSB University in Wrocław, Poland
Radosław Michalski	Wrocław University of Science and Technology, Poland
Peter Mikulecky	University of Hradec Králové, Czech Republic
Miroslava Mikusova	University of Žilina, Slovakia
Marek Milosz	Lublin University of Technology, Poland
Jolanta Mizera-Pietraszko	Opole University, Poland
Nurhizam Safie Mohd Satar	Universiti Kebangsaan Malaysia, Malaysia
Leo Mrsic	IN2data Ltd Data Science Company, Croatia
Agnieszka Mykowiecka	Institute of Computer Science, Polish Academy of Sciences, Poland
Pawel Myszkowski	Wrocław University of Science and Technology, Poland
Grzegorz J. Nalepa	AGH University of Science and Technology, Poland
Fulufhelo Nelwamondo	Council for Scientific and Industrial Research, South Africa
Huu-Tuan Nguyen	Vietnam Maritime University, Vietnam
Le Minh Nguyen	Japan Advanced Institute of Science and Technology, Japan
Loan T. T. Nguyen	Nguyen Tat Thanh University, Vietnam
Ngoc-Thanh Nguyen	Wrocław University of Science and Technology, Poland
Quang-Vu Nguyen	Korea-Vietnam Friendship Information Technology College, Vietnam
Thai-Nghe Nguyen	Cantho University, Vietnam
Yusuke Nojima	Osaka Prefecture University, Japan
Jerzy Paweł Nowacki	Polish-Japanese Academy of Information Technology, Poland
Agnieszka Nowak-Brzezińska	University of Silesia, Poland
Mariusz Nowostawski	Norwegian University of Science and Technology, Norway
Alberto Núñez	Universidad Complutense de Madrid, Spain
Manuel Núñez	Universidad Complutense de Madrid, Spain
Kouzou Ohara	Aoyama Gakuin University, Japan
Tarkko Oksala	Aalto University, Finland
Marcin Paprzycki	Systems Research Institute, Polish Academy of Sciences, Poland
Jakub Peksiński	West Pomeranian University of Technology, Poland
Danilo Pelusi	University of Teramo, Italy
Bernhard Pfahringer	University of Waikato, New Zealand

Bartłomiej Pierański	Poznan University of Economics and Business, Poland
Dariusz Pierzchała	Military University of Technology, Poland
Marcin Pietranik	Wrocław University of Science and Technology, Poland
Elias Pimenidis	University of the West of England, UK
Jaroslav Pokorný	Charles University in Prague, Czech Republic
Nikolaos Polatidis	University of Brighton, UK
Elvira Popescu	University of Craiova, Romania
Petra Poulova	University of Hradec Králové, Czech Republic
Om Prakash	University of Allahabad, India
Radu-Emil Precup	Politehnica University of Timisoara, Romania
Małgorzata Przybyła-Kasperek	University of Silesia, Poland
Paulo Quaresma	Universidade de Evora, Portugal
David Ramsey	Wrocław University of Science and Technology, Poland
Mohammad Rashedur Rahman	North South University, Bangladesh
Ewa Ratajczak-Ropel	Gdynia Maritime University, Poland
Sebastian A. Rios	University of Chile, Chile
Leszek Rutkowski	Częstochowa University of Technology, Poland
Alexander Ryjov	Lomonosov Moscow State University, Russia
Keun Ho Ryu	Chungbuk National University, South Korea
Virgilijus Sakalauskas	Vilnius University, Lithuania
Daniel Sanchez	University of Granada, Spain
Rafał Scherer	Częstochowa University of Technology, Poland
Juergen Schmidhuber	Swiss AI Lab IDSIA, Switzerland
Ali Selamat	Universiti Teknologi Malaysia, Malaysia
Tegjyot Singh Sethi	University of Louisville, USA
Natalya Shakhovska	Lviv Polytechnic National University, Ukraine
Donghwa Shin	Yeungnam University, South Korea
Andrzej Siemiński	Wrocław University of Science and Technology, Poland
Dragan Simic	University of Novi Sad, Serbia
Bharat Singh	Universiti Teknology PETRONAS, Malaysia
Paweł Sitek	Kielce University of Technology, Poland
Andrzej Skowron	Warsaw University, Poland
Adam Słowik	Koszalin University of Technology, Poland
Vladimir Sobeslav	University of Hradec Králové, Czech Republic
Kamran Soomro	University of the West of England, UK
Zenon A. Sosnowski	Białystok University of Technology, Poland
Chutimet Srinilta	King Mongkut's Institute of Technology Ladkrabang, Thailand
Bela Stantic	Griffith University, Australia
Jerzy Stefanowski	Poznań University of Technology, Poland
Stanimir Stoyanov	University of Plovdiv "Paisii Hilendarski", Bulgaria

Ja-Hwung Su	Cheng Shiu University, Taiwan
Libuse Svobodova	University of Hradec Králové, Czech Republic
Tadeusz Szuba	AGH University of Science and Technology, Poland
Julian Szymański	Gdańsk University of Technology, Poland
Krzysztof Ślot	Łódź University of Technology, Poland
Jerzy Świątek	Wrocław University of Science and Technology, Poland
Andrzej Świerniak	Silesian University of Technology, Poland
Ryszard Tadeusiewicz	AGH University of Science and Technology, Poland
Muhammad Atif Tahir	National University of Computing and Emerging Sciences, Pakistan
Yasufumi Takama	Tokyo Metropolitan University, Japan
Maryam Tayefeh Mahmoudi	ICT Research Institute, Iran
Zbigniew Telec	Wrocław University of Science and Technology, Poland
Dilhan Thilakarathne	Vrije Universiteit Amsterdam, The Netherlands
Satoshi Tojo	Japan Advanced Institute of Science and Technology, Japan
Bogdan Trawiński	Wrocław University of Science and Technology, Poland
Trong Hieu Tran	VNU University of Engineering and Technology, Vietnam
Ualsher Tukeyev	Al-Farabi Kazakh National University, Kazakhstan
Olgierd Unold	Wrocław University of Science and Technology, Poland
Natalie Van Der Wal	Vrije Universiteit Amsterdam, The Netherlands
Jorgen Villadsen	Technical University of Denmark, Denmark
Bay Vo	Ho Chi Minh City University of Technology, Vietnam
Gottfried Vossen	ERCIS Münster, Germany
Wahyono Wahyono	Universitas Gadjah Mada, Indonesia
Lipo Wang	Nanyang Technological University, Singapore
Junzo Watada	Waseda University, Japan
Izabela Wierzbowska	Gdynia Maritime University, Poland
Krystian Wojtkiewicz	Wrocław University of Science and Technology, Poland
Michał Woźniak	Wrocław University of Science and Technology, Poland
Krzysztof Wróbel	University of Silesia, Poland
Marian Wysocki	Rzeszow University of Technology, Poland
Farouk Yalaoui	University of Technology of Troyes, France
Xin-She Yang	Middlesex University, UK
Tulay Yildirim	Yildiz Technical University, Turkey
Piotr Zabawa	Cracow University of Technology, Poland
Sławomir Zadrożny	Systems Research Institute, Polish Academy of Sciences, Poland

Drago Zagar	University of Osijek, Croatia
Danuta Zakrzewska	Łódź University of Technology, Poland
Katerina Zdravkova	Ss. Cyril and Methodius University in Skopje, Macedonia
Vesna Zeljkovic	Lincoln University, USA
Aleksander Zgrzywa	Wroclaw University of Science and Technology, Poland
Jianlei Zhang	Nankai University, China
Zhongwei Zhang	University of Southern Queensland, Australia
Maciej Zięba	Wrocław University of Science and Technology, Poland
Adam Ziębiński	Silesian University of Technology, Poland

Program Committees of Special Sessions

Special Session on Cyber-Physical Systems in Healthcare: Applications and Challenges (CSHAC 2020)

Michael Mayo	University of Waikato, New Zealand
Abigail Koay	University of Waikato, New Zealand
Panos Patros	University of Waikato, New Zealand

Special Session on Advanced Data Mining Techniques and Applications (ADMTA 2020)

Tzung-Pei Hong	National University of Kaohsiung, Taiwan
Tran Minh Quang	Ho Chi Minh City University of Technology, Vietnam
Bac Le	VNU University of Science, Vietnam
Bay Vo	Ho Chi Minh City University of Technology, Vietnam
Chun-Hao Chen	Tamkang University, Taiwan
Chun-Wei Lin	Harbin Institute of Technology, China
Wen-Yang Lin	National University of Kaohsiung, Taiwan
Yeong-Chyi Lee	Cheng Shiu University, Taiwan
Le Hoang Son	VNU University of Science, Vietnam
Vo Thi Ngoc Chau	Ho Chi Minh City University of Technology, Vietnam.
Van Vo	Ho Chi Minh University of Industry, Vietnam
Ja-Hwung Su	Cheng Shiu University, Taiwan
Ming-Tai Wu	University of Nevada, Las Vegas, USA
Kawuu W. Lin	National Kaohsiung University of Applied Sciences, Taiwan
Tho Le	Ho Chi Minh City University of Technology, Vietnam
Dang Nguyen	Deakin University, Australia
Hau Le	Thuyloi University, Vietnam
Thien-Hoang Van	Ho Chi Minh City University of Technology, Vietnam
Tho Quan	Ho Chi Minh City University of Technology, Vietnam
Ham Nguyen	University of People's Security, Vietnam
Thiet Pham	Ho Chi Minh University of Industry, Vietnam

Nguyen Thi Thuy Loan	Nguyen Tat Thanh University, Vietnam
Mu-En Wu	National Taipei University of Technology, Taiwan
Eric Hsueh-Chan Lu	National Cheng Kung University, Taiwan
Chao-Chun Chen	National Cheng Kung University, Taiwan
Ju-Chin Chen	National Kaohsiung University of Science and Technology, Taiwan

Special Session on Computer Vision and Intelligent Systems (CVIS 2020)

Yoshinori Kuno	Saitama University, Japan
Nobutaka Shimada	Ritsumeikan University, Japan
Muriel Visani	University of La Rochelle, France
Heejun Kang	University of Ulsan, South Korea
Cheolgeun Ha	University of Ulsan, South Korea
Byeongryong Lee	University of Ulsan, South Korea
Youngsoo Suh	University of Ulsan, South Korea
Kang-Hyun Jo	University of Ulsan, South Korea
Hyun-Deok Kang	Ulsan National Institute of Science and Technology, South Korea
Van Mien	University of Exeter, UK
Chi- Mai Luong	University of Science and Technology of Hanoi, Vietnam
Thi-Lan Le	Hanoi University of Science and Technology, Vietnam
Duc-Dung Nguyen	Institute of Information Technology, Vietnam
Thi-Phuong Nghiem	University of Science and Technology of Hanoi, Vietnam
Giang-Son Tran	University of Science and Technology of Hanoi, Vietnam
Hoang-Thai Le	VNU University of Science, Vietnam
Thanh-Hai Tran	Hanoi University of Science and Technology, Vietnam
Anh-Cuong Le	Ton Duc Thang University, Vietnam
My-Ha Le	Ho Chi Minh City University of Technology and Education, Vietnam
The-Anh Pham	Hong Duc University, Vietnam
Van-Huy Pham	Tong Duc Thang University, Vietnam
Van-Dung Hoang	Quang Binh University, Vietnam
Huafeng Qin	Chongqing Technology and Business University, China
Danilo Caceres Hernandez	Universidad Tecnologica de Panama, Panama
Kaushik Deb	Chittagong University of Engineering and Technology, Bangladesh
Joko Hariyono	Civil Service Agency of Yogyakarta, Indonesia
Ing. Reza Pulungan	Universitas Gadjah Mada, Indonesia
Agus Harjoko	Universitas Gadjah Mada, Indonesia
Sri Hartati	Universitas Gadjah Mada, Indonesia
Afiahayati	Universitas Gadjah Mada, Indonesia

| Moh. Edi Wibowo | Universitas Gadjah Mada, Indonesia |
| Wahyono | Universitas Gadjah Mada, Yogyakarta, Indonesia |

Special Session on Multiple Model Approach to Machine Learning (MMAML 2020)

Urszula Boryczka	University of Silesia, Poland
Abdelhamid Bouchachia	Bournemouth University, UK
Robert Burduk	Wrocław University of Science and Technology, Poland
Oscar Castillo	Tijuana Institute of Technology, Mexico
Rung-Ching Chen	Chaoyang University of Technology, Taiwan
Suphamit Chittayasothorn	King Mongkut's Institute of Technology Ladkrabang, Thailand
José Alfredo F. Costa	Federal University (UFRN), Brazil
Ireneusz Czarnowski	Gdynia Maritime University, Poland
Fernando Gomide	State University of Campinas, Brazil
Francisco Herrera	University of Granada, Spain
Tzung-Pei Hong	National University of Kaohsiung, Taiwan
Konrad Jackowski	Wrocław University of Science and Technology, Poland
Piotr Jędrzejowicz	Gdynia Maritime University, Poland
Tomasz Kajdanowicz	Wrocław University of Science and Technology, Poland
Yong Seog Kim	Utah State University, USA
Bartosz Krawczyk	Virginia Commonwealth University, USA
Kun Chang Lee	Sungkyunkwan University, South Korea
Edwin Lughofer	Johannes Kepler University Linz, Austria
Hector Quintian	University of Salamanca, Spain
Andrzej Sieminski	Wrocław University of Science and Technology, Poland
Dragan Simic	University of Novi Sad, Serbia
Adam Słowik	Koszalin University of Technology, Poland
Zbigniew Telec	Wrocław University of Science and Technology, Poland
Bogdan Trawiński	Wrocław University of Science and Technology, Poland
Olgierd Unold	Wrocław University of Science and Technology, Poland
Michał Woźniak	Wrocław University of Science and Technology, Poland
Zhongwei Zhang	University of Southern Queensland, Australia
Zhi-Hua Zhou	Nanjing University, China

Special Session on Computational Imaging and Vision (CIV 2020)

Ishwar Sethi	Oakland University, USA
Moongu Jeon	Gwangju Institute of Science and Technology, South Korea
Jong-In Song	Gwangju Institute of Science and Technology, South Korea
Taek Lyul Song	Hangyang University, South Korea
Ba-Ngu Vo	Curtin University, Australia
Ba-Tuong Vo	Curtin University, Australia
Du Yong Kim	Curtin University, Australia
Benlian Xu	Changshu Institute of Technology, China
Peiyi Zhu	Changshu Institute of Technology, China
Mingli Lu	Changshu Institute of Technology, China
Weifeng Liu	Hangzhou Danzi University, China
Ashish Khare	University of Allahabad, India
Moonsoo Kang	Chosun University, South Korea
Goo-Rak Kwon	Chosun University, South Korea
Sang Woong Lee	Gachon University, South Korea
U. S. Tiwary	IIIT Allahabad, India
Ekkarat Boonchieng	Chiang Mai University, Thailand
Jeong-Seon Park	Chonnam National University, South Korea
Unsang Park	Sogang University, South Korea
R. Z. Khan	Aligarh Muslim University, India
Suman Mitra	DA-IICT, India
Bakul Gohel	DA-IICT, India
Sathya Narayanan	NTU, Singapore

Special Session on Intelligent Systems and Algorithms in Information Sciences (ISAIS 2020)

Martin Kotyrba	University of Ostrava, Czech Republic
Eva Volna	University of Ostrava, Czech Republic
Ivan Zelinka	VŠB – Technical University of Ostrava, Czech Republic
Hashim Habiballa	Institute for Research and Applications of Fuzzy Modeling, Czech Republic
Alexej Kolcun	Institute of Geonics, ASCR, Czech Republic
Roman Senkerik	Tomas Bata University in Zlin, Czech Republic
Zuzana Kominkova Oplatkova	Tomas Bata University in Zlin, Czech Republic
Katerina Kostolanyova	University of Ostrava, Czech Republic
Antonin Jancarik	Charles University in Prague, Czech Republic
Petr Dolezel	University of Pardubice, Czech Republic
Igor Kostal	The University of Economics in Bratislava, Slovakia
Eva Kurekova	Slovak University of Technology in Bratislava, Slovakia

Leszek Cedro	Kielce University of Technology, Poland
Dagmar Janacova	Tomas Bata University in Zlin, Czech Republic
Martin Halaj	Slovak University of Technology in Bratislava, Slovakia
Radomil Matousek	Brno University of Technology, Czech Republic
Roman Jasek	Tomas Bata University in Zlin, Czech Republic
Petr Dostal	Brno University of Technology, Czech Republic
Jiri Pospichal	The University of Ss. Cyril and Methodius (UCM), Slovakia
Vladimir Bradac	University of Ostrava, Czech Republic
Roman Jasek	Tomas Bata University in Zlin, Czech Republic
Petr Pavel	University of Pardubice, Czech Republic
Jan Capek	University of Pardubice, Czech Republic

Special Session on Internet of Things and Artificial Intelligence for Energy Efficiency-Recent Advances and Future Trends (IOTAI 2020)

Xiaohui Yuan	University of North Texas, USA
Andino Maseleno	Universiti Tenaga Nasional, Malaysia
Amit Kumar Singh	National Institute of Technology Patna, India
Valentina E. Balas	Aurel Vlaicu University of Arad, Romania

Special Session on Data Modelling and Processing for Industry 4.0 (DMPI-4.0 2020)

Jörg Becker	Westfälische Wilhelms-Universität, Germany
Rafał Cupek	Silesian University of Technology, Poland
Helena Dudycz	Wroclaw University of Economics and Business, Poland
Marcin Fojcik	Western Norway University of Applied Sciences, Norway
Du Haizhou	Shanghai University of Electric Power, China
Marcin Hernes	Wroclaw University of Economics and Business, Poland
Wojciech Hunek	Opole University of Technology, Poland
Marek Krótkiewicz	Wrocław University of Science and Technology, Poland
Florin Leon	Technical University Asachi of Iasi, Romania
Jing Li	Shanghai University of Electric Power, China
Jacek Piskorowski	West Pomeranian University of Technology Szczecin, Polska
Khouloud Salameh	American University of Ras Al Khaimah, UAE
Predrag Stanimirović	University of Nis, Serbia
Krystian Wojtkiewicz	Wrocław University of Science and Technology, Poland
Feifei Xu	Shanghai University of Electric Power, China

Special Session on Intelligent and Contextual Systems (ICxS 2020)

Adriana Albu	Polytechnic University of Timisoara, Romania
Basabi Chakraborty	Iwate Prefectural University, Japan
Chao-Chun Chen	National Cheng Kung University, Taiwan
Dariusz Frejlichowski	West Pomeranian University of Technology Szczecin, Poland
Diganta Goswami	Indian Institute of Technology Guwahati, India
Erdenebileg Batbaatar	Chungbuk National University, South Korea
Goutam Chakraborty	Iwate Prefectural University, Japan
Ha Manh Tran	Ho Chi Minh City International University, Vietnam
Hong Vu Nguyen	Ton Duc Thang University, Vietnam
Hideyuki Takahashi	Tohoku Gakuin University, Japan
Intisar Chowdhury	University of Aizu, Japan
Jerzy Świątek	Wroclaw University of Science and Technology, Poland
Józef Korbicz	University of Zielona Gora, Poland
Keun Ho Ryu	Chungbuk National University, South Korea
Khanindra Pathak	Indian Institute of Technology Kharagpur, India
Kilho Shin	Gakashuin University, Japan
Maciej Huk	Wroclaw University of Science and Technology, Poland
Marcin Fojcik	Western Norway University of Applied Sciences, Norway
Masafumi Matsuhara	Iwate Prefectural University, Japan
Min-Hsiung Hung	Chinese Culture University, Taiwan
Miroslava Mikusova	University of Žilina, Slovakia
Musa Ibrahim	Chungbuk National University, South Korea
Nguyen Khang Pham	Can Tho University, Vietnam
Plamen Angelov	Lancaster University, UK
Qiangfu Zhao	University of Aizu, Japan
Quan Thanh Tho	Ho Chi Minh City University of Technology, Vietnam
Rafal Palak	Wroclaw University of Science and Technology, Poland
Rashmi Dutta Baruah	Indian Institute of Technology Guwahati, India
Senthilmurugan Subbiah	Indian Institute of Technology Guwahati, India
Sonali Chouhan	Indian Institute of Technology Guwahati, India
Takako Hashimoto	Chiba University of Commerce, Japan
Tetsuji Kuboyama	Gakushuin University, Japan
Tetsuo Kinoshita	RIEC, Tohoku University, Japan
Thai-Nghe Nguyen	Can Tho University, Vietnam
Zhenni Li	University of Aizu, Japan

Special Session on Automated Reasoning with Applications in Intelligent Systems (ARAIS 2020)

Yuichi Goto	Saitama University, Japan
Shinsuke Nara	Muraoka Design Laboratory, Japan
Hongbiao Gao	North China Electric Power University, China
Kazunori Wagatsuma	CIJ Solutions, Japan
Yuan Zhou	Minjiang Teachers College, China

Special Session on Intelligent Supply Chains and e-Commerce (ISCEC 2020)

Carlos Andres Romano	Polytechnic University of Valencia, Spain
Costin Badica	University of Craiova, Romania
Davor Dujak	University of Osijek, Croatia
Waldemar Koczkodaj	Laurentian University, Canada
Miklós Krész	InnoRenew, Slovenia
Paweł Pawlewski	Poznan University of Technology, Poland
Paulina Golińska-Dawson	Poznan University of Economics and Business, Poland
Adam Koliński	Łukasiewicz Research Network – The Institute of Logistics and Warehousing, Poland
Marcin Anholcer	Poznan University of Economics and Business, Poland

Special Session on Intelligent Applications of Internet of Things and Data Analysis Technologies (IAIOTDAT 2020)

Goutam Chakraborty	Iwate Prefectural University, Japan
Bin Dai	University of Technology Xiamen, China
Qiangfu Zhao	University of Aizu, Japan
David C. Chou	Eastern Michigan University, USA
Chin-Feng Lee	Chaoyang University of Technology, Taiwan
Lijuan Liu	University of Technology Xiamen, China
Kien A. Hua	Central Florida University, USA
Long-Sheng Chen	Chaoyang University of Technology, Taiwan
Xin Zhu	University of Aizu, Japan
David Wei	Fordham University, USA
Qun Jin	Waseda University, Japan
Jacek M. Zurada	University of Louisville, USA
Tsung-Chih Hsiao	Huaoiao University, China
Tzu-Chuen Lu	Chaoyang University of Technology, Taiwan
Nitasha Hasteer	Amity University Uttar Pradesh, India
Chuan-Bi Lin	Chaoyang University of Technology, Taiwan
Cliff Zou	Central Florida University, USA
Hendry	Satya Wacana Christian University, Indonesia

Special Session on Current Trends in Artificial Intelligence, Optimization, Learning, and Decision-Making in Bioinformatics and Bioengineering (CTAIOLDMBB 2020)

Sajid Gul Khawaja	National University of Sciences and Technology, Pakistan
Tehmina Khalil	Mirpur University of Sciences and Technology, Pakistan
Arslan Shaukat	National University of Sciences and Technology, Pakistan
Ani Liza Asmawi	International Islamic University, Malaysia
Martin Augustynek	VŠB – Technical University of Ostrava, Czech Republic
Martin Cerny	VŠB – Technical University of Ostrava, Czech Republic
Klara Fiedorova	VŠB – Technical University of Ostrava, Czech Republic
Habibollah Harun	Universiti Teknologi Malaysia, Malaysia
Lim Kok Cheng	Universiti Tenaga Nasional, Malaysia
Roliana Ibrahim	Universiti Teknologi Malaysia, Malaysia
Jafreezal Jaafar	Universiti Teknologi Petronas, Malaysia
Vladimir Kasik	VŠB – Technical University of Ostrava, Czech Republic
Ondrej Krejcar	University of Hradec Kralove, Czech Republic
Jan Kubicek	VŠB – Technical University of Ostrava, Czech Republic
Kamil Kuca	University of Hradec Kralove, Czech Republic
Petra Maresova	University of Hradec Kralove, Czech Republic
Daniel Barvík	VŠB – Technical University of Ostrava, Czech Republic
David Oczka	VŠB – Technical University of Ostrava, Czech Republic
Dominik Vilimek	VŠB – Technical University of Ostrava, Czech Republic
Sigeru Omatu	Osaka Institute of Technology, Japan
Marek Penhaker	VŠB – Technical University of Ostrava, Czech Republic
Lukas Peter	VŠB – Technical University of Ostrava, Czech Republic
Alice Krestanova	VŠB – Technical University of Ostrava, Czech Republic
Chawalsak Phetchanchai	Suan Dusit University, Thailand
Antonino Proto	VŠB – Technical University of Ostrava, Czech Republic
Naomie Salim	Universiti Teknologi Malaysia, Malaysia
Ali Selamat	Universiti Teknologi Malaysia, Malaysia
Imam Much Subroto	Universiti Islam Sultan Agung, Indonesia

Lau Sian Lun	Sunway University, Malaysia
Takeru Yokoi	Tokyo Metropolitan International Institute of Technology, Japan
Hazli Mohamed Zabil	Universiti Tenaga Nasional, Malaysia
Satchidananda Dehuri	University Balasore, India
Pradeep Kumar Mallick	KIIT University, India
Subhashree Mishra	KIIT University, India
Cem Deniz	NYU Langone, USA
P. V. Rao	VBIT Hydrabad, India
Tathagata Bandyopadhyay	KIIT University, India

Special Session on Interactive Analysis of Image, Video and Motion Data in Life Sciences (SAILS 2020)

Artur Bąk	Polish-Japanese Academy of Information Technology, Poland
Grzegorz Borowik	Warsaw University of Technology, Poland
Wayne Brookes	University of Technology Sydney, Australia
Leszek Chmielewski	Warsaw University of Life Sciences, Poland
Zenon Chaczko	University of Technology Sydney, Australia
David Davis	University of Technology Sydney, Australia
Aldona Barbara Drabik	Polish-Japanese Academy of Information Technology, Poland
Marcin Fojcik	Western Norway University of Applied Sciences, Norway
Carlo Giampietro	University of Technology Sydney, Australia
Katarzyna Musial-Gabrys	University of Technology Sydney, Australia
Tomasz Górski	Polish Naval Academy, Poland
Adam Gudyś	Silesian University of Technology, Poland
Doan Hoang	University of Technology Sydney, Australia
Celina Imielińska	Vesalius Technologies LLC, USA
Frank Jiang	University of Technology Sydney, Australia
Henryk Josiński	Silesian University of Technology, Poland
Anup Kale	University of Technology Sydney, Australia
Sunil Mysore Kempegowda	University of Technology Sydney, Australia
Ryszard Klempous	Wroclaw University of Technology, Poland
Ryszard Kozera	The University of Life Sciences - SGGW, Poland
Julita Kulbacka	Wroclaw Medical University, Poland
Marek Kulbacki	Polish-Japanese Academy of Information Technology, Poland
Aleksander Nawrat	Silesian University of Technology, Poland
Jerzy Paweł Nowacki	Polish-Japanese Academy of Information Technology, Poland
Eric Petajan	LiveClips LLC, USA
Andrzej Polański	Silesian University of Technology, Poland
Andrzej Przybyszewski	UMass Medical School Worcester, USA

Joanna Rossowska	Polish Academy of Sciences, Poland
Jakub Segen	Gest3D LLC, USA
Aleksander Sieroń	Medical University of Silesia, Poland
Carmen Paz Suarez Araujo	University of Las Palmas, Spain
José Juan Santana Rodríguez	University of Las Palmas, Spain
Adam Świtoński	Silesian University of Technology, Poland
Agnieszka Szczęsna	Silesian University of Technology, Poland
David Tien	Charles Sturt University, Australia
Konrad Wojciechowski	Polish-Japanese Academy of Information Technology, Poland
Robin Braun	University of Technology Sydney, Australia

Special Session on Application of Intelligent Methods to Constrained Problems (AIMCP 2020)

Peter Nielsen	Aalborg University, Denmark
Paweł Sitek	Kielce University of Technology, Poland
Antoni Ligęza	AGH University of Science and Technology, Poland
Sławomir Kłos	University of Zielona Góra, Poland
Grzegorz Bocewicz	Koszalin University of Technology, Poland
Izabela E. Nielsen	Aalborg University, Denmark
Zbigniew Banaszak	Koszalin University of Technology, Poland
Małgorzata Jasiulewicz-Kaczmarek	Poznan University of Technology, Poland
Robert Wójcik	Wrocław University of Science and Technology, Poland
Arkadiusz Gola	Lublin University of Technology, Poland
Marina Marinelli	University of Leicester, UK
Masood Ashraf	Aligarh Muslim University, India
Ali Turkyilmaz	Nazarbayev University, Kazakhstan
Chandima Ratnayake	University of Stavanger, Norway
Marek Magdziak	Rzeszów University of Technology, Poland

Special Session on Privacy, Security and Trust in Artificial Intelligence (PSTrustAI 2020)

M. Ilhan Akbas	Embry-Riddle Aeronautical University, USA
Christoph Benzmüller	Freie Universität Berlin, Germany
Roland Bouffanais	Singapore University of Technology and Design, Singapore
Bernabe Dorronsoro	University of Cadiz, Spain
Rastko Selmic	Concordia University, Canada
Ronaldo Menezes	University of Exciter, UK
Apivadee Piyatumrong	NECTEC, Thailand
Khurum Nazir Junejo	Ibex CX, Pakistan
Daniel Stolfi	University of Luxembourg, Luxembourg

Juan Luis Jiménez Laredo	Normandy University, France
Kittichai Lavangnananda	King Mongkut's University of Technology Thonburi, Thailand
Jun Pang	University of Luxembourg, Luxembourg
Marco Rocchetto	ALES, United Technologies Research Center, Italy
Jundong Chen	Dickinson State University, USA
Emmanuel Kieffer	University of Luxembourg, Luxembourg
Fang-Jing Wu	Technical University Dortmund, Germany
Hannes Frey	University Koblenz-Landau, Germany
Umer Wasim	University of Luxembourg, Luxembourg
Christian M. Adriano	University of Potsdam, Germany

Intelligent Modeling and Simulation Approaches for Games and Real World Systems (IMSAGRWS 2020)

Alabbas Alhaj Ali	Frankfurt University of Applied Sciences, Germany
Costin Bădică	University of Craiova, Romania
Petru Cașcaval	Gheorghe Asachi Technical University, Romania
Gia Thuan Lam	Vietnamese-German University, Vietnam
Florin Leon	Gheorghe Asachi Technical University, Romania
Doina Logofătu	Frankfurt University of Applied Sciences, Germany
Fitore Muharemi	Frankfurt University of Applied Sciences, Germany
Minh Nguyen	Frankfurt University of Applied Sciences, Germany
Julian Szymański	Gdańsk University of Technology, Poland
Pawel Sitek	Kielce University of Technology, Poland
Daniel Stamate	University of London, UK

Contents

Artificial Intelligence, Optimization, and Databases in Practical Applications

Intelligent Applications of Internet of Things

Recommendation and User Centric Applications of Intelligent Systems

Advanced Big Data, Machine Learning
and Data Mining

On the Design of Profitable Index Based on the Mechanism of Random Tradings

Jia-Hao Syu[1]([⊠])(iD), Mu-En Wu[2](iD), Shin-Huah Lee[2], and Jan-Ming Ho[3](iD)

[1] Department of Computer Science and Information Engineering,
National Taiwan University, Taipei, Taiwan
r08922011@ntu.edu.tw
[2] Department of Information and Finance Management,
National Taipei University of Technology, Taipei, Taiwan
mnwu@ntut.edu.tw, a0955051298@gmail.com
[3] Institute of Information Science, Academia Sinica, Taipei, Taiwan
hoho@iis.sinica.edu.tw

Abstract. Designing profitable trading strategies is an issue of interest to many experts and scholars. There are thousands of strategies in financial markets, and almost all of them can be divided into two types: momentum-type and contrarian-type. However, there is no formal way to determine which type of strategies are suitable for each stock. This study proposes a method to quantify and classify the momentum-type and the contrarian-type stocks for investors, which makes the trading strategies more quantitative. Our approach uses the technique of random trading and the proposed profitable index to quantify the stock attributes. We take the constituted stocks of Taiwan's 50 (TW50) as research objects. According to the experimental results, there are 8 stocks in TW50 that are suitable for contrarian-type trading strategies, and the others 42 stocks are suitable for momentum-type trading strategies. We also use simple momentum and contrarian strategies to evaluate the effectiveness of the proposed algorithms and index. The results show the positive correlation between the momentum-type (contrarian-type) profitable index and the trading performance, and the correlation coefficient achieves 77.3% (80.3%). In conclusion, the scale of momentum-type and contrarian-type profitability index actually represents the profitability and the attribute of the stock.

Keywords: Profitable index · Random trading · Momentum · Contrarian

1 Introduction

There are different attributes for each stock, and can be divided into two main types: momentum and contrarian. In addition, trading strategies can also be divided into momentum-type and contrarian-type, and opposite types of strategies usually generate the opposite trading signals. Therefore, investors must know which type of trading strategies is suitable for the target stock.

© Springer Nature Singapore Pte Ltd. 2020
P. Sitek et al. (Eds.): ACIIDS 2020, CCIS 1178, pp. 3–12, 2020.
https://doi.org/10.1007/978-981-15-3380-8_1

In this paper, we use random trading mechanism to quantify the momentum and contrarian attributes of stock. Danyliv et al. [3] find the market price is not normal, and the random walk behavior is appropriate understating for the market. In order to make the research results objective and fit the unmoral distributed market price, we use the random trading to calculate the PI value. Hu et al. [5] also study the random trading, and find the degree of mean-reversion trading is proportionate to the degree of random trading, which means random trading is representative when the financial system stays partial stability. Further, we proposed a profitable index (PI) to quantify the overall trading performance of random trading and to quantify the stock attributes. Also, we use simple momentum and contrarian strategies to evaluate the effectiveness of the proposed index.

In view of this research, the proposed profitable index (PI) is an effective and efficient algorithm to quantify and classify the stock attributes. Accurate and objective classification can reduce the losses caused by subjective judgment. Further, investors should take investment risks and volatility into consideration. The PI takes volatility into account, therefore, PI can represent the stableness and riskiness of the strategy.

In this study, we use the constituted stocks of Taiwan's 50 (TW50) as the research target, and use the value of PI to classify each stock, and determined each stock is suitable for momentum-type or contrarian-type trading strategies. The constituted stocks of TW50 have larger market capitalization and public liquidity, and they are high-quality stocks that recognized by the government. The experimental results show that there are 8 stocks in TW50 that are suitable for contrarian-type trading strategies, and the other 42 stocks are suitable for momentum-type trading strategies. Further, the experiment shows that the PI is positively correlated with the profit factor (PF) of the specific strategy. Therefore, we believe the scale of PI can represent the profitability and the attribute of stock.

2 Literature Review

In this section we will introduce the attributes of trading strategies, performance of trading strategies, and time scale of stocks.

2.1 Momentum and Contrarian Attributes

The momentum trading is based on a concept of movement of the price is driven by momentum, which means the price will continue to move forward as the near past trend. Opening Range Breakout (ORB) is a basic momentum strategy, which can detect the price trend and generate trading signals. Holmberg et al. [4] access the profitability of the ORB strategy and find the normally distributed return on the day that the open range is broken. Tsai et al. [9] and Syu et al. [8] find that ORB strategy is profitable in Taiwan financial market.

The contrarian trading is based on a concept of mean reversion, which is in accordance with the Martingale Central Limit theorem [2]. It believes the price will fluctuate nearby the mean price. Even if there is a trend of the price, it will remain within a certain range. If the price is far from the mean and out of the certain range, the contrarian strategies expect the price will return to the mean. It is a concept opposite to the momentum strategy. Bollinger Band is a well-known technical index in the empirical trading and research field [7, 11]. Bollinger proposed the method of mean reversal strategy [1], which used to measure the volatility of stocks and the price trend over time. Typically, investors use the average closing price within 20 days as the trend line, with positive and negative of two times of standard deviations as the range of fluctuations.

We use the stop-loss and take-profit mechanisms to simulate the momentum and contrarian effect [10]. The stop-loss mechanism believes that if the price falls below the threshold, the price will continue to fall, and it will immediately close the position. Therefore, stop-loss is a momentum strategy. The take-profit mechanism believes that if the price rises above the threshold, the price will quickly fall back to the mean, and it will immediately close the position. Therefore, take-profit is a contrarian strategy. The stocks with different attributes are suitable for different type of strategies. Therefore, we want to quantify the stock attributes, and make it easier for investors to develop strategies.

2.2 Performance of Trading Strategies

A commonly-used performance indicator for trading is return, defined as (final accumulated profit - original accumulated profit)/final accumulated profit. However, the trading return isn't able to examine the details, and doesn't consider the risk during the trading period.

Therefore, we use the profit factor (PF) to measure the overall trading performance, which is widely use in financial researches [6]. The PF is defined as the gross profit divided by the absolute value of gross loss for the entire trading period. This indicator relates the amount of profit per unit of loss. With PF value greater than one, it indicates the strategy is profitable. If the PF less than one, it means the gross loss is greater than the gross profit, and it is a losing strategy.

2.3 Time Scale of Stocks

Wu, et al. [10] use trading mechanisms to investigate futures market, and we focus on the stock market instead. Unlike the high time-frequency of futures data, Taiwan Stock Exchanges (TWSE) only provides daily data for each stock, including opening price, highest price, lowest price, and closing price of the day. In this paper we call these four values as OHLC for short and convenience.

In this paper we use day-traded random trading strategy, which means we will take a position and close the position in each trading day. This strategy is not determined by any information or technical index, it is suitable to observe the pure attributes of the stocks and will not have the overfitting issue.

3 Methodology

We use the stop-loss and take-profit mechanisms to represent the momentum and contrarian strategies, and the random trading is utilized to investigate the attributes of the stocks. In this paper, we use the constituted stocks of Taiwan's 50 (TW50) from TWSE. The data is from 3 Nov. 2006 to 14 Dec. 2018, which contain 3,000 trading days including both bull and bear markets.

3.1 Random Trading Mechanism

There are 3,000 days in our data set, and we will take a position and close the position in each day. To simulate the random trading mechanism, flipping a coin is utilized to determine to take a long (buy) or short (sell) position in each day, and the position will be taken at the opening price. When studying momentum effect, a stop-loss mechanism will be implemented. On the other hand, when studying contrarian effect, a take-profit mechanism will be implemented. Once the stop-loss or take-profit condition is satisfied, the position will be immediately closed. Otherwise, the positions will be closed at closing price.

Algorithm 1: Algorithm for the Momentum-Type (MomRT)

Result: The probability density function (PDF) of the N PFs
Data: δ is the stop-loss threshold, N is the simulation times, TD is the OHLC
    data in trading period
Input ($\delta_{con_T P}$, N, TD)
while *Repeat N times sampling* **do**
  for *each trading day in TD* **do**
    Sample from the vector (0,1) uniformly;
    if *Sampling is 0* **then**
     | Long a position at the opening price
    else
     | short a position at the opening price
    if *Stop-loss condition is satisfied* **then**
     | Close the position immediately
    else
     | Close the position at the market closes

The momentum- and contrarian-type random trading algorithms are shown in Algorithms 1 and 2. The δ is the threshold of activating stop-loss or take-profit mechanism, and the TD is the OHLC price data for 3,000 days. Because there is randomness in random trading, we sample the trading for N times (3,000 days $\times N$ times) to obtain more reliable result.

For each day, we will flip a coin to determine to take a long or short position at opening price. During the day, if the stop-loss/take-profit mechanism is satisfied (price drop δ/price rise δ), the position will be immediately closed. Otherwise, the positions will be closed at closing price. By the above process, we can obtain returns of 3,000 days which determine a PF of that sampling. The sampling process will repeat N times, and we will obtain N PFs and a probability density function (PDF) of PF.

Algorithm 2: Algorithm for the Contrarian-Type (ConRT)

Result: The probability density function (PDF) of the N PFs
Data: δ is the take-profit threshold, N is the simulation times, TD is the
  OHLC data in trading period
Input $(\delta_{con_T P},\ N,\ \text{TD})$
while *Repeat N times sampling* **do**
 for *each trading day in TD* **do**
  Sample from the vector (0,1) uniformly;
  if *Sampling is 0* **then**
   | Long a position at the opening price
  else
   | short a position at the opening price
  if *Take-profit condition is satisfied* **then**
   | Close the position immediately
  else
   | Close the position at the market closes

3.2 Construct Profitable Index via Distribution of PF

The price scale of each stock is different, so some performance indicators will also have different scale. In order to measure the risk and the profitability of different stocks, we use PF to evaluate the trading performance, which standardizes the performance and is more reliable when evaluate different stocks. The PF is defined as the total profit divided by the absolute value of total loss.

We design the PI to be positively affected by profitability and be negatively affected by risk. The profitability can be represented by the mean of the PF, and the risk can be represented by the standard deviation (SD) of the PF. Therefore, we define the PI as the mean of PF minus 1, and divided by the standard deviation of PF. We subtract 1 from the mean of PF, science the PF lager (lower) than 1 means the strategy is profitable (non-profitable). Therefore, if PI is larger than 0, it means the strategy is profitable. On the other hand, if PI is lower than 0, it means strategy is loss. The better strategy will have higher mean and lower standard deviation, which shows the larger the PI, the better the strategy is. Assuming the MomRT or ConRT algorithm samples a set of PF $(PF_1,\ldots,PF_N)$, the PI is calculated as follows:

$$PI = \frac{(\frac{1}{N}\sum_{i=1}^{N} PF_i) - 1}{\sqrt{\frac{1}{N}\sum_{i=1}^{N}(PF_i - mean(PF))^2}} \tag{1}$$

Table 1. Profitable index for a stock from TW50

	Mean of PF	SD of PF	Profitable Index (PI)
RT_SL	1.0938	0.0442	2.1217
RT_TP	0.9150	0.0369	−2.3027

We take a stock from TW50 for example. In Table 1, RT_SL is the performance of random trading strategy with stop-loss mechanism. RT_TP is the performance of the random trading strategy with take-profit mechanism. The mean of PF of RT_SL is 1.0938, and the standard deviation of PF is 0.0442, and the momentum-type PI is 2.1217. The mean of PF of RT_TP is 0.915, and the standard deviation of PF is 0.0369, and the contrarian-type PI is −2.3027. From the above values, we find the stock has higher momentum-type PI value, which means it is more appropriate and profitable in RT_SL, and it will be classified into momentum-type stock.

4   Experimental Results and Analysis

We propose algorithms and a novel index to quantify the stock attributes of momentum and contrarian. In this section, we verify the effectiveness of the PI and whether the sampling time is sufficient, and calculate PIs for constituted stocks of TW50.

4.1   Robustness Under the Random Trading Mechanism

We use constituted stocks of TW50, which contain 3,000-days daily data. Because the algorithms take different position (long or short) in each 3,000 days, the random trading algorithms both have 2^{3000} different trading combinations. It is nearly impossible to be finished in the life time. Therefore, we attempt to use 10,000 times sampling to approach 2^{3000} possible combinations.

In this section, we want to verify whether the 10,000 samples are sufficient. We observe the first to the fourth moment differences to check whether the 10,000 samples are large enough to represent the 2^{3000} combinations. We will simulate 100 times (100 times × 10,000 samples) and plot the first to the fourth moment differences first to the fourth moment differences. We connect 100 times simulation, and hope the differences will not change significantly between simulations. If the lines are close to horizontal lines, we can believe the 10,000 samples are sufficient to represent the 2^{3000} combinations.

Figure 1 shows the results of 100 time simulations of the 10,000 samples for momentum (left) and contrarian (right) trading. The blue line is the expected value of PF (first moment), and the orange line is the variance of PF (second moment). The green line is the skew state (third moment), and the red line is the kurtosis (fourth moment). We find that the moves of the first and the second moments approach to the horizontal line. It indicates that the distribution of

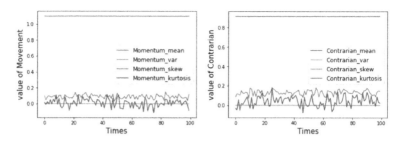

Fig. 1. 100 simulations of 10,000 samples of momentum (left) and contrarian (right) trading. (Color figure online)

10,000 samples is similar to the distribution of 2^{3000} combinations. Because the first and second order are the component of PI and remain stable during 100 simulations, we will use 10,000 samples to represent 2^{3000} combinations in order to calculate efficiently.

4.2 Momentum-Type and Contrarian-Type PI of Stocks in TW50

The results show that 8 stocks in TW50 have positive contrarian-type PI, which means they are suitable for contrarian trading strategies, including 2412.TW, 2880.TW, 2883.TW, 2884.TW, 2887.TW, 2890.TW 2891.TW, and 4904.TW..

42 stocks in TW50 have positive momentum-type PI, which means they are suitable for momentum trading strategies, including 1101.TW, 1102.TW, 1216.TW, 1301.TW, 1303.TW, 1326.TW, 1402.TW, 2002.TW, 2105.TW, 2207.TW, 2301.TW, 2303.TW, 2308.TW, 2317.TW, 2327.TW, 2330.TW, 2357.TW, 2382.TW, 2395.TW, 2408.TW, 2409.TW, 2454.TW, 2474.TW, 2633.TW, 2801.TW, 2823.TW, 2881.TW, 2882.TW, 2885.TW, 2886.TW, 2892.TW, 2912.TW, 3008.TW, 3045.TW, 3481.TW, 3711.TW, 4938.TW, 5871.TW, 5876.TW, 5880.TW, 6505.TW, 9904.TW..

4.3 Relationship Between PI and Trading Performance

In the experiment, we implement simple momentum and contrarian trading strategies to evaluate the effectiveness of PI. To more specifically, we want to know if higher momentum/contrarian-type PI implies higher performance of the stock under momentum/contrarian-type trading strategy. We will not calculate the transaction fee and tax to observe the pure attributes of the stocks and to verify the effectiveness of the PI.

The momentum trading strategy is defined as follows. If the opening price is higher (lower) than yesterday's closing price, take a long (short) position at the market opens. The momentum strategy has with 1% stop-loss mechanism, and if the stop-loss condition is not satisfied, closes the position at the market closes. The contrarian trading strategy is defined as follows. If the opening price is higher (lower) than yesterday's closing price, take a short (long) position at the market opens. The contrarian strategy has with 1% take-profit mechanism, and if the take-profit condition is not satisfied, closes all the position at the market closes.

Figure 2 is a scatter plot of the PF of trading performance and the PI values of the constituted stocks of TW50. The horizontal axis is the PI, and the vertical axis is the PF of the strategy. The green points are the PF under the contrarian strategy and contrarian-type PI of 50 constituted stocks. The green line is the linear regression line of the green points, which is positive correlation and the correlation coefficient achieves 80.3%. Under the contrarian trading strategy, the contrarian-type PI is positively correlated with the PF under the contrarian strategy, which means that when the contrarian-type PI is larger, the trading performance of the stock under the contrarian strategy is better.

The red points are the PF under the momentum strategy and momentum-type PI. The red line is the linear regression line of the red points, which is positive correlation and the correlation coefficient achieves 77.3%. The momentum-type PI is positively correlated with the PF under the momentum strategy, which means that when the momentum-type PI is larger, the trading performance of the stock under the momentum strategy is better. However, even if the momentum-type PI is larger than 0, the PF of momentum trading strategy is not necessary larger than one (profitable). We can only use the relative size not the absolute size of momentum-type PI to compare the profitability and attribute of different stock.

The PI we proposed is positively correlated with the PF of the strategy performance. Therefore, the size of PI can quantify and classify the stock attribute of momentum and contrarian.

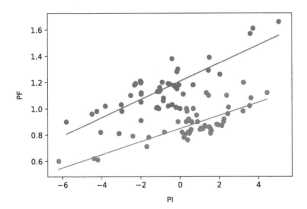

Fig. 2. The scatter plot of PF and PI of the TW50 component stocks with momentum and the contrarian trading strategy. The red (green) points are the pairs of momentum-type PI and PF of momentum trading strategy (contrarian-type PI and PF of contrarian trading strategy). (Color figure online)

5   Conclusions and Future Works

This paper proposes the profitable index (PI) by the random trading mechanism to identify the stock attributes, which can quantify and classify that the stock is suitable for momentum and contrarian strategies. It solves the problem of subjective way to determine stock attributes. We use stop-loss and take-profit mechanisms to represent momentum and contrarian strategies in financial markets. By repeating the random trading, it can get rid of the deviations from specific strategy and find the unique attributes of the stock. After understanding the stock attributes, the investors can further develop the suitable strategies, which makes it easier for the investors to get the desired performance.

The experimental results show that the PI we proposed can effectively quantify the probability of the PF distribution, measure the performance of the overall trading. The larger the PI, the better the overall performance is. Among the constituent stocks in TW50, only 8 constituent stocks of TW50 are suitable for the contrarian trading strategies, and the others 42 stocks are suitable for the momentum trading strategies.

Further, we design an experiment to verify the effectiveness of the PI. The PI is positively correlated with the trading performance. The correlation coefficient between momentum-type PI and PF of the momentum trading strategy achieves 77.3%. The correlation coefficient between contrarian-type PI and PF of the contrarian trading strategy achieves 80.3%. Therefore, the size of PI can represent the profitability of the strategy, and the attribute of momentum and contrarian. In the future, we will use the PI to help investors find appropriate trading strategies for each stock.

References

1. Bollerslev, T., Chou, R.Y., Kroner, K.F.: Arch modeling in finance: a review of the theory and empirical evidence. J. Econometrics **52**(1–2), 5–59 (1992)
2. Brown, B.M., et al.: Martingale central limit theorems. Ann. Math. Stat. **42**(1), 59–66 (1971)
3. Danyliv, O., Bland, B., Argenson, A.: Random walk model from the point of view of algorithmic trading. arXiv preprint arXiv:1908.04333 (2019)
4. Holmberg, U., Lönnbark, C., Lundström, C.: Assessing the profitability of intraday opening range breakout strategies. Finan. Res. Lett. **10**(1), 27–33 (2013)
5. Hu, W., Liu, G., Zhang, W., Wu, T.: Study on random trading behavior, herd behavior and asset price volatility. In: 2016 Chinese Control and Decision Conference (CCDC), pp. 3157–3163. IEEE (2016)
6. Huang, Z., Martin, F.: Pairs trading strategies in a cointegration framework: backtested on cfd and optimized by profit factor. Appl. Econ. **51**(22), 2436–2452 (2019)
7. Parambalath, G., Mahesh, E., Balasubramanian, P., Kumar, P.N.: Big data analytics: a trading strategy of NSE stocks using bollinger bands analysis. In: Balas, V.E., Sharma, N., Chakrabarti, A. (eds.) Data Management, Analytics and Innovation. AISC, vol. 839, pp. 143–154. Springer, Singapore (2019). https://doi.org/10.1007/978-981-13-1274-8_11

8. Syu, J.H., Wu, M.E., Lee, S.H., Ho, J.M.: Modified orb strategies with threshold adjusting on taiwan futures market. In: 2019 IEEE Conference on Computational Intelligence for Financial Engineering & Economics (CIFEr), pp. 1–7. IEEE (2019)
9. Tsai, Y.C., et al.: Assessing the profitability of timely opening range breakout on index futures markets. IEEE Access **7**, 32061–32071 (2019)
10. Wu, M.E., Wang, C.H., Chung, W.H.: Using trading mechanisms to investigate large futures data and their implications to market trends. Soft Comput. **21**(11), 2821–2834 (2017)
11. Yan, X.X., Zhang, Y.B., Lv, X.K., Li, Z.Y., et al.: Improvement and test of stock index futures trading model based on bollinger bands. Int. J. Econ. Finan. **9**(1), 78–87 (2017)

Real Estate Market Price Prediction Framework Based on Public Data Sources with Case Study from Croatia

Leo Mrsic$^{(\boxtimes)}$ ⓘ, Hrvoje Jerkovic, and Mislav Balkovic ⓘ

Algebra University College, Ilica 242, 10000 Zagreb, Croatia
{leo.mrsic,hrvoje.jerkovic,mislav.balkovic}@algebra.hr

Abstract. This study uses machine learning algorithms as a research methodology to develop a housing price prediction model of apartments in Zagreb, Croatia. In this paper we've analyzed Croatian largest real estate ad online service njuskalo.hr. In period from April to May we've collected several times all ads related to Zagreb area. Each time approximately 8 000–9 000 ads were analyzed.

To build predicting model with acceptable accuracy of housing price prediction, this paper analyzes the housing data of 7416 apartments in Zagreb gathered from njuskalo.hr portal. We develop an apartment price prediction model based on machine learning algorithms such as Random Forest, Gradient Boosting AdaBoost and popular XGBoost algorithms. Final outcome of this research is fully functional apartment price prediction model to assist a house seller or a real estate agent make better informed decisions based on house price valuation. The experiments demonstrate that the XGBoost algorithm, based on accuracy, consistently outperforms the other models in the performance of housing price prediction.

Keywords: Real estate price prediction · Machine learning · Real estate prices · Prices seasonality · Behavioral economics · Housing price prediction model · Machine learning algorithms

1 Introduction

Real estate markets experience boom and boost periods and Croatia is not an exception. Although offered price is often first selection factor, it is not true that a property sells just because of price but also based on value component. This paper is focused on easy-to-use analysis/prediction model aiming towards better market understanding and prediction of difference between market price and market value. Buyer and seller might not rate value equally, each side is driven by different factors while market price without viewing the property and the probability of that property being sold in predicted amount of days make data hard to compare, sometimes not possible at all. Market price is what a willing, ready and bank-qualified buyer will pay for a property and what the seller will accept for it. The transaction that takes place determines the market price, which will then influence the market value of future sales. Price is determined by local supply and demand, the property's condition and what other similar properties have sold for without

© Springer Nature Singapore Pte Ltd. 2020
P. Sitek et al. (Eds.): ACIIDS 2020, CCIS 1178, pp. 13–24, 2020.
https://doi.org/10.1007/978-981-15-3380-8_2

adding in the value component. On the other hand, market value is an opinion of what a property would sell for in a competitive market based on the features and benefits of that property (the value), the overall real estate market, supply and demand, and what other similar properties have sold for in the same condition. The major difference between market value and market price is that the market value, in the eyes of the seller, might be much more than what a buyer will pay for the property or it's true market price. Value can create demand, which can influence price. But, without the demand function, value alone cannot influence price. As supply increases and demand decreases, price goes down, and value is not influential. As supply decreases and demand increases, the price will rise, and value will influence price. Market value and market price can be equal in a balanced market. Fact is, in a buyer's market, or even a neutral market, price alone can beat most objections. In a buyer's market, where demand is lower, buyers will wait for the right deal. The economic downturn in the past has made buyers more cautious about their money and how they spend it. Buyers are more cautious, and they are taking more time to decide. In this paper we are looking to argue that such factors as sales techniques, marketing, increased exposure and staging can add more value and increase demand, which will cause a higher market price. In real estate most consumers looking in a particular area and price range know which properties are for sale and can determine price and value quickly while marketing is a function of price. Great marketing with the right message will drive more traffic to the property. But when the buyers can touch and feel the property, the property does have to "sell itself" to some degree. Real estate agents, marketing and even home staging can help bring those buyers to the property and entice interest; however, in the end the home has to be within a buyer's budget and provide value, and the home does have to "sell itself."

2 Related Work

To set the stage for our research, we will present a statistical summary of real estate purchase and sale data in Croatia. According to the study 536.811 transactions were performed on the real estate market in the period from 2012 to 2017, with the largest number of transactions relating to agricultural land, which recorded a total of 220,459 in the observed period. After the agricultural land, apartments have a total of 103,193, and construction land with 74,378 transactions. The total value of transactions in 2012 amounted to HRK 22.4 billion, while in 2017 the total value of transactions reached HRK 27.8 billion, representing 7.7% of the gross domestic product of the Republic of Croatia that year. The most significant share in the value of transactions in the real estate market is occupied by dwellings, which are related to 35.4% of the value of contracted transactions, followed by various real estate, construction land, other category and business premises. Single-family homes in the Adriatic are up to 18 times more expensive than inland. According to local real estate web portals and their survey of non-resident real estate claims, it showed that potential foreign buyers showed the greatest interest in homes (43% of inquiries) and apartments for sale (17%), and rental apartments (12.5%).

3   Background

3.1   Data Extraction and Data Collection Tasks

This part of the project is based on extracting data from the main category listing and from individual pages of ads. Data extraction is done using several python libraries dominantly BeautifulSoup for basic data and Selenium with Google Chrome driver for extraction of all other data from individual listings. Full feature list for each apartment consist. Final feature analysis showed that almost all additional features that we have extracted didn't make statistically significant effect on accuracy of prediction model, nevertheless it's valuable information to know with certainty that some features where not consistently entered while creating ad therefore their effects on final price of apartment could not be observed. After finalizing data extraction process, we had 48 features extracted for all of 7,416 apartments. Total number of ads for Zagreb area on njuskalo.hr for ads with images and prices more than 30,000 EUR is around 9,500 ads. After additional filtering of outliers and misclassified ads we got 7416 ads. Also we have to take into consideration that luxury apartments differ in prices for various reasons where many important features are missing from categorical entry but they are present in description of ads, also there is lack of such apartments per Zagreb counties so we don't have enough samples to train model for properly predicting prices of such apartments. We can consider same limitation is present for very cheap apartments. Raising filter limit for apartment prices to 40,000 EUR will omit only several dozen apartments which means that prices below 30,000 EUR are probably not apartments at all but garages or apartments with serious defects and therefore should not be taken into analysis. So price range between 30,000 and 350,000 EUR will give us solid population in that range. Further filtering of our dataset in order to get even better distribution was consequences of filtering any apartments with price or apartment size variating more than three standard deviations from mean value. So this is where we used z-score which is the number of standard deviations from the mean value of data points. All apartments where z-score was more than three for apartment price or apartment size were also filtered out which on the end gave us final dataset. Reason for this is that prediction intervals for normal distributions are easily calculated from the ML-estimates of the expectation and the variance and the 99.7%-prediction interval is between

$$[\mu - 3\sigma, \mu + 3\sigma]$$

Why applying same principle to apartment size and not only to apartment price – simply because that is simplest way of "partially" detecting heteroscedasticity which is unequal variability of a variable across the range of values of a second variable that predicts it. Since there is strongest correlation between prices and sizes of apartments it's logical to apply z-score to it as well (Table 1).

3.2   Data Cleaning and Transformations

We omitted some of the transformation steps like skewness and kurtosis control and various transformations and filtering based on that since they are somewhat obsolete because

Table 1. List of attributes

General attributes	Specific attributes
ID	Balcony
Price EUR	Loggia
Title	Terrace
Location	Used before
Street	Elevator
Type	Disabled person friendly
Levels	Gas
Number of rooms	Water
Floor	Sewerage system
Total floors	Heating
Space m2 total	Additional heating
Space m2 living space	Air condition
Year	Ownership
Parking places	Licensed
Energy certificate	Certified
Object reference	Garage
Swap option	Garage places
	Parking places type
	Orientation (NESW)
	Yard/Garden
	Barbicue
	Winter garden
	Pool
	Yard house

since we are not going to be focused on linear model but dominantly on models based on decision trees. Nevertheless, linearity of our data is basically already achieved with steps described in chapter 3.2 where we explained data selection process. Algorithms based on decision trees are completely insensitive to the specific values of features, they react only to their order. This means that we don't have to worry about "non-normality" of our features even if they are present it also means that by further trimming and winsorizing data we could discard information that might be meaningful for our regression problem. Before we got into feature analysis and building models, we needed to perform basic data cleaning steps. Data cleaning was tedious process since is required a lot of data preprocessing steps like splitting data to additional columns, string trimming, cleaning and transforming, number types conversions etc. We were also manually assigning number types of data to otherwise categorical types of data like "Where is apartments: in house/in flat". This and similar data were usually turned in numerical types in form of new variable called "In-house" which allowed us to use in house = 1, in not in house = 1 values. There were many other categorical features like that we manually turned into numerical so we could lessen number of columns. Similar mappings were applied to apartment floors with actual values corresponding to number of floors in apartment. This allowed us to fill missing values with mean value of all floor values.

3.3 Collinearity Problem

Another type of thing to lookout for is collinearity between some of the features. For example, feature "doesn't have heating" is either checked (1) or not (0) which would mean there is some kind of heating in apartment or there isn't. There is also "type of heating" feature which contains all possible types of heating options. So, in case that "doesn't have heating" feature is 0 it automatically means that all "type of heating" feature options would be 0 which means that there is direct collinearity which needs to be removed from features since some algorithms would not work properly with it. Decision trees are immune to collinearity and multi-collinearity. If we have for example 2 features which are 99% correlated, when deciding upon a split the tree will choose only one of them. Other models such as Logistic regression would use both the features so they would have problem called Dummy Variable Trap. The Dummy Variable trap is a scenario in which the independent variables are multicollinear - a scenario in which two or more variables are highly correlated; in simple terms one variable can be predicted from the others. This can produce singularity of a model, meaning model won't work. But since boosted trees (Gradient Boosting and XGBoost) use individual decision trees, they also are unaffected by multi-collinearity. However, it is a good practice to remove any redundant features from any dataset used for training, irrespective of the model's algorithm.

4   Data Exploratory Analysis and Feature Selection

Most important part of data exploratory analysis is feature correlation, especially in regard with price.

Figure 1 show feature correlation between most important features. Strongest correlation was between apartment size () and number of rooms and price but significant correlation was present between price and ad title length (0.13) which signifies that more expensive objects are usually more thoroughly described in title by ad owners.

Which can on other hand probably mean that ads were created by professional agency. Table 2 shows other relevant correlations many of which are including specific city regions since correlations where tested after we created dummy variables for categorical values (Fig. 2).

We have used sklearn ensemble class for feature selection which includes ensemble-based methods for classification, regression and anomaly detection and for that purpose we have used an Extra-trees classifier. This class implements a meta estimator that fits a

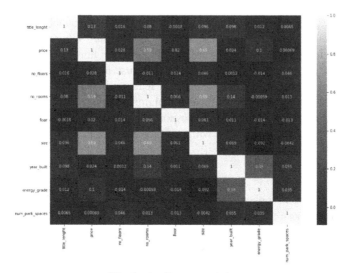

Fig. 1. Attribute correlation

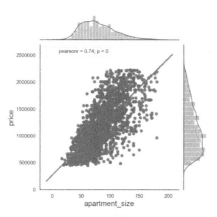

Fig. 2. Apartment size and price correlation (p = 0 is approximations since p is very low)

number of randomized decision trees (a.k.a. extra-trees) on various sub-samples of the dataset and uses averaging to improve the predictive accuracy and control over-fitting. This class implements method for feature importance which returns array with shape of n_features. The values of this array sum to 1, unless all trees are single node trees consisting of only the root node, in which case it will be an array of zeros. This is usual method of extracting features for predictive modeling. This method got us list of most important features which were: size in square meters, year of building, floor, number of rooms, number of floors, energy grade, location and possession of elevator, air conditioning, balcony, terrace and pool.

Table 2. Highest correlation for first 20 attributes

Attributes match	Correlation	Attributes match	Correlation
cityprt_pescenica vs price	− 0.126858	M2 vs price	0.732671
cityptr_podsused_vr vs price	− 0.116629	rooms vs price	0.591136
energy_calss vs price	0.107672	city vs price	0.220293
ctiyprt_crnomerec vs price	0.086252	cutyprt_nzgi vs price	− 0.193652
terrace vs price	0.086207	cityprt_dgrad vs price	0.170374
pool vs price	0.074356	cityprt_maksimir vs price	0.148492
cityprt_gdubrava vs price	− 0.057596	cityprt_nzgz vs price	− 0.146647
other vs price	− 0.049950	ctiyprt_podsljeme vs price	0.133797
balcony vs price	0.046320	cityprt_sesvete vs price	− 0.131062
cityprt_dubrava vs price	− 0.041156	cityprt_stenjevec vs price	− 0.127690

5 Machine Learning Models Evaluation

Number of machine learning models were tested in order to find best possible match. In our analysis presented here we'll focus on explaining how we approached usage and implementation of XGBoost algorithm options and decision trees regression models in general. Other algorithms were presented as mere comparison with XGBoost. All models were cross validated except linear regression. Authors are aware that linear regression without regularization is not acceptable model, but for our case we just wanted to display key metrics for pure (plain ordinary least squares) linear regression for the sake of comparison. Gradient Boosting and AdaBoost regressor were implemented as well with implementation of parameter cross validation. We have used the root mean squared error (RMSE) performance metric to check the performance of the trained models on the test set and R^2 (coefficient of determination) regression score function. Best possible score is 1.0 and it can be negative (because the model can be arbitrarily worse). A constant model that always predicts the expected value of y, disregarding the input features, would get a R^2 score of 0.0. Another definition or R^2 is "(total variance explained by model)/total variance." therefore we can call it variance score of model. Table 3 Shows final machine learning models comparison.

Table 3. Final machine learning models comparison

Model	Description	RMSE HRK	Variance	Rank
XGBoost - manual parameter tuning with cross validation	XG Boost Individual parameter tuning	176.500	0,83	1
Gradient Boosting	Best model after cross validation	177.321	0,83	2
AdaBoost Regressor	Best model after cross validation	180.306	0,82	3
XGBoost with GridSearchCV	Hyperparameter Tuning with GridSearchCV	184.345	0,82	4
XGBoost - basic	Basic automatic tuning	215.011	0,75	5
Linear regression	Plain Ordinary Least Squares (scipy.linalg.lstsq) wrapped as a predictor object	227.673	0,72	6
Decision Tree Regression	Best model after cross validation	252.677	0,65	7
KNN Regression	Best model after cross validation	253.218	0,65	8

In following chapters we'll focus on explaining of result obtained by using various techniques with XGBoost algorithm. We will also learn some of the common tuning parameters which XGBoost provides in order to improve the model's performance.

5.1 XGBoost Automatic Tuning

XGBoost builds model using trees as base learners (they are actually default base learners) using XGBoost's scikit-learn compatible API. XGBoost is an optimized distributed gradient boosting library designed to be highly efficient, flexible and portable. It implements machine learning algorithms under the Gradient Boosting framework. XGBoost provides a parallel tree boosting (also known as GBDT, GBM) that solve many data science problems in a fast and accurate way. The same code runs on major distributed environment (Hadoop, SGE, MPI) and can solve problems beyond billions of examples. In our first step we have implemented automatic tuning to see what performance XGBoost will achieve. In automatic mode algorithm is trying to find best model exhaustively from a collection of possible parameter values across multiple parameters simultaneously. For our given case training lasted about 1.5 h with final variance score of 75% and RMSE of 215.011 kn.

5.2 Automatic Hyperparameter Tuning with GridSearchCV

Our next step is implementation of automated search for best parameters which is usually done with GridSearchCV class.

Most common parameters that we can tune are:

- learning_rate: step size shrinkage used to prevent overfitting. Range is [0,1]
- max_depth: determines how deeply each tree is allowed to grow during any boosting round (more than 6 usually might cause overfitting)
- subsample: percentage of samples used per tree. Low value can lead to underfitting.
- colsample_bytree: percentage of features used per tree. High value can lead to overfitting.
- n_estimators: number of trees you want to build.
- objective: determines the loss function to be used like reg:linear for regression problems, reg:logistic for classification problems with only decision, binary:logistic for classification problems with probability (XGBoost also supports regularization parameters to penalize models as they become more complex and reduce them to simple (parsimonious) models)
- gamma: controls whether a given node will split based on the expected reduction in loss after the split. A higher value leads to fewer splits. Supported only for tree-based learners.
- alpha: L1 regularization on leaf weights. A large value leads to more regularization.
- lambda: L2 regularization on leaf weights and is smoother than L1 regularization.

In order to build more robust models, it is common to do a k-fold cross validation where all the entries in the original training dataset are used for both training as well as validation. Also, each entry is used for validation just once. XGBoost supports k-fold cross validation via the cv() method. We have to specify the nfolds parameter, which is the number of cross validation sets we want to build. Also, it supports other tunable parameters like:

- num_boost_round: denotes the number of trees we build (analogous to n_estimators)
- early_stopping_rounds: finishes training of the model early if the hold-out metric ("rmse" in our case) does not improve for a given number of rounds.

We've used two scikit-learn packages for hyperparameter tuning: GridSearchCV[1] and StratifiedKFold[2]. The first one is here to test out every specific combination of parameters we choose. The second one splits the data into n folds and trains the model n times, each time choosing different fold to be for testing. This prevents overfitting. We have used 12 splits (folds). There are lot of combinations, so training took approximately two hours for our given dataset. We have used following initial parameters combination as fllows.

We were tuning six most dominating parameters that are usually tuned and which have most significant effect on prediction model. We have used following values as startup values:

---

[1] https://scikit-learn.org/stable/modules/generated/sklearn.model_selection.GridSearchCV.html.

[2] https://scikit-learn.org/stable/modules/generated/sklearn.model_selection.StratifiedKFold.html.

```
params_grid =
{
"max_depth": [1, 2, 3, 4, 5, 6],
"n_estimators": [10, 25, 50, 100, 200],
"learning_rate": [0.001, 0.1, 0.25, 0.5],
"min_child_weight": [1, 3, 5, 7],
"gamma": [0.0, 0.1, 0.2, 0.3, 0.4],
"colsample_bytree": [0.3, 0.4, 0.5, 0.7]
}
```

Tuning each new parameter with their own corresponding value would exponentially increase training time therefore we opted to tune these six parameters. In next iterations after obtaining better results we tried to fine-tune certain parameter by changing parameter range around best obtained value from previous training. After several iteration of training for all parameters we have obtained final results.Best accuracy obtained was 0.8156 using parameters: colsample_bytree: 0.5; gamma: 0.0; learning_rate: 0.1; max_depth: 6; min_child_weight: 1; n_estimators: 200.

5.3 XGBoost with Individual Sets of Parameters Tuning with Cross Validation

With individual tuning method we are not going to do GridSearchCV which takes a lot of time but we'll try manually fine tune pairs of parameters which can be fine-tuned together and therefore testing for various combinations can yield results much faster.

However, this method doesn't allow us to change other parameters but we are keeping them fixed while tuning only pair of parameters. Each time we fine tune some parameter or set of parameters we will store them in parameters list and use it for fine tuning other parameters. We started with cross validating tuning of max_depth and min_child_weight parameters. Those parameters add constraints on the architecture of the trees. Max_depth is the maximum number of nodes allowed from the root to the farthest leaf of a tree. Deeper trees can model more complex relationships by adding more nodes, but as we go deeper, splits become less relevant and are sometimes only due to noise, causing the model to overfit. min_child_weight is the minimum weight (or number of samples if all samples have a weight of 1) required in order to create a new node in the tree. A smaller min_child_weight allows the algorithm to create children that correspond to fewer samples, thus allowing for more complex trees, but again, more likely to overfit. Thus, those parameters can be used to control the complexity of the trees. It is important to tune them first and tune them together in order to find a good trade-off between model bias and variance. In similar manner we have tuned other parameters and cross-validated results after testing of each parameter combination which gave us best sets of individual parameters. Respecting the order in which parameters where tuned we managed to get best results with final XGBoost RMSE 176500 and variance score of 83%.

5.4 Predicted vs Real Chart for XGBoost

Final XGBoost RMSE (176500) is little bit better than classical Gradient Boosting (177321) with equal variance score of 0.83. It's also worth noting that we got better results than with hyperparameter tuning with GridSearchCV where RMSE was 184345 and variance score 0.82. Our case is simple one where we found out that for classical gradient boosting might actually be faster to implement than XGBoost automatic GridSearchCV training with standard parameters (Fig. 3).

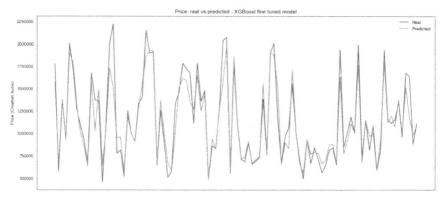

Fig. 3. Model final results (real vs predicted)

6 Conclusion

In this paper we have used several machine learning algorithms to develop a prediction model for apartment prices. We test for the performance of these techniques by measuring how accurately a technique can predict whether the closing price is greater than or less than the actual price. Following machine learning algorithms where used: Gradient Boosting, AdaBoost, Decision Trees, KNN, Linear regression and XGBoost. Selected algorithms where tested for which algorithm gives lowest error while predicting. We find that the performance of XGBoost is superior but only if fine-tuned manually. We can conclude that further research could be focused on defining specific business use cases and creating automated fine-tuning procedure for individual case such as real-estate market predictions for various real-estate objects. For such cases we can assume that algorithm like XGBoost could be more quickly fine-tuned and therefore much faster deployed in real world environment. Due to fact that there are no official registers of real estate prices that can be accessed for research or statistics purposes, market is supported by several web portals specialized for real estate. Being at the same time interested in their primary business (real estate agents) such statistics can be biased without relevant and larger data sample and validation. Understanding mechanics and dynamics of real estate market, understanding similarities and trend is one of the problems faced by the real estate market participants. Monitoring real estate prices is a more complex problem as portals are using freeform texts which are difficult to compare and also has a hierarchical structure containing different sections.

Acknowledgement. To conclude this research we were using data sample from most popular ecommerce site Njuskalo (https://www.njuskalo.hr/).

References

1. Mukhlishin, M.F., Saputra, R., Wibowo, A.: Predicting house sale price using fuzzy logic, artificial neural network and K-nearest neighbor. In: IEEE 2017 1st International Conference on Informatics and Computational Sciences (ICICoS) - Semarang, Indonesia 15–16 November 2017 (2017). https://doi.org/10.1109/icicos.2017.8276357
2. Park, B., Bae, J.K.: Using machine learning algorithms for housing price prediction: the case of fairfax county, Virginia housing data (2015). https://doi.org/10.1016/j.eswa.2014.11.040
3. Geltner, D., de Neufville, R.: Real estate price dynamics and the value of flexibility. SSRN Electron. J. (2017). https://doi.org/10.2139/ssrn.2998832
4. Edelstein, R., Liu, P., Wu, F.: The market for real estate presales: a theoretical approach. J. Real Estate Financ. Econ. **45**(1) (2012). https://doi.org/10.1007/s11146-011-9318-z
5. Kaplanski, G., Levy, H.: Real estate prices: an international study of seasonality's sentiment effect. J. Empir. Financ. **19**(1) (2012). https://doi.org/10.1016/j.jempfin.2011.11.004
6. Scott, L.O.: Do prices reflect market fundamentals in real estate markets?. J. Real Estate Financ. Econ. **3**(1) (1990). https://doi.org/10.1007/bf00153703
7. Salnikov, V.A., Mikheeva, O.M.: Models for predicting prices in the Moscow residential real estate market. Stud. Russ. Econo. Dev. **29**(1) (2018). https://doi.org/10.1134/S1075700718010136
8. Sternik, G.M., Sternik, S.G.: Mass estimation of real estate on the basis of discrete space-parametrical modeling of the market (on an example of townhouses of the western sector of near Moscow suburbs), Otsenochnaya Deyat. No. 2, pp. 22–27 (2010)

Music Classification by Automated Relevance Feedbacks

Ja-Hwung Su[1], Tzung-Pei Hong[2,3]([✉]), and Hsuan-Hao Yeh[3]

[1] Department of Information Management, Cheng Shiu University, Kaohsiung, Taiwan
[2] Department of Computer Science and Information Engineering,
National University of Kaohsiung, Kaohsiung, Taiwan
tphong@nuk.edu.tw
[3] Department of Computer Science and Engineering, National Sun Yat-sen University,
Kaohsiung, Taiwan

Abstract. Music recognition systems help users and music platform developers analyze what genre a music piece belongs to. In this paper, we propose an effective automatic music recognition system to help developers effectively tag music with genres. First, we extract Mel-Frequency Cepstral Coefficients (MFCCs) as the basic features. We then transform MFCCs into a set of conceptual features by Support Vector Machine (SVM). By the conceptual features, a automatic relevance feedback method is performed to generate a navigation model, which can be viewed as a recognition model. In the recognition phase, the proposed approach, called music classification by navigation paths (MCNP) uses these conceptual features to recognize the unknown music. The experimental results show that the proposed method is more promising than the state-of-the-arts on music classification.

Keywords: Music recognition · Acoustic features · Conceptual features · Relevance feedback

1 Introduction

Music is a part of life for most people around the world. Listening to music can relieve stress and reduce anxiety. However, music media devices have changed significantly with time. There are basically two ways to listen to music. One is to download the music to a personal device and then listen to it using apps or built-in music players. The other is to use an audio streaming platform such as Spotify or iTunes: this method is becoming more and more popular. This raises important issues for streaming platforms. For platform developers, efficiently and automatically tagging music genres is challenging. For users, how to efficiently find music they would like to listen to is also a challenge. Given the above concerns, what we need is to efficiently and accurately recognize music pieces.

Due to the popularity of digital music and the advanced development of mobile devices, demand has increased for music. Sometimes, people do not understand what a specific music genre is because the information is rarely included within the metadata for music pieces. Thus, experts are needed to tag music pieces with specific genres

© Springer Nature Singapore Pte Ltd. 2020
P. Sitek et al. (Eds.): ACIIDS 2020, CCIS 1178, pp. 25–34, 2020.
https://doi.org/10.1007/978-981-15-3380-8_3

on streaming platforms. To reduce the cost of manual tags, we here develop a system based on auto-classification to help platform developers classify large amounts of music efficiently and to help users understand music pieces genre. In addition, modern music recognition tasks and classifiers are still limited by what is termed the semantic gap, which describes the gap between music and the features extracted from music. This is what causes low accuracies in music recognition tasks. We propose novel features that take this problem into account. To solve these problems, we propose conceptual features (CF), a new kind of feature generated by any machine learning algorithm based on result probability and an efficient classifier based on navigation paths (NP) which is proposed to improve efficiency and effectiveness on genre classification tasks. NP tracks all music pieces in the database to iteratively produce automatic relevance feedback. The proposed approach is called music classification by navigation paths (MCNP).

2 Related Work

- Relevance feedback

Relevance feedback (RF) has been studied for a long time. RF is a mechanism that yields improved accuracy using iterative feedback. The basic notion of RF is to improve the accuracy or efficiency of retrieval using human judgment, a score calculated by a formula, or a set of system outputs. One RF method is query point movement (QPM). In QPM, a query on the feature space always moves to where the most relevant music is. For the detailed updating formula for QPM, refering to Rocchio [5]. Further, Su et al. [7] proposed an approach that realized the practice direction of using query notion and Chen [2] also proposed the model based QPM for music retrieval. Su et al. [8] proposed a fast music retrieval by using advanced acoustic features.

- Music Recognition and Classification

Linear discriminant analysis (LDA) is based on finding the linear transformation that best discriminates among classes. An early paper by Alexandre-Cortizo et al. in 2005 adopts LDA to classify speech and music using only two kinds of audio [1]. Their work shows preliminary results on the application of linear discriminant analysis. Support vector machines (SVMs) have long been a popular classification algorithm. The basic idea of SVM is to consider every example as a point in a hyperspace whose dimension depends on the number of attributes in the example. The focus is to find a hyperplane that separates the examples into their corresponding hyperspaces through mathematical models. SVM has been used in the context of genre classification [4, 10]. LIBSVM by Chang and Lin [9] is a simple, easy-to-use, and efficient tool for SVM classification. In the proposed approach, we adopt LIBSVM as our SVM classifier for conceptual features generation. Su et al. [6] presented a music classifier to classify the music by a progressive learning.

3   Proposed Method

To solve problems of semantic gap, in this paper, we propose a method named "music classification by navigation paths (MCNP)", a classifier based on automatic relevance feedbacks. As shown in Fig. 1, the proposed method can be divided into three phases, namely preprocessing phase, training phase and recognition phase.

- Preprocessing Phase

    The goal of this phase is to transform the low-level audio features into high-level conceptual features.

- Training Phase

    The goal of this phase is to construct a recognition model by the conceptual features and relevance feedbacks.

- Recognition Phase

    The goal of this paper is to classify the unknown music by the conceptual features and recognition model.

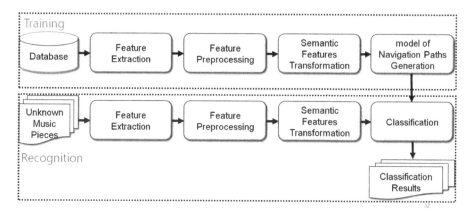

Fig. 1. Framework of proposed method.

3.1   Preprocessing Phase

MFCCs are first extracted as the basic features for comparison. Figure 2 shows the correspondence between frames and time in a music piece. Each frame corresponds to 20 ms to 30 ms of music and a n-dimension feature vector (where n is 26). To facilitate the use of these MFCCs features for classification, we use the following preprocessing. The first technique used is averaging. The feature matrix is transformed into a feature vector by averaging each column. The second technique is normalization. Normalization is a simple way to constrain all the data in a database to the range [0, 1]. Here we describe conceptual features (termed CF below). In this paper, conceptual features (lowercase) are a set of features produced by an CF model.

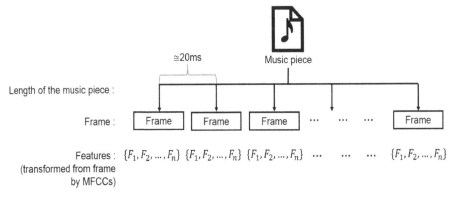

Fig. 2. The expected scenario of the progressive learning strategy.

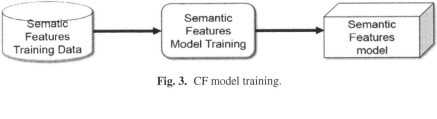

Fig. 3. CF model training.

Fig. 4. CF generation

Before this process, we must choose a specific classifier as a base with which to train the CF model: here we choose SVM as an example. In addition, because the CF model needs a training dataset, we need CF training data and classification training data. Figure 3 shows the first step of conceptual features: the CF training data is used to train the CF model, which is SVM model. This process mirrors that of the general classifier training process. Next, as shown in Fig. 4, the resultant CF model is used to generate conceptual features and the input classification training data. The CF generation process mirrors that of a classifier's classification process, but our purpose is to utilize the genre classification probabilities as features to represent the data. A set of conceptual features is defined in Definition 1.

Definition 1 (A set of conceptual features). Let n be the number of genres, and let the probabilities of every genre of the classification result be P_j for $j \in \{1, 2, \ldots, n\}$ A set of semantic features CFs is defined as a vector of P_j as

$$SFs = < P_1, P_2, \cdots, P_{n-1}, P_n > \tag{1}$$

$$\forall j \in \{1, 2, \ldots, n\}, P_j \in [0, 1] \wedge \sum_{j=1}^{n} P_j = 1 \tag{2}$$

3.2 Training Phase

In the training phase, the NP model generates a set of navigation paths. As shown in Fig. 5, a path is composed of chunks of feedback information, each of which consists of a number of positive and negative music pieces. Here, positive ones indicate that their genres are the same as that of the query (QP_1); the others are negative. In this paper, we distinguish between the Navigation Path (NP) approach and navigation path (lowercase) paths generated by the model.

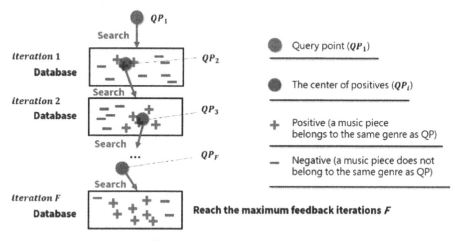

Fig. 5. Navigation path generation.

3.3 Training Phase

This is a fundamental but critical phase in this paper. Without successful training, the high quality of music classification is not easy to achieve. Basically, this phase can further be split into two steps, including generation of advanced features and construction of learning models. In the followings, this phase will be described step by step. Each music piece in the classification training dataset is used as a query point (QP_1), yielding a navigation path. The NP generation process consists of F iterations. In the first iteration, all other music pieces in the classification training dataset are located by comparing the

Euclidean-distance-based similarity between QP_1 and the classification training data as defined in Definition 2. The similarity measure used in the NP training and recognition phases is Euclidean distance, which is a simple way to represent the distance between two vectors or tensors in a hyperspace.

Definition 2 (Euclidean Distance). Let A and B be vectors in n-dimensional space; the Euclidean distance between A and B, $ED(A, B)$, is defined as

$$A = \{A_1, A_2, .., A_n\} \tag{3}$$

$$B = \{B_1, B_2, .., B_n\} \tag{4}$$

$$ED(A, B) = \sqrt[2]{\sum_{i=1}^{n} (A_i - B_i)^2} \tag{5}$$

First, the top-R music pieces are located with the highest similarities to QP_1. Of these, those that belong to the same genre as QP_1 are taken to be positive points, as represented by the plus marks in Fig. 4; otherwise, they are negative points, represented by the minus marks. The positives can be regarded as automatic relevance feedback for a search query (in the first iteration, QP_1). Then we take the averaged center of the positives as the query point for the next iteration. We expect the center to be more representative of the genre to which QP_1 belongs. Thus this center is QP_2 in the first iteration, the query point for the second iteration. The center of positives is defined below in Definition 3. It can be regarded as a virtual query generated as the arithmetic mean of positives.

Definition 3 (Center of positives). Let C is a center of positives (a virtual query generated by this process): there are n genres and p positives in this iteration. The SFs of the positives are $PSFs_i, i \in \{1, 2, \cdots, p\}$. The center of positives C is defined as

$$PSFs_i = \{PSF_{i1}, PSF_{i2}, \ldots, PSF_{in}\} \tag{6}$$

$$C = < CSF_1, CSF_2, \cdots, CSF_{n-1}, CSF_n > \tag{7}$$

$$\forall CSF_j, j \in \{1, 2, \cdots, n\}$$

$$CSF_j = \frac{\sum_{i=1}^{p} PSF_{ij}}{p} \tag{8}$$

This technique yields increasingly accurate virtual queries that represent the genre of the root query (QP_1). The sets of new queries generated by Definition 3 are recorded and used in the recognition phase. The new queries of all feedback chunks are the set of centers of the navigation path. In the next iteration, the query point is the new query (QP_2) and the same process is used until the preset maximum F-th iteration, at which point the process ends and the navigation path is complete. In our experiments, F was set to 6.

3.4 Recognition Phase

In the recognition phase, navigation paths are used to classify what genre an unknown music piece belongs to. Two kinds of sets of conceptual features are jointly used for classification via late fusion (also called co-training). Before describing navigation paths and late fusion, we describe music classification by navigation paths (MCNP), that is, navigation paths without late fusion. First, the unknown music piece is compared with the end center of each path C included in the NP tuples $<R, C, P>$, yielding the top-N paths with the highest similarity to the unknown music piece.

Next, for each genre, we count the number of positives in all paths (all positives in each P of the top-N paths; note that if there are repeated positives in different P sets of top-N paths, these positives are repeatedly counted) retrieved in the previous step. Finally, we take as the prediction result that genre with the largest number of positives. However, this approach uses only one kind of conceptual feature, we call this approach music classification by navigation paths (MCNP).

Table 1. Experimental data.

Type	Genre
Instrumental	Piano, saxophone, erhu, flute, harmonica, guitar, symphony, techno, zheng, violin, drum, soundtracks, harp, dulcimer, lounge music
Vocal	Rock, classical chorus, rap, disco dance, vocal, country, pop, latin, folk, blues, jazz, new age, metal, r&b, children's music

4 Experiments

All experiments were implemented in C++, and executed on a PC Intel® Core™ i5-3230 M CPU @ 2.60 GHz with 8 GB RAM. All music data used in the experiments were collected from the web and from CDs, and included 30 genres, of which 15 were purely instrumental and the remaining 15 included human singing. These genres are shown in Table 1 and the compared methods are shown in Table 2.

In the experiments, there were 30 genres G and 1500 music pieces in the *Music* corpus; thus each specific genre was represented by 50 pieces of music. The corpus was divided into three parts: *S_Train* (450 pieces) for CF model training, *NP_Train* (600 pieces) for navigation path generation, and *NP_test* (450 pieces) for MCFNP classification. *NP_Train* and *NP_test* were also used for the other compared approaches for 2-fold cross validation. Note that every such partition included a balanced amount of music for each genre. For example, as *NP_Train* included a total of 600 pieces, there were 20 pieces per genre for all 30 genres.

Table 2. Definitions of the compared methods.

Method	Name
BayesNet	BN
DecisionTree (C4.5)	DT
AdaBoost-DecisionTree (C4.5)	ADT
Support Vector Machine	SVM
RandomForest	RF
Music Classification by Navigation Paths	MCNP

In the comparisons, we chose 12 state-of-the-art classifiers as baselines to evaluate the effectiveness of the proposed approaches. The evaluation measure used in these experiments is accuracy. All machine learning approaches compared in this work were implemented as Java-based Weka packages, except SVM, for which we used Chang and Lin's LIBSVM [10] based on both C++ and Java sources. The deep learning approaches were implemented using the python-based Tensorflow. Owing to the considerable impact of different structures in deep learning approaches, we describe the structures of the deep learning approaches here. The neural network (NN) used here was composed of 2 hidden layers, each of which had 25 nodes. For the NN, the learning rate was set to 0.1, the learning step was set to 1000, softmax was used as the activation function, and Adam was used as the optimizer.

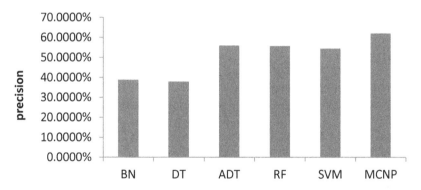

Fig. 6. Comparison with state-of-the-art classifiers.

Note that all machine learning methods used the acoustic features (MFCCs) as model inputs. In contrast, for the convolutional neural network (CNN) we did not use MFCCs, as CNNs require image or matrix input rather than acoustic features. For the CNN experiments, we followed Costa et al. [3] and transformed the music into spectrograms as the image inputs of the CNN model. We used the VGG16 structure for CNN: 16 2D-convolutional layers and 3 fully connected layers.

Figure 6 shows the experimental results. We observe that the proposed approaches significantly outperformed the state-of-the-art approaches. Among these, LDA also significantly outperformed other approaches. We note also that although the NN performance was slightly lower than other machine learning methods, it was still acceptable, surpassing that of VGG16. This was due to the difference in inputs. NN is a deep learning approach that still uses acoustic features as input, but CNN is not. This difference may lead to recognition difficulties even if VGG16 is a complex CNN structure.

5 Conclusion

Content-based music recognition has gained attention due to the popularity of audio streaming platforms. From a developer's point of view, especially, given the digital circulation of music, more people are becoming used to listening to music on audio streaming platforms rather than downloading music. Thus, music genres have become key to representing user preferences. An automatic and efficient recognition system would reduce the costs associated with manual tagging of music pieces by experts. In this paper, we propose music classification by navigation paths (MCNP), a music classifier based on automatic relevance feedback and navigation paths (NP). Additionally, we propose conceptual features and the more advanced music classification by fused navigation paths (MCFNP). We propose conceptual features to take the conceptual gap into account. Conceptual features can be regarded as conceptual features generated by a classifier. We propose navigation paths to improve classifiers often used in music recognition. Based on automatic relevance feedback, NPs make the system better by labeling related pieces in a music database as positives and calculating the center to determine a virtual music piece that well represents the target piece's genre. We also propose MCFNP, which further improves performance by combining NPs derived from two different kinds of conceptual features. Experiments show that MCFNP achieves higher music recognition accuracy than 5 state-of-the-art classifiers. In the future, there remain a number of works to do. First, more methods such as ResNet, Convolutional Neural Network and so on will be compared. Second, it will be mater materialized in real applications. Third, the proposed idea will be applied other multimedia data applications.

Acknowledgement. This research was supported by Ministry of Science and Technology, Taiwan, R.O.C. under grant no. MOST 107-2221-E-230-010.

References

1. Alexandre-Cortizo, E., Rosa-Zurera, M., Lopes-Ferreras, F.: Application of fisher linear discriminant analysis to speech/music classification. In: Proceedings of the International Conference on Computer as a Tool, Serbia (2005)
2. Chen, Y.T.: Music retrieval by learning from automated logs with semantic features. National Sun Yat-sen University (2017)
3. Costa, U.M.G., Oliveira, L.S., Silla Jr., C.N.: An evaluation of convolutional neural networks for music classification using spectrograms. Appl. Soft Comput. **52**, 28–38 (2017)

4. Lidy, T., Rauber, A.: Evaluation of feature extractors and psycho-acoustic transformations for music genre classification. In: Proceedings of the 6th International Conference on Music Information Retrieval (ISMIR), UK, pp. 34–41 (2005)

5. Rocchio, J.J.: Relevance feedback in information retrieval. In: Proceedings of the SMART Retrieval System – Experiment in Automatic Document Processing, pp. 313–323. Prentice-Hall (1971)

6. Su, J.H., Chin, C.Y., Hong, T.P., Su, J.J.: Content-based music classification by advanced features and progressive learning. In: Proceedings of the 11th Asian Conference on Intelligent Information and Database Systems, Yogyakarta, Indonesia, 8–11 April 2019

7. Su, J.H., Huang, W.J., Yu, P.S., Tseng, V.S.: Efficient relevance feedback for content-based image retrieval by mining user navigation patterns. IEEE Trans. Knowl. Data Eng. **23**(3), 360–372 (2011)

8. Su, J.H., Hong, T.P., Chen, Y.T.: Fast music retrieval with advanced acoustic features. In: Proceedings of IEEE International Conference on Consumer Electronics, Taipei, Taiwan (2017)

9. Xu, C., Maddage, N.C., Shao, X., Cao, F., Tian, Q.: Musical genre classification using support vector machines. In: Proceedings of IEEE International Conference on Acoustics, Speech, and Signal Processing, Hong Kong (2003)

10. http://www.csie.ntu.edu.tw/~cjlin/libsvm

Exploiting CBOW and LSTM Models to Generate Trace Representation for Process Mining

Hong-Nhung Bui[1,2(✉)], Trong-Sinh Vu[2,3], Hien-Hanh Nguyen[4], Tri-Thanh Nguyen[1], and Quang-Thuy Ha[1]

[1] Vietnam National University, Hanoi (VNU), VNU-University of Engineering and Technology (UET), Hanoi, Vietnam
nhungbth@hvnh.edu.vn, {ntthanh,thuyhq}@vnu.edu.vn
[2] Banking Academy of Vietnam, Hanoi, Vietnam
[3] Japan Advanced Institute of Science and Technology (JAIST), School of Information Science, Nomi, Japan
sinhvtr@jaist.ac.jp
[4] Foreign Trade University, Hanoi, Vietnam
hienhanh22@yahoo.com

Abstract. In the field of process mining, one of the challenges of the trace representation problem is to exploit a lot of potentially useful information within the traces while keeping a low dimension of the corresponding vector space. Motivated by the initial results of applying the deep neural networks for producing trace representation, in this paper, we continue to study and apply two more advanced models of deep learning, i.e., Continuous Bag of Words and Long short-term memory, for generating the trace representation. The experimental results have achieved significant improvement, i.e., not only showing the close relationship between the activities in a trace but also helping to reduce the dimension of trace representation.

Keywords: Process mining · Trace representation · Trace clustering · Deep learning · CBOW · LSTM

1 Introduction

Today's information systems are increasing in both scale and data. Most businesses deploy their own information systems to manage and operate the business processes, such as business management, customer relationship management, supply chain management, etc. The information about the activities, transactions of users when working with the information system is automatically saved in the event log which can provide a great deal of insights into the activities that have been carried out in the production and business processes.

A new data mining branch has arrived, i.e., *process mining* with three problems: *process discovery*, *process conformance*, and *process enhancement* using the useful information stored in the event logs to build a process model, identify process habits, check

© Springer Nature Singapore Pte Ltd. 2020
P. Sitek et al. (Eds.): ACIIDS 2020, CCIS 1178, pp. 35–46, 2020.
https://doi.org/10.1007/978-981-15-3380-8_4

compliance, identify implicit relationships or bottlenecks in processes. Such information can help to adjust and improve the business processes so that they can operate better in reality [1]. These processes will be updated back into the software system, forming an increasingly completely continuous life cycle that is always valuable to contribute to the addition of business process resources.

Process discovery is the first problem in process mining and has important direct effects on the two other problems, i.e., process conformance and process enhancement. Using an event log that recodes users' activity information when interacting with the information system as input data, process discovery can automatically generate a process model that accurately reflects the actual business activities that are taking place in the enterprise. This is very useful information to help businesses control their activities and have interesting insights about their actual business processes.

The quality of the generated process model depends heavily on the uniformity of the input event log; however, in practice, the execution processes are often highly flexible, and the number of records is large, so the corresponding event logs may be inconsistent, containing several different cases in the same process that are difficult to handle. Even if it can be processed, the process model received is very complex, difficult to read or understand, and misleading because it tries to merge unrelated cases in a single model [2]. Different procedures may occur in any business, such as medical, insurance, banking, aviation, etc. For example, in the medical field, the diagnosis and treatment process of patients requires coping capacity with unforeseen circumstances. Therefore, the implementation of the same process model can vary significantly, resulting in heterogeneity in the event log.

One approach to overcome this is that, instead of generating a large process model from all the traces in the event log to explain everything, the traces are grouped into a set of clusters, and sub-process models are generate from this set of sub-clusters. Therefore, sub-process models are created with easy-to-understand and easy-to-analyze analysis with high quality and low structural complexity (Fig. 1). Trace clustering is considered

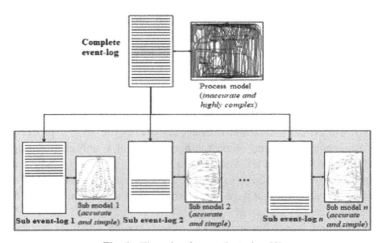

Fig. 1. The role of trace clustering [8]

to be a simple, flexible and effective method that reduces the complexity of the process detection problem [3–7].

One of the factors affecting the quality of the cluster problem is the trace representation method. Traditional trace representation methods describe the connection and relationship between trace elements. However, this relationship is expressed simply as binary numbers 0, 1 or integers, which are the frequency of occurrence of these relationships, and the representation space has a relatively large number of dimensions. In this paper, we propose two new representation methods using two advanced techniques in deep learning, i.e., Continuous Bag of Words (CBOW) and Long short-term memory (LSTM). The relationship between the elements in the trace is captured and described by the actual values in the range from 0 to 1, showing the different influence level of each element. The global optimization of CBOW and LSTM will better assign the weight of each activity in a trace, hence, the clustering will produce better results. In addition, the spatial representation space size and the quality of generated process model are also significantly improved.

The rest of this paper is organized as follows: In Sect. 2, we introduce some trace representation methods. In Sect. 3, the application of CBOW and LSTM model for trace representation are presented. Section 4 provides the experimental results. Finally, Sect. 5 shows some conclusions and future work.

2   Traditional Trace Representation Methods

Trace is a shortened representation of the event log, which only interested in the activity of events. A trace includes a set of events, having the same "case id", and ordered by timestamp.

There are some available approaches for trace representation, such as bag-of-activities, k-grams, maximal repeats, distance graph, compact trace [11]. Each trace representation method will describe the different relationship between the activities. The best representation method is one that both increases the relationship between the activities and reduces the dimension of the vector space.

Bag-of-activities method presents the appearance of activities without preserving the relationship between them in term of activity order. k-grams can preserve the order of k consecutive activities in a trace. Maximal repeats describe the relationship in term of a sequence of activities that always occur together in the event log. Distance graph can describe the order relationship between the two activities in the trace with a certain activity distance. Compact trace is a modern trace representation method using deep neural networks to generate compact representation.

Among the above performing methods, bag-of-activities and compact traces have low dimensions while the remaining methods have relatively large dimensions.

3   Deep Learning Application for Trace Representation

3.1   Application of CBOW Model in Trace Representation

CBOW, proposed by Mikolov et al. 2013 [9], is an advanced model of word embedding that is effectively used in natural language processing, especially in text processing.

CBOW is designed as a neural network consisting of 3 layers: 1 input, 1 hidden, and 1 output layers. The model uses surrounding words (previous and after) in a specified size window to predict the word in the middle. The main purpose of the model is to learn the representational weights of the word vectors.

In order to apply the CBOW model to the trace representation problem, we map each trace in the event log corresponding to a sentence in the text; Each activity in a trace corresponds to a word in a sentence.

Suppose that a trace v consists of five activities a, c, e, b and g, i.e., $v = acebg$. The trace activities represented by one-hot vectors having the following values: $a = (1, 0, 0, 0, 0)$; $c = (0, 1, 0, 0, 0)$; $e = (0, 0, 1, 0, 0)$; $b = (0, 0, 0, 1, 0)$; $g = (0, 0, 0, 0, 1)$. To predict activity e with window size $k = 2$, we get context of $2k$ activities $\{a, c, b, g\}$. The training model is designed as follows: An input class X consists of $2k$ elements x_i corresponding to four activities $\{a, c, b, g\}$; a hidden layer H and an output class Y consisting of an element y corresponding to the activity to be predicted e (Fig. 2).

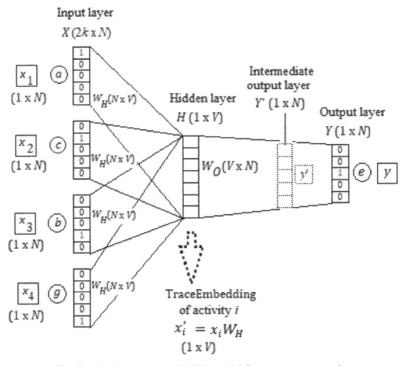

Fig. 2. The idea of using CBOW model for trace representation

At the input layer, the element x_i initially receives the value as a one-hot vector of the size $(1 \times N)$ of its corresponding activity, where N is the number of features in the vector space representing the trace. The initial weight matrix of the input-hidden W_H class is randomly generated with the size of $(N \times V)$, where V is a user defined value.

At the hidden layer, each the input value x_i will be multiplied by the input-hidden layer's weight W_H. The result is a hidden value h_i size $(1 \times V)$ which is calculated by the following formula:

$$h_i = x_i W_H \tag{1}$$

Finally, the hidden value H size $(1 \times V)$ of the hidden layer is calculated as the average of the hidden values h_i :

$$H = \frac{\sum_{i=1}^{2k} h_i}{2k} \tag{2}$$

Then the hidden value H is multiplied by the hidden-output layer's weight W_O, where the initial weight of the hidden-output matrix W_O is randomly generated with size $(V \times N)$. The result will be put it into a softmax function so that the output is a probability vector y' size $(1 \times N)$ which is the intermediate output value by the following formula:

$$y' = LogSoftmax(HW_O) \tag{3}$$

The output layer is a one-hot vector y with dimension $(1 \times N)$ representing activity to predict. The intermediate output value y' will be compared with the output value y of the model, and calculated error, based on this error the model will propagate backwards to update the values of the weight matrices W_H and W_O.

The weight matrix of input-hidden layer W_H after training is used to create trace representation (call *TraceEmbedding*) for activities. Let x_i' be the *TraceEmbedding* representation of the activity corresponding to the element x_i, x_i' calculated using the following formula:

$$x_i' = x_i W_H \tag{4}$$

It is clear that the *TraceEmbedding* x_i' is trained on not only on the information of the activity itself, but also on the information and relationship with its surrounding activities. According to the way the word embedding CBOW model works, input-hidden weight matrix W_H is best trained to transform the input layer x_i (i.e., the activity) from their initial values as binary numbers into real values containing information of the activities around it with the purpose of helping the model to accurately predict the output value y. Thus the amount of information in x_i' is much richer than x_i. Moreover, the size of x_i' is smaller than the size of the original x_i because of $V \ll N$. On the other hand, when using *TraceEmbedding* representation, the input trace is kept as the original list of activities without having to pre-convert to vector format, which also significantly reduces the computation time. This is the motivation for us to propose a new trace representation method named *TraceEmbedding* using CBOW model to improve the quality of trace performance problems, while improving the quality of the generated process model in the process model discovery step.

3.2 Application of LSTM Model in Trace Representation

Long-short term memory (LSTM) was introduced by Hochreiter and Schmidhuber in 1997 [10] and was later improved and popularized by many researchers around the world. LSTM is a special type of Recurrent Neural Network (RNN), which can overcome the problem of not learning RNN's remote dependencies.

The highlight of LSTM is that the cell state runs through all network nodes with linear interactions, so that information can easily be transmitted without loss or change. LSTM can discard or add information groups needed for the cell state, which are automatically regulated by gate groups. The ports in the model are combined by a sigmoid network layer σ and a multiplication that allows the screening of information passing through it. The sigmod layer gives an output within the range [0,1] specifying how much information can pass. A value of 0 means no information is allowed to pass, and a value of 1 means for all the information that goes through it. The gates include: forget gate to decide how much information to get from the previous cell state; input gate to decide how much information to get from the status value and the hidden value from the previous step. An output gate decides how much information to take from the cell state to become the output of the stealth mode. According to the mode of operation of the LSTM model, the input value at time t includes not only information about time t but also important information about the model memorized by the previous $t - 1$.

This advantage of the LSTM model is very suitable for the problem of trace representation in process mining. The activities in a trace are always closely influenced and interact with each other at long distances. An activity that can occur is derived from one or more activities that have taken place in the past. In other words, an activity that takes place is to solve problems that are being handled by previous activities. The existing trace representation methods also describe the relationship between activities in a trace but are usually limited to a defined distance, for example two or three activities before and after it. The LSTM model can learn the smooth relationship between activities in a spot with any distance, even from the beginning. This is the motivation for us to propose a new trace representation method using LSTM model.

To apply the LSTM model for trace representation, we map each activity hd in a trace as the input x of the model. The tth module describes the activity hd_t corresponding to the input x_t. The initial value of x_t is initialized by word embedding method $x_t = embedding(hd_t)$, resulting in a random real vector of size $(1 \times M)$.

Suppose that a trace v consists of five activities: $a, c, e, b,$ and g, i.e., $v = acebg$. The training model is designed to predict the tth activity based on the value x_t and the training information of the previous step $t - 1$ with the structure state t^{th} of the LSTM model is described in Fig. 3.

Input: x_t, h_{t-1}, c_{t-1} where x_t is the input of the state t; h_{t-1} is the output of the previous step; c_{t-1} is the state of previous step.

Output: h_t, c_t where h_t is the hidden state and c_t is the cellular state of state t.

The gates in the LSTM model are implemented as follows:

Forget gate: decides how much information to get from the output of the previous step:

$$f_t = \sigma\left(x_t U_f + h_{t-1} W_f\right) \tag{5}$$

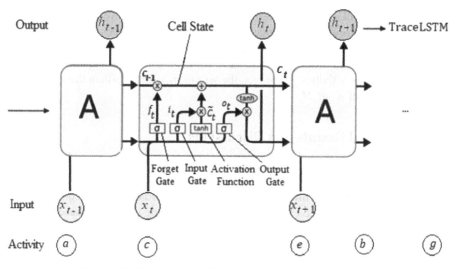

Fig. 3. The idea of using LSTM model for trace representation

Input gate: updates memory with the information about current activity, including *sigmoid* and *tanh* functions:

$$i_t = \sigma(x_t U_i + h_{t-1} W_i) \qquad (6)$$

$$\check{c}_t = tanh(x_t U_c + h_{t-1} W_c) \qquad (7)$$

From information received at the forget and input gates, the model calculates the value of the cell state that stores the selective information of all the activities considered up to now:

$$c_t = f_t c_{t-1} + i_t \check{c}_t \qquad (8)$$

Output gate: decides what the output information h_t that represents for the current activity. This information is combined from two sources, the current output o_t and the current cell state c_t.

$$o_t = \sigma(x_t U_o + h_{t-1} W_o) \qquad (9)$$

$$h_t = o_t tanh(c_t) \qquad (10)$$

The parameters involved in the model include: x_t is a real vector with size $(1 \times M)$ representing the initial activity t^{th}. The weight matrix U is randomly generated with the size of $(M \times K)$. The weight matrix W is randomly generated with the size of $(K \times K)$, where K is a value defined by user.

The hidden value h_t with the size of $(1 \times K)$ carries the information of the current activity and previous activities to pass on to the next operation. This is the mechanism that helps the LSTM model to learn the interrelated relationship between activities, the previous activities will affect the next ones. This mechanism is perfectly similar to the nature of business process implementation. In this paper, we propose the use h_t as a trace representation (called *TraceLSTM*) instead of the original representation x_t of the tth activity with richer information, particularly, in keeping the close and useful relation of hd_t to its previous activities. Moreover, the size of h_t is smaller than the size of the original x_t because of $K \ll M$.

4 Experimental Results and Discussions

4.1 Experimental Method

The paper followed the experimental framework [5] with two new traces representation TraceEmbedding and TraceLSTM. The framework including five steps: Trace processing; Training model; Clustering; Discovering process model and evaluation as described in Fig. 4.

The trace processing step represents the activities in each of the original traces into two data sets in the form of one-hot vectors (for CBOW) and embedding vectors (for LSTM).

Training model step trains two CBOW and LSTM models using PyTorch[1] framework corresponding to two input data sets 1 and 2. The experiments were carried out on Ubuntu 16.04, Python 2.7 with the function: $sigmoid = 1/(1 + e^{-x})$. Other hyperparameters of the model are as follows: learning rate $= 0.005$; iterations $= 10.000$; and the LogSoftmax is used.

In the Clustering step, a K-means clustering algorithm and a data mining tool, i.e., Rapid Miner Studio[2], were used. In the Discovering Process Model phase, we used α-algorithm (a plug-in in the process mining tool – ProM 6.6[3]) to get the generated process models from trace clusters.

The Evaluating Model phase determines the quality of the generated process models using two main measures Fitness and Precision [4]. The fitness measure determines whether all traces in the log can be replayed by the model from beginning to end. The precision measure determines whether the model has behavior very different from the behavior seen in the event log. Additional explanation about the fitness: consider an event log L of 600 traces, and MO is the correspondingly generated model. If only 548 traces in L can be replayed correctly in MO, then the fitness of MO is 548/600 $=$ 0.913. These two measures are in the range of [0,1], and the bigger the better. We used the "conformance checker" plug-in in ProM 6.6 to calculate the fitness and precision measure for each sub-model. Since there are more than one sub-model, we calculated the weighted average of the fitness and precision of all sub-models for comparison as follows:

$$w_{avg} = \sum_{i=1}^{k} \frac{n_i}{n} w_i \qquad (11)$$

---

[1] https://pytorch.org/.

[2] https://rapidminer.com.

[3] http://www.promtools.org/.

where w_{avg} is the average value of the fitness or precision measure; k is the number of models; n is the number of traces in the event log; n_i is the number of traces in ith cluster; and w_i is the fitness or precision score of the ith model, correspondingly.

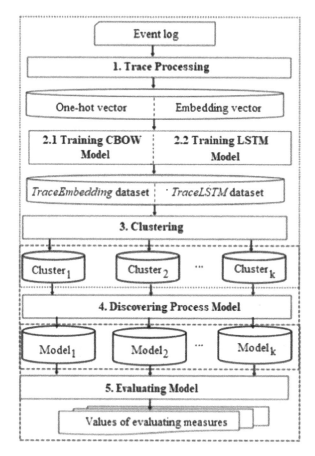

Fig. 4. The experimental framework

4.2 Experimental Data

In the experiments, we used three event logs Lfull[4], prAm6[5] and prHm6 (See footnote 5) in the process mining community with the statistical characteristics in Table 1.

---

[4] www.processmining.org/event_logs_and_models_used_in_book
[5] https://data.4tu.nl/repository/uuid:44c32783_15d0_4dbd_af8a-70b97bc3de49.

Table 1. The characteristics of three event logs

Event log	#cases	#events	Characteristics
Lfull	1391	7539	Several duplicated traces; Several repeated activities in a trace
prAm6	1200	49792	Few duplicated traces; No-repeated activities in a trace
prHm6	1155	1720	No-duplicated traces; No-repeated activities in a trace

4.3 Experimental Results

During the experiments, we changed the value of parameters V, M, and K with a set of $\{30, 40, 50, 60, 70, 80\}$. For the Lfull event log, the three best scores of experimental results correspond to $\{80, 40, 30\}$; for prAm6 it is $\{40, 40, 70\}$; for prHm6 it is $\{50, 50, 60\}$.

For evaluation, we compare the experimental results with some existing methods in Table 2, where *Dim* is the size of the trace; *Time* is the time (s-seconds, m-minutes, h-hours) to create a representation of a trace (Time); as well as fitness, and precision of process models. We show the results in three groups, i.e., group 1: the traditional trace representation including Bag-of-activities, k-grams, Maximal Repeats, Distance Graphs and CompactTrace [11]; Group 2: Trace the representation using CBOW model; Group 3: Trace the representation using LSTM model.

Table 2. The experimental results of TraceEmbedding and TraceLSTM representations

Event log	Method of trace representation	Measure			
		Dim	Time	Fitness	Precision
Lfull	Group 1: Traditional trace representations				
	Bag-of-activities	**08**	**0.1 s**	0.991	0.754
	k-grams	23	1.9 s	0.955	0.962
	Maximal repeats	50	2.0 s	0.950	**1**
	Distance graphs	43	1.9 s	0.992	**1**
	Compact trace (DNN)	50	17 s	0.99995	0.794
	Group 2: Using CBOW model				
	TraceEmbedding	80	60 s	0.99995	0.822
	Group 3: Using LSTM model				
	TraceLSTM	30	50 m	**1**	0.980
prAm6	Group 1: Traditional trace representations				
	Bag-of-activities	317	**0.3 s**	0.968	0.809
	k-grams	2467	76 s	0.968	0.809
	Maximal repeats	9493	8 h	0.968	0.332

(continued)

Table 2. (*continued*)

Event log	Method of trace representation	Measure			
		Dim	Time	Fitness	Precision
	Distance graphs	1927	93 s	0.968	0.809
	Compact trace (DNN)	**30**	43 s	0.973	0.911
	Group 2: Using CBOW model				
	TraceEmbedding	40	30 m	0.973	0.911
	Group 3: Using LSTM model				
	TraceLSTM	70	90 m	**0.974**	**0.920**
prHm6	Group 1: Traditional trace representations				
	Bag-of-activities	321	**0.2 s**	0.902	0.660
	k-grams	730	9.8 s	0.902	0.660
	Maximal repeats	592	59 s	0.897	0.730
	Distance graphs	1841	54 s	0.902	0.660
	Compact trace (DNN)	**30**	37 s	0.902	0.762
	Group 2: Using CBOW model				
	TraceEmbedding	50	22 m	0.922	0.730
	Group 3: Using LSTM model				
	TraceLSTM	60	93 m	**0.961**	**0.789**

Experimental results show that trace representation using deep learning models have proven their effectiveness compared to traditional methods. Although *TraceLSTM* trace method using LSTM model has a higher training time than other methods, the number of consistent results is always the highest of all experimental data sets. Especially for the Lfull dataset, *TraceLSTM* reaches the absolutely highest value of 1, meaning all actions in Lfull are represented by the model. For datasets with a large number of activities such as prAm6, prHm6, *TraceLSTM* always gives the best results on both fitness and precision. This is because its mechanism is able to learn the interrelated relationship between the activities of the LSTM model similar to that of a real business process.

For *TraceEmbedding* representation method using CBOW, the model only learns the relationship between activities in a specified window size, so the experimental results are lower than those of LSTM. However, the results are approximate or higher than those of the trace representation method using DNN in some cases.

5   Conclusions and Future Work

The paper proposes two new trace representation methods using the Continuous bag of words model and Long short-term memory model. With the learning mechanism that can remember the useful relationship between a set of activities, the experimental results have proved that the two our propose methods provide a effective trace representation solution. They not only reduce the size of the vector space but also increase quality of generated process models. This result has contributed an active part in the research flow of trace representation methods to improve the efficiency of process discovery problems in the process mining.

In the near future, we plan to apply the deep learning techniques in other problems of process mining such as process conformance and process enhancement.

References

1. van der Aalst, W.: Process mining manifesto. In: Daniel, F., Barkaoui, K., Dustdar, S. (eds.) BPM 2011, Part I. LNBIP, vol. 99, pp. 169–194. Springer, Heidelberg (2012). https://doi.org/10.1007/978-3-642-28108-2_19
2. Jagadeesh Chandra Bose, R.P., van der Aalst, W.: Trace alignment in process mining: opportunities for process diagnostics. In: Hull, R., Mendling, J., Tai, S. (eds.) BPM 2010. LNCS, vol. 6336, pp. 227–242. Springer, Heidelberg (2010). https://doi.org/10.1007/978-3-642-15618-2_17
3. de Medeiros, A.K.A., et al.: Process mining based on clustering: a quest for precision. In: ter Hofstede, A., Benatallah, B., Paik, H.-Y. (eds.) BPM 2007. LNCS, vol. 4928, pp. 17–29. Springer, Heidelberg (2008). https://doi.org/10.1007/978-3-540-78238-4_4
4. van der Aalst, W.M.P.: Process Mining: Discovery, Conformance and Enhancement of Business Processes. Springer, Heidelberg (2011). https://doi.org/10.1007/978-3-642-19345-3
5. Jagadeesh Chandra Bose, R.P.: Process Mining in the Large: Preprocessing, Discovery, and Diagnostics, PhD thesis, Eindhoven University of Technology, The Netherlands (2012)
6. Sun, Y., Bauer, B., Weidlich, M.: Compound trace clustering to generate accurate and simple sub-process models. In: Maximilien, M., Vallecillo, A., Wang, J., Oriol, M. (eds.) ICSOC 2017. LNCS, vol. 10601, pp. 175–190. Springer, Cham (2017). https://doi.org/10.1007/978-3-319-69035-3_12
7. Jablonski, S., Röglinger, M., Schönig, S.: Katrin maria wyrtki: multi-perspective clustering of process execution traces. Enterp. Model. Inf. Syst. Architect. 14, 1–22 (2018)
8. De Weerdt, J.: Business Process Discovery-New Techniques and Applications, PhD thesis, Catholic University of Leuven, Dutch (2012)
9. Mikolov, T., Chen, K., Corrado, G., Dean, J.: Efficient Estimation of Word Representations in Vector Space, ICLR (2013)
10. Hochreiter, S., Schmidhuber, J.: Long short-term memory. Neural Comput. 9(8), 1735–1780 (1997)
11. Bui, H.-N., Vu, T.-S., Nguyen, T.-T., Nguyen, T.-C., Ha, Q.-T.: A compact trace representation using deep neural networks for process mining. In: Proceeding of the 11th IEEE International Conference on Knowledge and Systems Engineering, pp. 312–316 (2019)

Construction of Virtual Metrology Cloud Platform with Machine Learning Tools for Providing Factory-Wide Manufacturing Service

Tang-Hsuan O[1], Min-Hsiung Hung[2]([✉]), Yu-Chuan Lin[1], and Chao-Chun Chen[1]

[1] IMIS/CSIE, NCKU, Tainan, Taiwan
{P96084087,chaochun}@mail.ncku.edu.tw, duke@imrc.ncku.edu.tw
[2] CSIE, PCCU, Taipei, Taiwan
hmx4@faculty.pccu.edu.tw

Abstract. In recent years, more and more high-tech manufacturing plants have used virtual metrology technology to monitor the production quality of machines and processes. The principle of virtual metrology operation consists of two phases: the off-line modeling stage and the on-line conjecture stage. In the off-line modeling stage, various calculation methods are used (such as neural networks, regression techniques etc.) to build a virtual metrology model. In the on-line conjecture stage, the established virtual metrology model can be used to instantly estimate the manufacturing quality of the workpiece or the health of the machine. Therefore, the virtual metrology can solve the measurement delay problem without increasing the measurement cost, and achieve the full inspection realm that the quality of each production workpiece can be monitored online and immediately. Microsoft Azure Machine Learning Studio (AMLS) is a cloud machine learning service developed by Microsoft. It integrates the tools needed for machine learning on a cloud platform and uses drag and drop to analyze machine learning related data, model building, performance testing and service building which greatly reduce the threshold for learning. For providing factory-wide manufacturing service, this research used AMLS machine learning services to construct a virtual metrology cloud platform, so that all production machines have the virtual metrology capability with a highly integration solution. Finally, the actual production data of the factory was used to conduct the integration test and performance evaluation of the system to verify the availability and industrial utilization of the research.

This work was supported by Ministry of Science and Technology (MOST) of Taiwan under Grants MOST 107-2221-E-006-017-MY2, 108-2218-E-006-029, and 108-2221-E-034-015-MY2. This work was financially supported by the "Intelligent Manufacturing Research Center" (iMRC) in NCKU from The Featured Areas Research Center Program within the framework of the Higher Education Sprout Project by the Ministry of Education in Taiwan.

P. Sitek et al. (Eds.): ACIIDS 2020, CCIS 1178, pp. 47–59, 2020.
https://doi.org/10.1007/978-981-15-3380-8_5

Keywords: Cloud manufacturing · Virtual metrology · Machine learning applications · System integration · Factory-wide service

1 Introduction

The manufacturing industry considers the cost and time of the workpiece measurement. Traditionally, the monitoring of the process is mostly carried out by sampling measurement. However, process monitoring by sampling measurement is not able to detect process or machine abnormalities in real time. If an abnormality occurs in the machine or process during the measurement delay period, many workpieces with defects may be produced during this period, which will cause great production loss.

In recent years, more and more high-tech manufacturing plants have used virtual metrology technology [1,2] to monitor the production quality of machines and processes. The principle of virtual metrology operation consists of two phases: the off-line modeling stage and the on-line conjecture stage. In the off-line modeling stage, the process data of the production machine and the corresponding metrology data are collected, and then various calculation methods are used (such as neural networks, regression techniques etc.) to build a virtual metrology model. In the on-line conjecture stage, once the processing data of a workpiece are obtained (such as integrated circuit, machine tool parts, etc.), the established virtual metrology model can be used to instantly estimate the manufacturing quality of the workpiece or the health of the machine. Therefore, the virtual metrology can solve the measurement delay problem without increasing the measurement cost, and achieve the full inspection realm that the quality of each production workpiece can be monitored online and immediately. The international SEMATECH manufacturing initiative ISMI has incorporated virtual metrology into its next generation semiconductor factory implementation blueprint [6]. At the same time, the semiconductor international technology blueprint ITRS [3] also set virtual metrology as one of the key areas of advanced process control (APC) for semiconductor factories.

Most of the virtual metrology literatures mainly focus on the use of different algorithms or mathematical methods to establish virtual metrology models of the process, and to display the error detection capability of the virtual metrology model, accuracy of prediction, and application to process control. The literature [4] proposed a virtual metrology model for CVD process. The literature [5] developed a virtual metrology model to perform error detection and classification to avoid the failure of copper interconnection in the system wafer. The literature [7] proposed to use the Dynamic-Moving-Window method to update the virtual metrology model to improve the prediction accuracy of the TFT-LCD process.

Traditionally, a computer is placed next to each production machine to collect data generated when the machine is producing workpieces, but this will cause cost increases. Once the number of production machine is very large, multiple computers need to be installed. There will be a huge amount of overhead, and in the initial construction, it is not easy to install due to the large number of computers, and maintenance work in the future is also a difficult problem. In order to save costs and the difficulty of installation and maintenance, we set up a microcomputer near the production machine. This computer can be connected to the Internet, which can transmit data to the Internet. Then, we combined cloud technology to develop a private cloud to upload data from this microcomputer to the private cloud. The benefit of a private cloud is the ability to use a large computer, coupled with microcomputers next to the production machine, to integrate data from the entire production plant, and to manage it more economically and efficiently. Finally, we used AMLS (Azure Machine Learning Studio, Microsoft) combined with private cloud technology to integrate into a cloud platform and developed a systematic operation method that allows users to easily operate and use the platform.

AMLS is a free machine learning cloud service, which contains various data processing and machine learning algorithms, and can publish the completed prediction model as a cloud service. Therefore, this research used the AMLS machine learning tools to construct a virtual metrology cloud platform, and then used the actual production data of the factory to conduct integrated testing and performance evaluation of the system to verify the availability and industrial utilization of the research.

2   Architecture of Virtual Metrology Cloud Service

Figure 1 is the architecture diagram of the virtual metrology cloud platform system in this research. The architecture consists of three parts: private cloud,

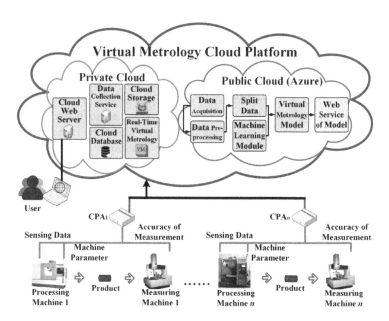

Fig. 1. Virtual metrology cloud platform system architecture.

public cloud, CPA (Cyber-Physical Agent, virtual and reality agent, also known as data collector). The details of each part will be explained one by one below.

2.1   Private Cloud for Real-Time Virtual Metrology Service

The private cloud, built in the lab (or factory), includes cloud web server, data collection service, cloud database, cloud storage, and real-time virtual metrology service. The cloud web server provides users to connect to the virtual metrology cloud service through a web browser. The data collection service can transfer historical process data of production machines, actual measurement data stored in the CPA to the cloud database to provide training and test dataset for training virtual metrology models. The cloud database is used to store historical process data, actual measurement data, and virtual metrology data of production machines. The cloud storage is used to store the data converted from the cloud database, Real-time virtual metrology service can instantly obtain the latest production machine process data from CPA, The process data are processed through the real-time virtual metrology service with a proper virtual metrology model, which needs to be trained in the public cloud for alleviating the resource pressure during factory manufacturing to obtain the corresponding virtual metrology values.

2.2   Public Cloud for Off-Line Virtual Metrology Service

We use AMLS in the public cloud to create models for the real-time virtual metrology service, and such service in the public cloud is called off-line virtual metrology service. With AMLS, certain functional modules are built, including data acquisition, data pre-processing, split data, machine learning module, and web services, to train the virtual metrology model and publish the model as a web service.

For creating a virtual metrology model, the client needs to upload the historical process data of the production machine and the actual measurement data to the "Acquisition Data Module", and then passes the data to the "Data Pre-Processing Module" for data pre-processing (e.g., removing missing values, outliers, etc.), obtains clean data, and then splits the data into training data and test data through the "Split Data Module" to carry out the next virtual metrology model training. The "Machine Learning Module" provides machine learning algorithms such as linear regression and neural network etc., or the machine learning algorithm written by Python/R which can also be applied to this module. Using the training data, test data and "Machine Learning Module", the virtual metrology model training can be started. After model training is completed, the virtual metrology model is released to the Microsoft Azure cloud through the "Web Service Module".

2.3   CPA (Cyber-Physical Agent)

The CPA is an internet-of-things (IoT) device for encapsulating production machines as internet accessible objects, so that factory machines can exchange data with other remote servers or machines. In this work, we implemented a CPA with a single-chip computer (Raspberry Pi), which is used to store the historical process data of the production machine and the actual measurement data. The CPA would periodically transmit data collected from processing machines and measuring machines to the public/private cloud with external network.

Figure 2 depicts a CPA framework, which includes communication services, CPA control kernel, data collection manager, application interface, equipment driver and so on. The Communication services facilitate communication between CPA and cloud services over the internet. The CPA control kernel is the communication core of all modules. The data collection manager processes and manages collection of data through device drivers. The application interface allows a CPA to add pluggable application modules (such as data pre-processing modules) in a plug-and-play manner. The equipment drivers enable a CPA to communicate with variety of sensors, devices, and machines for achieving data collection.

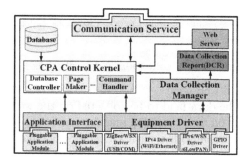

Fig. 2. CPA framework.

3 Core Designs for Virtual Metrology Cloud Service

According to Fig. 1, four key system operation processes are needed in virtual metrology cloud service: data collection, data conversion, offline build virtual metrology service, and real-time virtual metrology service. Each of them is presented in details in this section.

3.1 Data Collection

Figure 3 shows the system operation process for data collection. The data collection service requests the CPA to collect the historical process data of processing machines and measurement data of measuring machines.

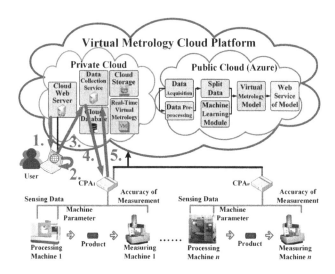

Fig. 3. System operation process for data collection.

The operational flow of data collection is described as follows.

Step 1: User download web page.
Step 2: User selects the data field to be collected on the web (sensing data and machine parameters on the processing machine) and data items (measurement items of the measuring machine, such as: center hole diameter, hubcap outer diameter etc.)
Step 3: User transmits the selected data fields and data item information to the data collection service.
Step 4: Data collection service requests specific data from CPA.
Step 5: CPA returns the specific data to the data collection service and stores it into the cloud database.

3.2 Data Conversion

Figure 4 shows the system operation process for data conversion. The data conversion service converts collected historical process data stored in the cloud database to the CSV (comma-separated values) format, which is the input of the AMLS programs.

The operational flow of data conversion is described as follows.

Step 1: User download web page.
Step 2: User selects the data field to be collected on the web (sensing data and machine parameters on the processing machine) and data items (measurement items of the measuring machine, such as: center hole diameter, hubcap outer diameter etc.)
Step 3: User transmits the selected data fields and data item information to the data collection service.

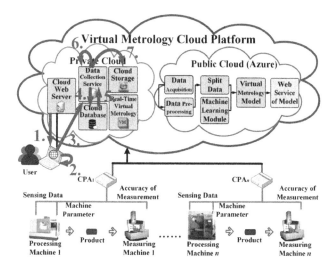

Fig. 4. System operation process of data conversion.

Step 4: The data collection service requests the specific data from the cloud database.

Step 5: The cloud database returns the specific data to the data collection service.

Step 6: The data collection service converts the specific data into a CSV format file.

Step 7: The data collection service stores the CSV format file to the cloud storage for users to download.

3.3 Off-Line Virtual Metrology Service

Figure 5 shows the system operation process of the off-line virtual metrology service. The off-line virtual metrology service creates virtual metrology model via AMLS-based training programs, and publishes the created model as a web service. After obtaining the web service request information, the information can be used to import the model to the real-time virtual metrology service.

The operational flow of the off-line virtual metrology service is described as follows.

Step 1: The user goes to the AMLS web page to operate.

Step 2: The user uploads the CSV format file (obtained through the data conversion service) to AMLS.

Step 3: The data acquisition transmits data to the data pre-processing and removes missing values and outliers from the uploaded file.

Step 4: The data pre-processing obtains clean data and spilts into training and test data.

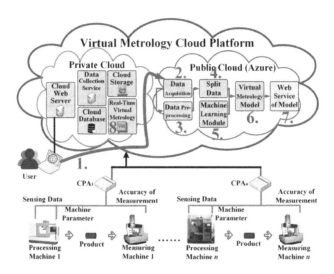

Fig. 5. System operation process of the off-line virtual metrology service.

Step 5: The machine learning module selects the machine learning algorithm that used to train the model.
Step 6: The machine learning module uses training data and machine learning algorithms. Then, test data is used to evaluate model accuracy and to obtain virtual metrology model.
Step 7: The virtual metrology model publishes the trained virtual metrology model as a web service.
Step 8: Input the request information of the virtual metrology model web service into the real-time virtual metrology service.

3.4 Real-Time Virtual Metrology Service

Figure 6 shows the system operation process of the real-time virtual metrology service. The real-time virtual metrology service immediately requests the CPA for the latest production process data in the processing machine (and the data has not been or can not be measured by the measuring machine), and is transmitted back to the real-time virtual metrology service to measure the virtual metrology value of the production workpiece.

The operational flow of real-time virtual metrology is described as follows.

Step 1: User download web page.
Step 2: User selects items on the web page for real-time virtual metrology (Such as: center hole diameter, hubcap outer diameter etc.)
Step 3: Pass the selected measurement items to the real-time virtual metrology service.
Step 4: The real-time virtual metrology service requests the CPA for the latest production workpiece data in the processing machine (different data requests according to the selected measurement items).

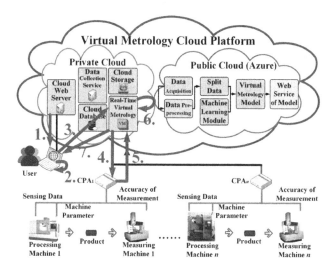

Fig. 6. System operation process of the real-time virtual metrology service.

Step 5: CPA returns data to real-time virtual metrology service.
Step 6: The real-time virtual metrology service requests the established virtual metrology web service to obtain the virtual metrology value of the production workpiece data.
Step 7: The virtual metrology value is passed back to the user.

4   Experimental Results

The application of applying virtual metrology to aluminum rim processing is illustrated in this work. We obtained the real-world data from aluminum rim production machines and built virtual metrology model using AMLS. Measure whether the specifications of the aluminum rim meets the standard through the virtual metrology model. We have a total of three measurement items, which are as follows:

1. Center Hole Diameter (CHD): The rim aperture mounted on the axle head of the car.
2. Hubcap Outer Diameter (HOD): Aperture of the outer cover of the aluminum rim.
3. Pitch Circle Diameter (PCD): The center of all bolt holes is rounded to the diameter of the circle.

We integrated the virtual metrology model into a virtual metrology cloud platform, providing real-time process data for production workpiece for on-line conjecture and monitoring of the quality of each production workpiece. The test steps of the user's operation for the virtual metrology cloud service are:

1. Download the file of "Aluminum rim production machine history process data and actual measurement data" from the cloud webpage.
2. Virtual metrology model implementation in AMLS.
3. Publish virtual metrology models to become web services.
4. Back to the webpage to establish a real-time virtual metrology service.
5. Start real-time virtual metrology.

4.1 Data Collection from Machines via CPA

Figure 7 shows the screenshot of data collection. The data collection web interface provides the user to select the machine (processing machine) and the measurement item (the item measured by the measuring machine), and also to input the upper/lower bounds of the measurement data, the start/end date of the data, and the data field (the field include the sensing data of the processing machine and the machine parameters etc.) After all required information is filled, the data collection cloud service in the private cloud would collect data from machines in the factory via a CPA.

Fig. 7. Screenshot of the data collection service.

4.2 Off-Line Virtual Metrology Service

The user goes to AMLS to offline build virtual metrology mode. Figure 8 shows the training steps of model creation with AMLS on public cloud in off-line virtual metrology service. The user uploads the data downloaded from Sect. 4.1 to AMLS and clears the missing values in the data through "Clean Missing Data"; "Select Columns In Dataset" selects training data and training target; "Split Data" divides the data into training and test data; Uses "Neural Network Regression" as the algorithm for training the virtual metrology models; "Train Model" starts training the model; "Score Model" uses test data to evaluate models; "Evaluate Model" calculate performance and accuracy for this model.

Fig. 8. Screenshot of creating off-line virtual metrology model.

4.3   Publishing a Virtual Metrology Model as a Web Service

Through the function of the web service deployed in AMLS, we can publish the model trained in Sect. 4.2 as a web service, so that required modules in the private cloud can access it with "API Key" and "Request URI". Figure 9 shows the screenshot of "API Key" and "Request URI" of a created virtual metrology model with our developed AMLS-based training procedure. Clients can use the information to access virtual metrology model.

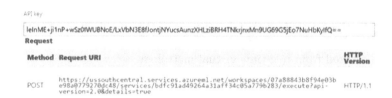

Fig. 9. Screenshot of the request information for Virtual metrology of web service.

Since the real-time virtual metrology service in the private cloud requires the associated virtual metrology model created in the public cloud, a connection needs to be built between public/private cloud and the web service for the virtual metrology model is the connection interface. Figure 10 shows that the completed virtual metrology model request information is used in the real-time virtual metrology service for creating a connection to the associated virtual model.

Fig. 10. Cloud web - virtual metrology service file creation.

4.4   Apply Virtual Metrology Service to Wheel Manufacturing

We apply virtual metrology service to wheel manufacturing, and the result is shown in Fig. 11. It can be seen that the actual measured value and the virtual metrology value are displayed in the graphical user interface, so that the user to easily see the error between the virtual metrology and the actual measurement. The purple curve is the virtual metrology value, and the orange curve is the actual measured value. We can also directly observe the production process data of the production workpiece that has not been measured, and monitor of the quality of each production workpiece through real-time process data, which is online conjectured from real-time virtual metrology.

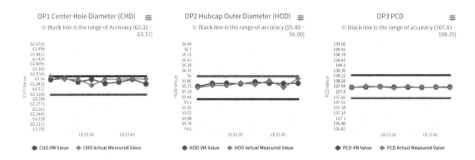

Fig. 11. Screenshot of the real-time virtual metrology results.

5   Conclusions

This research proposes a systematic method of virtual metrology cloud platform based on AMLS machine learning service, and uses aluminum rim processing data to verify the availability and industrial utilization. A technology for constructing a self-constructed virtual metrology of virtual measurement cloud platform is established. Future research involves implementing better machine learning algorithms and adding more sophisticated methods (such as standardizing data, filtering outliers etc.) to the AMLS cloud platform. We expect to obtain the better virtual metrology model to improve prediction performance.

Acknowledgment. Authors thank Yung-Chien Chou for her effort on revising the draft of this manuscript.

References

1. Cheng, F.T., Chang, J.Y.C., Huang, H.C., Kao, C.A., Chen, Y.L., Peng, J.L.: Benefit model of virtual metrology and integrating AVM into MES. IEEE Trans. Semicond. Manuf. **24**(2), 261–272 (2011)
2. Cheng, F.T., Kao, C.A., Chen, C.F., Tsai, W.H.: Tutorial on applying the VM technology for TFT-LCD manufacturing. IEEE Trans. Semicond. Manuf. **28**(1), 55–69 (2015)
3. Gargini, P.: The international technology roadmap for semiconductors (ITRS): "past, present and future". In: GaAs IC Symposium. IEEE Gallium Arsenide Integrated Circuits Symposium. 22nd Annual Technical Digest 2000. (Cat. No.00CH37084), pp. 3–5, November 2000
4. Hung, M.H., Lin, T.H., Cheng, F.T., Lin, R.C.: A novel virtual metrology scheme for predicting CVD thickness in semiconductor manufacturing. IEEE/ASME Trans. Mechatron. **12**(3), 308–316 (2007)
5. Imai, S., Kitabata, M.: Prevention of copper interconnection failure in system on chip using virtual metrology. IEEE Trans. Semicond. Manuf. **22**(4), 432–437 (2009)
6. Rothe, O.: ISMI Next Generation Factory. e-Manufacturing Workshop, SEMICON West 2008, USA, July 2008
7. Wu, W.M., Cheng, F.T., Kong, F.W.: Dynamic-moving-window scheme for virtual-metrology model refreshing. IEEE Trans. Semicond. Manuf. **25**(2), 238–246 (2012)

Data Collection for Natural Language Processing Systems

Patrik Hrkút[1][✉] [iD], Štefan Toth[1][✉] [iD], Michal Ďuračík[1][✉], Matej Meško[1][✉],
Emil Kršák[1][✉], and Miroslava Mikušová[2][✉]

[1] Department of Software Technologies, Faculty of Management Science and Informatics,
University of Žilina, Univerzitná 1, 010 26 Žilina, Slovakia
{patrik.hrkut,stefan.toth,michal.duracik,matej.mesko,
emil.krsak}@fri.uniza.sk
[2] Department of Road and Urban Transport, Faculty of Operation and Economics of Transport,
University of Žilina, Univerzitná 1, 010 26 Žilina, Slovakia
mikusova@fpedas.uniza.sk

Abstract. Any NLP system needs enough data for training and testing purposes. They can be split into two datasets: correct and incorrect (erroneous) data. Usually, it is not a problem to find and get a set of correct data because the correct texts are available from different sources, although they may also contain some mistakes. On the other hand, it is a hard task to get data containing errors like typos, mistakes and misspellings. This kind of data is usually obtained by a lengthy manual process and it requires annotation by human. One way to get the incorrect dataset faster is to generate it. However, this creates a problem how to generate incorrect texts so that they correspond to real human mistakes. In this paper, we focused on getting the incorrect dataset by help of humans. We created an automated web application (a game) that allows to collect incorrect texts and misspellings from players for texts written in the Slovak language. Based on the obtained data, we built a model of common errors that can be used to generate a large amount of authentic looking erroneous texts.

Keywords: Data collection · Typos · Automatic text correction · Spelling and typing model · Typing game

1 Introduction

Nowadays, systems with an artificial intelligence support are booming, especially in the human-machine environment. Chatbot systems are often used for such communication. If the chatbot communication is in a text-like form, it depends on the correct text input. If there are misspellings or grammatical mistakes in human communication, the text becomes incomprehensible, from a chatbot's point of view, and it is unable to respond to it correctly.

In this paper, we will deal with one of the necessary processes that must be implemented when creating an automated system for automatic correction in the text from the user - data collection. The use of the text correction system is not only bound to the

© Springer Nature Singapore Pte Ltd. 2020
P. Sitek et al. (Eds.): ACIIDS 2020, CCIS 1178, pp. 60–70, 2020.
https://doi.org/10.1007/978-981-15-3380-8_6

correction of mistakes in chatbot communication but will also find application in other areas, such as:

- speeding up typing with automatic correction and prediction
- correcting typing mistakes in emails
- correction of dictated text
- unknown text correction
- additional corrections after OCR scanning
- language teaching aid (mother tongue or foreign language).

As you can see, the use of such a system is very versatile. We are currently designing the system for the Slovak language. In the future, it will be possible to apply it to other languages after minor modifications.

1.1 State of the Art

The idea to use a game to get the data came by Rodrigues and Rytting [1] who developed a typing race game to create spelling mistakes corpora for English. The game was played by 251 participants through Amazon Mechanical Turk system. Each of players had to retype one of 100 words which was shown sequentially. Authors analyzed 15 300 words from 153 native English speaker participants. 4.65% of words contained mistakes.

Another word typing games were created by Tachibana and Komachi [2]. They implemented two word-typing games (common word-typing game and correctable word-typing game) for analysis of English spelling mistakes. The first game was played by 7 and the second game by 19 students of computer science. Authors collected and analyzed 26 192 words. Their experimental results showed that typing-game can be regarded as a good source of spelling mistakes.

There are many applications and games that have been developed for keyboard typing. Some of them were developed for fun, others for learning keyboard typing. Although these games were not created primarily for data acquisition, we can learn from them and use their ideas for our purpose, as we will show later in this paper.

The first example of the typing game is the Typing of the Dead videogame released by Sega in 1999 [3]. The goal of the game is to type correct words to kill zombies. Other game is the TypeRacer [4], which is a multiplayer typing game released in 2008. People are motivated to play through competition. When the game is over, the game displays score and typo statistics. It is available in 50 different languages including the Slovak language. Other example of a modern game is ZType [5], which is a galactic keyboarding adventure game by Dominik Szablewski released for web, iOS and Android. As other examples of typing games we can name Keyboard Jump, Keyboard Ninja and many others available at [6].

Obtaining erroneous data is possible in other ways as presented Grundkiewicz and Junczys-Dowmunt in [7], who processed the entire English Wikipedia revision history. The Mistake Corpus of Slovak CHIBY was based on this work for the Slovak language [8]. Since the Slovak Wikipedia is not as extensive as the English version, the created corpus is not large. Overall, there are not many Slovak incorrect datasets, so we decided to get it using a game.

2 System Overview

2.1 Steps for Creating a Text Correction System

Creating a system for an automatic text correction can be divided into several parts. The figure (see Fig. 1) shows what steps need to be taken to ensure that the result of the system is the correct text.

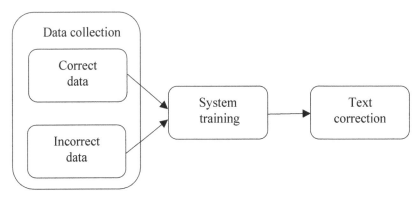

Fig. 1. Steps needed for text correction system building

The first step is to collect the correct data, texts that are written correctly (or with minimal number of mistakes). The source of these texts could be the Internet because there is a lot of freely available, mostly grammatically correct, text. We obtained these texts using our crawler, which automatically browsed and downloaded texts from selected websites. Of course, some texts could also contain mistakes. Subsequently, the downloaded documents were cleaned from irrelevant parts and the text without HTML tags was extracted.

A more complicated problem is obtaining incorrect (erroneous) data. If we would like to use the Internet again to retrieve this data (e.g. some publicly available forums), there is a problem that we cannot identify individual mistakes. We can manually annotate the mistakes, but it is an extremely time-consuming activity. Therefore, we designed a more sophisticated system for collecting erroneous data. It involves more users in data collection. The collection is implemented as part of the web game we proposed, where the player's task is to transcribe the text quickly. The game contains a ranking of the best players, which motivates them to play the game repeatedly.

After data collection, it is necessary to analyze what types of typos usually appear in the texts and categorize them. This allows us to create an automated application for generating typos and misspelling that matches real human mistakes.

Then, if we get enough correct and incorrect data, it will allow us to create e.g. a neural network that uses this data for training. Building a neural network requires a large amount of correct data and a certain amount of incorrect data. The more data becomes available, the better network we will be able to create, so our goal is to collect as much data as possible.

3   Collection of Data

3.1   Collection of Correct Data

The Internet is a very good data source because there is enough free available text. We downloaded a lot of texts from freely available news portals in Slovak language and other websites. Although we are aware that these resources may contain some mistakes because they were written by humans but with a collaborative approach, most mistakes are likely corrected.

Another data source for us was the Slovak Wikipedia database markup dump [9]. To obtain plain text, we used *WikiExtractor* Python script [10], which can create files containing text categorized by articles. However, the extracted wiki text contained various mistakes, and not all texts were successfully converted to the plain text. Unfortunately, the resulting text was not completely grammatically correct, there was a large amount of multiple white chars and misspelled or omitted words. E.g. tables found in texts caused many problems, often words from different table cells was merged into one word, etc.

We also processed the text from other sources such as free news portals, free newspapers and magazines, where we stripped HTML tags, left out uninteresting parts and saved the text for future use.

3.2   Collection of Incorrect Data

Gathering text data with annotated misspellings and typos is more difficult task. It is necessary to determine whether the found text is correct or contains mistakes. The simplest way is to manual annotate it, which is a very time-consuming job, and besides, it can also be the source of additional mistakes (a false mistake detection, or vice versa overlooking of a mistake). For this reason, we decided to create a web application that will help us to collect incorrect data. It was necessary to devise a concept of the application

Fig. 2. Screenshot of the application *Minútovka*

that would motivate users to insert texts with mistakes. Because we wanted to attract mainly young people, we created the application as an internet game where players will compete, who will transcribe the text faster and with as few mistakes as possible. The application is publicly available at https://minutovka.fri.uniza.sk/ (see Fig. 2). Since we focused on Slovak texts, the whole web application is only localized to the Slovak language. The name of the game is *Minútovka* and was chosen according to the duration of the game, which is exactly one minute.

The goal of the game is to transcribe as many words in the correct form as possible within a predetermined time (60 s). The text is gradually displayed on the screen and the player must transcribe a word highlighted in bold into the input field. As time is limited, the player tries to write down the text as soon as possible to send the maximum number of words. Obviously, there are a lot of misspellings, which are usually not corrected by the player, because he would be unnecessarily delayed and lowered his score. If the player corrects the mistake, the application not only records the word itself, but also the keystroke sequence that the player used to type. This way we got misspellings, even in the words appeared as the correct ones, but the player made a mistake as he typed. For example, if he was supposed to write the Slovak word *ktorý*, but he wrote *ktorz*, and then he corrected it, the application remembers the following sequence of pressed characters with timestamps (Fig. 3):

```
{"word":"ktorý",
 "playerWord":"ktorý",
 "answerparts":[
   {"word":"","timeStamp":2784,"trigger":"keypress","data":"k"},
   {"word":"k","timeStamp":3161,"trigger":"keypress","data":"t"},
   {"word":"kt","timeStamp":3680,"trigger":"keypress","data":"o"},
   {"word":"kto","timeStamp":3999,"trigger":"keypress","data":"r"},
   {"word":"ktor","timeStamp":4872,"trigger":"keypress","data":"z"},
   {"word":"ktorz","timeStamp":6799,"trigger":"keypress","data":"Backspace"},
   {"word":"ktor","timeStamp":6993,"trigger":"keypress","data":"ý"}
 ],
 "duration":7600}
```

Fig. 3. Sequence of characters recorded by application

Based on the words we have received from the players and the originally sent words we can determine what typos the players made. We analyzed and divided these misspellings into categories. We ignored mistakes that were useless and irrelevant to us. To assess them, we used the metric introduced by V. I. Levenshtein to measure the editing distance in the space of text strings. In other words, it determines how many simple operations like adding a character, deleting a character, or swapping a character for another are needed to get a new string from the original one (Fig. 4).

The Levenshtein distance between two strings a, b (of length $|a|$ and $|b|$ respectively) is given by $lev_{a,b}(|a|, |b|)$ where

In the formula $1_{(a_i \neq b_j)}$ is the indicator function equal to 0 when $a_i = b_j$ and equal to 1 otherwise, and $lev_{a,b}(i, j)$ is the distance between the first i characters of a and the first j characters of b. i and j are 1-based indices.

$$lev_{a,b}(i,j) = \begin{cases} \max(i,j) & \text{if } \min(i,j) = 0, \\ \min \begin{cases} lev_{a,b}(i-1,j)+1 \\ lev_{a,b}(i,j-1)+1 \\ lev_{a,b}(i-1,j-1)+1_{(a_i \neq b_j)} \end{cases} & \text{otherwise.} \end{cases}$$

Fig. 4. Levenshtein distance definition

Examples of determining the Levenshtein distance for a pair of words can be found in the following table:

Table 1. Levenshtein distance between two words (slovo = word)

Original word	Misspelled word	Levenshtein distance
slovo	slavo	1
slovo	solvo	2
slovo	slloovo	2
slovo	slloovoo	3
slovo	sklloovoo	4

As can be seen from Table 1, if the Levenshtein distance between the original and the misspelled word is greater than 3, the word is significantly different from the original. This is evident for short words (up to 7 characters), but for longer words, the higher value of the Levenshtein distance is allowed, e.g. Slovak words *juhokórejského* and *juhokňorejskeňeho* have the Levenshtein distance equal to 5 and still, the misspelled word resembles the original one. Therefore, it should be included in the group of words suitable for analysis. Therefore, as a measure for including a word in a set of words suitable for analysis, we included those words for which:

$$lev_{(a,b)} <= \frac{|a|}{2} + 1 \qquad (2)$$

where $lev_{a,b}$ is the Levenshtein distance, a is the original word, b is the player word and $|a|$ is the length of the word a.

Levenshtein distance serves here as a context that allows us to differentiate between words that should be included in planned analysis and those which should not. Our method uses a contextual method to filter out a large amount of insignificant data, because without such data reduction, words that are meaningless for our application would be processed as well.

We deployed the application on the faculty server and promoted it among students. We have noticed the total number of players and games in the 4 weeks since the game was started (see Table 2):

The other statistics show the average mistake rate per game (Table 3). As the table shows, the number of mistakes made by one player in a game is not big, so we need many players to get enough data for our purposes.

Table 2. Statistics of played games

Parameter	Value
Games played	2 329
Number of players	608
Written words	71 900
Incorrect words	11 346
Words corrected during typing	7 650

Table 3. Statistics of a game

Parameter	Value
The average number of words written by a player	31.26
The average number of misspelled words per player	5.27
Average time to write one word	1.63 s

The following chart shows the most frequent number of mistakes made by a player makes during a game (see Fig. 5).

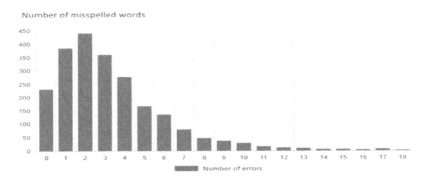

Fig. 5. Number of misspelled words per one player in *Minutovka* game

3.3 Evaluation of Mistakes Found

Using the app, we managed to collect typos and mistakes that players made while playing the game. We stored the mistakes in a database and made them available for web-based processing for our other applications. The next step was to filter out the data that were not suitable for the analysis.

First, we excluded words where punctuation marks (dot, comma after a word) were missing only, then words where the words differed only by missing diacritics. The

Levenshtein distance was the last criterion we used to filter the data. If the distance was bigger than the value computed in the Eq. (2), we omitted the word from the misspelled list because this word was too different from the original. In total, we received from players 11 346 words with some mistakes. Finally, 5 361 words remained after applying the mentioned filters. After that, we analyzed the individual mistakes and found the following mistake categories that could be generalized (Table 4):

Table 4. Categorization of mistakes

Mistake category	Count	%	$Lev_{(a,b)}$	$D_{(a,b)}$
One incorrect character	1 744	32.53	1	0
One incorrect character added	1 053	19.64	1	1
One character dropped	1 079	20.13	1	−1
Two incorrect characters	196	3.66	2	0
Two characters swapped	364	6.79	2	0
One incorrect, one character added	262	4.89	2	1
One incorrect, one character dropped	141	2.63	2	−1
Two incorrect characters added	86	1.60	2	2
Two incorrect characters dropped	106	1.98	2	−2
Combination of 3 mistakes	237	4.42	3	−3..3
More than 4 mistakes	93	1.73	4+	N/A

The meaning of the columns in the Table 4 is as follows:

- *Column 1 (Mistake category)* – the type of a mistake
- *Column 2 (Count)* – number of mistakes of the given type (out of all mistakes)
- *Column 3 (%)* – percentage of mistakes from total
- *Column 4 ($Lev_{(a,b)}$)* – Levenshtein distance between original and misspelled word in the given category
- *Column 5 ($D_{(a,b)}$)* – the difference in the number of characters between the misspelled and the original word in the given category

The Table 4 shows that 98.27% of all mistakes have a Levenshtein distance of less than 4. The analyzed data also showed that if a player made 4 or more mistakes in a word, the reason was, that he gave up the attempt to type the correct word and pressed random keys or sent the unfinished word. Another interesting fact that emerged from the analysis is that most misspellings and mistakes are not accidental but arose for these main reasons:

1. The player remembers the word visually but transcribes it by heart and makes a spelling mistake (e.g. *Výnimku* ⇨ *Výnymku*). Very often it is just an exchange of characters *y* and *i*, for which the Slovak language has special rules.

2. The player had set a different keyboard than usual. A typical case is the exchange QWERTY and QWERTZ Slovak keyboards, where *z* and *y* keys are exchanged (63 such mistakes in data). Another example is that the player did not notice that he had set a different keyboard than the Slovak one (typos like *bl9zkom* ⇨ *blízkom*). However, easy algorithms can remove these typos.

3. The player misreads the word and transcribes it (e.g. *nákladné* ⇨ *základné*). However, the number of such cases is negligible.

4. Another set of mistakes is caused by typing the same character as required, but the player uses a lowercase character where capital one was expected and vice versa (e.g. *Ostrov* ⇨ *ostrov*). These mistakes represent 11.12% of all misspelled words. However, this kind of mistakes can be eliminated algorithmically.

5. The most common mistakes found in data were typing mistakes, such as pressing another key, respectively pressing an extra key. Such typing mistakes rate is 53.60% of all mistakes collected. Our hypothesis was, that the typing mistakes are mostly generated by pressing one of the adjacent keys to correct key. An example of adjacent characters to the character *j* can be seen in Fig. 6.

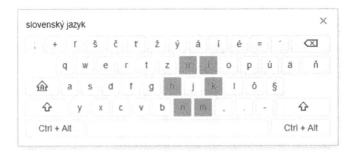

Fig. 6. Adjacent keys to key *j*

According to the collected data, only 32.55% of misspellings come from these adjacent characters. Our hypothesis was not confirmed.

Collecting data in collaboration with players is a very good method of getting erroneous data. However, it is necessary to have a large amount of data. Experimental knowledge allows us to create an application that generates misspelled words that are close to the human mistakes. We learnt that the following prerequisites must be considered when creating an automatic mistake generator:

- Words with 1 or 2 mistakes make up 94.12% of the incorrect words.
- Words with 3 mistakes represents 4.17% of the incorrect words.
- Only 1.71% of misspelled words has 4 or more mistakes.
- We can omit mistakes related to incorrect diacritics since we can fix them programmatically by our automatic diacritic restoration system [11].
- We can also fix mistakes caused by a mistakenly set keyboard.
- Incorrectly typed or added character mistakes are not significantly bound to adjacent keys.

4 Discussion

We focused on collecting typos using a web game. We realize that when writing texts (theses, essays, longer texts) in common situations where the writer is neither under time stress nor competing, other types of errors may occur. Of course, such errors are much more natural and more precisely show what errors usually writers do. On the other hand, collecting such data is very tedious and complicated process. It would require the collection of texts, their manual correction by human and the subsequent annotation of errors. It would be necessary to have the original text with errors as well as the corrected one. The source of such texts could be e.g. written projects of students and the versions corrected by their teacher, but even so we would not avoid manually transcribing errors into electronic form. Despite these imperfections, we believe that our way of obtaining errors is a sufficient method to create a model for correction of grammatical errors in texts.

5 Conclusion

In our paper, we dealt with collecting data for the purposes of automatic correction of the text. We experimentally verified what types of mistakes people make during writing. Based on the collected data and after their analysis, it will be possible to create an automatic misspelling and mistake generator similar to the human way of creating them. This generator is necessary for creating a larger set of data eligible for training and testing the entire system for the correction of Slovak grammar, which is our primary goal for further research.

Acknowledgment. This article was created in the framework of the National project IT Academy – Education for the 21st Century, which is supported by the European Social Fund and the European Regional Development Fund in the framework of the Operational Programme Human Resources.

References

1. Rodrigues, P., Rytting, C.A.: Typing race games as a method to create spelling error corpora. In: International Conference on Language Resources and Evaluation (LREC), Istanbul (2012)
2. Tachibana, R., Komachi, M.: Analysis of English spelling errors in a word-typing game. In: Proceedings of the Tenth International Conference on Language Resources and Evaluation (LREC 2016), Portorož, Slovenia (2016)
3. The International Arcade Museum: The Typing Of The Dead, WebMagic Ventures. https://www.arcade-museum.com/game_detail.php?game_id=10244. Accessed 27 Sept 2019
4. TypeRacer. https://data.typeracer.com/misc/about. Accessed 27 Sept 2019
5. Szablewski, D.: ZType - Typing Game - Type to Shoot. https://zty.pe/. Accessed 27 Sept 2019
6. Typing.com: Typing Games. https://www.typing.com/student/games. Accessed 27 Sept 2019
7. Grundkiewicz, R., Junczys-Dowmunt, M.: The WikEd error corpus: a corpus of corrective wikipedia edits and its application to grammatical error correction. In: Przepiórkowski, A., Ogrodniczuk, M. (eds.) NLP 2014. LNCS (LNAI), vol. 8686, pp. 478–490. Springer, Cham (2014). https://doi.org/10.1007/978-3-319-10888-9_47

8. Ľ. Štúr Institute of Linguistics of the Slovak Academy of Sciences: Error Corpus of Slovak CHIBY, 05 Aug 2019. https://www.juls.savba.sk/errcorp_en.html
9. The Wikimedia Foundation: skwiki dump. https://dumps.wikimedia.org/skwiki/latest/
10. Attardi, G.: WikiExtractor - Python script that extracts and cleans text from a Wikipedia database dump. https://github.com/attardi/wikiextractor
11. Navarro, G.: A guided tour to approximate string matching. ACM Comput. Surv. (CSUR) **33**(1), 31–88 (2001)

BDmark: A Blockchain-Driven Approach to Big Data Watermarking

Swagatika Sahoo[1(✉)], Rishu Roshan[2], Vikash Singh[2], and Raju Halder[1]

[1] Indian Institute of Technology Patna, Patna, India
{swagatika_1921cs03,halder}@iitp.ac.in
[2] Indian Institute of Information Technology Guwahati, Guwahati, India
rishuroshan.1998@gmail.com, vik625singh@gmail.com

Abstract. Big data, as a driving force to the business growth, creates a new paradigm that encourages large number of start-ups and less-known data brokers to adopt data monetization as their key role in the data marketplace. As a pitfall, such data-driven scenarios make big data prone to various threats, such as ownership claiming, illegal reselling, tampering, etc. Unfortunately, existing watermarking solutions are ill-suited to big data due to a number of challenging factors, such as V's of big data, involvement of multiple owners, incremental watermarking, large cover-size and limited watermark-capacity, non-interference, etc. This paper presents a novel approach BDmark that provides a transparent immutable audit trail for data movement in big data monetizing scenarios, by exploiting the power of both watermarking and blockchain technologies. We describe in detail how our approach overcomes the above-mentioned challenging factors. As a proof of concept, we present a prototype implementation of the proposed system using Java and Solidity on Ethereum platform and the experimental results on smart contracts show a linear growth of gas consumption w.r.t. input data size. To the best of our knowledge, this is the first proposal which deals with watermarking issues in the context of big data.

Keywords: Digital watermarking · Big data · Blockchain · Smart contract

1 Introduction

With explosive increase of global data over the last decade, big data has become a powerful resource which is playing a leading role in the transformation of existing business models [3]. This targets not only business analytics process, but also academic, research, and other decision making activities. Thanks to the growth of social media, the increasing number of smart connected devices, ubiquitous network access, and many others. This new paradigm, on the other hand, offers an establishment of large number of start-ups companies who sell and purchase our personal data on a daily basis. Few, among many others, include Datacamp,

P. Sitek et al. (Eds.): ACIIDS 2020, CCIS 1178, pp. 71–84, 2020.
https://doi.org/10.1007/978-981-15-3380-8_7

Datawallet, Dawex, etc.[1]. Even most of us are unknown about the existence of less-known data-brokers who gain profit by gathering, aggregating, analyzing, hoarding, commodifying, trading or using personal data without our knowledge or consent [11]. There are many other situations where data monetization is an integral and indispensable part of a system in the form of data-as-a-service model [14]. Some interesting fields spawned and co-existing with the use of big data are machine learning, deep learning, artificial intelligence, data-science, etc., which may demand training dataset in a pay-per-use fashion. In this context, example like census data collection shows its relevancy, where the task is outsourced to a large number of organizations in a hierarchical fashion to collect data locally at individual-levels and then to combine them together towards the higher levels, covering data-collection over a large geographical areas.

The above data driven scenarios give rise to a major concern related to our fundamental right to privacy and security. Moreover, such data is prone to various activities, such as piracy, illegal reselling, tampering, illegal redistribution, ownership claiming, forgery, theft, misappropriation, etc. Digital watermarking has emerged as a promising technique to address these challenges [4]. A watermark is considered to be some kind of information that is embedded into underlying data and is extracted later to prove the absence of above-mentioned activities. In this process, a watermark W is embedded into an original data-piece using a private key K which is known only to the owner. On receiving any suspicious data-piece, the owner may perform a verification process using the same private key K by extracting and comparing the embedded watermark (if present) with the original watermark information W.

There are large number of watermarking approaches exist in the literature, targeting a variety of digital contents such as databases, images, audio, video, text data, etc. [4,5,7], however they are found unfit to adopt to the case of big data watermarking due to the following challenges: V's of big data, involvement of multiple owners, incremental watermarking, large cover-size and limited watermark-capacity, non-interference, etc. [3]. On the other hand, four contributions [6,8,15,16] in the literature exist, which target specific kind of big data (such as social network data, geographical big data, and large data algebraic graph) as a cover to watermark. However, we observed that none of them addresses the above-mentioned challenges. In recent years, blockchain technology [10] has become a source of new hope with its broad spectrum of applications in practice. Examples include supply-chain, insurance, real-estate, financial services, and many more [12,13]. We are witnessing its footstep in digital watermarking as well. Few recently proposed watermarking solutions using blockchain technology are reported in [1,2,9,17]. Although, the use of blockchain in the above-mentioned proposals fulfils a common interest to improve the verifiability of the ownership in a distributed settings, unfortunately they are not meant for big data scenarios. In [16], although the proposal keeps watermarked data

---

[1] https://www.datacamp.com, https://www.datawallet.com/, https://www.dawex.co m/en/.

sharing records in blockchain, this lacks in various aspects, such as this has not taken care of big data properties, access control, etc.

As observed, none of the techniques in the literature shows its competence to be applied directly in the realm of big data watermarking by respecting the challenges we already highlighted before. To fill this research gap, in this paper we propose a novel approach BDmark that provides a transparent immutable audit trail for data movement in big data monetizing scenarios, by exploiting both watermarking and blockchain technologies power. To the best of our knowledge, this is the first proposal which deals with watermarking issues in the context of big data. To summarize, our main contributions in this paper are:

- We consider a complex big data monetization scenario where multiple actors are involved in data collection, aggregation, storage, selling, and purchasing.
- We propose a novel approach which provides a transparent immutable audit trail for data movement, by exploiting the power of both watermarking and blockchain technologies.
- We devise an access control mechanism to ensure the legitimate buyers, on receiving data-seller's permission, can get access to the target data-piece.
- We show in detail how the approach overcomes the present challenging factors in big data watermarking settings.
- Finally, as a proof of concept, we present a prototype implementation of the proposed system using Java and Solidity on Ethereum platform and report experimental results.

The structure of the paper is organized as follows: Sect. 2 describes the related works in the literature. In Sect. 3, we identify the challenging factors involved in big data watermarking. The detail description of our proposed approach is presented in Sect. 4. The attack analysis is performed in Sect. 5. Section 6 presents proof of concept and experimental results. Finally, Sect. 7 concludes our work.

2   Related Works

The authors in [6] proposed a reversible watermarking of social network data. The approach, before watermark encoding, adopted a data pre-processing phase, where features of numeric and non-numeric datasets are selected and encoded into the generated watermark. Moreover, the Genetic Algorithm in case of the numeric dataset and two operations - hashing and permutations - for the non-numerical dataset are applied. [15] presented the watermarking of large data algebraic graphs using a deep belief network. Aiming to solve the problem of interpretation attack, a zero-watermarking scheme for vector map, a type of geographical big data, is proposed in [8] based on the feature points of vector maps. In [17], the authors introduced BMCProtector, a prototype implementation based on blockchain and smart contracts, to protect music copyright issues and to ensure income rights/incentives to original holders or owners. The deployed smart contract is responsible to share the copyright parameters of the music owners and to transfer cryptocurrency to their wallet when purchasing events take place. A new design approach for copyright management of image files based on digital watermarking and blockchain is proposed in [9]. The approach stores owner's digital signatures along with images' cryptographic hashes in the blockchain and the corresponding blocks information along with watermarked images in an interplanetary file system. In [2], the authors designed a proof of concept prototype which provides an online verification platform to verify the integrity of the recorded video. With the help of blockchain technology, the approach stores cryptographic hashes of video contents in a chronological chained link to establish an irrefutable database. A blockchain-based multimedia watermarking framework is proposed in [1]. This allows the retrieving of either the transaction trails or the modification histories of an image and preserves retrievable original media content identifying the edited/tampered regions. The framework proposed in [16] facilitates the sharing of watermarked data, keeping records in the underlying blockchain, which is limited to numerical data only. A Comparative Summary in this direction, as compared to BDmark, is depicted in Table 1 where BC stands for Blockchain.

Table 1. A comparative summary w.r.t. literature

Proposals	Metric					
	Is BC-based?	Cover type	Blockchain type	Storage type	Support access control?	Dealing BigData?
[6]	N	Social network dataset	NA	NA	N	Y
[15]	N	Algebric graph	NA	NA	N	Y
[8]	N	Vector map	NA	NA	N	Y
[2]	Y	Video	Ethereum	Android devices + BC	N	N
[9]	Y	Image	NA	IPFS + BC	N	N
[17]	Y	Music	Ethereum	IPFS + BC	Y	N
[1]	Y	Multimedia	Ethereum	Media database server + BC	N	N
[16]	Y	Numerical data	Fabric	BC	N	Y
BDmark	Y	All types of data	Ethereum	IPFS + BC	Y	Y

3 Challenges in Big Data Watermarking

Let us identify a number of challenging factors that lie with the big data watermarking [3,4]:

1. **Capacity.** The most important challenge in big data watermarking is *capacity*. It determines the optimum amount of data that can be embedded in a cover and the optimum way to embed and extract this information. Due to *"volume"* property of big data, this needs to be ensured that the embedded watermark is spread over all parts of the data. Moreover, if multiple marks are inserted into such large cover of big data, they should not interfere with each other.

2. **Incremental Watermarking.** The second property *"velocity"* of big data gives rise to another challenge: the generation of streaming data requires an adoption of incremental watermarking approach to ensure that the watermarking algorithm should consider only the newly added or modified data for the watermark, keeping the unaltered watermarked-data untouched.

3. **Usability.** This is quite natural to assume that more than one actors participate in the process of big data collection. In addition to the original data-owners (who collects the data from the environment at individual levels), a number of data-collectors are also involved. The sole responsibility of data-collectors is to collect and aggregate data coming from either original data-owners or other data-collectors. Notably, in a more generic practical situation, data-collectors may also claim the ownership of the collected data, in addition to original data-owners. In such complex situation, the embedding of large number of ownership signatures, each corresponds to individual data-owner or -collector, may degrade the usability of big data.

4. **Security.** The involvement of large volume of data and many ownerships make it a natural choice to embed multiple signatures into the big data. Such setting pushes watermarked-data towards a number of attacks, including subset attack, superset attack, collusion attack, etc.

5. **Public Verifiability.** The major drawback in private watermarking scheme is single-time verifiability, due to the possibility of revealing private parameters during the verification process to take place for the first time. In contrary, watermarking scheme based on public parameters overcome such limitations and anyone can verify the ownership at any time publicly. Big data watermarking requires a public treatment because of huge cover-size and multiple ownership involved, especially when big data can be split, aggregated and shared in pieces among many actors.

6. **Trust.** Big data collection, storage, sharing, etc., requires the support of cloud-based infrastructure. In such case, trust is a concern when we are providing watermark solution to big data and at the same time relying on semi-trusted or even untrusted third party cloud service provider.

7. **Traceability.** Traditional watermarking approaches do not support traceability. Although this may not be required in case of simple and restrictive scenarios involving single owner and limited sized data, this of course carries an important and impactful role in a complex scenarios like our case.

4   BDmark: A Blockchain-Driven Big Data Watermarking

The proposed system involves the following actors: (1) Data-owners, (2) Data-collectors, and (3) Data-buyers. Data-owners are those persons or organizations who are responsible to generate data from the environment. The task of data-collectors is to collect data either from data-owners or from other data-collectors and to transfer them further to another set of data-collectors. Since we are considering data as purchasing and selling items, there exist many data-buyers in the system who need data to buy either

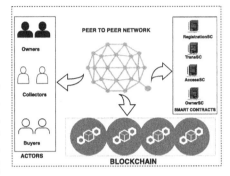

Fig. 1. A pictorial representation of the overall system components

from the original owner or from the data-collectors. All these actors are connected in a peer-to-peer network which maintains a blockchain and records all kinds of interactions among the actors. The overall system components are shown pictorially in Fig. 1. The smart contracts deployed in the blockchain are responsible to perform crucial functionalities, such as registration, traceability, access control, etc. Our proposed approach BDmark comprises of the following phases: Joining to Blockchain Network, Registration, Data Collection and Storage and Data Monetization. Figure 2 depicts the interactions among data-owners, data-collectors and smart contracts which take place during the phases 2 and 3, whereas Fig. 4 depicts the same among data-buyers and smart contracts which take place during phase 4. Let us now describe below each of the phases in detail.

4.1   Joining to Blockchain Network

The first and foremost step for an actor to participate in the system is to join the blockchain network through specially designated nodes, known as seed nodes. This simply starts by exchanging joining messages between new node and any one seed node. As a result, the seed node returns addresses of its neighbouring nodes with whom the new node can establish peer to peer connections. This process is repeated until a satisfactory number of peers is found.

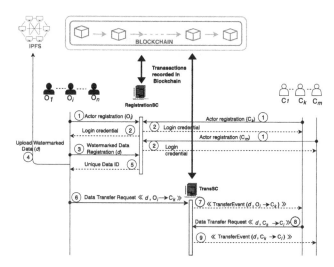

Fig. 2. Interaction-diagram among owners, collectors and smart contracts

4.2 Registration

This phase is responsible to provide a unique credential to all actors who participate in the system. This is crucial to ensure that only legitimate actors are performing only those transactions for which they are allowed. Observe that additional use of biometric-based authentication through national identity database may improve the security of the registration process. The smart contract RegistrationSC is responsible for the registration process. The interactions among data-owners O_i, data-collectors C_k and data-buyers B_j with RegistrationSC are indicated by the steps ① and ② in Figs. 2 and 4 respectively.

4.3 Data Collection and Storage

This is the core phase in our approach to ensure the copyright protection of big data. We assume the presence of multiple actors (owners and collectors) in the process of big data collection, aggregation and storage. The data-collection from the environment would be performed by data-owners who then transfer the collected data-pieces to another collectors. After aggregating the incoming data-pieces, a collector may send it to another set of collectors as well. In contrast to the data-aggregation operation, the approach also supports data-splitting when a collector needs to transfer different segments of the collected-data to different collectors. Let us now describe all the activities separately which are involved in this phase:

Watermarking of Owner's Data. After collecting data from the environment, an owner must embed his/her signature (as watermark information) into the data. This enables the owner to claim the ownership of his/her data anytime later. Assuming the size of the collected data-pieces at individual level is limited, one can apply any suitable existing watermarking technique [4] for this purpose.

Registering Watermarked-Data. After successful watermark embedding, data-owners register their watermarked-data by invoking `RegistrationSC` and by uploading it on the IPFS. Like actor's registration, this step also assigns an unique identity to the watermarked-data in the form of two-tuple $\langle uniqueID,$ $data\text{-}hash \rangle$. These interactions are shown by the steps ③, ④ and ⑤ in Fig. 2. Please note that, from now onwards, we use the terms 'data' and 'watermarked-data' interchangeably when there is no ambiguity in the context.

Data Transfer. This phase allows the transfer of data either from an owner to a collector, or from a collector to another collector. The interactions are shown by the steps ⑥–⑨ in Fig. 2. The smart contract `TransSC` is responsible for these tasks. To improve the scalability of the system, the operations on data, such as aggregation and splitting, are achieved with the help of token creation. Figure 3 depicts a scenario involving various operations on data through token generation. For example, $Token_1$: $\langle d_1, d_2, d_3 \rangle$ represents a new token (named as $Token_1$)

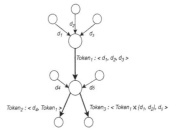

Fig. 3. Data transfer scenarios involving data-collection, aggregation and splitting through token generation

which consists of three data units d_1, d_2 and d_3. On the other hand, $Token_3$ consists of d_1, d_2 and d_5 where d_1 and d_2 are obtained from $Token_1$. Formally, we denote by '$\langle \ \rangle$' as data-aggregation operation, whereas '$\succ_\in\{ \ \}$' as data-splitting operation. The symbol ':' denotes 'named as' operation. Observe that a token may contain another token as well. The overall algorithm to perform data-transfer and data-traceability is depicted in Algorithm 1.

Let us now briefly describe the algorithmic steps. The algorithm takes as inputs the unique identifiers of sender and receiver (which are generated in the registration phase) and the collection D of data for which ownership needs to be transferred.

Algorithm 1: TransferOwnership

Input   : Sender A_i, Receiver A_j,
          Data-collection D
Output: Transfer id, Token id

```
1  flag=true;
2  S=∅;
3  for all basic data block dᵢ ∈ D do
4  ⌊   S=S ∪ dᵢ;
5  for all token tᵢ ∈ D do
6      X =getBasicDataBlocks(tᵢ);
7  ⌊   S=S ∪ X;
8  for all splittedtoken dⱼ ∈ t⋈φ do
9      X =getBasicDataBlocks(φ);
10 ⌊   S=S ∪ X;
11 for all basic data block dₖ ∈ S do
12     if Aᵢ ∉ getCurrentOwner(dₖ) then
13         flag=false;
14 ⌊   ⌊   exit();
15 if flag==true then
16     for all basic data block dₖ ∈ S do
17         replace Aᵢ by Aⱼ in the current
           owner getCurrentOwner(dₖ);
18 ⌊   ⌊ Append Aⱼ to the list
           InheritOwners(dₖ);
19 Create a new token l to uniquely identify D;
20 Store the token id t corresponding to D
   denoted t:D with ownership Aⱼ and the
   transfer id h;
21 Create a new Transfer id h;
22 Store the token id t corresponding to D
   denoted t:D with ownership Aⱼ and the
   transfer id h;
23 Return h and t;
```

Algorithm 2: GetWatermarkedData

Inputs : Buyer's identity B_i, Data Collection D
Output: Hash links to download D

```
1  Bᵢ requests to the smart contract AccessSC to
   purchase data D;
2  AccessSC interacts with the smart contracts
   RegistrationSC and TransSC to check whether Bᵢ and
   D are registered, and gets the list of D's owners
   L_owner and their personal smart contract
   addresses and names L_SC;
3  if Bᵢ is valid buyer then
4      if D is registered data then
5          Ask Bᵢ to select one owner Oⱼ from the
           list L_owner of eligible owners;
6          Addr:= getOwnerSCaddress(Oⱼ, L_SC);
7          Name:= getOwnerSCname(Oⱼ, L_SC);
8          flag:=true;
9          Generate an unique interaction id I;
10         τ=getCurrentTime();
11         Store a new tuple ⟨I, Bᵢ, D, Oⱼ, τ,
           Addr, Name, flag⟩ into LookTab;
12 ⌊   ⌊ Return Addr to the buyer;
13 Bᵢ invokes OwnerSC, deployed to the address Addr,
   with inputs ⟨Bᵢ, D, Oⱼ⟩;
14 OwnerSC contacts AccessSC by passing ⟨Bᵢ, D, Oⱼ⟩;
15 AccessSC checks the look-up table LookTab;
16 if ∃ ⟨ Bᵢ, D, Oⱼ, τ, Addr, Name⟩ ∈ LookTab then
17     τ₁=getCurrentTime();
18 ⌊   Return interaction id I to OwnerSC;
19 OwnerSC sends I to the buyer Bᵢ;
20 Bᵢ requests AccessSC for D supplying ⟨I, Bᵢ, D,
   Oⱼ⟩;
21 τ₂=getCurrentTime();
22 if τ₂ - τ₁ ⩽ δ then
23     if Verify(⟨I, Bᵢ, D, Oⱼ⟩, LookTab)==success then
24         if flag≠ false then
25             return IPFS hash link of D to Bᵢ;
26 ⌊   ⌊   ⌊ Set flag:= false;
```

Observe that the data-collection may contain basic data blocks or previously generated tokens or splitted tokens representing other data-collections. Steps 3 to 7 identify a set S of all basic data blocks belonging to D by enumerating it recursively, whereas steps 11 to 12 verify whether the transfer request is issued by legitimate owner A_i by checking the current ownership of all data blocks in S as per the record in blockchain smart contract state variables. On successful verification, *flag* variable remains *true*, and steps 15 to 18 updates the ownership. Observe that, in addition to the current ownership change at step 17, the algorithm maintains a trace of ownership changes by appending all new owners to a list. Finally, a token identifier representing this data-collection and a transaction identifier are generated and stored.

4.4 Data Monetization and Access Control

This phase is designed to enable data-owners or data-collectors to sell their data to registered data-buyers. The interaction diagram is depicted in Fig. 4. As usual, to participate in the system, data-buyers first register themselves by invoking RegistrationSC, depicted by steps ① and ②. Whenever a data-buyer wants to buy a chunk of data, the whole process must pass through an access control mechanism involving the steps ③–⑮ among data-buyers and two smart contracts AccessSC and OwnerSC. A look-up table LookTab is maintained by

AccessSC to record some crucial information, like unique identifier for a particular data request, the time-stamp when the request is made, etc. The overall algorithm is depicted in Algorithm 2. Let us now explain the algorithmic steps and the corresponding interactions in detail. When a legitimate data-buyer B_i requests for registered data D to AccessSC, on successful verification in steps 3 and 4 through invocation of RegistrationSC and TransSC, an entry containing a unique interaction id, buyer-seller information, time-stamp of the request, and details of data-owner's smart contract are stored in LookTab in step 11. These are shown by the steps ③ and ④ in Fig. 4. Observe that the *flag* value indicates whether the current request is already fulfilled or yet to fulfill. On receiving the address of owner's smart contract OwnerSC, the data-buyer invokes it by passing the request information $\langle B_i, D, O_i \rangle$ in step 13. In order to check weather to give permission or not, OwnerSC will contact AccessSC to check the validity of the request in step 14. These are shown by the steps ⑤, ⑥ and ⑦ respectively in Fig. 4. If an entry corresponding to this request is found in LookTab (step 16), the validity is ensured and therefore AccessSC returns the corresponding I to OwnerSC who then passes it to the buyer as an indication of "data access permission". These are shown in algorithmic steps 17 to 19 and by steps ⑧, ⑨, ⑩ and ⑪ in Fig. 4. Finally, on producing the same interaction id by the buyer in step 20, AccessSC determines that owner has given the permission and the hash links to download D from IPFS are therefore provided. Accordingly, the value of *flag* is set to *false*, in order to prevent the repeated download of the same data against the same I. These interactions are shown by the steps ⑫ to ⑯ in Fig. 4. Observe that δ represents the maximum time gap, starting from the receiving of I to the production of the same to AccessSC by the data-buyer.

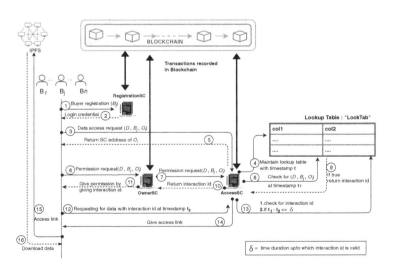

Fig. 4. Interaction-diagram between data-buyers and smart contracts.

5   Attack Analysis

In this part, we discuss few relevant attacks and their preventive-measures addressed by the proposed approach.

- **Denial-of-Service (DoS) attack.** DoS attacks may take place in the system aiming to prevent data access services to other legitimate buyers. A flood of data request messages may intentionally be sent to the corresponding smart contract AccessSC keeping it throughout busy. The thawrt of DOS attacks is achieved by discouraging the attackers as Gas price is involved in every execution of AccessSC. Where gas price is the total cost of a transaction.
- **Man in the middle attack.** Man in the middle attack is possible when an attacker intercepts the communication between buyer and owner, and get access to the interaction id which she may present later to the smart contract AccessSC in order to get data-access. This is impossible in the proposed framework because of the following factors: (1) The login mechanism using pre-approved credentials, (2) The sharing of interaction id through registered media, *e.g.* mobile, (3) One time use of generated interaction id for a given owner-buyer combination at a specific time-stamp, (4) The access restriction within a predefined time interval.
- **Attacks on Watermark:** Big data is highly susceptible to the following attacks: (a) Subset Attack, (b) Superset Attack, (c) Collusion Attack, (d) Value Modification Attack, etc. The proposed system takes care of big data ownership by embedding watermarks in basic data blocks at fine-grained granularity level after collected by data-owners at individual levels. We rely on the security strength of the existing watermarking techniques, to ensure the success of ownership claim in future. Moreover, in addition to this, the association of hash value of basic data blocks during registration also helps to perform tamper detection. Since the blockchain network is pseudonymous, this is an advantageous step to weaken the collusion attacks.

6   Proof of Concept and Experimental Results

We have implemented a prototype to analyze the feasibility of the proposal. The programming languages we used in the implementation are Java and Solidity. We have created a simple Ethereum DApp using Web3.js and Truffle and set up monitoring of the API transactions sent to the blockchain. We have used Truffle framework, as it provides a set of tools and boilerplate code for scaffolding DApps for Ethereum. In the current implementation, we have provided the complete functionalities in the form of two Smart Contracts: (i) RegistrationTransSC which implements the functions of both the Smart Contracts RegistrationSC and TransSc, that includes Actors Registration, Data Registration, and Ownership Transfer. (ii) AccessOwnerSC which implements the functions of AccessSC and OwnerSC, that includes Data Request, Access Policy, Buyer's Validation, and Permission. We have designed a web interface to interact with the contracts

Table 2. Transaction gas costs for remaining smart contract functionalities

Sl. no.	Functions	Gas used	Actual cost (*Ether*)	*USD* ($)
1	$RegistrationTransSC$	4724439	0.009448878	2.92
2	$AccessOwnerSC$	568945	0.001137890	0.35
3	$createUser$	114041	0.000228082	0.07
4	$newData$	190189	0.000380378	0.11
5	get_data_owners	22888	0.000045776	0.014
6	$getdata\_tracking\_ids$	22954	0.000045780	0.014
7	$getdata\_trackindes$	25435	0.000050870	0.015
8	$userLogin$	27857	0.000055714	0.017
9	$getdetails$	239230	0.000478460	0.14
10	$concatenateInfoAndHash$	29603	0.000059206	0.018

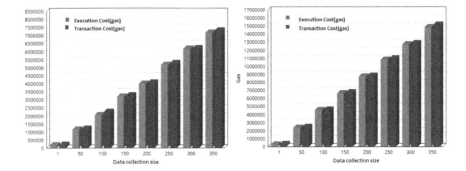

Fig. 5. Gas price analysis of TransferOwnership and GetWatermarkedData

that assume three roles: Actors Registration, Data Registration, and Data Monetization. Each has its own view (page) and we keep them separated to better demonstrate how different actors could use the contracts. Figures 5(a) and (b) depict the experimental results which show the variation of gas cost for the execution of the modules in RegistrationTransSC and AccessOwnerSC corresponding to TransferOwnership (Algorithm 1) and GetWatermarkedData (Algorithm 2) respectively w.r.t. various size of data collection D. Observe that the gas cost complexity is linear w.r.t. the input data collection size. Table 2 depicts the transaction gas costs for the remaining functionalities where input (and hence gas cost) remains same all the time.

7   Conclusion

This paper presents a novel approach to provide transparent immutable audit trail for data movement in big data monetizing scenarios. The proposal addresses a number of common data breaches in the world of big data by strengthening the use of blockchain technology on top of existing watermarking techniques at fine-grained levels. Interestingly, the approach is immune to several common attacks and its feasibility is established through a proof of concept. To the best of our knowledge, this is the first proposal which deals with watermarking issues in the context of big data.

References

1. Bhowmik, D., Feng, T.: The multimedia blockchain: a distributed and tamper-proof media transaction framework. In: Proceedings of 22nd International Conference on Digital Signal Processing (DSP), London, UK, pp. 1–5. IEEE, August 2017
2. Billström, A., Huss, F.: Video Integrity through Blockchain Technology. KTH Vetenskap Och Konst, Stockholm, Sweden, August 2017
3. Chen, M., Mao, S., Liu, Y.: Big data: a survey. Mob. Netw. Appl. **19**(2), 171–209 (2014)
4. Halder, R., Pal, S., Cortesi, A.: Watermarking techniques for relational databases: survey, classification and comparison. J. Univers. Comput. Sci. **16**(21), 3164–3190 (2010)
5. Hartung, F., Girod, B.: Watermarking of uncompressed and compressed video. Signal Process. **66**(3), 283–301 (1998)
6. Iftikhar, S., Kamran, M., Munir, E.U., Khan, S.U.: A reversible watermarking technique for social network data sets for enabling data trust in cyber, physical, and social computing. IEEE Syst. J. **11**, 197–206 (2017)
7. Kamaruddin, N.S., Kamsin, A., Por, L.Y., Rahman, H.: A review of text watermarking: theory, methods, and applications. IEEE Access **6**, 8011–8028 (2018)
8. Liu, Y., Yang, F., Gao, K., Dong, W., Song, J.: A zero-watermarking scheme with embedding timestamp in vector maps for big data computing. Clust. Comput. **20**, 3667–3675 (2017)
9. Meng, Z., Morizumi, T., Miyata, S., Kinoshita, H.: Design scheme of copyright management system based on digital watermarking and blockchain. In: Proceedings of IEEE 42nd Annual Computer Software and Applications Conference (COMPSAC), Tokyo, Japan, pp. 359–364. IEEE, July 2018
10. Nakamoto, S.: Bitcoin: A peer-to-peer electronic cash system, March 2009. http://bitcoin.org/bitcoin.pdf
11. Parra-Arnau, J.: Optimized, direct sale of privacy in personal data marketplaces. Inf. Sci. **424**, 354–384 (2018)
12. Pilkington, M.: Blockchain technology: principles and applications. In: Handbook of Research on Digital Transformations. Edward Elgar (2016)
13. Sahoo, S., Fajge, A.M., Halder, R., Cortesi, A.: A hierarchical andabstraction-based blockchain model. Appl. Sci. **9**(11), 2343 (2019)
14. Terzo, O., Ruiu, P., Bucci, E., Xhafa, F.: Data as a service (DaaS) for sharing and processing of large data collections in the cloud. In: Proceedings of Seventh International Conference on Complex, Intelligent, and Software Intensive Systems, Taichung, Taiwan, pp. 475–480. IEEE, July 2013

15. Wangming, Y.: The digital watermarking algorithm based on the big data algebra graoh. In: Proceedings of International Conference on Robots & Intelligent System, Huaian, China, pp. 342–345. IEEE, November 2017
16. Yang, J., Wang, H., Wang, Z., Long, J., Du, B.: BDCP: a framework for big data copyright protection based on digital watermarking. In: Wang, G., Chen, J., Yang, L.T. (eds.) SpaCCS 2018. LNCS, vol. 11342, pp. 351–360. Springer, Cham (2018). https://doi.org/10.1007/978-3-030-05345-1_30
17. Zhao, S., O'Mahony, D.: BMCProtector: a blockchain and smart contract based application for music copyright protection. In: Proceedings of International Conference on Blockchain Technology and Application, USA, pp. 1–5. ACM, December 2018

Efficient Approaches for House Pricing Prediction by Using Hybrid Machine Learning Algorithms

Sruthi Chiramel$^{(\boxtimes)}$, Doina Logofătu$^{(\boxtimes)}$, Jyoti Rawat$^{(\boxtimes)}$,
and Christina Andersson$^{(\boxtimes)}$

Department of Computer Science and Engineering,
Frankfurt University of Applied Sciences, 60318 Frankfurt a.M., Germany
{chiramel,rawat}@stud.fra-uas.de, {logofatu,andersso}@fb2.fra-uas.de

Abstract. To own a house is dream of many. However, in this age of inflation and sky rocketing housing prices, its not always easy to find dream home within the constrained budget. Also, in addition to budget, there are several other factors that contributes towards finding the right home-location, ease of access, transportation etc. In such a scenario, a house price predicting system will be helpful for both buyers and sellers. This research aims to predict house prices in IOWA state, USA using regression analysis. The prediction is arrived at by help of various explanatory variables such as area of the property, location of the house, material used for construction, age of the property, number of bedrooms and garages and so on. This paper elaborates on the performance of Linear regression and Ridge regularization for model prediction. It also details the machine learning techniques used and its significance pertaining to the results.

Keywords: Linear regression · Ridge regularization · Machine learning

1 Introduction

Housing industry or real estate industry, caters to one of the basic needs of human- shelter. Due to this, housing accounts to high percentages of national transactions per year [1]. Over the years various factors have contributed to the variation of housing prices. These variations are dependent on the value of property and various extrinsic and intrinsic factors affecting the same. Land and property are main components of real estate whose value varies due to demand and supply conditions [2]. In this paper, we have made an attempt to analyze the existing data set, its parameters or explanatory variables and come up with an efficient machine learning algorithm to predict the price of the house.

There are several approaches that can be used to determine the price of the house. The first approach is a quantitative prediction. A quantitative approach is an approach that utilizes time-series data [3]. We have used Linear regression in combination with ridge regularization to predict the results.

© Springer Nature Singapore Pte Ltd. 2020
P. Sitek et al. (Eds.): ACIIDS 2020, CCIS 1178, pp. 85–94, 2020.
https://doi.org/10.1007/978-981-15-3380-8_8

2   Problem Description

The real estate industry is an illustrious business which should be both beneficial for the buyer and the seller. The problem faced by the buyer and the seller respectively are as follows:

House buyer: The buyer wants to buy a good property at a reasonable price. They would consider various factors such as location, size of house, garden, garage etc and would compare if the quoted price is reasonable to them.

House seller: The seller is always interested in profit making. They typically want to buy a house at a low price and invest on the features that will give the highest return.

In this paper, we have tried to predict the Sale price of houses by analysing the dependent variables that influence the sale price of the house. In our dataset, there are 79 explanatory variables describing various attributes of residential homes in Ames, Iowa. We have tried to predict the sale price accurately using hybrid machine learning techniques.

3   Related Research

In the past couple of decades, the steep increase in the demand for property and the fluctuating economic conditions have propelled scientists and researchers to develop prediction models that estimates prices without biases. Building a predictive model not just requires expertise in data science software but also the knowledge of various socio-economic factors that forms a part of the data pool. In this paper, we have gained inspiration from the below mentioned research works.

For instance, In his research Rahadi, [4] has divided these factors into three main groups- physical condition, concept and location. Physical properties of house are those which is visible to the human eye, including the size of the house, the number of bedrooms, the structure of kitchen, availability of garage and garden, the area of land and buildings, and the age of the house [5], while it also depends how the seller markets the property claiming new age minimalism, energy conservation, sustainable properties etc. Krol [6] analysed the relationship between the price of an apartment on the criteria based on its features resulting from hedonic analysis in Poland, Wilhelmsson [7] derived the weights of the relative importance of location features that influence the market values of apartments in Donetsk, Ukraine and Ottensmann [8] analysed housing preferences based on the proximity to employment location in Indianapolis, Indiana, USA. Also, housing price fluctuations can occur during financial crisis. One such research has been based on German real estate industry by considering the GDP of the nation [14]. This research has been built by analysing the data over a period of 6 months from the one of the most trusted housing internet platform ImmobilienScout24. The prediction was made using Autoregressive distributed lag model (ARDL) and Vector auto regressive (VAR) models.

4   Proposed Approaches

Machine learning is the science in which machines are taught to perform a particular activity by training them using algorithms. There are numerous algorithms that can be used for model prediction such as K Means Clustering Algorithm, Support Vector Machine Algorithm, Linear Regression, Logistic Regression, Random Forests, Decision Trees. The choice of algorithm to be used is dependent upon factors such as the category of data, type of the response or target variable etc. In this paper we have presented a hybrid approach via the analysis of Linear modelling and ridge regularization on the Ames, Iowa, USA housing data set (Fig. 1).

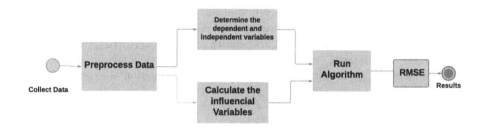

Fig. 1. Work flow diagram

4.1   Linear Regression

Linear regression is the statistical method of predicting the value of a dependent/response variable from an independent/explanatory variable. The response variable is predicted against one or more independent variables. Linear regression analysis is the most commonly used statistical techniques [11]. The linear regression analysis uses the mathematical slope-intercept equation, i.e., y = mx + c. This equation describes the line of best fit for the relationship between y (dependent variable) and x (independent variable) [11].

Coefficient of Determination, R^2
The coefficient of determination is the level of the total variation in the response/target variable that can be explained by varying in explanatory variable(s). When R^2 is +1, there exists a perfect linear relationship between x and y. When it is $0 < R^2 < 1$, there is a weaker linear relationship between x and y, i.e., some, but not all of the variation in y is explained by variation in x [11].

$$R^2 = [correl(y, ypred)]^2$$

It is the squared correlation between the observed and the predicted values.

4.2   Ridge Regularization

Regularization is the technique used to avoid over-fitting by penalizing high-valued regression coefficients i.e it reduces the number of parameters and makes the model more compact. Ridge regularization is used when the explanatory variables are highly co-linear. Regularization works by biasing data towards particular values (such as small values near zero). The bias is achieved by adding a tuning parameter to encourage those values [12]. Ridge regularization adds an L2 penalty equal to the square of the magnitude of coefficients. L2 will not yield sparse models and all coefficients are shrunk by the same factor (none are eliminated) [12].

Similar to least-squares methods ridge regularization aims at minimizing the loss function that includes the sum of squared regression residuals. However, opposed to least squares, the loss function also includes a term consisting of positive penalty parameter λ times the model complexity, measured by the sum of squared regression weights [13]. This penalty prevents over-fitting by shrinking the weights towards zero.

More formally, predictor y in terms of ridge regularization is expressed as:

$$y = X\beta + Z\gamma + \epsilon$$

where β is the vector of coefficients linking X and Y variables, γ the vector of coefficients linking Z and Y variables, and ϵ the error.

5   Implementation Details

We have followed the below mentioned hierarchy to arrive at our results for housing price prediction:

- Gathering data.
- Data Cleansing and Feature Engineering
- Defining model.
- Training, testing model and predicting the output.

5.1   Gathering Data

In the Ames, Iowa housing data set, there are 1460 instances of training data and 1460 of test data. Total number of attributes equals 81, of which 36 is quantitative, 43 categorical + Id and SalePrice.

Quantitative: 1stFlrSF, 2ndFlrSF, 3SsnPorch, BedroomAbvGr, BsmtFinSF1, BsmtFinSF2, BsmtFullBath, BsmtHalfBath, BsmtUnfSF, EnclosedPorch, Fireplaces, FullBath, GarageArea, GarageCars, GarageYrBlt, GrLivArea, HalfBath, KitchenAbvGr, LotArea, LotFrontage, LowQualFinSF, MSSubClass, MasVnrArea, MiscVal, MoSold, OpenPorchSF, OverallCond, OverallQual, PoolArea, ScreenPorch, TotRmsAbvGrd, TotalBsmtSF, WoodDeckSF, YearBuilt, YearRemodAdd, YrSold.

Qualitative: Alley, BldgType, BsmtCond, BsmtExposure, BsmtFinType1, BsmtFinType2, BsmtQual, CentralAir, Condition1, Condition2, Electrical, ExterCond, ExterQual, Exterior1st, Exterior2nd, Fence, FireplaceQu, Foundation, Functional, GarageCond, GarageFinish, GarageQual, GarageType, Heating, HeatingQC, HouseStyle, KitchenQual, LandContour, LandSlope, LotConfig, LotShape, MSZoning, MasVnrType, MiscFeature, Neighborhood, PavedDrive, PoolQC, RoofMatl, RoofStyle, SaleCondition, SaleType, Street, Utilities.

5.2 Data Cleansing and Feature Engineering

As the first step to data cleansing, we have removed the outliers. Feature engineering is the process of using domain knowledge of the data to create features that make machine learning algorithms work. It is a crucial step in machine learning and predictive modelling. It involves the transformation of given feature space, typically using mathematical functions, with the objective of reducing the modeling error for a given target [9].

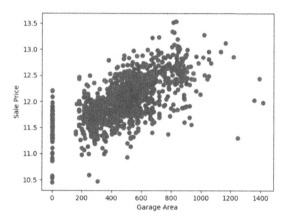

Fig. 2. Outliers in Garage Area

On closer analysis of the data, we came to a conclusion that certain variables have an higher impact on the Sale price. Hence we created a subset of main data keeping the following variables:
MSZoning, Utilities, Neighborhood, BldgType, HouseStyle, OverallQual, OverallCond, YearBuilt, ExterQual, ExterCond, BsmtQual, BsmtCond, TotalBsmtSF, Heating, HeatingQC, CentralAir, Electrical, GrLivArea, BedroomAbvGr, KitchenAbvGr, KitchenQual, TotRmsAbvGrd, Functional, Fireplaces, FireplaceQu, GarageArea, GarageQual, GarageCond, OpenPorchSF, PoolArea Fence, MoSold, YrSold, SaleType, SaleCondition, SalePrice

Also, 19 attributes have missing values, 5 over 50 % of all data. Most of times NA means lack of subject described by attribute, like missing pool, fence, no garage and basement. We have used the method of interpolation to deal with the missing values. This method replaces the missing values with an average value and then assign the results to data.

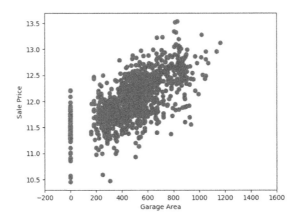

Fig. 3. Outliers removed

Figures 2 and 3 depicts the graphs before and after the outlier removal.

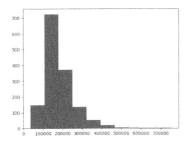 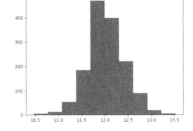

(a) Right skewed distribution   (b) Normal distribution after log transformation

Fig. 4. Effect of log transformation on target variable

From Fig. 4, It is apparent that SalePrice doesn't follow normal distribution, the distribution of our target variable-Sale Price is heavily right skewed. Thus, a log term of Sale Price has been performed before performing regression. Similarly, Also none of quantitative variables have normal distribution; hence, they were transformed as well. Performing log transformation of sale price has normalized it and the skewness has reduced from 1.88 to 0.12133. Log transformations helps to analyse the data better, however, one should always exponentiate it back during the prediction. Also, we have observed two houses with huge living areas and low SalePrices and this can seem to be outliers. However, we have not removed them, as this could lead to false results. For instance, a low score on the Overall Quality could denotes a low price. But, it has been observed that, these two houses scores maximum points on Overall Quality.

Since our model needs numerical data, we have also used one-hot encoding to transform the qualitative data into quantitative data.

Eg. As shown in Fig. 5, The partial sale condition is considerably higher than other sale conditions, Hence we have Boolean encoded partial condition to 1 and rest to zero.

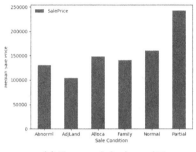
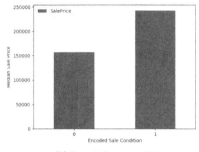

(a) Non-encoded sale conditions   (b) Encoded sale-conditions

Fig. 5. One-hot encoding for transformation of qualitative data

5.3   Defining and Training Model

Linear Regression and Ridge regularization has been used for training the data set and creation of a predictive model. Regularized regression techniques for linear regression have been created the last few ten years to reduce the flaws of ordinary least squares regression with regard to prediction accuracy [10]. Before performing the linear regression and ridge regularization, we have partitioned the data. This helped us to evaluate how our model might perform on unknown data. If we had train the model on all of the test data, it will have been difficult to analyse for the data over-fitting.

Multicollinearity
On checking for collinearity among the explanatory variables, the following variables displayed a high degree of collinearity:

OverallQual, GrLivArea, GarageCars, GarageArea, TotalBsmtSF, 1stFlrSF, FullBath.
This high degree of correlation, makes this data set an ideal candidate for the application of ridge regularization (Fig. 6).

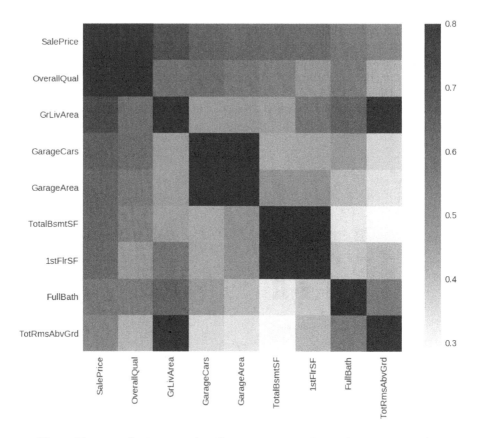

Fig. 6. Heatmap depicting multicollinearity among the explanatory variables

6   Results and Discussion

We have used the parameters R^2 and RMSE for evaluating the performance of the model.

R^2 (multiple R-squared): It is the called regression measure or fit-measure, equivalently defined as: $R^2 = [correl(y, ypred)]^2$ i.e squared correlation coefficient between observations and predictions. Higher the value of R^2, better is the fit.

RMSE (Root mean square error): The root mean square error (RMSE) has been used as a standard statistical metric to measure model performance. Most of times, a low value of RMSE is preferred for better performance of models

$$\text{RMSE} = \text{RMSE} = \sqrt{\frac{1}{n} \Sigma_{i=1}^{n} \left(y_o - y_p \right)^2}$$

y_o = observed target variable (Sale price)
y_p = predicted target variable (Sale price)

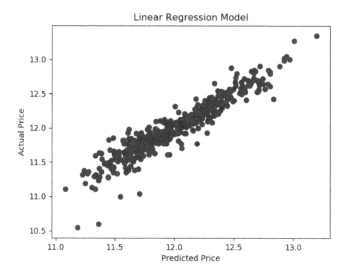

Fig. 7. Linear modelling

As results, we have obtained the following values for R^2 and RMSE for both Linear regression and using ridge regularization varying the α value:

Using Linear Regression
R^2 for Linear Modelling training set = 0.8926335399061596
R^2 for Linear Modelling test set = 0.8882477709262525
RMSE for Linear Modelling = 0.01784179451956801

Using Ridge Regularization
R^2 for Ridge Regularization training set = 0.8893871564635024
R^2 for Ridge regularization test set = 0.8869291173077205
RMSE for Ridge regularization = 0.018052324073200527

Linear regression was the first mode of approach used by us. Figure 7 depicts the Linear modelling results for the predicted test set values and the actual test set values. It shows a fairly good fit. While the R^2 of the linear modelling training set and test set values being comparable, depicts our algorithm performance good as well. RMSE of 0.01784179451956801 shows the model predicts the target variable with an error factor of 0.0178%. A lower RMSE value is always preferable

As we wanted to improve the model using a different approach given the high degree of co-linearity among the explanatory variables, Ridge regularization has been considered. However, there was no statistical improvement in the results. The value of α was varied from 0.01 until 100.

7   Conclusion

Using a data set of 1,460 houses from Ames, Iowa, this paper addresses the following questions:

1. Can the models proposed in this paper be improved?
2. What are the most important attributes that affect sold price?
3. Can the 79 explanatory values be reduced since there is high level of co-linearity between certain variables?

The assessment of the results suggests that linear regression gives satisfactory results and the observed and predicted values are fairly accurate. Ridge regularization did not help in improving the model. Moreover, it would be interesting to observe how the model will perform without running the risk of over-fitting of some of the correlated variables are omitted.

Finally, for future work, it would be interesting to see what results could be yielded from applying random forest and gradient descent on the same data set and by how much degree it is better than linear modelling.

References

1. Ioannides, Y.M.: Interactive property valuations. J. Urban Econ. **53**, 145–170 (2003)
2. French, N.: Valuation of specialized property - a review of valuation methods. J. Prop. Invest. Financ. **22**(6), 533–541(9) (2004)
3. Ghodsi, R.: Estimation of housing prices by fuzzy regression and artificial neural network. In: Fourth Asia International Conference on Mathematical/Analytical Modelling and Computer Simulation, no. 1 (2010)
4. Rahadi, R.A., Wiryono, S.K., Koesrindartotoor, D.P., Syamwil, I.B.: Factors influencing the price of housing in Indonesia. Int. J. Hous. Mark. Anal. **8**(2), 169–188 (2015)
5. Limsombunchai, V.: House price prediction: hedonic price model vs. artificial neural network. Am. J. Appl. Sci. **1**(3), 193–201 (2004)
6. Król, A.: Application of hedonic methods in modelling real estate prices in Poland. In: Lausen, B., Krolak-Schwerdt, S., Böhmer, M. (eds.) Data Science, Learning by Latent Structures, and Knowledge Discovery. SCDAKO, pp. 501–511. Springer, Heidelberg (2015). https://doi.org/10.1007/978-3-662-44983-7_44
7. Kryvobokov, M., Wilhelmsson, M.: Analysing location attributes with a hedonic model for apartment prices in Donetsk, Ukraine. Int. J. Strat. Prop. Manag. **11**(3), 157–178 (2007)
8. Ottensmann, J.R., Payton, S., Man, J.: Urban location and housing prices within a hedonic model. J. Reg. Anal. Policy **38**(1), 19–35 (2008)
9. Khurana, U., Samulowitz, H., Turaga, D.: Feature engineering for predictive modeling using reinforcement learning. In: The Thirty-Second AAAI Conference on Artificial Intelligence (AAAI 2018) (2018)
10. Doreswamy, Vastrad, C.M.: Performance analysis of regularized linear regression models FOR oxazolines and oxazoles derivates descriptor dataset. Int. J. Comput. Sci. Inf. Technol. (IJCSITY) **1**(4) (2013)
11. Kumari, K., Yadav, S.: Curric. Cardiol. Stat. **4**, 33–36 (2018)
12. Statistics How to. http://www.statisticshowto.datasciencecentral.com/ridge-regression. Accessed 14 Oct 2019
13. Hoerl, A.E., Kennard, R.W.: Ridge regression biased estimation for nonorthogonal problems. Technometrics Am. Soc. Qual. **12**, 55–67 (1970)
14. an de Meulen, P., Micheli, M., Schmidt, T.: Forecasting House Prices in Germany. Ruhr Economic Papers, vol. 294 (2011)

Design and Implementation of Business Intelligence Dashboard for Project Control at the Port Harbor-Company

Ford Lumban Gaol[1][✉], Arsyan Syahir[2][✉], and Tokuro Matsuo[3][✉]

[1] Computer Science Department, BINUS Graduate Program – Doctor of Computer Science, Bina Nusantara University, Jakarta, Indonesia
fgaol@binus.edu
[2] Computer Science Department, BINUS Graduate Program – Master of Information System, Bina Nusantara University, Jakarta, Indonesia
Arsyan.syahir@binus.ac.id
[3] Advanced Institute of Industry Technology, Tokyo, Japan
matsuo@aiit.ac.jp

Abstract. This study aims to assist resource management and the project controller at Port Harbor Company. Port Harbor Company is an IT Consulting. Problems that often occur in IT Consulting are related to the project cost, resource management and control of each project. Problems that occur at the Port Harbor Company are poor resource management, spending costs that exceed a predetermined budget and how to see the status of ongoing projects. Using Business Intelligence and the dashboard as a front end will help the project controller and resource management manage resources, manage project costs and monitor ongoing projects. In this study, the development and implementation of Business Intelligence and dashboards using the ASAP method are expected to be more structured and can solve the Port Harbor Company problem.

Keywords: Business Intelligence · Business Object · ERP · Project Management

1 Introduction

The Port Harbor Company is a multinational IT company engaged in consulting, transactional services and information technology services. The Port Harbor Company was founded in 2009 and is still operating today. The company offers solutions in the field of Enterprise Resource Planning (ERP) to clients which the company uses SAP (SAP Application Production) as its tools. SAP itself is an application used to process data used by companies to manage the resources they have. SAP itself has many modules in it such as Finance, Control, Material Management, Logistics, Factory Maintenance, Project Systems, Fund Management, Business Planning Consolidation, Production Planning, Sales Distribution, Human Resource Management, Business Intelligence Business Objects, SAP Fiori, SAP Leonardo, SAP Success Factor. The Port Harbor Company itself has successfully carried out many ERP implementations both in government agencies, and

© Springer Nature Singapore Pte Ltd. 2020
P. Sitek et al. (Eds.): ACIIDS 2020, CCIS 1178, pp. 95–105, 2020.
https://doi.org/10.1007/978-981-15-3380-8_9

private, Port Harbor Company has also successfully implemented in oil and gas companies in Brunei Darussalam, Malaysia, Australia, and several other countries. Until now some of the biggest revenue is still obtained from domestic projects, which is around 90% and 10% from projects originating from abroad.

Of the many projects that have been implemented by the Port Harbor Company, it does not necessarily run smoothly. Some projects have failed and also been detrimental. There are many factors why implementation is not going well as project control is not going well. The Project Manager cannot properly manage the project team so the deliverables from each phase are delayed and this results in costs incurred that will exceed what was set at the beginning of the project. Then there are not enough resources assigned to the project to handle a project. The Project Management Resource Management team often has problems monitoring which resources are on board and which resources are idle. There should be a reminder system to see the scheduled start and end dates for the consultant's assignment. This is also a problem that the Port Harbor Company management is facing right now assignment. This is also a problem that the Port Harbor Company management is facing right now.

The scope of the project's problems is not far from resource, timeline and cost issues where these three factors will affect deliverables to users from each phase. Regarding resources, the Port Harbor Company management still has a big problem with this. Management does not have a system to monitor consultants who are on board and consultants who are idle where this is seen per module and per level. Current resource settings use the manual method by looking at operational systems. This requires quite a time and a quick decision in resource management. Then management and resource management also want to see resource utilization per division where this will be needed if there are modules that have the idlest resources. The resume can be shared with other modules if there are modules that require additional resources and this will also be utilized in ongoing projects. This will make consultants more productive than they must be idle.

Then the second problem is related to the project cost. This project cost is related to cost, revenue, and margin. Cost plans, revenue plans, and margin plans will be determined by the sales and project controller which will be compared with the actual ones. There is concern about this where this will affect the revenue that will be obtained. The problem that often occurs with the cost is where there is rework and so requires additional mandays. The consumption of these mandays will affect the revenue per month. Then other costs such as residential accommodation, patty cash, and entertainment costs are also charged to the project cost. If not controlled then this will also affect revenue later. In running its business, the Port Harbor Company also not only provides consulting services but also sells licenses, Annual Maintenance Services (AMS), hardware, migration, and non-SAP. At present management and the project, the controller wants to see financial status such as total revenue plan, total cost plan, margin plan, total actual revenue, total actual cost, forecast cost, forecast margin. All components want to be seen per project type.

The third is related to the project timeline. There is no status of ongoing project monitoring loading the Project Controller must check the timeline and status of the ongoing project. Project management and controller requires a project status monitoring system that contains the total project, complete project, ongoing, on Schedule, canceled project, Project On Scope. Later here will be very petrified management and resource management to see which projects are not on schedule and see what's on the project. This will have an impact on the cost and also the resources needed. At present, there is no system to control all of these components so it takes time to do analysis and decision making.

In reality, there are external factors that also influence the success or failure of a project. Factors of political conditions in the country where the implementation and also the condition of the company or user also greatly affect the success or not implementation. The key user mutation process will also hamper the work because they will know more about the business processes at their company and also they will be faster to process the required data. In addition, management changes such as directors in the implementation company will also affect the policies taken and will indirectly affect the project network. In 2016, the Port Harbor Company experienced problems with this. Projects that have been going on until the realization phase, suddenly there are advantages in the management of the user side to stop the project so the project must be stopped.

Currently, the Port Harbor Company also uses SAP ERP to record their daily transactions. One module that is used to control projects and resources is the SAP PS (Project System) module. All data related to actual costs, cost plans, actual revenue, revenue plans, actual margins, margin plans and also work orders or mandays per consultant are recorded by the project system module. However, with this data, the Port Harbor Company does not use this data as a project monitoring media. Actually, the project system module has standard reports related to costs, resources and also the timeline but they do not yet have reports or monitoring tools and media for quick decision making. Therefore, the authors suggest using Business Intelligence and Dashboard as the front end for controlling the project being worked on and also the resources by the Port Harbor Company. Besides, the use of business intelligence is to utilize data that is already transactional so that the data has an important role for the company.

Some Key Performance Indicators (KPI) needed to conduct an analysis are project on schedule, project on budget, project on scope, actual Cost, plan cost, revenue actual, revenue plan, margin actual, margin plan, resource utilization per level and model fulfillment of information needs quickly and realtime related to the Project System can be met to make strategic, operational and predictive decisions to make project control run well and efficiently, especially with project controller and resource management.

This dashboard will be very petrified later if management, project controller and resource management want to do a review of each The Port Harbor Company project and also as a warning if there are projects that indicate a loss. Besides, can see which projects are profitable or not and also see what causes the project to be unprofitable. Also, this dashboard will also help to manage the timeline and ongoing resources so that, making the project manager, PCRM and management especially Boss Of Director analyze to optimize profits and reduce the cost of each project. The making of this paper aims to provide knowledge and description related to the application of business intelligence for project controlling, especially related to cost control. This paper can be an illustration of the application of project control for specialized IT consulting firms.

2 Literature Review

In the progress of information technology today many companies are implementing business intelligence technology. Business intelligence implemented by the company aims to assist management in decision making. At present almost every company that has an integrated information system or ERP supports the transactional activities of business processes. This transactional data will increase in volume each year and the greater the management will have difficulty in processing the data into information. Companies that have implemented each module have a standard report but the report is not a report that is used as a media analysis because ERP is OLTP (Online Analytical Processing). Therefore, the data contained in ERP is replicated in the data warehouse to be processed as information because business intelligence is OLAP (Online Analytical Processing). The characteristic of business intelligence is the ability to provide representative management with high-level information strategic activities such as goal setting, planning, and forecasting, and also tracking performance, to collect, analyze, and integrate internal and external data to become dynamic profiles of key performance indicators. Based on every information needed by management where business intelligence can view historical information such as historical data 5 years before to see trends every year. Business Intelligence can also receive data sources that do not originate from ERP systems and can even come from other information systems where this combination is sometimes needed by management to be seen as important information in decision making. Table 1 differences between ERP standards and business intelligence reports [3].

Table 1. Comparison of ERP reports and Business Intelligence reports

Characteristic	ERP reports	Business intelligence
Objectivities	Used to report daily and internal activities of each department	Analyze the company's key performance indicators and also focus on internal and external factors of the company
Level of decision	Operational	Strategic
User involved	Operational management	Executive management
Data management	Relational database	Data warehouse/OLAP
Typical operation	Report	Analyze
Number of records transaction	Limited	Huge
Data orientation	Record	Cube
Level of detail	Detailed, summarized, preaggregate	Aggregate
Age of data	Current	Historical/current/prospective

Based on the explanation above is ERP only transactional and not analytical tools because ERP is OLTP (Online Analytical Processing) concept. The use of business intelligence makes the data contained in ERP and information systems make the data can be visualized in the form of a dashboard that becomes an interesting information tool. Business Intelligence is based on innovative technology such as data warehousing, OLAP, data mining, graphical user interface, integrating tools that can collect, process, store and retrieve data from different sources.

2.1 Data Warehouse

Data and information are the most important assets for any company. Almost every company has a transactional system as a tool to store their operational data. Data stored in a transactional system will be difficult as a management analysis tool, therefore there is business intelligence to support it all. Characteristically the data management business intelligence report uses a data warehouse. Data warehouse is used to accommodate transactional data and is processed into information and knowledge. The operational system will record and store data every day related to customers, goods entering and leaving the warehouse, logistics, and others. This operational data will later be replicated in the data warehouse. Data warehouse is not at all times or its activities are not like an operational system because data warehouses in replicating data are usually set when the data must be replicated.

The data stored in the data warehouse is very many, even millions of records in it. The number of records will be an answer to management in decision making. Some of the goals of data warehouse like as [1]

- Data warehouse helps companies to facilitate them in getting information assembled internal and external conditions of the company.
- Data warehouse presents data that is consistent and valid.
- Data warehouse as a tool and foundation as a basis for decision making.

2.2 Integration Business Intelligence and ERP

Business intelligence is a tool that aims to modify, create, explore data, connect data and data source links and make it a report that can be seen trend information displayed in the form of history and realtime so that information can be used for decision making. ERP system that processes and stores transaction data from various internal and external sources. Integrated BI and ERP will be very useful for companies to make decisions and increase the effectiveness of the use of information systems in companies in utilizing and processing company data. Some benefits of the BI and ERP systems are integrated [4].

- Enabling and helping companies to monitor the condition of their companies.
- Help departments in the company to work together to improve performance between departments.
- Shorten the time to make a management report.
- Improve management analysis and see business trends that occur in the corporate environment.

Many benefits of integration between BI and ERP. However, many considerations must be prepared to carry out this integration related to technological innovation, size, reliability and availability, efficiency, and system flexibility. Business intelligence systems must be able to support ERP systems in reporting because basically ERP systems are not a tool for analytic reporting. The data stored in the ERP system will certainly continue to increase in volume where this system certainly will not be able to process that much data for fast reporting. The company will continue to grow every day and the data stored will also be more and more. Therefore, the BI system specifications will certainly require large specifications to accommodate and process the replicated data and make information that can be analyzed and used in management decision making [5].

2.3 Related Work

In several studies relating to the application of business intelligence where there is a study entitled Business Intelligence System for Banking and Finance where the use of business intelligence in banks is to help banks get a competitive advantage over its various products [1]. Reports are presented in context so you can make informed decisions rather than losing time to argue what action should be taken. where the focus of the application of business intelligence in this industry is relationship marketing, performance management, risk management, assets, and compliance [2]. Then in another study, An Enterprise Resource Planning (ERP) for a construction company along with Business Intelligence (BI) where construction companies in this study used ERP before to manage the company's resources. The business intelligence system in construction companies helps assist managerial staff in decision making. the use of business intelligence in construction companies is related to CRM to see customer feedback according to the customer's location and development [6].

In this study, researchers developed business intelligence to control projects in terms of project status, cost and revenue using the ASAP method where the phases are project preparation, business blueprint, realization, final preparation and go-live support. In this study, only a few discussed the development of business intelligence using the ASAP method. This research data source used is SAP ERP with the main module is SAP PS and some data from SAP SD and SAP FI. This data source will be replicated in a data

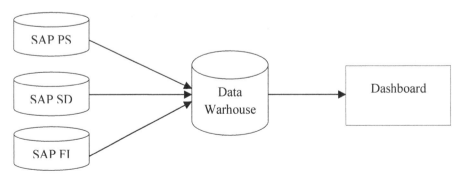

Fig. 1. Business intelligence project controlling architecture

warehouse whose data will be stored and processed into information. Data that has been processed in the data warehouse will be visualized in the form of a dashboard. The following architecture researchers use from ERP, Data Warehouse and Dashboard data sources (Fig. 1).

There are still not too many papers and studies that develop business intelligence using the ASAP method. In a paper entitled A model for Business Intelligence Development 'where the paper explains that there are 5 phases of development namely feasibility study, project planning, business analysis, design, and construction. In other studies related to project monitoring entitled The Development of Project Monitoring Information System (Case Study: PT Permanundi Prima Kelola) where this research is almost the same as the research paper related to monitoring and controlling, but in the previous research paper used Microsoft Excel to monitor the progress of projects that are operating and making the system using PHP, MySQL, XAMPP Apache HTTP Server, PHP MyAdmin, Adobe Dreamweaver, Internet Explorer, and Google Chrome which is different from the research that researchers are working on using business intelligence to monitor and control projects [7].

3 Method

The research methodology is the next step used to design the project implementation plan. This research methodology uses Accelerated SAP (ASAP) which is the SAP methodology for implementation developed by the German SAP AG software company to improve quality, reduce time and optimizing other resources. The ASAP methodology has 5 phases as shown below [8] (Fig. 2).

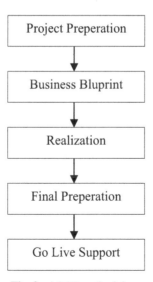

Fig. 2. ASAP methodology

Project preparation includes all activities required before the project starts with a discussion of needs. The main activities in this phase are developing project charter, including details of project plans, defining team and project roles, kick-off meeting, determining deliverable documents, project guidelines and procedures. The purpose of the project preparation stage is to have good project planning and preparation.

Business blueprint aims to carry out a series of requirements and processes with all major project resources to ensure an effective, efficient and complete design. Most of the time will be spent discussing data integration and master topics. The main activities in this phase are the blueprint workshop, making blueprints with agreed-upon requirements, signing off blueprints, landscape architecture system design, Installing server development.

In the realize phase, the system is configured based on the blueprint document defined in the blueprint phase. Initially the basic configuration, which represents the settings of the core business processes, was carried out and confirmed. Through a series of cycles, the final configuration is done and confirmed. The main activities in this phase are configuration, conducting a user acceptance test (UAT), conducting key user training (KUT).

In the final preparation phase, system integration testing (SIT) is now complete and all systems are known to function correctly. Technically, all integration problems must now be resolved. Transition, migration and cutover plan. The main activities in this phase are creating end-user manuals, developing role and matrix authorization, go-live checklist.

4 Result

Based on the methodology used in which there are 5 phases, we get the results of data warehouse modeling and dashboards that illustrate information related to costs and revenues such as Fig. 3.

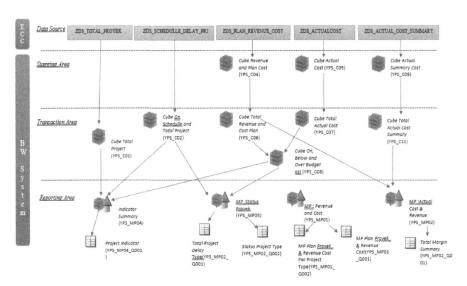

Fig. 3. Data warehouse modelling design

In the picture Fig. 3 is a data warehouse modeling design. There is 5 data source to get the project status ongoing, on schedule and delay. Besides this modeling is also to get the actual cost, cost plan, actual revenue, revenue plan, below budget, on budget and over budget per project type. This modeling is based on a logic that has been created by functional and obtained a design like a picture above.

In the above design, there are 3 levels of layers were staging, transaction and reporting. At the level of staging here, the author aims to accommodate the replication of data originating from the data source and do some logic manipulation on each ETL cube level stagging. Then the cube at the transaction level also has some logic manipulation and some not. At the reporting level, some cubes are combined and some are not, because several cubes contain data cost plans and actual plans, and therefore different cubes must be combined. Queries to be mapped on the dashboard component based on cube and multi provider (a combination of two or more cube) at the reporting level. From this research, six queries were made and the queries were mapped to the dashboard component and the results such as Fig. 4.

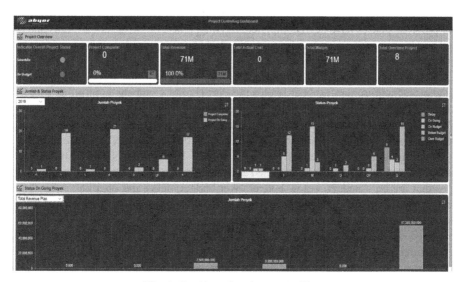

Fig. 4. Dashboard project controlling

From the dashboard image above displays some information, namely overall project status indicator, project complete, total revenue, total actual cost, total margin, and overtime. There are three charts, namely the number of projects chart, project status chart and cost revenue chart. On the chart, the number of projects displays the number of projects that have been completed and are currently running per project and can be filtered annually. Then the project status chart displays the project type which is over budget, on budget, below budget, ongoing and delay. Then at the bottom of the chart, cost and revenue show the actual total cost, total cost plan, actual total revenue, total revenue plan, forecast margin, and margin.

5 Conclusions

The application of business intelligence at Port Harbor Company is presented in this paper. It uses the ASAP (Accelerated SAP) method in which there are five phases, namely project preparation, business blueprint, realization, final preparation, and go-live support. In the project preparation phase which determines the timeline, the resources involved and also the roles and documents needed such as project charters and others. Then in the business blueprint phase wherein this phase creates a blueprint document and conducts a group discussion forum with all stakeholders involved. Then in this phase where the writer makes a mockup based on the problems that have been discussed in the forum group discussion and the authors together functionally discuss the related logic of how to retrieve the data needed and also the table. The author's realization activity makes ETL modeling to the dashboard. Final Preparation where all objects such as cubes, data sources, queries, and dashboards are migrated to the production server and create a list of users to authorize. In this phase, there is a UAT (user acceptance test) where whether the ETL modeling and dashboard are made until the information displayed on the dashboard is appropriate and answers the problems faced by the project controlling team. After the four previous phases have been completed, the final phase of the dashboard runs and is used and monitors the data warehouse to the dashboard information that comes out to ensure there are no problems.

This research is based on the project which is expected that the implementation of the project controller dashboard helps the Port Harbor Company controlling project team to control the Port Harbor Company project quickly so that the project controlling and management team can take an action quickly if the worst case occurs in a project. The dashboard displays overall project status, total project complete, total revenue, total cost, total margin and the number of project delays. Then the dashboard also displays the number of projects that are completed and those that are still running and see project types that are on a budget, below budget, over budget, delay and ongoing. After that, the dashboard displays the actual total revenue, total revenue plan, total actual cost, total plan, forecast margin and margin per project type. In this dashboard, it can be further developed. In the next development, the researchers hope that the dashboard can be developed to see the resources that are being idle or those that are in the project and how long the resource is in the project or the customer so that the project controller team can manage the recommendations better.

References

1. Vaidya, T., Ahirrao, S., Kadam, K., Lugade, K.: Business intelligence system for banking and finance. Int. J. Comput. Sci. Inf. Technol. 5(3), 4336–4349 (2014)
2. Ouda, G.K.: Application of business intelligence in the financial services industry. Int. J. Innov. Sci. Res. 26(1), 135–145 (2016)
3. Bara, A., Botha, I., Diaconita, V., Lungu, I., Velicanu, A., Velicanu, M.: A model for business intelligence systems' development. Inform. Econ. 13(4), 99–108 (2009)
4. Nofal, M.I., Yusof, Z.M.: Integration of business intelligence and enterprise resource planning within organizations. Procedia Technol. 11, 658–665 (2013). https://doi.org/10.1016/j.protcy.2013.12.242

5. Rahimia, E., Rostami, N.A.: Enterprise resource planning and business intelligence: the importance of integration. Int. J. Manag. Acad. **3**(4), 7–14 (2015)
6. Kadoli, S., Patil, D., Mane, A., Shinde, A., Kokate, S.: An enterprise resource planning (ERP) for a construction enterprise along with business intelligence (BI). Int. J. Innov. Res. Sci. Eng. Technol. **3**(2), 9487–9493 (2014)
7. Sari, D.P., Putra, S.J., Rustamaji, E.: The development of project monitoring information system (Case study: PT Tetapundi Prima Kelola). In: International Conference on Cyber and IT Service Management, CITSM 2014 (2014). https://doi.org/10.1109/citsm.2014.7042172
8. Jingga, F., Limantara, N.: The implementation of ERP systems using ASAP methodology: (Case study: OpenERP 9.0 application on sales & distribution module at PT. XYZ). In: International Conference on Information Management and Technology, ICIMTech 2016 (2016). https://doi.org/10.1109/icimtech.2016.7930296

Industry Applications of Intelligent Methods and Systems

Association Rules Extraction Method for Semantic Query Processing Over Medical Big Data

Ling Wang, Jian Li, Tie Hua Zhou$^{(\boxtimes)}$, and Wen Qiang Liu

Department of Computer Science and Technology, School of Computer Science,
Northeast Electric Power University, Jilin 132000, China
{smile2867ling,thzhou}@neepu.edu.cn, jonkiwork@gmail.com,
lwq1107076853@163.com

Abstract. With the rapid development of online medical platform, data mining algorithms can effectively deal with an amount of online medical data and solve the complex semantic relationships among these data. However, traditional data mining algorithms may directly remove some professional terms as interference words, because professional medical terms account for a small proportion of online medical data. Therefore, we proposed TRSC algorithm to extract keywords and semantic relationships among online medical data, which support to add these words to keywords libraries based on their semantic weight. Furthermore, it can provide a complete keyword library for semantic relation extraction. Experiments show that TRSC algorithm can effectively recognize the low-frequency keywords and extend medical keywords library, it accurately mined the semantic relationships.

Keywords: Medical text data · Association rules · Semantic queries

1 Introduction

Large amounts of data are routinely created in the fields of science, industry, entertainment, medicine and biology [1–3]. Getting knowledge from data has always been a hot topic in the field of computer research. Association rule extraction technology is an important technology to obtain knowledge from data. It can naturally combine the data according to the original attributes of the data for relational extraction [4, 5]. Making full use of the data of the online medical service platform and mining the potential relationships can improve the service quality of such platform and help users to search useful knowledge more quickly.

In order to make better use of the explosive growth of medical data sets, more and more enterprises begin to share data, such as PatientsLikeMe, PubMed, and WebMD. Although data sharing is convenient for users to obtain information, users still need to spend a lot of time browsing potentially irrelevant information [6]. The research and innovation of relational extraction algorithm can discover the internal connection between data and improve the accuracy of information obtained [7–9]. The significance of this research can be summarized as follows:

© Springer Nature Singapore Pte Ltd. 2020
P. Sitek et al. (Eds.): ACIIDS 2020, CCIS 1178, pp. 109–120, 2020.
https://doi.org/10.1007/978-981-15-3380-8_10

(1) Extracting keywords from three types of text and retaining low-frequency words.
(2) Matching the keywords extracted from the three types of text, removing the redundant keywords, and constructing the keyword library.
(3) Avoiding multiple scans of the original transaction database, improving the efficiency of medical data mining and accuracy of mining results.

The overall process as follows:

Step1: preprocessing the original data and getting three kinds of text;
Step2: extracting keywords and constructing keyword library;
Step3: extracting the correlation relationship through the weight of keywords.

The data preprocessing of the algorithm has two main functions: text denoising and text classification. The main tasks of keywords extraction process are: reserving low-frequency words, matching text keywords and removing redundant keywords, constructing keyword library according to keyword weight. The retention of low-frequency words ensures the integrity of the keywords library, and the removal of redundant keywords ensures the accuracy of the keywords library. Finally, obtaining the text relevance by analyzing the weight of keywords in the keywords library.

2 Related Work

Based on literature studies at home and abroad, the current research on the extraction of association rules in the direction of data is summarized as follows:

Robert Moskovitch and Yuval Shahar introduced the KarmaLego algorithm for frequent sign interval correlation pattern (TIRPs) [10]. KarmaLego algorithm has advantages in running speed over several existing most advanced algorithms in the case of large data sets and low level of minimum vertical support. Mohamed abdel-basseth and his team proposed a new association rule mining method and studied a new neural network association rule algorithm [11]. The algorithm uses a new method is used for by processing the membership, the relationship between the uncertainty and non-members function of the project, to generate association rules by taking into account all fuzzy factors for effective decision-making. Association rules Bagherzadeh - Khiabani and others shows some variable selection method commonly used in data mining application in epidemiological studies [12]. Xika Lin, Stephen Tu, Jaroslaw Szlichta et al. optimized the Apriori algorithm for its disadvantages such as too many database scans, more intermediate item sets and unique support [13–16].

Yang et al. in order to avoid the expensive cost and noisy results brought by the existing data annotation schemes to large data sets, they used an economical and effective annotation method and focused on the generation of label rules. The purpose of this problem is to generate high-quality rules and greatly reduce the label cost while maintaining the quality [17]. Square differentiation et al. proposed a graphical pattern association rule (GPAR) for social media marketing. GPAR extended the association rules of the project set to help it find the rules between entities in the social graph and identify potential customers by studying the social impact [7]. Zeng et al. optimized the FP-Growth algorithm for memory bottlenecks or failures due to the limitation of hardware resources [18–21].

In general, algorithms for association relation extraction can be divided into three categories: rule-based, supervised learning, and semi-supervised and unsupervised learning combining algorithms, such as Bootstrap, remote Supervision and unsupervised learning. The advantage of a silicon-based association relation extraction algorithm is that it is accurate and suitable for some specific scenarios. However, its disadvantages are obvious, such as low recall rate, high labor cost, and difficulty in designing such an algorithm due to rule conflict and overlap. Some preparatory work should be done before using a supervised learning class algorithm to extract association relations. For example: define relationship types, define entity types, and training data, including entity annotation and relationship annotation between entities, and extract relationships after completion of these preparations. Although the extracted correlation is more accurate, this kind of algorithm is less flexible, and its preparation is different for different data types. Compared with the supervised algorithm, the semi-supervised algorithm abandons some accuracy, but greatly reduces the preparation time in the early stage and improves the flexibility of the algorithm.

3   TRSC Algorithm

3.1   Motivation

The rise of online health services has produced a wealth of medical data. How to extract the valuable information hidden in the medical data has always been a hot topic in various research institutes. Traditional data mining algorithms cannot meet the requirements of online medical data processing. For example, the Apriori algorithm scans the database too many times, producing more intermediate item sets and unique support degree, etc. FP-Growth algorithm may encounter memory bottleneck or failure due to the limitation of hardware resources, etc. The traditional TF-IDF algorithm only considers two statistical information of words and makes little use of text information. The feature space dimension of the LSA algorithm is large and the calculation efficiency is low.

Based on this, the advantages of the TRSC algorithm is: (a) text preprocessing. The data is divided into two parts, and the whole text and the sub-text are extracted with keywords, it can better remove redundant and useless keywords, retain valuable keywords, extract keywords and relations more accurate and complete; (b) data can be changed dynamically, and the keywords and association relationships obtained will be changed accordingly; (c) the algorithm also performs well in time complexity.

3.2   TextRank-Separate-Combination Algorithm

The algorithm flow chart of this algorithm is shown in Fig. 1:

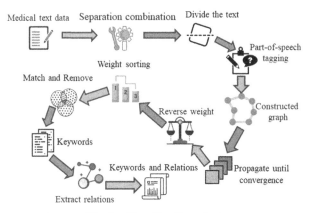

Fig. 1. Algorithm flow chart

Algorithm 1 is a pseudo-code about TRSC algorithm and the symbols in pseudo-code 1 are shown in Table 1.

Algorithm 1: TRSC

Input: Medical text data
Output: keywords and rules
1: Segmenting medical text into p, d and pd
2: Dividing t into s
3: **For** each $wd \in s$
4:     Marking wd with part of speech
5: **if** $wd \in qw$ **then**
6:     Extract the keywords
7:        **if** $kw \in noun$ or adj **then**
8:            add kw to t_{kw}
9:            add w to t_w
10:           **end if**
11:    **end if**
12:    **For** each $kw \in t_{kw}$
13: **if** $kw = kt_p \cap kt_d \cap key_{pd}$ **then**
14:     add kw to T_{KEY}
15:     add w of the T_{KEY} to T_{weight}
16: **end if**
17: **For** each $kw \in T_{KEY}$
18: **if** $w1 \text{-} w2 <= 0.00025$ **then**
19:     add $w1, w2$ to *rules*
20: **end if**
21: Clean failed *rules*
22: Retain the union T_{KEY} and *rules*

Table 1. Notations table

Symbol	Definition
p	Question text
d	Answer text
pd	Combination of p and d text
t	Text floorboard
s	Sentence
wd	Words
qw	Qualitative
kw	Keywords
w	Weight
t_{kw}	Text of keywords
t_w	Text of weight
kt_p	Patient of keywords
kt_d	Doctor of keywords
kt_{pd}	General keyword text
T_{KEY}	Final keyword text

The following is the execution process of Fig. 1, which can be divided into four modules:

(1) Text preprocessing phrase

- Input: Medical text data
- Main Works: splitting and combining the original text.
- Specific Instructions of Works: according to the characteristics of conversational recording of online medical data, mark the questions of patients with *"question"* and mark the answers of doctors with *"answer"*. The original medical text was extracted and combined according to different labels to obtain the text of doctor, the text of patient and the processed total text.

$$T_{doctor} = \{T_{answer1}, T_{answer2}, \ldots, T_{answern}\} \tag{1}$$

$$T_{patient} = \{T_{question1}, T_{question2}, \ldots, T_{questionn}\} \tag{2}$$

$$T = T_{patient} + T_{doctor} \tag{3}$$

T_{doctor} is the sum text of all answers of doctors, $T_{patient}$ is the sum text of all patient problem descriptions, and T is the sum of the text for T_{doctor} and $T_{patient}$.

(2) Using TextRank algorithm to Extracting keywords

- Input: $T_{doctor}, T_{patient}, T$
- Main Works: Divide text, Part-of-speech tagging, Constructed graph, Propagate until convergence, Reverse weight, Weight sorting
- Specific Instructions of Works:

(a) Dividing the text into sentences: $P = [S_1, S_2, S_3, \ldots S_n]$.
(b) Parting of speech tagging the words in each sentence S_i, then removing the stop word and retaining the qualitative word:

$$S_i = \left[t_{i,1}, t_{i,2}, t_{i,3}, \ldots, t_{i,n}\right] \tag{4}$$

$$t_{i,j} \in S_j \tag{5}$$

(c) Constructing an undirected graph $G = (V, E)$, V is a set of nodes composed of nouns and adjectives and E is the edge between any two nodes constructed by the co-occurrence relation. Divide all reserved words into fixed length K, and the value of K in this experiment is 5. The formula for TextRank algorithm is as follows:

$$WS(V_i) = (1 - d) + d * \sum_{v_j \in In(V_i)} \frac{W_{ji}}{\sum_{V_k \in Out(V_j)} W_{jk}} ws(v_j) \tag{6}$$

For a given point V_i, $In(V_i)$ is the number of edges that point to i, and $Out(V_j)$ is the number of edges of j points to others. W_{ji} is the weight of j, and its initial value is set to 1. W_{ji} is the TR value. The Fig. 2 is the specific calculation process of TR:

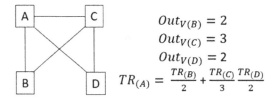

$$Out_{V(B)} = 2$$
$$Out_{V(C)} = 3$$
$$Out_{V(D)} = 2$$
$$TR_{(A)} = \frac{TR_{(B)}}{2} + \frac{TR_{(C)}}{3} + \frac{TR_{(D)}}{2}$$

Fig. 2. TR calculation process

(d) According to formula 6, the weight of each node is iteratively calculated until convergence, and the weight of the node is sorted in reverse order, from which the most important t words are obtained as top-t keywords. Finally, the keywords are classified and the low-frequency words are retained.

- Output: keywords library: $Key_{doctor}, Key_{patient}, Key_{pd}$
  $Key_{doctor}, Key_{patient}, Key_{pd}$ represents the Key words extracted from the doctor text, the patient text, and the doctor-patient text.

(3) Contracting keywords library

- Input: Key_{doctor}, $Key_{patient}$, Key_{pd}
- Main Works: Matching keywords and removing redundant keywords
- Specific Instructions of Works: Conducting keyword matching and screening for the processed doctor text keywords, patient text keywords and doctor-patient text keywords, extract the same keywords, and find keywords with similar weights according to the weight of these keywords. This way of processing has a good reservation effect on keywords with less weight, and provides a good basis for later extraction of relations:

$$Key = Key_{doctor} \cap Key_{patient} \cap Key_{pd} \qquad (7)$$

$$Key_{Dif} = Key_{doctor} - Key \qquad (8)$$

- Output: Key_{Dif}, Key
  The Key is the intersection of Key_{doctor}, $Key_{patient}$, Key_{pd}

(4) Extracting relations

- Input: Key_{Dif}, Key
- Main Works: Extracting and optimizing correlation
- Specific Instructions of Works: Calculating W_d for Key according to formula 9. If $W_d \leq 0.00025$, add the R_i to the association library. If $P \geq 0.3$, add the Key_{Dif} to R_i.

$$W_d = Weight_{keyi} - Weight_{keyj} \qquad (9)$$

$$R_i = keyi, keyj \qquad (10)$$

$$P = Max : P(W_{ki}|W_{kD}), P\left(W_{kj}|W_{kD}\right), P(W_{kD}|W_{ki}), P\left(W_{kD}|W_{kj}\right) \quad (11)$$

R_i is an association made up of the words $keyi$ and $keyj$. For the formula 9, W_d represents the difference between two weights, $key_i \in Key$, $key_j \in Key$. For the formula 10, the W_{ki} and W_{kD} is the weight of keyword in the Key_{doctor}.
- Output: R_i

3.3 Experimental Data Analysis

The data of this algorithm comes from online medical services of WebMD, HealthTap, eHealth and the following Table 2 is part of the output data under the window size K = 5 (the weight is increased by 1000 times):

Table 2. Key weight

Key	Doctor weight	Patient weight	Doctor-patient
Symptoms	4.93395	1.72585	3.27793
Pregnancy	2.76851	1.29911	2.22258
Diet	2.59491	2.23686	2.43701
Weight	2.26964	2.95170	2.31739
Baby	2.04568	2.01859	1.94567
Cancer	1.80747	2.01362	1.84916
Age	1.62248	1.95477	1.65153
Month	1.58101	3.02621	1.46034
Surgery	1.51306	2.06803	1.65431
Exercise	1.44522	1.80939	1.44733
Pressure	1.41753	1.78459	1.43568
Food	1.30437	3.02596	1.29233
Breast	1.26358	1.46719	1.01102

Table 3 shows the partial relationships extracted based on key phrases. The following conclusions can be drawn from the analysis of experimental data:

(1) By preprocessing the original text, the medical texts of doctors and patients were extracted, the same keywords was extracted, and the weight features in the Keywords list of each Key were analyzed and found: Doctors medical data for the use of jargon in the text, as the above list of the *Pregnancy* is about other keyword weight twice, and patients in medical text for the use of time significantly more frequent, similar to the *year*, weight more than 0.005, the *month*, higher than 0.003, the *week*, *weeks* above 0.002. By comparing the key words related to time, you can see the more accurate time, the less appears in the text. This proves that the extracted keywords and their weights are relatively accurate. By comparing the data with the original text, the proportion of patients' consultation on health problems in the original data was small. Therefore, the separation of the original data is beneficial to the extraction of keywords.

(2) By sorting the weight of the same keywords in the three medical texts, it can be found that the general trend of keyword weight change of the keywords in the doctor data text and the original medical texts is generally consistent. According to the analysis of the original data, the main reason is that there are fewer vocabularies in patients' questions, while doctors' answers to patients will further describe patients' questions, then explain them, and finally give Suggestions. The sentence length is longer than that of patients' questions.

(3) By comparing the extracted doctor medical text with the patient's medical text keywords can be found that patients have put forward question in the text to life

language use more frequent, such: food, feel the work, coffee, and the doctor answer for symptoms described in the text of the professional term used more frequently, such as: pregnant, diet, pressure, such words are many, describes the cause of the adverse reactions in patients with and how to deal with the discomfort.

Figure 3 shows the trend chart of the weight relationship among the $Doctor_{words}$, $Doctor_{words}$ and $Doctor - patient_{words}$.

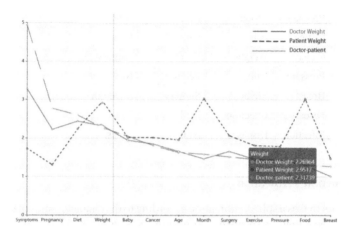

Fig. 3. Weight trend diagram

3.4   The Example Analysis

According to the association relationship in Table 3 and the original medical text data, the source corresponding to the association relationship can be found in the original text. For example:

- The relationship that can be extracted from *"vision", "eye", "disorders"* is as follows: vision disorders.
  Extract relevant data items from the original data according to the above keywords and correlation relations. The following is part of the original data extracted:
- The specific *verification of visual* impairment in the original data are: *your concern is regarding the recurrent chalazia that your wife is having especially when she is planning for chemo/stem cell transplant. a chalazion is an accumulation of material in the eyelid as a result of a blocked oil gland and there is no underlying cause for the same. for recurrent chalazia your wife can use pre-moistened eyelid cleansing wipes to maintain hygiene. other than that regular use of topical or oral antibiotics can also be prescribed to prevent any further recurrence. however if the size is big or it is obstructing field of vision then it may need to be removed surgically. patients with underlying conditions such as rosacea seborrheic dermatitis or blepharitis are more prone to multiple and recurrent chalazia so your wife needs to get evaluated*

for these conditions also as they may be responsible for recurrent chalazia. it is very difficult to precisely confirm a diagnosis without examination and investigations and the answer is based on the medical information provided. for exact diagnosis you are requested to consult your doctor. i sincerely hope that helps. take care.;.

Table 3. Key correlation

Key	Doctor word	Patient word	Doctor-patient word
Pregnancy	Blood	Diet	Null
Coffee	Pain	Null	Breast
Cancer	Weight	Hair	Surgery
Pressure	Null	Feeling	Null
Breast	Medical	Surgery	Infection
Disease	Infection	Null	Null
Infection	Disease	Null	Breast

3.5 Experimental Verification

TRSC algorithm makes a split combination according to the characteristics of the original data and processes them respectively to ensure the quality of the output data in the preprocessing stage. The removal of redundant keywords and the retention of low-frequency words by TRSC algorithm ensure the integrity and accuracy of the keyword library, providing a prerequisite for the subsequent extraction of relationships. Finally, the weight is used to optimize and supplement the relation, so as to ensure the accuracy of the extracted relation. Figure 4 is the comparison diagram of the accuracy of relation extraction. It can be seen from Fig. 4 that the accuracy of TRSC algorithm in relation extraction is more accurate than the other three algorithms.

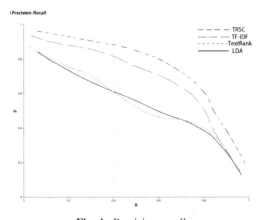

Fig. 4. Precision-recall

4   Conclusion

Some traditional algorithms pay more attention to the extraction of high-frequency words and ignore the processing of low-frequency words in the keyword extraction stage, which makes the keyword database constructed incomplete. TRSC contains 3 phases: separating and combining the original data, extracting keywords from the separated text and the total text, and matching keywords and adding low-frequency words to the keyword library. According to the weight of keywords to extract the relationship between keywords and remove the redundant relationship to ensure keywords and the relationships are more accurate and complete. TRSC algorithm does not directly delete low-frequency words but uses weights to find the relationship between low-frequency words, which has a good retention effect for low-frequency words.

Acknowledgment. This work was supported by National Natural Science Foundation of China (No. 61701104), and by the Natural Science Foundation of Jilin Province of China (No. 20190201194JC).

References

1. Dong, X.L., Srivastava, D.: Big data integration. In: 2013 IEEE 29th International Conference on Data Engineering (ICDE), pp. 1245–1248. IEEE (2013)
2. Eldawy, A., Mokbel, M.F.: The era of big spatial data. In: 2015 31st IEEE International Conference on Data Engineering Workshops, pp. 42–49. IEEE (2015)
3. Bifet, A.: Mining big data in real time. Informatica **37**(1), 15–20 (2013)
4. Song, S., Chen, L., Cheng, H.: On concise set of relative candidate keys. Proc. VLDB Endow. **7**(12), 1179–1190 (2014)
5. Milo, T., Novgorodov, S., Tan, W.C.: Rudolf: interactive rule refinement system for fraud detection. Proc. VLDB Endow. **9**(13), 1465–1468 (2016)
6. Ji, X.: Social data integration and analytics for health intelligence. In: Proceedings VLDB PhD Workshop (2014). http://www.vldb.org/2014/phd_workshop.proceedings_files/Camera-Ready%20Papers/Paper%201285/p1285-Ji.pdf
7. Fan, W., Wang, X., Wu, Y., Xu, J.: Association rules with graph patterns. Proc. VLDB Endow. **8**(12), 1502–1513 (2015)
8. Lin, X., Mukherji, A., Rundensteiner, E.A., Ruiz, C., Ward, M.O.: PARAS: a parameter space framework for online association mining. Proc. VLDB Endow. **6**(3), 193–204 (2013)
9. Abedjan, Z., Akcora, C.G., Ouzzani, M., Papotti, P., Stonebraker, M.: Temporal rules discovery for web data cleaning. Proc. VLDB Endow. **9**(4), 336–347 (2015)
10. Moskovitch, R., Shahar, Y.: Fast time intervals mining using the transitivity of temporal relations. Knowl. Inf. Syst. **42**(1), 21–48 (2015)
11. Abdel-Basset, M., Mohamed, M., Smarandache, F., Chang, V.: Neutrosophic association rule mining algorithm for big data analysis. Symmetry **10**(4), 106 (2018)
12. Bagherzadeh-Khiabani, F., Ramezankhani, A., Azizi, F., Hadaegh, F., Steyerberg, E.W., Kjalili, D.: A tutorial on variable selection for clinical prediction models: feature selection methods in data mining could improve the results. J. Clin. Epidemiol. **71**, 76–85 (2016)
13. Tu, S., Kaashoek, M.F., Madden, S., Zeldovich, N.: Processing analytical queries over encrypted data. Proc. VLDB Endow. **6**(5), 289–300 (2013)

14. Szlichta, J., Godfrey, P., Golab, L., Kargar, M., Srivastava, D.: Effective and complete discovery of order dependencies via set-based axiomatization. Proc. VLDB Endow. **10**(7), 721–732 (2017)
15. Bedini, I., Elser, B., Velegrakis, Y.: The Trento big data platform for public administration and large companies: use cases and opportunities. Proc. VLDB Endow. **6**(11), 1166–1167 (2013)
16. Bergamaschi, S., Guerra, F., Interlandi, M., Trillo-Lado, R., Velegrakis, Y.: QUEST: a keyword search system for relational data based on semantic and machine learning techniques. Proce. VLDB Endow. **6**(12), 1222–1225 (2013)
17. Yang, J., Fan, J., Wei, Z., Li, G., Liu, T., Du, X.: Cost-effective data annotation using game-based crowdsourcing. Proc. VLDB Endow. **12**(1), 57–70 (2018)
18. Zeng, Y., Yin, S., Liu, J., Zhang, M.: Research of improved FP-Growth algorithm in association rules mining. Sci. Program. **2015**, 6 (2015)
19. Feng, W., Zhu, Q., Zhuang, J., Yu, S.: An expert recommendation algorithm based on Pearson correlation coefficient and FP-growth. Cluster Comput. **22**, 7401–7412 (2018)
20. Chang, H.Y., Lin, J.C., Cheng, M.L., Huang, S.C.: A novel incremental data mining algorithm based on FP-growth for big data. In: 2016 International Conference on Networking and Network Applications (NaNA), pp. 375–378. IEEE (2016)
21. Wang, C.H., Zheng, L., Yu, X., Zheng, X.: Using fuzzy FP-growth for mining association rules. In: 2017 International Conference on Organizational Innovation (ICOI 2017). Atlantis Press (2017)

Popular Disease Topics Mining Method for Online Medical Community

Tie Hua Zhou, Wen Qiang Liu, Ling Wang[✉], and Jian Li

Department of Computer Science and Technology, School of Computer Science, Northeast Electric Power University, Jilin 132000, China
{thzhou,smile2867ling}@neepu.edu.cn, lwq1107076853@163.com, jonkiwork@gmail.com

Abstract. With the rapid development of intelligent medical, mobile medicine, health management self-diagnosis, big data management and analysis have become hot research areas. In this paper, we proposed a medical text-based processing method (TLC algorithm), which can enhance feature semantic associations without losing useful information, and effectively discovery the potential value knowledge in medical texts. It can adaptively classify the topics of disease based on specific terms, construct disease-department lexicons according to the weighted coefficients. Our proposed algorithm will effectively mine the underlying disease topics in the mass medical community text data, which can discover the patients high concerned diseases and symptoms, provide the reference of pathological symptoms to doctors, and support the decision-making treatment programs.

Keywords: Medical text analysis · Disease classification · Topic mining

1 Introduction

In the recent years, netizens often use the Internet to acquire health-related knowledge. Traditional health-related websites usually restrict users only to obtain relevant information, and the online medical community allows users with the same disease or treatment experience to communicate in a timely manner, promoting the sharing of high-quality medical resources, making medical treatment more convenient, personalized, and diversified. But this also arises a problem, such as a large amount of data in text form accumulated in the database in the form of text. A significant portion of this data is recorded manually, so it is unstructured and requires semantic analysis [1–3]. The unstructured clinical record contains a wealth of insight into patients that aren't available in the structured record. Zhu propose an analysis framework on social health that would provide a semantic integration data model, which represents the semantic relationship of stream data from distributed health data sources. Monitoring and extracting social media data involve a large amount of data in a highly unstructured format [4]. Lee propose a data analysis model of healthcare for user database based on a neural network algorithm, which is mainly applied to "database marketing" through customer database analysis [5]. Topics are actually dimensionality reduction representation of text. Commonly used dimensionality reduction methods are tf-idf and lda [6–8].

© Springer Nature Singapore Pte Ltd. 2020
P. Sitek et al. (Eds.): ACIIDS 2020, CCIS 1178, pp. 121–132, 2020.
https://doi.org/10.1007/978-981-15-3380-8_11

In this paper we propose a disease topic mining and classification model for the online medical community, which has the following advantages:

(1) According to the medical text processing method proposed in this paper, features with close semantic relations can be mined without losing useful information.
(2) By mining the underlying disease topics in the mass medical community text data, we can better discover the diseases and symptoms that are of high concern to patients. It can also help the medical community to provide targeted services to different patient groups.

2 Related Work

At present, the research on disease topic mining is mainly summarized as follows: Ma et al. proposed a feature selection algorithm of two-stage text to solve the problem of high feature dimension disaster in the field of text feature selection. Firstly, based on the mutual information algorithm, five indexes including balance factor, frequency, concentration, part of speech and word position in the text are introduced to calculate the mutual information value [9]. Zhou et al. proposed an advanced TF-IDF feature extraction method for traditional TF-IDF ignore text structure information, and calculated the importance value of nodes based on the text network and improved Page Rank algorithm [10]. Ping considered the different problems of concurrent words and proposed an improved TF-IDF algorithm to extract feature items bases on the traditional TF-IDF and in combination with the location features and length features [11]. Chen et al. by combining Word2vec and TF-IDF, re-weighted each feature word to achieve text classification [12].

Wang et al. put forward an advanced FP - Growth, such as association rule model to extract the theme of the model, the model can be used in a large number of Chinese medical literature. First of all, medical record literature will be divided into several keywords of medical literature item set document, then use the FP - Growth algorithm to calculate keywords of frequent item sets, and generate the pathological dictionary, finally extracted text diseases subject [13]. Wang et al. proposed to construct a co-word network with Weibo as the node based on whether the micro-blog contained same keywords, next conducted text topic mining in combination with the Louvain community detection algorithm [14]. Yin et al. used thematic modeling to mine clinical texts to discover disease characteristics, clinical treatment path patterns and clinical risk assessment [15]. Yang et al. explored the clinical pathway treatment model with the theme mining method, optimized the clinical treatment path and improved the medical service level [16].

Calin et al. added a fast increment feature to the LDA model as the observed value, and obtained a model in which the theme model rapidly declined and converged with the increment [17]. Siddiqi et al. combined LDA with a generalized dynamic linear model (GLDM) to overcome the influence of time variation, so that the model could be adjusted according to the time lapse [18]. Ji et al. used the latent semantic analysis (LSA) with the hidden Markov model to freely define the effect of topics of interest without annotation [19].

At present, there are two main research methods for topic recognition of medical texts: theme-based model method and text-based clustering method. The topic model, also known as a probabilistic topic model, is a kind of statistical model widely used in document modeling in data mining and natural language processing. This kind of model can divide the words in the document set or corpus according to the semantics, obtain a set of topics composed of semantically related words, and express the documents as the mixed probability on these topics. Given a set of documents, the topic model can mine the core topics discussed by the set of documents and the distributed probability of the topics covered by each document. Then a series of applications such as prediction, classification, and clustering can be made with the acquired topics. The essence of theme recognition based on text clustering is that the text groups formed after the text automatically clustered represent the prototype of the theme [20]. The basic idea of text clustering is that documents with the same topic are more similar, while documents with different topics are less similar.

3 TLC Algorithm

3.1 Motivation

With the continuous development of the medical community, the accumulation of a large number of online medical texts make it particularly difficult to extract key information from them. How to mine disease information from massive medical text data is a research hotspot. The traditional methods based on association rule analysis, clustering analysis which lack of efficiency and accuracy. Based on this, we propose the TLC algorithm, which can better retain the characteristics of medical text, and improve the accuracy of target text classification by mining the underlying disease topics of the text.

3.2 TFIDF-LDA-Classification Algorithm

The flow chart of this algorithm is shown in Fig. 1:
    The main steps of this model are as follows:

(1) Mine the initial feature set from the medical text dataset.
(2) Filter the features below the threshold by calculating the score of each feature in the feature set.
(3) Generate potential disease topics and determine the optimal partition granularity.
(4) Construct disease department lexicons based on the features of the disease topic.
(5) Extract related disease features of the target text.
(6) Match the target text with the disease department lexicons iteratively and calculate the match rate.

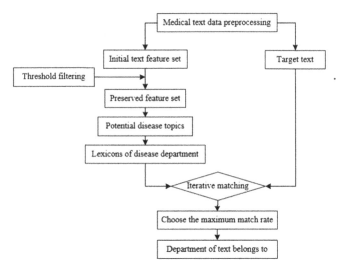

Fig. 1. Flow chart of TLC algorithm

The notation table and details of TLC algorithm are as follows (Table 1):

Table 1. Notations table

Symbol	Definition
p	Phrase of medical text
T	Medical text
$d\alpha$	Degree of dispersion
$d\beta$	Degree of aggregation
s(p)	Score of phrase
lex_i	Lexicon of disease-department i
kw	Keyword of target text
x_i	Counter
ω_{lex_i}	Total number of features of lex_i
θ_i	Rate of match

Algorithm 1: TLC Algorithm

```
1:Input: Medical text, target text
2:Output:dept of target text
3:Segmenting medical text into p
4:for each p ∈ T
5:    calculate dα, dβ of p
6:    if p contains one character
7:      dβ==0
8:        s= dα+ dβ
9:    end if
10: if s(p)>9.0
11:   retain p
12: end if
13:Generate topics and lexᵢ
14: For kw in target text
15:if kw in lexᵢ
16:   xᵢ++
17:   θᵢ=xᵢ/ωₗₑₓᵢ
18:end if
19: If θᵢ ∈ lexᵢ and max(θᵢ)
20: Return deptᵢ
21:end if
```

3.2.1 Mine Initial Disease Features Set

In the context of Chinese grammar, the description of disease symptoms is usually longer than them in English, and lack of professional disease dictionaries. Therefore, before word segmentation we need to find these phrases, which combined with the characteristics of Chinese medicine-related vocabulary, we mainly consider the prefix and suffix of phrases, disease described in Chinese suffixes are usually "inflammation", "disease", and a noun prefix of body parts expression such as "shoulder" should be contained. Since Chinese phrases are composed of characters, if there is no concept of characters, statistics on texts with N words will get N! word combination. Therefore, we set the length of phrase to 6, and the initial candidate phrase set obtained, which can retain the Chinese disease characteristics to a great extent.

$$T = \{w_1, w_2, \ldots\ldots w_n\} \tag{1}$$

The T is the candidate phrase set.

Definition 1. The degree of dispersion of word E_{w_i}.

$$E_{(w_i)} = -\frac{1}{n} \sum_{w \in T} \text{Fre}(w, w_i) \log \frac{\text{Fre}(w, w_i)}{n} - \frac{1}{n} \sum_{w \in T} \text{Fre}(w_i, w) \log \frac{\text{Fre}(w_i, w)}{n} \tag{2}$$

The w_i represents word in T, and the Fre represents word frequency, and n is the word frequency of w_i.

Definition 2. The aggregation degree of word M.

$$M = \log \frac{p(w_i, w_j)}{p(w_i)p(w_j)} \tag{3}$$

In particular, set the aggregation degree of each single character to 0. We sum and score dispersion degree and aggregation of each phrase, set a threshold to 9.0, retain phrases that exceed the threshold. Part disease-related phrases that need to be retained as features shown in Table 2:

Table 2. Part of disease-related phrases

Retained phrase	Score
Weak of limbs	9.06
Heart damage	9.42
Vomit and diarrhea	10.12
Persistent high fever	10.31
Pimple on back	11.41
Weak positive hepatitis B antibody	12.63
Fracture of tibia	13.77
Skin allergies	14.28
Irregular menstruation	14.97

Some words that appear frequently but have no practical meaning in the text called stop words. They should be regarded as noise to remove. Although there are some common Chinese stop word lists, given the medical texts have certain professionality, IDF measures need to be used to identify stop words. A lower IDF value for a word indicates that it tends to appear in a large number of texts. In this experiment, stop words are set by using professional stop word lists and manual addition.

After word segmentation and a stop list is set up, which is screened for partial stop words, as shown in Table 3.

3.2.2 Extract and Process Medical Text Feature

In this section, based on the feature words in the previous section, we need to calculate the weight of the features and extract them from medical text, the importance of a word is proportional to the frequency of its appearance in the file and the frequency of its appearance in the corpus decrease inversely, It should be noted that to prevent low

Table 3. Part of stop words list.

Stop word	IDF
Outer	2.14
Small	2.56
And	3.43
Feel	4.21
The	4.45
Injury	5.28
Inflammation	5.66
Doctor	5.78

frequency features from being ignored, we need to use a smoothing-based approach. The calculation method is as follows:

$$\text{TF} - \text{IDF} = (1 + \log(\text{tf})) * (\ln((p + 1)/(p')) + 1) \qquad (4)$$

The tf represents the frequency of feature words, p represents the total number of texts, and p' represents the number of texts containing the feature.

Next, we need to conduct text vectorization, that is to convert the keywords in the data set into a column. For example, if there are two sentences: *I have a fever. I have a headache.* We extract the following characteristics: *I, have, a, fever, headache,* and convert the above two sentences into Table 4:

Table 4. Example of vectorization matrix

I	have	a	fever	headache
1	1	1	1	0
1	1	1	0	1

The vectorization matrices are [1, 1, 1, 1, 0] and [1, 1, 1, 0, 1], and the corresponding matrices can be obtained for data clustering analysis. In this experiment, when constructing the keyword set of corpus, if the text frequencies of a certain word is more than 0.4 threshold or less than 10 times, it will be ignored directly.

3.2.3 Disease Topics Mining and Target Text Classification

In this section, we mine potential topics hidden under text features by using LDA algorithm, and divide the mined topics into different disease departments, extract pathological features under each department to construct disease department lexicons.

Our goal is to find the topic distribution of each text and the distribution of feature in each topic. Firstly, in order to better explore potential topics, we use perplexity to determine the number of topics of potential disease. Secondly, divide disease topics into different disease departments and construct lexicons of disease department. Finally, classify the target text into a specific disease department according to its pathological characteristics.

Specifically, the top n disease features of each subdivision subject of each department are extracted to construct the disease department lexicons, the calculate TF-IDF values of each feature of target text, then select the top k feature words to form feature set d_i. Features in d_i are screened out to match with features which in department's lexicons, the ratio between the feature words matched successfully and the characteristic feature in d is denoted as the matching rate θ_i, the department to which $Max(\theta_i)$ belongs is the category to which the classification belongs.

$$d_i = \{f1, f2, \ldots, fk\} \tag{5}$$

The d_i represents the feature set of target text. f_i represents features of target text.

4   The Experimental Analysis

In this section we use the medical text which from a well-known online medical community in China called Sanjiu Health Network [21]. From the experiment, we found that the suitable number of topics can be obtained according to the position of the inflection point in Fig. 2. Divided into 50 subdivided topics, datasets with the best discrimination between each topic, and the least number of redundant features in each topic. Because the lower the perplexity of a model, the more certain the distribution of features in the model is. After the number of topics exceeds 50, the perplexity does not decrease significantly as the number of topics increases, and gradually converges. In addition, too many topics will causes confusion for subsequent analysis, so we take the value at k = 50 as the optimal value.

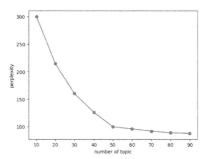

Fig. 2. The Perplexity of topic number

We can extract the topics distribution situation of the current text, as shown in Fig. 3. On the left side of the figure, circles represent different topics. The size of circles represents the number of texts contained in each topic, and the distance between circles represents the degree of correlation between each topic. The themes expressed by circles in the same quadrant are often more similar, just like topic 7, topic 15, and topic 30 in the fourth quadrant. The right side of the figure lists the 30 most frequent keywords. The text in the Fig. 3 are "pregnancy", "symptoms", "hemorrhoids", "baby"," child", "time", "surgery", "onset", "child", "menstruation period", "cough", "fetus", "anus", "stool", "problem", "never", "few days", "no", "fracture", "cold", "lacking strength", "whole body", "curative effect", "previous", "dizziness", "once", "eyes", "fever", "hurt" "whether". It can be seen that diseases and symptoms such as obstetrics and gynecology, anorectal, and colds have attracted much attention.

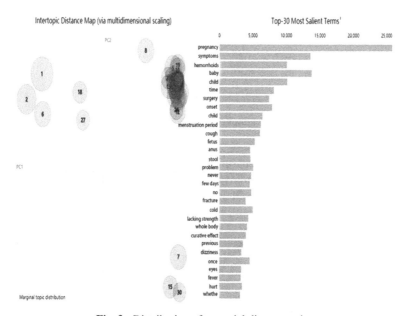

Fig. 3. Distribution of potential disease topics

As shown in Fig. 4, the current distribution is under topic 7. The text in Fig. 4 are "nausea", "vomiting", "dizziness", "tumor", "gastritis", "bloodshot", "chemotherapy", "detection", "hours", "cervical", "spondylosis", "bad breath", "granules", "fatigue", "abdomen", "neck", "tumor", "puffiness", "long-term", "period", "years", "late period", "unconscious", "hours", "father", "lump", "superficial", "tongue coating", "strength", "on the high side", "become thin". It can be seen that the main symptoms of the disease under this theme are mainly long-term chronic diseases, and the main disease sites are the head and chest cavity.

From the above figures, it can be observed that some subdivisions have an aggregation phenomenon. Therefore, similar subjects are merged into different large departments, and 50 subdivisions are eventually divided into 10 disease departments. In this case, the corresponding disease departments of each topic are classified into orthopedics department, thoracic department, gynecology department, ophthalmology department, general

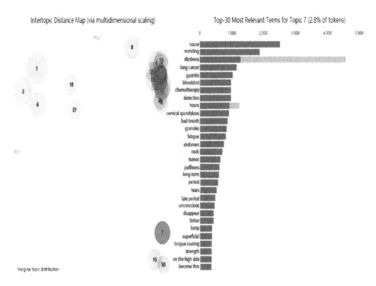

Fig. 4. Features distribution of Topic 7.

surgery department, dermatology department, irritability department, pediatrics department, proctology department and cardiovascular department. The types and proportions of various diseases are shown in Fig. 5:

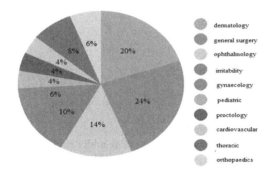

Fig. 5. The topic belongs to the department and the proportion of departments.

On the premise of knowing certain disease departments, this model can classify the disease combination contained in the selected labeled target text, and finally obtain the category of the disease department to which it belongs. This is a multi-classification problem, by comparing with TLC algorithm and two traditional classification algorithms to evaluate the performance of our algorithm, we applied the measures precision, recall and F1-measure, which emphasized the performance of the algorithm on the degree of confidence listed in Table 5.

As shown in Table 5, our proposed TLC algorithm has higher precision, recall and F1-measure, which proves its accuracy. Our method can overcome xx to some extent,

Table 5. Classification accuracy

Method	Precision	Recall	F1-Measure
TLC	0.87	0.92	0.89
ID3	0.80	0.86	0.82
Bayesian	0.76	0.83	0.78

because we fully consider low-frequency phrases and words, and preserved integrity of medical text features. In addition, we mine potential topics with reasonable granularity, and built fine-grained disease-department lexicon, which improved the accuracy of the target text which department belongs to.

5 Conclusion

This paper proposes a model that classify online medical texts by potential disease topics and disease departments. In this method, the medical first processed medical description texts and convert medical texts into feature representations, then mines potential disease topics of online medical community that have received widespread attention and merges them into different disease departments, and classifies target texts into above disease departments by matching ratio of features. TLC algorithm retains the integrity of medical text features as much as possible while eliminate interference of unnecessary words. The experiments are conducted on real data sets, and demonstrate the effectiveness of the results by comparative analysis, to improve the accuracy of classification and reduce the interface of redundant features will be our next research direction.

Acknowledgment. This work was supported by National Natural Science Foundation of China (No. 61701104), and by the Natural Science Foundation of Jilin Province of China (No. 20190201194JC).

References

1. Mihai, G.: Recommendation system based on association rules for distributed e-learning management systems. Acta Univ. Cibiniensis. Tech. Ser. **67**(1), 99–104 (2016)
2. Yang, S., Mohammed, K., Khalifeh, J., Natarajan, T.G.: Combining content-based and collaborative filtering for job recommendation system: a cost-sensitive Statistical Relational Learning approach. Knowl.-Based Syst. **136**, 37–45 (2017)
3. Zhang, Z., Zheng, X., Zeng, D.D.: A framework for diversifying recommendation lists by user interest expansion. Knowl.-Based Syst. **105**, 83–95 (2016)
4. Zhu, X., Tian, M., Shi, Y.: Status quo of research on classification system of medical adverse events at home and in abroad. Chin. Nurs. Res. (2013)
5. Lee, K., Jung, H., Song, M.: Subject-method topic network analysis in communication studies. Scientometrics **109**(3), 1761–1787 (2016)
6. GibbLDA-v.1.0 [EB/OL]. https://sourceforge.net/projects/gibbslda/. Accessed 10 Nov 2018

7. Shi, M., Liu, J.X., Zhou, D.: WE-LDA: a word embedding augmented LDA model for Web services clustering. In: IEEE International Conference on Web Services. Honolulu, USA: IEEE Computer Society, pp. 9−16 (2017)

8. Chu, Z., Yu, J., Wang, J.Y.: Construction method of mobile application similarity matrix based on latent Dirichlet allocation topic model. J. Comput. Appl. **37**(4), 1075–1082 (2017)

9. Ma, J.H., Liu, G.S., Yao, S., Yang, Z.: Feature selection and text representation for short text. Comput. Modernization (03), 95–101+126 (2019)

10. Zhou, Y., Liu, H.L., Du, P.P., Liao, L.: Study on text classification model based on improved TF-IDF feature extraction. Inf. Sci. **35**(05), 111–118 (2017)

11. Ping, N., Huang, D.G.: Research on automatic extraction of Chinese keywords based on TF-IDF and rules. Small Comput. Syst. **37**(4), 711–715 (2016)

12. Chen, J., Chen, C., Liang, Y.: Document classification method based on Word2vec. Comput. Syst. Appl. **26**(11), 159–164 (2017)

13. Wang, M., Ji, H.M., Wu, C.Q.: Research on automatic extraction of diseases from massive texts. Digit. Technol. Appl. **37**(05), 74–75 (2019)

14. Wang, Y.D., Fu, X.K., Li, M.M.: A social media data topic mining method based on co-word network. J. Wuhan Univ. (Inf. Sci. Ed.) **43**(12), 2287–2294 (2018)

15. Yin, L.Y., Dong, W., Huang, Z.X., et al.: Detection and analysis of medical behavior change trend oriented to clinical path. Chin. J. Biomed. Eng. **34**(3), 272–280 (2015)

16. Yang, X., et al.: Analyzing health insurance claims on different timescales to predict days in hospital. J. Biomed. Inform. **60**, 187–196 (2016)

17. Calin, R.T., Luke, D., Russo, A., Krysia, B.: Probabilistic abductive logic programing using Dirchlet priors. Int. J. Approximate Reasoning **78**(c), 223–240 (2016)

18. Siddiqi, S., Sharan, A.: Keyword and keyphrase extraction techniques: a literature review. Int. J. Comput. Appl. **109**(2), 18–22 (2015)

19. Ji, G., Lu, Y., Chen, W., Qin, Z.G.: An improved text categorization algorithm based on VSM.C. In: International Conference on Computational Science and Engineering. IEEE (2014)

20. Trstenjak, B., Mikac, S., Donko, D.: KNN with TF-IDF based framework for text categorization. J. Procedia Eng. **69**(1), 1356–1364 (2014)

21. https://www.39.net

An Adaptive Algorithm for Multiple Part Families Manufacturing Selection in Reconfigurable Flow Lines

Masood Ashraf[1], Arkadiusz Gola[2(⊠)], Faisal Hasan[3], and Ali S. AlArjani[1]

[1] College of Engineering, Prince Sattam bin Abdulaziz University, Al-Kharj, Saudi Arabia
mashrafalig@outlook.com, a.alarjani@psau.edu.sa
[2] Faculty of Mechanical Engineering, Department of Production
Computerisation and Robotisation, Lublin University of Technology, Lublin, Poland
a.gola@pollub.pl
[3] Department of Mechanical
Engineering, Zakir Husain College of Engineering and Technology, Aligarh Muslim University,
Aligarh, India
f.hasan.me@amu.ac.in

Abstract. Reconfigurable manufacturing systems (RMSs) are designed to satisfy for the requirements of a part family by amending changes in its hardware and software components rapidly in response to the quick fluctuations in the market demands. In the present work, a key RMS planning aspect has been considered and corresponding methodology and solutions are proposed for solving the problem. A Multiple Part Families Manufacturing (MPFM) problem has been considered for RMS. It involves selection of optimal reconfiguration policy while switching from production of one part family to another. This policy involves the evaluation of optimal sequences to be adopted for MPFM, which are evaluated on the basis of performance measures like number of reconfiguration set-ups involved, total reconfiguration cost and total reconfiguration time, while switching from one RSPFL set-up to another.

Keywords: RMS · Reconfigurable Manufacturing System · Reconfiguration Policy · Multiple Part Families Manufacturing · Reconfiguration cost · Reconfiguration time

1 Introduction

The mounting pressure of the competition forces the enterprises to maximise their efforts in constant upgrading and optimising the effectiveness of conducted processes [1–3]. Therefore, scheduling production jobs remains the crucial element in the field of production organisation and management [4, 5]. Sequencing jobs on technological machines affects both the completion time of production jobs, as well as the degree to which the production capabilities of a given enterprise are utilised [6].

Conventionally, any modification in the method of functioning of an industry implied an added consumption of resources [7–9]. These industries are incapable to cope up

© Springer Nature Singapore Pte Ltd. 2020
P. Sitek et al. (Eds.): ACIIDS 2020, CCIS 1178, pp. 133–144, 2020.
https://doi.org/10.1007/978-981-15-3380-8_12

with these modification requirements, enforced by such a competitive manufacturing environment [10, 11]. Hence, the responsive production systems with new configurations are needed to introduce novel products in the market, thus reconfigurability aspect of manufacturing systems is a matter of importance [12, 13].

Past two decades back, the concept of reconfigurability in manufacturing systems was introduced by Koren et al. [14] and it was termed as Reconfigurable Manufacturing System (RMS). Reconfigurability can be defined as the ability of a manufacturing system to be reconfigured cost effectively in a short period of time [12]. It is an ability that allows the addition, rearrangement or removal of system modules and functions to better cope up with high product range and rapid fluctuations in market demand in a profitable manner [13]. The RMS was designed to deal with situations where both productivity and ability of system can be changed in order to meet with large variations in product demand in combination with the ability to respond to market fluctuations [15–17]. Also, the output for RMS has adjustable functionality in order to introduce new products as and when needed [2, 18].

A RMS is a system which is designed around a part family and manufactures all the members of the part family [19–21]. A part family can be defined as a group of products having some common design or manufacturing features [21]. Conclusively, a RMS is a system designed at the outset for quick changes in its structure, as well as in its software and hardware modules, in order to rapidly modify the functionality and production capacity [22].

Since, the concept of RMS revolves around manufacturing of part families, the parts are made to group into respective part families according to their similarity levels. Once the products are grouped into respective part families, these families are required to be produced one after another on the RSPFL. In a shop floor environment, manufacturers have to produce wide-ranging number of orders for multiple part families, and after producing the orders of a particular part family, they are required to change over to the orders of a different part family [21]. A RSPFL is a production flow line which comprises of several production stages, each stage is equipped with RMTs for performing a specific kind of operation. In case of Multiple Part Family Manufacturing (MPFM), when RMS finishes the production of one part family, the whole system needs to be reconfigured/changed from its previous configuration setup to the next suitable one as per its requirements, for the processing of subsequent part family. Thus, RSPFL is needed to be reconfigured before initiating the production of the next part family. This can be done by reconfiguring the existing RMT configurations installed on the production stages into new RMT configurations. As industries generally produce multiple part families; a sequence of reconfiguration decisions i.e. Reconfiguration Policy (RP) is required to be made at production stages of a RSPFL to work productively. The RP has to be wisely selected for the reconfiguration capacity of RMSs which makes the decision-making process for controlling the production disturbances more difficult [23]. Thus, an efficient change-over is to be wisely performed while switching from one configuration set up to another.

While switching from production of one part family to another, the reconfiguration set-up change-over involves Set-up times, Reconfiguration cost and effort which is required for changing tools, fixtures and configuration of a RMT on one or more platforms of RSPFL [24]. The shop floor environments require frequent set-up change-overs, which involves certain features in between producing the two part families. It plays a crucial role and are taken as more significant than production/processing times [24]. During the production phase, each part family involves a set of operations to be performed at different stages on a RSPFL. Each stage usually installed with a RMT which is capable to carry out several operations by reconfiguring it, as per need arises at the expense of reconfiguration cost, time and effort. Though, the nature of operations to be executed at each stage on a RSPFL are not considerably dissimilar and the consecutive operations performed at a given station can be of same type and hence, sometimes requiring no set-up changes at all [24]. Therefore, reconfiguration cost, time and effort involved in between two set up change-overs can be optimized by pre-planning the sequence of production of part families that are required to be produced on a RSPFL. Hence, an optimal RP is required for selecting the appropriate production sequence of MPFM. This is done in order to optimize the performance parameters involved while switching from production of one part family to another.

The present work proposes a novel methodology of RP selection for MPFM on a RSPFL having stochastic orders of production. The RP selection model is developed taking into consideration the total number of reconfiguration set-ups occurred, total Reconfiguration cost and time occurred in processing all the part families considered in the problem. Some of the related works pertaining to the RP under multiple part families are discussed in the succeeding sections.

The rest of this paper is presented as follows: Sect. 2 presents a literature review on the aspects of reconfiguration policy selection in RMS. Section 3 provides the problem description and general description of proposed algorithm. Section 4 presents the way of sequences selection using the presented approach. Section 5 summarizes the paper and indicates research that will be provided to evaluate the proposed algorithm and make it more and more effective.

2 Literature Review

Since then, the concept of RMS has revolved around the family of parts formation (PFF), which consists of conceptually grouping products into a family of products based on certain similarities in product characteristics. An important problem that arises after PFF is the formation of optimal RP for MPFM, which must be recognized to improve the productivity of RMS. After the creation of the parts families, they must be produced on RSPFL one after the other. Once a family of parts is produced, the following family of parts can be created after reconfiguring RMT configurations already installed on RSPFL. With regards to this issue, Moghaddam et al. [25] considered an RMS configuration design problem, with a variable demand for a single product all over its product life cycle, and the system configuration changes based on demand with minimal cost. A reconfiguration link between dynamic market demands and the capacity and functionality of manufacturing systems was developed to group products into part families before starting its manufacturing. Another problem was to determine the optimal configuration of a RMS server for the production of multiple part families. Research has suggested an optimal production order for parts families to get the most out of a given system configuration [16]. Abdi and Labib [26] proposed a hierarchically structured framework for choosing the part families during each configuration phase. Navaei and Elmaraghy [24] considered the effect of setup changes that occur between the production of two consecutive product variants. The research goal was to find the best sequence of product variants to minimize changes/costs/times in the entire machine setup. An index of performance named as service level was proposed and modelled by Hasan et al. [27] for MPFM in RMS. In order to identify the best time to reconfigure the RMS, a dynamic complexity-based RMS reconfiguration point decision method was proposed by Huang et al. [28]. Ashraf and Hasan [29] developed a framework for the selection of a Manufacturing Flow line (MFL) configuration and demonstrated the problem using the non-dominated genetic sorting algorithm II (NSGA-II). Likewise, a dynamic maintenance strategy was also proposed for reconfigurable structures of RMS [30]. A planning problem based on MPFM took into account the costs of reconfiguration to switch over the set-up from one part family to another; the problem was solved to improve the efficiency of the work of a RCMS [31]. Musharavati et al. [32] developed a process planning evaluation model for MPFM on a criterion based on minimizing the total processing costs. An optimal policy was proposed by Matta et al. [33] in order to decide when and how to reconfigure the manufacturing system under uncertain market demand and product features. Under stochastic market demand, Matta et al. [34] considered an optimal capacity problem and proposed a RP for adaptable capacity. Similarly, a capacity reconfiguration problem has been proposed to allow capacity exchange between the manufacturing lines based on the performance of the due date [23]. Deif and ElMaraghy [35] also developed a capability-scalability modelling approach, which has shown that RMS can manage their scalability of system-level capacity cost-effectively. An optimization problem related to an optimal selection policy based on a stochastic model was formulated and two resolution procedures were defined to solve the problem [36]. In order to utilize the RMS, Xiaobo et al. [37] proposed a selection policy whereby the manufacturer chooses a family of parts to manufacture ordered products that fit the selected family of parts.

As far as research gaps are concerned, several literatures like [21, 38, 39] reported that very few RMSs are designed around several families of parts. In addition, the literature identified revealed that work on the selection of reconfiguration policy is limited. Some work is based on problems with RMS reconfiguration, capacity reconfiguration, and reconfiguration time. However, no past work has addressed reconfiguration policy selection issues considering factors such as the total number of reconfiguration set-up change-overs, reconfiguration time, and reconfiguration cost that have been reported in this work.

3 Problem Description and Solution Approach

Take the example of a RSPFL that operates according to RMS principles and is able to produce several families of parts one after the other. Consider a manufacturing company producing multiple families of parts say, $PF_1, PF_2, PF_3 \ldots PF_n$ that are to be produced one after another on a RSPFL. Each family of parts has its own operating requirements, as shown in Table 5. The RSPFL must be reconfigured according to the requirements of these parts families. When a partial family is in production, the other families are waiting for production on RSPFL. Since the operating requirements of the parts families differ from each other, it is necessary to reconfigure the RMT configurations at the production stages before starting the production of the next part family. As soon as RSPFL gets reconfigured according to the operating requirements of the next part family then only its processing gets started. The complete RSPFL reconfiguration can only be performed once the production of each part family has been completed and this process continues until RSPFL has completed the production of the last remaining part family.

Since, it is quite possible that the same operation can be performed by several RMT configurations; it is necessary to study and select the RMT configuration which has the lowest cost of installation and/or reconfiguration and which can also be reconfigured as quickly as possible. Thus, an RP gives a reconfiguration path that must be adopted when passing a production configuration corresponding to a family of parts to another. Table 1 defines several parameters and their corresponding notations that are considered in the present problem.

Table 1. Nomenclature

Parameter definition	Notation
Production stage number on a RSPFL	$S_i \mid i \in \{1, 2, \ldots\}$
Part family to be produced on the RSPFL	$PF_j \mid \forall_j \in \{1, 2, \ldots\}$
RMT	$M_i \mid \forall i \in \{1, 2, \ldots 4\}$
Feasible RMT configurations	$M_i^k \mid \forall i \in \{1, 3, 4\}, k \in \{1, 2\};$ $\forall \{i\} \in \{2\}, \{k\} \in \{1, 2\}$
Operation p to be performed on the jth part family	$O_p^j \mid p \in \{1, 2, \ldots\}, \ j \in \{1, 2, \ldots, N\}$
Reconfiguration time (in hours) required in switching from one RMT configuration set-up to another	$\tau_{i \to i'}^{k \to k'} \mid \forall \{i, i'\} \in \{1, 3, 4\}, \{k, k'\} \in \{1, 2\};$ $\forall \{i, i'\} \in \{2\}, \{k, k'\} \in \{1\}$
Cost (in 1000 €) occurred in switching from one RMT configuration set-up to another	$C_{i \to i'}^{k \to k'} \mid \forall \{i, i'\} \in \{1, 3, 4\}, \{k, k'\} \in \{1, 2\};$ $\forall \{i, i'\} \in \{2\}, \{k, k'\} \in \{1\}$
Installation and removal cost of a RMT configuration on a RSPFL (in 1000 €)	$[\ ]_{ik}^{(I, R)} \mid \forall \in \{1, 3, 4\}, \{k\} \in \{1, 2\};$ $\forall \{i\} \in \{2\}, \{k\} \in \{1\}$
Production rate (parts/hr) of a RMT configuration for performing the pth operation on the ith stage of a RSPFL	$R_{i_k}^p \mid \forall \in \{1, 3, 4\}, \{k\} \in \{1, 2\};$ $\forall \{i\} \in \{2\}, \{k\} \in \{1\}, p \in \{1, 2, \ldots, 8\}$
Total number of reconfiguration set-ups required on i^{th} stage while switching from one RMT configuration set-up to another	$n_{j \to j'}^i \mid i \in \{1, 2, \ldots, 4\};$ $j \ \& \ j' \in \{1, 2, 3\}, \forall j \neq j'$

The production rates of RMT configurations (in parts/hour) and their respective capabilities to perform several operation is defined in Table 2. Table 3 defines the time required to reconfigure τ_i^k (in minutes) from one configuration set-up to another and so its corresponding reconfiguration cost C_i^k (in 1000 €). The costs of installing and removing the RMT configuration (in 1000 €) are listed in Table 4. The sequence of operations to be performed for the production of parts families is shown in Table 5. The candidate RMT configurations capable to perform operations required for processing the part families are shown in Table 6.

Table 2. Production rates (in parts/hour) for performing operations

$O_p \rightarrow$ $M_i^k \downarrow$	O_1	O_2	O_3	O_4	O_5	O_6	O_7	O_8
M_1^1	14	–	16	–	18	–	–	–
M_1^2	–	20	–	17	–	–	12	–
M_2^1	–	–	20	–	–	13	–	16
M_3^1	–	15	–	–	–	–	18	–
M_3^2	14	–	–	15	–	–	17	–
M_4^1	–	12	15	–	–	10	–	20
M_4^2	–	–	–	–	16	–	–	19

Table 3. Reconfiguration time (in minutes) and cost (in 1000 €) for switching from one configuration set-up to another

$M_i^K \rightarrow$ $\downarrow$	M_1^1	M_1^2	M_2^1	M_3^1	M_3^2	M_4^1	M_4^2
M_1^1	(0, 0)	(40, 10)	.....	.....	.....	.....	.....
M_1^2	(40, 10)	(0, 0)	(50, 36)	.....	.....	.....	.....
M_2^1	.....	(50, 36)	(0, 0)	(80, 44)	.....	.....	.....
M_3^1	.....	.....	(80, 44)	(0, 0)	.....	.....	.....
M_3^2	.....	.....	.....	.....	(0, 0)	.....	.....
M_4^1	.....	.....	.....	.....	.....	.....	.....
M_4^2	.....	.....	.....	.....	.....	.....	.....

Figure 1 shows the flow chart of RP generation for MPFM in RMS. First, the families of parts and their processing orders must be identified. An inquiry is made, whether all families of parts are already produced or not. Otherwise, the first part family of unfinished parts must be produced. Before starting the production, a check is made to determine if the configuration change is required at the production stages. If so, the configuration change must be made according to the instructions below:

Table 4. Installation and removal cost of RMT

M_i	M_i^k	Installation and removal cost of configurations on RSPFL (in 1000 €)
M_1	M_1^1	(60, 40)
	M_1^2	(50, 45)
M_2	M_2^1	(65, 35)
M_3	M_3^1	(45, 20)
	M_3^2	(55, 35)
M_4	M_4^1	(70, 25)
	M_4^2	(75, 30)

Table 5. Operation sequences for producing the part families

$O_p^j \rightarrow$ / $PF_j \downarrow$	O_1	O_2	O_3	O_4	O_5	O_6	O_7	O_8
PF_1		1 ⇒ 2 ⇒ 3 ⇒ 4						
PF_2	1 ⇒		2 ⇒		3 ⇒		4	
PF_3	1 ⇒					2 ⇒	3 ⇒	4
.....								
PF_n	.....			.....	.....			.....

Table 6. RMT configurations capability to perform operations on part families

$O_p^j \rightarrow$ / $PF_j \downarrow$	O_1	O_2	O_3	O_4	O_5	O_6	O_7	O_8
PF_1	–	M_1^2 M_3^1 M_4^1	M_1^1 M_1^2 M_4^1	M_1^2 M_3^2	–	M_2^1 M_4^1	–	–
PF_2	M_1^1 M_3^2	–	M_1^1 M_2^1 M_4^1	–	M_1^1 M_4^2	–	M_1^2 M_3^1 M_3^2	–
PF_3	M_1^2 M_3^1 M_4^1	–	–	–	–	M_2^1	M_1^2 M_3^1 M_3^2	M_2^1 M_4^1 M_4^2
.....	.....		.....		.....		.....	
PF_n		.....		.....	.....			.....

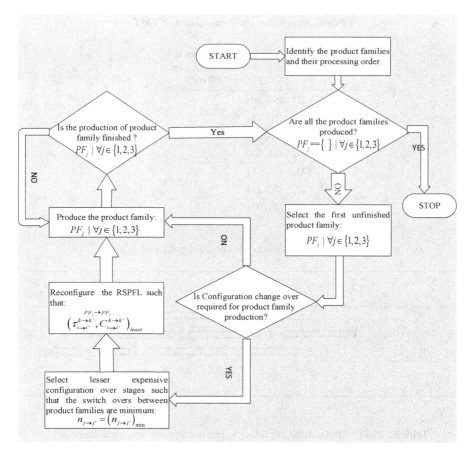

Fig. 1. Flow diagram for reconfigurable policy selection for multi-part families manufacturing

(a) The number of set-up changeovers should be minimum.
(b) If there is a need of set-up changeover, then it should be performed in such a way that the number of reconfiguration set-ups, reconfiguration time and/or reconfiguration cost should be minimum.

Part families have to be produced by opting comparatively lesser expensive RMT configurations, which are capable to perform the required operations.

If configuration change on RSPFL is not required, the part family must be produced with the existing configuration. Otherwise, the configuration change must be made in accordance with the three directives mentioned above. The part family must be created after the configuration change on the RSPFL. Once production of the parts family is complete, a new check must be made to determine if all families of parts are produced. This process continues until the production of the last part family is complete.

4   Sequences Selection of MPFM Using the Adaptive Algorithm

Consider four production stages of a RSPFL where, the three part families are to be produced in a several order of production i.e. $\{PF_l \rightarrow PF_m \rightarrow PF_n \rightarrow \ldots\}$. Each part family requires certain operations to be performed on them. Part families differ from each other from the aspect of type of operations to be performed, their corresponding sequence of operations (Table 5) and with respect to multiple RMT configurations capable of meeting these operation requirements (Table 6). Since it is quite possible that the same operation can be performed by several RMT configurations on production steps at different production rates (Table 2) and with different installation/removal costs (Table 4). Since, the best possible configuration of RMT must be selected for the same thing. Once a part family production gets complete after performing several operations, another family of parts is ready for processing. Since, the operations to be performed on the next part family are totally different from the previous family of parts, it is necessary to reconfigure the configurations on the production steps in accordance with the appropriate requirements of the subsequent part family. Since, the selection of reconfiguration time and reconfiguration cost (Table 3) largely effects the reconfiguration effectiveness of RMS. Hence, while switching from production of one part family to another, the three aforementioned guidelines need to be followed.

Consider, one of the MPFM sequence i.e., $\{PF_l \rightarrow \ldots PF_m \rightarrow \ldots PF_n \rightarrow \ldots\}$ which is required to be processed on the four stages of RSPFL. These stages are equipped with suitable RMT configurations, capable enough to perform the necessary operations. A multi-level RP for e.g. (i) $\{PF_l \rightarrow PF_m\}$ (ii) $\{PF_m \rightarrow PF_n\}$ is adopted as per the three guidelines mentioned in the previous section. The corresponding least reconfiguration time and cost occurred has been presented in the same. Likewise, the reconfiguration policies for other possible orders of MPFM are suggested.

Due to some part family processing constraints, there are certain circumstances occur when the sequence of MPFM is not fixed. In such a case, the part families are required to be produced in different orders. The RSPFL set-up is required to be changed partly or completely for each MPFM sequence with regards to the performance criterion (i.e. number of reconfiguration set-ups, reconfiguration time and reconfiguration cost) considered in the present work. The part families having similar operation sequence can be produced consecutively with minor change-overs or absolutely no change-over at all. However, the part families which are entirely different with respect to their production features, require major set-up change-overs on the RSPFL that raises the number of reconfiguration change-overs required, reconfiguration time and cost on a RSPFL.

5   Summary and Future Research

The present work proposes a novel methodology for MPFM which are to be processed on RSPFL i.e. the course of action of RMS while producing the multiple part families on a RSPFL. Several dissimilar part families are considered to be produced by executing different set of operations on the production stages, under different sequences. The part families undertaken in this problem are dissimilar with respect to operations and/or operation sequences performed on the production stages. The RSPFL when it is needed to be reconfigured, it can be done by reconfiguring the existing RMT configurations installed on the production stages into the new RMT configurations. This is to be done in between finishing the production of a part family and before initiating the production of another part family. The criterion for MPFM involves the selection of best feasible sequence of part family production which is to be made on the basis of number of reconfiguration set-ups, reconfiguration time and reconfiguration cost.

In future, this work can further be extended for determining the optimal sequence of MPFM for seasonal part families that can further be modelled and solved by using programming software's like Enterprise Dynamics, Tecnomatix Plant Simulation and MATLAB.

Funding. The project/research was financed in the framework of the project Lublin University of Technology-Regional Excellence Initiative, funded by the Polish Ministry of Science and Higher Education (contract no. 030/RID/2018/19).

References

1. Terkaj, W., Gaboardi, P., Trevisan, C., Tolio, T., Urgo, M.: A digital factory platform for the design of roll shop plants. CIRP J. Manufact. Sci. Technol. **26**, 88–93 (2019)
2. Ashraf, M., Hasan, F.: Product family formation for RMS: a review. In: National Conference on Mechanical Engineering-Ideas, Innovation & Initiatives, vol. 1, pp. 37–40 (2016)
3. Gola, A.: Economic aspects of manufacturing systems design. Actual Probl. Econ. **156**(6), 205–212 (2014)
4. Burduk, A., Musial, K., Kochanska, J.: Tabu search and genetic algorithm for production process scheduling problem. LogForum **15**(20), 181–189 (2019)
5. Sobaszek, Ł., Gola, A., Kozłowski, E.: Application of survival function in robust scheduling of production jobs. In: Proceedings of the 2017 Federated Conference on Computer Science and Information Systems (FEDCSIS), pp. 575–578. IEEE, New York (2017)
6. Sitek, P., Wikarek, J.: A multi-level approach to ubiquitous modeling and solving constraints in combinatorial optimization problems in production and distribution. Appl. Intell. **48**(5), 1344–1367 (2018)
7. Sitek, P., Wikarek, J.: Capacitated vehicle routing problem with pick-up and alternative delivery (CVRPPAD) – model and implementation using hybrid approach. Ann. Oper. Res. **273**(1–2), 257–277 (2019)
8. Gola, A., Kłosowski, G.: Development of computer-controlled material handling model by means of fuzzy logic and genetic algorithms. Neurocomputing **338**, 381–392 (2019)
9. Bocewicz, G., Wójcik, R., Banaszak, Z.: AGVs distributed control subject to imprecise operation times. In: Nguyen, N.T., Jo, G.S., Howlett, R.J., Jain, L.C. (eds.) KES-AMSTA 2008. LNCS (LNAI), vol. 4953, pp. 421–430. Springer, Heidelberg (2008). https://doi.org/10.1007/978-3-540-78582-8_43
10. Jasiulewicz-Kaczmarek, M., Gola, A.: Maintenance 4.0 technologies for sustainable manufacturing – an overview. IFAC PapersOnLine **52**(10), 91–96 (2019)
11. Antosz, K., Pasko, L., Gola, A.: The use of intelligent systems to support the decision-making process in lean maintenance management. IFAC PapersOnLine **52**(10), 148–153 (2019)
12. Lee, G.H.: Reconfigurability consideration design of components and manufacturing systems. Int. J. Adv. Manuf. Techol. **13**(5), 376–386 (1997)
13. Maganha, I., Silva, C., Ferreira, L.M.D.F.: Understanding reconfigurability of manufacturing systems: an empirical analysis. J. Manuf. Syst. **48**, 120–130 (2018)

14. Koren, Y., et al.: Reconfigurable manufacturing systems. CIRP Ann. **48**(2), 527–540 (1999)
15. Dashchenko, A.I.: Reconfigurable Manufacturing Systems and Transformable Factories. Springer, Heidelberg (2006). https://doi.org/10.1007/3-540-29397-3
16. Hasan, F., Jain, P.K., Kumar, D.: Machine reconfigurability models using multi-attribute utility theory and power function approximation. Procedia Eng. **64**, 354–1363 (2013)
17. Deif, A.M., Eimaraghy, W.H.: Dynamic modelling of reconfigurable manufacturing planning and control systems using supervisory control. Int. J. Manuf. Technol. Manage. **17**(1), 82–102 (2009)
18. Gola, A.: Reliability analysis of reconfigurable manufacturing system structures using computer simulation methods. Eksploatacja I Niezawodnosc – Maint. Reliab. **21**(1), 90–102 (2019)
19. Koren, Y., Shpitalni, M.: Design of reconfigurable manufacturing systems. J. Manuf. Syst. **29**(4), 130–141 (2011)
20. Katz, R.: Design principles of reconfigurable machines. Int. J. Adv. Manuf. Technol. **34**(5), 430–439 (2007)
21. Hasan, F., Jain, P.K., Kumar, D.: Optimum configuration selection in reconfigurable manufacturing system involving multiple part families. Opsearch **51**(2), 297–311 (2014)
22. Abbasi, M., Houshmand, M.: Production planning and performance optimization of reconfigurable manufacturing systems using genetic algorithm. Int. J. Adv. Manuf. Techol. **54**(1–4), 373–392 (2011)
23. Renna, P.: Capacity reconfiguration management in reconfigurable manufacturing systems. Int. J. Adv. Manuf. Techol. **46**(1–4), 395–404 (2010)
24. Navaei, J., Elmaraghy, H.: Grouping and sequencing product variants based on setup similarity. Int. J. Comput. Integr. Manuf. **30**(6), 664–676 (2016)
25. Moghaddam, S.K., Houshmand, M., Fatahi, V.O.: Configuration design in scalable reconfigurable manufacturing systems (RMS): a case of single-product flow line (SPFL). Int. J. Prod. Res. **56**(11), 3932–3954 (2018)
26. Abdi, M.R., Labib, A.W.: Grouping and selecting products: the design key of reconfigurable manufacturing systems (RMSs). Int. J. Prod. Res. **42**(3), 521–546 (2004)
27. Hasan, F., Jain, P.K., Kumar, D.: Service level as performance index for reconfigurable manufacturing system involving multiple part families. Procedia Eng. **69**, 814–821 (2014)
28. Huang, S., Wang, G., Shang, X., Yan, Y.: Reconfiguration point decision method based on dynamic complexity for reconfigurable manufacturing system (RMS). J. Intell. Manuf. **29**(5), 1031–1043 (2017)
29. Ashraf, M., Hasan, F.: Configuration selection for a reconfigurable manufacturing flow line involving part production with operation constraints. Int. J. Adv. Manuf. Technol. **98**, 2137–2156 (2018)
30. Xia, T., Xi, L., Pan, E., Ni, J.: Reconfiguration-oriented opportunistic maintenance policy for reconfigurable manufacturing systems. Reliab. Eng. Syst. Saf. **166**, 87–98 (2017)
31. Eguia, I., Racero, J., Guerrero, F., Lozano, S.: Cell formation and scheduling of part families for reconfigurable cellular manufacturing systems using Tabu search. Simulation **89**(9), 1056–1072 (2013)
32. Musharavati, F., Ismail, N., Majid, A., Hamouda, S., Ramli, A.R.: A metaheuristic approach to manufacturing process planning in reconfigurable manufacturing systems. Jurnal Teknologi **48**, 55–70 (2008)
33. Matta, A., Tomasella, M., Clerici, M., Sacconi, S.: Optimal reconfiguration policy to react to product changes. Int. J. Prod. Res. **46**(10), 2651–2673 (2008)
34. Matta, A., Tomasella, M., Valente, A.: Impact of ramp-up on the optimal capacity-related reconfiguration policy. Int. J. Flex. Manuf. Syst. **19**(3), 173–194 (2007)
35. Deif, A.M., Elmaraghy, W.: Investigating optimal capacity scalability scheduling in a reconfigurable manufacturing system. Int. J. Adv. Manuf. Technol. **32**(5–6), 557–562 (2007)

36. Xiaobo, Z., Wang, J., Luo, Z.: A stochastic model of a reconfigurable manufacturing system Part 2: optimal configurations. Int. J. Prod. Res. **38**(12), 2829–2842 (2000)
37. Zhao, X., Wang, J., Luo, Z.: A stochastic model of a reconfigurable manufacturing system. Part 3: optimal selection policy. Int. J. Prod. Res. **39**(4), 747–758 (2001)
38. Galan, R., Racero, J., Eguia, I., Garcia, J.M.: A systematic approach for product families formation in reconfigurable manufacturing systems. Robot. Comput. Integr. Manuf. **23**(5), 489–502 (2007)
39. Rakesh, K., Jain, P.K., Mehta, N.K.: A framework for simultaneous recognition of part families and operation groups for driving a reconfigurable manufacturing system. Adv. Prod. Eng. Manag. **5**(1), 45–58 (2010)

Time Series Analysis and Prediction of Geographically Separated Accident Data

Katherina Meißner$^{(\boxtimes)}$, Florian Pal, and Julia Rieck

University of Hildesheim, Universitätsplatz 1, 31141 Hildesheim, Germany
{meissner,palflo,rieckj}@uni-hildesheim.de

Abstract. Road accidents are one of the most common causes of death in many countries, so it is imperative that police and local authorities take appropriate measures to prevent them. Accident circumstances vary depending on place and time. Therefore, a determined geographical and temporal analysis is needed in order to predict and interpret future accident numbers. Our study shows how such an analysis can be carried out using geographical segmentation. In particular, we take into account the different accident circumstances and their influence on the number of road accidents in the context of time series analysis.

Keywords: ARIMA · Data mining application · Geographical analysis

1 Introduction

Almost five fatal accidents happen on average every day on British roads. In Germany, nearly nine fatal accidents occur daily. In addition, around 6,300 property damages (but not personal injury) are recorded per day in Germany (cf. [16]). Due to the large numbers and the increasing trend of accidents over time, an analysis of accident data is of great importance for local authorities, cities, and the police. The analysis provides answers to questions such as: Where do most accidents happen? Are there geographical differences? What are the environmental conditions for most accidents? What conclusions can be drawn for the future of accidents from historical data?

In our approach, we first separate the data by geographical regions in order to identify spatial differences. Then, we calculate the number of accidents over time and interpret the data as *time series*. The resulting time series have a behavior that is usually determined by various influencing factors or *attributes* (e.g., day, weather, urban or rural area, and road type). An interaction of different influencing factors leads to a behavior of the time series which shows, e.g., a trend (long-term basic direction of a time series; upward or downward), periodic annual fluctuations (due to seasonal effects) or regular and irregular movements, caused by significant events. In order to analyze and forecast time series data, the combined consideration of the time series of the individual attributes can be an important instrument. In this way, we obtain a collection of time series that

© Springer Nature Singapore Pte Ltd. 2020
P. Sitek et al. (Eds.): ACIIDS 2020, CCIS 1178, pp. 145–157, 2020.
https://doi.org/10.1007/978-981-15-3380-8_13

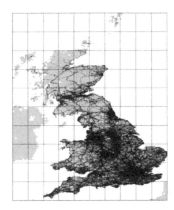

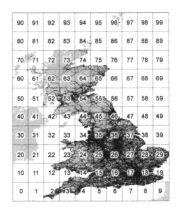

Fig. 1. Accidents in GB

Fig. 2. Numbered grid cells

corresponds to the measurements of attributes spanning the same time interval (*multivariate time series*, cf. Cheng et al. [2]).

In the following, the accident data of Great Britain is exemplary taken into account. The decision for this data is influenced on the one hand by the fact that Great Britain is characterized by large cities, long country roads, sparsely populated areas, rolling hills, and coastal roads and thus shows a high degree of heterogeneity (see accident locations indicated by black dots in Fig. 1). On the other hand, the British road accident data is available at a very detailed level and can be inspected publicly [4]. The study under consideration is based on traffic accident data from 2012 to 2017, which show about 840,000 accidents in 72 months. Obviously, the procedure discussed below for analyzing the data can also be applied to other regions and countries.

Accident data is usually recorded by the police. Thereby, as much information as possible is stored so that local authorities, cities, and the police can subsequently take appropriate measures to prevent accidents. Typically, detailed *accident circumstances* are provided including time and day, condition at accident location (e.g., road surface, weather, lighting conditions, special hazards), and a location description (e.g., road type, speed limit, junction control, pedestrian crossing). *Personal circumstances* refer to age and gender of the persons involved, vehicle type, and a detailed description of the course of events, usually structured in different attributes with predefined categories. Not included in the police data are *exogenous variables* that can also be used to support the analysis. This data is typically characterized by the fact that it does not address a specific geographical position; the exogenous data often refers to certain areas. Examples are *socio-demographic data* such as unemployment rate, population density, and age structure, *detailed weather information* including temperature, wind speed, and direction or data related to traffic in general, like petrol prices.

The paper's contribution is to perform a comprehensive analysis and prediction of accident time series data, composed of several attribute time series. Within the analysis, a special focus is made on the geographical location of accidents and the respective accident circumstances (i.e., neither personal circumstances nor exogenous data are considered in our study). In order to distinguish the approach from other studies, a literature review is given in Sect. 2. Section 3 describes the procedure of the analysis. Section 4 discusses the results obtained by a case study and Sect. 5 ends with a summary and an outlook.

2 Literature Review

In this section, we provide an overview of articles in which accident numbers are predicted on the basis of accident time series. The analysis of time series refers either to entire countries or cities or to smaller geographical separations of these. In addition, attributes or exogenous variables are considered in some articles.

Quddus [14] analyses data on road accidents in Great Britain. A forecasting of future accident numbers is performed using integer autoregressive models at different aggregation levels (e.g., years and months, the whole of Great Britain and individual street levels etc.). Karlis et al. [11] discuss time series models for accident prediction, in particular state-space models (flexible approaches that can be reduced to, e.g., AutoRegressive Integrated Moving Average (ARIMA) if suitable parameters are selected). A focus is given to models that allow for disaggregate analysis, i.e. analysis on, e.g., different age categories (young vs. elderly drivers), different genders or different road types (motorway, regional road, and local road).

Kumar et al. [12] consider accident time series of 13 different districts in India. The resulting time series are grouped using clustering methods in order to find similar districts. Moreover, a (simple) trend analysis is carried out for each cluster. Dong et al. [5] focus on the identification of spatial and temporal patterns in Florida. In their study, they use a Bayesian ranking model to determine similar areas with different accident numbers over time and different areas with similar accident trends (rising or falling) and are thus able to find areas that could become accident hot spots in the future. Fawcett et al. [6] identify hot spots in the city of Halle (in Germany). The authors divide the city into small areas (a kind of grid formation). Then, the numbers of accidents over time are determined and a Bayesian hierarchical modeling is used for forecasting. In the area of crime analysis, Huddleston et al. [8] introduce a top-down forecasting approach that considers the differences between subregions to forecast future crime hot spots within the city of Pittsburgh. The subregions are not defined on the basis of jurisdictional boundaries. Instead, the authors place a fine grid over the city, measure the density of events in each grid cell, and use a kernel density function to accurately position the hot spots (and their offshoots) in a grid. The time series of crime events are predicted with ARIMA and Holt-Winter, using only a single model (assuming all sub-regions have the same trend and seasonal effects).

Commandeur et al. [3] show that time series analysis methods such as ARIMA (compared to simple linear regression methods) are efficient in predicting future trends in road accidents. The study is based on Norwegian, British as well as French data and take exogenous variables such as petrol price, temperature, rainfall etc. into account. In this way, statements can be made, such as an increase in the petrol price by 1% leads to a reduction in fatalities or serious injuries in accidents by 0.3%. In addition, the effects of major safety campaigns (e.g., the introduction of safety belts) are analyzed. Other authors also confirmed the applicability of ARIMA for accident forecasting in different countries (e.g., Nigeria [1], Iran [15,19], India [17], and Malaysia [18]). Ihueze et al. [10] also refer to road traffic crashes in Nigeria and develop ARIMA and ARIMAX models (ARMIA with eXogenous variables) for forecasting crash frequencies. The results show that ARIMAX, which considers accident and personal circumstances like over speeding, weather or brake failure, produces a robust predictive model.

3   Time Series Analysis and Prediction

In order to obtain an overview of the geographical distribution of accidents, the accident frequencies within specific areas, and the relevant attributes, we first separate the data. For this purpose, a 10×10 *grid* is laid over the map of Great Britain which also includes the islands on the Scottish coast (cf. Fig. 2 and Subsect. 3.1). After the grid separation, we determine the accident time series for each grid cell (cf. Subsect. 3.2). The generated time series are used to predict future trends (cf. Subsect. 3.3). With the forecasting result, we identify interesting cells for which the analysis of attribute relationships and the derivation of accident prevention measures is performed (cf. Subsect. 3.4). Therefore, the relevant attributes for the cells are identified and attribute time series are created. There may be dependencies between various attributes, some of them only become apparent in an individual view of the attribute time series. For example, an almost constant time series can consist of attribute time series that have opposite seasonal effects. These relationships interest the communities and the local police. Figure 3 shows the individual steps of our approach (i.e., (a) geographical separation, (b) time series generation, forecasting and scoring, as well as (c, d) determining attribute relationships).

3.1   Geographical Separation

The *geographical separation* of the underlying region implies that accidents are not evenly distributed over all cells. In rural areas, the individual accidents on the road network can be easily distinguished, whereas in urban areas, with more than 50 inhabitants per hectare, an accident has occurred at almost every conceivable location in the six years under consideration (cf. Fig. 1). The use of a fixed grid is necessary in order to examine individually the geographical situations of accidents and identify specific preventive measures. For example, there seems to be a lot of slight accidents in cities, while there are relatively many fatal accidents in rural areas with a low population structure. Moreover, using a grid scheme instead of, e.g., local jurisdictions allows us to identify interesting areas that might not have attracted attention due to a separation into different local jurisdictions. The grid-size was chosen to ensure a certain amount of accidents

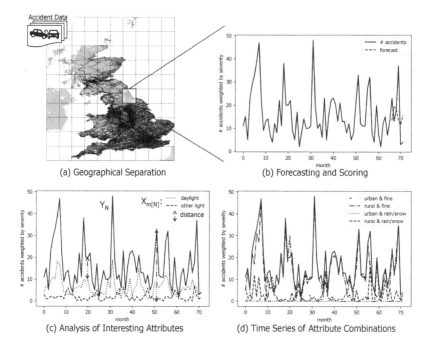

Fig. 3. Visual abstract of our research method

even in sparsely populated cells. Otherwise, slight differences in the number of accidents would lead to large fluctuations in the time series of these cells. Due to the grid scheme, some cells (exactly 38) are located completely in the North Sea and are of course accident-free.

3.2 Time Series Generation

Once the grid has been determined, accident time series can be identified for the individual cells. Although our evaluation should not concentrate on predicting different severity levels of accidents, the severity needs to be considered in the analysis. Therefore, we generate a *time series* for each grid cell by quantifying the number of accidents for each month and including the severity of every accident as a weight. In this way, we ensure that the very rarely occurring accidents with a high severity level are sufficiently considered during the analysis. Analogously to the Belgian approach for detecting risky road segments (cf. [7]), we multiply the number of accidents classified as serious (i.e., with hospital stay) by a weight of 3, while a fatal accident (i.e., with death) is adjusted with a weight of 10. Slight personal injuries are taken into account with a weight of 1. Figure 3(b) shows a resulting weighted time series of one grid cell. We use a month-based scaling of the time axis so that a sufficient number of accidents appear in a period. A finer scaling would often lead to time series containing zeros when no accidents have occurred. Moreover, the safety measures must be planned and implemented by the police. This is usually done several months in advance, which is why a finer scaling of the time series is also not necessary from a police point of view.

A weighted time series can now be decomposed in order to obtain weighted time series for individual, specific attributes. By overlaying the original time series and the *times series of attributes* (e.g., for road type "single carriageway", fine or rainy weather), a multivariate time series is generated. On the basis of this *multivariate* time series, attributes can be identified that significantly determine the behavior of the underlying accident time series.

In addition to the consideration of individual attribute time series, the combined influence of attributes on weighted accident data should be considered. For this purpose, we generate time series for different attribute combinations (e.g., for fine weather and road type 'single carriageway'). The British accident data contains up to 18 different attributes with varying values describing the accident circumstances, which can be meaningfully combined to more than 5,000 attribute combinations (cf. [13]). Thus, a distinction must be made between attribute (itemset) time series that are relevant and those that are non-relevant and can be neglected. We detect meaningful combinations by applying frequent itemset mining to the accidents of one grid cell and thereby obtain frequently occurring itemsets I consisting of several attributes (e.g., attributes i_1, i_2, i_3).

Through our grid scheme and our decomposition, we obtain $10 \times 10 = 100$ severity-weighted time series $y_0, \ldots, y_{99}$ with $t = 1, \ldots, 72$ timestamps each (for six years). Furthermore, corresponding time series for relevant itemsets are identified for every time series $y_N, N \in \{0, \ldots, 99\}$. Since the number of relevant itemsets can vary, we assume that time series y_N has $m[N]$ relevant itemset time series $x_{1[N]}, \ldots, x_{m[N]}$.

3.3 Forecasting and Scoring

By studying the accident numbers in a grid cell, it is possible to identify cells that show a recurring course of accidents, which means that a forecast does not yield any significant surprises. For these cells, the police can easily adjust the degree of prevention measures to the frequency of accidents. Locations with accident black spots (i.e., many accidents) are usually already known to the police and are covered by appropriate measures. Cells of particular interest are therefore those where the behavior is not easy to anticipate. These cells or the corresponding regions are of particular interest for the police and also for the local communities, although they may not show an accident black spot. In order to identify the "interesting" cells, a scoring procedure is introduced which rates these cells with a high score value.

In what follows, we assume that a forecast is made for each time series using statistical methods. In preliminary studies, ARIMA has proven to be suitable for forecasting, as the time series of the British data are either rather constant, have a trend or follow a seasonal effect. ARIMA supports these characteristics by an integrated season-trend-decomposition. Other statistical methods, such as exponential smoothing, can also reflect trend and seasonality, but were dominated by ARIMA regarding forecasting accuracy.

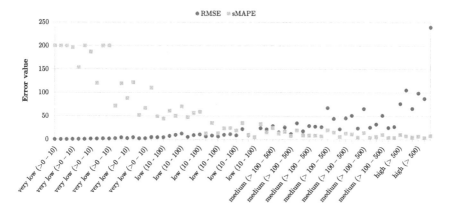

Fig. 4. RMSE and sMAPE values by cell size category

We use the first 66 months of the univariate time series of accidents with weighted severity to estimate the parameters for ARIMA. Afterwards, a forecast for the remaining 6 months is performed, allowing a comparison of the predicted and actual accident numbers. The worse the accident numbers could be predicted, the more "interesting" the time series is, since no pattern can be found for the time series. Preventive measures are thus particularly difficult to apply as it is impossible to assess whether they will be effective.

In order to determine ARIMA's *accuracy*, the Root Mean Squared Error (RMSE) is chosen. RMSE is calculated as the square root of the average of squared differences between the predicted and actual values (see, e.g., [9]). Due to the squaring of differences, RMSE is very sensitive to outliers, making it highly applicable for our scoring procedure. Other known error measures, such as MASE (Mean Absolute Scaled Error) or sMAPE (symmetric Mean Absolute Percentage Error), were excluded by preliminary tests for determining a meaningful score value. In particular, the property of MASE to set the prediction error in relation to the naive forecast is most unsuitable for our application, which shows trend and seasonality. The sMAPE $\in [0\%, 200\%]$ is also not applicable, as it strongly emphasizes the poorly predictable outliers in the time series of grid cells with few accidents, as illustrated in Fig. 4 and Table 1. The RMSE is inherently not scaled, so the forecast errors for cells with many accidents are naturally higher

Table 1. RMSE and sMAPE for ARIMA forecast (for 62 non-empty cells)

	∅ monthly accidents	Score (bias = 10)	RMSE ARIMA	sMAPE
Mean	298.188	0.078	25.109	50.723
Standard deviation	487.391	0.099	37.271	64.946
Min	0.014	0.002	0.015	3.403
Max	2,803.000	0.471	239.601	200.000

than the RMSE values for cells with fewer accidents. To scale it appropriately, the RMSE value is divided by the monthly-average accident number weighted by the severity $\bar{y}_N$. Moreover, we add a bias term of $b = 10$ to the denominator in order to ensure that cells with few accidents are not overweighted. This results in the following formula for the score of cell $N \in \{0, \ldots, 99\}$ (cf. Table 1), where $\hat{y}_N(t)$ is the predicted number of accidents at timestamp t and $T = 72$:

$$\text{score}_N = \frac{\sqrt{\frac{1}{6}\sum_{t=T-6}^{T}(\hat{y}_N(t) - y_N(t))^2}}{b + \frac{1}{T}\sum_{t=1}^{T} y_N(t)}. \tag{1}$$

The bias $b = 10$ in Eq. 1 was determined in a preliminary study, in which the score values were compared to the average monthly observation values $\bar{y}_N$. Figure 5 shows for some selected bias values the scores of the cells sorted and grouped by accident severity and number of accidents. This reveals that small bias values (e.g., $b = 0, b = 0.5, b = 1$) result in a high score for cells with very few accidents and a low severity, as the prediction accuracy is very poor due to the low number of accidents. For a bias of $b = 10$, significantly concentrated score values were found in the interval $[0, 0.5]$. Here, cells with the highest score values can be identified for cells with a higher monthly average $\bar{y}_N$. For larger bias values, the same cells receive a high score value as for $b = 10$, but the score interval becomes too small and thus too little distinguishable (e.g., $b = 100$).

Figure 6 visualizes the ordered score values of all 62 non-empty grid cells. The darker a point, the more accidents occurred within the corresponding cell. The figure shows a cutoff value for an "interesting" cell with a score of 0.3, since a clear jump in the scores can be seen here. The thus selected eight grid cells are indicated in Fig. 7. Please note that despite our scoring procedure, cells with few accidents become visible (mainly in Scotland). These cells are particularly interesting and need to be examined further.

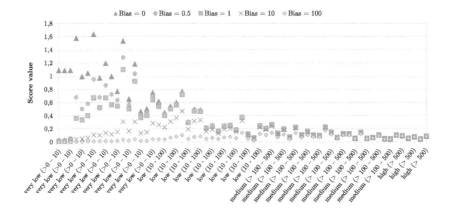

Fig. 5. Score values for different bias terms

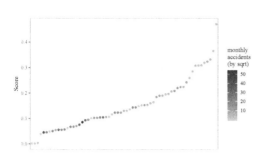

Fig. 6. Score values for all non-empty grid cells (the color scale for indicating the number of accidents is adjusted by the square root, while maintaining the monotony)

Fig. 7. 8 selected grid cells, with score greater than 0.3

3.4 Analysis of Interesting Attributes

Once an interesting cell has been determined from the score or one has been chosen within the geographical area of responsibility, it is crucial for the local police to know which attributes of an accident have the greatest influence on the temporal pattern of the accident numbers. Only then can they plan and implement the appropriate measures.

To estimate the influence of an itemset time series $x_{m[N]}$, we make use of different *influence indicators*. First, we calculate the euclidean distance between the time series $x_{m[N]}$ and the weighted severity time series y_N. In this way we discover whether the temporal course of the two time series is similar. The higher the distance $d_{eucl}(x_{m[N]}, y_N)$, the weaker is the influence of $x_{m[N]}$ on y_N. For better comparability, we also center all time series by subtracting their mean values. The (centered) euclidean distance is defined as follows:

$$d_{eucl}(x_{m[N]}, y_N) = \sqrt{\sum_{t=1}^{T} (x_{m[N]}(t) - y_N(t))^2} \qquad (2)$$

$$\text{center\_}d_{eucl}(x_{m[N]}, y_N) = \sqrt{\sum_{t=1}^{T} ((x_{m[N]}(t) - \bar{x}_{m[N]}) - (y_N(t) - \bar{y}_N))^2} \qquad (3)$$

To analyze time series dependencies, one of the most widely used approaches is to calculate the cross-covariance or cross-correlation between the series (cf., e.g., [10]). Due to our setup, we can assume that no causality can ever exist between a weighted severity value of a certain month in time series y_N and a previous month in time series $x_{m[N]}$. Therefore, we only calculate the cross-correlation and the normalized cross-correlation between the aligned time series (a high value indicates similar shapes). Please note that the normalization has a comparable effect as the centering for the euclidean distance.

$$\text{cross\_corr}(x_{m[N]}, y_N) = \sum_{t=1}^{T} x_{m[N]}(t) * y_N(t) \tag{4}$$

$$\text{norm\_cross\_corr}(x_{m[N]}, y_N) = \frac{\text{cross\_corr}(x_{m[N]}, y_N)}{\sqrt{\sum_{t=1}^{T} x_{m[N]}(t)^2 * \sum_{t=1}^{T} y_N(t)^2}} \tag{5}$$

4   Results of a Case Study

Using our presented forecasting and scoring procedures, eight interesting cells could be found in Great Britain. One of these cells (number 63 with the highest score value) is selected to present and discuss the results in form of a case study. In Table 2, we show different values of the influence indicators (2)–(5) for several itemset time series $x_{m[63]}$ of grid cell 63. All four indicators depict the same trend and favor the "urban" time series as the most influential one, followed by road type "other road" (i.e., all road types excluding "single carriageway"). For the other seven interesting cells, the indicators behave in the same way.

As the normalized cross-correlation value is the most suitable influence indicator, we focus on this measure for further analysis of itemsets with more than one item. Table 3 contains the most frequent itemsets for grid cell 63, which is located in the Scottish Highlands and shows only an average of 15 accidents in one month. The most influential combination is the time series of accidents on rural roads at fine weather conditions. Please note that this particular combination has a higher normalized cross-correlation than both individual time series, indicated in Table 2. The police can use this information to carry out preventive measures. Obviously, driving in fine weather in rural areas (possibly on undeveloped roads) causes drivers to drive too fast or too carelessly, which leads to accidents. Possible police measures now would be the use of speed cameras in such weather conditions and/or the installation of moving design elements to break the monotony of driving.

Table 2. Comparison of different influence measures for itemset time series $x_{m[63]}$

Attribute	Value	d_{eucl}	center_d_{eucl}	cross_corr	norm_cross_corr
light	daylight	281	254	21,241	0.895
light	other light	880	543	5112	0.322
weather	fine	947	580	3423	0.146
weather	rain/snow	239	225	2,2310	0.906
area	*urban*	93	104	25,889	0.968
area	rural	1,110	592	464	−0.093
road type	single carriageway	1,063	576	1648	0.218
road type	*other road*	148	150	24,705	0.951

Table 3. Normalized cross-correlation for itemset time series with more than one item

Weather	Light	Area	Road	norm_cross_corr $(x_{m[63]}, y_{63})$	norm_cross_corr $(x_{m[28]}, y_{28})$
fine	*daylight*			0.849	0.294
rain/snow	daylight			0.236	0.338
fine	other light			0.376	0.538
rain/snow	other light			0.005	0.342
	daylight	urban		−0.037	0.276
	other light	urban		−0.208	0.457
	daylight	*rural*		0.902	0.369
	other light	rural		0.335	0.506
fine		urban		−0.034	0.605
rain/snow		urban		−0.173	0.259
fine		*rural*		0.912	0.726
rain/snow		rural		0.196	0.449
fine	*daylight*	*rural*		0.854	0.287
fine	*daylight*		*s. carriagew.*	0.831	0.292
fine		urban	s. carriagew.	0.009	0.572
rain/snow	daylight	urban	other road	−0.134	0.142
fine	other light	rural	s. carriagew.	0.409	0.494

In order to assess the results of cell 63 more clearly, we additionally present the data of a different cell in Table 3. Cell 28 has the highest score of all cells in the size category "medium", i.e., 295 accidents per month and a score of 0.21. The itemsets of cell 63 are also frequent here, but the influence of the itemset time series on the severity weighted accident numbers is different for cell 28, with exception of the most influential. This result clearly demonstrates why it is important to first segment the data geographically and then examine the influence of the accident attributes, as this can vary greatly at different locations.

5   Discussion and Future Research

We have presented a procedure for analyzing accidents, which initially segments the accident data geographically. The areas, where accident numbers are most difficult to predict, are then examined further, as these are the areas in which police measures are very promising. To determine the appropriate road safety measures, we perform an analysis of the time series for individual accident attributes and combinations of attributes. If these are cross-correlated with the course of the accident numbers in the segment under consideration, the police gains insight in the main accident causes and can derive measures.

In ongoing developments of our approach, we aim to improve geographic segmentation by not rigidly specifying the size of grid cells, but by reducing the size of cells in areas with more accidents and enlarging them in others. This also optimizes the scoring process, as the number of accidents between cells will no longer vary so much. Moreover, we will use the automatically detected dependencies between accident attributes to enhance the forecasting by performing a multivariate prediction based on ARIMAX.

References

1. Balogun, O.S., Oguntunde, P.E., Akinrefon, A.A., Modibbo, U.M.: Comparison of the performance of ARIMA and MA model selection on road accident data in Nigeria. Eur. J. Academ. Essays **2**(3), 13–31 (2015)
2. Cheng, H., Tan, P.N., Potter, C., Klooster, S.: Detection and characterization of anomalies in multivariate time series. In: Park, H. (ed.) Proceedings of the 9th SIAM International Conference on Data Mining, pp. 413–424. SIAM, Philadelphia (2009)
3. Commandeur, J.J.F., Bijleveld, F.D., Bergel-Hayat, R., Antoniou, C., Yannis, G., Papadimitriou, E.: On statistical inference in time series analysis of the evolution of road safety. Accid. Anal. Prev. **60**, 424–434 (2013)
4. Department for Transport: Road safety data (2019). Published under Open Government Licence. https://data.gov.uk/dataset/cb7ae6f0-4be6-4935-9277-47e5 ce24a11f/road-safety-data. Accessed 10 Sept 2019
5. Dong, N., Huang, H., Lee, J., Gao, M., Abdel-Aty, M.: Macroscopic hotspots identification: a Bayesian spatio-temporal interaction approach. Accid. Anal. Prev. **92**, 256–264 (2016)
6. Fawcett, L., Thorpe, N., Matthews, J., Kremer, K.: A novel Bayesian hierarchical model for road safety hotspot prediction. Accid. Anal. Prev. **99**, 262–271 (2017)
7. Geurts, K., Wets, G.: Black spot analysis methods: literature review. Policy Research Centre for Traffic Safety 2002–2006 (2003)
8. Huddleston, S.H., Porter, J.H., Brown, D.E.: Improving forecasts for noisy geographic time series. J. Bus. Res. **68**(8), 1810–1818 (2015)
9. Hyndman, R.J., Athanasopoulos, G.: Forecasting: Principles and Practice, 2nd edn. OTexts, Melbourne (2019). OTexts.com/fpp2
10. Ihueze, C.C., Onwurah, U.O.: Road traffic accidents prediction modelling: an analysis of Anambra State, Nigeria. Accid. Anal. Prev. **112**, 21–29 (2018)
11. Karlis, D., Hermans, E.: Time series models for road safety accident prediction. Policy Research Centre for Mobility and Public Works (2012)
12. Kumar, S., Toshniwal, D.: A novel framework to analyze road accident time series data. J. Big Data **3**(1), 1–11 (2016)
13. Meißner, K., Rieck, J.: Data mining framework to derive measures for road safety. In: Perner, P. (ed.) Machine Learning and Data Mining in Pattern Recognition - Proceedings of the 15th International Conference, MLDM, NY. ibai Publishing (2019)
14. Quddus, M.A.: Time series count data models: an empirical application to traffic accidents. Accid. Anal. Prev. **40**(5), 1732–1741 (2008)
15. Razzaghi, A., Bahrampour, A., Baneshi, M.R., Zolala, F.: Assessment of trend and seasonality in road accident data: an Iranian case study. Int. J. Health Policy Manag. **1**(1), 51–55 (2013)

16. Statistisches Bundesamt (Destatis): Verkehr - Verkehrsunfälle 2018: Fachserie 8 Reihe 7 (2019). https://www.destatis.de/DE/Themen/Gesellschaft-Umwelt/Verke hrsunfaelle/Publikationen/Downloads-Verkehrsunfaelle/verkehrsunfaelle-jahr-208 0700187004.pdf
17. Sunny, C.M., et al.: Forecasting of road accident in Kerala: a case study. In: International Conference on Data Science and Engineering (ICDSE). IEEE, Piscataway (2018)
18. Wai, A.H.C., Seng, S.Y., Fei, J.L.W.: Fatality involving road accidents in Malaysia. In: Proceedings of the 2nd International Conference on Mathematics and Statistics - ICoMS 2019, pp. 101–105. ACM Press, New York (2019)
19. Yousefzadeh-Chabok, S., Ranjbar-Taklimie, F., Malekpouri, R., Razzaghi, A.: A time series model for assessing the trend and forecasting the road traffic accident mortality. Arch. Trauma Res. 5(3), e36570 (2016)

Method of Defining Diagnostic Features to Monitor the Condition of the Belt Conveyor Gearbox with the Use of the Legged Inspection Robot

Pawel Stefaniak$^{(\boxtimes)}$ ⓘ and Sergii Anufriiev ⓘ

KGHM Cuprum Research and Development Centre, Wrocław, Poland
pkstefaniak@cuprum.wroc.pl

Abstract. This paper presents the results of constructing the inspection robot serving as a tool to define the conditions of technical infrastructure in deep mine. The project has been conducted as the part of the European "THING - subTerranean Haptic INvestiGator" project. The challenge of managing the dispersed deep mine machine park in the conveyor transport network has been discussed in the paper. One of the functions of the inspection is to evaluate the technical condition of the conveyor gearbox. Thus, the haptic robot leg has been designed to perform non-invasive vibration measurements on the gearbox housing. The inspection robot has been designed to consequently perform the necessary monitoring processes currently performed by human, which proves to be troublesome in the mining industry worldwide. The aim of the paper is to suggest the complete method of collecting field measurements and defining diagnostic features based on time-frequency analysis. Such an approach would facilitate full mobility and automatization of defining diagnostic features process with the robot, what is crucial in the harsh mining conditions.

Keywords: Inspection robot · Deep mine · Belt conveyor · Gearbox · Condition monitoring

1 Introduction

Belt conveyors which transport material are subject to numerous adverse incidents resulting from faulty construction, inappropriate selection of material properties, faulty assembly or incorrect exploitation. Such incidents, leading to breakdowns or repairs of the machines, generate substantial additional costs [1, 2]. Therefore, in order to enhance the performance of the belt conveyor transportation system, the servicing costs are considered to be more important than the costs of initial investments. The shift towards the quality approach to the issues of exploiting belt conveyors might be observed. This change is aided by the constant development of measurement techniques in technical diagnostics and of methods and tools supporting the exploitation decision process [3, 4]. SCADA software implemented for the daily operation provides the important data on mining performance. However, considering technical diagnostics, the software analyzes

© Springer Nature Singapore Pte Ltd. 2020
P. Sitek et al. (Eds.): ACIIDS 2020, CCIS 1178, pp. 158–167, 2020.
https://doi.org/10.1007/978-981-15-3380-8_14

current or temperature data, which are insufficient for the complete insight into technical condition of vibrating parts, such as gearbox, bearing or drum. Commonly implemented SCADA software is limited to signal acquisition and raw data visualization [5–7]. Large mining enterprises often face difficulties in interpreting raw signals because of multiple stoppages and complexity of monitored processes [8]. More advanced online conveyor monitoring systems are expensive and arduous to maintain, taking into account the number of objects (>200), the spatial dispersion of machines (up to >100 km^2) and harsh environmental conditions in mines (temperature, dust, humidity, salinity). Therefore, advanced systems are implemented only at specific and critical locations.

The "THING - subTerranean Haptic INvestiGator" project has been initiated to respond to the expectations of contemporary users of belt conveyors. The project covers the construction of inspection robot used for evaluating the machine condition and the technical infrastructure of deep mines. It has been assumed that the inspection robot will take over the necessary monitoring processes currently performed by human (for example operating the conveyor). The robot might prove to be the indispensable tool particularly in harsh environmental conditions in deep mines which are subject to temperature and gaseous hazards. Considering harsh mining conditions, the crucial goal of the project is to ensure the proper robot's perception in terms of defining material and road surface (condition evaluation, location, mapping, identification of the environment in which the robot operates) [10, 11] (see Fig. 1).

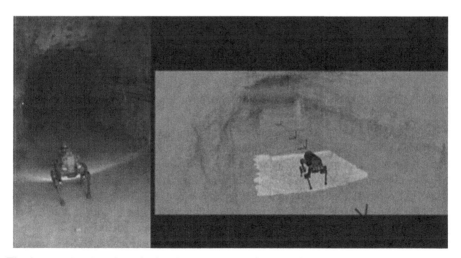

Fig. 1. Functional testing of robot in the tunnel (left), visualization depicting mapping of the passage while the robot moves in the tunnel (right) [14].

The main focus of the inspection mission concerns the methodology of vibration measurements on the belt conveyor gearbox and of defining diagnostic features. Obtaining the measurements of vibration signal, its processing, further analysis and concluding on the features of vibration signal are inevitable to properly evaluate the condition. The simplest example of concluding follows: *if* **value of a feature** *is greater than* **alarming level,** *apply* **alarm status**; *if not, apply* **correct status**. Indeed, ongoing tracking of the level of diagnostic features can be used for estimation of residual lifetime of gearbox in the future. For better comprehension, Fig. 2 shows the general idea of determining decision thresholds.

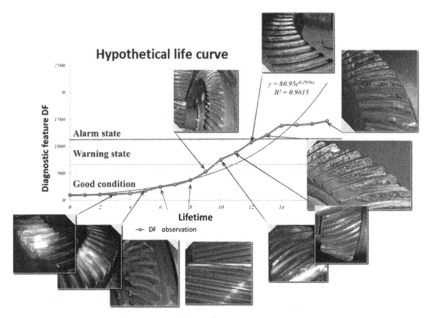

Fig. 2. Hypothetical life curve based on proposed diagnostic features [12].

The detailed description of the assumptions of the diagnostic mission is shown in [9].

The paper is divided into 6 parts. In Sect. 1 the authors introduce current knowledge on belt conveyors' monitoring systems, the objectives of THING project and challenges in evaluating the condition of the conveyor gearbox. The construction and characteristics of belt conveyors are presented in Sect. 2, while the construction and anticipated functions of inspection robot designed by THING team are described in Sect. 3. Section 4 covers the goals of the diagnostic mission and the procedure of measuring the diagnostic parameters on the belt conveyor gearbox. Section 5 describes the method of identifying diagnostic features from diagnostic signal. Section 6 is the conclusion.

2   Construction and Characteristics of Belt Conveyor

A single belt conveyor is the part of the whole horizontal continuous transport system. It operates continuously (on 24-h basis irrespective of short service breaks). The conveyor transports material on its looped belt. The belt constitutes the closed loop, thus, there are two sides, upper - carrying side (top link) and bottom - return side, separated by front and backing drums. The belt loop is located on respective roller bearings - idlers and drums between the front station and turning station of the conveyor. The points are located respectively at the front and back of the conveyor. The section between one point and the other is called a conveyor route. The conveyor route consists of the load bearing structure. This structure supports conveyor's components and balances pressures resulting from belt tensions and the weight of material and the belt itself. Alike the front point, the backing point is the separate construction. It supports components which construct the back part of the conveyor. At that point the material is placed on the belt. A drive unit propelling the belt is assembled at the front point. Depending on its function and length, the drive consists of 1–4 engines usually featuring the same technical parameters. The single drive unit is built of an engine, coupling and gearbox (usually two-stage or three-stage). The combination of rigid coupling and fluid coupling is commonly used to dampen the sudden load shocks during exploitation. Figure 3 depicts the construction of the drive unit.

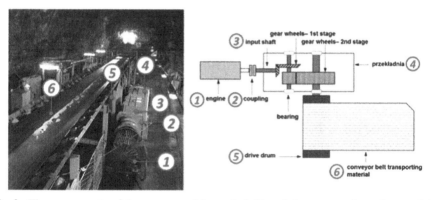

Fig. 3. The components of the conveyor drive unit (left) and the construction scheme of the conveyor drive unit (right) [12, 15].

3 Construction and Anticipated Functions of Inspection Robot

The robot is a four-legged (Fig. 4), module platform intended for inspection underground works (condition evaluation, emergency actions etc.) which are performed remotely and autonomously with the use of wireless connection. The robot is powered with a lithium-ion polymer battery. The whole sensory layer on the platform weighs no more than 5 kg. There are the following sensors:

- inertial sensors (3-axis accelerometers, gyroscope, magnetometer)
- adaptive feet,
- LIDAR scanning,
- laser scanner,
- head with a tilted panel and a high-quality, infrared zoom camera,
- thermal camera,
- sensors for environmental parameters and toxic gases detection (CO, H_2S).

Fig. 4. ANYmal legged robot used in the project [14].

Because of the carbon fibre construction, the robot weighs approximately 30 kg. The main body and the drive units are water- and dustproof. There are 12 actuators on the robotic legs, which allow collecting touch interactions with the surrounding, based on the techniques of full robotic body control and performing dynamic movements, such as jumping and running. In the course of THING project, the focus has been directed towards kinematic robot design to obtain full mobility for both agile passing through obstacles and stairs and convenient transportation, mainly of compactly stored elements. "360° rotation" in all joints facilitates the robot's climbing all kinds of obstacles and getting up once fallen. The robot is controlled by designed algorithm which steers its activity, namely the configuration of its legs and the position of its steps in line with the real-time parameters collected by the sensory layer. Regarding hardware, there are three independent computers connected by the intranet. The first computer (movement) controls the motor unit. The second computer (navigation) controls the perception of surrounding (mapping), location, navigation and autonomic performance of the mission. The third computer (inspection) controls the conditions of quarry, drivers and conveyor route and identifies abnormal phenomena/events.

4   Diagnostic Mission - Diagnostic Parameters Measurement Recorded on the Belt Conveyor Gearbox

Consequently, the robot is designed to perform inspection of the whole conveyor, including the condition of mining excavation. The detailed description of inspection, challenges in retaining functionality of the conveyor and the expected results of the robot's functioning are included in [9]. The main objective of this paper is only the diagnostic inspection of the conveyor drive unit gearbox, specifically the method of measurement and identification of diagnostic, damage-oriented features.

The mission of the robot is to perform the work of maintenance employee which constitutes evaluating technical condition of the pairs of kinematic gearboxes by vibration diagnostic technique. Currently this process is performed with the use of portable measurement unit with 3 vibration sensors and tachometer probe which measures rotational speed of the engine (Fig. 5).

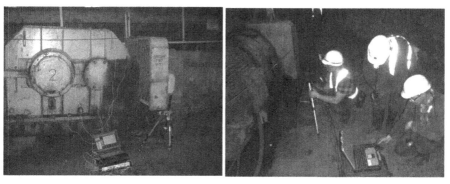

Fig. 5. Maintenance inspection for conveyor gearbox in underground mine - vibration measurement [9, 12].

The implementation of the robot aims at completely eliminating the human role in evaluating the gearbox's condition. The measurement procedure depicted in Fig. 6a and b indicates the measurement points. This measurement method does not require assembling sensors to the drive unit. The measurement is performed with haptic sensing.

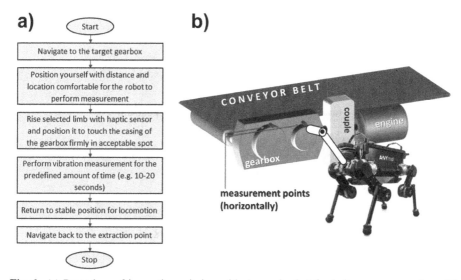

Fig. 6. (a) Procedure of inspection mission with Anymal robot for belt conveyor gearbox, (b) measurement points [9].

5 Method of Identifying Diagnostic Features to Examine Shafts, Gearings and Bearings of the Conveyor Gearbox

Diagnostic features of multistage gearboxes can be identified by transforming signal into frequency domain, and further defining, in its spectrum, components relative to the specific vibration elements (shafts, gearing, bearings) (Fig. 7c). Thus, the comprehensive condition of the components of the gearbox under inspection might be obtained. Figure 7 shows examples of vibration signals and their spectra from gearboxes in good and bad condition.

The solution suggested in the paper is a modifying method proposed by Bartelmus described in [13] and employs the broadband Fourier transform to translate the signal into frequency domain. The methodology adopted the vibration measurement for 20 s. Next, the raw signal was evenly segmented into 20 sections. Repetitively, each consecutive

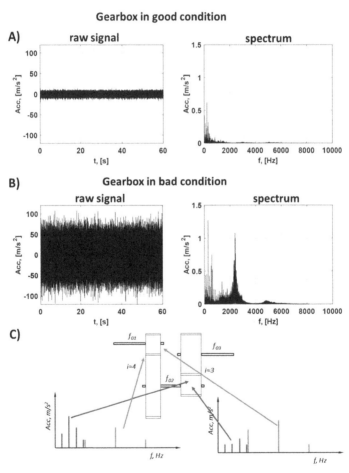

Fig. 7. Vibration signal and its spectrum from the conveyor gearbox in (a) good condition and (b) bad condition, (c) Signal spectrum components as diagnostic features [based on 16].

1-s section of vibration signal was converted into frequency domain and all obtained sections were totalled within three bands of spectrum frequency (for shafts: 10–100 Hz, for gears: 100–3500 Hz, for bearings: 3500–10000 Hz), Fig. 8.

The measurement results in 20-s time series (with sample period of 1 s) of diagnostic features sDF (shafts diagnostic feature), gDF (gearbox diagnostic feature) and bDF

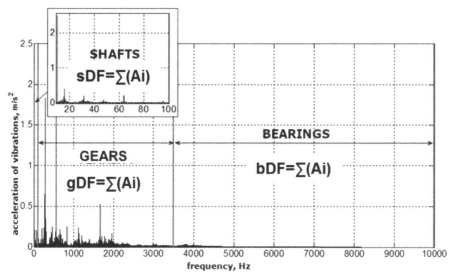

Fig. 8. Three key spectrum bands for determining diagnostic features for shaft, gearing and bearings [13].

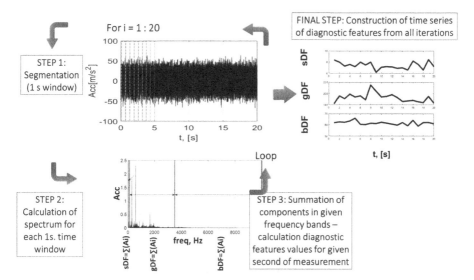

Fig. 9. The methodology of identifying diagnostic features from vibration signal spectrum [12].

(bearings diagnostic feature) which define the condition of, respectively, shafts, gears and bearings, Fig. 9.

6   Conclusion

The paper presents the general objectives of diagnostic mission of the legged inspection robot for monitoring mining belt conveyors. The challenge of managing the conveyor transport network has been discussed herein. It has been recommended to perform the diagnostics mission with the legged diagnostic robot. Thus, the complete procedure of vibration measurements on the gearbox housing of the conveyor has been performed. The main objective of the mission was to identify faulty diagnostic features within the vibration signal. The paper outlines the set of shafts, gearing and bearing features and algorithm to define the diagnostic features.

Acknowledgments. This work is a part of the project which has received funding from the European Union's Horizon 2020 research and innovation programme under grant agreement No 780883.

References

1. Stefaniak, P., et al.: Some remarks on using condition monitoring for spatially distributed mechanical system belt conveyor network in underground mine-a case study. In: Fakhfakh, T., Bartelmus, W., Chaari, F., Zimroz, R., Haddad, M. (eds.) Condition Monitoring of Machinery in Non-stationary Operations, pp. 497–507. Springer, Heidelberg (2012). https://doi.org/10.1007/978-3-642-28768-8_51
2. Stefaniak, P., Wodecki, J., Zimroz, R.: Maintenance management of mining belt conveyor system based on data fusion and advanced analytics. In: Timofiejczuk, A., Łazarz, B.E., Chaari, F., Burdzik, R. (eds.) ICDT 2016. ACM, vol. 10, pp. 465–476. Springer, Cham (2018). https://doi.org/10.1007/978-3-319-62042-8_42
3. Wei, Y., Wu, W., Liu, T., Sun, Y.: Study of coal mine belt conveyor state on-line monitoring system based on DTS. In: Proceedings of SPIE - The International Society for Optical Engineering, vol. 8924, Article number 89242I (2013)
4. Kuttalakkani, M., Natarajan, R., Singh, A.K., Vijayakumar, J., Arunan, S., Sarojini, L.: Sensor based effective monitoring of coal handling system (CHS). Int. J. Eng. Technol. 5(3), 2432–2435 (2013)
5. Eliasson, J., Kyusakov, R., Martinsson, P.-E., Eriksson, T., Oeien, C.: An Internet of Things approach for intelligent monitoring of conveyor belt rollers. In: 10th International Conference on Condition Monitoring and Machinery Failure Prevention Technologies 2013, CM 2013 and MFPT 2013, vol. 2, pp. 1096–1104 (2013)
6. Sadhu, P.K., Chattopadhyaya, S., Chatterjee, T.K., Mittra, D.K.: Online monitoring and actuation for curing of rubber conveyor belts. J. Inst. Eng. (India) Mech. Eng. Div. **89**, 31–35 (2008)
7. Keerthika, R., Jagadeeswari, M.: Coal conveyor belt fault detection and control in thermal power plant using PLC and SCADA. Int. J. Adv. Res. Comp. Eng. Technol. (IJARCET) **4**, 1649–1652 (2015)

8. Sawicki, M., et al.: An automatic procedure for multidimensional temperature signal analysis of a SCADA system with application to belt conveyor components. Procedia Earth Planet. Sci. **15**, 781–790 (2015)
9. Zimroz, R., Hutter, M., Mistry, M., Stefaniak, P., Walas, K., Wodecki, J.: Why should inspection robots be used in deep underground mines? In: Widzyk-Capehart, E., Hekmat, A., Singhal, R. (eds.) Proceedings of the 27th International Symposium on Mine Planning and Equipment Selection - MPES 2018, pp. 497–507. Springer, Cham (2019). https://doi.org/10.1007/978-3-319-99220-4_42
10. Käslin, R., Kolvenbach, H., Paez, L., Lika, K., Hutter, M.: Towards a passive adaptive planar foot with ground orientation and contact force sensing for legged robots. In: 2018 IEEE/RSJ International Conference on Intelligent Robots and Systems (IROS), Madrid, pp. 2707–2714 (2018)
11. Bednarek, J., Bednarek, M., Wellhausen, L., Hutter, M., Walas, K.: What Am I touching? Learning to classify terrain via haptic sensing. In: 2019 IEEE International Conference on Robotics and Automation (ICRA), Montreal (2019)
12. Stefaniak, P.: Modeling of exploitation processes of spatially distributed continuous transport system. Ph.D. thesis (2016). (in Polish)
13. Bartelmus, W.: Condition monitoring of open cast mining machinery. Oficyna Wydawnicza Politechniki Wrocławskiej (2006)
14. http://www.rsl.ethz.ch/robots-media/anymal.html
15. http://inova.pl/
16. Zimroz, R.: Metoda diagnozowania wielostopniowych przekładni zębatych w napędach przenośników taśmowych z zastosowaniem modelowania. Ph.D. thesis, Wrocław (2002)

Road-Quality Classification and Motion Tracking with Inertial Sensors in the Deep Underground Mine

Pawel Stefaniak[1]($\boxtimes$) [iD], Dawid Gawelski[1] [iD], Sergii Anufriiev[1,2] [iD], and Paweł Śliwiński[2] [iD]

[1] KGHM Cuprum Research and Development Centre, Wroclaw, Poland
pkstefaniak@cuprum.wroc.pl
[2] KGHM Polska Miedz SA, Lubin, Poland

Abstract. For many years now the mining industry has seen boost in exploring and developing the systems for monitoring operational parameters of mining machines, in particular of load-haul-dumping machines. Therefore, further researches on algorithmics have also advanced dynamically regarding effective performance management as well as predictive maintenance. Nonetheless, the issue of road conditions is still being neglected. That issue has substantial impact on both the overall operator's convenience, their performance and machinery reliability, especially its construction node and tyres damages. Moreover, such negligence pertains also to the maintenance of mine infrastructure, including the network of passages. The paper explains the use of the portable inertial measurement unit (IMU) in evaluating road conditions in the deep underground mine. The detailed descriptions of the road quality classification procedure and bump detection have been included. The paper outlines the basic method of tracking motion trajectory of vehicles and suggests the method of visualisation the results of the road conditions evaluation. This paper covers the sample results collected by the measurements unit in the deep underground mine.

Keywords: Inertial sensors · Road-quality classification · Bump detection · Motion tracking · Load-haul-dumping machines

1 Introduction

In copper ore mines, where mining is performed in room and pillar method, passages constitute the main transportation infrastructure for both crew and autonomous mining machines operating in mining areas. The quality of passages is subject to the number of machines exploited in a mining department and harsh environmental and exploitation conditions. Damaged, bumpy passages often cause increased dynamic overloads of machines, resulting in hindering the parts' durability and their damaging. Construction node damages in the machine prove to be the severe problem. Neglecting the issue of deteriorating road conditions may completely thwart the possibility to rebuild a passage. The awareness of the transportation surface conditions facilitates pre-planning of the

© Springer Nature Singapore Pte Ltd. 2020
P. Sitek et al. (Eds.): ACIIDS 2020, CCIS 1178, pp. 168–178, 2020.
https://doi.org/10.1007/978-981-15-3380-8_15

optimal haulage routes for self-propelled machines, repairing activities and increasing pro-active motivation of road maintenance staff. It has been proved that using monitoring system to reward operators for their high-quality work contributes to considerable reduction of maintenance issues and improves the key performance indicators. Hence, ongoing tracking of road surface parameters (bumps and other abnormalities) may avail convenience and secure working conditions of the crew and of the machines' reliability. Road quality analysis shows dynamic overloads impacting the working machine, what may constitute the valuable information for the constructors to redesign respective machine units and adjust them to unique exploitation conditions. Currently, measuring departments of mines use common cartographic and laser scanning methods.

There have been new road-quality tracking methods acknowledged in luxurious passenger cars. Besides, the more common smartphones, the more popular the method of surface condition detection with the use of integrated inertial sensors. Suggested procedures are perfect solutions for collecting data, their validation, statistical evaluation and road condition classification [6, 10, 15, 23].

The literature elaborates on automated road condition classification methods, such as machine learning, heuristic approach, Euclidean distance, processing videos and photos or laser scanning [1, 8, 21].

Apart from evaluating road conditions, inertial measurements can be successfully applied to estimate road grade with measurements collected by the machine during driving that road. The issue of estimating road grade has been already widely discussed in the literature. Most of publications concern four-wheel vehicles: [3, 11] especially heavy duty vehicles varying in weight [7, 17, 18].

Next practical use of IMU is mapping the motion trajectory of a vehicle. This subject has been constantly advancing in robotics, sports, rehabilitation and film industry [2, 5, 14, 16, 22].

The paper outlines the basic method of obtaining the road surface analysis by the read-out of Z-axis accelerations on accelerometer. Prior to the presentation of results, the motion trajectory of self-propelled machine had been specified outlining the parameters of velocity and angle velocity in Z axis. The route had been further covered with road surfaces of different, 3-scale quality levels. The variations in operating the machine with empty and filled cargo box had to be taken into consideration.

2 Construction of the Machine and Anticipated Results of the Project

2.1 Investigated Machine - Haul Truck

Haul truck is used to haul material, including hauling from mining faces to department preloading points secured with grids. There are a few types of haul trucks operating in mines. They vary mainly in the capacity of cargo boxes. Haul trucks are designed and constructed to operate under harsh mining conditions. Both maintaining the proper stability of the machine and choosing the matching parameters of the drive unit contribute to satisfactory haulage performance of the machine even in passages with longitudinal grades up to $8°$. In case of transversal grades, the upper grade limit equals $5°$. The best manoeuvrability of the truck depends on a joint of two basic units of the machine: a drive unit (tractor) and a transportation unit (trailer/cargo box). There are two degrees of freedom in the joint of the haul truck. Two hydraulic actuators assembled between the above-mentioned units control the turning mechanism. This mechanism eases passing over perpendicular drifts (90° angle). Cargo box - trailer is the part of the machine operation unit. Operator uses the hydraulic unit to control the trailer operation unit. The cargo box is designed so that it allows free load and dump of material. The most common type of haul trucks are trucks with fixed cargo box and lid. Material is dumped through the sliding hydraulic partitions (Fig. 1).

Fig. 1. Investigated machine - haul truck.

2.2 Characteristics of Load-Haul Procedure

As already mentioned, haul trucks are designed to haul material from mining faces to department preloading points in which there are grids and hydraulic hammers to break oversized rocks. Single haulage cycle encompasses four basic procedures: (a) loading of the cargo box of the machine at the mining face, (b) hauling material to the dumping point, (c) dumping material, (d) returning to the loading zone at the mining face.

While loading, ore is directly preloaded from the bucket to the cargo box of the haul truck. Cargo box capacity is decisive for the selection of optimal loader type. It has been assumed that fully loaded cargo box of the machine requires 3 full haulage cycles. The haulage route of the haul truck does not exceed 1500 m. The speed of the truck passing through the sectioned passages should not exceed 12 km/h. Haulage process is usually short and lasts less than a minute (Fig. 2).

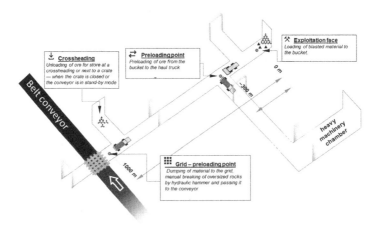

Fig. 2. Operation of LHD machines in mining area.

2.3 Identifying Operation Cycles - Key Variables

Typically, haul trucks perform basic operations - they drive from point A to point B, where their boxes are respectively loaded and dumped. In order to identify their operation cycles and individual procedures: loading, hauling, dumping and returning, the data were collected from the on-board monitoring system mounted on the machine. The key data crucial for identifying procedural components of the haulage operation regimes are:

- Torque of engine (ENGRPM),
- Speed (SPEED),
- Instantaneous fuel consumption (FUELUS),
- Current gear and movement direction (SELGEAR), (Fig. 3).

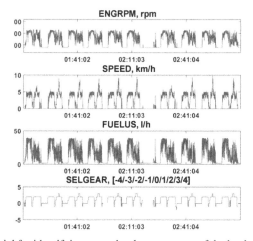

Fig. 3. Key data crucial for identifying procedural components of the haulage operation regimes.

The detailed description of the system has been included in [24]. Sampling frequency of signals equals 1 Hz. Recorded signal features cyclical variations, namely variables act alike in the consecutive cycles. The variability of signals is highly dependable on the haulage route, road conditions, number of machines in the mining department and operator's driving style.

2.4 Inertial Sensors

The project used the portable Inertial Measurement Unit described in [4]. The measurement unit is equipped with 3-axis accelerometer, gyroscope and magnetometer - the device for measuring magnetic field strength. Thus, 9 axes of freedom can be measured, and the location can be specified with the known starting point. Besides, the unit measures barometric pressure, temperature and humidity. The source data used in this project are:

- Z-axis gyroscope (range: ±2000°/s; resolution (min Δ): 0.06°/s; sampling frequency: 50 Hz)
- Vibration acceleration sensor on Z axis (range: ±16 g; resolution (min Δ): 490 μ; sampling frequency: 50 Hz)

Suggested mounting location of IMU is depicted in Fig. 4a. Figure 4b illustrates the 3-dimensonal orientation of IMU sensors.

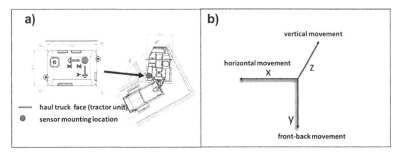

Fig. 4. (a) sensor mounting location, (b) 3-dimensonal orientation of IMU sensors.

2.5   Underground Experiment and Measurement Data

The experiment was conducted during the regular haulage operation in G-63 mining unit in one of the copper ore mines. During one shift, the machine operated along two routes (Figs. 5 and 6).

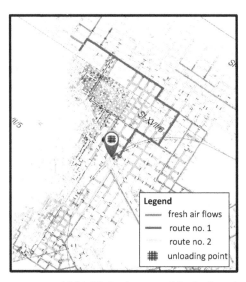

Fig. 5. Map of mining passages with highlighted routes of the haul truck during the experiment.

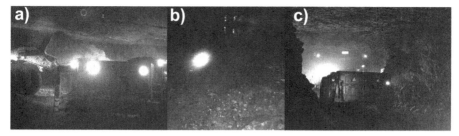

Fig. 6. (a) loading of the haul truck with the use of the wheel loader, (b) a part of the road surface - dip covered with mud, (c) driving with empty cargo box.

3   Methodology

3.1   Synchronizing Inertial Data and Data from On-Board Monitoring System

The analysed data have been obtained from two sources: the on-board monitoring system and the inertial measurement unit. The first steps are data validation, outliers' removal and completing missing data. Next, the data from different sources need to be rescaled. The IMU data are densely sampled whereas the data from the on-board monitoring system are sampled with 1-Hz frequency. Therefore, the data interpolation is necessary to calibrate the data to 50-Hz frequency.

3.2   Defining Work Cycles with Signal Segmentation

In order to define the work cycles of the machine, the patterns of operational data in specific operation regimes are to be acknowledged. The next step is to segment signals based on the recommended statistical parameters and condition classification principles. Algorithm with blind source separation approach described in [20] has been recommended herein. The issue of signal segmentation is omitted in this paper. For further information, please refer to [9, 12, 13].

3.3   Road-Quality Classification

The key variable considered in classifying the road condition was the signal from Z-axis accelerometer. First, 1-value was deducted from the data obtained from accelerometer to level out the speed of gravity. Afterwards, the data were overlapped with modulus. Python library, including cut function from pandas module, was used to section the road condition. Thus, the signal was segmented into 3 different sections matching the following road quality classes: good, fair and poor. Analyses are suggested to be performed individually for filled and empty cargo boxes. To correctly identify dynamic overloads, it is recommended to analyse the data of empty cargo box rides. The data may be supplemented with the statistical description of each cycle.

3.4   Calculating the Motion Trajectory

The method suggested herein has been developed with the use of the common inertial navigation system and AHRS (Attitude and Heading Reference System). Using trapezoidal rules for approximating integrals from Z-axis gyroscope, it has been possible to calculate the tilt angle of the machine. The x, y positions of the machine in time are determined by its speed and movement direction. Therefore, the route may be depicted as a graph, and thereafter - as 3-dimensional visualisation of the route driven and of the surface quality in various configurations (such as animation).

Procedure description:

STEP 1: Cycle segmentation,
STEP 2: Using trapezoidal rules for approximating integrals from Z-axis gyroscope, individually from each cycle to calculate the tilt angle of the machine,
STEP 3: Change of mathematical symbol of SPEED variable (driving speed), when SELGEAR (current gear and driving direction) is negative,
STEP 4: Defining x, y in t time by trapezoidal rules for approximating integrals of SPEED and the given angle, Fig. 7.

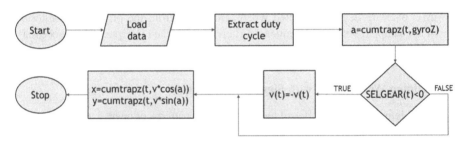

Fig. 7. Block schema of the algorithm for calculating the motion trajectory.

Trajectories calculated for individual haulage cycles have indicated the same route shape but some angular shifts (Fig. 8a). Such shifts resulted from gyroscope drift and signal noise, while the signal integration procedure has resulted in summing up the mistakes. The authors had endeavoured to improve the results merging the data with Kalman filter [19] and quaternion. That method failed due to a steel cover of the sensor used in the underground experiment - magnetometer was not able to properly read the data. Hence, future developments of alternative algorithmics in that issue are presumed. The developed algorithm allows also to depict animated route (Fig. 8b).

3.5   Filled and Empty Cargo Box Drives

Trajectories of driving with filled and empty cargo box should be presented concerning the quality of the road specified in line with the methodology described in 3.3 of this paper (Road-quality classification). The proper colour coding of the route with the use of 3 colours facilitates 3-dimensional presentation of the road and indicates the damaged spots which need repairing.

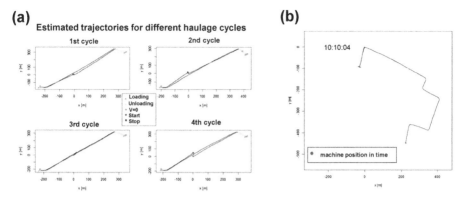

Fig. 8. (a) Estimated trajectories for a few haulage cycles, (b) Exemplary animation.

4 Results

The experiment lasted one working shift. Six hours of operational parameters from on-board monitoring system of the haul truck and mobile IMU sensor were registered. Additionally, the whole procedure was recorded with a camera. The data were then merged analytically and validated, including time synchronization in line with the method outlined in 3.1. Next, the signal segmentation with algorithm was performed [20] and the main procedure of evaluating the road condition and calculating the 2-dimensional route commenced. The analysis considered the following variables: SPEED, SELGEAR, ACC Z, GYRO Z. A sample section of signals from two haulage cycles is shown in Fig. 9.

All variables have demonstrated patterns characteristic for individual operation regimes. Indeed, while driving with empty cargo box the increase of signal power from Z-axis accelerometer has been observed. The signal is unstable and depends on many factors (for example self-vibration of the machine, road condition and grade, driving speed, motor capacity, tyres traction, load carried by the machine, noise or human factors). It is advised to check the accelerometer read-outs while idling the machine (ENGRPM ≈750 rpm) for reference value. Another good practice is to note ACCZ and GYROZ variables for the consecutive 3 dumps of material from the bucket of the wheel machine at the loading points.

In the next step, in order to apply the road surface classification: good, fair or poor, we analysed the data from Z-axis accelerometer.

Route trajectories for individual cycles of driving with filled or empty cargo box have been mapped. The results are shown in Fig. 10. Figure 7b illustrates high-frequency vibrations in the exploitation area resulting from the stand-by and loading of the machine, not from road conditions. Because of the low thill, the loader hit the roof and pushed down the machine during loading.

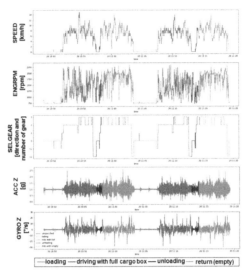

Fig. 9. Key timelines analysed after segmentation: driving speed (SPEED), current gear and movement direction (SELGEAR), Z-axis accelerometer (ACC Z), Z-axis gyroscope (GYRO Z). Operational regime is colour coded. Changeable torque (ENGRPM) is added to facilitate the interpretation of the data.

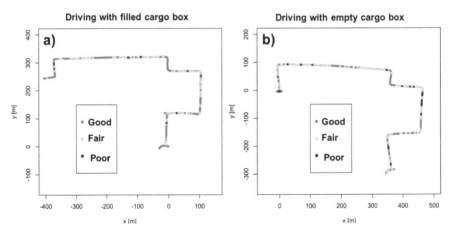

Fig. 10 Results of classifying the road conditions: (a) driving with filled cargo box, (b) driving with empty cargo box.

5 Summary

The paper outlines the basic method of using the inertial sensors for evaluating the road condition and mapping the trajectory of the machine's movement calculated by the IMU signals registered in the underground mine. The suggested algorithm operates on data from the on-board monitoring system - variables: speed, direction and the data from Z-axis accelerometer and Z-axis gyroscope. The experiment was conducted in the deep underground mine, on the haul truck and lasted one working shift. Next, the collected data were analysed. The route has been mapped on 2-dimensional map with the respective symbols indicating the road surface condition. The experiment showed the increased vibration of the machine during the rides with empty cargo box.

Acknowledgment. This work is supported by EIT RawMaterials GmbH under Framework Partnership Agreement No. 17031 (MaMMa-Maintained Mine & Machine).

References

1. Van Geem, C., et al.: Sensors on vehicles (SENSOVO)-Proof-of-concept for road surface distress detection with wheel accelerations and ToF camera data collected by a fleet of ordinary vehicles. Transp. Res. Procedia **14**, 2966–2975 (2016)
2. Hol, J.D., Schön, T.B., Luinge, H., Slycke, P.J., Gustafsson, F.: Robust real-time tracking by fusing measurements from inertial and vision sensors. J. Real-Time Image Proc. **2**(2–3), 149–160 (2007)
3. Hsu, L.Y., Chen, T.L.: Estimating road angles with the knowledge of the vehicle yaw angle. J. Dyn. Syst. Measur. Control **132**(3) (2010)
4. https://x-io.co.uk/
5. Huang, Y.C.: Calculate golf swing trajectories from IMU sensing data. In: Parallel Processing Workshops (ICPPW) (2012)
6. Eriksson, J., Girod, L., Hull, B., Newton, R., Madden, S., Balakrishnan, H.: The pothole patrol: using a mobile sensor network for road surface monitoring. In: Proceedings of the ACM 6th International Conference on Mobile System Application, Services, pp. 29–39 (2008)
7. Johansson, K.: Road Slope Estimation with Standard Truck Sensors. KTH, Sweden (2005)
8. Mohan, P., Padmanabhan, V.N., Ramjee, R.: Nericell: rich monitoring of road and traffic conditions using mobile smartphones. In: Proceedings of the 6th ACM Conference on Embedded Networking Sensor System, pp. 323–336 (2008)
9. Polak, M., Stefaniak, P., Zimroz, R., Wyłomańska, A., Śliwiński, P., Andrzejewski, M.: Identification of loading process based on hydraulic pressure signal. In: International Multidisciplinary Scientific GeoConference: SGEM: Surveying Geology & mining Ecology Management, vol. 2, pp. 459–466 (2016)
10. Ryu, S.-K., Kim, T., Kim, Y.-R.: Image-based pothole detection system for its service and road management system. Math. Problems Eng. **2015**(9) (2015). Art. no. 968361
11. Sebsadji, Y., Glaser, S., Mammar, S., Dakhlallah, J.: Road slope and vehicle dynamics estimation. In: American Control Conference, pp. 4603–4608. IEEE (2008)
12. Stefaniak, P., Śliwiński, P., Poczynek, P., Wyłomańska, A., Zimroz, R.: The automatic method of technical condition change detection for LHD machines - engine coolant temperature analysis. In: Fernandez Del Rincon, A., Viadero Rueda, F., Chaari, F., Zimroz, R., Haddar, M. (eds.) CMMNO 2018. ACM, vol. 15, pp. 54–63. Springer, Cham (2019). https://doi.org/10.1007/978-3-030-11220-2_7
13. Stefaniak, P., Zimroz, R., Obuchowski, J., Sliwinski, P., Andrzejewski, M.: An effectiveness indicator for a mining loader based on the pressure signal measured at a bucket's hydraulic cylinder. Procedia Earth Planet. Sci. **15**, 797–805 (2015)
14. Tao, Y., Huosheng, H., Zhou, H.: Integration of vision and inertial sensors for 3D arm motion tracking in home-based rehabilitation. Int. J. Robot. Res. **26**(6), 607–624 (2007)
15. Tedeschi, A., Benedetto, F.: A real-time automatic pavement crack and pothole recognition system for mobile android-based devices. Adv. Eng. Inform. **32**, 11–25 (2017)

16. Tessendorf, B.G.: An IMU-based sensor network to continuously monitor rowing technique on the water. In: Intelligent Sensors, Sensor Networks and Information Processing (2011)
17. Vahidi, A., Druzhinina, M., Stefanopoulou, A., Peng, H.: Simultaneous mass and time-varying grade estimation for heavy-duty vehicles. In: Proceedings of the American Control Conference, pp. 4951–4956 (2003)
18. Vahidi, A., Stefanopoulou, A., Peng, H.: Experiments for online estimation of heavy vehicles mass and time-varying road grade. In: Proceedings IMECE DSCD, 19th IFAC World Congress Cape Town, South Africa, 24–29 August 2014, 6300 (2003)
19. Welch, G., Bishop, G.: An introduction to the Kalman filter (1995)
20. Wodecki, J., Stefaniak, P., Śliwiński, P., Zimroz, R.: Multidimensional data segmentation based on blind source separation and statistical analysis. In: Timofiejczuk, A., Chaari, F., Zimroz, R., Bartelmus, W., Haddar, M. (eds.) Advances in Condition Monitoring of Machinery in Non-Stationary Operations, pp. 353–360. Springer, Cham (2018). https://doi.org/10.1007/978-3-319-61927-9_33
21. Yu, X., Salari, E.: Pavement pothole detection and severity measurement using laser imaging. In: Proceedings of the IEEE International Conference on Electro/Informatics Technology, May 2011, pp. 1–5 (2011)
22. Zhou, S., Fei, F., Zhang, G., Liu, Y., Li, W.: Hand-writing motion tracking with vision-inertial sensor fusion: calibration and error correction. Sensors **14**(9), 15641–15657 (2014)
23. Zimroz, R., et al.: Mobile based vibration monitoring and its application to road quality monitoring in deep underground mine. Vibroengineering PROCEDIA **19**, 153–158 (2018)
24. Zimroz, R., Wodecki, J., Król, R., Andrzejewski, M., Sliwinski, P., Stefaniak, P.: Self-propelled mining machine monitoring system–data validation, processing and analysis. In: Drebenstedt, C., Singhal, R. (eds.) Mine Planning and Equipment Selection, pp. 1285–1294. Springer, Cham (2014). https://doi.org/10.1007/978-3-319-02678-7_124

Safe and Secure Software-Defined Networks for Smart Electricity Substations

Filip Holik[1]([✉])[iD], Matthew Broadbent[2][iD], Mislav Findrik[3], Paul Smith[3],
and Nicholas Race[2][iD]

[1] Faculty of Electrical Engineering and Informatics, University of Pardubice,
Pardubice, Czechia
`filip.holik@upce.cz`
[2] School of Computing and Communications, Lancaster University, Lancaster, UK
[3] AIT Austria Institute of Technology, Vienna, Austria

Abstract. The next generation of *smart* electricity substations and grids are on the horizon. Part of the drive behind this movement is a need to improve safety and security. In parallel, software-defined networking has been proposed as a disruptive approach when deployed in these environments, presenting the opportunity to deploy novel functionality alongside existing forwarding behaviour. The benefits of software-defined networking are clear. Yet, if this technology is deployed without due care and attention, then it has the potential to reduce the safety and security of energy systems. In this paper we identify the aspects that must be considered to maintain the stringent requirements imposed by substation networks. With these as a basis, we provide recommendations for the successful deployment of software-defined networking technologies in these environments. We then demonstrate how additional functionality can be brought to the network without violating these requirements.

Keywords: ACL · Electricity substation · Safety and security
requirements · SDN · Smart Grid

1 Introduction

Electrical grids are evolving into next-generation Smart Grids. These address a number of challenges faced by current infrastructures, including mitigating peak energy demands, integrating renewable energy resources, improving grid resiliency to disruptions and increasing the cyber-security of critical infrastructures. Electrical substations are one of the most important elements in this electrical grid, with responsibility for voltage transformations and delivery of energy to end users. A Substation Automation System (SAS) is the central and most important component of a substation; realizing protection functions for circuit breaker tripping in the case of electrical faults, monitoring functions for collecting grid information, as well as various control functionalities for actuating the switchgear devices.

© Springer Nature Singapore Pte Ltd. 2020
P. Sitek et al. (Eds.): ACIIDS 2020, CCIS 1178, pp. 179–191, 2020.
https://doi.org/10.1007/978-981-15-3380-8_16

Traditionally, SASs have been built using wired copper cables, with industrial data exchange protocols (such as DNP3 and Modbus) used to facilitate inter-device communication. Modern substations use the latest generation of SASs, which are based on the Ethernet-IP/IEC 61850 communication standard [10]. When deploying in such an environment, consideration needs to be given to the design of the Ethernet network, including considering stringent reliability and availability requirements. Moreover, due to the open technologies that are used in the modern substations, and the growing need for greater information access (used to build emerging smart grid services), cyber-security is becoming a major concern for grid operators. The need for cyber-security has never been greater.

The process of meeting the requirements of safety *and* security is necessary in order to prevent accidents and outages caused by a network or security mis-configuration. Considering cyber-security as an aspect of this, it is necessary to minimise the vulnerabilities for a potential attacker to exploit. However, this is matched with the simultaneous need to ensure that any measures do not threaten the availability of legitimate substation functions, including the addition of new devices or services.

Software-defined networking (SDN) is a recently popularized paradigm which mandates the separation of data and control planes within computer networks. It is seeing increased adoption in a number of novel networking environments, and Smart Grids (SG) are no exception. However, deploying this technology without careful consideration can violate some of the established requirements in these topologies. Moreover, most of the security implications of deploying SDN are practically unexplored as the current work in this area address mostly resiliency [3,11] and performance [4] issues. There is consensus [5,7,12] that the following areas require further effort: improving reliability of the SDN controller, understanding the effect of network latency on SG reliability, vulnerability of the control network via switches and intelligent end devices, and conformance to security standards.

In this paper, we examine the core safety and security requirements in these networks. We reconcile these occasionally contradictory requirements to estab-lish recommendations for the safe and secure deployment of SDN in SG. We then show how a fundamental element of cyber-security defense, an access control ser-vice, can be deployed using SDN. Finally, we evaluate how the aforementioned recommendations impact the operation of this service, particularly under a num-ber of pertinent failure conditions.

2   Safety and Security Requirements

Substations are at the heart of the power transmission and distribution sys-tem used for delivering electricity to commercial, industrial and residential con-sumers. The IEC standard *Communication networks and Systems in Substa-tions* [1] brings open, inter-operable systems and flexible architectures to the substation automation domain. The interoperability is possible through the def-inition of communications protocols, data formats and a common configuration language. Moreover, the standard specifies OSI-7 layer based Ethernet communication systems. The communications hardware and software based on Ethernet are much less expensive than proprietary alternatives. Also, installation and maintenance of Ethernet networks is well understood. This reduces deployment, maintenance and operation costs. The standard defines two buses based on Ethernet technology: (i) the station bus and (ii) the process bus. The logical architecture of this standard is shown in Fig. 1.

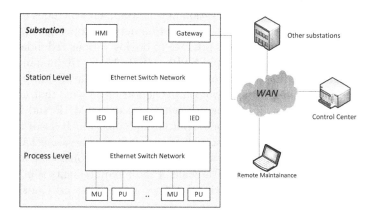

Fig. 1. Logical network architecture of IEC 61850 substations

However, from a security perspective, open systems are more inviting to malicious parties, since their implementation and vulnerabilities are publicly available. This is in contrast to proprietary systems, which are less well-understood and more diverse, thus protected with by a *security through obscurity* defense layer. Ethernet-based communication networks also need to ensure the safety of critical substation automation applications. This includes considerations of reliability, availability and performance. We summarize these requirements in the context of electrical substations based on the aforementioned IEC standard (and other, related standards).

Security Requirements. The landscape of substation automation systems is changing due to the acceptance of the IEC standards [1] by vendors. It is also driven by the increased need for cyber-security in these systems. Cyber-security has become one of the most important topics in the SG. A recently published technical specification IEC 62351 [2] covers information security for power system control operations. In parts 3–6 of the standard, measures for the security of communication protocols are defined. Besides specifying the measures for securing the SG protocols, parts 7–9 define end-to-end security involving security policies, access control mechanisms, key management, audit logs, and other critical infrastructure protection aspects. Part 8 defines a Role-Based Access Control

(RBAC) concept for users and automated agents. In general, these standards raise the need for access controls and define measures for securing communication, handling network and system management, as well as procedures for key management.

Safety Requirements. According to the IEC standard [1] reliability requirements, there should be no single point of failure that will cause the substation to move to an inoperable state. This standard specifies network redundancy that fulfills the requirements of substation automation. This includes the station and process bus. For different types of substation network topologies (star, ring, multi-ring and double network) it is possible to deploy various redundancy technologies. These include RSTP (Rapid STP), MRP (Media Redundancy Protocol), PRP (Parallel Redundancy Protocol) and HSR (High-availability Seamless Redundancy). PRP and HSR are two complementary protocols that are able to overcome the failure of a link or switch with zero delay. MRP and RSTP on the other hand are based on networks containing loops, which use a reconfiguration mechanism to recover the network from a failure. These mechanisms are necessary for mission-critical applications, such as substations, that have strict limitations on end-to-end latency. The scale of these requirements is in the order of few milliseconds up until hundreds of milliseconds for less critical substation functionalities [1].

3   Safe and Secure SDNs for Smart Substations

Safety and security are important facets in a substation environment. On the face of it, the use of SDN may initially seem to introduce an increased level of risk; the inclusion of additional components with dependencies could present potential points of failure. In this section, we examine the considerations for deploying SDN technology in a substation environment in regards to the previously defined requirements.

Fail Safe Modes. SDNs rely on a software-based controller. This creates a point of failure, which can occur when a controller becomes unresponsive, disconnected or the underlying hardware fails. If these events should occur then the forwarding elements, which rely on the controller to determine their behaviour, are left without specific instruction. Depending on the cause, this disconnection may only be temporary, with connectivity to the controller re-established soon afterwards. Upon reconnection, the controller may then remove and reinsert all of the prescribed flows, or simply retrieve the current state of the network without any changes being applied.

In cases where the controller remains disconnected, the switches need to behave in a consistent and predictable way. OpenFlow, the predominant SDN technology, includes two methods of achieving this. The first is *fail-standalone*, in which a switch simply reverts to its default switching behaviour. In this mode, once disconnection occurs, all existing OpenFlow rules are removed. Packets will be forwarded in the same way as if OpenFlow was not being used, using the hardware-based logic found in the switch. It is important to note that *fail-standalone* is only available on switches with *legacy* forwarding capability offered by the hardware itself. Software-based switches, such as Open vSwitch, do not provide this. It is therefore crucial to consider failure scenarios in these cases, as it is not possible to fall back to any default behaviour.

When using *fail-standalone*, configuration of forwarding should be established and tested before the switch ever reaches this state. This is especially the case if particular switching techniques need to be used (such as spanning trees for redundancy) or explicit topologies need to be considered (such as those with loops). Failure to complete this process may result in unintentional network behaviour if the fall-back state is reached, exacerbating the situation beyond the initial failure.

The other failure mode present in the OpenFlow specification is *fail-secure*. In this mode, the switch does not revert to legacy forwarding, and instead continues to utilise the flows (inserted by the controller previously) that are already present in the switch. These flows will continue until such a time as they expire or timeout. When this occurs (and if the controller has not created any flows with unlimited, non-expiring, timeouts), then the switch will drop all incoming packets. This will prevent any forwarding from occurring in the network. Evidently there needs to be some consideration given to the length of these timeouts, particularly so that basic forwarding can occur even if a controller is disconnected for an extended period of time.

Hybrid SDN. The use of OpenFlow in a *Hybrid SDN* (HSDN) mode provides an ideal compromise. It enables the coexistence of SDN functionality alongside legacy forwarding capability. In this configuration, packets will first traverse the SDN-enabled flow tables contained within a switch. Then, through either explicit action or default behaviour, a packet can be pushed into the standard networking stack. At this point, the packet can no longer be modified or forwarded by the SDN controller. HSDN therefore relies on the correct configuration of the underlying network, which can also be fully utilised in failover scenarios, ensuring that packets will always be forwarded as desired. This HSDN mode is available on a number of hardware-based OpenFlow switches and grants the flexibility and configurability inherent in SDN technology, whilst also enabling the accelerated forwarding and use of optimised forwarding protocols (such as RSTP, TRILL and OSPF).

Using existing protocols significantly reduces the complexity of building a fully compliant equivalent in an SDN controller. This has been a fundamental limitation of existing efforts, which has largely evaluated controller-based implementations of protocols such as STP [6,9]. This work does not take advantage of the hardware-accelerated forwarding present in these switches, nor does it consider the complexity found in the implementation of similar, but more performant, protocols.

Controller Replication and Roles. The positioning of controllers within a network and the impact this placement has on the overall network performance has been a key area of research [8], leading to the development of controllers that can be distributed and replicated. Within a substation environment, it would be possible to deploy multiple redundant controllers, offering resiliency. Controllers employ distributed state replication algorithms to ensure a consistent state is maintained. In a distributed controller environment, OpenFlow defines roles that each controller can take, however the mechanism for handover between controllers is not specified and left up to controller implementations. When multiple controllers are present, each switch is responsible for connecting to all controllers. In the default case, each controller is granted an *equal* role, in which every controller is capable of observing and modifying switch behaviour. Alternatively, controllers may be configured in a *master-slave* arrangement. This way, a controller defined as a *master* can view, modify the switching behaviour and send packets, whilst those in the *slave* role can only observe the state of the switch.

This role allocation process is entirely controller driven, with the controllers informing the switch as to their current role. Only a single controller can assume the *master* role at any one time; by indicating this role, the switch will automatically change the role of other connected switches to a *slave*. A controller can determine its role from the switch's perspective using a simple request message. Together, these roles offer a lightweight approach to assist in the election process, with controllers still requiring configuration and coordination between themselves to correctly allocate roles.

Flow Rule Persistence. SDN either uses *reactive* or *proactive* flow insertion. In the *reactive* case, flow rules are inserted only after a first packet from the specific flow is sent to the controller. Controllers will determine the destination for this packet, and insert a flow rule to ensure subsequent packets are handled in the same way. In the *proactive* case, rules are inserted into flow tables in advance, without needing the first packet to be forwarded to the controller.

The rule insertion method is tightly linked to the way in which rules are expired. Each flow rule has two timeouts: a *hard timeout* and an *idle timeout*. The *hard timeout* specifies the time after which a flow is always removed, regardless of its current state. An *idle timeout* is only triggered if no matching packets are received in the allotted time-frame. Setting of these timeouts depends on the application, and it is important to set these according to the requirements.

There are number of aspects to consider when building controller logic and setting values for these two timeouts. There is an associated latency when using reactive forwarding; the first packet must always be sent to the controller, and thus will incur additional link latency as well as any delay introduced by the controller's processing. This can be avoided through the use of proactive forwarding, where the controller must actively poll for state.

In scenarios where the controller is providing the main forwarding behaviour in the network, then the number of flow rules in a switch becomes an important factor. The number of flows that any one switch can contain is finite; the enforced expiry of flows ensures that only flows that are currently being used are present in the network. However, in a HSDN scenario, where the switch is still providing the underlying forwarding behaviour, then this limit presents less of an issue. This is because the controller does not have to provide the forwarding, and has the full flow table to realise any additional functionality.

These factors also have influence over the behaviour of the switch when the controller disconnects. If the switch is operating in a *fail-secure* mode, then it awaits a controller reconnection. In the meantime, any flows will expire as normal. This includes flows set with an infinite timeout, which will never expire. These can therefore be used to create persistent forwarding, and may be used to describe a *default* forwarding behaviour, such as pushing packets to the legacy forwarding stack (if available). In this way, it enables *fail-standalone*-like behaviour whilst maintaining controller-defined functionality for a period of time.

Connectivity. SDN technology typically relies on the connectivity between each switch and the controller(s). This can be provided in two main ways. *In-band* control traffic is included alongside the regular traffic that is traversing the network, and subject to the same latency and congestion. *Out-of-band* control traffic is separated from other traffic by either physical or virtual means, avoiding the associated impairments.

OpenFlow, as a specification, also defines *auxiliary* connections. These offer supplementary connectivity that can be used as an alternative transport mechanism for certain types of messages. The transport mechanism and type of messages sent over this channel are at the discretion of the controller. Importantly, they allow a form of load-balancing, which aims to reduce traffic on the *main* channel, increasing the likelihood of successful delivery in times of congestion.

4 A Substation Security Essential: An SDN-Based Access Control Service

Substation computer networks tend to have a relatively stable topology. Occasionally, new devices are connected, e.g., when an engineer introduces their computer for maintenance purposes or new devices (e.g., Intelligent Electronic Devices (IEDs)) are installed. For safety and security reasons, the connection of devices is tightly controlled; the introduction of unauthorised devices (for malicious reasons or otherwise) could have undesirable side-effects. One tool to support this control are network Access Control Lists (ACLs): a security mechanism for permitting and denying network access between specified devices.

An ACL can be configured to allow communication between specific devices using predefined protocols (such as GOOSE), and deny all other traffic. Consequently, an ACL reduces the potential network-borne attacks that can be implemented in a substation network. A key exception is when an attacker knows the address of a permitted device. With this knowledge, they can perform a *MAC spoofing attack*, changing their address to that of a known device. A typical ACL is unable to mitigate this form of attack, resulting in the attacker being able to send traffic with malicious application-level values or launch a Denial of Service (DoS) attack.

4.1   Realising an SDN-Based ACL Service

We have implemented a prototype SDN-based ACL service, using a whitelist of permitted communications between devices and protocols. All other communication is denied by default. In addition, to mitigate the effects of DoS attacks, it performs rate-limiting of traffic. ACLs are installed on all networking devices, e.g. switches and routers, which can make their configuration difficult and potentially error-prone. This task can be greatly simplified with the use of SDNs, which naturally hold a centralized view of the network. The ACL service is composed of two main components: a Ryu-based controller, that contains ACL modules, and a Web-based application, based on the Flask Web server. The Ryu controller interfaces with SDN devices using OpenFlow v1.3.

The controller component functions in the following way: when the controller services start, predefined topology information and initial ACL rules are loaded. All traffic that is not specified in these rules is blocked. In order to be able to monitor traffic and manage the ACL rules, traffic must be sent to the controller. To avoid a DoS attack on the controller, we have implemented a solution that sends only the first packet from a flow to the controller. At the same time, the controller inserts a deny rule on the switch, with a predefined *idle timeout* interval. All the subsequent packets from the same flow are thus discarded in hardware. If the flow remains in place for the duration of the *idle timeout*, the flow rule is removed, and the controller is notified. Meanwhile, using the Web-based application, an operator can decide whether to permit or deny further flows of this sort.

The Web-based application contains two parts: *(i)* a server that is used to communicate with operators via a web interface; and *(ii)* a client that sends translated ACL rule requests from operators to a module of the Ryu-based controller. The application provides the following features: topology status, flow tables, manual rules insertion (can be permitted in a uni- or bi-directional fashion), and statistics about allowed flows.

To mitigate a potential DoS attack, the following DoS protection is implemented: as soon as the number of packets of a permitted flow exceed a specified limit, the traffic is blocked and the operator is notified via the web application. The operator can then decide if further traffic should be allowed or not. The functionality of the DoS protection mechanism is shown in Fig. 2. It shows an increase in traffic, which is part of a DoS attack, that is throttled as soon as the traffic volume reaches a specified limit of 100 packets per second.

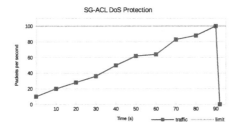

Fig. 2. Operation of the DoS protection function

5   Experimental Evaluation

In this section, we experimentally explore the implications of the deployment parameters that we have discussed in Sect. 3 using the prototype ACL service and a number of failure scenarios.

To conduct these experiments, we have created a substation network testbed. The topology reflects a typical substation environment, in which a ring topology with redundancy between switches is present. Such a topology is specified in the IEC 61850 standard [1]. IEDs are implemented as Linux VMs with the open-source IEC 61850 library [13] installed, which was used to generate and collect GOOSE control messages. Hewlett Packard (HPE) 3800 switches (running software version KA.15.17.0008) were installed and configured to operate with a Ryu controller (version 3.9). Flow rules, which implement the ACL behaviour, are configured to persist indefinitely.

5.1   Controller Loss

In this scenario, the controller was permanently disabled, simulating a controller failing or the connection to the controller being impaired – the root cause of this could be unintentional (a failure) or malicious.

Initially, we performed this experiment with the HPE switches in *fail-standalone* mode. No data from the ACL-permitted traffic was lost during the experiment; upon detecting the controller loss, the switch removed all the ACL-related flow rules and continued to forward frames. With the switches' default timeout settings, it takes approximately 28 s before the flow rules are removed and the transition to the *fail-standalone* mode is complete.

Clearly, this is desirable behaviour when considering network availability, which is necessary for ensuring safety requirements are met. This is the case if the cause of the controller loss is non-malicious. However, with knowledge of this behaviour, an attacker could use it to gain uninhibited network access in a substation. This can be done by intentionally denying access to the switches' controllers. In this way, in *fail-standalone* mode, all security services that are supported by the controller would be disabled. Denying switches access to controllers could be implemented using a relatively straightforward MITM attack.

To address this problem, and ensure availability and security, the *fail-secure* mode was employed in combination with the use of the HSDN approach. In this case, when the controller loss is detected, frames destined to the controller are dropped, while the current ACL rules persist in the flow table until their timeout (*idle* or *hard*) expires. In the application, the ACL rules have infinite *idle timeouts*, so they will remain active while all the other traffic will be discarded. This ensures the network remains secure until the root cause of the problem can be identified and mitigated.

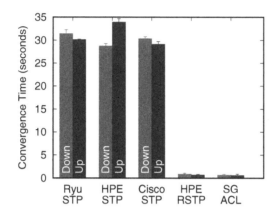

Fig. 3. A comparison of STP and RSTP implementations

5.2   Network Failures

As discussed above, a primary motivation for using a HSDN approach for substation networks is to be able to leverage the mature implementations of services that ensure network availability, such as STP and RSTP. In the following subsection, we illustrate the importance of this issue through experimentation. We examined the convergence times of different STP and RSTP configurations under two common conditions: link failure and link restoration. The configurations that we examined included the use of a standard Ryu controller (bundled with an implementation of the STP, which we used for the experiments) in conjunction with *(i)* the aforementioned HPE switch; *(ii)* the same HPE switch in HSDN mode; and *(iii)* a non-SDN Cisco 2960 switch (software version 15.0(2)SE4).

The results of our experiments are shown in Fig. 3. The convergence times were measured using ICMP messages sent between the two devices. This indicates the length of time it takes for a link to become available, after it is taken down or up. The results shown are average values over ten runs. It can be seen from these experiments that STP convergence times are similar, regardless of whether it is realised on the switch or in the controller. Based on the requirements that are presented in Sect. 2, it is clear that convergence times of approximately thirty seconds are inadequate. The HPE switch's implementation of RSTP converges in the order of seconds, making RSTP a better choice for network availability in substation networks. We conducted the same experiment with the SDN-based ACL operating (shown as SG ACL in Fig. 3). It can be seen that its presence does not impair the operation of RSTP on the switch, offering line-rate performance whilst benefiting from the protection of the ACL.

5.3 Summary of Recommendations

In Table 1 we summarized our recommendations for safe and secure SDN deployment in electrical substation networks based on the requirements and configuration options for the SDN features mentioned in Sect. 3.

Table 1. Recommended SDN configuration for substation networks

SDN Feature	Configuration
Fail Safe Mode	Fail-secure
Hybrid/Pure SDN	Hybrid SDN
Controller Replication	Recommended
Connectivity	Out-of-band
Flow Rule Insertion mode	Reactive
Allow Rule Idle Timeout	Infinity
Deny Rule Idle Timeout	30 s
Flow Rule Hard Timeout	Infinity

A Hybrid SDN is a viable and recommended configuration for the substation networks. It allows coexistence of well-established forwarding protocols which enable fast failover (e.g. RSTP), as well as integration of additional security functionalities such as ACLs. Since the substations are required to have highly reliable networks, other features should be configured such that they do not hinder availability of legitimate flows. For that reason out-of-band connectivity, controller replication, infinite idle timeouts and fail-secure modes are recommended. Moreover, due to a static nature of substation network topologies reactive flow insertion mode is recommended in order to reduce frequent interaction with network administrators once the network has been configured. Lastly, the idle timeout for deny rules is set to 30 s. This is a compromise between controller load and the ability to notify the application about denied traffic.

6 Conclusion

This paper discussed opportunities that SDN may bring to the electrical substation in the Smart Grid for improving their cyber-security without hindering stringent requirements necessary for their safe functioning. SDN technology offers various design options which have to be carefully considered in co-engineering of safety and security in the critical infrastructures. Our research shows that even simple security measures require deep investigation for proper integration in the substation environments. The discussed security aspects culminated in recommendations for safely integrating this technology into critical infrastructures. Furthermore, we showed how, when successful, SDN can provide essential security functionality without violating the strict performance requirements imposed in such environments. This was illustrated through an in-depth evaluation using realistic traffic generation, topologies and equipment.

References

1. IEC 61850–5: Communication networks and systems in substation, Geneva, Switzerland (2003). https://webstore.iec.ch/publication/6012
2. IEC TC57 WG15: IEC 62351 Security Standards for the Power system Information Infrastructure (2016). http://iectc57.ucaiug.org/wg15public/Public%20Documents/White%20Paper%20on%20Security%20Standards%20in%20IEC%20TC57.pdf
3. Al-Rubaye, S., Kadhum, E., Ni, Q., Anpalagan, A.: Industrial internet of things driven by SDN platform for smart grid resiliency. IEEE Internet Things J. **6**(1), 267–277 (2019). https://doi.org/10.1109/JIOT.2017.2734903
4. Cokic, M., Seskar, I.: Analysis of TCP traffic in smart grid using SDN based QoS. In: 2018 26th Telecommunications Forum (TELFOR), pp. 1–4, November 2018. https://doi.org/10.1109/TELFOR.2018.8611800
5. Dorsch, N., Kurtz, F., Georg, H., Hägerling, C., Wietfeld, C.: Software-defined networking for smart grid communications: applications, challenges and advantages. In: 2014 IEEE International Conference on Smart Grid Communications (SmartGridComm), pp. 422–427, November 2014. https://doi.org/10.1109/SmartGridComm.2014.7007683
6. Fang, S., Yu, Y., Foh, C.H., Aung, K.M.M.: A loss-free multipathing solution for data center network using software-defined networking approach. IEEE Trans. Magn. **49**(6), 2723–2730 (2013). https://doi.org/10.1109/TMAG.2013.2254703
7. Genge, B., Graur, F., Haller, P.: Experimental assessment of network design approaches for protecting industrial control systems. Int. J. Crit. Infrastruct. Prot. **11**(C), 24–38 (2015). https://doi.org/10.1016/j.ijcip.2015.07.005
8. Heller, B., Sherwood, R., McKeown, N.: The controller placement problem. In: Proceedings of the First Workshop on Hot Topics in Software Defined Networks, HotSDN 2012, pp. 7–12. ACM, New York (2012). https://doi.org/10.1145/2342441.2342444
9. Huang, Y.Y., Lee, M.W., Fan-Chiang, T.Y., Huang, X., Hsu, C.H.: Minimizing flow initialization latency in software defined networks. In: 2015 17th Asia-Pacific Network Operations and Management Symposium (APNOMS), pp. 303–308, August 2015. https://doi.org/10.1109/APNOMS.2015.7275444
10. Lee, R.M., Assante, M.J., Conway, T.: Analysis of the cyber attack on the Ukrainian power grid (2016). http://www.nerc.com/pa/CI/ESISAC/Documents/E-ISAC_SANS_Ukraine_DUC_18Mar2016.pdf

11. Rehmani, M.H., Akhtar, F., Davy, A., Jennings, B.: Achieving resilience in SDN-based smart grid: a multi-armed bandit approach. In: 2018 4th IEEE Conference on Network Softwarization and Workshops (NetSoft), pp. 366–371, June 2018. https://doi.org/10.1109/NETSOFT.2018.8459942
12. Sydney, A., Ochs, D.S., Scoglio, C., Gruenbacher, D., Miller, R.: Using GENI for experimental evaluation of software defined networking in smart grids. Comput. Netw. **63**, 5–16 (2014). https://doi.org/10.1016/j.bjp.2013.12.021
13. Zillgith, M.: libIEC61850 - open source library for IEC 61850 (2016). http://libiec61850.com/libiec61850/about/

Industrial Network Protection by SDN-Based IPS with AI

Filip Holik$^{(\boxtimes)}$ and Petr Dolezel

Faculty of Electrical Engineering and Informatics, University of Pardubice,
Studentska 95, 532 10 Pardubice, Czech Republic
`filip.holik@upce.cz`

Abstract. This paper analyses requirements of industrial networks in relation to usability of the software-defined networking concept. This modern approach to centralized software management of data networks can bring many advantages, especially in security area, into industrial networks. These networks, originally based on proprietary protocols, are nowadays being transformed into standard IP-based networks. This transition promises significant cost saving and operation simplification, but it makes industrial networks more vulnerable to modern security threats. These threats are now using automation and distributed resources to increase the number of successful security incidents.

The paper defines requirements for a software-defined network-based protection system to mitigate these threats. Based on these requirements, the system is designed and implemented. To cope with complex security threats, the system implements a functionality of artificial intelligence, which can autonomously perform various filtering operations. The system is evaluated with a positive result as the artificial intelligence achieves a success rate of over 99%.

Keywords: AI · Industrial networks · IPS · Neural networks · SDN

1 Introduction

Industrial networks are experiencing a revolution. These networks are nowadays being transformed from originally private and closed networks, often based on proprietary communication technologies, into standardized IP networks, which are connected to the Internet. Such a transformation can support the use of cloud centers, Internet of Things (IoT) devices, mobile devices and can also achieve better network management and supervision.

This transformation, on the other hand, significantly increases network traffic heterogeneity, complexity and therefore complicates security. This trend is evident from interconnection of IoT devices. Their large number - in 2018 it reached 7 billion and it is expected to grow to 10 billion in 2020 [12] - increases the possible attack surface. Moreover, IoT devices often have limited security capabilities and can be therefore easily attacked. If they become compromised,

© Springer Nature Singapore Pte Ltd. 2020
P. Sitek et al. (Eds.): ACIIDS 2020, CCIS 1178, pp. 192–203, 2020.
https://doi.org/10.1007/978-981-15-3380-8_17

they might stay undetected for a long time and meanwhile act as *zombies* or *swarms* causing massive damage.

Another significant security issue is increasing sophistication of attacking tools, which can use artificial intelligence (AI), automation, polymorphism and machine learning. These tools can often be used without any expert knowledge and can be very hard to detect as each attack can be different. In 2018 alone, a single security solution detected 24 000 malware variants [6]. According to [17], 93% of malware and 95% of potentially unwanted applications in 2017 were unique.

This presents a demanding challenge for security solutions. Manual approaches to security management are now obsolete and inefficient. According to [8], the average time of a malicious attack detection in 2018 was 221 days. The threat containment phase took additional 81 days. During that time, each day significantly increases the cost connected with the attack.

The response of security solutions to these increasing challenges is in automation. Unfortunately, only 15% of companies in 2018 had fully deployed security automation, while 34% of companies had it deployed partially. On the other hand, 38% of companies were seriously considering its implementation during 2019, while only 13% of companies do not consider security automation at all [8].

These results clearly show the importance of efficient, reliable and automated security solutions. One of the best approaches to achieve such a level of automation is utilization of AI. Luckily, the transition of industrial networks to traditional IP-based networks brings an opportunity to utilize many innovative software approaches such as software-defined networking (SDN), network function virtualization, and infrastructure-as-a-service platforms. These concepts promise more flexibility, better efficiency and dynamic configurability.

2   SDN Integration with Industrial Networks

The most promising approach to network softwarization is SDN - the concept of separation of forwarding and control planes, where the control plane is represented by a software application running on a centralized server. The continuous rise of SDN usage is expected, as it is finding its way into more specialized domains such as smart cities and industrial networks.

2.1   Industrial Network Requirements and SDN

Industrial networks are defined as networks containing specialized devices, which provide automation of industrial control processes [9]. While these networks vary significantly from business to business, they have several common specific requirements as described in [16]. These requirements can be met with SDN, if a suitable controller and OpenFlow protocol version are selected.

Component Lifetime - a typical equipment in industrial networks has a very long life expectancy of 15–20 years. During this period, the communication network compatibility has to be ensured. **SDN** can ensure this compatibility, as it supports various low-level and high-level APIs and it uses standardized header fields of the TCP/IP model. This compatibility also enables network functionality modifications via software updates.

Critical Infrastructure - industrial networks can operate critical services (energy, transportation, healthcare etc.). Reliability of such networks has to be ensured at all times by proper monitoring and management tools. **SDN** can deliver these features via the controller, which represents the centralized point for management of the entire network, and can provide a human-friendly topology visualization.

Fault Tolerance - industrial networks must be resilient to failures according to regulatory requirements. They also have to prevent loss of life and equipment damage. **SDN** with a centralized control can perform more effective traffic monitoring than traditional networks. This can detect network anomalies; and automatically react to prevent further damage and to ensure human safety.

High Availability - most of the industrial processes are continuous and the production in these cases (power plants, chemical plants etc.) cannot be stopped. This eliminates the use of techniques such as a device reboot or an unplanned network outage. An infrastructure update has to be carefully planned in advance so it will not affect the network operation. This requires use of redundant components, pre-deployment testing and intelligent control. **SDN** can achieve high availability by deployment in the distributed architecture mode with multiple controllers. In this mode, a controller can be updated and rebooted, as another controller can substitute its functionality. The dynamic module loading feature provides an option to install or remove features without the need of restarting the controller. SDN can also more efficiently utilize redundant links, when compared to traditional networks (for example with adaptive load-balancing techniques).

Limited Component Access - industrial components might be physically located in remote or hard to access locations. This means, that the devices cannot be easily reset or checked for damage or malicious tampering. These devices have to be therefore well protected and remotely monitored. **SDN** can efficiently monitor network behavior and automatically detect any non-standard communication patterns which could indicate a spoofed device. SDN can then control traffic flows coming from and to these devices.

Non-upgradability - industrial devices often contain OS or firmware, which cannot be updated for the entire lifetime of the component. This can make them vulnerable for various attacks if a vulnerability is discovered. **SDN** can help in securing these devices by monitoring and controlling their communication. Protection on this level is independent of the end device type and it ensures future-proof compatibility.

Performance - industrial networks often work with time-critical information and require real-time operation. The most strict performance requirement is therefore on low latency and jitter, while throughput and bandwidth requirements are not so strict as in classical data networks. **SDN**, if configured properly, can achieve the same performance as traditional networks. This includes use of fast hardware-based chips for storing flow rules, the proactive flow rule insertion method and use of multiple flow tables. Performance requirements can be defined by implementation of the QoS functionality, which is supported from OpenFlow version 1.3. More information about SDN latency performance can be found in [7].

Proprietary Communication Protocols - industrial networks can use non-typical protocols, which might be unknown for traditional protection systems. **SDN** can mirror such a traffic to specific ports, where specialized monitoring devices might be used for advanced offline monitoring.

System Certification - critical industrial networks require official certification of safe and secure operations. This might forbid the use of specific 3rd party components, or components with a proprietary source code. **SDN** can use open-source code, which can be checked and verified by certification organizations. The security can be strengthened by features such as AAA (authentication, authorization and accounting) and protocol encryption.

2.2 Related Work

Most of industrial networks rely on a traditional combination of several security solutions such as firewalls, service gateways (IDS and IPS) and end-nodes antivirus software. To cope with the advancing level of current threats, these security solutions have started to implement innovative functionalities based on cloud and AI technologies. The current research in this area also targets pattern recognition [11] and prevention of man-in-the-middle types of attacks [15].

The utilization of SDN in these security areas is still being researched. Traditional firewalls were implemented in SDN in many works [3,5,10,13], but AI-based firewalls, on the other hand, were researched only in one work. The paper [4] presented a firewall with machine learning for securing cloud data centers. This firewall supported L7 data inspection, but it performed filtering based only on allow or deny operations. Such a solution cannot be considered for a complex security IPS.

Work done in the SDN-based IPS area then does not utilize AI at all. Examples of such solutions are: *SDNIPS* [18], *real-time alerting system* [2] and *lightweight IPS* [14]. Our solution is therefore, to the best of our knowledge, the first approach which interconnects domains of SDN, IPS and AI.

3   Industrial Network Protection System

This section describes design and development of the IPS with AI for protection of industrial networks. This solution will be further called **INPS** (Industrial Network Protection System). The goal of the system is to provide complex security features of traditional security solutions within a single system.

3.1   Protection System Features

A protection system for industrial networks should comply with the requirements summarized in Sect. 2.1. In order to cope with the modern security threats and to replace the traditional security solutions mentioned in Sect. 2.2, the system should provide the following features:

1. Basic firewall features - the system should provide efficient real-time traffic monitoring and an option to allow or deny selected traffic flows. The configured firewall state should be exportable and importable for even more effective management. Other standard features include the configurable *implicit deny* function and an option to allow only IP addresses from a selected range.
2. Advanced traffic handling - in addition to the basic firewall functionality (allow and deny), the system should perform more advanced traffic features, such as:
   (a) Application layer inspection - the system should support the payload inspection of selected messages. This inspection can be done only by the controller. The software processing can, however, be very demanding on controller resources. The inspection can detect potential tampering with industrial devices (abnormal values, malicious code), analyze proprietary communication protocols and store messages for logging purposes.
   (b) Traffic mirroring - the system should provide a function to copy a selected data flow to an additional port. Such a port typically leads to a dedicated device, which can perform detailed offline inspection (of encrypted traffic or proprietary protocols) and logging.
   (c) QoS control - the system can optionally provide setting or modification of DSCP values of selected data flows in order to apply performance restrictions on the network (such as to ensure minimal latency).
3. Automated filtering - in addition to the manual firewall operation, the system should be able to optionally perform this filtering automatically. The best implementation of this feature is via integration with some type of AI. Based on the setting and the AI complexity, this filtering can cover only the basic firewall features or the advanced traffic handling as well.

3.2   INPS Design

The INPS was developed to comply to all requirements stated in Sect. 2.1. For this purpose, the ONOS SDN controller was selected as the foundation technology. This decision was based on the analysis of four controllers: RYU, Floodlight, OpenDaylight and ONOS. Only the ONOS controller supported all the described requirements. Other controllers lack these features:

- RYU - critical infrastructure, high availability and system certification.
- Floodlight - high availability.
- OpenDaylight - high availability (only the dynamic module loading).

3.3   INPS Architecture

The INPS architecture is composed from four main parts, which are shown in Fig. 1. These parts are:

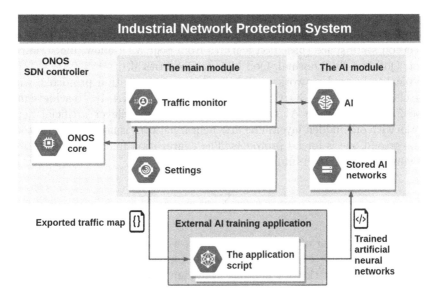

Fig. 1. INPS architecture

1. The main module - it contains the INPS application and related functionalities such as a web graphical user interface. The module is implemented within the ONOS controller and it uses ONOS's internal interfaces to communicate directly with the distributed core.
2. The AI module - is implemented in the AI class within the ONOS controller. The class uses a dedicated package, which contains supporting libraries and functions. The module also uses files of artificial neural networks, which contain learned network control behavior.

3. The ONOS SDN controller - it handles basic networking functions such as routing and forwarding and it also provides the default web graphical user interface.
4. External AI training application - it is implemented independently on the INPS application in the form of a *Matlab* script. The application performs a one-time offline training of artificial neural networks based on a provided network traffic map (traffic flows with corresponding firewall setting). Generated files can then be imported into the AI module, which can then perform autonomous network control.

3.4   Artificial Intelligence in the INPS

The INPS by default works in the manual operation mode. The AI functionality can be turned on in the settings page. This requires uploading of trained neural networks, which can be created in the external application (otherwise default ones - included in the system - are used). Upon the activation, the system starts to automatically perform filtering operations based on the learned behavior.

The AI functionality in the INPS is based on a decision element. This element evaluates incoming flow characteristics and assigns one of the following flags from the decision state space (based on features from Sect. 3.1): allow, block, mirror, inspect, QoS low, QoS normal, QoS high or QoS critical.

Typical industrial networks utilize various communication protocols, which can be classified by used ISO/OSI layer - typically L3 and L4 [1]. To achieve more precise functionality, the AI uses two feedforward multilayer artificial neural networks with one hidden layer. The first neural network is used for L3 protocols and the second one is for L4 protocols. The aggregation function of all neurons is the sum of all weighted inputs:

$$y_a = \sum_{i=0}^{R} w_i x_i \tag{1}$$

Where R is the number of inputs, w_i are input weights, $x_0 = 1$ is a threshold of each neuron and x_i for $i = 1, 2...R$ are neuron inputs.

The activation function for neurons in hidden layers is:

$$y = \tanh y_a \tag{2}$$

The function used for neurons in output layers is the *softmax* activation function. This function was selected based on the decision function. Both artificial neural networks were designed by the bottom-up approach and topology for the L4 traffic as shown in Fig. 2. The topology for L3 traffic was the same, but contained only 10 inputs and 3 outputs.

Both neural networks use these same inputs: source IP, destination IP and packets per second. Every octet in IP addresses is considered to be a unique input. The L3 network additionally uses *icmp type* and the L4 network uses source and destination ports instead of the *icmp type*.

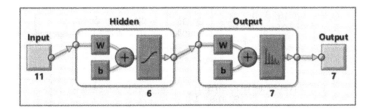

Fig. 2. Artificial neural network for L4 traffic (TCP, UDP)

3.5 Integration of the AI Functionality

The AI module becomes active if the system is configured in the autonomous mode. The main module then starts to automatically notify the AI module in the following two conditions:

1. A change in traffic flows - if a new traffic is detected or a flow expired.
2. Periodically - every time statistics are collected from networking devices. The interval is fully configurable and it is set to 5 s by default.

This notification is implemented in the AI function *evaluate Traffic* call, which takes the up-to-date traffic flow map as a parameter. This map represents an image of the entire traffic of the network. It is created from active OpenFlow rules located on all connected networking devices and from OpenFlow *packet-in* events processed by the controller.

The AI module sequentially compares (in a separate thread, so the system latency is not negatively influenced) all traffic flows and decides, if the current output action is still valid, or if it has to be changed. Any changes are then returned to the main module, which applies them to designated networking devices in the form of new OpenFlow rules. The traffic flow map is also accordingly updated.

4 Protection System Evaluation

The INPS was evaluated in several emulated networks and in one physical topology. Emulated networks were created in the *Mininet* tool and their scale simulated a typical size of industrial networks (tens of networking devices and end nodes).

The second scenario tested the INPS on a real physical network of a smaller scale. This topology is shown in Fig. 3. The topology corresponded to a typical Smart Grid network of an electrical substation as defined in [1]. The INPS and the ONOS controller were deployed on the physical server, which was connected to two SDN-enabled switches (through a traditional L2 switch). This out-of-band connection is displayed with red links. Remote access to the server was represented by the wireless AP. Two end hosts were connected to each SDN-enabled switch to simulate industrial nodes.

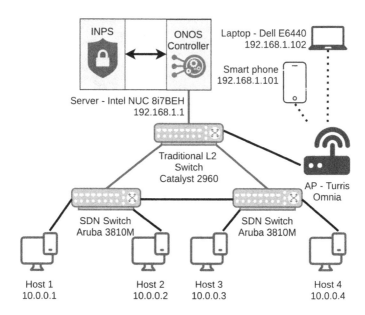

Fig. 3. Physical topology for system evaluation

4.1   Training of Neural Networks

The INPS was tested on data traffic, which simulated typical Smart Grid substation flow patterns and communication protocols [1]. Several firewall rules were defined to test all features of the INPS. These rules are shown in Table 1.

Table 1. Data traffic rules for the INPS evaluation

Scenario	Type of traffic	Action
Normal ICMP traffic	Allowed IP range	Allow
Normal L4 traffic	Random source/destination L4 port	Allow
ICMP DoS attack	ICMP, more than 100 PPS	Block
TCP DoS attack	TCP, more than 100 PPS	Block
UDP DoS attack	UDP, more than 100 PPS	Block
HTTP traffic	HTTP, destination TCP port 80	Inspect
HTTPS traffic	HTTPS, destination TCP port 443	Mirror
QoS, maximum priority	Destination TCP port 5060	QoS critical
QoS, minimum priority	Source/destination port of 20/21/69/115	QoS low
QoS, high priority	Destination TCP port 37	QoS high
ICMP type 3 - unreachable	ICMP type 3	Mirror

Under typical conditions, the rules used in the system would have to be manually configured. A created traffic map could then be exported and used for training of neural networks. A reliable training can be achieved only with high versatility, heterogeneity and a large amount of these traffic flows. Such a configuration, when done manually, might be too time-consuming and difficult.

To ensure maximum training reliability, we created a custom-made traffic pattern generator, which allowed us to simulate a highly utilized industrial network. The generated traffic map contained 110 000 unique data patterns according to the scenarios defined in Table 1. Each scenario therefore contained 10 000 unique data patterns. Trained artificial neural networks were then provided to the AI module and were also included in the INPS as the default AI files.

4.2   Evaluation Results

The INPS was tested in two modes: manual and autonomous. The defined topology (Fig. 3) was used for the final evaluation. All traffic patterns defined in Table 1 were consequently tested by manual generation of traffic flows. These traffic flows were generated using the *ping* tool (normal traffic, ICMP DoS attack, ICMP type 3), *iperf* (normal L4 traffic, TCP and UDP DoS attacks) and *curl* (HTTP, HTTPS traffic and QoS scenarios).

Manual Mode. Firstly, the AI functionality was turned-off and the system was used for traffic monitoring and manual control. The features of the system as defined in Sect. 3.1 (except automated filtering) were tested on generated traffic. Each feature of the system provided the expected functionality (ex. block the traffic, mirror the traffic, or set a QoS value).

The GUI was also tested from mobile devices (a smartphone and a laptop), which were connected to the tested topology within the management IP address range and used the out-of-band connection. All the features were tested again to verify, if the system can be fully controlled from these devices. All input controls and features were working in the same way, as in the normal test.

Autonomous Mode. In this scenario, the AI functionality was turned-on. The goal was to observe, if the AI performs the same filtering operations as if a person would be controlling the network manually. The default neural network files were used. The network was consequently loaded with generated traffic flows and the AI responses were recorded. The experiment was repeated 10 times. From the total number of 110 tests (10 repetitions of 11 scenarios), the AI failed only in one scenario and therefore achieved the success rate of 99.1%.

The failure scenario was testing the QoS setting and in this case, the AI set an incorrect QoS value (high priority instead of low priority). This error should not pose a critical problem in industrial networks, as it could only potentially affect the network performance - and only if the network would be highly utilized. Such a mistake is significantly less dangerous than, for example, a substitution of allow and deny operations, which could make the network inoperable.

5   Conclusion

The paper evaluated feasibility of an SDN-based protection system deployment in industrial networks. Firstly, requirements of industrial networks were analyzed. Based on the analysis, the system was designed and implemented. To cope with modern security threats, the system implemented autonomous traffic filtering operations based on AI with neural networks. The performed testing confirmed, that the system can achieve the complete level of automation with a very reliable rate of traffic filtering. The system can therefore improve industrial network security especially against modern vulnerabilities. The system can also significantly reduce network management load as trained neural networks can be used in network topologies, which have the same security policies and similar traffic patterns. In these cases, no network configuration is needed and the system is able to handle traffic filtering automatically by the AI.

On the other hand, it is important to consider, that even in cases when the AI is trained thoroughly, it can sometimes bring unexpected results. The AI's biggest advantage is in its flexibility to adapt to similar networking conditions without the need of any network reconfiguration. If the network requires strictly defined security policies with 100% repeatability in all cases, more traditional approaches such as ACLs might have to be used.

References

1. IEC 61850-5: Communication networks and systems in substation, Geneva, Switzerland (2003). https://webstore.iec.ch/publication/6012
2. Alsmadi, I.M., AlEroud, A.: SDN-based real-time IDS/IPS alerting system. In: Alsmadi, I.M., Karabatis, G., AlEroud, A. (eds.) Information Fusion for Cyber-Security Analytics. SCI, vol. 691, pp. 297–306. Springer, Cham (2017). https://doi.org/10.1007/978-3-319-44257-0_12
3. Bakhareva, N., Polezhaev, P., Ushakov, Y., Shukhman, A.: SDN-based firewall implementation for large corporate networks (2019). https://doi.org/10.1109/ICAICT.2017.8687088
4. Cheng, Q., Wu, C., Zhou, H., Zhang, Y., Wang, R., Ruan, W.: Guarding the perimeter of cloud-based enterprise networks: an intelligent SDN firewall. In: 2018 IEEE 20th International Conference on High Performance Computing and Communications; IEEE 16th International Conference on Smart City; IEEE 4th International Conference on Data Science and Systems (HPCC/SmartCity/DSS), pp. 897–902, June 2018. https://doi.org/10.1109/HPCC/SmartCity/DSS.2018.00149
5. Fiessler, A., Lorenz, C., Hager, S., Scheuermann, B.: Fireflow - high performance hybrid SDN-firewalls with OpenFlow, October 2018, pp. 267–270 (2019). https://doi.org/10.1109/LCN.2018.8638090
6. Fortinet: Threat landscape report Q2 2018 (2018). https://www.fortinet.com/demand/gated/q2-2018-threat-landscape-report.htmll
7. Holik, F.: Meeting smart city latency demands with SDN. In: Huk, M., Maleszka, M., Szczerbicki, E. (eds.) ACIIDS 2019. SCI, vol. 830, pp. 43–54. Springer, Cham (2020). https://doi.org/10.1007/978-3-030-14132-5_4
8. IBM Security and Ponemon Institute: 2018 cost of a data breach study. Technical report (2018)

9. Knapp, E.D., Langill, J.T.: Chapter 2 - About industrial networks. In: Knapp, E.D., Langill, J.T. (eds.) Industrial Network Security, pp. 9–40, 2nd edn. Syngress, Boston (2015). https://doi.org/10.1016/B978-0-12-420114-9.00002-2

10. Li, H., Wei, F., Hu, H.: Enabling dynamic network access control with anomaly-based IDS and SDN, pp. 13–16 (2019). https://doi.org/10.1145/3309194.3309199

11. Lin, K.-S.: A pattern recognition based FMEA for safety-critical SCADA systems. In: Nguyen, N.T., Gaol, F.L., Hong, T.-P., Trawiński, B. (eds.) ACIIDS 2019. LNCS (LNAI), vol. 11432, pp. 26–39. Springer, Cham (2019). https://doi.org/10.1007/978-3-030-14802-7_3

12. Lueth, K.L.: State of the IoT 2018: number of IoT devices now at 7B - market accelerating. https://iot-analytics.com/state-of-the-iot-update-q1-q2-2018-number-of-iot-devices-now-7b/

13. Mahamat Charfadine, S., Flauzac, O., Nolot, F., Rabat, C., Gonzalez, C.: Secure exchanges activity in function of event detection with the SDN. In: Mendy, G., Ouya, S., Dioum, I., Thiaré, O. (eds.) AFRICOMM 2018. LNICST, vol. 275, pp. 315–324. Springer, Cham (2019). https://doi.org/10.1007/978-3-030-16042-5_28

14. Neu, C.V., Tatsch, C.G., Lunardi, R.C., Michelin, R.A., Orozco, A.M.S., Zorzo, A.F.: Lightweight IPS for port scan in OpenFlow SDN networks. In: NOMS 2018–2018 IEEE/IFIP Network Operations and Management Symposium, pp. 1–6, April 2018). https://doi.org/10.1109/NOMS.2018.8406313

15. Nguyen, D.T., Le, M.T.: A new method for establishing and managing group key against network attacks. In: Nguyen, N.T., Hoang, D.H., Hong, T.-P., Pham, H., Trawiński, B. (eds.) ACIIDS 2018. LNCS (LNAI), vol. 10752, pp. 287–296. Springer, Cham (2018). https://doi.org/10.1007/978-3-319-75420-8_27

16. Stouffer, K.A., Falco, J.A., Scarfone, K.A.: Sp 800–82. guide to industrial control systems (ICS) security: Supervisory control and data acquisition (SCADA) systems, distributed control systems (DCS), and other control system configurations such as programmable logic controllers (PLC). Technical report, Gaithersburg, MD, United States (2011)

17. Webroot: Threat report. Technical report (2018). https://www-cdn.webroot.com/9315/2354/6488/2018-Webroot-Threat-Report_US-ONLINE.pdf

18. Xing, T., Xiong, Z., Huang, D., Medhi, D.: SDNIPS: Enabling software-defined networking based intrusion prevention system in clouds. In: 10th International Conference on Network and Service Management (CNSM) and Workshop, pp. 308–311, November 2014

Vertical Integration via Dynamic Aggregation of Information in OPC UA

Sebastian Schmied[1](✉)⬤, Daniel Großmann[1], Selvine G. Mathias[1], and Suprateek Banerjee[2]

[1] Zentrum für Angewandte Forschung, Technische Hochschule Ingolstadt, 85049 Ingolstadt, Germany
{Sebastian.Schmied,Daniel.Grossmann,SelvineGeorge.Mathias}@thi.de
[2] VDMA Robotik + Automation, Verband Deutscher Maschinen- und Anlagenbau, 60528 Frankfurt am Main, Germany
Suprateek.Banerjee@vdma.org

Abstract. Vertical and horizontal integration of manufacturing systems is an important part of the Industry 4.0 concept.

The provision of actual implementation strategies for manufacturing systems not following the hierarchy levels of the automation pyramid is still a challenge that needs to be solved. In a traditional production environment data exchange happens through strictly defined interfaces that are not easily changeable or extendable. Within the shop-floor, OPC UA is a communication technology already used for the widespread exchange of information. OPC UA offers a technology that allows data exchange using unified interfaces. Information can be organized and provided in a more effective way. This provision requires an information model as semantic description of the data, and a strategy to integrate data from different sources.

This paper presents an approach for information model creation and demonstrates an implementation approach in order to create a single OPC UA address space from multiple physical and digital devices. This is done via creation of OPC UA servers for all production entities and dynamically linking them via intelligent aggregation.

Keywords: OPC UA · Interoperability · Aggregation

1 Introduction

To enable a manufacturing process constantly changing information has to be exchanged between the different process steps. This includes for example information about orders or more specific manufacturing information like programs to control milling machines (nc-programs). Every type of information is saved in its specialized system like Enterprise Resource Planning (ERP)-systems, Manufacturing Execution Systems (MES), specialised databases or on manufacturing machines. Along the process chain, during the manufacturing process,

P. Sitek et al. (Eds.): ACIIDS 2020, CCIS 1178, pp. 204–215, 2020.
https://doi.org/10.1007/978-981-15-3380-8_18

the information exchange happens through strictly defined interfaces between these systems. These interfaces can only be read by permanently defined senders and receivers. In some cases, the transfer of information generates a media break if for example the transfer happens through paper. An example for a strictly defined interface is the exchange of tool offset data between measuring machine and CNC-machine. Usually there is a direct exchange of information between the two machines, that does not allow further examination. If such information would be available it could be used to better predict tool live and avoid tool breakdown during use.

Therefore, interoperability is only partially given. Information models that offer semantic descriptions of the manufacturing systems are not defined. This limits the possibilities for integration of new software components, or the exchange of already used systems. The creation of evaluations using data from different sources requires additional effort.

OPC UA is a communication technology offering a unified interface for information exchange. It integrates information models to semantically describe the exchanged data [11]. But as the data has various sources, it is a challenge to integrate this data into one common address space. On the one hand, because prior integration a common information model has to be designed and on the other hand because an implementation strategy needs to be developed to actually create the common address space.

This paper describes how information can be uniformly integrated into OPC UA. This enables interoperability between all project steps, avoids media discontinuities and thus increases the overall efficiency of the manufacturing system. In addition, software systems used in the process can be easily exchanged because uniform interfaces are defined.

For this purpose, a concept is presented where data from various sources is first made available in OPC UA and then summarized in a structured manner using an aggregation server. The aggregation takes place dynamically to cope with ever-changing data.

The presented approach displays information as nodes in a OPC UA address space. These nodes are dynamically connected via references. Depending on the actual status of the manufacturing system these references can automatically change according to a given set of conditions. This enables browsing of the complete information structure and makes it easier for clients to read relevant information. Example use cases are the linking of the ERP-data like purchasing cost and MES-data like the manufacturing time. This enables the accounting department to determine relevant costs directly. Another use case is the linkage of tool offset data or nc-programs to the order, this enables manufacturing machines to read all relevant information from one source.

2   State of the Art

At first a brief outlook about OPC UA, vertical integration and aggregation is provided.

2.1   OPC UA

OPC UA, is a platform-independent middleware and information modelling technology. It provides a service-oriented publish-subscribe and client-server architecture communication between different devices and systems independent from the used operating systems and platforms [5]. Integral parts of OPC UA are mechanisms for a robust and reliable communication structure. The detection and handling of lost messages and the support of redundant systems are examples of this structure. OPC UA can sign and encrypt messages and facilitates security with for example user administration [4,11].

It uses an object-oriented architecture to provide inheritance and type hierarchies and enables information modelling [5]. The OPC UA address space is a network of object-oriented entities called nodes. Nodes are identified by a namespace index and a node name, the combination of these two elements is called nodeid. With hierarchical and non-hierarchical references semantic relationships between the nodes are described and an information model is created [2]. The OPC UA specification describes different node classes, such as objects, variables and methods. Predefined references and node types can be extended by subtypes, reference types or methods [9]. Instances of node types contain information about the data type they contain and additionally may entail information about the unit of measurement [13]. Information models are maintained by servers and can be read by clients without the necessity of the client knowing the model [2].

2.2   Vertical Integration

Due to increasing demands for individualization and therefore the requirement for more flexible manufacturing systems, vertical integration of information within the production system is necessary. The different layers as for example ERP-, management- and shop-floor layer have to be able to communicate directly and on the basis of a common communication standard [7]. Vertical Integration allows direct access to management, planning and field information. It triggers the end of the automation pyramid [14].

On the shop-floor layer new devices with an increased range of function and expanded ability for information exchange are used. To fully use the benefit of such devices models and concepts for information exchange are necessary [3].

A constraint during interaction of these layers is the different information they contain. The higher layers, like management and ERP level contain long time data from actual, past and future manufacturing operations. Long time planning and historical data is saved in these layers. Whereas the shop-floor layer supplies real-time information of the actual status of the machines or short time planning and short-time historic information. Besides the different information structure the software architecture of these layers is divers. The prior named challenges lead to a need for a well-defined possibility to exchange information between these layers [5,8].

2.3 Aggregation

Devices within the production environment are becoming more and more digitalized. That leads to a scenario, where every component of the production system is having its own communication interface. To access data of these devices, it is either possible to have various clients, that connect to multiple devices or having a central software that aggregates the information and supplies it to various clients.

Using a direct connection between clients and the devices leads to a situation, where the servers have connections to multiple clients. Every client needs to know the addresses of every device it needs to connect to. This leads to a complex mesh of server and client connections [6].

Alternatively a central aggregation software can be used. It connects to all available servers within the manufacturing environment and displays them to the clients. This has the benefit, that a client just needs to know the address of the aggregation server. Information about adding or changing a system component just needs to be implemented on the aggregation software. The aggregation server can manage security policies and connections to the aggregated devices [6,16,17].

3 Dynamic Aggregation of Manufacturing Information

Instead of querying data from ERP, MES or other IT systems, this approach aims at representing all relevant information within a OPC UA address space. This includes not only information about order quantities or time constraints, but also manufacturing information like nc-programms or tool offset data.

The information is usually stored and provided in different sources. The concept makes every source available as a OPC UA server and makes every information object available as an instance in the OPC UA address space.

Based on the overall information model, references are added to the nodes to establish links between the different objects of the information model. For instance, a nc-program is linked with an "is programmed for" reference to a manufacturing order. This way, a mesh of information is created which is browsable by every OPC UA client.

The following chapter presents a prototypic implementation of such a system. It also describes the necessary preparation steps.

4 Prototypic Implementation

This chapter describes seven relevant steps necessary for the implementation of the demonstrator. The manufacturing of a milling part was chosen as a sample use case.

4.1   Identification of Information Objects

The first step is the identification of information objects. To limit the scope, a relevant business process needs to be defined. A business process produces a valuable output based on a defined input by executing a certain number of process steps. An exchange of objects in form of digital information and physical assets occurs between the process steps [12]. Under these boundary conditions a clear definition of inputs, outputs and the relevant business process is needed. For every process step the exchanged physical assets and informations need to be denominated [15]. A possible technique to document this is the Supplier, Input, Process, Output and Customer Analysis (SIPOC). The whole business process as well as the identified subprocesses are examined and a SIPOC sheet is created for every process step.

Department: Work Planning

Supplier	Input				Process	Output				Customer
	Object	Attribute	Type	Unit		Object	Attribute	Type	Unit	
Work preparation	Order (Email)	earliest start Date	Date		Machine Planning	Suborder	Machine Name	String		Machine Park
		latest end Date	Date				NC Program	File		
		Product Name	String				Suborder ID	String		
...	...	...	...	...	...	...	...	...	...	....

Fig. 1. Sipoc analysis

Figure 1 shows an example of a SIPOC-Sheet. On the right side, the attributes that are needed for the creation of the suborder can be seen. Additionally to the name of the attribute, the datatype and the unit of the attribute is documented.

Based on the SIPOC analysis information objects can be determined. Every digital collection of attributes can be considered as an information object, for example a suborder, or a nc-programm.

The information objects of the demonstration scenario and their corresponding attributes can be seen in Fig. 2.

4.2   Identification of References and Linking Attributes

After defining the information objects, it is necessary to know how the information objects are linked to each other, and based on which attributes these links can be established. Generally it can be distinguished between hierarchical and non-hierarchical references. Hierachical references describe top-down relationships like order and suborder, whereas for non-hierachical references the level is irrelevant. References additionally can be described by a string in order to increase semantic readability. For example the "organizes" reference can be a subtype of a hierarchical reference.

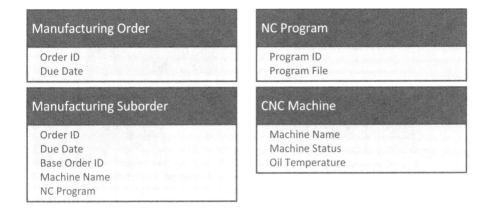

Fig. 2. Identified information objects

It is assumed that every information object has at least one reference to another object. The reference is established based on one or more attribute values of the object. An orientation, on how to design the references, can be the organization of information in the ERP or MES system. References should be discussed with experienced workers, to ensure their correctness.

If the references are denominated, attributes have to be found that enable a computer system to know which objects have to be linked with a certain reference. Such attributes are identifiers that are the same in both information objects. This is similar to a key in a relational database. In this paper these attributes will be called linking attributes.

In our example the "Order ID" of the order object and the "Base Order Id" of the suborder object are linked with an hierarchical "organize" reference. A nc-programm is especially written for a specific order. Based on the linking attribute "Program ID" in both the nc-programm node and in the suborder a non-hierachical "uses" reference is established.

The references of the use case can be seen in Fig. 3. To simplify the illustration, only the linking attributes and their corresponding references are shown.

4.3   Creation of the Information Model

The prior identified information objects and their attributes are linked according to the identified references and plotted following to the OPC UA information model notation. Every single information object is represented as a type in the information model [10].

The information model of the presented use case can be seen in Fig. 4. The linking attributes must not be shown in the information model, as the implicit knowledge of how the nodes are connected to each other was translated into explicit machine-readable information.

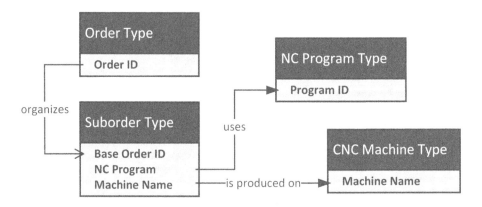

Fig. 3. References and linking attributes

To create a machine-readable information model, a .xml file containing all information model related information must be created. This is done by following the OPC UA standard [10].

4.4 Provision of Information in OPC UA

It is determined where the information objects are stored so far. The aim is to create an OPC UA server for every physical or digital entity containing data about the identified information objects. From a technical point of view this requires the creation of adaptors for the different field devices and databases if these adaptors are not available from the machine vendors. The use case was performed in a legacy environment where no OPC UA interfaces were available for the used machines and systems. To create the address space three different OPC UA adaptors had to be created. One for the milling machine, one for the order database and one for the database containing nc-programs.

As the utilized CNC-Machine is using a Haidenhain controller, the OPC UA server was created using the RemoToolsSDK from Haidenhain. It offers a communication interface to the machine in the .net programming language. A OPC UA server using the Unified Automation .net SDK was integrated into the Haidenhain software. All the information defined in the information model can be read from the machine.

For access to the database, the OPC UA java SDK from Prosys was used. An SQL connector was developed to create a OPC UA node for every dataset of the database.

In order to make the nc-files available in the address space, the .net SDK from unified Automation was used. All nc-files are present in a specific file location on the same computer that is running the OPC UA Server. Every nc-file is made available as a single node in the OPC UA address space.

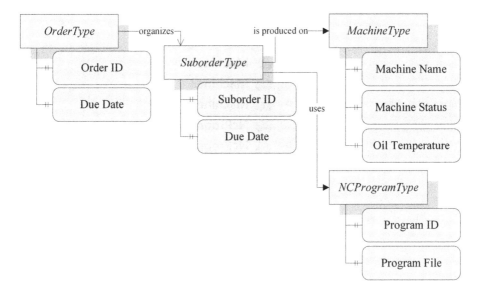

Fig. 4. Information model

4.5   Aggregation of the OPC UA Servers

Based on previous work of Banerjee [1] an aggregation server was created. This server adds OPC UA servers defined in a configuration file and creates a common address space. The base aggregation is flat and adds every OPC UA server on the same level. Figure 5 shows how the OPC UA address space looks after aggregation.

4.6   Adding Additional References to the Aggregation Server

Additionally, to the flat aggregation, an agent was created that adds the prior defined references to the different nodes within the OPC UA servers. It dynamically adds references to the instances of the information objects based on their type and linking attribute values. An overview about the dynamically aggregated address space can be seen in Fig. 6.

To enable the structuring of the address space, during the aggregation lists of the nodeids, their types and their corresponding linking attributes are created. In a second step the lists are compared to each other and the references are added.

A challenge is to detect changes is the address space. This is necessary if a new information is added, removed or assigned to a different entity of the system. For example a manufacturing order is shifted from one machine to another. If the address space changes, it becomes necessary to trigger a re-browse within the aggregation server and the linking agent to ensure that the correct address space is shared with the client.

Fig. 5. Flat aggregation

In the demonstrator this was solved by rebrowsing in fixed intervals, e.g. during shift breaks and at night. In the future, the OPC UA model change event can be used to trigger a re-browse.

4.7 Validation

Since the legacy systems are preserved, it is now possible to check whether the OPC UA structure correctly represents all data as expected. The structure, that was created in the first step is used.

Comparing the database, the nc-files and the machine information manually, showed that all information was correctly added and shown in the OPC UA address space. It has to be noticed, that the shown use case is only a small example and for big complex automation system the expenditure for validation is higher. For further development of this approach it is necessary to develop standard procedures for validation.

What was noticed during the testing phase is, that the aggregation and re-browse of a large address space requires a considerable amount of time. The aggregation server is not reachable during this period. Depending on the use case this can lead to restrictions on system availability. A re-browse is needed if e.g. the model changes because a new order was added. It must be clarified whether the aggregation system that created the OPC UA adress space will be able to react quickly to changes in the data. Above all, it is interesting, whether the model is changed sufficiently quick if data is added or changed.

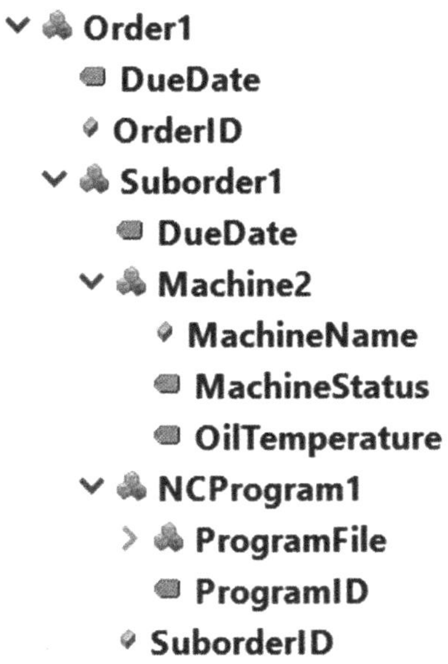

∨ ⚙ **Order1**
 　　⬗ **DueDate**
 　　◈ **OrderID**
 ∨ ⚙ **Suborder1**
 　　⬗ **DueDate**
 　∨ ⚙ **Machine2**
 　　　◈ **MachineName**
 　　　⬗ **MachineStatus**
 　　　⬗ **OilTemperature**
 　∨ ⚙ **NCProgram1**
 　　＞ ⚙ **ProgramFile**
 　　　⬗ **ProgramID**
 　　◈ **SuborderID**

Fig. 6. Intelligent dynamic aggregation

5 Conclusion

An approach for dynamic aggregation of manufacturing information was shown in this paper. It leads to a common information model and an OPC UA address space containing all relevant manufacturing attributes and their references. This way it is possible for clients to self discover the address space by connecting to the aggregation OPC UA server.

By fully implementing manufacturing information via dynamic aggregation in OPC UA, all interfaces to different components of the manufacturing system are defined as part of an information model. Systems can be viewed independently of each other. As data and information is transmitted with a standard communication protocol, programs can be seen independent of their communication abilities. This leads to further opportunities as the access to data is easier, and all parts of the system communicate with the same communication protocol. Therefore, previously not possible applications can be introduced into the manufacturing system. With a fully defined information model it is also easier to exchange legacy systems. New system components only need to fullfill the OPC UA requirements and display their information according to the defined information model.

Acknowledgement and Outlook. The presented paper was elaborated within the research project InMoFlex. This project is founded by the Federal Ministry of Education and Research of Germany. The present approach was developed within the competence field "Production and Automation Engineering" of the Technical University Ingolstadt.

In a manufacturing environment the permanent availability of information is very important. Therefore, it is relevant to integrate functions that ensure high availability, as for example redundancy, to the aggregating server. Additionally, functions for security like a central certificate store have to be implemented.

References

1. Banerjee, S., Großmann, D.: Aggregation of information models—an OPC UA based approach to a holistic model of models. In: 2017 4th International Conference on Industrial Engineering and Applications - ICIEA 2017, pp. 296–299. IEEE, Piscataway (2017). https://doi.org/10.1109/IEA.2017.7939225
2. Derhamy, H., Ronnholm, J., Delsing, J., Eliasson, J., van Deventer, J.: Protocol interoperability of OPC UA in service oriented architectures. In: 2017 IEEE 15th International Conference on Industrial Informatics (INDIN), pp. 44–50. IEEE, Piscataway (2017). https://doi.org/10.1109/INDIN.2017.8104744
3. Diedrich, C., Lüder, A., Hundt, L.: Bedeutung der interoperabilität bei entwurf und nutzung von automatisierten produktionssystemen. at - Automatisierungstechnik **59**(7), 426–438 (2011). https://doi.org/10.1524/auto.2011.0937
4. Enste, U., Mahnke, W.: OPC unified architecture. Automatisierungstechnik **59**(7), 397–404 (2011). https://doi.org/10.1524/auto.2011.0934
5. Faller, C., Höftmann, M.: Service-oriented communication model for cyber-physical-production-systems. Procedia CIRP **67**, 156–161 (2018). https://doi.org/10.1016/j.procir.2017.12.192
6. Großmann, D., Bregulla, M., Banerjee, S., Schulz, D., Braun, R.: OPC UA server aggregation—the foundation for an internet of portals. In: IEEE International Conference on Emerging Technologies and Factory Automation (ETFA), pp. 1–6. IEEE, Piscataway (2014). https://doi.org/10.1109/ETFA.2014.7005354
7. Hoffmann, M., Meisen, T., Schilberg, D., Jeschke, S.: Multi-dimensional production planning using a vertical data integration approach: a contribution to modular factory design. In: 10th International Conference and Expo on Emerging Technologies for a Smarter World (CEWIT), pp. 1–6. IEEE, Piscataway (2013). https://doi.org/10.1109/CEWIT.2013.6713754
8. International Electrotechnical Commission: IEC 62264–1, enterprise-control system integration - Part 1: models and terminology (2013)
9. International Electrotechnical Commission: IEC 62541–3 OPC unified architecture - Part 3: Address Space Model. International standard Norme internationale, vol. IEC 62541–3. International Electrotechnical Commission, Geneva, 2.0 edn. (2015)
10. International Electrotechnical Commission: IEC 62541–5 OPC unified architecture - Part 5: Information Model. International Standard International Electrotechnical Commission, Geneva, 2.0 edn. (2015)
11. International Electrotechnical Commission: IEC TR 62541–1 OPC UA Part 1: Overview and Concepts. International standard, International Electrotechnical Commission, Geneva, 2.0 edn. (2016)
12. Irani, Z., Hlupic, V., Baldwin, L.P., Love, P.E.: Re-engineering manufacturing processes through simulation modelling. Logist. Inf. Manag. **13**(1), 7–13 (2000). https://doi.org/10.1108/09576050010306341
13. Mahnke, W., Leitner, S.H., Damm, M.: OPC Unified Architecture, 1st edn. Springer, Berlin (2009). https://doi.org/10.1007/978-3-540-68899-0

14. Schlick, J., Stephan, P., Loskyll, M., Lappe, D.: Industrie 4.0 in der praktischen anwendung. In: Vogel-Heuser, B., Bauernhansl, T., ten Hompel, M. (eds.) Handbuch Industrie 4.0, vol. 3, pp. 1–27. Springer, Heidelberg (2016). https://doi.org/10.1007/978-3-662-45537-1_46-1
15. Schmied, S., Grosmann, D., Denk, B.: A systematic top-down information modelling approach for workshop-type manufacturing systems. In: IEEE Conference on Emerging Technologies & Factory Automation (ed.) Proceedings, 2019 24th IEEE International Conference on Emerging Technologies and Factory Automation (ETFA), pp. 1305–1308. IEEE, Piscataway (2019). https://doi.org/10.1109/ETFA.2019.8869377
16. Seilonen, I., Tuovinen, T., Elovaara, J., Tuomi, I., Oksanen, T.: Aggregating OPC UA servers for monitoring manufacturing systems and mobile work machines. In: 2016 IEEE 21st International Conference on Emerging Technologies and Factory Automation (ETFA), pp. 1–4. IEEE, Piscataway (2016). https://doi.org/10.1109/ETFA.2016.7733739
17. Wang, H., Ma, Y., Yu, F.: An OPC UA multi-server aggregator with cache management. In: CAC (ed.) Proceedings, 2018 Chinese Automation Congress (CAC). pp. 68–73. IEEE, Piscataway (2018). https://doi.org/10.1109/CAC.2018.8623689

Assessing Industry 4.0 Features Using SWOT Analysis

Ahmad Reshad Bakhtari[1], Mohammad Maqbool Waris[1(✉)], Bisma Mannan[1],
Cesar Sanin[2], and Edward Szczerbicki[3]

[1] Sharda University, Greater Noida, UP, India
ahmadreshadbakhtari@yahoo.com, MohammadMaqbool.Waris@uon.edu.au,
bismamannan@gmail.com
[2] The University of Newcastle, Callaghan, NSW, Australia
cesar.sanin@newcastle.edu.au
[3] Gdansk University of Technology, Gdansk, Poland
esz@zie.pg.gda.pl

Abstract. This paper assesses some features of industry 4.0 by using SWOT analysis that affects the adoption and implementation of industry 4.0. The paper identifies the strengths, weaknesses, opportunities, and threats related to industry 4.0. By the consideration of these four groups of factors, the industrial practitioners can understand how to implement industry 4.0. Moreover, industrial practitioners can use the strengths/opportunities offered by industry 4.0 to take strategic decisions to decrease the effect of the threats/weaknesses that come along with industry 4.0.

Keywords: Industry 4.0 · SWOT analysis · Knowledge management · Cyber-physical systems

1 Introduction

As the days pass, life on our earth changes and develops. In the same manner, the business, manufacturing, services, and industry is evolving and developing. We have already experienced the three industrial revolutions so far and we are on the verge of the fourth industrial revolution (see Fig. 1).

With the ability to continuously monitor [1] and control the products and real time data processing due to new advancements in information technology (IT), the next (fourth) industrial revolution will be adopted by industries very soon. The fourth industrial revolution (industry 4.0) is a concept proposed by an association of representatives from academia, business and politics to increase strength and competitiveness in the German manufacturing industry in 2011 [2]. Industry 4.0 is a concept that tries to make the industries more intelligent, dynamic and flexible.

Industry 4.0 is based on the integration of IT systems with physical systems to create a cyber-physical system, which then creates a virtual reality of the real world [3], or industry 4.0 is the merged form of the real and virtual world in a cyber-physical system [4].

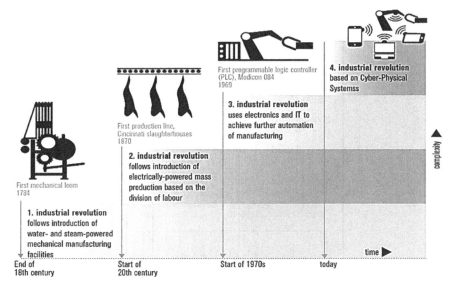

Fig. 1. Industry 4.0 –The 4th industrial revolution with CPS [2]

Cyber-physical systems stand for the systems that have integrated computational and physical capabilities to allow interaction between physical objects (man and machines) [5]. In industry 4.0 three levels form the cyber-physical systems [6]: physical objects (data generation and acquisition), cloud (computation and aggregation of acquired data) and services (decision-support) (see Fig. 2).

Industry 4.0 connects all the physical objects and allows them to generate and share their data and information using sensors, actuators and a network connection. This well-connected system in industry 4.0 provides solutions to overcome the issues in industries. For example, in most industries, the main reason that causes the breakdown of the digital chain is the lack of traceability [7] that can be solved by the implementation of industry 4.0.

Traceability is the identification of the product, and its situation at each step of the manufacturing process, starting from raw material input to the finished product output. Traceability is an important aspect of production monitoring, product quality control, customer satisfaction and competitiveness of the industry. Therefore, a proper information flow allows the system to have good traceability of the resources, processes, and functions required and all of these can be achieved by the implementation of the industry 4.0.

Industry 4.0 runs based on continuous communication using the internet that creates a platform for continuous interaction and exchange of information, not just between humans and machines, as well as the machines themselves [8]. These communication interactions need a proper knowledge management system, as from the last 25 years knowledge management has become a vital source to raise efficiency and competitive abilities for the industries [9, 10] and lack of a proper knowledge management system could act as a barrier to the adoption of industry 4.0 [11].

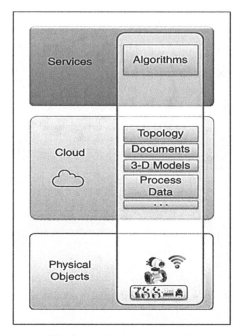

Fig. 2. CPS in industry 4.0 [6]

Knowledge management is a tool for identifying and acquiring the collective knowledge in an organization to help the organization compete [9] and a proper knowledge management system in industry 4.0 leads to the establishment of a communication channel that allows continuous exchange of information regarding an individual's (product) needs and situation in real-time that helps in the continuous improvement it. For example, due to the tight competition among similar manufacturing organizations and high customer expectation to have quality products at lower costs, product innovation is needed regularly [12]. Product innovation is mainly driven by knowledge and previous experiences. These previous experience and knowledge are acquired through the platform that the knowledge management system provides for the industry 4.0. Smart Innovation Engineering (SIE) [12], which is an experienced-based product innovation system for industry 4.0, works by the past experiences and formal decisional events related to the product innovation. SIE is the extension of the Virtual Engineering Object (VEO) concept proposed by Shafiq et al. [13]. VEO is a specialized form of cyber-physical system for the industry 4.0. VEO concept is an experienced-based knowledge representation of engineering objects, which is based on knowledge management and knowledge engineering. SIE and VEO are examples of the knowledge management application in industry 4.0 and shows how knowledge management act as an enabler of industry 4.0.

By emerging of every industrial revolution there was optimism and pessimism from the society and industry because the industrial revolution changes the way industries run [14]. Industry 4.0 which stands for the fourth industrial revolution is also not exceptional. One of the major concern about industry 4.0 is the global job loss because the majority of the people in developed and developing countries are scared of the technological development that threats their jobs [15], as of a survey done by the World Economic Forum (WEF) in 2016 if the industry 4.0 would become adopted completely there will be a loss of more than 5 million jobs globally [16]. In the same manner industry, 4.0 threatens the future of public administration as the emergence of new technology tends to replace human labor, in the long run, same as the third industrial revolution [17]. But industry 4.0 can help local and central governments to give better services using new and developed technologies [18].

In addition to all weaknesses and threats of industry 4.0, there are lots of opportunities that industry 4.0 offers. Sustainability and sustainable development is the phenomenon that should be considered in the industry, as per the report of the UN World Commission on Environment and Development 'Our Common Future' 1987 Sustainable Development "Is development that meets the needs of the present without compromising the ability of future generations to meet their own needs" [19]. Industry 4.0 can play a vital role in sustainable development, like by the adoption of industry 4.0 the industries can have interoperability which will increase the machine life cycle, decrease industrial waste and helps to have more efficient processes [20].

This paper presents clearly the benefits and measures to be considered by the industries to prosper in the near future in order to become smart factories of Industry 4.0 era. To understand industry 4.0 and its impact on the industry, by using SWOT analysis this paper studies industry 4.0 to identify its strengths and opportunities as well as weaknesses and threats that can lure industries to embrace industry 4.0. There is some doubt especially in the mind of present business community whether to advance for Industry 4.0. Representatives from the politics are also concerned about the job loss that may arise in adopting Industry 4.0.

The next section presents a brief introduction of SWOT analysis and then presents the strengths, weaknesses, opportunities, and threats related to industry 4.0. It is also discussed how Industry 4.0 will provide various benefits as compared to some disadvantages (rather hurdles). In fact most of these hurdles will controlled directly or indirectly by its benefits.

2 SWOT Analysis for Industry 4.0

SWOT analysis stands for the short form of four words; Strength, Weaknesses, Opportunities, and Threats (see Fig. 3). SWOT analysis is a technique to identify the internal strengths and weaknesses and external opportunities and threats. It was first introduced by Albert Humphrey, a research scholar and a research project team leader at Stanford University in the 1960s and 1970s. Humphrey had a research team known as the Team Action Model (TAM). The team identified some important areas and the tool used to investigate each of these areas was called **SOFT** analysis. They used the categories "What is good in the present is **S**atisfactory, good in the future is an **O**pportunity; bad in the present is a **F**ault and bad in the future is a **T**hreat." [21].

SWOT analysis is categorized into two parts; internal and external analysis (see Fig. 4). The internal analysis identifies resources, capabilities, core competencies, and competitive advantages inherent to the organization. The external analysis is used to identify market opportunities and threats by looking at competitors' resources, the industry environment, and the general environment. The main objective of the SWOT analysis is to use the knowledge an organization has about its internal and external environments and to formulate its strategy accordingly.

Industry 4.0 is a new concept in the industry, which stands for the fourth industrial revolution. It was first proposed in 2011, by an association of representatives from business, politics, and academia in Hanover Fair as an approach to strengthening the competitiveness of the German manufacturing industry [2].

Industry 4.0 is still in its initial phase and needs to be studied and analyzed because currently many industries are worried about its adoption and adaptation impacts on their internal and external environment like labor, security, competitiveness, profit, etc. This paper mainly focuses on the usage of SWOT analysis to identify the internal and external impacts of Industry 4.0 in four categories (Strengths, Weaknesses, Opportunities, and Threats).

In the literature, authors studied different aspects of industry 4.0 and some of them have focused on the challenges and opportunities offered by industry 4.0. The challenges and opportunities related to the industry are studied from different points of view,

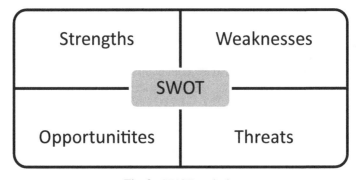

Fig. 3. SWOT analysis.

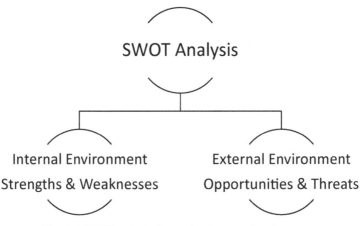

Fig. 4. SWOT analysis: internal and external environment.

economic, social [17], industrial [3], country-based [11], sustainability [19], etc. Like one has focused on how industry 4.0 design principles (interoperability, decentralization, virtualization, real-time capability, and modularity and service orientation) will help industries to have a sustainable production system, which will promise energy-efficient and low waste production system [19]. But none of the authors have presented the strengths, opportunities, threats, and weaknesses of the industry 4.0 in one paper.

This paper mainly focuses on the identification of the industry 4.0's weaknesses, opportunities, strengths and threats and tries to offer solutions to the identified threats and weaknesses of it. Table 1 shows all the strengths, weaknesses, opportunities and threats related to industry 4.0. The upper left box shows the strengths, the upper right box shows the weaknesses, the lower-left box shows the opportunities and the lower right box shows the threats.

3 Managerial Implications

The outputs and findings of the current study offer a lot of implications to the industry practitioners. First, it identifies the weaknesses and threats of the industry 4.0. The practitioners can focus on these weaknesses and threats and try how to decrease their effect and find a solution for them. Secondly identifies the strengths and opportunities of the industry 4.0 that could help the industry practitioners to cope up with the weaknesses and threats of the industry 4.0. Like proper knowledge management which is an inseparable part of the industry 4.0 and the Practitioners should think and develop models and systems in which they can implement and adopt industry 4.0 easily. Another important point that this study provides to the industry practitioners is the improvement of their staff's skills to implement industry 4.0. The staff should go through a program of training and skills development by which they can achieve improvement in their soft and hard skills.

4 Results and Discussion

Through the extant literature review, this study identified the factors of industry 4.0 in four categories. The SWOT analysis was applied to categorize the factors of industry 4.0 into strengths, weaknesses, opportunities, and threats. From the analysis, it is observed that industry 4.0 offers more advantages to the industry than its disadvantages. Table 1 shows the strengths and opportunities of industry 4.0 as well as its weaknesses and threats.

Some of the major strength of Industry 4.0 are making industries more efficient, increased productivity, more flexibility in production system, ease of customization and customer satisfaction. Apart from that, it also provides various opportunities that adds more value to its overall benefits like sustainable development, direct interaction with the customer, reduction in energy consumption, waste reduction, faster connectivity and creating new business models. Most of the weaknesses and threats can be controlled and/or used as a competitive advantages over other industries by proper approach and planning.

Table 1. Strengths, weaknesses, opportunities, and threats offered by industry 4.0

S	W
-Interoperability: enables the industries to share or exchange their machines and equipment which perform the same functions. -Decentralization: industry 4.0 increases the ability of machines, operational personal and local companies to make the decision faster and data-driven. -Increased real-time capability: increases the response rate and enables the machines to bring changes to the product as per customer request. -Modularity: enables the production system to be flexible with changes that happen in product design or during seasonal changes. -Service orientation: allows the business, human and CPS to have interactions with each other through the internet oft hings and internet of services for creating much better value for the consumers. -Industry 4.0 increases the efficiency that results in the conservation of energy and raw materials. -Industry 4.0 increases productivity due to the integration ofi ntelligentt echnologies, which are more productive. -Industry 4.0 increases the flexibility of production systems due to cyber-physical systems usage. -Industry 4.0 integrates the customer with the production cycle through a network and increases customer satisfaction.	-Operators training and improvement oft heir softskills to manage digital jobs. -Equipping of operators with new skills and workforce transformation to enable them to manage the required task digitally. -Data and information sharing among differenti ndustries that compete. -High investment required to make all the Industry components smart. -Security of computer data and the communication between intelligent systems to avoid leakage of confidential data, which affects the competitiveness of the organization.

SWOT Analysis

O	T
-Industry 4.0 can have a big contribution to sustainable development and eco-sustainable production due to increase in efficiency, productivity and flexibility oft he industries. -Industry 4.0 will increase customer satisfaction with the directi nteraction oft he customer. -With the increase in efficiency and productivity in industry 4.0 the product cost will decrease. -Industry 4.0 will help in removing barriers between investors and markets. -Industry 4.0 will help to have better customization of products and services. -Industry 4.0 will help in waste reduction and reduction of energy consumption due to higher efficiency. -Shorter lead times due to better connectivity and fast information flow. -Industry 4.0 creates new business models. -Due to high efficiency the cost of production will decrease.	-Job losses, industry 4.0 will replace low skilled and low wage jobs by computers and digitization. Thus increases the social tensions and pessimistic ideas againsti ndustry 4.0. -In industry 4.0 data and knowledge will play the most important role so the security of data and information is a big concern. -Cyber-terrorism, hacking and cyber-crimes are the realities, which can act as a barrier towards the implementation ofi ndustry 4.0. -Social beliefs and perceptions againstt he digitalization and connection of everything through the internet of things, which threats customer privacy. -Lack of proper and applicable framework to implement industry 4.0 in industry. -Lack of proper knowledge management systems and platforms. -The development of algorithms to deal with data due to collection and production of massive data.

Detailed analysis of Strengths, Weaknesses, Opportunities and Threats is used to formulate appropriate strategies that help in achieving the goal of Industry 4.0.

SO Strategy (Strengths - Opportunities): pursue opportunities that match the company's strengths. For example strength like flexibility in production system and faster and efficient CPS help industries to get benefitted by opportunities like customization and faster services.

WO Strategy (Weaknesses - Opportunities): overcome weaknesses to make good use of opportunities. For example weakness such as training of operator and equipping with new skills will cause initial investment but result in faster information flow as an opportunity that helps in better connectivity and shorter lead times.

ST Strategy (Strengths - Threats): identify How to use advantages and strengths to minimize risks caused by the external environment. For instance, the implementation of industry 4.0 causes job loss due to high automation and digitization and may cause a global crisis. To decrease the effect of job loss the industries can use the opportunity of new business models offered by industry 4.0 to create new job opportunities.

WT strategy (Weaknesses - Threats): establish a "defense plan" to avoid the weak points being more seriously affected from the outside environment. For example weakness like data and information sharing among different industries concern about hacking and cyber-crimes that may act as a barrier towards the implementation of industry 4.0. This can be avoided by implementing the proper and efficient Knowledge Management System.

More detailed strategies will be conducted in future research as a next step. The achieved result is useful to the industries and identifies the possible challenges and opportunities offered by industry 4.0. The analysis result shows the factors that should be considered during the implementation of the industry 4.0 and the barriers and challenges may disrupt the industry 4.0 adoption.

5   Conclusion

As the world moves forward, the effect of industry 4.0 or the fourth industrial revolution on the industry, society, and economy increases and everyone is worried that how industry 4.0 will affect them. Industry 4.0 will be implemented by the industries in the upcoming years and it allows to have more productivity, flexibility, and customization to satisfy the customer. But with these, all benefits, industry 4.0 will also bring challenges and problems with itself like changes to the job market and radical changes to the industry. In this paper, we presented a study on industry 4.0 by using SWOT analysis and identified the strengths, weaknesses, opportunities, and threats related to industry 4.0.

The paper discusses how industry 4.0 can help industries to overcome contemporary problems in industries. The findings were based on a review of the literature. The importance of knowledge management and knowledge management systems in industry 4.0 were discussed and showed how knowledge management can act as an enabler of industry 4.0.

Industry 4.0 is established on the idea of the cyber-physical systems, which allows the connection between man and machine. In the cyber-physical systems, the information and data are generated by physical objects and flows to the cloud, the cloud then allows all the connected objects to use the available data or information. These stored data and information are later used for the continuous improvement and optimization of products, to do so industry 4.0 needs to have proper knowledge management and knowledge management system. Lack of proper platform and systems to manage data knowledge would act as a barrier to implementation and adoption of industry 4.0 and beside the proper platform for knowledge management, the risk of hacking and data leakage (cyber-security) is to be considered.

The main concern about industry 4.0 is the job loss or jobs would not be needed anymore or would be replaced by the machine and technology as it will be implemented. This can be overcome by use of opportunity of new business models offered by Industry 4.0 that results in job creation.

Industry 4.0 besides all of its weaknesses and challenges has a lot to offer for the industry like an increase in flexibility, productivity, and customization of the product. With higher productivity and flexibility industry 4.0 will help to have a sustainable product production that can decrease the usage of the energy due to higher efficiency offered by the industry 4.0.

Industry 4.0 is a concept that soon or later will bring everything under its territory and there is no way to go back, so the organizations and industries should prepare themselves accordingly. Industries should provide training to their staff and should improve their skills. Industry 4.0 or the fourth industrial revolution is irreversible and everyone should prepare themselves accordingly.

In future this research may be further extended for detailed strategies planning that provide a clear and technical understanding of Industry 4.0 concept.

References

1. Park, N., Song, Y.: AONT encryption based application data management in mobile RFID environment. In: Pan, J.-S., Chen, S.-M., Nguyen, N.T. (eds.) ICCCI 2010. LNCS (LNAI), vol. 6422. Springer, Heidelberg (2010). https://doi.org/10.1007/978-3-642-16732-4_16
2. Henning, K.: Recommendations for implementing the strategic initiative Industrie 4.0 (2013)
3. Petrillo, A., Felice, F. D., Cioffi, R., Zomparelli, F.: Fourth industrial revolution: current practices, challenges, and opportunities. Digit. Transform. Smart Manuf. 1–20 (2018). https://doi.org/10.5772/intechopen.72304
4. Capgemini Consulting.: Digitizing Manufacturing Ready, Set, Go! (2014). https://www.de.capgemini-consulting.com/resource-fie-access/resource/pdf/digitiz-ing-manufacturing_0.pdf
5. Baheti, R., Gill, H.: Cyber-physical systems. Impact Control Technol. **12**(1), 161–166 (2011)
6. Drath, R., Horch, A.: Industrie 4.0: hit or hype? [industry forum]. IEEE Ind. Electr. Mag. **8**(2), 56–58 (2014)
7. Meski, O., Belkadi, F., Laroche, F., Furet, B.: Towards a knowledge-based framework for digital chain monitoring within the industry 4.0 paradigm. Procedia CIRP **84**, 118–123 (2019)
8. Cooper, J., James, A.: Challenges for database management in the internet of things. IETE Tech. Rev. **26**(5), 320–329 (2009)
9. Von Krogh, G.: Care in knowledge creation. Calif. Manag. Rev. **40**(3), 133–153 (1998)
10. Roblek, V., Meško, M., Krapež, A.: A complex view of industry 4.0. Sage Open **6**(2), 2158244016653987 (2016)

11. Kamble, S.S., Gunasekaran, A., Sharma, R.: Analysis of the driving and dependence power of barriers to adopt industry 4.0 in Indian manufacturing industry. Comput. Ind. **101**, 107–119 (2018)
12. Waris, M.M., Sanin, C., Szczerbicki, E.: Smart innovation engineering (SIE): experience-based product innovation system for industry 4.0. In: Wilimowska, Z., Borzemski, L., Świątek, J. (eds.) ISAT 2017. AISC, vol. 657. Springer, Cham (2018). https://doi.org/10.1007/978-3-319-67223-6_36
13. Shafiq, S.I., Sanin, C., Szczerbicki, E., Toro, C.: Virtual engineering object/virtual engineering process: a specialized form of cyber physical system for Industrie 4.0. Procedia Comput. Sci. **60**, 1146–1155 (2015)
14. Lasi, H., Fettke, P., Kemper, H.G., Feld, T., Hoffmann, M.: Industry 4.0. Bus. Inf. Syst. Eng. **6**(4), 239–242 (2014)
15. Shank, P.: The Fourth Industrial Revolution: What Happens With Employment? (2016). https://www.td.org/Publications/Blogs/Learning-ExecutiveBlog/2016/05/The-Fourth-Industrial-Revolution-What-Happens-withEmployment. Accessed 10 Sept 2019
16. World Economic Forum (WEF).: Five Million Jobs by 2020: The Real Challenge of the Fourth Industrial Revolution (2016). https://www.weforum.org/press/2016/01/five-million-jobs-by-2020-the-real-challenge-of-the-fourth-industrial-revolution. Accessed 15 Sept 2019
17. Shava, E., Hofisi, C.: Challenges and opportunities for public administration in the Fourth Industrial Revolution. Afr. J. Pub. Aff. **9**(9), 203–215 (2017)
18. McKinsey, C.: Public sector-information technology. McKinsey & Company, Chicago (2016)
19. Wced, S.W.S.: World commission on environment and development. Our Common Future **17**, 1–91 (1987)
20. Carvalho, N., Chaim, O., Cazarini, E., Gerolamo, M.: Manufacturing in the fourth industrial revolution: a positive prospect in sustainable manufacturing. Procedia Manuf. **21**, 671–678 (2018)
21. Thompson, A.A., Strickland, A.J., Gamble, J.E.: Crafting and Executing Strategy-Concepts and Cases, 15th edn. McGraw-Hill/Irwin, USA (2007)

Lean Based and Artificial Intelligence Powered Support Framework for Independent Screen Entertainment Creators

Ivan Spajic Buturac, Leo Mrsic$^{(\boxtimes)}$ ⓘ, and Mislav Balkovic ⓘ

Algebra University College, Ilica 242, 10000 Zagreb, Croatia
ispajic@gmail.com, {leo.mrsic,mislav.balkovic}@algebra.hr

Abstract. Our research is focused in helping new entrants into online comedy business and propose a solution that would enable them to enter a "virtuous cycle of success" very early on using digital technologies. We focus on these independent creators as they represent an enormous potential in future of the industry. Named, screen entertainment, term refers to audiovisual entertainment formats that were traditionally represented by movies and TV series, but have since gone through a transformation in the era of online entertainment, where format boundaries have become blurred. As part of our research, we are using many learnings from traditional movie and TV, acknowledging that the online screen entertainment is much more fluid and diverse. In paper, we first present the problem and run an overview of industry history in order to highlight existing business models and challenges they represent. Next, we provide an overview of existing methods already used in screen entertainment industries. Then, based on all the learnings we aim to propose solution most beneficial to independent creators. Our concept is inspired by Lean methodology, in which we approach early stage comedy in a similar fashion one might approach early stage startup companies using the Lean methodology: by introducing content with just enough features (or qualities) to analyze and test the market potential very early in the process.

Keywords: Lean methodology · Screen entertainment · Online video creators · Advanced analytics · Video content analysis · Test screening

1 Introduction

One of the most important aspects of marketing is content. Content is used to engage, create emotional connection and sell products and services. Brands continuously look for movies and shows that interconnect with culture of their consumers and, metaphorically speaking, "hijack" those connections. And yet, content on its own continually struggles to generate income for its creators. The perceived value of content in the eyes of the viewer is a very complex issue, emerging from the history of the industry. As we will show in this paper, screen entertainment industry in fact has a widening value gap for creators, in spite of constant development in both production accessibility and distributions channels. This gap is primarily located in three areas: quality, willingness of viewers to pay and ability to fund production. When speaking about the quality gap, we address the fact that most

© Springer Nature Singapore Pte Ltd. 2020
P. Sitek et al. (Eds.): ACIIDS 2020, CCIS 1178, pp. 226–237, 2020.
https://doi.org/10.1007/978-981-15-3380-8_20

screen entertainment today is created for efficiency, not quality. Screen entertainment has a number of limitations deriving from both its historical development and financing models. Most entertainment financing models lead to "pandering to fans", i.e. creating "more of the same" in order to prolong the success of a "winning formula" for as long as possible, especially in large entertainment companies. This has often led to market oversaturation and development of such concepts as "least objectionable content", that sacrifice innovation and quality for the sake of reaching larger market shares. Digital screen entertainment channels and advancement of digital production tools have only partially offset this problem, since current marketing and financing models involved in online success still aren't favorable for new and unproven entrants or those not proficient in marketing. This is especially true for creators who desire to independently create higher quality content, with higher production costs or niche markets, since these creators have a larger cash flow gap. Another type of gaps that we introduce into discussion is "reputational gap". By this term we describe a cultural artefact of the entertainment culture [1–3]. A "reputational gap" is a position very normal in any line of business: a person or business entering the market has to endure a period of time underpricing their work, in order to gain enough reputation and references in the market to start being perceived as a trustworthy market participant. In general business, market entry strategies such as "price dumping" or promotions, are used to bridge this gap. Content creators are no exception to this position, and the entertainment industry has a long tradition of expecting creators to create free of charge or for minimum wages, for a very long time before they establish their reputation. It is standard practice for screenwriters to send their scripts to studio script readers or for cartoon illustrators to send their work for editors of magazines for years without any success. Key two issues that any creator faces in this model is that (a) they need to fund themselves through other means while attempting to enter the "circle" and (b) once they do enter, they will still work for minimum wages. Success of YouTube has proven that independent content has the biggest growth within industry and tapping into this segment presents great business potential. By empowering creators to gain access to resources and insights currently available only to large studios, we believe that a large portion of that value could be captured and sustained. The end goal of this paper is to help address the gaps and propose a technological solution that could help reposition creators when it comes to proving their content's market worth and increasing the perceived value of content. To do that, we propose a novel solution, inspired by some of the best practices in the IT industries. IT industry, unlike entertainment industry, has shown a strong resilience to marginalization of its creators. IT has shown an immense willingness to consort, standardize and develop their eco-system. One such attempt to improve the quality of developing startups was Eric Ries' "Lean startup". Based on a set of best/worst practices and a scientific approach so familiar to IT, "Lean startup" methodology successfully helps founders resolve some of the greatest issues they face as they start building their enterprise. It is based on what he calls "build-measure-learn loop", an experimental method that allows founders to validate their (mis)conceptions about their products and the market, and learn how to either improve existing ideas or completely pivot in their strategies [4, 5].

2 Introducing "Lean Startup" Methodology for Independent Screen Entertainment Content Creators

Goal of this research is to propose a "lean" solution for the process of independent online screen entertainment. Eric Ries developed his business framework "Lean Startup" as a criticism of some misconceptions about startups he believed were dangerous for aspiring founders. One was that if founders only possessed determination, brilliance, great timing and a great product, they were destined to succeed. Another, related to that one, was the notion that ideas were precious and should be well hidden. Based on his experience as a founder and advisor to other founders, he argued that the real issue lay in the execution of business ideas [6, 7]. So, he proposed several mechanisms to cope with building a startup. The one we will focus on is the "build-measure-learn feedback loop". The idea behind this concept is that planning and forecasting are only useful when operations of a business have been rather stable and where the environment is static. Startups have neither of these. Planning for several months and releasing a product only after many thousands of hours of perfecting it, is a game of very high stakes. As he illustrates, the most dangerous thing to do is to build something on time, within budget and according to specifications, only not to have anyone use it. Many entrepreneurs, just like video creators, have realized this and as a consequence, derived that the only alternative was to operate in chaos, without any planning. As a result, many startups lasted only as long as their founder's passion. In our terminology, the reputational gap was too wide to cross it with limited resources. Fortunately, Ries proposed a feasible alternative to both approaches were quickly going through cycles the build-measure-learn feedback loop [8].

The goal of a startup, he argues, is to figure out the right thing to build - that customers want and will pay for - as quickly as possible. Founders must be capable of quickly removing anything that which doesn't make sense, and double down on that which does. The process he proposes moves backwards, from learning to building. He argues that founders should always first define what they want to learn, state a hypothesis. This hypothesis should revolve around the target consumers. For example, IKEA's hypothesis could be stated as "People are willing to assemble their own furniture at home". As trivial as these hypotheses might seem, any business model that relies on them should verify them. After formulating these hypotheses comes the process of validating or rejecting them. Ries argues that the only real/service validation point in business is to test if customers would be willing to pay for the product. He encourages startups to "get out of the building" approach in a phase called "customer development" to test their hypotheses. They should go out and ask potential users, purchasers, and partners for feedback on all elements of the business model, including product features, pricing, distribution channels, and affordable customer acquisition strategies. The emphasis is on nimbleness and speed: new ventures should rapidly assemble new experiments and immediately elicit customer feedback. Then, using customers' input to revise their assumptions, they start the cycle over again. During the experiment, they should focus on observing the customer behavior as much as possible rather than just asking. The idea is that customers usually don't even know what they want, but if they see a product, they will know if they are interested in it [9].

There are three types of "engine of growth" from which the company should choose. The idea is to select just one at a time and focus on improving the metrics connected to it. Otherwise, he argues, company will lose focus and "drown" under the variety of parallel activities. The three engines of growth are a way to focus the energy of the startup in the right place. They are also often embedded into the product itself, as is the case with most of the viral examples below [10].

First "engine" is the "sticky engine", which is a fit for companies that are designed to attract customers for the long term. The two metrics for this type are customer acquisition rate through Word of mouth (WOM) and customer churn rate, the number of customers who failed to stay with the company. As long as the WOM generates an acquisition rate higher than the churn rate, these companies will grow [11].

The second type is "viral". These companies spread by a rate comparable to an epidemic. The idea behind this "engine" is that for every person that joins, they should invite one person or more. For these products, invites happen as a necessary side effect of product usage, unlike in "sticky engine", where WOM is a result of satisfaction. Success is measured in the "viral coefficient", which we already discussed. The "viral engine" of growth is used by, for example, social networks and by multi-level marketing businesses, among others [12].

And finally, companies that need to focus on advertising to reach customers are using the "paid engine". A company using the paid engine of growth realizes that primarily, it will have to focus on advertising in some form to reach customers. The two most useful metrics to a company of this kind are CPA (short for cost per acquisition), and LTV (short for lifetime value), the difference between how profitable a customer is over their entire lifetime, minus the cost of acquiring a customer, that will determine the growth rate of such a company. An example is e-commerce businesses.

What this means, is that the entrepreneur either perseveres with the general hypothesis and changes various elements or makes a pivot, a change in overall strategy on how to achieve the vision that you have for the startup. The goal is to find the right balance between not giving up to easily and being overly stubborn. If the decision is to pivot, the pivot can occur in different areas: customer segment, financing model (e.g. selling application vs advertising on them), company growth methods, etc. The key ending notion is that pivoting should not be considered a failure, but a useful and timely discovery of what doesn't work and what might [13].

2.1 Prototype Design

With all the guideline in hand, we set out to create the first prototype for our tool. We decided to first test out in live surroundings, in order to collect both quantitative and qualitative data. 12 respondents at Zagreb Faculty of Economics were shown a series of short videos of different comedy types. Videos varied in subgenre and level of production. We showed clips of stand-up comedy shows, sketch shows, humorous advertisements, scenes from TV shows and adult cartoons. Most of the videos were in fully finished version, but we also created 2 storyboards based on finished versions of TV ads, in order to test out what an MVC might look like. One of the storyboards had the original soundtrack and the storyboard images were exchanging as the soundtrack moved along (Storyboard proposal), while the other one had a narrator explain what was happening in the video, while the storyboard images were exchanging (Storyboard Insurance). To adhere to the "observe, don't ask" principle, 2 cameras were used, recordings were cut into clips and each of the respondent reactions was extracted manually. The clips were then analyzed using Microsoft Cognitive services Emotion API, at a frame rate of 5 frames per seconds, measuring 8 basic emotions: anger, contempt, disgust, fear, happiness, surprise, sadness and neutral state (Fig. 1).

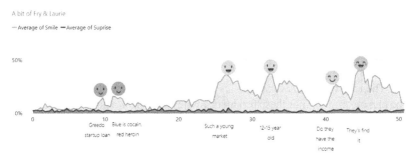

Fig. 1. Example of the reactions report based on emotional reactions of respondents.

Results were shown as displayed above showing aggregated reactions of all the respondents in a line graph, for two of the positive emotional reactions: laughter and surprise. Additionally, emoticons were added for better explanation of the results, and a set of bar charts was present that displayed average reaction score for each of the respondents. Notes were also taken on respondent reactions to the screening.

2.2   Interviews

After the prototype was complete, we decided to seek out professionals from the industry. Through different channels, we contacted 4 interviewees: 3 were comedians. All had experience with stand-up comedy and 1 was at the time a professional screenwriter. We the added another interview, with a founder of a novel UK based website, attempting to grow the business of independent online comedians through connections, educations and promotion.

2.3   Creating an Actionable Set of Insight

To be useful in improving crowdfunding campaigns, the test needs to gain insights that can be used in a very practical manner. Since we've found that Facebook is a preferred method in prelaunch testing, since it enables audience targeting both by demographics, preferences and similarity to existing user base, we will focus on building a dataset that could instantly be used in their advertising system. We hypothesize that our best course of action is to attempt to create a set of items that would differentiate those respondents who give good ratings on a test from others, as well as to identify the next potential segments. One approach might be to screen respondents before the actual tests, in order to segment them immediately. Another might be to leave the initial group random and then as we test the content, look for a "bucket" of preferences specific to that test. The advantage of the second approach is that we can work with a smaller question set. This is relevant, both because of test pricing and respondent fatigue. So, our goal is to generate a network of items that are as dissimilar between themselves as possible, while at the same time representative of a wider group of content that might be used in targeting [14–16].

2.3.1 Clustering Objects

The survey was conducted via Clickworker.com. Clickworker.com is a Germany based service portal that connects anonymous respondents with researchers, for a fee. It currently hosts over 1.2 million respondents worldwide, located in 136 countries. The purpose of using the service was to find sufficient respondents from United Kingdom ready to participate in the longitudinal research with camera recordings. United Kingdom was selected because of native English speakers, since all the tested content was in English (Fig. 2).

Fig. 2. Eigenvalues show that 21 factors are required to explain 75% of variance.

Survey was conducted on a sample of 1.600 respondents, age 18–69 from UK. An elimination question was used to make sure respondents weren't simply clicking through the survey, and 26 participants were eliminated, leaving 1584 respondents. For the UK population of 66,2 million, this provides us with a confidence interval of 2,46 at confidence level of 95%. Demographic data for total respondent population shows detailed information about respondent demographics. Respondents were displayed 44 questions, not including the elimination question. Questions were grouped into 2 groups: demographic questions and preferences about entertainment. For preference testing, a Likert scale of 1 to 7 was used, where 1 was "Extremely dislike" and 7 "Extremely like". Due to the length of the survey, questions about preferences were divided into 4 groups and these groups were rotated in 4 populations of 400 respondents, to reduce the effect of survey fatigue. The preference items were selected based on a University of Cambridge preference-based personality test [17]. We selected this set because, while the direct mechanism of the test wasn't available to us, we believed at the time that items on the list presented a spectrum of opposing tastes, considering how they originally measured opposite personalities. While we didn't leave room for "haven't watched/haven't heard of it" in our survey, we covered it with an option of middle rating, 4, which stated that the user had no opinion on the item (Fig. 3).

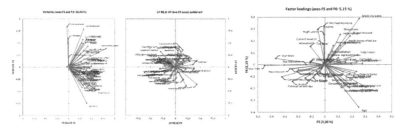

Fig. 3. Factors in 2-dimensional representation

2.4 Attribute Based Segmentation

After analyzing the initial study, we conducted a follow-up survey. Due to budgetary restrictions, we were only able to survey 89 respondents from study 1. In this survey we asked the respondents to answer additional questions. The goal was to test out whether we could explicitly ask correspondents questions about content in order to better understand how their taste was defined. We hypothesized that this might help in finding the right items to place into our item network. We asked them to rank in order of priority attributes that were important to them in a show. To split the task, we asked them a question on things they liked and another about things they disliked. To further test what the undiscovered variables are, we also asked additional questions about respondent demographics and habits [18] (Fig. 4).

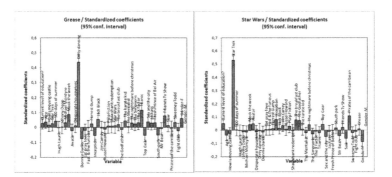

Fig. 4. ANCOVA standardized coefficients

2.5 Key Research Findings

We will now analyze the key point of our research by following the "Lean Startup" order. In order to address the value gap and raise pledge levels above 20$, content in development needs to find viewers with the greatest appreciation so they can later apply the concierge MVP process on them. To connect the recruited audience as closely as possible with a wider population, we proposed to build a preference network for our respondents and enable the creators to understand various details about the potential viewers, including how to reach them using the Facebook targeting system. The key factor will be the proper level of generalization, as research showed that lower level entities or exemplars, such as individual movies may be too specific and unfamiliar to respondents. Also, unlike higher order categories, such as genre or subgenre, exemplars tend to outdate we also expanded on our initial logic of using personality types, since significant correlation has been found between personality types and genre preference (Listening, Watching, and Reading). Considering how we are attempting to build an affordable solution; the recruited respondent numbers should be relatively low. This, of course brings to the question statistical confidence, so developing a solution that could be both accurate and remain affordable will be key to developing a reliable tool. For this purpose, we will investigate using the Bayesian truth serum algorithm, which enables higher accuracy with lower number of predictors. We've concluded that the hypotheses in entertainment comes on two levels: overall premise and individual segments. Either of these might reduce the viewer satisfaction. Our correspondents noted that to improve a segment, it was vital for them to hear feedback on why something didn't work for the audience, not just that it didn't. The solution, therefore, could include a way to include the points within content where individual jokes are located, like we did in our prototype [19–21]. Based on the reaction or the lack of it, system could go back and address the point that didn't work. Same applies if we get an indication that the user showed no interest from the very start or that we lost him at some point. As explained, experiments would be performed on two levels, inside the sandbox environment of "grinder", where we could gain deep insights and then in the prelaunch environment. The respondents are paid through a 3d-party platform and we do not have direct contact with them. As the number of projects and channels grows, it might be better and more cost efficient to create own survey panel. We proposed to use face recording and emotion recognition system to observe respondent reactions in real time. While there was worry about the willingness of respondents to participate, during Study 1, we asked respondents if they would be willing to participate in such a test, and 59,3% opted for "Yes". Next, based on their reactions during live screening, we conclude that the "grinder" should include a stress-relief mechanism. Regardless of whether respondents will be recorded or asked to react directly, two factors could alleviate the stress: prelaunch content and habit [22]. By prelaunch content we mean that, if uninterrupted, the second or third video in a row may suffer from far less stress influence than the first one and that we should show content not relevant to the test first, perhaps even something very familiar to viewers. By habit, we are referring to the "exposure effect", the psychological phenomenon in which people express undue liking for things merely because they are familiar with them (science daily). By having respondents participate in more than one test of this type, their stress levels would possibly decrease simply because of familiarity. In regards to the low level of emotional reaction with some participants, we propose several possible solutions might help. First is to benchmark each user, with short form content, in order to calculate the difference between the emotional reaction and opinion. Second is to include personality traits into the screening process and see if there is a correlation between different personality types and their responses. Third is to use screening to filter out the most expressive respondents. This, however, carries a level of risk, because we might intentionally skew the results. During the live test, we found there was potential in the voiceover with storyboard version. Based on the existing practices in the industry, we believe that a trailer might be a good fit, since it describes the premise and includes examples of humor. Also, viewers are used to the form. The level of completeness of the trailer is a matter for further research. Since the concierge MVC implies paying close attention to the select group, and on the long run it would be more cost efficient to move away from the "paid engine" to "sticky engine", we should also consider levels of experiments for testing and optimizing the actual series once it goes into production. To this purpose, we believe that a table read with low level visual assistance might suffice, since these viewers are now already familiar with characters and premise, and might find it easier to follow. Finally, considering the reputational gap of the new creators, and how the prelaunch strategies operate, the only real option creators have in the beginning is the "paid engine". However, as mentioned above, a concierge approach could give good results since it could provide strong fan loyalty. Similar to crowdfunding agencies, we might find it very cost-efficient to build and maintain a satisfied user base. Another very valuable element of experimentation could be benchmarking against other tested content. This may prove particularly useful in early stages of development, when prelaunch test might not be an option. By using benchmarking, creators will get a general reference as to how they are doing compared to other users [21–23] (Fig. 5).

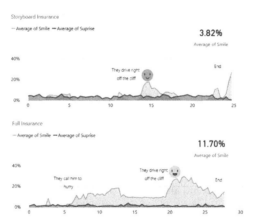

Fig. 5. Searching for the MVC: captured reactions of live audience to storyboards with voice-over, compared to reactions to their final versions.

Our hypothesis was that just like in IT, independent entertainment could benefit from taking a "leaner" approach to product testing and positioning. The assumption was that, essentially, a video production project is in many ways similar to launching new technology startups. However, as we initially anticipated, we've learned during our research of some of the key differences between IT and screen entertainment, and the barriers that emerge from history of television and film. Business models greatly differ: while an IT product is most often an end to itself and capable of generating revenue, entertainment has a deeply rooted value perception issue, or a value gap. Viewers, as we have seen throughout the history, aren't as ready to pay directly for entertainment as they are for other products, even digital ones, like games or apps. Almost a century of free TV has made an impact on both how screen entertainment is consumed and funded. This has made screen entertainment much more dependent on large industry leaders, be they TV networks, movie distributors or production companies. Online channels are the area with the lowest entry barrier for creators. However, the value gap remains and the reputational gap grows further in the online environment. From our interview with the distribution startup representative, we have learned that tools for optimization only make sense if there is an environment in which the optimization leads to better funding. Without such an environment, YouTube creators have a very low cashflow and need resort to low production standards. They would therefore be reluctant to invest into production unless they could see the concrete potential for generating more revenue in the short or midterm. We concluded that the best solution would need to include both the tool and a funding model that would justify use of the tool. In our opinion, the best existing candidate for such a model is crowdfunding. It is a form of selling direct to consumer, making it sustainable. We also already utilize an existing methodology of prelaunch testing and allows for sequential development; a trailer can be basis for funding of an entire series, a prelaunch can be basis for selecting to go live with the trailer, and the recruited audience test can be the basis of selecting the right segments for the trailer. To build on it, we propose that our "grinder" solution needs to be more cost efficient than the current prelaunch test, capable of validating more detailed hypotheses inside the content and provide actionable insights about the target audience, in order to use prelaunch testing only for validation, rather than for segmentation purposes. In terms of the need for a more supportive environment, this solution could in combination with the prelaunch test provide a set of metrics indicating its market potential. With this validation, creators could pitch for micro investments needed to launch a crowdfunding campaign. This process would both return immediate profits to the investor after a successful campaign and enable the content to be produced and distributed on online channels. Then, regardless of the revenue generating model that the channel employ, the product would immediately be profitable and from there continue to creative a long-term passive income both for creators and the investors. In this scenario, the investors would enter the role of producers to a certain extent. Potential candidates for investors, aside from us, are the new channels looking for quality content, production companies or pure capital investors. Another group of candidates might be crowdfunding marketing agencies, which often already possess a large user database and could use it for cost efficient campaigns. Alternatively, since the early funding is used to attract viewers to crowdfund, a large global community of potential fans/funders could also have a good impact. To conclude, just like in IT, the framework itself is only a part of the story. As we've hopefully shown, there is a lot of potential for developing cost-efficient and precise tests, but just like in launching a startup, validation is often useless without a solid financing eco-system. From a business point of view, full development of this eco-system could have a disruptive and transformative effect on the market. As we've seen, the standard production models haven't changed a lot throughout the last century. By focusing on serving the creators as they search for the right audience-content fit, and enabling them to "jump" over the value and reputational gaps, we would essentially shift the very center of power in the industry.

3 Conclusion

In this framework, the value is fully measured and increased from earliest phases, and as we decrease investment risks, creators are able to maintain a retain larger ownership throughout the production cycle, maintain better fan resonance and reinvest into themselves and new projects. Introducing this type of bottom-up solution would present a new business model, one where production and funding would be a tool/service, rather than the initiator. Once the content is present and fan communities prove their loyalty, long term revenue will also start to become less of a challenge, considering the speed at which new media are penetrating the global market. In just the last 5 years, number of internet users has grown by more than 75% or 1,9 billion people. Out of these 405 billion, 92% watch videos online and 58% stream TV content via internet. This implies that around 4 billion people watch are consuming video content online, compared to 6 billion people that have a television set at home. User interest for quality content is large, and movies are the third most popular search category while, comedy and cartoon fall into the top 20. We conclude, therefore, that there is ample demand for quality and unique content, tailored to fan tastes, both on the consumer and business side of the market and that our framework presents the missing link to bridge the last gap in this massive transformation.

References

1. Agarwal, A., Balasubramanian, S., Zheng, J., Dash, S.: Parsing screenplays for extracting social networks from movies (2014). http://www.imsdb.com
2. An Important Note About Funny Or Die, From The Folks At Funny Or Die - Funny Or Die (n.d.). https://www.funnyordie.com/2018/8/20/17784670/an-important-note-about-funny-or-die-from-the-folks-at-funny-or-die. Accessed 5 May 2019
3. Arnold, M.: Think pink: the story of DePatie-Freleng. BearManor Media, Albany (2015)
4. As algorithms take over, YouTube's recommendations highlight a human problem (n.d.). https://www.nbcnews.com/tech/social-media/algorithms-take-over-youtube-s-recommendations-highlight-human-problem-n867596. Accessed 5 May 2019
5. Booker, C.: The seven basic plots : why we tell stories. Continuum (2004). https://www.bloomsbury.com/us/the-seven-basic-plots-9780826452092/
6. Cai, Q., Chen, S., White, S.J., Scott, S.K.: Modulation of humor ratings of bad jokes by other people's laughter. Curr. Biol. CB **29**(14), R677–R678 (2019). https://doi.org/10.1016/j.cub.2019.05.073
7. Caiani, M., della Porta, D., Wagemann, C.: Mobilizing on the Extreme Right Germany, Italy, and the United States. Oxford University Press (2012). https://doi.org/10.1093/acprof:oso/9780199641260.001.0001
8. Chaffee, J., Crick, O.: The Routledge Companion to Commedia dell'Arte. Routledge, Abingdon (2017)
9. Covington, P., Adams, J.: Deep Neural Networks for YouTube Recommendations. https://doi.org/10.1145/2959100.2959190
10. DeFino, D.J.: The HBO effect (2013). https://www.bloomsbury.com/uk/the-hbo-effect-9781441180438/
11. Digital 2019: Global Digital Overview—DataReportal – Global Digital Insights (n.d.). https://datareportal.com/reports/digital-2019-global-digital-overview. Accessed 11 October 2019

12. DNA's Comedy Lab | Comedy Lab (n.d.). https://www.dnascomedylab.com/#about. Accessed 5 October 2019
13. How Does the YouTube Algorithm Work? A Guide to Getting More Views (n.d.). https://blog.hootsuite.com/how-the-youtube-algorithm-works/. Accessed 4 May 2019
14. Is This the End of the TV Writers' Room as We Know It? | Vanity Fair (n.d.). https://www.vanityfair.com/hollywood/2018/08/the-end-of-the-tv-writers-room-as-we-know-it-mini-rooms. Accesses 3 October 2019
15. Margarat Valentine, M., Kulkarni, V.: A model for predicting movie's performance using online rating and revenue. Int. J. Sci. Eng. Res. **4**(9) (2013). http://www.ijser.org
16. Murtagh, F., Ganz, A., McKie, S.: The Structure of Narrative: the Case of Film Scripts. Royal Holloway, University of London (2018). https://arxiv.org/pdf/0805.3799.pdf
17. New Changes to YouTube Monetization in 2018 to Better Protect Creators (n.d.). https://digitalready.co/blog/new-changes-to-youtube-monetization-in-2018-to-better-protect-creators. Accesses 5 May 2019
18. Ries, E.: The Lean Startup: How Today's Entrepreneurs Use Continuous Innovation to Create Radically Successful Businesses, 1st edn. Crown Business, New York (2011)
19. Shatz, M., Helitzer, M.: Comedy Writing Secrets: The Best-Selling Guide to Writing Funny & Getting Paid for It. Penguin, New York (2016)
20. The 20 types of YouTube videos with most views in the UK (n.d.). https://blog.printsome.com/top-20-types-of-videos-with-most-views-on-youtube/. Accesses 4 May 2019
21. The golden age of YouTube is over - The Verge (n.d.). https://www.theverge.com/2019/4/5/18287318/youtube-logan-paul-pewdiepie-demonetization-adpocalypse-premium-influencers-creators. Accessed 4 October 2019
22. Why You Must Unlearn What You Know About the YouTube Algorithm (n.d.). https://www.searchenginejournal.com/youtube-algorithm-findings/296291/#close. Accessed 5 May 2019
23. Why you should have a pre-launch campaign (n.d.). https://www.thrinacia.com/blog/post/why-you-should-have-a-pre-launch-campaign. Accessed 5 October 2019

A Proposal of Optimal Wavelet Based Smoothing for EGG Signal Trend Detection

Jan Kubicek[✉], Jana Kosturikova, Dominik Vilimek, Marek Penhaker,
Martin Augustynek, Martin Cerny, David Oczka, and Daniel Barvik

FEECS, VSB-Technical University of Ostrava, K450, 17. Listopadu 15,
Ostrava-Poruba, Czech Republic
{jan.kubicek,jana.kosturikova.st,dominik.vilimek,marek.penhaker,
martin.augustynek,martin.cerny,david.oczka,daniel.barvik}@vsb.cz

Abstract. Despite knowing the electrogastrography (EGG) for many years, there are still open issues regarding its measurement and processing. In the comparison with other electrophysiological signals, like is electrocardiography (ECG), we still miss a unified scheme for the placement of electrodes and EGG evaluation. In this paper, we analyze the possibilities of the Wavelet transformation for elimination of the ECG influence in the EGG records with the goal to obtain the EGG trend signal. In our analysis, we tested different settings of Wavelet based smoothing to evaluate an optimal setting for the Wavelet based smoothing filter. In this study, we bring an objective evaluation of the comparative analysis of individual Wavelet filters with the goal the EGG trend detection. EGG activity was measured via standardized laboratory conditions with system g.tec. All the measurements were done for set of 10 volunteers who consumed predefined same food to observe the gastric waves as for an empty stomach, and specific groceries.

Keywords: EGG · Smoothing filter · Wavelet transformation · Objective evaluation · Gastric waves

1 Introduction

EGG, also called electrogastrography, has recently gained a significant attention due to many benefits. At first, it is a non-invasive approach for evaluation of the gastric activity [1, 2]. This method enables recording slow gastric waves, representing the gastric function. Also, based on the interpretation of this method, it is possible to track and evaluate acute and chronical gastric disorder. Since this method has been well known for many years, it is still attractive for a wide research community [1, 3]. From the clinical point of the view, it is important to define world-wide clinically acceptable standards for EGG evaluation and interpretation. From the technical point of the view, there are a lot of open issues which are challenging for the research community. Firstly, it is hardware platform for detection and measurement of the EGG signal. In this context, there is not a unified standard for the hardware requirements [4–6].

© Springer Nature Singapore Pte Ltd. 2020
P. Sitek et al. (Eds.): ACIIDS 2020, CCIS 1178, pp. 238–248, 2020.
https://doi.org/10.1007/978-981-15-3380-8_21

Regarding measurement procedure, based on the most studies, it is recommended to use the conventional ECG surface electrodes for detection and recording the EGG activity. A significantly challenging issue of EGG analysis is placing the EGG electrodes. For this task, we have not had a unified electrodes placement, like is in the case of ECG. Based on the recent literature, there are some recommended electrode schemes which can detect the EGG activity [6–8]. The most common configuration represents a unipolar scheme where the active electrodes are placed on the stomach wall in short distance between each other, and the reference electrode should be placed somewhere where we can either exclude, or completely eliminate electromyographical artifacts. It is recommended a spur of the hip bone or sternal bone [8, 9]. Such configuration can detect the slow gastric waves, which can be observable in the characteristic EGG frequencies. In such configurations, we must consider of the influence of other electrophysiological signals, especially including ECG activity. Since we measure EGG activity close to the heart, the ECG spikes may be significantly presented in the EGG signal and should be eliminated [10, 11].

The most significant issue in EGG analysis is signal processing. We should be aware that the gastric activity is commonly influence by surrounding electrophysiological signals, especially ECG and EMG activity. These phenomena have tendencies to influence morphological properties of the EGG signal thus, modify its frequency spectra, yielding to distortion of the slow wave's activity. In this context, signal smoothing is challenging to remove the ECG artefacts and noise, which do not have the EGG origin, and in the same time perceive the EGG signal trend. For this task, the Wavelet transformation appears to be a suitable alternative for signal smoothing due to plenty settings which make from Wavelet robust method for the EGG smoothing. On the other hand, we have to deal with selection of the most suitable wavelet settings which removes the aforementioned artifacts, and in the same time perceives the EGG trend. EGG signal after smoothing enables extraction of clinically important parameters for classification and tracking the significant EGG events, often linked with the pathological disorders of stomach [1, 10, 11].

2 Related Work

In this chapter, we state the recent advances and notes which are known for the EGG signal measurement and analysis. In spite of EGG signal has been known for more than 100 years, it is still challenging issue for the research community due to not defining standards as for the measurement and for the EGG evaluation [1, 2].

EGG is a diagnostic method, which records bioelectrical stomach potentials by using electrogastrograph. The most common target is an examination of gastrointestinal tract (GIT). The resulting time-depend recording is called electrogastrogram [12, 13]. We recognize invasive (intracranial stomach) and non-invasive (percutaneous) detection of the stomach activity [11, 12].

For the EGG processing, we lack any standardization for detection and evaluation, when comparing with different methods, like is ECG or EEG. Even there is not a unified approach to evoke GIT function. Regarding the EGG measurement, in many applications they use Smithe and Hain electrod placement, utilizing eight-channel bipolar measurement. Individual electrodes are placed in one diagonal line within the stomach area [12, 13].

A membrane cell potential of smooth muscles is in the range: -60mV$:-75$mV and -20mV$:-40$mV. A spontaneous electrical activity of the stomach begins in the pacemaker area within creation of a so-called basal electrical rhythm – slow waves. In the EGG signal we recognize two types of the activity: ECA – controlling activity, which is not a consequence of the smooth muscles, and ERA, which is denoted as response activity, as a result of the smooth muscles contraction. This activity is noticeable nearly after ECA activity [14–16]. The greatest complication in these activities is the amplitude range. While the peak values of in vitro cells reach up to $0.1-10$mV, in the case of the percutaneous detection it is only $10-500\mu$V. For such detection it is needed to have sensitive amplifier and consider the influence of adjacent bio signals, like is the ECG, whose amplitudes multiple overcome the EGG signal. Therefore, the EGG filtration is one of the most common and important procedures for the EGG processing [17–19].

3   Design of Experimental EGG Measurement

In this experiment, 10 volunteers within the age range 23–25 years participated. We performed the EGG measurement with two meals. This scheme was selected due to analysis how the food stiffness can influence the stomach function and manifestation of the EGG signal.

The measurement was realized four-channel, with using of the ECG electrodes (Ag/AgCl) and amplifier g.USBamp from g.tec company, connected with software MATLAB. In the Simulink, we designed the measuring procedure (Fig. 1) for the real-time EGG signal processing and evaluation. The g.tec amplifier has 16 monopolar channels and 4 independent grounds, which may be connected among each other. This system also contains 24-bit A/D convertor. For the EGG measurement, we set the following parameters:

- Selected channels
- Sampling frequency: 128 Hz or 256 Hz (we use 128 Hz)
- NOTCH filter for elimination of 50 Hz site noise

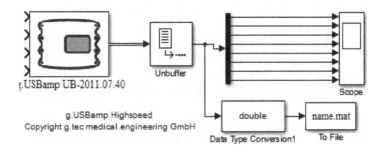

Fig. 1. Simulink environment for real-time measurement and analysis of EGG signal

The EGG measurement was divided into two parts with consuming predefined food. We were aimed to compare a food intake against an empty stomach activity as a reference level. Firstly, we tested a cream yoghurt (1017 kJ = 243.063 kcal), in the second phase we tested sandwich (2x dark toast bread, 2x slice of 30% cheese and 1x slice of ham: together approximately 1065 kJ = 254.535 kcal). In the both cases, volunteers were given a small cup with warm tea. We required several rules before the EGG measurements:

- Having an empty stomach at least 6 h before the measurement
- Not drinking 2 h before the measurement
- Reduce (at least 2 days before the measurement) all the medicaments, may influence the stomach motility

Before the measurement, skin was cleaned with a cosmetic tampon in the area of electrode placement. Consequently, a conductive gel was applied, which was penetrated into the skin. The reference electrode was placed between the processus xiphoideus and navel. The active electrodes were placed in a square configuration, as it is seen in the Fig. 2. The ground electrode was placed on the flank. We recorded 17-min pre-prandial EGG activity and 30-min post-prandial activity.

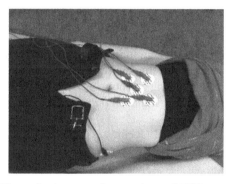

Fig. 2. Electrode placement for experimental EGG measurement

4   Wavelet-Based Smoothing of EGG Signal

In this chapter, we describe the process of the Wavelet transformation for EGG signal smoothing. As we expected, the ECG signal represents a significant problem for the EGG activity measurement. The ECG spikes are linked with the ECG signal trend, which makes the ECG signal badly evaluable. Therefore, we test and analyze various settings of the Wavelet based filtration for the EGG signal smoothing. The Wavelet transformation allows the signal decomposition into predefined levels, corresponding with certain frequency bands. By using this assumption, we can classify the EGG activity from other artifacts and noise. The basis formulation of the Wavelet transformation is following:

$$WT(\tau, s) = \frac{1}{\sqrt{s}} \int_{-\infty}^{\infty} f(t) \overline{\psi\left(\frac{t-\tau}{s}\right)} dt \tag{1}$$

Where $f(t)$ is the analyzed signal, ψ is a wave, s is the scale and τ represents the wave's shift within the time axis. By using the Wavelet transformation, we can decompose the EGG signal into individual levels (l). Localization of the signal components is controlled by using a suitable Wavelet function. In our analysis, we tested six wavelets: Haar, Daubechies (Db), Mayer, Coiflet, Symlet and Biorthogonal wave.

Result of the Wavelet transformation is a sequence of the Wavelet coefficients, representing the EGG signal in the time-frequency domain. In the case of the Wavelet coefficients we suppose that some of these coefficients represent the EGG signal, others represent noise and artifacts. In this context, we need to perform thresholding of these coefficients to detect the EGG trend. In the EGG trend detection, we define the following parameters, determining the process of the EGG smoothing.

- **Thresholding rule:** versatile thresholding (*sqtwolog*), thresholding with using minima and maxima (*minimaxi*), heuristic (*heursure*) Stein balanced estimation of mean quadratic error.
- **Thresholding type:** soft thresholding, which utilizes the fuzzy logic (s) or hard thresholding (*h*). The soft thresholding (Eq. 2) eliminates discontinuities, in the comparison with the hard thresholding.

$$w' = \begin{cases} sgn(w) * (|w| - th), |w| \geq th \\ 0, |w| < th \end{cases} \tag{2}$$

Where $sgn(w)$ denotes to the signum function and th is the set threshold.

- **Multiplicative scale change and thresholding:** we test an alternative with no scale (*one*), with a scale change, utilizing one noise estimation based on the coefficients of I. level (*sln*) or more noise level estimation (*mln*).

The Second part of the proposed EGG filter is the median filter. This statistical filter is used for smoothing of rapid oscillations which are not suppressed by the Wavelet filtration. This filter works on the principle of a moving window, going through the EGG signal an compute median for each shift of this window. We experimentally set the window length 50 samples.

5 Testing and Evaluation

In this section, we present the results of EGG signals and methods for evaluation of effectivity and robustness of the proposed filter for EGG trend detection. Each volunteer was measured two signals to compare individual activity, evoked by specific food. Shorter EGG signal on an empty stomach (pre-prandial signal) against longer (post-prandial 30 min) EGG signal, representing the stomach function after consuming some food. Post-prandial should be generally longer due to detection the activity, representing food processing, which exhibit differently and various time in each individual. In Fig. 3, we present an extract of the EGG signals.

The main issue, which we tackle with, is selection of the most suitable Wavelet for identification of the EGG trend signal. As we aforementioned, we tested 6 mother's wavelets (Haar, Daubechies (Db), Mayer, Coiflet, Symlet and Biorthogonal wave). These wavelets seem to be appropriate for the EGG analysis due to similar morphological features with the EGG signal. A robustness of the proposed scheme was tested by using additive synthetic noise with dynamic power applied on the raw EGG signals. We used the Gaussian white noise (Fig. 4) with the power: 100, 150 and 200 μW. Thus, raw EGG signal represents reference signal for testing each mother's wavelet.

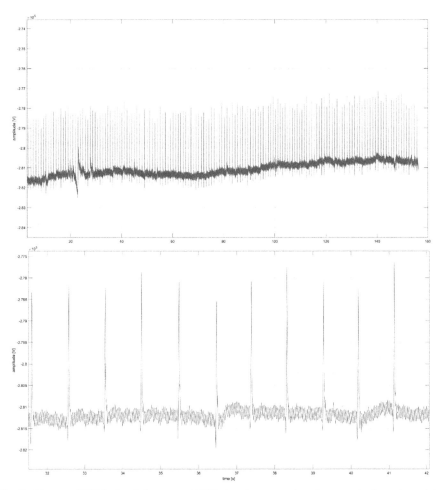

Fig. 3. Extract of EGG signal: long-term EGG signal representing slow trend of gastric activity and dominant peaks, representing R waves of ECG signal (up) and short extract of the ECG signal (below)

On such noise-modified signals we applied the Wavelet based smoothing procedure completed with the median filter. We performed testing for all the six types of wavelets. For each wavelet, we tested various levels of decomposition: $l = 3, 5, 7, 11, 15$. This Wavelet scheme was tested for the thresholding settings: thresholding rules and types

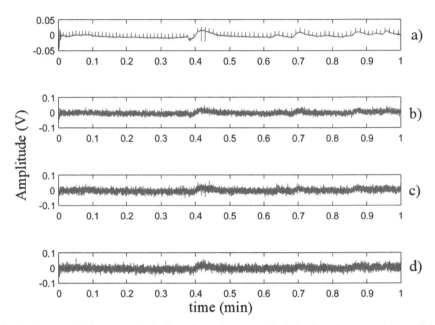

Fig. 4. Process of adding synthetic Gaussian noise to test the Wavelet robustness: (a) raw EGG record, (b) Gaussian noise with 100 μW, (c) Gaussian noise with 150 μW and (c) Gaussian noise with 200 μW

and multiplicative scale change and thresholding. Evaluation of each such thresholding scheme was done based on the objective measurement. The following parameters for evaluation were considered:

- **Correlation coefficient (Corr)** measures the level of a linear dependency between raw EGG signal and the EGG signal with the Gaussian noise. This parameter has the standardized range within: [0; 1] where 0 indicates no similarity between the signals, while 1 stands for the full correlation. Higher values indicate better result.
- **Mean Squared Error (MSE)** indicates average quadratic difference between EGG signals. This parameter compares signals samples in the same positions. Lower values indicate better result. MSE is given by following term:

$$MSE = \frac{1}{N} \sum_{i=1}^{N} (y_r - y_t)^2 \tag{3}$$

where $y_r - y_t$ represents variance of the estimation.

- **Euclidean distance (ED)** represent the Euclidean metric. By using this parameter we measure a distance between each two samples in 2D cartesian space by the following equation:

$$ED(y_r, y_t) = \sqrt{(y_{rx} - y_{tx})^2 + (y_{ry} - y_{ty})^2} \tag{4}$$

As well as in the previous case lower values indicate better results.

Each Wavelet and its setting were applied on the EGG signals of all 10 volunteers. Individual parameters were averaged. In the Fig. 5, we report median values for the best Wavelets settings (for each type of Wavelet).

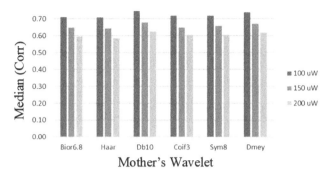

Fig. 5. A comparative analysis of correlation for best settings for correlation between raw EGG signal (reference) and EGG signal corrupted with Gaussian noise for different noise power

Apparently higher noise power more deteriorates EGG signal. This trend is also declared in the Fig. 5 by descending tendency of correlation. Based on the comparative analysis, we evaluated the mother's wave Daubechies 10 (Db 10) with the thresholding settings: heuristic soft thresholding. In the Table 1, we report results for Db 10 with level of the decomposition 7 for all the parameters, which were used for evaluation. Contrarily, in the Table 2, we report same comparative analysis for Db 10, but with the level of decomposition 15. Such high level of decomposition significantly suppress signal components, which is also observable on the evaluation parameters.

Table 1. Averaged evaluation results for Db 10 ($l = 7$) wave for different noise power

Gaussian power (μW)	Corr (%)	MSE (-)	ED (-)
100	73	0.009	2.14
150	66	0.015	2.65
200	59	0.084	2.98

In the combination with Wavelet based transformation, we use the median filter for the EGG signal smoothing. Since the Wavelet transformation is sometimes unable to remove oscillating components (glitches), median-based statistical filtration is aimed on removing such components and performs the last stage of the EGG filtration. In the Figs. 6 and 7, we report results of the Wavelet-based and median filtration to EGG trend detection.

Table 2. Averaged evaluation results for Db 10 ($l = 15$) wave for different noise power

Gaussian power (μW)	Corr (%)	MSE (-)	ED (-)
100	61	0.08	4.11
150	48	0.11	5.25
200	32	0.81	6.74

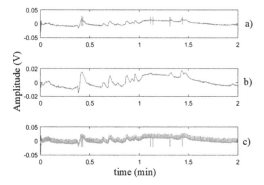

Fig. 6. A process of hybrid wavelet-based filtration method for EGG trend detection: (a) Wavelet based smoothing with Db 10 and $l = 7$, (b) median filtration and (c) hybrid Wavelet-based and median filter for EGG trend detection, indicated as green (Color figure online)

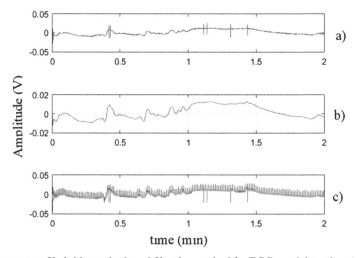

Fig. 7. A process of hybrid wavelet-based filtration method for EGG trend detection: (a) Wavelet based smoothing with Db 10 and $l = 15$, (b) median filtration and (c) hybrid Wavelet-based and median filter for EGG trend detection, indicated as green (Color figure online)

6   Discussion

In this paper, we present a hybrid filtration system, comprising Wavelet transformation and median filter for smoothing the EGG signal. EGG signal does not have standard for measurement and evaluation; therefore, it is still challenging issue for the research community. In this paper, we are focused on the fact that the EGG signal is commonly affected with adjacent electrophysiological signals, where the most dominant influence can be expected on ECG and EMG due to investigating the stomach area, which is close to the heart. Such signals significantly impair the EGG signal and make impossible the EGG evaluation.

We prose a hybrid filter, taking advantage the features of Wavelet transformation and median filter. In the context of the Wavelet transformation, we usually solve a crucial task which relates to suitable Wavelet's settings and filtration procedure to detect the signal trend, and simultaneously suppress the signal noise and artifacts. We publish a comparative analysis of six selected mother's wavelets, levels of decomposition and the thresholding settings to select the most suitable Wavelet settings. We did this analysis within applying the additive Gaussian noise with dynamic noise power. As a part of our analysis, we compared the EGG signals on empty stomach and after food consumption. In this context, we compared average power in this signals. In this analysis, we measured a higher power after food consumption.

The main limitation of the Wavelet transformation is an effective approach of the Wavelet selection. We publish comparative analysis of selected Wavelet settings, nevertheless, other mother's wavelets and settings may be included in the analysis. Such testing procedure is time demanding furthermore, when perform testing in a large EGG database. Therefore, in the future time, the main attention should be paid to incorporating intelligent methods, like is the genetic algorithms or evolutionary computing to build an optimization procedure, which will be able to find the most suitable Wavelet settings.

Acknowledgement. The work and the contributions were supported by the project SV450994/2101Biomedical Engineering Systems XV'. This study was also supported by the research project The Czech Science Foundation (GACR) 2017 No. 17-03037S Investment evaluation of medical device development run at the Faculty of Informatics and Management, University of Hradec Kralove, Czech Republic. This study was supported by the research project The Czech Science Foundation (TACR) ETA No. TL01000302 Medical Devices development as an effective investment for public and private entities.

References

1. Al-Tae, A.A., Al-Jumaily, A.: Electrogastrogram based medical applications an overview and processing frame work. In: Madureira, A.M., Abraham, A., Gandhi, N., Varela, M.L. (eds.) HIS 2018. AISC, vol. 923, pp. 511–520. Springer, Cham (2020). https://doi.org/10.1007/978-3-030-14347-3_50
2. Popović, N.B., Miljković, N., Stojmenova, K., Jakus, G., Prodanov, M., Sodnik, J.: Lessons learned: gastric motility assessment during driving simulation. Sensors **19**(14) (2019). Article no. 3175

3. Popović, N.B., Miljković, N., Popović, M.B.: Simple gastric motility assessment method with a single-channel electrogastrogram. Biomed. Tech. **64**(2), 177–185 (2019)

4. Kubicek, J., et al.: A proposal of optimal wavelet filter design for EGG signal decomposition based on modified ABC evolutionary optimization. In: SAMI 2019 - IEEE 17th World Symposium on Applied Machine Intelligence and Informatics, Proceedings, pp. 83–88 (2019). Article no. 8782785

5. Matsuura, Y., Takada, H.: Comparison of electrogastrograms in a seated posture with those in a supine posture using wayland algorithm: for the evaluation of motion sickness induced by stereoscopic movies. In: 13th International Conference on Computer Science and Education, ICCSE 2018, pp. 804–808 (2018). Article no. 8468840

6. Mika, B., Komorowski, D., Tkacz, E.: Assessment of slow wave propagation in multichannel electrogastrography by using noise-assisted multivariate empirical mode decomposition and cross-covariance analysis. Comput. Biol. Med. **100**, 305–315 (2018)

7. Homaeinezhad, M.R., Ghaffari, A., Rahmani, R.: Review: multi-lead discrete wavelet-based ECG arrhythmia recognition via sequential particle support vector machine classifiers. J. Med. Biol. Eng. **32**(6), 381–396 (2012)

8. Lentka, Ł., Smulko, J.: Methods of trend removal in electrochemical noise data – overview. Meas. J. Int. Meas. Confed. **131**, 569–581 (2019)

9. Al Kafee, A., Akan, A.: Analysis of gastric myoelectrical activity from the electrogastrogram signals based on wavelet transform and line length feature. Proc. Inst. Mech. Eng. Part H J. Eng. Med. **232**(4), 403–411 (2018)

10. Poscente, M.D., Mintchev, M.P.: Enhanced electrogastrography: a realistic way to salvage a promise that was never kept? World J. Gastroenterol. **23**(25), 4517–4528 (2017)

11. Gharibans, A.A., Kim, S., Kunkel, D.C., Coleman, T.P.: High-resolution electrogastrogram: a novel, noninvasive method for determining gastric slow-wave direction and speed. IEEE Trans. Biomed. Eng. **64**(4), 807–815 (2017). Article no. 7488203

12. Okkesim, S., et al.: Line length feature of the electrogastrogram for delayed gastric emptying diagnosis. In: 2016 IEEE International Conference on Signal and Image Processing, ICSIP 2016, pp. 462–465 (2017). Article no. 7888305

13. Reynolds, G.W., Lentle, R.G., Janssen, P.W.M., Hulls, C.M.: Continuous wavelet analysis of postprandial EGGs suggests sustained gastric slow waves may be slow to develop in infants with colic. Neurogastroenterol. Motil. **29**(3) (2017). Article no. e12948

14. Komorowski, D., Pietraszek, S.: The use of continuous wavelet transform based on the fast fourier transform in the analysis of multi-channel electrogastrography recordings. J. Med. Syst. **40**(1), 1–15 (2016). Article no. 10

15. Curilem, M., et al.: Comparison of artificial neural networks an support vector machines for feature selection in electrogastrography signal processing. In: 2010 Annual International Conference of the IEEE Engineering in Medicine and Biology Society, EMBC 2010, pp. 2774–2777 (2010). Article no. 5626362

16. Yacin, S.M., Manivannan, M., Chakravarthy, V.S.: On non-invasive measurement of gastric motility from finger photoplethysmographic signal. Ann. Biomed. Eng. **38**(12), 3744–3755 (2010)

17. Levine, M.E., Koch, S.Y., Koch, K.L.: Lipase supplementation before a high-fat meal reduces perceptions of fullness in healthy subjects. Gut Liver **9**(4), 464–469 (2015)

18. Khan, M.F., Atteeq, M., Qureshi, A.N.: Computer aided detection of normal and abnormal heart sound using PCG. In: ACM International Conference Proceeding Series, pp. 94–99 (2019)

19. Wang, Z.S., Elsenbruch, S., Orr, W.C., Chen, J.D.Z.: Detection of gastric slow wave uncoupling from multi-channel electrogastrogram: Validations and applications. Neurogastroenterol. Motil. **15**(5), 457–465 (2003)

Development of Smartphone Application for Evaluation of Passenger Comfort

Juraj Machaj[1](✉) ⓘ, Peter Brida[1] ⓘ, Ondrej Krejcar[2] ⓘ, Milica Petkovic[3] ⓘ, and Quingjiang Shi[4]

[1] Faculty of Electrical Engineering and Information Technology, Department of Multimedia and Information-Communication Technology, University of Zilina, Univerzitna 1, 010 26 Zilina, Slovakia
{juraj.machaj,peter.brida}@feit.uniza.sk
[2] Center for Basic and Applied Research, Faculty of Informatics and Management, University of Hradec Kralove, Rokitanskeho 62, 500 03 Hradec Kralove, Czech Republic
ondrej.krejcar@uhk.cz
[3] Faculty of Technical Sciences, University of Novi Sad, Trg Dositeja Obradovića 6, 21000 Novi Sad, Serbia
milica.petkovic@uns.ac.rs
[4] School of Software Engineering, Tongji University, 4800 Cao an Road, 201804 Shanghai, China
shiqj@tongji.edu.cn

Abstract. Nowadays, smartphones are not utilized for communications only. Smartphones are equipped with a lot of sensors that can be utilized for different purposes. For example, inertial sensors have been used extensively in recent years for measuring and monitoring performance in many different applications. Basically, data from the sensors are utilized for estimation of smartphone orientation. There is a lot of applications which can utilize these data. This paper deals with an algorithm developed for inertial sensors data utilization for vehicle passenger comfort assessment.

Keywords: Inertial sensors · Smartphones · Passenger comfort · Transport systems

1 Introduction

In recent time transport systems are facing significant changes in the behaviour of passengers. This might be caused by increased awareness about pollution generated by cars, as well as the development of new services allowing shared mobility. The idea of shared mobility is that a group of passengers share a single vehicle for their journey.

With the development of intelligent transport system, there is a large amount of data that can be used to improve provided services and thus comfort levels of passengers. However, passengers comfort levels can be decreased by aggressive driving.

In order to keep the passengers safe and satisfied drivers of shared cars, or any other service like UBER, DiDi etc., should not drive aggressively and dangerously. If such

© Springer Nature Singapore Pte Ltd. 2020
P. Sitek et al. (Eds.): ACIIDS 2020, CCIS 1178, pp. 249–259, 2020.
https://doi.org/10.1007/978-981-15-3380-8_22

drivers are present in the system, they should be identified and denied to provide further service. This can be done by collecting feedback from the passengers. However, passengers might be in a hurry or not willing to provide feedback in the mobile application.

In this paper, we propose a solution for the automatic evaluation of passenger comfort, which can run on a smartphone device. The motivation is to allow the collection of information about driver behaviour on a widely used platform. A similar system was used to analyze the impact of different materials used to build transport infrastructure on the comfort level of passengers in [1, 2]. However, this system was based on a device specifically designed to provide the required data. Since this specialized device has to be implemented in all tested vehicles, its implementation on a greater scale would be financially ineffective. Therefore, we proposed a solution to use data from the Inertial Measurement Unit (IMU) inbuilt in the majority of current smartphones. This should allow wide adoption of the solution without any hardware costs since smartphones are used ubiquitously.

The rest of the paper is organized as follows, the next section will describe IMU and individual sensors that could be used for the purpose of comfort level assessment, Sect. 3 will introduce the proposed solution. Analysis of the achieved results will be provided in Sect. 4 and Sect. 5 will conclude the paper.

2 Inertial Measurement Units

The inertial measurement unit consists of multiple sensors that are used to detect and measure external forces applied to the device. Typically, IMU consists of Accelerometer, Gyroscope and Magnetometer sensors [3–12]. These sensors are used to measure acceleration using gravitational force, orientation and variations of a magnetic field, respectively. Variations of a magnetic field can be used to estimate heading of the device with respect to North, however, measurements are affected by disturbances of a magnetic field caused by metal objects. Since in the proposed solution data from accelerometer and gyroscopes are used, these will be described in more detail.

2.1 Accelerometer

The accelerometer can be used to measure acceleration using inertial parameters of objects. In case when an object is still, the accelerometer will report acceleration equal approximately to 9.81 ms^{-1} which represent the gravitational force of the Earth. The accelerometer cannot separate gravitational force from other acceleration forces affecting the device, therefore the gravitational force has to be compensated in the application.

Accelerometers implemented in the smartphones are using micro-electro-mechanical systems (MEMS). Their accelerometers can measure acceleration only in one direction, perpendicular to axis od the matrix. Therefore, in order to provide measurements in all axes, three MEMS accelerometers must be implemented.

2.2 Gyroscope

Gyroscope is a device able to sense an angular velocity of the object. A triple-axis gyroscope can measure rotation around three axes: x, y, and z. There are MEMS gyros implemented in smartphones because the quality is sufficient at a reasonable price. The gyroscope sensor within the MEMS is very small (between 1 to 100 μm). If the gyro is rotated, a small resonating mass is shifted as the angular velocity changes. The principle is based on Coriolis force

$$\mathbf{F_{cor}} = 2m(\boldsymbol{\omega} \times \mathbf{v}), \tag{1}$$

where m is the weight of a vibrating element, $\boldsymbol{\omega}$ is angular velocity, $\mathbf{v}$ is the speed of the element and $\mathbf{F_{cor}}$ is Coriolis force.

2.3 Measurement Errors

The measured data from the sensors are influenced by measurement errors. The physical properties of these sensors change over time which results in different characteristics over time. Following phenomenon should be considered when IMU measurements are used:

- Repeatability: It is the ability of the sensor to deliver the same output for the same repeated input, assuming all other conditions are the same
- Stability: It is the ability of the sensor to deliver the same output, over time, for the same constant input.
- Drift: It is the change of the output over time (zero drift is the change over time with no input).
- Bias: For a given physical input, the sensor outputs a measurement, offset by the bias.
- Noise: the random fluctuation of the output data, can be reduced by filters.

For example, when input rotation is null, the output of the gyro could be nonzero. The equivalent input rotation detected is the bias error. Depending on sensor usage the internal sensor biases may increase over time. In order to compensate these errors, the gyroscope must be calibrated. This is usually done by keeping the gyroscope still and zeroing all the readings.

3 Proposed System

In the proposed system data from both gyroscope and accelerometer sensors are used in order to detect and events that have a negative impact on passenger comfort level, i.e. detection of high acceleration, hard braking, uneven roads, etc. Data from the sensors are, however, affected by noises coming from multiple sources. For example, in Fig. 1 raw data from the accelerometer in the vertical axis during the ride on a road are presented. Under ideal conditions, these data should have constant value as it impacts of gravitational force. However, the acceleration value fluctuates quite significantly. This might be caused by multiple factors, one of them being an uneven road which might have an impact on comfort levels of passengers. Other parameters that can cause fluctuations of the acceleration inv vertical axis include vibrations from the engine, the setting of the car suspension that should reduce the impact of the uneven road but also introduce some secondary fluctuations.

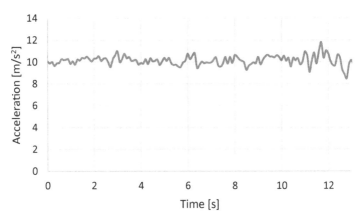

Fig. 1. Vertical acceleration from the raw data

Therefore, to reduce detection error low pass filter was used to smoothen raw data from the IMU. The implemented filter can be described as

$$out(i) = out(i - 1) + \alpha(input(i) - out(i - 1)), \qquad (2)$$

where α is defined as the time constant of filter t divided by the sum of the time constant and time of individual accelerations provided by sensor dT:

$$\alpha = \frac{t}{t + dT}. \qquad (3)$$

Since low past filter should remove high-frequency noises the filtered value should include only changes in acceleration caused by uneven road, the acceleration on vertical axes after filtration is shown in Fig. 2. However, the data are still affected by noises generated by the sensor itself as described in the previous chapter.

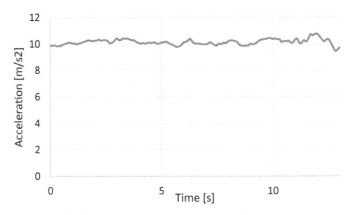

Fig. 2. Vertical acceleration from the filtered data

On the other hand, data from the horizontal plane are not affected by gravitational force in case that vehicle is not going uphill or downhill. In horizontal plane data from 2 axes are collected. Accelerometer data from x-axis represent the change in the speed of the vehicle, as it measures positive or negative acceleration in case of accelerating or slowing down. The data from the y-axis, on the other hand, represent a centrifugal force that is affecting vehicle while driving thru a curve.

These data are not affected by the quality of the road, however, can provide crucial information about the behaviour of the driver. On the other hand, the data are affected by vibrations caused by the vehicle engine. Therefore, the same filtering approach as for vertical axis was applied on both axes in the horizontal plane. In case that driver is driving more aggressively, forces affecting accelerometer will be higher and thus can provide feedback about reckless driving.

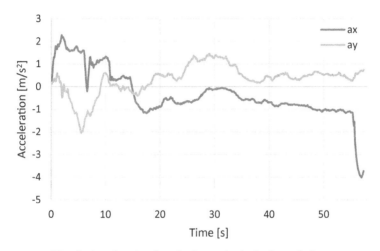

Fig. 3. Acceleration from both axes in the horizontal plane

In Fig. 3 accelerometer data from both axes in the horizontal plane are shown. Data ax is from x-axis that shows acceleration or braking of the car, and ay represents the impact of centrifugal force when the car is driving thru the curve.

When it comes to the data from the gyroscope, the rotation on vertical z-axis gives information about the rotation of the vehicle when driving thru the curve. Rotation on y-axis give information about ascend or descend of the vehicle and rotation on x-axis gives information about uneven roads.

The axes should be fixed to the vehicle and not to the smartphone device, that might have axes shifted due to the position of the device within the vehicle. Therefore, it is required to map axes of the smartphone to axes of the vehicle. This can be done using a transformation matrix for conversion between different coordinate systems. The transformation matrix is defined as:

$$\begin{bmatrix} x^v \\ y^v \\ z^v \end{bmatrix} = \left(R_z^{-1} \left(R_y^{-1} \right) R_x^{-1} \begin{bmatrix} x \\ y \\ z \end{bmatrix} \right), \tag{4}$$

where [x, y, z] are values on axes of the smartphone, x^v, y^v, z^v are axes of vehicle and R_x, R_y, R_z are rotation matrices.

In the first step vertical alignment is performed. To perform vertical alignment 2 approaches were implemented. The first approach is angular velocity method. This method can be applied when the vehicle is going thru the curve. In such case the angular velocity is given by the velocity of vehicle and diameter of the curve and can be expressed as:

$$\omega = \frac{v}{r}. \tag{5}$$

When axes of the gyroscope are mapped to the axes of the car, the vertical z-axis should have significantly higher angular velocity than any other axis. However, if the gyroscope is not aligned with axes of the vehicle the fact that car is turning can be determined based on total angular velocity, given by:

$$\omega_t = \sqrt{\omega_x^2 + \omega_y^2 + \omega_z^2}. \tag{6}$$

Components of the rotation matrix R used for alignment in the vertical axis can be calculated using:

$$\begin{bmatrix} R_x^v \\ R_y^v \\ R_z^v \end{bmatrix} = \frac{1}{\sqrt{\omega_x^2 + \omega_y^2 + \omega_z^2}} \begin{bmatrix} \omega_x \\ \omega_y \\ \omega_z \end{bmatrix}. \tag{7}$$

In Fig. 4 gyroscope data transformed into vehicle coordination system using Eq. (7) are shown.

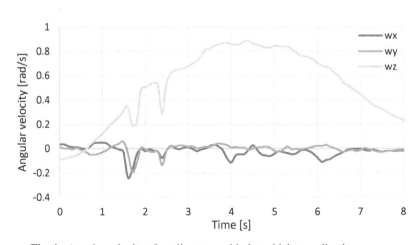

Fig. 4. Angular velocity after alignment with the vehicle coordination system

From the figure, it is obvious that angular velocity on the z-axis is significantly higher than angular velocities recorded on horizontal axes, which are oscillating around 0.

Vertical alignment using angular velocity is suitable when the vehicle is moving on the curve, however, in a situation when the vehicle is not moving or is moving on the straight section of road it is required to use a different approach for alignment of the vertical axis. Under these conditions, gravitational alignment method can be used. In this method data from accelerometers are used. Moreover, it is assumed that the only force that is affecting the IMU measurements is a gravitational force, therefore, this approach work when the vehicle is still or is moving with constant speed on a straight section of the road. In such a case, the total acceleration is given by:

$$a_t = \sqrt{a_x^2 + a_y^2 + a_z^2}, \tag{8}$$

and should be equal to the impact of gravitational force. However, even in a case when the vehicle is moving on the constant speed the acceleration fluctuates due to the uneven surface of the road. Unfortunately, the frequency of this fluctuation cannot be determined, therefore it is not possible to remove it using low pass filter. Anyhow, the rotation matrix for transformation between coordinate systems using gravitational method can be defined as:

$$\begin{bmatrix} R_x^v \\ R_y^v \\ R_z^v \end{bmatrix} = \frac{1}{\sqrt{A_x^2 + A_y^2 + A_z^2}} \begin{bmatrix} A_x \\ A_y \\ A_z \end{bmatrix}, \tag{9}$$

where A_x, A_y, A_z are values of acceleration measured by accelerometers on individual axes.

Horizontal alignment can be performed under two scenarios as well. In the first scenario, the vehicle is accelerating, and the acceleration vector is the same as the direction of the movement. On the other hand, if the vehicle is driving thru the curve on constant speed, then acceleration vector will be perpendicular to the direction of vehicle movement and therefore it will be mapped on the y-axis of the vehicle.

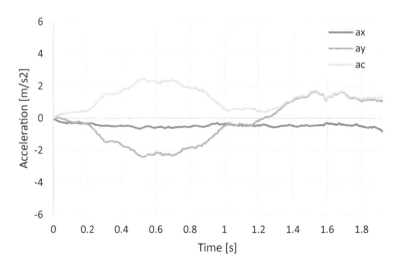

Fig. 5. Measured and calculated acceleration in the horizontal plane

In Fig. 5 real data measured by accelerometers in horizontal plane a_x and a_y are presented together with combined acceleration ac given by:

$$a_c = \sqrt{a_x^2 + a_y^2}. \tag{10}$$

To align horizontal axes, it is required to estimate forces caused by acceleration (or breaking) of the vehicle and map these to x-axis and acceleration caused by centrifugal force that should be mapped to the y-axis. From the figure, it can be seen that the vehicle is moving on the constant speed since acceleration on the x-axis is close to 0. Then, the value of a_c is close to the absolute value of acceleration on the y-axis.

The other option is to align the horizontal axes during vehicle acceleration. The basic assumption is that the vehicle is moving straight forward. In such case value of ac is actually the value of acceleration in the x-axis.

After the data extraction, reduction of data dimensions is performed using Principal Component Analysis (PCA). The goal is to find interconnection between variables. In the first step, the covariance matrix is calculated. In our case relation between vertical and horizontal acceleration is investigated using:

$$\text{cov}(x, y) = \frac{\sum_{i=1}^{n}(x_i - \bar{x})(y_i - \bar{y})}{(n - 1)} = \mathrm{E}[xy] - \mathrm{E}[x]\mathrm{E}[y]. \tag{11}$$

For multiple variables the covariance can be calculated for each pair individually and then covariance matrix can be formed as follows:

$$\mathbf{C} = \begin{pmatrix} \text{cov}(x, x) & \text{cov}(x, y) & \text{cov}(x, z) \\ \text{cov}(y, x) & \text{cov}(y, y) & \text{cov}(y, z) \\ \text{cov}(z, x) & \text{cov}(z, y) & \text{cov}(z, z) \end{pmatrix}. \tag{12}$$

Using equations above it is possible to calculate eigenvalues and eigenvectors. The outcome of PCA is eigenvector $\mathbf{m}$, which represent direction, in which the covariance is the highest, i.e. direction of vehicle movement.

Therefore, it is possible to estimate angle ϕ using:

$$\phi = atan2(m_2, m_1), \tag{13}$$

where m_2 and m_1 are values of eigenvector $\mathbf{m}$.

4   Testing and Evaluation

In order to evaluate the comfort level of passengers in the vehicle, we need to define events that reduce comfort. In this work we have focused on four types of events, namely, fast acceleration, hard braking, hitting potholes on a road, and driving thru curves on high speed.

Each of these events has a different signature on readings from the IMU sensors implemented in the smartphones. In the first step, we had to find threshold values to trigger the detection of the given event. This has been done by test drives with multiple passengers while the driver was driving the same stretch of the road with a different

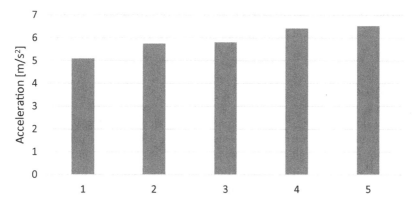

Fig. 6. Thresholds for acceleration marked by 5 passengers

pace. In Fig. 6 the thresholds marked by 5 passengers for acceleration speed that makes them uncomfortable is shown.

From the figure, it is clear that passengers provided different acceleration levels as thresholds for the comfort level, which was expected. However, the settings of the system should consider the lower value of the threshold since, to provide the best results in general. Therefore, the threshold for acceleration was set to 5 m/s^2.

In the next scenario impact of the turning was examined, input provided by passengers is shown in Fig. 7.

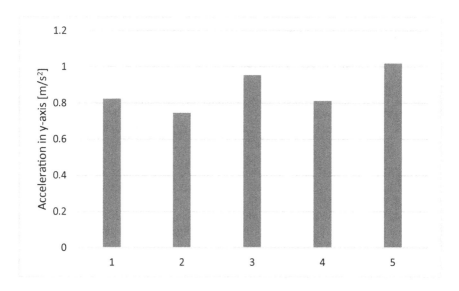

Fig. 7. Thresholds for acceleration on y-axis marked by 5 passengers

From the figure, it is obvious that in y-axis significantly lower acceleration is required to lower the comfort level of passengers. In this case, the acceleration threshold was set to 0.75 m/s^2.

5 Conclusion

In the paper development of a smartphone-based system for automatic evaluation of passenger comfort was described. The system is using data from the IMU implemented in all currently used smartphones. The developed app was tested on multiple passengers to set up thresholds for event detection. However, different passengers reported different threshold values for accelerations on both x and y axes. Therefore, the lowest value was set as a threshold in order to satisfy the preferences of most of the passengers.

In the future we will perform more tests aimed at detection of potholes, that should be visible on changes of acceleration at the vertical axis.

Acknowledgement. This work has been partially supported by the Slovak VEGA grant agency, Project No. 1/0626/19 "Research of mobile objects localization in IoT environment" and European Union's Horizon 2020 research and innovation programme under the Marie Skłodowska-Curie grant agreement No 734331.

References

1. Bodini, I., Lancini, M., Pasinetti, S., Vetturi, D.: Techniques for on-board vibrational passenger comfort monitoring in public transport. ACTA IMEKO **3**(4), 32–37 (2014)
2. Simonyi, E., Fazekas, Z., Gáspár, P.: Smartphone application for assessing various aspects of urban public transport. Transp. Res. Procedia **3**, 185–194 (2014)
3. Passaro, V., Cuccovillo, A., Vaiani, L., De Carlo, M., Campanella, C.E.: Gyroscope technology and applications: a review in the industrial perspective. Sensors **17**(10), 2284 (2017)
4. Davidson, P.: Algorithms for autonomous personal navigation system. Juvenes Print TTY, Tampere (2013). ISBN: 978-952-15-3174-3
5. Renaudin, V., Combettes, C., Peyret, F.: Quaternion based heading estimation with handheld MEMS in indoor environment. In: IEEE/ION Position, Location and Navigation Symposium, May 2014, pp. 645–656 (2014)
6. Penhaker, M., Geyerova, R., et al.: Weariness and vigilance data mining using mobile platform assessment. In: 5th IIAI International Congress on Advanced Applied Informatics (IIAI-AAI), pp. 13–18. IEEE (2016)
7. Bobkowska, K., Inglot, A., Mikusova, M., et al.: Implementation of spatial information for monitoring and analysis of the area around the port using laser scanning techniques. Pol. Marit. Res. **24**(1), 10–15 (2017)
8. Torres-Sospedra, J., Moreira, A.: Analysis of sources of large positioning errors in deterministic fingerprinting. Sensors **17**(12), 2736 (2017)
9. Sevcik, P., Zak, S., Hodon, M.: Wireless sensor network for smart power metering. Concurrency Comput. Pract. Experience **29**(23), e4247 (2017)
10. Racko, J., Brida, P., Perttula, A., Parviainen, J., Collin, J.: Pedestrian dead reckoning with particle filter for handheld smartphone. In: 2016 International Conference on Indoor Positioning and Indoor Navigation (IPIN), pp. 1–7. IEEE (2016)

11. Jimenez, A.R., Seco, F., Prieto, C., Guevara, J.: A comparison of pedestrian dead-reckoning algorithms using a low-cons MEMS IMU. In: IEEE International Symposium on Intelligent Signal Processing, pp. 37–42 (2009)
12. Corrales, J.A., Candelas, F., Torres, F.: Hybrid tracking of human operators using IMU/UWB data fusion by a Kalman Filter. In: 2008 3rd ACM/IEEE International Conference on Human-Robot Interaction (HRI), pp. 193–200. IEEE (2008)

Improving the Robustness of the Cross-Domain Tracking Process

Bede Ravindra Amarasekara$^{(\boxtimes)}$ ⓘ, Anuradha Mathrani ⓘ, and Chris Scogings ⓘ

School of Natural and Computational Sciences, Massey University, Albany, New Zealand
{b.amarasekara,a.s.mathrani,c.scogings}@massey.ac.nz

Abstract. HTTP-cookie based tracking technologies provide efficient and reliable tracking capabilities across web domains on the internet. Different entities track user activity for various purposes. E-commerce practitioners need a reliable tracking system to quantify and reward visitor traffic generators. Business analytic providers track user interactions to generate customer behavioral insight that assist targeted marketing capabilities. Governments and security agencies track user activity to prevent national security threats. In a previous research study, the authors uncovered instances when tracking efforts can fail due to technical limitations, and instances where tracking results can be skewed fraudulently for monetary gain. In this research, we have examined additional tracking techniques that can be combined with the existing tracking methods to improve the robustness of the cookie-based tracking process. Following design science methodology, a domain-based network environment setup with bespoke web server software has been used to investigate the usability and robustness of the proposed tracking techniques.

Keywords: Cross-domain · Tracking · Affiliate marketing · HTTP cookie · XDT

1 Introduction

Cross-domain tracking involves the process of tracking a user's online activity across multiple web domains. In an inherently stateless ecosystem, HTTP protocol has provided the ability to maintain state using HTTP cookie, which still remains the primary method to track online activity [1]. When a webserver sends an HTTP cookie to a client browser with a unique identifier for each visitor, the cookie is saved into the cookie cache of the client's browser. On all subsequent requests to that specific webserver the client browser returns the said cookie, which allows the web server to identify the visitor uniquely on each visit. The HTTP cookie-based tracking system provides an easy, reliable and lightweight tracking technology. Previous research from the authors have explored instances where cookie-based tracking system can fail [2], and also instances in which the cookies can be fraudulently manipulated to deceive the tracking data [3, 4].

This research explores the usability of alternative state management techniques that could supplement HTTP cookie based cross-domain tracking capabilities, to improve the robustness of the underlying technology. A review of existing literature has revealed

© Springer Nature Singapore Pte Ltd. 2020
P. Sitek et al. (Eds.): ACIIDS 2020, CCIS 1178, pp. 260–270, 2020.
https://doi.org/10.1007/978-981-15-3380-8_23

some alternative state management techniques, though they have not been originally designed for that purpose. A test environment for simulation was set up to experiment which of those techniques would be relevant and useful today.

Cross-domain tracking technologies are used in multitude of e-commerce applications and within security and defense contexts, some of which are presented in the next section. Therefore, our research findings can be applied across diverse application environments and lead to more elegant tracking designs that have a great significance in the improvement of reliability and robustness of the underlying technology.

2 Related Literature

Hypertext Transport Protocol (HTTP) is inherently stateless by design. Application "state" is not maintained between calls to an HTTP server. With the development of the Internet and e-commerce activities, a mechanism to manage state was required, and HTTP-cookie was introduced [1]. Most e-commerce applications need a persistent state management mechanism, as it is vital to "remember" choices of individual customers, and to gather behavioral data related to customers habits and preferences. With the ability to persist data within the client computer HTTP-cookie became the de facto tracking technology of choice.

By design, when an HTTP-cookie is received by a client browser from a web server, any subsequent requests to the same web server will be accompanied by the said cookie. The lifespan of the cookie is set by the server. This enables the server to place a cookie on a client browser and track a visitor's interaction with the website over a long period. With HTML5, "Local Storage" was introduced as another reliable method to store data locally within a client browser [5]. As a client-side technology, the webserver cannot interact with the "Local Storage" directly; therefore, all interactions are managed by JavaScript. A unique identifier for each visitor can be stored in "Local Storage". It is less versatile than an HTTP-cookie when used as a tracking technology, as it was not intended for that purpose. It requires extra effort to manage communication between the server and client browsers. Nevertheless, researchers found that "Local Storage" can be utilized for tracking purposes [6, 7]. With the introduction of E-tag as a web cache validation mechanism [8], it was discovered that E-tags too can be used as a tracking mechanism, though it was not the purpose of E-tag either [9].

Flash-cookie or the local storage of adobe flash application, officially named "Local shared objects" has been successfully used in the past as a "super-cookie"; previous research considered it to be almost indestructible as it is not managed by the browser [7, 9, 10]. Blocking of HTTP-cookies on the browser, deleting of cookies, browser cache or browsing history did not have any effect on the Flash-cookie. Even switching to "in-private" browsing could not disable it either, as it is not part of the browser infrastructure. Its purpose was to provide "Local Storage" to Adobe Flash applications. Since the widespread use by third parties for tracking purpose, and the release of since the release of Adobe Flash Player version 10.1, it has been brought in sync with the browser's settings, by blocking access during "in-private" browsing and also when cookies are blocked [11]. Even without the "super-cookie" function, it still would function similar to "Local Storage" provided by HTML5, but it is usability is restricted. This is because

Flash Player is disabled by default in modern browsers and requires explicit user consent. Therefore, flash-cookies were not considered in this research.

As all alternative tracking methods discussed above, except the HTTP cookie were not originally meant for tracking purpose, the evolution of the original requirements they were deemed to serve, will change their usability as a tracking mechanism over time. This research presents the current usability state of those alternative tracking methods and explore the ability to use any of those methods that might still be valid today to supplement the efficacy of cookie-based tracking.

Cross-domain tracking capabilities are useful for different purposes. While tracking information is very useful for commercial and governmental entities who gather data, it can intrude the user's privacy. But it may not always be a negative experience for internet users, as it can improved online user-experience by presenting information that is relevant and remembering user preferences. Some tracking scenarios are a technical necessity as an underlying technology, which do not capture Personally Identifiable Information (PII), which are not considered a privacy threat. Others capture online behavioral data that is combined with PII to create comprehensive user profiles that invade the privacy of users, without their explicit permission. Some usage scenarios are:

- Affiliate Marketing model, which is one of the most cost-efficient online marketing methods available to e-marketing practitioners. It needs the capability to track visitors who are viewing and clicking on advertisements placed on affiliates' websites [12, 13]. The tracking mechanism traces clicks and successful outcomes; and pays commissions to affiliates.
- From an e-commerce perspective, an e-marketer can personalize advertisements that are presented to visitors, depending on the visitor's recent interests, that are determined by the recent browsing history [14]. Without this capability, internet users will feel hassled, when products and services that the internet users are not even vaguely interested in, is displayed at most of the websites they visit [15]. Also, the advertisers will be wasting their marketing budget on audiences that do not yield them any positive outcomes.
- Customer behavioral data within an e-commerce site (e.g. duration spent on site and on specific pages, products perused, success rate, etc.) are useful for a marketer, and can be easily generated within the e-commerce application. By subscribing to an external business analytics provider, such data can be combined with customer demographics obtained through insights over interactions beyond the boundaries of the practitioner, to generate precise information useful for a marketeer [16].
- Security establishments who identify people who are deemed a security threat are monitored across multitude of websites to monitor their activities.
- Companies such as Cambridge Analytica profiles people with the help of their social media affiliations and interests. By using such profiling methods, they are capable of undertaking nefarious activities such as political and elections manipulations in many countries around the globe [17].

3   This Study

This research will focus the study on an e-commerce scenario. Most of the modern e-commerce sites depend on multiple channels to generate visitor traffic. Search Engines and e-marketing strategies using a large network of affiliates require reliable tracking technology to discover the source of the traffic, quantify and to pay the fees and commissions to the advertisers. While some large e-commerce practitioners such as e-bay, amazon.com, etc. manage the tracking process in-house, others choose to entrust it to specialist tracking service providers (TSP).

An Affiliate Marketing Network (AMN) is a typical example of a large network of affiliates who generate web traffic e-commerce sites. Affiliates are popular websites based on diverse themes, that already have a large audience of web traffic. They agree to display advertisements of e-commerce sites for a fee. Some advertisers pay a set fee to affiliates for simply displaying advertisements, while others pay only if a visitor clicks on an advertisement to arrive at the e-commerce site. Yet others pay a commission to affiliates, only if a visitor makes a purchase. A tracking pixel of TSP will be placed on affiliate's webpage, which is usually a small piece of JavaScript, which will cause the visit to be registered on the TSP's tracking server. In case of commission-based advertising, another "conversion-pixel" is placed on the e-commerce site's payment confirmation page, which will cause the TSP's tracking server to register the total prices and the commission amounts due to the affiliate. In spite of the transaction originating and ending at vastly different web domains, possibly over different geographical locations and over a longer time span, the HTTP cookie based tracking process enables the TSP to accurately recognize the affiliate who displayed the advertisement to the customer and reward the affiliate with the correct amount of commission or fee.

But there are instances that the cookie-based tracking process can fail. We discuss some of those scenarios and present methods to make the HTTP based tracking process more robust by supplementing the HTTP cookie-based technology with other technologies that we encountered in our previous research work.

4   Methodology

Information systems research fall broadly in to two research paradigms; behavioral research and design science research. The purpose of design science research is to solve an existing industry problem by producing design artefacts as outputs [18, 19]. Our research aims to solve an existing industry problem on how to make the online cross domain tracking processes more robust. We believe our design science approach has resulted in the elegant design of an artefact that solves an ongoing real-world problem related to cross-domain tracking. The artefact is discussed in the following four sub-sections [18, 20].

4.1   Setting up of Test Environment

An experiment on cross-domain tracking requires multiple domain-based networks on separate IP segments that are interconnected with same network technologies and topologies to mirror the internet settings. From the cross-domain tracking scenarios discussed above, a simulation of an Affiliate Marketing Networks (AMN) was chosen for this experiment, which comprises a minimum of four separate domains. A multi-domain network environment was created using virtual servers as shown in Fig. 1. Each domain based virtual network consisted of a Primary Domain Controller (PDC), Domain Name Server (DNS), a Web Server, a Database Server. Each domain was connected via virtual network infrastructure that allowed inter-domain routing using TCP-IP protocol.

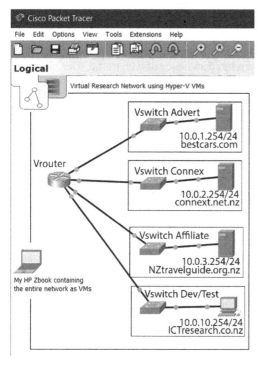

Fig. 1. Virtual network diagram

Only one instance of a tracking server is required to track visitor interactions across all participating domains. Though one instance per each of the other three types of domains (e-commerce, affiliate & visitor) is sufficient to experiment cross-domain tracking functionality, we extended the experiments by adding multiple instances of each of the three categories except the tracking server. Having multiples of each category allowed us to simulate different real-world scenarios that use such cross-domain tracking technology. It allowed us to simulate a real-world AMN that provides tracking services to multiple e-commerce sites. It further allowed us to simulate business analytics services such as Google Analytics, which can gather information relating to customer interactions across diverse network domains. The risks associated with rogue Content Delivery Networks (CDN) were experimented using the multiple domain configuration. Similarly, multiple e-marketing domains allowed us to simulate AMN's with multiple affiliates who display advertisements and generate traffic for the e-commerce sites.

By using virtual servers, adding more e-commerce networks or affiliate networks entailed only making a copy of the master copy of the relevant configuration and setting up the Primary Domain Server to a new domain name and setting the IP address segment to a new segment.

Participating network domains were classified based on their functionalities within a cross-domain tracking scenario into four groups. Each group has then been configured with bespoke software to carry out their specific roles as follows:

1. Domain (connex.net.nz) was configured as a tracking server, with a bespoke software that had the function and ability to track user activities within all other e-commerce domains.
2. Domain EcoTourismPNG.com was added as an e-commerce server.
3. Domain NZtravelguide.org.nz was configured as an e-marketing advertiser for EcoTourismPNG.com simulating an affiliate marketing network.
4. Test computers and mobile devices in Dev domain used to carry out the experiments were placed outside all above domains.

Above bespoke software for the e-commerce sites and for the tracking server were developed as part of this research. This allowed the researchers to add and upgrade functionality during the experiments to suit and incorporate any changing needs.

4.2 Configuration of Tracking Domain

Tracking domain connex.net.nz is at the heart of the tracking process in this study. Multitudes of e-commerce domains and e-marketing domains subscribe to the tracking services provided by the tracking domain. "Pixel-codes" embedded in the webpages belonging to e-commerce and e-marketing sites cause visitor-browsers to "ping" the tracking server at connex.net.nz. This enabled us to test tracking service capabilities for AMNs based on different affiliate marketing models, e.g. display advertising, click advertising and revenue-share advertising models.

4.3 Configuration of E-Commerce Domains

A bespoke e-commerce application was developed with only those functionalities that were needed for conducting the experiment. It contained a basic landing page that displayed products with a payment button which when clicked would register the transaction details in the back-end database. A payment confirmation page was presented to the visitor containing a "conversion pixel" code, which does not have a visual representation, but causes a "ping" at the tracking server at connex.net.nz.

Though the conversion pixel is usually a small JavaScript code provided by the tracking technology provider, the simplest form of conversion pixel can be any kind of resource request from the tracking web server. Apart from an <imp> resource, we successfully tested other requests, such as an iframe, a CSS file, a JavaScript file, etc.

Tracking services can also be used to monitor online customer behavioral activity for the purpose of generating business analytics. In this case the practitioner will embed a pixel in every page that the practitioner wants to include in the analytics data, and thereby monitor page by page navigation and customer interactions. Some service providers instead could use a small JavaScript code that can extract more information from the page as well as any data used by a competitor (using cookies or local storage) and post back a much richer dataset to the tracking server. Such information can also include uniquely identifiable information of the visitor.

4.4   Configuration of Affiliate (E-Marketing) Domains

Affiliates are third-party websites that display advertisements of e-commerce practitioners, for a fee. They are usually simple static websites on popular topics, blogs, music, etc. To track and quantify visitor-traffic generated by each affiliate, the tracking services provider makes available a customized "click-pixel" as a banner advertisement to be embedded into affiliate's webpages. "Display-advertising pixel" codes are set to trigger automatically without any visitor action, at the opening of a page in the browser. Instead of simple HTML pages, our test affiliates were equipped with a combination of server pages and static pages. This allowed us to test through simulation, different fraudulent techniques some affiliates use to defraud the tracking system.

4.5   Configuration of Client Devices

Multiple laptop and desktop computers, and three mobile phones were used as client devices. The computers had Windows 10, Mac OSX and Linux operating systems to verify behavior under each operating system. Each computer had multiple web browsers installed, including Google Chrome, Internet Explorer, Edge, Opera, Safari and Firefox. Experiments were executed using the browsers in standard mode, and "private mode", which allows us to simulate a new visitor originating at a previously known IP address. We also used simulation modes within the browsers, that can simulate different devices such as a mobile device of a specific manufacturer or an operation system, as well as different sized display capabilities. Apart from these simulation capabilities provided by the browser, we also executed our tests using real hardware, using Apple iPhone, Windows Phone environment on a Nokia mobile phone and Android mobile phone.

HTTP cookie and E-tags are both designed for communication between the server and the client browser, primarily for the consumption of the server. E-tags carry the version identifier of a specific resource and entrust the client browser to return it with every request for the same resource, back to the server. The server then compares the returned version identifier with the version identifier currently in possession of the server. If they match, the server sends a result code "304 Not Modified", so that the client browser can use the copy of the resource in its cache. If the E-tags do not match, the Server will send the new version of the resource. As both HTTP-cookies and E-tags are designed for communication of information, the client browsers always send them back to the server. But the purpose of "Local Storage" is to provide web applications ability to store any user-specific data that it may require for its operation locally on the user's computer. As such data does not need to be shared with the server, there is not easy mechanism to send the unique visitor identifier back to the server. Therefore, the interaction between the application and the local storage is through JavaScript, using which we can extract the identifier from local storage and use one of the few different methods to send that information to the server.

4.6   Test Setup

The following test parameters were defined to measure the success of cross-domain tracking. Using HTTP-cookies the following capabilities were ascertained as a baseline for the test environment. Following seven tests were conducted:

- Test 1: Loading a page or clicking a banner on any of the tracked pages of the e-marketing domains causes a visit to be accurately registered on the tracking server.
- Test 2: The ability for payment confirmation pages of e-commerce sites to accurately and reliably transmit the affiliate identifier and total price of the good purchased to the tracking server. These two test capabilities encompass the tracking process needed for an affiliate marketing network.
- Test 3: Ability to simultaneously maintain visitor identity between two windows of the same browser.
- Test 4: Ability to simultaneously maintain visitor identity between two tabs within the same window of a browser.
- Test 5: Despite the "private browsing" mode of a browser, the tracking server has ability to identify a user with a previously saved identifier instead of recording them as a new user.
- Test 6: Ability to identify a visitor uniquely by different browsers within the same device. Usually, browsers do not share cookies, therefore will appear as a new visitor for each browser.
- Test 7: Ability to continue to identify a visitor even after the browser cookies are deleted, using facilities provided by the browser or third-party utilities.

4.7 Experiment Using Local Storage

HTTP-cookie usage was disabled in this experiment. Our aim was to achieve similar or more reliable tracking capability results, as defined by the test parameters above, without the use of HTTP-cookies. As the data stored in the local storage is not automatically sent back to the server, we need some extra effort to make it a part of the client-server communication. All the communication between a webpage and the local storage happens using a JavaScript file that attaches to each tracked webpage for checking the local storage of a previously saved unique identifier. If no unique key/value pair was found, it is considered a first visit to the website, therefore a unique identifier is obtained from the webserver and saved into the client's local storage. If an identifier is found, the visitor is identified, and webserver is notified using a method that fits the requirement. If the web page contents need to be customized dynamically for each visitor, then asynchronous communication (AJAX) is used to transmit the visitor identifier to the webserver, and to receive the customized content by the browser. If the identifier is used only for tracking process, it can be saved into a hidden field within a webform, which becomes available to the server on the next post-back action.

4.8 Experiment Using Entity Tags (E-Tags)

Unlike "Local storage", E-tags are inherently a mode of communication between server and client browsers, like HTTP-cookies. The cookie usage was disabled for this experiment to simulate the tracking mechanism, by only using E-tags.

Tracking-pixels were assigned with the URL of the tracking service. Click-pixels, Conversion-pixels and other tracking-pixels caused the client browsers to send an HTTP-request to the server. As the first step, the server examines the headers for an "If-None-Match" header, which if present indicate the existence of a tracking E-tag. The value of this is the unique identifier of the user and can be used in place of the value read from an HTTP-cookie, in a cookie-based tracking process. If no "If-None-Match" header is found, it indicates the start of a new tracking process, in which case the server adds two new headers to the HTTP-response: "Cache-control" header enabling caching on client and "Etag" header with the visitor's unique identifier as the value.

The same E-tag must be sent repeatedly on every response during all future communication between the webserver and the client browser. Else, a response without an E-tag and Cache-Control header or a directive will cause the browser to not use the previous browser cache, thereby losing the tracking capability of the E-tag.

5 Discussion

The state management methods discussed here are not by design, technologies invented for tracking purposes. HTTP-cookies have nevertheless been used for tracking purposes over a long period and has become the de-facto tracking mechanism. Methods that allows automatic transfer of small amounts of data with each HTTP-request back to the server, without having to implement specific code for such functionality is a good candidate for tracking purpose. It helps establish reliable communication channel between the server and client browser. By design, both HTTP-cookie and E-tags fulfil this condition. Server sets the cookie or the E-tag, and on subsequent requests looks for the cookie (by the name) or the E-tag (by the value). It is the browser's responsibility to send it to the server, with every request. Whereas "Local Storage" is not designed to send its values back to the server. It is meant to be used by the code running on client browser. Therefore, additional efforts are required to extract the information from the local storage and post it back to the server.

The tests have confirmed that the "super cookie" techniques mentioned in the literature do not have the same effects anymore, although they have been effective a few years ago. As these additional techniques for tracking were by design not meant for that purpose, further development of some technologies will inadvertently make them unusable for tracking purposes. Other technologies such as "Adobe Flash Local shared objects" commonly known as "Flash cookies" have been intentionally upgraded, to prevent them being used as tracking technologies. By default, access to flash content is disabled and require user's explicit permission. Ayenson et al. [9] found that E-tag retained their identifier values even when the cookies were blocked in a browser and when using "Private browsing mode". The above results show that all the browsers now block E-tags and Local storage, in both of the above scenarios. Therefore, keeping abreast with current developments of these technologies will enable researchers to adapt to these changes and modify the techniques to keep abreast with these changing technologies.

However, our results in Table 1 show that tracking capabilities using "Local Storage" perform equally well as HTTP-cookie based traditional tracking technologies. Most common browsers have visual indicators on the browser window to show the use of HTTP-cookies within a site. For example, Chrome has a small cookie icon at the end of the URL address bar at the top of the windows. On clicking it, even the least-tech savvy users can delete or even block the cookies to that specific site, thereby failing the tracking process within that browser completely.

Table 1. Test results

	Cookies	Local storage	E-tags
Test 1	Success	Success	Success
Test 2	Success	Success	Success
Test 3	Success	Success	Success
Test 4	Success	Success	Success
Test 5	Fail	Fail	Fail
Test 6	Fail	Fail	Fail
Test 7	Fail	Fail	Partial success

In contrary, the use of local storage is not as visible to the user; therefore, to view the data in the local storage, requires user to dig deeper, such as use the "Developer Tools" that are accessible to users with more technical sophistication. Nevertheless, deleting HTTP-cookies now deletes local storage too, in newer versions of modern browsers.

E-tags have an advantage over the other two methods, as E-tag values are meant for the caching engines and therefore not easily visible to the general user. Also, the tools that are readily accessible on the user interface to remove or block cookies, do not delete the E-tags, though they affect both the HTTP-cookies and local storage. But by removing browsing data including cache history, all identifiers can be removed.

Though we have displayed how these methods could be used without using cookies, for tracking purpose, we are not presenting them as alternatives for HTTP-cookies. While using cookies as the primary means for tracking, we wish to present other methods that we can use in combination with cookie-based tracking, to make the process more robust.

Tests conducted in this study are publicly accessible at connex.net.nz

6 Future Direction

As these methods discussed in this research are not by design meant for tracking purpose, they can change over time. Though HTTP-cookies were originally meant for the purpose of saving application state, it has over time become the de-facto technology also for the purpose of online tracking. Therefore, it can be rightfully expected that any future developments to state-management technologies would still adhere to this requirement too. Similar research efforts can increase the robustness of the tracking technology by supplementing with alternative non-traditional technologies. In this research we have used stateful tracking technologies. It will be useful to investigate how stateless tracking technologies can add to the robustness of the above tracking methods [6, 7, 21]. As those alternative technologies keep changing their capability to be used as a tracking technology, continuous research work adapting to these changes can drive the efficacy of cross-domain tracking capabilities.

References

1. Kristol, D.M.: HTTP State Management Mechanism (RFC 2109). Internet RFCs **2109** (1997)
2. Amarasekara, B.R., Mathrani, A.: Exploring risk and fraud scenarios in affiliate marketing technologies from the advertiser's perspective. In: Australasian Conference in Information Systems 2015, Adelaide (2015)
3. Chachra, N., Savage, S., Voelker, G.M.: Affiliate crookies: characterizing affiliate marketing abuse. In: IMC 2015 Proceedings of the 2015 ACM Conference on Internet Measurement Conference, pp. 41–47. ACM, New York (2015)
4. Edelman, B., Brandi, W.: Risk, information, and incentives in online affiliate marketing. J. Market. Res. **LII**, 1–12 (2015)
5. W3C: W3C Recommendation - Web Storage (2013). 20130730. https://www.w3.org/TR/2013/REC-webstorage-20130730/
6. Englehardt, S., Narayanan, A.: Online tracking: a 1-million-site measurement and analysis. In: Proceedings of the ACM SIGSAC Conference on Computer and Communications Security. Association for Computing Machinery (2016)
7. Laperdrix, P., Rudametkin, W., Baudry, B.: Beauty and the beast: diverting modern web browsers to build unique browser fingerprints. In: 37th IEEE Symposium on Security and Privacy, San Jose (2016)
8. Fielding, R., Reschke, J.: Hypertext Transfer Protocol (HTTP/1.1): Conditional Requests. Internet RFCs **RFC 7232** (2014)
9. Ayenson, M.D., Wambach, D.J., Soltani, A., Good, N., Hoofnagle, C.J.: Flash cookies and privacy II: now with HTML5 and ETag respawning. In: World Wide Web Internet and Web Information Systems (2011)
10. Soltani, A., Canty, S., Mayo, Q., Thomas, L., Hoofnagle, C.J.: Flash cookies and privacy. In: AAAI Spring Symposium: Intelligent Information Privacy Management, pp. 158–163 (2010)
11. Adobe: Adobe Flash Player - Local Settings Manager (2015). https://help.adobe.com/archive/en_US/FlashPlayer/LSM/flp_local_settings_manager.pdf
12. Brear, D., Barnes, S.J.: Assessing the value of online affiliate marketing in the UK financial services industy. Int. J. Electron. Finance (2008)
13. Norouzi, A.: An integrated survey in affiliate marketing network. In: Press Academia Procedia, pp. 299–309 (2017)
14. Libert, T.: Exposing the invisible web: an analysis of third-party HTTP requests on 1 million websites. Int. J. Commun. (2015)
15. Hoofnagle, C.J., Urban, J., Li, S.: Privacy and modern advertising: most us internet users want 'Do Not Track' to stop collection of data about their online activities. In: Amsterdam Privacy Conference (2012)
16. Baumann, A., Haupt, J., Gebert, F., Lessmann, S.: The price of privacy: an evaluation of the economic value of collecting clickstream data. Bus. Inf. Syst. Eng., 1–19 (2018)
17. Richterich, A.: How data-driven research fuelled the Cambridge Analytica controversy. Open J. Sociopolitical Stud. **11**(2), 528–543 (2018)
18. Hevner, A.R., March, S.T., Park, J., Ram, S.: Design science in information systems research. MIS Q. **28**(1), 75–105 (2004)
19. March, S.T., Smith, G.: Design and natural science research on information technology. Decis. Support Syst. **15**(4), 251–266 (1995)
20. Nunamaker, J., Chen, M., Pruding, T.D.M.: Systems development in information systems research. J. Manag. Inf. Syst. **7**(3), 89–106 (1991)
21. Eckersley, P.: How unique is your web browser? In: Atallah, M.J., Hopper, N.J. (eds.) PETS 2010. LNCS, vol. 6205, pp. 1–18. Springer, Heidelberg (2010). https://doi.org/10.1007/978-3-642-14527-8_1

Artificial Intelligence, Optimization, and Databases in Practical Applications

Currency Recognition Based on Deep Feature Selection and Classification

Hung-Cuong Trinh[1], Hoang-Thanh Vo[2], Van-Huy Pham[1], Bhagawan Nath[1], and Van-Dung Hoang[2(✉)]

[1] Faculty of Information Technology, Ton Duc Thang University, Ho Chi Minh City, Vietnam
{trinhhungcuong,phamvanhuy,bhagawanNath}@tdtu.edu.vn
[2] Quang Binh University, Dong Hoi City, Vietnam
thanhhv@qbu.edu.vn, zunghv@gmail.com

Abstract. Advanced technology has played an important role in the circulation of the banknote counterfeit and currency value recognition. This study proposes an approach for the currency recognition based on the fundamental image processing and deep learning for the extraction characteristics and recognition of currency values. The large capacity of traditional techniques was proposed for currency recognition based on infrared spectrometer and chemometrics using special devices. This paper presents a recognition method to detect face values from currency paper and. The proposed method can recognize some kinds of currency values and national currencies. The study investigated and proposed the deep neural network, which reaches appropriate accuracy rate and reduces consumption time. In order to improve accuracy of recognition model, data augmentation techniques are also investigated for training data preprocessing. The experimental results show that the proposed approach is applicable to the practical applications.

Keywords: Currency recognition · Deep feature extraction · Deep learning

1 Introduction

In recent years, object detection and recognition systems have been applied in many fields of intelligent systems such as smart supermarkets, automatic currency exchange machines, security surveillance systems, intelligent human-machine interaction and other industrial applications. However, there are many challenges in banknote recognition procedures such as various appearances, different face and background values, lighting conditions, occlusion for detecting fake material. There are many solutions in the field of currency recognition and authentic ones such as [1–3]. An approach for authentic and counterfeit banknotes based on information on infrared spectroscopy was presented in [1]. The authors have been investigated for discrimination using near-infrared spectroscopy with a portable instrument associated with principal component analysis (PCA) and partial least squares. Similarly, the authors presented an approach for the extraction of characteristics using spectra from neighboring infrared spectrometers, independent soft models of class analogy and associated models of linear discriminant analysis are

© Springer Nature Singapore Pte Ltd. 2020
P. Sitek et al. (Eds.): ACIIDS 2020, CCIS 1178, pp. 273–281, 2020.
https://doi.org/10.1007/978-981-15-3380-8_24

applied for counterfeit and currency value recognition [2]. Unlike the two previous methods, a method used low resolution multispectral images for the detection of counterfeit banknotes [3]. The method used low-resolution images has become difficult for banknote recognition. The limitations of these approaches use special sensors for feature extracting, which is expensive while the multispectral images are able to use as a solution of the counterfeit banknote problem.

In the field of banknote recognition based on image processing in [4] a currency recognition approach based on color SIFT and grayscale SIFT algorithms was presented. The article developed a data set for automatic recognition using the scale-invariant feature transform (SIFT) technique based on color information and gray information. The color image information provides significant functionality for the descriptor, while the gray image support to reduce the number of data dimensions. The experimental results show that an approach using the SIFT method based on color images exceeds the gray images in terms of precision. Another group of researchers [5] presents a banknote recognition system that uses a sensor to discern the image to recognize its naming and anti-counterfeiting characteristics to address some problems such as the recognition of banknotes, the detection of counterfeit banknotes, the recognition of the serial number and the classification of suitability [5]. Some advantages and disadvantages of the methods presented in those studies with both high computational costs and insufficient precision to recognize nominal values and different notes of a specific country. In our approach, the currency recognition system is not limited by any banknote country.

This document focuses on a deep neural construction network for the extraction of functions and the recognition of banknotes. The mosaic of information on paper currency is analyzed to discover the aspect relationship to distinguish the characteristics of a similar currency mosaic. Furthermore, the data increase activity supports the need to make training data sufficiently large and to cover conditional CNN learning situations that significantly improve the results of currency forecasting. In this study, we plan to improve the results based on the distinction between feature extractions and CNN deep classification.

2 Proposal System for Currency Recognition

The currency recognition system is based on a general idea that uses deep learning. The deep learning architecture was created to extract distinctive visual feature of banknotes and recognize currency values. Some signs for the recognition of the nominal value of the currencies and the anti-counterfeiting are illustrated in Fig. 1. It is hard to recognize this every kind and all values of the real banknote or counterfeit note. This study proposes methodologies for the currency recognition in the two main problems of recognize currency values, detect of counterfeit banknotes. The banknote inspection is built on several main modules, which consist of learning the banknote model, extracting features, currency recognition. We also implement the system using deep CNN to extract face visual features and recognize of currency values and detect face material. An overview of the recognition system is presented in Fig. 2.

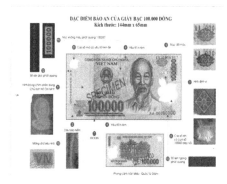

Fig. 1. Some special signals for currency recognition based on visualized information.

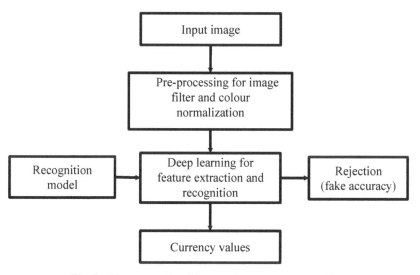

Fig. 2. The proposed architecture for currency recognition

3   Implement Recognition Model

In this study, we proposed a new approach for the CNN model for currency recognition for feature extraction and classification. The CNN model relies heavily on multiple CNN channels and four building blocks, which leverage the benefits of extracting local and global features. The CNN model for feature extraction is shown in Fig. 3. Some kinds of deep learning architectures can be used such as AlexNet, R-CNN, GoogleNet, VGG and so on. Directed graph architecture of CNN is a well-known model developed base on the GoogLeNet [7]. In this study, we implemented the input layer with the size $100 \times 250 \times 3$, which is appropriated for real time processing on color images. In this investigation, we proposed the deep learning architecture based on CNN technique as depicted in Fig. 3. We assessed that CNN was used for both tasks of the feature extraction and recognition of currency value. The network architecture is composed of 66 layers.

Fig. 3. The details of deep learning architecture

The set of training and evaluation data corresponds to the uniformity of the frame image of 100×250 pixels. The input data consists of an original image of 100×250. Convolutional filters at the first input layer are 3 channels corresponding to 3 colors of the R-G-B image. The details of the currency recognition architecture are illustrated Table 1. Difference to method in [14], the proposed method using smaller and simple architect with 66 layers to compare with 75 layers, and the input image size is 100×250 pixels instead of 200×450 pixels. Evidentially, this model should be faster the previous model. The results of the training showed that the accuracy of recognition system reaches 97.85% rate.

The imbalance and small data problem of training task is solved by the used of data augmentation technique processing. This task is important to provide balance and enough data to define powerful parameters of the recognition system. The problem of increasing data means that it increases the number of image data sets. There are many ways to increase data, for example rotation processing, normalizing lighting conditions, different directions, flipping, blurring. Thus, for an image, different subsamples can be generated. There are two types of augmentation applied in this study, such as geometric transformation and color processing. Training game images are enhanced to create a larger

Table 1. Detail of deep neural network parameters

1	Input	$100 \times 250 \times 3$ images	34	In2ReLu2	Rectified linear unit
2	Conv1	64 7×7 convolutions	35	In2Conv3	96 7×7 convolutions
3	ReLu1	Rectified linear unit	36	In2ReLu3	Rectified linear unit
4	Maxp1	3×3 max pooling	37	In2Conv4	96 5×5 convolutions
5	CrossCh1	normalization	38	In2ReLu4	Rectified linear unit
6	Conv2	64 7×7 convolutions	39	In2Conv5	96 7×7 convolutions
7	ReLu2	Rectified linear unit	40	In2ReLu5	Rectified linear unit
8	Conv3	64 7×7 convolutions	41	In2Maxp1	3×3 max pooling
9	ReLu3	Rectified linear unit	42	In2Conv6	96 5×5 convolutions
10	CrossCh2	normalization	43	In2ReLu6	Rectified linear unit
11	Pool0Maxp3	2×2 max pooling	44	In2Conc6	Concatenation 4
12	In1Conv1	96 5×5 convolutions	45	Pool2Maxp3	3×3 max pooling
13	In1ReLu11	Rectified linear unit	46	In3Conv1	96 5×5 convolutions
14	In1Conv12	96 3×3 convolutions	47	In3ReLu11	Rectified linear unit
15	In1ReLu1	Rectified linear unit	48	In3Conv12	96 3×3 convolutions
16	In1Conv2	96 5×5 convolutions	49	In3ReLu1	Rectified linear unit
17	In1ReLu2	Rectified linear unit	50	In3Conv2	96 5×5 convolutions
18	In1Conv3	96 7×7 convolutions	51	In3ReLu2	Rectified linear unit
19	In1ReLu3	Rectified linear unit	52	In3Conv3	96 7×7 convolutions
20	In1Conv4	96 5×5 convolutions	53	In3ReLu3	Rectified linear unit
21	In1ReLu4	Rectified linear unit	54	In3Conv4	96 5×5 convolutions
22	In1Conv5	96 7×7 convolutions	55	In3ReLu4	Rectified linear unit
23	In1ReLu5	Rectified linear unit	56	In3Conv5	96 7×7 convolutions
24	In1Maxp1	3×3 max pooling	57	In3ReLu5	Rectified linear unit
25	In1Conv6	96 5×5 convolutions	58	In3Maxp1	3×3 max pooling
26	In1ReLu6	Rectified linear unit	59	In3Conv6	96 5×5 convolutions
27	In1Conc6	Concatenation 4	60	In3ReLu6	Rectified linear unit
28	Pool1Maxp3	3×3 max pooling	61	In3Conc6	Concatenation 4
29	In2Conv1	96 5×5 convolutions	62	FinalPool	3×3 average pooling
30	In2ReLu1-1	Rectified linear unit	63	FinalDrop1	50% dropout
31	In2Conv1-2	96 3×3 convolutions	64	FC1	8 fully connected layer
32	In2ReLu1	Rectified linear unit	65	SoftMax1	Softmax
33	In2Conv2	96 5×5 convolutions	66	Classifier	Crossentropyex

dataset for training. There are many resampling techniques such as rotation, stretching, shearing: random rotation with an angle between $-1°$ and $1°$, random shear with an angle between $-1°$ and $1°$, random shear stretching with a stretching factor between $1°$ and $2°$ and reversal, a Gaussian blur with sigma values of 1.2 and 1.5 is applied. The color enhancement processing is also applied because the images are recorded with different light sources, different lighting conditions and different scanners. Therefore, it is important to normalize image coloring, blur noise.

4 Experiment and Evaluation

For evaluation of the proposed method, we collected image data set from real currency. It is separated two sets with 60% training data and 40% evaluation data. The training and evaluation data sets consist of two scenarios. The first scenario is a set of images that have been collected from actual banknotes in many face values, such as images of 10,000, 20,000, 50,000, 100,000, 200,000, and 500,000 VND. In total, there are 9,736 samples of actual banknotes, 1,083 samples of counterfeit banknotes and 1,548 non-monetary images. All samples were normalized to the same resolution of 100×250 pixels. Some real and fake banknotes are shown in Tables 2 and 3.

Table 2. Some kinds of paper currency classes.

Currency values	Front	Backside
10,000		
20,000		
50,000		
100,000		
200,000		
500,000		

In the training task, there are many approaches to build a deep neural network, which can be applied to currency recognition. Some pretraining models may also be applied in the case of the banknote recognition. In this study, a directed graph based on an initial traditional CNN is used to implement the learning architecture. The input image

Table 3. Some types of different fake banknotes.

Banknotes on fake material	Front	Backside
10,000		
20,000		
50,000		
100,000		
200,000		
500,000		

is set to small size for reducing consuming time. The input layer processes with 100×250 neural with 3 channels on color image. In order to detect banknote counterfeit, we collected currency counterfeit in different materials to created training data for learning a recognition model (Fig. 4).

Cross validation results show that the accuracy of the system can reach an accuracy rate of 97.85% on average money values. The result also illustrated that the proposed architecture conducting model outperforms. Some results are shown in Table 4. This approach is appropriate for an application in general condition of a realistic banknote.

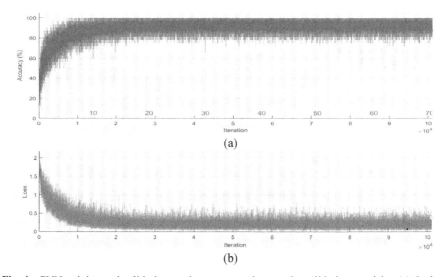

(a)

(b)

Fig. 4. CNN training and validation on the monetary dataset: the validation precision (a) the loss function values (b) converged towards the expected values after several periods.

Table 4. Cross-verification matrix of prediction results

Data	10k	20k	50k	100k	200k	500k	Fake	Non-money
10k	**99.72%**	0.00%	0.10%	0.00%	2.05%	0.09%	0.09%	3.88%
20k	0.05%	**97.01%**	0.00%	0.24%	0.00%	0.00%	0.37%	1.10%
50k	0.00%	0.00%	**98.76%**	0.00%	0.00%	0.00%	1.39%	0.78%
100k	0.05%	0.25%	0.00%	**99.37%**	0.00%	0.35%	0.00%	0.00%
200k	0.05%	0.00%	0.00%	0.00%	**97.86%**	0.00%	0.00%	0.00%
500k	0.05%	2.09%	0.00%	0.39%	0.00%	**99.48%**	0.00%	0.00%
Fake	0.05%	0.65%	1.14%	0.00%	0.00%	0.00%	**97.60%**	1.42%
Non-money	0.05%	0.00%	0.00%	0.00%	0.09%	0.09%	0.55%	**92.83%**

5   Conclusion

This article presents a currency recognition approach based on deep learning. Instead of using infrared spectrometer and chemometrics as features for the currency recognition, this study developed method based on RGB image and artificial intelligent technique for learning visual mosaic of currency paper. In this model, the normal camera can be used to digitize currency paper, fed to learn recognition model. The deep learning model is used for both tasks feature extraction, values recognition of currency paper. In this study, some learning architectures were investigated to select an appropriate architecture, which is smaller than the previous one, while maintaining the accuracy of the recognition rate.

References

1. Correia, R.M., et al.: Banknote analysis by portable near infrared spectroscopy. Forensic Chem. **8**, 57–63 (2018)
2. da Silva Oliveira, V., Honorato, R.S., Honorato, F.A., Pereira, C.F.: Authenticity assessment of banknotes using portable near infrared spectrometer and chemometrics. Forensic Sci. Int. **286**, 121–127 (2018)
3. Baek, S., Choi, E., Baek, Y., Lee, C.J.D.S.P.: Detection of counterfeit banknotes using multispectral images. Digit. Signal Proc. **78**, 294–304 (2018)
4. Nammoto, T., Hashimoto, K., Kagami, S., Kosuge, K.: High speed/accuracy visual servoing based on virtual visual servoing with stereo cameras. In: IEEE/RSJ International Conference on Intelligent Robots and Systems, pp. 44–49. IEEE (2013)
5. Hoang, V.-D., Le, M.-H., Tran, T.T., Pham, V.-H.: Improving traffic signs recognition based region proposal and deep neural networks. In: Nguyen, N.T., Hoang, D.H., Hong, T.-P., Pham, H., Trawiński, B. (eds.) ACIIDS 2018. LNCS (LNAI), vol. 10752, pp. 604–613. Springer, Cham (2018). https://doi.org/10.1007/978-3-319-75420-8_57
6. Dollar, P., Wojek, C., Schiele, B., Perona, P.: Pedestrian detection: an evaluation of the state of the art. IEEE Trans. Pattern Anal. Mach. Intell. **34**(4), 743–761 (2012)
7. Doush, I.A., AL-Btoush, S.: Currency recognition using a smartphone: comparison between color SIFT and gray scale SIFT algorithms. J. King Saud Univ. Comput. Inf. Sci. **29**(4), 484–492 (2017)
8. Tran, D.-P., Nhu, N.G., Hoang, V.-D.: Pedestrian action prediction based on deep features extraction of human posture and traffic scene. Intell. Inf. Database Syst. **10752**, 563–572 (2018)
9. Wahyono, Hoang, V.-D., Kurnianggoro, L., Jo, K.-H.: Scalable histogram of oriented gradients for multi-size car detection. In: 10th France-Japan/ 8th Europe-Asia Congress on Mecatronics, pp. 228–231 (2014)
10. Lee, J.W., Hong, H.G., Kim, K.W., Park, K.R.J.S.: A survey on banknote recognition methods by various sensors. Sens. J. **17**(2), 313 (2017)
11. Hoang, V.-D., Jo, K.-H.: Joint components based pedestrian detection in crowded scenes using extended feature descriptors. Neurocomputing **188**, 139–150 (2016)
12. Lee, J.W., Hong, H.G., Kim, K.W., Park, K.R.: A survey on banknote recognition methods by various sensors. Sensors **17**(2), 313 (2017)
13. Szegedy, C., Vanhoucke, V., Ioffe, S., Shlens, J., Wojna, Z.: Rethinking the inception architecture for computer vision. In: Computer Vision and Pattern Recognition (CVPR), pp. 2818–2826 (2016)
14. Hoang, V.-D., Vo, H.-T.: Hybrid discriminative models for banknote recognition and anti-counterfeit. In: 5th NAFOSTED Conference on Information and Computer Science, pp. 394–399. IEEE (2018)

Design and Life Cycle Data Analysis for Smart Metering

Josef Horalek and Vladimir Sobeslav[✉]

Faculty of Informatics and Management, University of Hradec Kralove, Hradec Kralove,
Czech Republic
{josef.horalek,vladimir.sobeslav}@uhk.cz

Abstract. The presented article introduces an issue of data processing in the Smart
Metering from the life cycle analysis persepctive. The life cycle of data has been
identified and formalized; based on the results, the methodology for control and
usage of the data in the Smart Metering area has been proposed. The methodology
has been verified in three chosen pilot projects realized by a company owning
licence for electric power distribution in the Czech Republic. On the grounds of
verification, the fundamental areas that seem to be critical for effective usage of
Smart Metering and AMM in distribution system are formulated.

Keywords: AMM · Smart grid · Smart metering · Methodology · Data
processing

1 Introduction

Smart Grid concept is nothing new in energy industry. Many professional associations,
teams of specialists, and creators of regulations work on creating and updating architecture, communication technologies, and communication protocols definitions. Yet, there
is a gap available for improvement in the area of data processing obtained from the smart
networks, and their usage for effective operation of the whole distribution system. Smart
Grid system and perhaps Smart Metering in their basic concept bring a lot of data, which
opens a whole field of opportunity for their utilization. In this context it is not only data
processing, reading electric meters and incorrect measures, but it is a complex view on
data in general. Smart Grid can classify the importance of data and determine which
should be subtracted, which should realize connection between the failure of data readout and current status of the distribution network, take error messages etc. Therefore,
it is the determination of the extent of automatization while using the expert systems
over AMM (multi-agent system), mapping of activity of the trained operator in order to
prevent failures in readouts or electric energy supply, discovering the cause of technology failure, sophisticated validation, or automatic changes of reading task according to
current situation in the distribution network. These are the greatest challenges in Smart
Grid and Smart Metering concepts because this is evolutionary extension and a logical
step after long years of testing and debugging readouts on verification installations of
intelligent electric meters all over the world.

© Springer Nature Singapore Pte Ltd. 2020
P. Sitek et al. (Eds.): ACIIDS 2020, CCIS 1178, pp. 282–295, 2020.
https://doi.org/10.1007/978-981-15-3380-8_25

The aim of the present article is to map and identify potential areas to work with the data for automatization installation, mechanical learning, smart validation and the supporting process, so that in the future it would be possible to deal with the growth of the processed data volume in smart measuring areas. The limits on the side of human operators are often reached already and it is unimaginable to expect that – with increased need for data processing from the wide population of newly installed electrometers without advanced data work techniques – the standards even in only key areas of their work aspects will be kept. The article proposes formalization of data life cycle in form of methodology aimed at data processing from Advanced Metering Infrastructure/Smart Grid. This formalization aims to identify the key areas to improve the state of AMM data processing and it is tested on three pilot projects.

The issue of Smart Grind has been a long-term interest of many authors, mostly in the area of communication safety [1], where they enter and define general outputs like [2]. Another area of the research is data transfer quality with the results published in [3, 4]. Smart Grid communication safety has been examined widely by many authors [5, 6]. Another area important factor for solving the quality of the data life cycle are outputs focused on incorrect AMM readouts [7, 8]. While discussing the definition of the data life cycle in Smart Metering most thorough publications are [9–11]; however, these researches approach Smart Metering data same way as Big data, which in many cases, when Smart Metering and Smart Grid area are realized on limited sample within pilot projects, the data registered cannot be considered as Big data. For this reason, the data life cycle and method for their formalization introduced below can be considered innovative, which is verified in the analysis of real project in the area of distribution of electric power.

2 Data Life Cycle Proposal in Smart Metering

Implementation of Smart Metering brings about significant increase in the volume of processed data because they are its natural need. This also means increased requirements for the processing so that the acquired data were effectively used and processed. The issue here is to optimize the processing method of gathered data amount to eliminate the increased expenses brought by the increased volume, but also to ensure the effective data usage. For this reason, it is necessary to realize the state of the art analysis and to recommend optimization of the data life cycle in Smart Metering. Based on the results obtained from Local Optimization of Distribution System (LODIS) project, it can be stated that AMM electrometer records 1 191 360 registers and approximately 7 300 events during one year. If we approach it as to existing electrometer C measuring, a non-progressive measurement used for measuring offtake of electric power in households and small costumers, it means that it is necessary to have two figures of registers for invoicing - consumption in low and high rate. The reader then checks whether the electrometer does not show signs of damage or attack. Furthermore, the reader checks whether the display of the electrometer does not identify error with inner controlling mechanism of the electrometer. For AMM electrometer this control function is performed by readout of registers in which the electrometer transfers the same information as the display of the electrometer. To simplify, it is possible to state that this information is sufficient for invoicing of consumed energy and to accomplish the primary function that electrometer installed in electro installation at customer has. It is apparent that this approach does not use the full potential of the Smart Grid concept without meeting the requirements of Smart Metering. Measured data are used not only for invoicing, but they find wide usage within balance calculations, unauthorized offtake detection, also evaluation of qualitative parameters of the network focused on asymmetries in phases, idle components, factor power etc. The data is also used for detection in solutions of operating problems like electrometer malfunction, communication failure or quality of electric energy supply.

Based on these realities it is possible to propose work-in-progress data life cycle below within a closed infinite cycle that can be described by thought process coming from the need to know what data are important, readout these data, process them and if necessary, enrich them, properly represent them and gain knowledge Fig. 1.

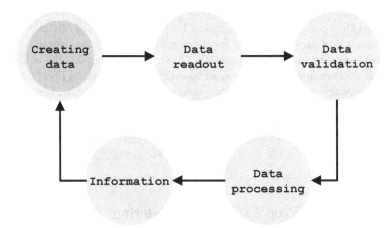

Fig. 1. Data life cycle

2.1 Data Creation

Primary sources of the data in Smart Grid are different types of sensors. In case of AMM the main sources are intelligent electrometers installed at offtake sites and variably quality meters or summative electrometers installed at the side of low voltage in distribution station (DTS). These are not an exclusive data source because it is also necessary to include the data generated within the operation, i.e. logs, communication records and results of infrastructure monitoring.

Considering the use of information, it is essential to have the data in processable form, in standardized format without differences in information value from the source the data are coming from. This task is currently not finalized despite it being the aim of standardized work groups, including National Institute of Standards and Technology (NIST) [12], The Institute of Electrical and Electronics (IEEE) [13], The International Electrotechnical Commission (IEC) [14], The International Telecommunication Union (ITU) [15]. In the area of communication with intelligent electrometer, one of the most perspective communication protocols is DLMS/COSEM, which is an often-used set of IEC 62056 norms specializes in utility data measuring and transfer.

The first step of the data life cycle is their creation. Within the methodology it is necessary to process in what way and in what format the data in AMM infrastructure are created. As a source of the data we consider intelligent electrometers, quality meters, concentrators. Data is created in standardized format i.e. according to IEC 62056. Categorization of the data type or the identification here is about the data measuring, events from the electrometers, etc. Within methodology it is necessary to evaluate:

- data source determination
- data format definition
- data type definition

2.2 Data Readout – Data Flow Control

In its basic functionality an advanced readout central allows to administer readout tasks, to plan them and display their progress and results. This all is in the setting of operation mode. It shows that it would be convenient to at least partly automize these processes as described in [16], where based on events identified by the system the behaviour of readout tasks changes. Current trends are headed this way when readout of all accessible information that electrometers and concentrators record are required. Results from the implemented pilot projects suggest that fulfilment of these tasks is limited by current communication throughput of implemented technology, and the operator is thus forced to compromise between data requirements and the communication infrastructure. Here it is necessary to find an algorithm that would secure that the most valuable data are read first when the value of the data depends on the amount of potential of their next use. From the data life cycle point of view there is evaluation of the way and possibilities of the data central to read the data. First it is necessary to identify functionality of reading tasks and then map control of the data flow and existence of integration to neighbouring systems. It is necessary to take in account if the push reading is initialized by electrometer on the event base or the time period. Next it is necessary to determine whether the full reading of the electrometer is actively addressed by the concentrator or the reading central. Regarding reading tasks, it is necessary to establish whether it is possible to set the level of data central possibilities with the help of the user interface or if the system settings is used for the configuration of central reading, yet it is not possible to influence them by user; simultaneously whether it is possible to set times for readings at the reading central. An important element is also the prioritization possibility of individual reading tasks based on the defined parameters, the data type or the task type. Relevant requirements for reading central in area of personalization of the reading task is equally seminal, therefore task determination of what will be read and identification of the status of the reading task, hence whether GUI data central allows to monitor development of individual reading tasks. For AMM it is then necessary that reading functions support the smart reading functions allowing the data centre to use inner logic to connect readings to previous results i.e. for adding unread data. For effective and fully-fledged use of AMM in Smart Grid network it is relevant to require a control of the data flow therefore requirement that the data centre allows to actively control data flow and by that react to current communication situation during data reading and communication to neighbouring systems. Within methodology it is necessary to evaluate:

- Push reading possibilities.
- Pull reading.
- Reading tasks user definition.
- Reading tasks start up definition.
- Reading task prioritization possibilities.
- Reading task settings possibilities.
- Reading task status monitoring possibilities.
- Smart reading function definition and support.
- Data control possibilities:

  - During data reading.
  - During communication with neighbouring systems.

2.3 Validation

The aim of the validation is to verify gained data intergrity. In AMM we understand the data validation as their quality improvement which can be reached by removing gross errors of reading, compensation of the system reading errors, and minimalization of random errors influence during reading. Methods of similarity with exactly valid mathematical and physical models are used for this approach for AMM data validation. The aforementioned results suggest that all data in the system must be validated so that their use is relevant and usable within next processes using the measured data. This method can be called the technical validation. Currently individual occurrences are mostly validated in the isolated way. Within validation it is relevant to demand extension of validation usage with connected processes and services, which would allow hidden connections to be found or e.g. possibly to decide data validity based on different values or sets within cooperation processes.

Regarding the data life cycle and defined methodology, it is evaluated whether implemented data centre allows some form of validation. From the methodological control perspective, we can differentiate two types of validation. The first type is so called technical validation that detects whether the measured values are not influenced by a technical error coming e.g. from the electrometer malfunction or if the measured value corresponds to the format. Another type of validation is the user validation which is based on the existence of possibility to specify set of validation rules that are set for the measured data. Typical example is control of the measured values that are not zero of electric power production registers on the consumer offtake site. The last validation parameter is context validation that can work with context of other connected parameters. As a typical example we can provide the validation whether the measured value of production from the electrometer installed on a photovoltaic power station is labelled as invalid in the case when they are read at night and therefore additional information of the processed data sentence about time context is validated. Within methodology it is necessary to evaluate:

- Determination of possibilities to start data validation.
- Technical validation is used.
- Technical validation with possibility for setting of business rules is used.
- Contextual validation is used.

2.4 Data Processing

Data processing from the Smart Grid networks and AMM perspective has wide reach and it is necessary to include a complex set of operations with data and clear aim of evolutionary developed data driven company and its processes in compliance with [17]. As an example from the energetics area it is useful to mention possibilities of algorithm prediction in the area of the wind energy according to [18], where due to instability of this source it is apparently not possible to fully accept predictions usually based on historical data. This is an exemplary issue with unbalanced class in the area of mechanical learning and therefore different methods of data selection have to be implemented to allocate the correct context. From the life cycle perspective and their methodical process it is possible to narrow the issue into two areas: the first requires to evaluate whether the implemented system allows predication of the data and substitute values processing and within the second area it allows to define possibilities within aggregation and readings. These possibilities need to be considered:

- Possibilities of the data prediction and data steps that are allowed by the data centre.
- Substitute values process definition.
- Aggregation and readings of the data centre possibilities.

2.5 Information

According to [19] the information is better understood from the DIKW hierarchy perspective, i.e. from the view of the information model explaining the structure and functional relationship between data, information, knowledge and wisdom. Should we arrange these data into numerical vector, we create a vector image arranged to image space. Recognition task can be then divided into two parts – in the first part we define processing of data measured at the object (image processing) so the discrimination ability is maximized during minimalization of the data. In the second part we connect class indicators to individual descriptions gained in preceding part which is considered its own qualification that is realized using the clasificator under which we understand system that realizes classification algorithms. The clasificator displays a set of vector signs to set of names (indicators) of classes and defines decision-making rules. The clasificator can be set in two ways – by analysis of the problem and definition of decision-making rule before classification, or by setting decision-making rule while using the objects where correct classification is known in advance. Here it is necessary to consider that having the data does not mean having the information and without processing we only have a large amount of data that fill up the data bank. Based on evaluation of the relevant AMM pilot solutions we can say that the issue of data processing from AMM in ČEZ is currently on the level of figuring out reasons that caused an event. Within the evaluation of the measured data the focus is currently on the site of informed and experienced operator of the data centre and the evolutionary sophisticated analytical methods are not used effectively. From the methodical perspective basic methods of acquiring knowledge from the data are evaluated. The first method uses identification whether the implemented system supports creation of reports that mediate information to the operator. Next, following the methodological framework, it is necessary to evaluate possibilities of using advanced mathematical methods for data processing therefore whether it is possible to use and identify statistical characteristics and automatically identify anomalies. Next it is necessary to identify whether it is possible to process acquired data by clusters or to subject them to automatic classification. The last point of methodology is evaluation whether the used system supports smart functionality acquiring information from the data therefore whether it is possible to implement algorithms that react to the new information in form of feedback by Smart Grid infrastructure or to the user. It is the highest algorithms adaptation form based on the context work and feedback.

3 Data Flow Control and Data Evaluation in Selected Projects

Analytical approach of the data life cycle in Smart Metering with suggested crucial parts of data processing methodology described above is now possible to use practically within analysis of the data flow and the evaluation of data on selected projects realized in the Czech Republic by one of the three companies providing electricity distribution.

3.1 WPP AMM Pilot Project

Within the development of the solution possibilities in Smart Grid network several smaller projects were realized. They provided valuable preliminary data; however, a set of deployed AMM electrometers was insignificant. Based on these elementary attempts a project focused on verification of accessible technologies for AMM took place from 2010 to 2013. It included 35 000 smart electrometers, communication between readers and the central and connection to control, invoice and financial systems. The implementations took place in three locations that represented different characters of the distribution network including different operation, geographical, demographical and meteorological conditions. In the pilot there are three data centres installed – one of them reads technology installed on the distribution station (DTS) and another two are set to read electrometers installed at offtake sites. These data centres are also integrated on the information system of the company, due to which it is possible to receive technical fundamental data identifying offtake site where the electro meter was installed and join the provision of the measured data for invoicing based on electronic requirement from the distributor's customer system. The aim of the project is to gain experience and as possible to and accurately simulate real operation of complex AMI/AMM system under real circumstances of distribution network.

The methodology described above was used at reading centre that reads electrometers of all customers after the project.

To create the data, it is necessary that the electrometers are not interoperable. The communication and the form of data reading is therefore defined by the distributor. In one case it is possible to control electrometers of two distributors with one concentrator. Within the data reading and the data flow control the reading is realized based on set reading tasks that the control can parametrize from the point of view of group of read electrometers and start up time. The user is able to set automatic repetition. The functionality of the smart reading task is implemented within the data centre. After one set of reading it is automatically evaluated which data are already in the data centre and the next reading is created only for the set of unknown data. It is possible to follow the progress of every task. The reading centre was integrated into distributor's systems. The integration was realized as automatic data transfer based on the requirement for reading as electronic work order are given data for invoicing to distributor's customer system. In case of data validation, the user validation in the data centre is used. Validation standards can be set by the user. Technical validation is realized based on database requirements where incorrect format will not be saved. The user has no control over this process and they are not informed about it. During data processing it was identified that the data centre does not allow prediction and creation of replacement values; in other words, the creation of replacement values was not implemented to operate with real readings within the project. The data centre supports aggregation and data reading. Integration of the data centre to GIS allowed to test automatized calculation of balances for set DTS. Furthermore, the data centre supports full scale information reporting. Advanced user can create SQL questions and display required data based on them. Advanced analytical methods are not supported, but the system for advanced correlation of events was implemented in the open case of electrometer and work tasks wrote on service intervention of the controller of the company. In case that the event matches with values of electronic work order, the electrometer report about attack is automatically closed. Overall evaluation of the WPP AMM project according to the life cycle and methodical questions described above is introduced in Table 1.

Table 1. Evaluation of the WPP AMM pilot project

Life stage	Methodological areas	WPP AMM
Creating data	Data source	Electricity meters
	Data format	Proprietary
	Data type	Measurement data technical data
Data readout	Push	Yes
	Pull	Yes
	Subtraction tasks can be customized	Yes
	Read tasks can start with time settings	Yes
	Read jobs can be run with time settings	Yes
	Subtraction tasks can be set to subtraction type	Yes

(*continued*)

Table 1. (*continued*)

Life stage	Methodological areas	WPP AMM
	It is possible to monitor the status of the reading task	Yes
	Smart read function	Yes
Flow control	When reading data	Partially active
	While communicating with neighboring systems	Passive
Data validation	Allows you to validate data	Yes
	Technical validation	No
	User validation	Yes
	Contextual validation	No
Data processing	Data prediction	No
	Processing of substitute values	Not implemented
	Aggregations, conversions	Yes
Information	Reporting	Yes
	Statistical characteristics	No
	Identifying anomalies	No
	Clustering	No
	Data classifiers	No
	Smart functionality	Partly

3.2 LODIS

The second project selected is the localized distribution system information. Its aim was to prove that with help of the predication control of readings it is possible to balance overflows caused by photovoltaic electro station installed under the set DTS. Due to this the reading centre of the main component was not implemented so the functionality implemented to the reading centre are not comparable with WPP AMM solutions. Data creation investigation is not relevant. The electrometers and concentrators used in this project are from the same manufacturer and therefore the solution is not interoperable with different on the market. The data reading and the control of data flow are realized based on internally set reading tasks without possibility to change the operator of the data centre. Functionality of the reading is already implemented in core of the data centre. Paradoxically, the inability to influence the reading task did not create problems with readings. On the other hand, only one DTS in set location was read so it was impossible for readings to collide on one communication channel. The reading centre is integrated for reception of Time/Table of Use (TOU tables) for turning on tariffs in electrometers on the Centre of performance control. The validation of the data is realized by using basic technical validations implemented in the core of the data centre. The data centre controller has no way to influence the validation and user validation cannot be set. Within the project the user validation is implemented to the core of the system for correctness of TOU definitions that are acquired from the Centre of performance control. The data was processed based on the historical experience with behaviour, and models of behaviour for individual offtake sites and their groups are calculated by the progress of consumption. Based on current reading and weather forecast the prediction is set every day. Based on this prediction TOU table is automatically calculated and automatically remotely loaded into selected electrometer. The information is then reflected by the data centre to support new forms of visualization of the measured data and the events read from electrometers by head map form. In this form the status of reading is reported. The interface of the data centre does not allow to create classical reports. Within the project only one report is implemented to display status and start-up time of high and low tariff for possible customer request about the progress of the start-ups. Overall evaluation of LODIS project according to the life cycle and methodical questions described above is introduced in Table 2.

Table 2. Evaluation of the LODIS pilot project

Life stage	Methodological areas	LODIS
Creating data	Data source	Electricity meters concentrators
	Data format	Proprietary
	Data type	Measurement data technical data
Data readout	Push	Yes
	Pull	No
	Subtraction tasks can be customized	No
	Read tasks can start with time settings	No
	Read jobs can be run with time settings	No
	Subtraction tasks can be set to subtraction type	No
	It is possible to monitor the status of the reading task	No
	Smart read function	Yes
Flow control	When reading data	Active
	While communicating with neighboring systems	Passive
Data validation	Allows you to validate data	Yes
	Technical validation	Yes
	User validation	Yes
	Contextual validation	No

(continued)

Table 2. (*continued*)

Life stage	Methodological areas	LODIS
Data processing	Data prediction	Yes
	Processing of substitute values	Not implemented
	Aggregations, conversions	Not implemented
Information	Reporting	Yes
	Statistical characteristics	No
	Identifying anomalies	No
	Clustering	Yes
	Data classifiers	No
	Smart functionality	No

3.3 KODA

The last project that underwent the analysis is project KODA whose task was to process the data from the previous projects (LODIS and WPP AMM) and test advanced analytical methods of the data processing. The data for the project was provided in the form of data dumps from the previous data centres. For this reason, it is not relevant to discuss the area of data creation because the used data was read from the previous projects. This also applies to the data reading area and the data from control because the electrometer reading was not implemented. Within the project the technical and the user-set validation of the measured data and events from the electrometers were verified. In the data processing area 15 algorithms were verified for the evaluation and the setting of alternate values and data predication. The results were compared with process custom used in current data processing in the company. The project provided advanced analysis of the read data which was analysed and verified. Automatic reporting was not implemented, however, all individual results from the project were reported and consulted with the company workers. This step of the data life cycle was fully met. Project KODA is partially evaluated only in Smart functionality because analytical methods of i.e. clasificators are not implemented to the data centre and during the project they did not support feedback. Functionality of the clasificators was evaluated (Table 3).

Table 3. Evaluation of the KODIS pilot project

Life stage	Methodological areas	LODIS
Creating data	Data source	Electricity meters concentrators
	Data format	Proprietary
	Data type	Measurement data technical data

(continued)

Table 3. (*continued*)

Life stage	Methodological areas	LODIS
Data readout	Push	Not implemented
	Pull	Not implemented
	Subtraction tasks can be customized	Not implemented
	Read tasks can start with time settings	Not implemented
	Read jobs can be run with time settings	Not implemented
	Subtraction tasks can be set to subtraction type	Not implemented
	It is possible to monitor the status of the reading task	Not implemented
	Smart read function	Not implemented
Flow control	When reading data	Not implemented
	While communicating with neighboring systems	Not implemented
Data validation	Allows you to validate data	Yes
	Technical validation	Yes
	User validation	Yes
	Contextual validation	Yes
Data processing	Data prediction	Yes
	Processing of substitute values	Not yes
	Aggregations, conversions	Not yes
Information	Reporting	Not implemented
	Statistical characteristics	Yes
	Identifying anomalies	Yes
	Clustering	Yes
	Data classifiers	Yes
	Smart funcionality	Partly

4 Conclusion

The present article has introduced methodology of data flow control and evaluation of the data acquired within Smart Metering management via Smart Grid infrastructure. The methodology departs from the thought concept based on the data life cycle. The thought concept stems from the process of recognition and acquiring information in the data cycle and contains key components that can be summed up followingly: It is necessary to know vital elements ➜ correctly read (acquire) them ➜ process them correctly ➜ enrich the data with more information and sources ➜ correctly interpret and represent the results ➜ acquire knowledge that can be used in the final form or as entrance to another round of the data life cycle i.e. in form of clarification of what the data are necessary for the next processing. Based on this methodology, the realized projects were evaluated, used for testing and data evaluation and AMM technological solution were realized within the distributor. From the realized analysis results the high significance for data processing and the distributor is aware of this issue and they are taking steps to prepare for the jump in the processing data amount. Using the proposed methodology, the evaluation of the project shows relatively wide space for development and improvement of the current state with possibility to implement business intelligence elements. In this context it is possible to state that to this day no proposed concept or pilot project has tested complex data approach, only partial proposed data life cycle. Using advanced analytical functions and automatic clasificators in extensive installations can help significantly with their safe operation. This issue also includes SW solution providers who begin to realize this fact, and the data centres of new generation start to work with requirements for reading and processing of huge data volume and integrate these requirements to suggested solutions. Based on the long-term research in this area, it is necessary to formulate few suggestions via the introduced analysis. In the area of the data creation it is vital to focus on standardization and interoperability of individual technologies. Currently every manufacturer uses proprietal implementation of set communication protocols that causes electrometers communicate only with concentrator of said manufacturer and consequently the technology is unusable in this amount. In the case of the measured data usage of advanced methods and functionalities of the reading tasks reacting to reading process can be proposed due to its success rate. This issue is connected with data flow control. The data centre and installed technology must support prioritization of the reading and integrating tasks. The suggestion for data processing is the use advanced mathematic methods to process high volumes of data focused on data prediction and creation of alternative values. Regarding reading outage, the subsequent systems, e.g. systems of the electric energy market operator, will need credible and precise data. Acquiring information was identified as the greatest potential for improvement of state of the art because the current identification is based on expert knowledge of the controller, which is not sufficient with massive installation and large data volume. Thus it is necessary to determine knowledge base for automatization of this process in accordance to possibilities, views and forms of data processing which Smart Metering and Smart Grid concepts bring. The proposed and tested methodology aims to contribute to clear data control within AMM and possibilities for setting distribution system control effectivity.

This work and the contribution were supported by a Specific Research Project, Faculty of Informatics and Management, University of Hradec Kralove, Czech Republic. We would like to thank to Hana Svecova, Matej Drdla, Jakub Pavlik and Jan Stepan – Ph.D. candidates at Faculty of Informatics and Management, University of Hradec Kralove.

References

1. Horalek, J., Sobeslav, V., Krejcar, O., Balik, L.: Communications and security aspects of smart grid networks design. In: Dregvaite, G., Damasevicius, R. (eds.) ICIST 2014. CCIS, vol. 465, pp. 35–46. Springer, Cham (2014). https://doi.org/10.1007/978-3-319-11958-8_4

2. Kabalci, Y.: A survey on smart metering and smart grid communication. Renew. Sustain. Energy Rev. **57**, 302–318 (2016). https://doi.org/10.1016/j.rser.2015.12.114. ISSN 1364-0321

3. Sobeslav, V., Horalek, J.: Communications and quality aspects of smart grid network design. In: Wong, W.E. (ed.) Proceedings of the 4th International Conference on Computer Engineering and Networks, pp. 1255–1262. Springer, Cham (2015). https://doi.org/10.1007/978-3-319-11104-9_143

4. Komarek, A., Pavlik, J., Mercl, L., Sobeslav, V.: Hardware layer of ambient intelligence environment implementation. In: Nguyen, N.T., Papadopoulos, G.A., Jędrzejowicz, P., Trawiński, B., Vossen, G. (eds.) ICCCI 2017. LNCS (LNAI), vol. 10449, pp. 325–334. Springer, Cham (2017). https://doi.org/10.1007/978-3-319-67077-5_31

5. Zhou, Z., Gong, J., He, Y., Zhang, Y.: Software defined machine-to-machine communication for smart energy management. IEEE Commun. Mag. **55**(10), 52–60 (2017). https://doi.org/10.1109/MCOM.2017.1700169

6. Xu, S., Qian, Y., Qingyang Hu, R.: Reliable and resilient access network design for advanced metering infrastructures in smart grid. IET Smart Grid **1**(1), 24–30 (2018). https://doi.org/10.1049/iet-stg.2018.0008

7. Rawat, D.B., Bajracharya, C.: Detection of false data injection attacks in smart grid communication systems. IEEE Signal Process. Lett. **22**(10), 1652–1656 (2015). https://doi.org/10.1109/LSP.2015.2421935

8. Horalek, J., Sobeslav, V.: Analysis of the error rate in electrometers for smart grid metering. In: Nguyen, N.T., Gaol, F.L., Hong, T.-P., Trawiński, B. (eds.) ACIIDS 2019. LNCS (LNAI), vol. 11432, pp. 533–542. Springer, Cham (2019). https://doi.org/10.1007/978-3-030-14802-7_46. SCIACCA, Samuel C. IEEE 2030 ® Smart Grid Interoperability Standards What is Smart Grid ? [online]. 2012, 1–20 [vid. 2019-04-03]

9. Zhang, Y., Huang, T., Bompard, E.F.: Energy Inform **1**, 8 (2018). https://doi.org/10.1186/s42162-018-0007-5

10. Murray, D.M., Stankovic, L., Stankovic, V., Espinoza-Orias, N.D.: Appliance electrical consumption modelling at scale using smart meter data. J. Cleaner Prod. **187**, 237–249 (2018). https://doi.org/10.1016/j.jclepro.2018.03.163. ISSN 0959-6526

11. Yao, H.-W., Wang, X.-W., Wu, L.-S., Jiang, D., Luo, T., Liang, D.: Prediction method for smart meter life based on big data. Procedia Eng. **211**, 1111–1114 (2018). https://doi.org/10.1016/j.proeng.2017.12.116. ISSN 1877-7058

12. IEC: IEC - Smart Grid Standards Map [vid. 2018-04-01]. http://smartgridstandardsmap.com/

13. ITU: SG15: Smart Grid [vid. 2019-04-03]. https://www.itu.int/en/ITU-T/studygroups/Pages/sg15-sg.aspx

14. Wang, J., Zhou, P., Huang, G., Wang, W.: A data mining approach to discover critical events for event-driven optimization in building air conditioning systems. Energy Procedia **143**, 251–257 (2017). https://doi.org/10.1016/j.egypro.2017.12.680. ISSN 1876-6102

15. Tao, F., Qi, Q., Liu, A., Kusiak, A.: Data-driven smart manufacturing. J. Manufact. Syst. (2018). https://doi.org/10.1016/j.jmsy.2018.01.006

16. Takahashi, Y., Fujimoto, Y., Hayashi, Y.: Forecast of infrequent wind power ramps based on data sampling strategy. Energy Procedia **135**, 496–503 (2017). https://doi.org/10.1016/j.egypro.2017.09.494. ISSN 1876-6102

17. Intezari, A., Pauleen, D.J., Taskin, N.: The DIKW hierarchy and management decision-making. In: 2016 49th Hawaii International Conference on System Sciences (HICSS), Koloa, HI, pp. 4193–4201 (2016). https://doi.org/10.1109/hicss.2016.520

18. Jennex, M.E.: Big data, the internet of things, and the revised knowledge pyramid. SIGMIS Database **48**(4), 69–79 (2017). https://doi.org/10.1145/3158421.3158427

19. Burnay, C., Jureta, I.J., Linden, I., et al.: Softw. Syst. Model. **15**, 531 (2016). https://doi.org/10.1007/s10270-014-0417-1

A Cloud Services Security Analysis

Tomas Svoboda[1], Josef Horalek[2], and Vladimir Sobeslav[2(✉)]

[1] Faculty of Electrical Engineering and Informatics, University of Pardubice, Pardubice,
Czech Republic
`tomas.svoboda5@student.upce.cz`
[2] Faculty of Informatics and Management, University of Hradec Kralove,
Hradec Králové, Czech Republic
`{josef.horalek,vladimir.sobeslav}@uhk.cz`

Abstract. The aim of the article is the analysis of cloud services and data stored
into cloud infrastructure. At first, history and principles of cloud computing technology are introduced. This is flowed by the introduction of security threats related
to the use of cloud computing technology for storing data into cloud infrastructure
managed by a third-party subject, whose infrastructure is different from that of
the owner of the stored data. Based on the identification of security threat identification, tools designated for encryption of data saved into cloud, and allowing
for increased security and mitigation of threats related to cloud data storing are
showcased. Furthermore, these tools are compared using a comparative analysis
in terms of workload on system and network adapter resources while encrypting
and storing the data into cloud. As part of the comparative analysis, a comparison
of encryption and saving of a single 1-GB file and 10,000 .txt files was performed.
In the last part of the article, the results of the comparative analysis are interpreted
visually and with the description of the measured values.

Keywords: Cloud computing · Security · Public cloud · Boxcryptor · AxCrypt ·
Folder Lock

1 Cloud Computing a Security of Cloud Services

The term of cloud computing and cloud services is already well-known nowadays. Cloud
computing can be defined as a parallel and distributed computer system comprised of
a series of interconnected and virtual computers that are dynamically secured and presented as one or more unified computing resources based on the Service-Level Agreement (SLA) established between the service provider and the consumers, or, according
to a more general definition, it is hardware and software of the data center that provides
the services [1].

Security and ethical aspects are one of the critical factors of successful cloud service
operation as the data is often very sensitive, confidential, and limited by the laws or other
policies. In [8], three main challenges present in this area are distinguished. First, compliance and responsibility for a wide scale of data or policies related to the consumer, such
as data retention duration, erasure process, backup plans, sharing policies, access monitoring systems, consumer accounting, activity logging etc. Second, security and privacy,

© Springer Nature Singapore Pte Ltd. 2020
P. Sitek et al. (Eds.): ACIIDS 2020, CCIS 1178, pp. 296–307, 2020.
https://doi.org/10.1007/978-981-15-3380-8_26

i.e. mechanisms intended for lowering security threats such as unauthorized access, data segregation, virtual networks, system isolation, error explosions, multi-layered security, backup mechanisms, or cryptography. The last question is the legislation. There are many legislative factors that affect the use of cloud computing. Nowadays, this topic is frequently discussed as these issues are often neglected and personal data are stored in cloud services [9]. The transfer of private data into uncontrolled Internet areas is highly complex.

Security of data and information in the area of cloud computing is seminal [10]. Its intention is to create a safe platform for operating systems and services. This area has been researched by a wide range of authors (Cloudbuzz 2013; Ballantine 2012; Bisong et al. 2011; Dupre et al. 2012; ENISA 2012; Grimes 2013; Jansen et al. 2011; Wheeler 2013). Private data security damage or breach, be it loss, damage, or abuse, is a very sensitive topic for many organizations [11, 12]. Cloud services are based on three main pillars: virtualization, computer networks, and web/mobile technologies. Every single of these areas is unique in terms of its technology and security. In the area of virtualization, there are hypervisor attacks, such as use of cache memory, virtual instance switching, processor instructions abuse (see e.g. SYSRET), malicious hypervisors, network communication breach, virtual image faking, VM escape attacks, etc. [13]. In the area of computer networks, there exist mainly DHCP snooping, man-in-the-middle attacks, VLAN hopping, communication wiretapping, encrypted channel breaching, ARP spoofing, and many others. Web and mobile technologies serve as proxies while accessing cloud services. The typical threats are DDOS attacks, authentication and authorization system breaching, attacks through communication channel between the user and the front-end (SSH, TLS, SSL protocols), SQL injection, HTTP relation modifications, cross-site scripting, unsecured web components attacks, etc. Therefore, the matter of cloud security is a very wide area [14].

In order to eliminate threats leading to abuse of the data being stored in the cloud, the most important factor serving to this purpose is data encryption [15]. If the data is transferred in an unencrypted form, the danger of their abuse is many times higher than while using encryption mechanisms [16]. For this purpose, programs that help the user to encrypt the data on the client's side even before their transfer to the cloud infrastructure. These programs encrypt the data so it can be read only using a key owned by its proper owner, and therefore, it prevents third parties from accessing the private data. Given the matters related to the lack of knowledge of the infrastructure and concrete protection of servers and cloud storages on the provider's part, these third-party tools help the user (or organization) to protect their data even in case of a loss, theft, or unwanted data access.

2 Methodology of Cloud Services Security Tools Analysis

For the methodology of cloud services security and encryption of data being stored in the cloud, analysis of third-party tools serving for encryption of data transferred to the cloud was chosen. Comparative analysis of these tools was based on the comparison of usage of the system resources, i.e. processor, memory, HDD, and network adapter during the process of encryption and transfer of the data into a uniform cloud storage.

2.1 Chosen Data Encryption Tools

Folder Lock
This application was developed by NewSoftwares.net, a company developing security applications. It serves for securing the data via AES-256 standard, where the user chooses the location of a "safe" folder, where the encrypted data is to be stored, and then Folder Lock creates a new drive partition, where the data could be viewed. Installation of this product does not require any registration. After installation, the application requires setting up the main password of any length and strength. The "safe" folder is created in a Dropbox folder, which automatically creates new drive partition Z; which is connected directly to the safe and all the operations with the data are performed directly in this partition. Therefore, a folder dedicated solely to storing encrypted data is located in the Dropbox. Data encryption and decryption is performed upon opening or closing the safe, which means that the data can be worked with immediately.

AxCrypt
This application was developed by a Swedish company called AxCrypt AB. It automatically connects to the cloud storage whose application is installed on the device and creates AxCrypt folder. End-to-end encryption is used here as well, and in case of a password loss, the data cannot be recovered. Data is encrypted using symmetrical encryption algorithm of AES-128 or AES-256 standard, depending on the application version. RSA-4096 public key for file sharing and private key for syncing between the devices, and which serves as a security means in case of loss of the device.

Boxcryptor
Developed by a German company called SecombaGmbH, this software is very widespread and popular for its very user-friendly interface. It checks the data via end-to-end encryption, and therefore, the encrypted data can be read only by the user to whom it belongs. Boxcryptor connects to chosen cloud storage and creates a virtual drive partition in the user's device (in Windows, it is "X:" drive by default), in which the user inserts data, which is in turn transferred to the cloud in the encrypted form. It is necessary to keep encfs6.xml file, which Boxcryptor creates in Boxcryptor.bc folder in the cloud storage. This file contains the encryption key, and if it were moved, deleted, or damaged, the data could not be decrypted. Boxcryptor uses a combination of asymmetrical and symmetrical encryption. RSA algorithm is used for asymmetrical encryption, and AES algorithm with 256-bit encryption key is used in symmetrical encryption. This method guarantees that every file is assigned a unique and random encryption key. Currently, Boxcryptor is compatible with thirty cloud storage providers. The compatible services include e.g. Dropbox, Google Drive, OneDrive, Box, Amazon Cloud Drive, iCloud, and others.

2.2 Tool Analysis Means

While performing the analysis of data encryption tools, Dropbox cloud storage at current version 67.4.83 was used.

Device used to perform the analysis of used system resources while using the encryption tools was Asus laptop with the following configuration:

- OS: Windows 7 Home Premium (64-bit) Service Pack 1
- CPU: AMD A4-3300 M 1,9 GHz 2 Core
- RAM: 6 GB
- HDD: 1x HDD 750 GB divided into two partitions
- Actual Internet connection speed: about 7 Mbit/s both download and upload

To monitor the used system resources, SysGauge System Monitor software was utilized. This monitoring tool was used to log the information about system resource workload during given time period with frequency of one log entry per second. SysGauge was utilized to log CPU, RAM, and HDD workloads. Another used tool was Windows Resource Monitor, which is a part of Windows OS, and which provided measured data about network adapter workload.

Data that was encrypted and transferred to the cloud storage was represented by generated sample data. For this purpose, one Excel (.xlsx) file of 1 GB size and 10,000 text (.txt) files of 12 kB size were generated. In the next step, encryption and testing data syncing with the use of the introduced products was analyzed.

All the measuring was performed using the tools immediately after starting data encryption. This data was synced into the cloud storage in order to simulate conditions of actual cloud service use. Given the requirements of Internet data transfer and data syncing, measuring was performed in maximum five 1-min intervals. If the process finished sooner, monitoring was terminated. This interval was sufficient for the measuring and to depict the results of the three products' performance in the charts. Measuring with all the products was performed using identical length encryption key: AES – 256 bit.

3   Analysis Results

3.1   FolderLock

Figure 1 depicts the workload of the system resources during the encryption of the 1 GB file. Maximum workload reached 80% of the CPU, 42% of the RAM, and 100% of the HDD. Average CPU workload was 32.8%, average RAM workload was 40.5%, and average HDD workload stayed at 100%.

In the recorded system resources workload, mode (i.e. the most often occurring value) was counted as well. The mode was 15% for the CPU, 40% for the RAM, and 100% for the HDD. Median (i.e. medium value) workload was 19% for the CPU, 40% for the RAM, and 100% for the HDD as this value was constant and the HDD was constantly under maximum workload.

Figure 2 showcases the network adapter workload during the encryption of the 1 GB file. The average workload was 11.4%. Both the mode and the median were 0%. The adapter workload was at 100% for only 10 s during the whole testing.

Figure 1 manifests the workload of the system resources during the encryption of the 10,000 .txt files. Maximum workload reached 70% of the CPU, 44% of the RAM, and 100% of the HDD. Average CPU workload was 63.1%., average RAM workload was 44%, and average HDD workload stayed at 61.6%.

In the recorded system resources workload, the most often occurring value (mode) was 15% in CPU, 44% in RAM, and 61.6% in HDD.

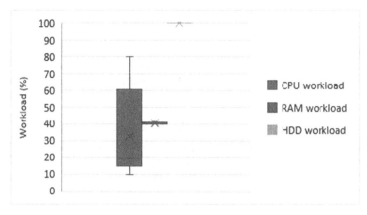

Fig. 1. Folder Lock system workload – 1 GB file. Source: authors

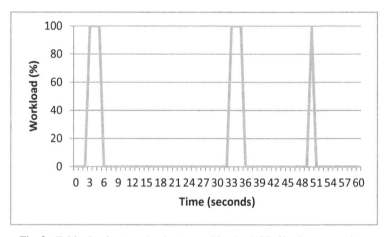

Fig. 2. Folder Lock network adapter workload – 1 GB file. Source: authors

Median (i.e. medium value) workload was 63% for the CPU, 44% for the RAM, and 55.5% for the HDD (Fig. 3).

Figure 4 showcases the network adapter workload during the encryption of the 10,000 .txt files. Here, the same as in the previous case, the average workload was counted to be 13.9% and the mode 0%. Median network adapter workload was 14%.

3.2 AxCrypt

Figure 5 depicts the values measured while working with SysGauge tool during the encryption of the 1 GB file. In this chart, the maximum reached workloads are showcased, with the highest value being 73% of the CPU performance. In the case of the RAM, the maximum workload was 42%. In the case of HDD, workload reached 100%.

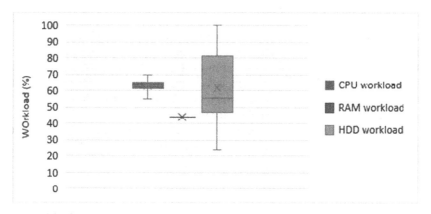

Fig. 3. Folder Lock system workload – 10,000. txt files. Source: authors

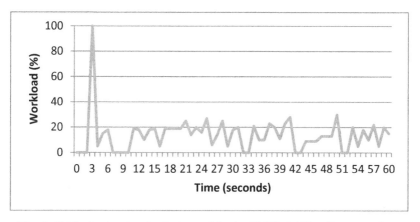

Fig. 4. Folder Lock network adapter workload – 10,000 .txt files. Source: authors

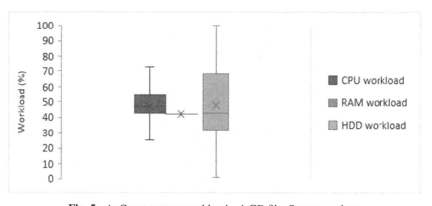

Fig. 5. AxCrypt system workload – 1 GB file. Source: authors

The average CPU workload value was 46.8%, the RAM workload was 42% in average, and the HDD workload was 48% in average. In the case of the HDD activity, high variance was observed with the values of 1% minimum and 100% maximum.

During this testing, the CPU workload mode was 47%, the RAM workload mode was again 42%, the same as the average and the maximum value. Mode of the HDD activity was 43%. Median of the values, which can be observed from the chart, was 47% for the CPU, 42% for the RAM, and 43% for the HDD.

Figure 6 showcases the network adapter workload during the encryption of the 1 GB file. The average workload was 27.5%, the mode was 0%, and the median was 20%.

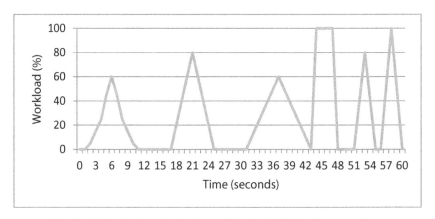

Fig. 6. AxCrypt network adapter workload – 1 GB file. Source: authors

Figure 7 depicts the workload of the system resources during the encryption of the 10,000 .txt files using AxCrypt. In this case, maximum workload, i.e. 100%, of the CPU was reached. In the case of the RAM, the maximum was 31% and 76% in the case of HDD. The average CPU workload value was 78%, workload of the RAM was 30.6% in average, and the average HDD workload was only 10.3%.

Mode for the CPU was 65%, 30.5% for the RAM, and 5% for the HDD. CPU workload median was 77%, in the case of RAM, it was 30.5%, and the HDD activity median was 5%.

Figure 8 shows the network adapter workload during the encryption of the 10,000 .txt files. Here, the average workload was 36.5%, mode was 0%, and median reached 25%.

3.3 Boxcryptor

Figure 9 portrays the values obtained during the encryption of the 1 GB file using Boxcryptor tool. In the chart, maximum workloads are shown – the values reached 100% of CPU performance. In the case of the RAM, the maximum workload was 47%. In the case of HDD, the maximum reached activity was 100%.

The average value of the CPU workload was 81.3%, the RAM workload was 46,7% in average, and the HDD workload averaged 61.8%. In the HDD'S activity, high variance was detected, as the minimum value was 4%, while the maximum was 100%.

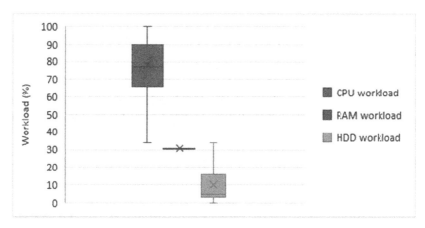

Fig. 7. AxCrypt system workload – 10,000 .txt files. Source: authors

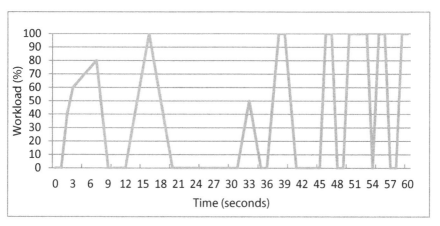

Fig. 8. AxCrypt network adapter workload – 10,000 .txt files. Source: authors

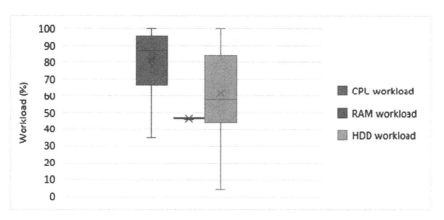

Fig. 9. Boxcryptor system workload – 1 GB file. Source: authors

During this testing, the mode reached the value of 100% in the case of the CPU, for the RAM it was again 47%, the same as the average and the maximum value. The HDD workload mode was 100%.

The median values, which can be observed in the chart below, were 87% for the CPU, 47% for the RAM, and 57.5% for the HDD.

Figure 10 depicts the network adapter workload during the encryption of the 1 GB file. Here, the average workload was 69.2%, the mode was 70%, and the median value was 71%.

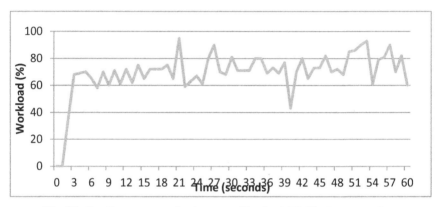

Fig. 10. BoxCryptor network adapter workload – 1 GB file. Source: authors

Figure 11 indicates the workload of the system resources during the encryption of the 10,000 .txt files using Boxcryptor. The maximum reached workloads are displayed here, and which reached values of 100% for the CPU performance, 54% for the RAM, and 78% for the HDD. The average value of the CPU workload was 81.4%, the average for the RAM was 53.3%, and for the HDD it was merely 25.1%.

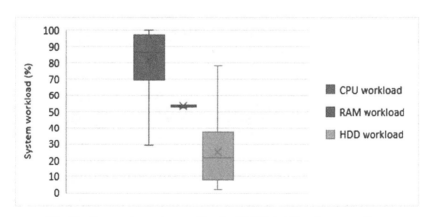

Fig. 11. Boxcryptor system workload – 10,000 .txt files. Source: authors

In the case of the CPU, the mode was 99%, for the RAM it was 54%, and for the HDD 8% only. The median value of the CPU workload was 87%, for the RAM it was 53.5%, and the HDD activity median value was 22%.

Figure 12 presents the network adapter workload during the encryption of the 10,000 .txt files. The average workload was 3.4%. The mode and the median values were identical in this case as both remained at 0%.

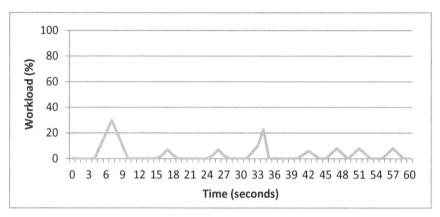

Fig. 12. Boxcryptor network adapter workload – 10,000 .txt files. Source: authors

4 Conclusion

The aim of the article was to perform a comparative analysis of the tools used to encrypt the data saved into the cloud, and therefore increase security and mitigate hazards related to storing the data into the cloud without using encryption mechanisms. First, the hazards related to storing the data into the cloud administered by a subject different from the owner of the data were identified. Then, tools suitable for data encryption stored into the cloud by their owner were introduced. These tools have been used to perform a series of measuring system resources used during encryption and transfer of a single 1 GB file and 10,000 .txt files.

The best results while encrypting the 1 GB file were achieved with AxCrypt, where the average CPU workload was 46.8%, and mode, as well as median value, were 47%. The RAM workload was constantly 30.6% and the HDD workload was 48% in average, while the mode and the median value were 43%. The variance of the measured values was the lowest of all the tested tools. This tool also proved itself to have the lowest variance in values of the workload of the system resources, i.e. CPU, RAM, and HDD.

In the case of encryption of the 10,000 .txt files, the best results were achieved with FolderLock. The average workload values were at 63.1% for the CPU, with the mode and the median values being 70% and 63%, respectively. The RAM workload stayed constantly at 44% and the HDD workload was, 61.6% in average. The mode and the median values were 100% and 55%, respectively. Given the lowest variance of the values among all the tested tools, FolderLock proved itself to be an ideal tool for encryption of a high number of small files (around several MB). The limitation of FolderLock is, however, that the free version can be used only for several launches, therefore, purchasing the full version is necessary. There is also a possibility to use AxCrypt, which reached worse values than FolderLock, although its results while encrypting the 10,000 .txt files were better than Boxcryptor's.

This work and the contribution were supported by a Specific Research Project, Faculty of Informatics and Management, University of Hradec Kralove, Czech Republic. We would like to thank to Hana Svecova, Matej Drdla, Jakub Pavlik and Jan Stepan – Ph.D. candidates at Faculty of Informatics and Management, University of Hradec Kralove.

References

1. Mell, P., Grance, T.: The NIST Definition of Cloud Computing (Draft): Recommendations of the National Institute of Standards and Technology (2011). http://csrc.nist.gov/publications/nistpubs/800-145/SP800-145.pdf
2. HADA: Introduction of Cloud Computing (2014). https://www.slideshare.net/rahulhada/introduction-of-cloud-computing
3. Sen, J.: Security and privacy issues in cloud computing. In: Cloud Technology, Management Association, Information Resources, ed., pp. 1585–1630. IGI Global (2015). https://doi.org/10.4018/978-1-4666-6539-2.ch074. ISBN 9781466665392. http://services.igi-global.com/resolvedoi/resolve.aspx?doi=10.4018/978-1-4666-6539-2.ch074
4. Villari, M., Fazio, M., Dustdar, S., Rana, O., Ranjan, R.: Osmotic computing: a new paradigm for edge/cloud integration. IEEE Cloud Comput. **3**(6), 76–83 (2016). https://doi.org/10.1109/mcc.2016.124. ISSN 2325-6095. http://ieeexplore.ieee.org/document/7802525. Accessed 29 Sept 2019
5. Lu, P., Sun, Q., Wu, K., Zhu, Z.: Distributed online hybrid cloud management for profit-driven multimedia cloud computing. IEEE Trans. Multimedia **17**(8), 1297–1308 (2015). https://doi.org/10.1109/tmm.2015.2441004. ISSN 1520-9210. http://ieeexplore.ieee.org/document/7116597/. Accessed 29 Sept 2019
6. Chou, D.C.: Cloud computing: a value creation model. Comput. Stan. Interfaces **38**, 72–77 (2015). https://doi.org/10.1016/j.csi.2014.10.001. ISSN 09205489. https://linkinghub.elsevier.com/retrieve/pii/S0920548914000981
7. Cloudbuzz:. Is cloud computing experiencing the same security threats as enterprise computing? (2011). https://cloudtweaks.com/2013/04/is-cloud-computingexperiencing-the-same-security-threats-enterprise-computing. Accessed 22 Mar 2017.
8. Selig, G.J.: Implementing Effective IT Governance and IT Management. van Haren Publishing, 's-Hertogenbosch (2015). ISBN 9789401805728
9. Wheeler, A., Winburn, M.: Cloud Storage Security: A Practical Guide. Elsevier Science, Amsterdam (2015). ISBN 9780128029312
10. Ballantine, R.: Cloud Computing: Security Compliance and Governance. BookBaby, Philadelphia (2012). ISBN 9781618429971
11. Rhoton, J., De Clercq, J., Novak, F.: OpenStack Cloud Computing: Architecture Guide. Recursive Press (2014). ISBN 9780956355683
12. Qi, H., Li, K.: Software Defined Networking Applications in Distributed Datacenters. SECE. Springer, Cham (2016). https://doi.org/10.1007/978-3-319-33135-5

13. Dupré, L., Haeberlen, T.: ENISA, Cloud computing benefits, risks and recommendations for information security (2012). https://resilience.enisa.europa.eu/cloud-security-andresilience/publications/cloud-computing-benefits-risks-and-recommendations-forinformation-security
14. Chen, J., Zhang, Y., Gottschalk, R.: Handbook of Research on End-to-End Cloud Computing Architecture Design. IGI Global, Hershey (2017). ISSN 2327-3453
15. Gai, K., Qiu, M., Zhao, M., Xiong, J.: Privacy-aware adaptive data encryption strategy of big data in cloud computing. In: IEEE 3rd International Conference on Cyber Security and Cloud Computing (CSCloud), pp. 273–278. IEEE (2016) . https://doi.org/10.1109/cscloud.2016.52. ISBN 978-1-5090-0946-6. http://ieeexplore.ieee.org/document/7545931/
16. Velumadhava, R., Selvamani, K.: Data security challenges and its solutions in cloud computing. Procedia Comput. Sci. **48**, 204–209 (2015). https://doi.org/10.1016/j.procs.2015.04.171. ISSN 18770509. https://linkinghub.elsevier.com/retrieve/pii/S1877050915006808

Genre-ous: The Movie Genre Detector

Amr Shahin and Adam Krzyżak[✉]

Department of Computer Science and Software Engineering, Concordia University,
1455 Boulevard de Maisonneuve West, Montréal, QC H3G 1M8, Canada
amrnablus@gmail.com, krzyzak@cs.concordia.ca

Abstract. The advent of Natural Language Processing (NLP) and deep learning allows us to achieve tasks that sounded impossible 10 years ago. One of those tasks is text genre classification such as movies, books, novels, and various other texts, which, more often than not, belong to one or more genres. The purpose of this research is to classify those texts into their genres while also calculating the weighted presence of this genre in the aforementioned texts. Movies in particular are classified into genres mostly for marketing purposes, and with no indication on which genre predominates. In this paper, we explore the possibility of using deep neural networks and NLP to classify movies using the contents of the movie script. We follow the philosophy that scenes make movies and we generate the final result based on the classification of each individual scene.

Keywords: NLP · HAN · Genre classification

1 Related Work

Brezeale and Cook [1] used combination of closed captions[1] and visual features to detect the genre of a video using a support vector machine (SVM). The authors used 81 movies from the MovieLens project[2] and were able to achieve 89.71% accuracy when using closed captions as the feature vector inputted to the SVM. It however is not clear, how the authors calculated the accuracy when the movie belongs to multiple genres. Moreover, the usage of classical machine learning algorithms like SVM and bag of words does not scale well when working with a larger dataset. The authors also pointed out that the closed captions "typically won't include references to non-dialog sounds", we found that using the original script of the movie circumvents this problem as not only it includes the actual speech, but also the "general feeling" of the scene.

Similar to our approach, Tsaptsinos [2] used a hierarchical attention networks to classify songs into genres based on their lyrics. The author tested the model with over 117-genre dataset and a reduced 20-genre dataset and concluded that the HAN outperforms both non-neural models and simpler neural models whilst

---

[1] https://en.wikipedia.org/wiki/Closed_captioning.
[2] https://grouplens.org/datasets/movielens/.

© Springer Nature Singapore Pte Ltd. 2020
P. Sitek et al. (Eds.): ACIIDS 2020, CCIS 1178, pp. 308–318, 2020.
https://doi.org/10.1007/978-981-15-3380-8_27

also classifying over a higher number of genres than previous research. Moreover, the HAN model has the ability to visualize the attention layers of the HAN model. While on the surface, it may seem that this problem is identical to ours, however, a deeper look debunks this assumption. It is very easy to notice that the genres differ greatly between songs and movies, additionally, a song belongs to a single genre which makes dataset gathering simpler, and finally, a trained model can be used directly to predict unseen data unlike our case, where the model is used to classify scenes that are used to classify the full script.

Aside from the aforementioned papers to our best knowledge there was no other research that directly works with text genres using the movie script. In the rest of this paper we will be presenting research done on text classification in general.

2   Dataset

One of the biggest challenges we were faced with while writing this paper was finding a suitable dataset that contains proper training data. The form of data we were looking for is a sentence mapped to a single genre (i.e: [But you step aside for the good of the party; people won't forget. The President and I won't let them] belongs to the genre 'politics', [He's in love with you. I've only ever seen him look at one other girl the way he looks at you] is 'romance', etc ...). Unfortunately, such dataset does not exist.

2.1   Available Datasets and Their Issues

We considered using The Internet Movie Script Database which contains the full script of most movies and parsing its contents, however, this leaves us with a large text corpus that belongs to multiple genres, which presents two issues: 1. The resources required to run a Recurrent Neural Network (RNN) to handle a corpus of this size are enormous and 2. Training a NN on a text that belongs to multiple genres will lead to the network learning the joint probability of the genres which is not desired in our experiment. Another option was using a news dataset which contains texts mapped to a certain news category such as https://www.kaggle.com/crawford/20-newsgroups or https://www.kaggle.com/therohk/india-headlines-news-dataset, we found that there is no clear one-to-one mapping between a news class and a movie genre aside from politics and sports, which will cause our model not to scale well should we decide to add more genres to our work.

2.2   Building a Custom Dataset

Due to the above-mentioned reasons, we decided to build our own dataset consisting of five genres: action, comedy, drama, politics, and romance to collect data for. We experimented with two types of textual contents:

Movie Quotes. Our process starts with scraping Google search using the queries: "Top <genre> movies" and "Top <genre> series"[3]. Out of the search result, we manually selected a collection of movies and series that we felt represent the selected genre best for the list of movies and series. Using this set of movies and series, we built a tool that scrapes the API of https://en.wikiquote.org/ collecting quotes belonging to this set.

This method provided us with the data we needed properly formatted. As the number of samples per genre varied greatly, we additionally scraped https://www.goodreads.com/quotes in order to have matching numbers in our five genres. We managed to collect 3000 samples for each genre which we have used both for training and testing.

Movie Plots. Using the same set of movies and series in the aforementioned method, we scraped https://www.imdb.com/ collecting plot synopsis of the movies and series we selected, an example of a synopsis can be found at https://www.imdb.com/title/tt0068646/plotsummary. Unlike the previous method, we were able to assemble a balanced dataset, complementing was unnecessary.

2.3 Data Preparation

In order to convert words into a form the network can understand, we first tokenize the sentences into individual words, which in turn got converted into integers each representing a unique index corresponding to each word present in the corpus. The resulting tokenized sequences were padded to be all of the same lengths, the sequence length is a parameter that will be specified for each model in the corresponding section.

The embedding layer is the other part of the input, which consists of the word embeddings of the form <unique word index>:<word embedding vector>. This is used as a look-up table for the neural network in order to map integers to vectors. We chose GloVe embedding of size 100 for in our experiments.

3 Methods

3.1 Attention

Self Attention (AKA Bahdanau or Intra Attention). Self-attention proposed by Bahdanau et al. [3] works by assigning an alignment score between the input as position i and the output based on how much the input affects the output. Self attention works by training a feed-forward networks with a single hidden layer along side the main network, thus, the loss function for attention neural network will be:

---

[3] Thus, looking up the genre "Romance" will result in queries: "Top romance movies" and "Top romance series".

$$score(s_t, h_i) = v_a^T \tanh\left(W a[s_t; h_i]\right)$$

where W_a is the weight of the attention layer.

Luong Attention. Luong et al. [4] proposed the idea of global and local attention, the global attention is similar the aforementioned Bahdanau attention where the attention vector moves freely over the input, while the hard attention is a mix of soft attention and hard attention where only part of the inputs can have the attention at a given time step, the model is preferred over hard attention as it's differentiable.

3.2 Word Representation

Machine Learning and Deep Learning architectures are incapable of processing text directly as input. In the case where the input is a text, pre-processing is needed in order to convert the text into numbers. In this section, we present the various methods to do so.

One-Hot Encoding. A one-hot encoding, in general, is a representation of categorical variables as vectors. Each integer value is represented as a binary vector that is all zero values except the index of the integer, which is marked with a 1, for example, applying One-Hot to an input vector consisting of: ['drama', 'comedy', 'sports'] will result in the following encoding [[1 0 0], [0 1 0], [0 0 1]].

While One-Hot encoding does work in the sense that they convert words to numbers, however, they fail to capture the relations between various words, the word "Ottawa" could be represented using to the 1000th column, while the word "Amman" could be the 1st column, although both words represent capitals and should have smaller distance. For this reason, One-Hot encoding is not widely used in NLP.

3.3 Word Embedding

A Word Embedding format generally maps a word to a vector. One important property of the vector representation of a single word is that its distance from other similar words[4] is less than that of less similar words. The resulting vector has the property that cosine similarity between words is higher for more similar words. This property is very important when training a neural network as it helps the network determine the nature of words it did not see during training.

$$a \cdot b = \|a\|\|b\| \cos\theta$$

$$\cos\theta = \frac{a \cdot b}{\|a\|\|b\|}$$

---

[4] Similar here means the words appear in the same context.

Word2Vec. Mikolov et al. [5] used skip-gram model to generate embeddings and circumvented some of the training challenges using negative sampling [6]. The main idea behind this method is that you train a model on the context of each word, so similar words will have similar numerical representations.

Word2vec model learns the weights by feeding a pair of input word and a target word to a neural network with one hidden layer of size [embedding dimension, vocabulary size] and an output layer of dimension [vocab size] consisting of softmax units. The hidden layer represents the probability that the word it represents will appear in the same context as the target word.

When the network training is done the output layer is dropped and the hidden layer will be used as the word vector.

GloVe: Global Vectors for Word Representation. Pennington et al. [7] presented the idea of learning embeddings by constructing a co-occurrence matrix (words X context) that counts how frequently a word appears in a context[5].

3.4   Hierarchical Attention Networks (HANs)

HANs consist of stacked recurrent neural networks on word level followed by an attention model to extract important to the classification of the sentence and aggregate the representation of those informative words to form a sentence vector. Then the same procedure is applied to the derived sentence vectors which then generate a vector that carries the meaning of the given document and that vector can be passed further for text classification as shown in Fig. 1

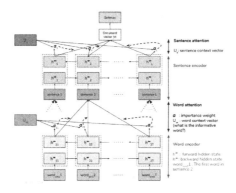

Fig. 1. HAN structure (image source: Fig. 1 Yang et al. [8])

---

[5] Context here is user-defined, in the literature it is usually chosen to be whether or not a word appears within X number of words of the target word.

4   Experiments

4.1   Model Architecture and Configuration

The HAN model is easier to be explained when thought of as two separate models, the first part (the encoder) consists of conventional recurrent neural network (RNN) built with a bi-directional long short-term memory (BLSTM) layer followed by an attention layer of the same size, this model is responsible for encoding the input data, it takes the word embeddings as input, and outputs an encoded representation of the words based on the hidden states of the BLSTM cells. The output of the encoder is then fed to the second part of the model, which in turn starts off with a time-distributed layer, this layer is the core of the HAN network, the purpose of the time-distributed layer is to run a copy of the encoder on each input sentence, the time-distributed layer is followed by a BLSTM layer of and an attention layer of the same size. Finally, the model adds a softmax fully connected layer as the output layer.

5   Discussion

5.1   Results

The HAN model achieved a test accuracy of 90% after training for 100 epochs on the quotes dataset and a testing accuracy of 93% on the plots dataset. The model out-performs, in terms of accuracy, both the traditional bi-directional LSTM with an accuracy of 50% and the one-dimensional CNN model with an accuracy of 75% as summarized in Table 1. It is worth mentioning, however, that the model is 2x times slower to train than the CNN model and about 1.5x times slower than the bi-directional LSTM. Another interesting feat to this model is that splitting the quotes in fewer sentences with higher maximum sentence length leads to better results compared to using more sentences with shorter sentence length. Hyper-parameter tuning was done on the validation dataset, we found that using Adam optimizer [9], a dropout [10] rate of 0.5, and an LSTM l2 regularizer with rate $1e^{-5}$ yield the best results.

Table 1. Models' testing accuracies

Model	Dataset	Accuracy
HAN	Quotes	90%
CNN	Quotes	75%
BLSTM	Quotes	51%
HAN	Plots	93%
CNN	Plots	86%
BLSTM	Plots	N/A

Looking at the confusion matrix exhibited in Table 1, we can see that the confusion is distributed evenly across genres. The only exception being comedy and romance, which is understandable since the romance movies tend to have the comedy genre as well, this example taken from the movie "The little mermaid" shows a potential source of confusion: "Scuttle: This, I haven't seen this in years. This is wonderful! A banded, bulbous snarfblatt.". The quote is more likely to be classified to the comedy genre by a human than it is likely to be classified as romance although it belongs to the romance genre, keeping in mind that the data was not manually labelled and that the HAN model can mitigate this issue as we explain the following section, we decided that this sort of data is an acceptable noise and does not affect the final results of this research.

Table 2. Confusion matrix of the HAN model on quotes

Genre	Action	Comedy	Drama	Politics	Romance
Action	370	7	6	12	3
Comedy	5	313	8	15	**38**
Drama	6	10	399	14	5
Politics	4	7	9	352	15
Romance	3	15	6	9	369

5.2 Rationale

To understand why HAN performs better than the other models, let us take a look at the following examples taken from our dataset:

Example 1: A text from Dr. House

> Dr. House: [to Dr. Cameron] Is he Canadian?
> Dr. Cameron: He's a low priority.
> Dr. House: Is that a yes?

Example 2: A text from Godfather

> Don Vito Corleone: [Sobs for a moment before he regains his composure] I want no inquiries made. I want no acts of vengeance. I want you to arrange a meeting with the Heads of the Five Families. This war stops now.

Looking closely at the above examples, it is clear that, not only, the second sentence contributes much more to the drama genre than the first one, but also, there are particular keywords like "sobs", "vengeance" and "war" in the second example that give clearer clues to the drama genre. The Hierarchical attention networks excel in such cases as they utilize two attention vector, the first works as a conventional attention vector over single words as described in Sect. 3.1 and the other works as an attention vector for the whole sentence.

5.3   Plots VS. Quotes

At the first glance, it looks that using the trained model to do the final classification of the full movie script makes more sense as all the three models performed better when using this dataset. However, when we tested both models, it turns out that the model trained on quotes was much more successful classifying movies correctly, the reason being is that the script text is more similar in structure to the quotes than it is for plots. We discuss the classification of full movie scripts in the following sections.

5.4   Attention Visualization

Another important feature of the attention networks in general is that the values of the attention can be visualized, we selected two examples from our dataset to show the attention for, the example, taken from the movie "The Rosa Parks Story" of the drama genre, is a very good example of attention as we can see that words that carry dramatic features such as "civil rights", "leaders" and "unmarried" got high attention values as shown in Fig. 2[6].

Fig. 2. Attention values for a drama genre example

Using the Trained Model for Genre Prediction. While building this model, we theorized that if the model can classify a single scene correctly, it would be able to be able to detect the overall genre, the testing process goes as follows: the movie script is downloaded from "The internet movie script database", the script gets parsed and broken into individual scenes. Next, the words are converted into their corresponding indexes, it's important to preserve the indexes to match the previously used indexes so that the embedding layer maps the correct vector to the word. The scenes are then padded to match the training data, and finally, the scenes are classified individually and the weighed sum of the probabilities is considered to be the full corpus' genre probability.

---

[6] It is also worth mentioning that although the attention is visualized on words, in reality the attention is applied to the RNN states which carry the meaning of the current word along with the surrounding words.

5.5   The Problem of Unseen Words

One challenging issue we faced is that a lot of words that appear in the testing data do not actually appear while training, which causes them to be dropped and could dramatically affect the predictions, to circumvent this, the model needs to be altered as follows[7]:

1. Remove Kera's embedding layer.
2. Add a Kera's input layer of type float, the shape of the model should be (max sentence length x embedding dimension).
3. The input to the trained model should be changed to be word embeddings rather than word ids.

6   Testing

Testing the model is particularly challenging due to non-existent data to evaluate with, we decided to rely in our experience with well-know movies as well as comparing the results with IMDB's genre classification, following are some of the predictions we made using the trained model:

1. "**Godfather**" (full script: http://www.dailyscript.com/scripts/The_Godfather.html), the two most dominating genres were: action with 24% of the total scenes and drama with 32% of the total scenes, we feel it matches the movie genre and it matches IMDB's genre tags.
2. "**Dumb and Dumber**" (full script: https://www.imsdb.com/scripts/Dumb-and-Dumber.html) had 63% of the scenes belonging to the comedy genre and about 10% for all other genres, which is pretty accurate depiction of the movie, it matches IMDB.
3. movie "**Lincoln**" (full script: https://www.imsdb.com/scripts/Lincoln.html) had 64% scenes classified as politics and 17% as action, we feel this is an accurate classification, we were unable to compare to IMDB as they don't have the politics genre.

7   Future Work

First and foremost, we would like to collect a more empirical testing data to evaluate our model, against, while we did put a lot of effort into manual testing, having an empirically labeled dataset would be very helpful especially in highly-subjective matter such as genres.

We also would like to predict the movie genre using an LSTM network, where the spacial input is the scene genre classification, the output would be similar to our existing input.

And finally, we predict that integrating the model's predictions into a movie recommendation engine is expected to lead to higher accuracy, which an experiment we are working on.

---

[7] For more details: https://amrnablus.github.io/blog/word_embedding.html.

8   Conclusions

In this research, we explored the possibility of using hierarchical attention network (HAN) architectures targeting of building a model capable of predicting a genre of a text corpus. Our dataset consists of quotes from famous movies from each genre taken mainly from wikiquote.com website and complemented from goodreads.com.

Upon looking at the confusion matrix in Table 2, we see that "romance" and "comedy" have high confusion, leading us to conjecture that generally the romance movies have comedy as a sub-genre, keeping in mind that the dataset we used consists of quotes picked up from movies without any sort of manual correction. In general, the comedy genre is difficult to detect by machines as it can be very context-dependent and thus often being a source of confusion.

Acknowledgement. We would like to thank Prof. Charalambos Poullis of the Department of Computer Science and Software Engineering, Concordia University for suggesting movie plots as an input to our model which gave us a good basis for comparing the results of two independent models.

References

1. Brezeale, D., Cook, D.J.: Using closed captions and visual features to classify movies by genre. In: Poster Session of the Seventh International Workshop on Multi-media Data Mining (MDM/KDD2006) (2006)
2. Tsaptsinos, A.: Lyrics-based music genre classification using a hierarchical attention network. In: Proceedings of the 18th International Society for Music Information Retrieval Conference, ISMIR 2017, Suzhou, China, 23–27 October 2017, pp. 694–701 (2017)
3. Bahdanau, D., Cho, K., Bengio, Y.: Neural machine translation by jointly learning to align and translate. arXive-prints, abs/1409.0473, September 2014
4. Luong, T., Pham, H., Manning, C.D.: Effective approaches to attention-based neural machine translation. In: Proceedings of the 2015 Conference on Empirical Methods in Natural Language Processing, pp. 1412–1421. Association for Computational Linguistics (2015)
5. Mikolov, T., Chen, K., Corrado, G.S., Dean, J.: Efficient estimation of word representations in vector space. Computing Research Repository, abs/1301.3781 (2013)
6. Mikolov, T., Sutskever, I., Chen, K., Corrado, G.S., Dean, J.: Distributed representations of words and phrases and their compositionality. In: Burges, C.J.C., Bottou, L., Welling, M., Ghahramani, Z., Weinberger, K.Q. (eds.) Advances in Neural Information Processing Systems, vol. 26, pp. 3111–3119. Curran Associates Inc. (2013)
7. Pennington, J., Socher, R., Manning, C.: GloVe: global vectors for word representation. In: Proceedings of the 2014 Conference on Empirical Methods in Natural Language Processing (EMNLP), pp. 1532–1543. Association for Computational Linguistics (2014)

8. Yang, Z., Yang, D., Dyer, C., He, X., Smola, A., Hovy, E.: Hierarchical attention networks for document classification. In: Proceedings of the 2016 Conference of the North American Chapter of the Association for Computational Linguistics: Human Language Technologies, pp. 1480–1489. Association for Computational Linguistics (2016)
9. Kingma, D.P., Ba, J.: Adam: a method for stochastic optimization. In: Bengio, Y., LeCun, Y. (eds.) 3rd International Conference on Learning Representations, ICLR 2015, San Diego, CA, USA, 7–9 May 2015, Conference Track Proceedings (2015)
10. Srivastava, N., Hinton, G., Krizhevsky, A., Sutskever, I., Salakhutdinov, R.: Dropout: a simple way to prevent neural networks from overfitting. J. Mach. Learn. Res. **15**(1), 1929–1958 (2014)

The Solution of the Problem of Unknown Words Under Neural Machine Translation of the Kazakh Language

Aliya Turganbayeva[iD] and Ualsher Tukeyev[(✉)][iD]

Al-Farabi Kazakh National University, Almaty, Kazakhstan
turganbayeva16@gmail.com, ualsher.tukeyev@gmail.com

Abstract. The paper proposes a solution to the problem of unknown words for neural machine translation. The proposed solution is shown by the example of a neural machine translation of a Kazakh-English language pair. The novelty of the proposed technology for solving the problem of unknown words in the neural machine translation of the Kazakh language is the proposed algorithm for searching of unknown words in the vocabulary of a trained model of neural machine translation using the dictionary of synonyms of the Kazakh language. A dictionary of synonyms is used to search for words that are similar in meaning to the unknown words, which was defined. Moreover, the found synonyms are checked for the presence in the vocabulary of a trained model of neural machine translation. After that, a new translation of the edited sentence of the source language is performed. The base of words-synonyms of the Kazakh language is collected. The total number of synonymous words collected is 1995. Software solutions to the unknown word problem have been developed in the python programming language. The proposed technology solution to the problem of unknown words for neural machine translation was tested on the two source parallel Kazakh-English corpus (KAZNU Kazakh-English parallel corpus and WMT19 Kazakh-English parallel corpus) in both variants: baseline and with using of the proposed technology.

Keywords: Neural machine translation · Unknown words · Kazakh language

1 Introduction

The Kazakh language belongs to the Turkic group of languages. About 13 million people use the Kazakh language according to Wikipedia, who live in Kazakhstan, Russia, China, Uzbekistan, Mongolia, and Turkmenistan. According to linguistic resources, the Kazakh language belongs to low-resource languages. Especially few linguistic resources are available for parallel corpora. This situation significantly affects the interaction of citizens of various countries with Kazakhstan.

For Kazakhstan, the problem of machine translation is very relevant as Kazakhstan is currently actively integrated into the global space and the needs of the translation of modern information in various fields of politics, economics, industry, and the social

P. Sitek et al. (Eds.): ACIIDS 2020, CCIS 1178, pp. 319–328, 2020.
https://doi.org/10.1007/978-981-15-3380-8_28

sphere are growing exponentially every year. The urgent issue is the timely translation of modern textbooks and scientific and technical literature into the Kazakh language as the Kazakh language begins to prevail in the educational sphere. The corps of translators of Kazakhstan, on the one hand, is not large enough to cover the ever-increasing needs of translation from leading world languages into the Kazakh language, and on the other hand, it is necessary to increase the productivity of translation by using machine translation programs. In this connection, the relevance of high-quality systems of machine translation of the Kazakh language is very important, especially languages relevant for Kazakhstan, like English and Russian. Since the problem of machine translation has not yet been solved at a sufficiently high level, close to professional translation, the problem of machine translation is very relevant. It should be noted that solving the problem of machine translation can open the way for solving other very important problems of artificial intelligence, such as understanding natural language.

Recently, the best results of machine translation have been shown by an approach based on neural networks, namely, neural machine translation. However, the quality of neural machine translation is not yet approaching professional translation. The main problem of neural machine translation is the need for large volumes of parallel enclosures necessary for learning neural machine translation. This is especially true for low-resource languages, which include the Kazakh language. Ways to solve this problem are either the creation of natural parallel corpora by professional interpreters, or the creation of synthetic parallel corpora. The first case is a very resource-consumer process; in the second case, various approaches to the generation of synthetic parallel packages are possible. The quality of neural machine translation is also affected by the problem of unknown words, i.e. words that are outside the dictionary of a machine translation system (Out Of Vocabulary - OOV).

The quality of a neural machine translation substantially depends on solving the problem of unknown words. This problem is associated with the concepts of "in-domain" (in the domain) and "out-of-domain" (outside the domain). By "in-domain" domain is meant a selection of source data on which neural machine translation is trained. If during testing or during a real translation, words that did not appear in the "in-domain" come across, then these will be unknown words. Some machine translation systems leave these unknown words untranslated, either replace them with the abbreviation "UNK", or translate them with words that are close in meaning. Accordingly, the last decision, namely, finding a word that is close in meaning, is also a difficult task.

This paper describes an approach to solving the problem of unknown words for a neural machine translation of a Kazakh-English pair, based on proposed algorithm for searching of unknown words in the vocabulary of the trained model of neural machine translation using the dictionary of synonyms of the Kazakh language.

2   Related Works

To solve the problem of unknown words in the literature, several approaches have been proposed that can be divided into three categories. The first category of approaches focuses on improving the speed of calculating the output of softmax tool so that it can support a very large vocabulary. The second category uses information from the context.

In particular, in relation to the problem of machine translation in [1], the system learns to indicate some words in the original sentence and copy them to the target sentence. In [2], when setting up the answer to a question in context, placeholders for named objects were used. The third category of approaches changes the input/output unit itself from words to a lower resolution, such as characters [3] or byte codes [4]. Although this approach has the main advantage that it can suffer less from the problem of unknown words, learning usually becomes much more difficult as the length of the sequences increases significantly.

In traditional machine translation, many off-vocabulary words still remain during testing, and they greatly reduce translation performance. In [5], when solving the problem of extra-vocabulary, attention is paid to how to correctly translate extra-vocabulary words. For this, additional resources such as comparable data and thesaurus of synonyms are used. One notable exception is the work [6, 7], which also focuses on the syntactic and semantic role of off-vocabulary words and suggest replacing off-vocabulary words with similar words during testing.

An effective method for solving the problem of unknown words is proposed and implemented in [1]. The authors trained the NMT system on data that was supplemented by the output of the word alignment algorithm, which allowed the NMT system to display for each out-of-dictionary word in the target sentence the position of its corresponding word in the original sentence. This information was later used in the post-processing phase, which translates each out-of-dictionary word using a dictionary.

In [8], a method is proposed for processing rare and unknown words for models of neural networks using the attention mechanism. Their model uses two softmax layers to predict the next word in conditional language models: one predicts the location of the word in the original sentence, and the other predicts the word in the short list dictionary. At each time step, the decision about which softmax layer to use is adaptively taken by the multilayer perceptron, which is context-specific.

To solve the problem of unknown words, in [9] a replacement-translation-recovery method is proposed. At the substitution stage, rare words in the test sentence are replaced by similar dictionary words based on the similarity model obtained from monolingual data. At the stages of translation and restoration, the sentence will be translated with a model trained in new bilingual data with the replacement of rare words, and finally, the translations of the replaced words will be replaced by the translation of the original words.

In [10], a method for processing unknown words in the NMT is proposed, based on the semantic concept of the source language. First, the authors used the semantic concept of the semantic dictionary of the source language to find candidates for dictionary words. Secondly, they proposed a method for calculating semantic similarities by integrating the source language model and the semantic concept of the network to get a better word replacement.

In [11] the problem of low-frequency content words was proposed to decide by incorporating discrete, probabilistic translation lexicons as an additional information source into neural machine translation. The proposed lexicon integration methods on the automatic, manual, and hybrid lexicons is achieved increases on 2.0–2.3 in BLEU metric.

3 Description of Method

The technology (method) for solving the problem of unknown words in the neural machine translation of the Kazakh language has been developed, which consists of the following steps:

1. Segmentation of the source text of the Kazakh language.
2. An algorithm for searching for unknown words in the vocabulary of a trained model of neural machine translation.
3. For each unknown word in the source text of the test corpus, a search is made for its synonyms in the dictionary of synonyms.
4. The defined unknown words are replaced with synonymous words.
5. Repeat the machine translation of the modified source text.
6. The base of words-synonyms of the Kazakh language, consisting of different parts of speech, is collected.

The novelty of the proposed technology for solving the problem of unknown words in the neural machine translation of the Kazakh language is the proposed algorithm for searching of unknown words in the vocabulary of the trained model of neural machine translation using the dictionary of synonyms of the Kazakh language for the Kazakh-English language pairs. To find words that are close in meaning to an unknown word, a dictionary of synonyms is used. In this case, an additional check is made for the presence of this synonym word in the dictionary of the trained model. These steps of the proposed technology for solving the unknown word problem are essentially actions that convert the out-of-vocabulary words of the source text into dictionary words, i.e. out-of-domain words are converted to in-domain words.

Below is a more detailed description of the stages of the proposed technology for solving the problem of unknown words in the neural machine translation of the Kazakh language.

3.1 Segmentation of the Source Text of the Kazakh Language

Segmentation of the Kazakh language source text is performed by the method proposed by the authors. This segmentation method is based on the definition of the complete set of endings of the Kazakh language. The Kazakh language ending system is divided into two groups: nominative endings (nouns, adjectives, numerals) and verb endings (verbs, participles, gerund, mood and voice). In the Kazakh language, a word is formed using 4 types of affixes. These species are: C-case, T-possessive, K-plural, J-personal. Kazakh language endings can be represented as all kinds of combinations of these basic types of affixes. All kinds of combinations of the basic affix types consist of combinations of the one type, combinations of two types, combinations of three types and combinations of four types. The total number of combinations is determined by the formula: $A_{nk} = n!/(N - k)!$.

Then the number of combinations (placements) will be determined as follows: $A_{41} = 4!/(4 - 1)! = 4$; $A_{42} = 4!/(4 - 2)! = 12$; $A_{43} = 4!/(4 - 3)! = 24$; $A_{44} = 4!/(4 - 4)! = 24$.

A total of 64 possible placements for the nominative base words. However, not all combinations of placements are semantically valid. The endings of combinations of the same type (K, T, C, J) are semantically valid. The endings of the combinations of the two types are as follows: KT, TC, CJ, JK, KC, TJ, CT, JT, KJ, TK, CK, JC. A semantic analysis of the combinations of the two types of endings shows that only six combinations are allowed (KT, TC, CJ, KC, TJ, KJ), and the remaining combinations are unacceptable. For combinations of three and four types of endings, the definition of acceptable combinations of endings is carried out in accordance with the rule: if within this combination there is an invalid combination of two types, then this combination is unacceptable. Then the correct combinations of the endings of the three types will be 4 (KTC, KTJ, TCJ, KCJ), and the correct combinations of the endings of the four types are 1. Given the semantic permissibility of the placements, the number of all possible placements for the name base is reduced to 15.

Similarly, the definition of all kinds of placements for endings with a verb stem was made, which amounted to 55 semantically acceptable types of endings. In general, the total number of ending types for nominal bases plus the total number of ending types for words with a verb stem is 70. In accordance with these types of endings, finite sets of endings are constructed for all the main parts of the Kazakh language. So, for parts of speech with nominal bases, the number of endings is 1213 (all plural variants are taken into account), and the number of endings of parts of speech with oral bases is: verbs - 432, participles - 1582, adverb - 48, moods - 240, voices - 80. In total - 3565 [12, 13].

The morphological segmentation algorithm of the Kazakh language words includes two stages:

(1) allocation of the basis and endings of words;
(2) segmentation of word endings into suffix segments.

The stage of dividing the base and endings of a word is performed using a stemmer, also based on the use of the complete Kazakh ending system. At the second stage, a simple transducer model is used, using the table of the complete ending system, in which the output is a segmented ending divided into suffixes. The table of the complete Kazakh ending system contains two columns: the column of endings of words of the

Table 1. Kazakh endings with segmented suffixes (fragment)

The endings of word	Sequences of suffixes
дарымызбенбіз (darymyzbenbiz)	дар@@ы@@мыз@@бен@@біз
дарымызбенмін (darymyzbenbin)	дар@@ы@@мыз@@бен@@мін
дарымызбенсіз (darymyzbensiz)	дар@@ы@@мыз@@бен@@сіз
дарымызбенсің (darymyzbensin)	дар@@ы@@мыз@@бен@@сің
лерменбіз (lermenbiz)	лер@@мен@@біз
лерменмін (lermenmin)	лер@@мен@@мін
лерменсіз (lermensiz)	лер@@мен@@сіз
лерменсің (lermensin)	лер@@мен@@сің

Kazakh language and the column of a sequence of suffixes corresponding to this ending. The Table 1 below shows the fragment of the table of Kazakh endings with segmented suffixes. The symbol @ @ is affix separation symbol.

3.2 An Algorithm for Searching for Unknown Words in the Vocabulary of the Trained Model

An algorithm is developed for searching unknown words in the vocabulary of a trained model of neural machine translation for the Kazakh-English pair of languages. The main idea of this algorithm for searching unknown words in the vocabulary of a trained model is as follows: for the sentence of the target language, where there is a symbol "unk", in its equivalent sentence of the source language, all words are checked for the absence of a trained model in the dictionary. Since it is assumed that if the word is not in the vocabulary, then it is not translated. Then, it is proposed to find its synonym, i.e. another word close in meaning. For this, it is proposed to use the dictionary of synonyms of the Kazakh language.

3.3 Define Synonyms of an Unknown Word

To determine the synonyms of an untranslated (unknown) word, a dictionary of synonyms of the Kazakh language has been compiled. The total volume of the synonym dictionary is 1995. Each word contains at least one synonym word, maximum 35 synonyms. Since there can be several synonyms for each word, it is necessary to check for the presence in the vocabulary of a trained model. For this, an algorithm has been developed that sequentially checks for the presence of synonyms of an untranslated word in the vocabulary of a trained model. The first synonym found in the vocabulary of the trained model is taken as a synonym for this unknown word.

3.4 Replace an Unknown Word by a Found Synonym

The synonym of the untranslated word found at the previous stage is substituted into the source text instead of the unknown word that was not translated, i.e. word that was "out-of-domain".

For all the above stages of solving the unknown word problem, software solutions have been developed in the Python 3 programming language.

3.5 Translation of the Modified Source Text

The resulting adjusted source text is submitted to the machine translation stage.

4 Experimental Part

4.1 Training Data

For the training is used two Kazakh-English parallel corpora: one is KAZNU Kazakh-English with a volume of 143 262 sentences (Table 2), second is WMT19 Kazakh-English with a volume of 140 870 sentences (Table 3). Before dividing to training and testing, the general text was shuffled to prevent learning the same structures. Both two corpora are checked on duplicates of sentences, therefore the KAZNU Kazakh-English corpus have volume 140 851 parallel sentences and the WMT19 Kazakh-English corpus have volume 140 000 parallel sentences (Table 4).

Table 2. KAZNU Kazakh-English parallel corpora

Corpus name	Number of sentences
OPUS	4 480
New World Bible	38 358
Lab IIS	5 925
Akorda	24 148
TED	6 120
Zakon.kz	20 961
Other sites	43 270
Total	143 262

Table 3. WMT 2019 Kazakh-English corpora

Corpus name	Number of sentences
News commentary	9535
Wiki titles v1	114453
The KazakhTV	16882
Total	140 870

The KAZNU Kazakh-English was divided on training set 132 983 sentences, development set 4 868 sentences and test set 3 000 sentences.

The corpus WMT19 Kazakh-English was divided on training set 135 000 sentences, test set 3 500 sentences and development set 1500 sentences.

Table 4. Total volume of corpora after assembling and duplicate sentences cleaning: KAZNU Kazakh-English and WMT19 Kazakh-English

Corpus name	Number of sentences
KAZNU Kazakh-English	140 851
WMT19 Kazakh-English	140 000

The vocabulary is created from frequently used words in corpus (occurring more than 3 times).

The vocabulary for the KAZNU Kazakh-English corpus training set is 16 878 words in Kazakh and 19 124 words in English (files: origvocab.kaz, origvocab.eng).

The vocabulary for the WMT19 Kazakh-English training set is 48 154 words in Kazakh and 20 957 words in English (files: vocab.kaz, vocab.eng).

To evaluate the results of the translation, the BLEU score was used.

In the Table 5 below provides the description of the source data for the training and testing of the NMT of the Kazakh-English language pairs for the proposed technology (method) of solving the problem of unknown words.

Table 5. Description of source data for training and testing of the NMT of the Kazakh-English language pairs for the proposed technology of solving the problem of unknown words.

KAZNU Kazakh-English parallel corpus with volume 140 851 sentences		WMT19 Kazakh-English parallel corpus with volume 140 000 sentences	
Training data: origtrain.kaz, origtrain.eng	132 983	Training data: train.kaz, train.eng	135 000
Test data: kazen-test1.kaz, kazen-test1.eng	3 000	Test data: test.kaz, test.eng	3 500
Development test data: kazen-test2.kaz, kazen-test2.eng	4 868	Development test data: test2.kaz, test2.eng	1 500
Vocabulary of Kazakh (words): origvocab.kaz	16 878	Vocabulary of Kazakh (words): vocab.kaz	48 154
Vocabulary of English (words): origvocab.eng	19 124	Vocabulary of English (words): vocab.eng	20 957

Table 6. Estimates of machine translation of the Kazakh-English language pairs of the baseline version and version using the proposed method for solving the problem of unknown words.

Corpus name	BLEU baseline NMT	BLEU NMT with preprocessing
KAZNU Kazakh-English parallel corpus with volume 140 851 sentences	8.9	8.9
WMT19 Kazakh-English parallel corpus with volume 140 000 sentences	13.2	13.6

Table 6 presents estimates of the machine translation of the Kazakh-English language pairs of the baseline version and the version using the proposed method for solving the problem of unknown words.

Table 7 presents number of unknown words in the text in baseline version of NMT processing and in the NMT with proposed method.

Table 7. Number of unknown words in the text in baseline version of NMT processing and in the NMT with proposed method.

Text volume	Number of unknown words in the text without preprocessing	Number of unknown words in the text after preprocessing
Text with volume 13 sentences	20	14
Text with volume 25 sentences	35	34
Text with volume 36 sentences	23	19
Text with volume 275 sentences	344	336

The application of this technology does not provide such a significant improvement, since only synonyms are used for rare (unknown) words and it may be that synonyms themselves are rare words or rare (unknown) words do not have synonyms.

5   Conclusion and Future Work

The Kazakh language is a low-resource language, especially few parallel corpora for machine translation. Therefore it very important to research the problems improving the quality of machine translation, such as problem of unknown words. In this work proposed technology improving the solution of this problem by the definition of unknown words in the source text by the search them in the vocabulary of the trained model, then define its synonyms by the dictionary of synonyms, after replace an unknown word by this found synonym and repeat translation.

The experiments shows improving of results by the decreasing numbers of un-known words in output text, but the quality of translation by BLEU metric is very little improving. In our opinion that results are explained by (1) the volume of synonyms dictionary is not enough; (2) meanings of synonyms using for replacing of unknown words is not quite suitable.

Therefore, future works are planned to improve the quality and volume of the synonyms dictionary. Also in the future planned to apply statistical methods to determine the position of unknown words in the source text and to use the word2vec model for replacing rare words with words that are meaning close.

Acknowledgments. This work was carried out under grant No. AP05131415 "Development and research of the neural machine translation system of Kazakh language" and grant No. AP05132950 "Development of an information-analytical search system of data in the Kazakh language", funded by the Ministry of Education and Science of the Republic of Kazakhstan for 2018–2020.

References

1. Luong, M.T., Sutskever, I., Le, Q.V., Vinyals, O., Zaremba, W.: Addressing the rare word problem in neural machine translation. In: Proceedings of the 53rd Annual Meeting of the Association for Computational Linguistics and the 7th International Joint Conference on Natural Language Processing, pp. 11–19 (2015)
2. Hermann, K.M., et al.: Teaching machines to read and comprehend. In: Proceedings of the 28th International Conference on Neural Information Processing Systems, pp. 1693–1701 (2015)
3. Generating sequences with recurrent neural networks. https://arxiv.org/pdf/1308.0850.pdf. Accessed 27 Aug 2019
4. Sennrich, R., Haddow, B., Birch, A.: Neural machine translation of rare words with subword units. In: Proceedings of the 54th Annual Meeting of the Association for Computational Linguistics, pp. 1715–1725 (2016)
5. Marton, Y., Callison-Burch, Ch., Resnik, Ph.: Improved statistical machine translation using monolingually-derived paraphrases, In: Proceedings of the 2009 Conference on Empirical Methods in Natural Language, pp. 381–390 (2009)
6. Zhang, J., Zhai, F., Zong, Ch.: Handling unknown words in statistical machine translation from a new perspective. In: Proceedings of the First CCF Conference Natural Language Processing and Chinese Computing, pp. 176–187 (2012)
7. Zhang, J., Zhai, F., Zong, Ch.: A substitution-translation-restoration framework for handling unknown words in statistical machine translation. J. Comput. Sci. Technol. **28**(5), 907–918 (2013)
8. Gulcehre, C., Ahn, S., Nallapati, R., Zhou, B., Bengio, Y.: Pointing the unknown words. In: Proceedings of the 54th Annual Meeting of the Association for Computational Linguistics, pp. 140–149 (2016)
9. Li, X., Zhang, J., Zong, C.: Towards zero unknown word in neural machine translation. In: Proceedings of the International Joint Conference on Artificial Intelligence, pp. 2852–2858. AAAI Press (2016)
10. Li, Sh., Xu, J., Miao, G., Zhang, Y., Chen, Y.: A semantic concept based unknown words processing method in neural machine translation. In: Proceedings of the 6th CCF International Conference on Natural Language Processing, pp. 233–242. NLPCC (2017)
11. Arthur, Ph., Neubig, G., Nakamura, S.: Incorporating discrete translation lexicons into neural machine translation. In: Proceedings of the 2016 Conference on Empirical Methods in Natural Language Processing, pp. 1557–1567. Association for Computational Linguistics (2016)
12. Tukeyev, U.: Automaton models of the morphology analysis and the completeness of the endings of the Kazakh language. In: Proceedings of the International Conference Turkic Languages Processing, TURKLANG 2015, pp. 91–100 (2015)
13. Tukeyev, U., Sundetova, A., Abduali, B., Akhmadiyeva, Z., Zhanbussunov, N.: Inferring of the morphological chunk transfer rules on the base of complete set of Kazakh endings. In: Nguyen, N.-T., Manolopoulos, Y., Iliadis, L., Trawiński, B. (eds.) ICCCI 2016. LNCS (LNAI), vol. 9876, pp. 563–574. Springer, Cham (2016). https://doi.org/10.1007/978-3-319-45246-3_54

Comparative Analysis of Selected Geotagging Methods

Sichen Mu, Mateusz Piwowarczyk⬤, Marcin Kutrzyński⬤,
Bogdan Trawiński⁽✉⁾⬤, and Zbigniew Telec⬤

Faculty of Computer Science and Management,
Wrocław University of Science and Technology, Wrocław, Poland
{mateusz.piwowarczyk,marcin.kutrzynski,bogdan.trawinski,
zbigniew.telec}@pwr.edu.pl

Abstract. Geotagging is a rapidly growing technology in digital photography and searching for specific landmarks, and helps everyone in our daily lives. Navigation applications and travel guides put a number of geotagged photos on the maps, providing a good overview of the destination. Recently, the development of photo geotagging methods has become a popular issue. Implementations of the SIFT and SURF algorithms and training of convolutional neural networks to obtain image classification for landmark images are presented in this paper. Based on the results of the classification of images and geotags of other similar images, geotags have been assigned to the target images. In addition, the results of image classification obtained using feature detection algorithms and neural networks were compared and analyzed.

Keywords: Geotagging · Landmark recognition · SIFT algorithm · SURF algorithm · Convolutional neural network

1 Introduction

Searching through a huge collection of images based only on their filenames could be very inefficient. Also other metadata assigned to pictures manually or automatically (e.g. coordinates of where photo is taken by camera build-in or connected GPS systems) could not be sufficient for many applications. Process of attaching geospatial identification metadata to media files such as images, videos, e-books and social media posts is called geotagging. Geotag is a form of geospatial metadata. Such data usually contains information about geolocation, timestamp, sometimes it also has GPS track information. Geotagging could be replaced by georeferencing and geocoding. Georeferencing is defined as specifying the geographic location of an object like image or movie. Geocoding is the process of finding a mathematical representation of geolocation. Generally, a geotag consists of latitude and longitude reference. In addition, the geotag may also contain legal place names. By searching through geotags, users can find different types of information at a particular location. For example, if you want to take

© Springer Nature Singapore Pte Ltd. 2020
P. Sitek et al. (Eds.): ACIIDS 2020, CCIS 1178, pp. 329–341, 2020.
https://doi.org/10.1007/978-981-15-3380-8_29

a brief look at the Great Wall view, you can easily get many images online by typing in the "Great Wall" image search engine. Geotagging is starting to gain popularity, among others thanks to social media. People want to include photo location information to show other people where they spend their holidays or just let others find their photos by entering the place name. Much of this information is very useful in applications such as Google Street View or Bing Maps Streetside Photos. Images with geospatial tags can be also very helpful for landmark recognition from untagged images [23] to automatically recognize photos of landmarks that were not annotated with proper metadata. One of the main questions that arise when building such systems is how to geotag images with geospatial information? Most images on the Internet are not geotagged images. This means that they do not have specific coordinate metadata for themselves. If we want to geotag it manually, it can be very difficult because the number of information appearing on the Internet every second [1] is much faster than the reasonable number of people who could manually assign geotags to this data and will grow in subsequent years together with the development of the Internet of Things technology. Moreover, these people could potentially not have detailed knowledge about each individual landmark and could not correctly recognize the landmark in each photo. On the other hand, some of the landmark images are tagged and available online. Thanks to modern image recognition techniques and recent improvements in computer vision [9], we can try to classify not geotagged images as a specific landmark of which we have geospatial data, and set these data to untagged images.

One example of approaches to such a task was presented by Song et al. [20]. They achieved landmark recognition through the use of the SURF algorithm [5]. They also compared performance between the SIFT algorithm and the SURF algorithm. Thanks to their use, landmark recognition accuracy reaches 84.5% for matching and downloading landmark images. In addition, Azhar et al. [3] applied the SIFT feature extraction and achieved the accuracy of batik image classification for normal, rotated and scaled images 97.67%, 95.47% and 79% respectively. Horak et al. [8,10] detected characteristic points using the SURF algorithm and use supervised learning algorithms such as Linear Discriminant Analysis (LDA) [4], Quadratic Discriminant Analysis (QDA) [13] and Naive Bayes [17] to the feature points. They reached 99.8% accuracy in classifying vehicle license plates. Khan et al. [11] and Juan and Gwun [10] compared performance between the SIFT and SURF algorithms. According to their conclusion, SIFT performance is as good as SURF, but SURF is much faster than SIFT. Among the problems we have to deal with when recognizing landmarks is that images can have objects other than landmarks, such as cars, birds, trees and people. In addition, there are both long-view and close-up images for landmarks. Using the SIFT algorithm or the SURF algorithm, it is possible to adjust the close-up view function to the image in the view with long exposure times and it is possible to match the image with part of the landmark to the image with the entire view of the landmark.

In this article, we present two approaches to classifying and geotagging images based on 927 photos of 17 landmarks located in Barcelona. After classification, we assigned landmarks category geotags to individual photos. The first approach was to detect image features using the SIFT algorithm [15] and the SURF algorithm [5]. By matching image features, the image class was predicted. The second approach relied on convolution neural networks (ConvNet) as the main classifiers. This approach was chosen due to a huge increase in accuracy in image classification tasks using ConvNet in recent years [12]. Images with geotags were divided into training and validation sets. After predicting a class of photos without geotags, the prediction accuracy was calculated. Then, for correctly selected images, we assigned the average geolocation of known landmark images appropriately to images in various landmark classes. A series of experiments compared the performance of the SIFT and SURF algorithms in terms of feature extraction time, feature matching time, and accuracy of landmark class prediction. The accuracy of prediction was also compared among convulsive neuron networks with different training parameters. Moreover, the accuracy between these two approaches was also compared. Based on the results of comparative experiments, Wilcoxon paired tests were performed among SIFT, SURF and convolution neural networks to check if the differences between the algorithms are statistically significant.

2   Method Description

In this section, we will briefly present two approaches to photo classification used in our research. The first is based on the extraction of image features and for this approach we used two different methods: SIFT and SURF. These methods were used because of their great ability to extract the image features and the easy way to match these features with other images to find out if they are images of the same object. One of the cones of this method is that we must additionally use a certain matching policy to determine if there are enough matching points to classify images as images of the same object. The second approach was based on the use of a convolutional neural network. This methods allows both the extraction of image features and image classification. The modified architecture of the VGG16 convolutional neural network was applied, and this selection was dictated by its high accuracy in classifying photographic images [18,22].

2.1   SIFT Algorithm

The SIFT (Scale-Invariant Feature Transform) algorithm is commonly used to detect, create and describe local features in photos [16]. It was published by Lowe [15] in 2004. The SIFT algorithm is mainly focused on detecting and finding feature points and extreme points. It also calculates the orientation of each feature point to create a descriptor for each feature point. The features extracted by the SIFT algorithm are invariant with respect to image translation, image scaling and image rotation transformation. It is also partially invariant to illumination changes. There are four main steps in the SIFT algorithm:

1. Scale-space extrema detection.
2. Key point localization.
3. Orientation assignment.
4. Key point descriptor.

The results of the SIFT algorithm are shown in Figs. 1 and 2.

Fig. 1. SIFT feature points on target image

2.2 SURF Algorithm

The SURF (Speed Up Robust Features) algorithm is a local feature detector and descriptor. The SURF algorithm is mainly used for object recognition, image classification and image registration tasks. It is partly inspired by the SIFT algorithm and is also considered a refinement of this algorithm because it works faster than it. The SURF algorithm was presented Bay et al. in 2006 [5]. It has also four main steps. It has also has four main steps and the main differences between SIFT and SURF algorithms are indicated below:

1. Scale-space extrema detection. SURF uses the Hessian Matrix to detect and extract extremes, while SIFT uses the Difference of Gaussians.
2. Key point localization.

Fig. 2. An example of matching result of SIFT algorithm

3. Orientation assignment. Instead of creating a gradient histogram, SURF uses wavelet responses horizontally and vertically in an adjacent circle and uses appropriate Gaussian weights.
4. Key point descriptor.

The results of the SURF algorithm are illustrated in Figs. 3 and 4.

2.3   Convolutional Neural Network

Convolutional neural network (CNN or ConvNet) is a class of deep neural network. ConvNet networks are often used for image classification, image recognition and other problems related to image analysis in computer vision [6,14,21]. Convolutional neural network are based on a mathematical operation called convolution, which is a type of linear operation. They are used to multiply the matrix in at least one of the layers of the artificial neural network. In our research, we used VGG16 (Very Deep Convolutional Networks for Large-Scale Image Recognition) [19]. It is a kind of model of a convolutional neural network proposed by Simonony and Zisserman which achieves 92.7% of test accuracy on the ImageNet data set [7]. This is a well-known data set for comparative analysis of algorithms and for comparing their performance for tasks related to 2D images. The VGG16 architecture consists of the following group of layers:

1. Image input layer - for inputting images of specific size.
2. Feature learning layers - consist of convolution layer, ReLU layer and pooling layer. It learns the features of images and reduces their size.

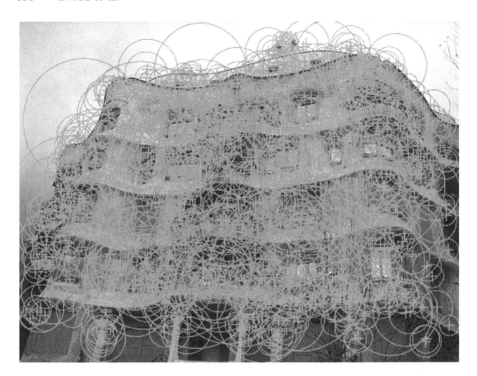

Fig. 3. SURF feature points on target image.

Fig. 4. An example of matching result of SURF algorithm.

3. Classification layers - consists of a few fully connected layers, softmax layer. The task of classification layers is assigning the input image to a specific class.

3 Dataset

We used in our research a subset of the European Cities 1M (EC1M) data set [2]. This collection contains 927 photos of Barcelona landmarks in 17 categories and geotags for each photo. The maximum size of each image was no more than 500×500 pixels. Categories of data sets were not well balanced. Four categories contained more than 100 images, and the next four comprised approximately 20 images. The number of images in the other 9 categories ranged from 30 to 70. This might affect the classification results for classes with fewer images, but most categories included over 50 images. Since the latitude and longitude provided for each photo in the data set were the coordinates of the place where the photos were taken, we had to calculate the average latitude and longitude for each category. These average coordinates were used as the final location of each landmark.

4 Experimental Setup

Workflow of geotagging using image feature extraction algorithms and classification based on these features and the Convolutional Neural Network learning process for the same task is shown in Fig. 5. To obtain image classification for target images, the Match Feature Points and Convolutional Neural Network approaches were used in parallel. The method of comparing feature points used the SIFT algorithm and the SURF algorithm separately.

We decided on two approaches to image classification: SIFT and SURF algorithms as one approach based on separately extracted image features and the convolutional neural network as a method for both extracting features and image classification. After extracting the features, the next step was the process of classifying target images and assigning geotags to images with the predicted landmark class. The image classification flow for new landmark images with the first approach consists of four main steps as below:

1. Target image extraction function by SIFT/SURF
2. Comparison and matching of functions with images in the dataset
3. Assigning the candidate class for the target image to a specific class
4. Determining the class of target image

A modified convolutional architecture of the VGG16 neural network was used to perform image classification. The input image was set to 224×224 with 3 channels. We used two approaches to training, the first with the number of filters from 8 to 64 and the second from 16 to 128. The initial learning rate was set to 0.01, the maximum epochal training rate was 50 epochs. During training the validation process was performed every 30 iterations. The entire training process was carried out on multiple CPUs.

After matching features between target image and images used for training, the number of matched feature points can be calculated. To select candidate class for the target image, we need to compare the number of matched feature

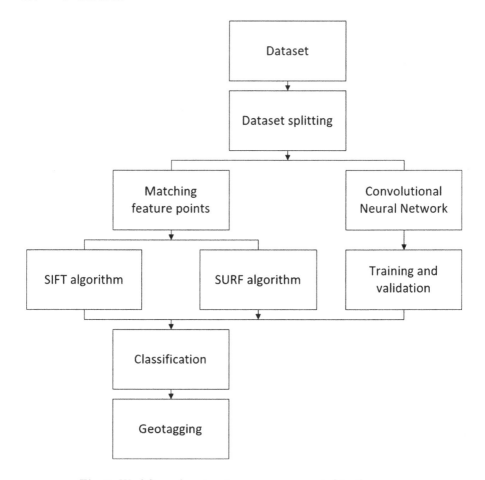

Fig. 5. Workflow of geotagging process presented in the paper.

points with a assumptive threshold value (match threshold). If the number of matched feature point is greater than the matching threshold, the class to which the matching image belongs will be selected as the candidate class and saved in the candidate class matrix (candidate matrix). However, how to set the match threshold value is problematic. If the threshold value is too high, it may turn out that there is no selected candidate class and the candidate matrix will be empty. So you will not be able to specify the target image class. If the threshold is too low, images that do not have many matching feature points will also be considered as candidates, and the classes to which they belong will also be calculated in the number of each candidate class. Because the number of images for each class is not the same in the database, it can happen that most candidate classes do not have many matching points. In the meantime, the right class, which has more points matched than others, can be ignored. Thus, the target image would be misclassified. To set a better match threshold value, match matrices were created that represent the number of matched points in one image for all other images in the data set. According to these matrices, the average number of matched points for each image is first calculated. However, the result has huge differences, even for images in the same class. The lowest average value was only about 3, while the highest average value could reach 50 or more. The reason for this may be that the landmark photos are taken from different perspectives, and the perspective of the currently classified photo can only match a certain subset of all photos of a given landmark in the training set. Thus, setting the average number of matched points as the match threshold is rejected. Since it is not possible to use the average number of matched points, we observed each match matrix and found a set of laws:

- The number of matched points varies a lot among different images. Images in one class that matches well with each other usually have more than 15 matched points.
- If we match an image with images in other classes, the number of matched points is usually less than 10.
- There exist a few results that different classes match more than 10 points. However, this case does not occur often.

As observed, two match threshold values: 10 and 15 were set separately. The value set as the final decision was chosen based on the tests carried out on the new photos. To determine the target image class after receiving the candidate matrix, we applied two approaches to class selection. The first was to choose the class with the most frequent occurrences (*Most*). The second approach was to choose the class with the highest number of matching points (*Top*). In most cases, photos in the same class had a greater number of matched points among them than matches with other classes. This ensured that the correct class of the target image had more instances than other classes. If the class appears in the candidate list the most frequently, it is more likely to be the correct class for the target image. That is why the *Most* method was considered. On the other hand, the more points the two images match, the more similar these two images are and the higher probability that they belong to the same class. Given this reason, if one of the images has the largest number of matching points compared to all other images, this image may be the most similar to the target image, and the image class may be the correct target image class. That is why the *Top* method was considered. There were, however, situations in which either the *Most* method or the *Top* method could not select the correct class for the target image. To test which of the two cases was more likely to be the case, which approach was more accurate, a new set of 170 images was created along with the test that better matches the matching threshold. There were 10 images randomly downloaded from Google Image Search and Baidu Search results in each class. None of them have been geotagged. Considering all the results of our tests, we could state that:

- SIFT algorithm generally performs better than SURF algorithm
- SURF feature extraction is faster than SIFT
- The *Most* approach had higher accuracy than the *Top* approach

– The accuracy was higher with match threshold equal to 10

According to the tests, match threshold was set to 10 and *Most* approach for predicting classes was selected.

5   Results

The basic compared attributes for SIFT and SURF were: descriptor dimensions, number of feature points extracted, average extraction time, average matching time, and prediction accuracy. Table 1 summarizes the results of the comparison of the application of the SIFT and SURF methods, and Table 2 shows the comparison between the SIFT and SURF algorithms and convolutional neural networks on test images.

By comparing the number of characteristic points extracted by SIFT and SURF, the SIFT algorithm extracted more characteristic points than SURF. We also see that the SURF algorithm was much faster than SIFT. This result is consistent with [10,11,20]. SIFT had more dimensions in the descriptor, which took more time to calculate. This may also be the reason why the SIFT prediction accuracy was higher than SURF. For both *Top* and *Most* methods, the SIFT algorithm outperformed SURF. However, the differences were statistically significant only for the *Top* method. For the *Most* method no statistically significant differences were observed between the SIFT and SURF.

Table 1. Comparison between SIFT and SURF algorithm.

Attributes	SIFT	SURF
Dimensions of descriptor	128	64
More number of points extracted	886/927	41/927
Average time for extracting	9.0122 s	0.0282 s
Average time for matching	0.0790 s	0.0034 s
Accuracy of prediction (arithmetic mean)	61%	47%
Accuracy of prediction (median)	60%	50%

Table 2. Comparison between SIFT/SURF and convolutional neural networks on test images.

Method	Accuracy (arithmetic mean)	Accuracy (median)
SIFT	61%	60%
SURF	47%	50%
vgg16_81.72	52,4%	60%
vgg16_79.03	47,6%	50%
vgg16_77.78	50%	50%

Considering the results and statistical tests, the performance of SIFT algorithm, SURF algorithm and CNN do not differ significantly.

6 Conclusions

In this paper, landmark image classification and geotagging landmark images was accomplished using SIFT, SURF algorithms and convolutional neural networks. First, a set of data was prepared with images of landmarks located in Barcelona. In addition, a set of 170 images (10 images in each class) was downloaded from the Internet to create a test set. Next, image feature detection algorithms: SIFT and SURF were used separately and three convolutional neural networks were trained to classify landmark images. Comparative experiments were conducted to select a match threshold and better approach to class selection. Tests were also carried out using convolutional neural networks to check their performance over new images. The accuracy of image classification in the experiments was calculated. Paired Wilcoxon tests were conducted to check if the differences were statistically significant.

The following conclusions were drawn from our preliminary results. The median accuracy of image classification by using SIFT, SURF, and VGG16 algorithms was 60%, 50%, and 50%, respectively. The performance of the SIFT and SURF algorithms was the best when the match threshold was set 10 and the *Most* approach was selected for choosing the predicted class from candidate classes. The performance of SIFT, SURF, and VGG16 algorithms did not differ significantly.

Further research should be conducted to improve our preliminary results. The scope of the project should be extended to include landmark images from all over world. The number of images in the dataset should be larger and the number of classes should be extended. Moreover, the number of photos in each class should be balanced. Algorithms that can remove outliers should be considered and applied to the results of matching features. Other methods such as k-nearest neighbour, naive Bayes, or support vector machine can be used to classify images based on SIFT/SURF features. Other convolutional neural networks such as GoogLeNet, ResNet, or Inception could be applied In addition, the long-view and close-up landmark images could be split into two classes to obtain better results of training. Due to the fact that averaging coordinates from all pictures of landmark loses some valuable information, a more accurate method of locating images in space should be used to assign them appropriate and exact coordinates. Other image matching methods could be also applied and tested.

References

1. Alansari, Z., et al.: Challenges of Internet of Things and big data integration. In: Miraz, M.H., Excell, P., Ware, A., Soomro, S., Ali, M. (eds.) iCETiC 2018. LNICST, vol. 200, pp. 47–55. Springer, Cham (2018). https://doi.org/10.1007/978-3-319-95450-9_4

2. Avrithis, Y., Kalantidis, Y., Tolias, G., Spyrou, E.: Retrieving landmark and non-landmark images from community photo collections. In: Proceedings of the 18th ACM International Conference on Multimedia, pp. 153–162. ACM (2010)

3. Azhar, R., Tuwohingide, D., Kamudi, D., Suciati, N., et al.: Batik image classification using SIFT feature extraction, bag of features and support vector machine. Procedia Comput. Sci. **72**, 24–30 (2015)

4. Balakrishnama, S., Ganapathiraju, A.: Linear discriminant analysis-a brief tutorial. Inst. Signal Inf. Process. **18**, 1–8 (1998)

5. Bay, H., Tuytelaars, T., Van Gool, L.: SURF: speeded up robust features. In: Leonardis, A., Bischof, H., Pinz, A. (eds.) ECCV 2006. LNCS, vol. 3951, pp. 404–417. Springer, Heidelberg (2006). https://doi.org/10.1007/11744023_32

6. Chellapilla, K., Puri, S., Simard, P.: High performance convolutional neural networks for document processing (2006)

7. Deng, J., et al.: ImageNet: a large-scale hierarchical image database. In: 2009 IEEE Conference on Computer Vision and Pattern Recognition, pp. 248–255. IEEE (2009)

8. Horak, K., Klecka, J., Bostik, O., Davidek, D.: Classification of surf image features by selected machine learning algorithms. In: 2017 40th International Conference on Telecommunications and Signal Processing (TSP), pp. 636–641. IEEE (2017)

9. Ioannidou, A., Chatzilari, E., Nikolopoulos, S., Kompatsiaris, I.: Deep learning advances in computer vision with 3D data: a survey. ACM Comput. Surv. (CSUR) **50**(2), 20 (2017)

10. Juan, L., Gwon, L.: A comparison of SIFT, PCA-SIFT and SURF. Int. J. Signal Process. Image Process. Pattern Recogn. **8**(3), 169–176 (2007)

11. Khan, N.Y., McCane, B., Wyvill, G.: SIFT and SURF performance evaluation against various image deformations on benchmark dataset. In: 2011 International Conference on Digital Image Computing: Techniques and Applications, pp. 501–506. IEEE (2011)

12. Krizhevsky, A., Sutskever, I., Hinton, G.E.: ImageNet classification with deep convolutional neural networks. In: Advances in Neural Information Processing Systems, pp. 1097–1105 (2012)

13. Lachenbruch, P.A., Goldstein, M.: Discriminant analysis. Biometrics, 69–85 (1979)

14. Le Callet, P., Viard-Gaudin, C., Barba, D.: A convolutional neural network approach for objective video quality assessment (2006)

15. Lowe, D.G.: Distinctive image features from scale-invariant keypoints. Int. J. Comput. Vis. **60**(2), 91–110 (2004). https://doi.org/10.1023/B:VISI.0000029664.99615.94

16. Luo, J., Ma, Y., Takikawa, E., Lao, S., Kawade, M., Lu, B.L.: Person-specific SIFT features for face recognition. In: 2007 IEEE International Conference on Acoustics, Speech and Signal Processing-ICASSP 2007, vol. 2, pp. II-593. IEEE (2007)

17. Murphy, K.P., et al.: Naive Bayes classifiers, vol. 18, p. 60. University of British Columbia (2006)

18. Qassim, H., Verma, A., Feinzimer, D.: Compressed residual-VGG16 CNN model for big data places image recognition. In: 2018 IEEE 8th Annual Computing and Communication Workshop and Conference (CCWC), pp. 169–175. IEEE (2018)

19. Simonyan, K., Zisserman, A.: Very deep convolutional networks for large-scale image recognition. arXiv preprint arXiv:1409.1556 (2014)

20. Song, X., Liu, J., Tang, X.: Image retrieval-based landmark recognition system. Electron. Des. Eng. (12), 54 (2012)

21. Szarvas, M., Yoshizawa, A., Yamamoto, M., Ogata, J.: Pedestrian detection with convolutional neural networks. In: Intelligent Vehicles Symposium, pp. 224–229 (2005)
22. Yu, X., Zhou, F., Chandraker, M.: Deep deformation network for object landmark localization. In: Leibe, B., Matas, J., Sebe, N., Welling, M. (eds.) ECCV 2016. LNCS, vol. 9909, pp. 52–70. Springer, Cham (2016). https://doi.org/10.1007/978-3-319-46454-1_4
23. Zheng, Y.T., et al.: Tour the world: building a web-scale landmark recognition engine. In: 2009 IEEE Conference on Computer Vision and Pattern Recognition, pp. 1085–1092. IEEE (2009)

Use of Ontology Learning in Information System Integration: A Literature Survey

Chuangtao Ma$^{(\boxtimes)}$ and Bálint Molnár$^{(\boxtimes)}$

Department of Information Systems, Faculty of Informatics, Eötvös Loránd
University, Budapest, Hungary
machuangtao@caesar.elte.hu, molnarba@inf.elte.hu

Abstract. Ontology-based information integration is a useful method to integrate heterogeneous data at the semantic level. However, there are some bottlenecks of the traditional method for constructing ontology, i.e., time-consuming, error-prone, and semantic loss. Ontology learning is a kind of ontology construction approach based on machine learning, it provides a new opportunity to tackle the above bottlenecks. Especially, it could be employed to construct ontologies and integrate large-scale and heterogeneous data from various information systems. This paper surveys the latest developments of ontology learning and highlights how they could be adopted and play a vital role in the integration of information systems. The recent techniques and tools of ontology learning from text and relational database are reviewed, the possibility of using ontology learning in information integration were discussed based on the mapping results of the aforementioned bottlenecks and features of ontology learning. The potential directions for using ontology learning in information systems integration were given.

Keywords: Information system integration · Ontology learning · Relational database · Literature survey

1 Introduction

The main aim of information system integration is to achieve the centralized storage and full access of the data from various information systems, share the workflow and provide an integrated information system for collaborative business. It is a common phenomenon that various conflicts, e.g., diverse format, naming conventions and semantic heterogeneity will occur when we manage to integrate heterogeneous information from different information systems [1]. Hence, the key task of information system integration is to eliminate the heterogeneity of the data and workflow between different information systems.

Ontology is one of the essential knowledge representation methods that have been widely adopting in the fields of data fusion and information system integration due to its high machine-readable and semantic interoperability. Especially, ontology could represent semantic interoperability within different concepts, instances relations and axioms related to the specified domain [2], which

© Springer Nature Singapore Pte Ltd. 2020
P. Sitek et al. (Eds.): ACIIDS 2020, CCIS 1178, pp. 342–353, 2020.
https://doi.org/10.1007/978-981-15-3380-8_30

provide an opportunity to integrate the heterogeneous data and information systems at the semantic level. Hence, an ontology-based information integration approach has been playing a critical role in the integration of the information system. Traditionally, the process of ontology construction is a time-consuming task that requires a lot of manpower and effort [3]. There is no doubt that the efficiency of the ontology-based information integration was limited by the automation degree of the ontology construction.

Ontology learning (OL) is a kind of ontology construction approach based on the machine learning technique [4]. It was proposed to (semi-)automatically extract the knowledge from the text document or database for constructing ontology efficiently [5]. In recent years, there is a great technological advancement in the fields of ontology construction, ontology mapping and semantic integration accompanied by the development of machine learning and computational intelligence [6]. Consequently, several novel approaches and techniques, e.g., automated ontology notation, dynamic ontology mapping, ontology refinement and so forth, have been applying in the fields of machine translation and question answering system [7]. In contrast to the aforementioned fields, the integration of the information system based on ontology learning is a new topic.

This survey paper focuses on how ontology learning could be adopted and play a vital role in the integration of information systems. The rest of this survey paper is structured as follows. Initially, the previous surveys on the topic of ontology-based information integration and ontology learning are concluded in Sect. 2. Then, the recent techniques and tools that support ontology learning from text and relational database are presented in Sect. 3. After that, the possibility of using ontology learning in information integration was analyzed based on the mapping results between the features of ontology learning and bottleneck problems of ontology-based information integration in Sect. 4. The potential directions of using ontology learning in information system integration and the conclusion of this paper were discussed and summarized in Sect. 5 and Sect. 6 respectively.

2   Summary of Previous Surveys

The previous surveys focused on the major bottlenecks of semantic integration, e.g., ontology mapping, formal representation and reasoning of mappings, from the perspective of ontology-based integration.

2.1   Ontology-Based Information Integration

Ontology-based information integration could achieve the integration at the semantic level, hence, Noy [8] surveyed the ontology-based approaches for semantic integration. The conclusion was drawn that automated mapping will be conducive to alleviate the constraints of ontology-based information integration, hence heuristic-based approaches of ontology mappings, e.g., machine learning, ontology learning, and so forth, should be studied further for improving the automation of ontology mapping.

Ontology-based information extraction is a critical component in the ontology-based integration framework, which provides the source of the information and knowledge for constructing ontology. Thus, Wimalasuriya et al. [9] surveyed and classified existing ontology-based information extraction (OBIE) approaches, from the technological perspective, e.g., linguistic rules, finite-state automata, classification, the partial parse tree, web-based search, tools and performance measures. They concluded that existing approaches to information extraction mainly rely on the linguistic rules that identified manually. Besides, the availability of the existing methods for measuring the performance is limited by the efficiency of identifying instance and property values.

Ontology mapping could support information integration by representing the relationship between global ontology and local ontology, hence ontology mapping is also a critical technique for ontology-based information integration. Thus, Hooi et al. [10] surveyed the existing ontology mapping techniques and tools. They focus on the analysis of existing mapping techniques and matching algorithms, which highlight the matcher is a core component of ontology mapping. They concluded that the majority of the matcher is designed on a specific domain, in this situation, the re-usability of mapping tools is restricted.

2.2   Ontology Learning

The model of ontology learning is usually built based on the techniques from machine learning, NLP (Natural Language Processing) and information retrieval [11]. The techniques of ontology learning could be classified into the statistical approach, natural language processing approach, and integrated approach.

To investigate the existing techniques of ontology learning, Biemann [12] surveyed the techniques of ontology learning from unstructured text, e.g., clustering, distributional similarity, co-occurrence matrix, decision tree. The conclusion was drawn that the majority of the existing approaches to ontology learning from unstructured text use only nouns and ignore the relationship between various words and classes. The past decade has witnessed tremendous progress regarding the techniques of machine learning and the semantic web. To investigate the recent techniques of ontology learning, Asim et al. [6] systematically classified the methodology of ontology learning into three categories: linguistics techniques, statistical techniques, and inductive logic programming. They compared the performance of each ontology learning techniques, and the accuracy of the ontology learning based on inductive logical programming up to 96%.

The conclusion could be drawn that the majority of aforementioned surveys on the topics of ontology-based information integration and ontology learning were conducted separately, there is rare work that surveys the opportunity of using ontology learning in information integration. However, in recent years, some bottlenecks of the traditional method for constructing ontology are emerging, i.e., time-consuming, error-prone, and semantic loss, which bring the unprecedented challenges of the traditional ontology-based information integration. OL probably provides a new perspective to tackle the above issues, thus, this survey paper aims to investigate the potential opportunity of using ontology learning in information system integration.

3   Ontology Learning Techniques

The majority techniques of ontology learning were borrowed from the NLP and data mining. The typical techniques of the terms and entities extraction are originated from NLP, e.g., tagging, syntactic segmentation, parsing, and so forth. The alternative approaches for implementing the NLP including machine learning and statistical inference. Moreover, the representative techniques of the relationship extraction were proposed based on the data mining algorithm, e.g., clustering algorithms, association rule mining, occurrence analysis.

3.1   Ontology Learning from Text

The mainstream techniques of ontology learning from the text could be classified into linguistics approach, machine learning, and the combination of the linguistics and machine learning. The representative works of the ontology learning from texts were summarized as follows.

To generate the ontologies from Web, Venu et al. [13] proposed a framework, they extracted the terms and relations by using of HITS (Hyperlink-Induced Topic Search) algorithm and Hearst Patterns respectively. The resource description framework (RDF) was adopted to store the extracted terms and their relations, then the ontology was constructed based on the RDF. OWL (Web Ontology Language) is a formal language for representing ontologies, which provides richer semantic representation than RDF. Thus, Petrucci et al. [14] developed a system to translate natural language into description logic (DL) based on the neural network. Based on the aforementioned work, Petrucci et al. [15] designed an ontology learning model based on a recurrent neural network (RNN) to extract OWL from a textual document. They focused on improving the performances of ontology learning, i.e., domain independence, accuracy, and so forth.

In addition to the machine learning techniques, the linguistics techniques were also utilized to construct ontology, Rani et al. [16] studied a semi-automatic terminology ontology learning approach based on LSI (Latent Semantic Index) and SVD (Singular Value Decomposition). This approach could semi-automatically create a terminological ontology based on the topic modeling algorithm by using Protégé[1]. To extract the terms and relation from cross-medial text automatically, Hong et al. [17] proposed a domain ontology learning method based on LDA (Latent Dirichlet Allocation) model. In this model, the NLPIR (Natural Language Process Information Retrieval) and LDA subject models were adopted to extract the terms and their relations respectively.

---

[1] https://protege.stanford.edu/, accessed on October 7, 2019.

To improve the dynamic of ontology learning, Dutkowski et al. [18] disclosed a framework of the ontology-based dynamic learning from text data. In this patent, the inference techniques were adopted to extract the relation between entities from the data. Besides, the statistical techniques, i.e., entities measurement, and relation score were applied to extend the ontology learning from static learning to dynamic learning. Considering the weak interactivity of the existing algorithm, Ghosh et al. [19] built an ontology learning experimental platform based on the Text2Onto[2] for learning the domain knowledge from text semi-automatically. In this work, the TF-IDF (Term Frequency-Inverse Document Frequency) concept extraction algorithm and relation extraction algorithm based on Subcat Frames were adopted to extract the terms and their relations respectively. The extraction techniques of the term, relation, and the input & output of the aforementioned works could be summarized in the Table 1.

Table 1. Summary of the techniques of ontology learning from text.

Paper	Techniques		Approach	Input & Output
	Term extraction	Relation extraction		
[13]	HITS algorithm	Hearst patterns	Linguistic	Corpora ⇒ RDF
[14]	Recurrent neural network		Machine learning	Text ⇒ OWL
[15]	Single neural network		Machine learning	Text ⇒ DL
[16]	LSI	Frequency analysis	Machine learning	Text ⇒ Ontology
[17]	NLPIR	LDA	ML & Linguistic	Text ⇒ Ontology
[18]	Text mining	Inference engine	Machine learning	Text ⇒ Ontology
[19]	TFIDF	Subcat	ML & Linguistic	Text ⇒ OWL

Based on the above summaries, the conclusion could be drawn that the majority of the OL model from the text was built based on machine learning techniques and linguistics techniques. The outputs of the model could be classified into three categories, formal ontology, semi-formal ontology, and information ontology. However, the existing ontology learning tools are semi-automatic which is limited by the performance of the algorithms.

3.2   Ontology Learning from Relational Database

Relational database (RDB) has been the majority source of the knowledge, which could provide the conceptual model and the metadata model for constructing ontology [20]. Hence, how to construct the ontology from the RDB efficiently and effectively has attracted the attention of the researcher. To tackle the aforementioned issues, ontology learning from RDB was investigated in recent years.

---

[2] http://neon-toolkit.org/wiki/1.x/Text2Onto.html, accessed on October 7, 2019.

There are two critical phases of constructing ontology from RDB based on ontology learning. In the first phase, the RDB schema is usually transformed into RDFS (RDF Schema) based on the DL and rule mapping. In the second phase, the semantic relationships are extracted and the ontology is generated from RDB by using semantic measurement and machine learning. The specified techniques of ontology learning from RDB could be depicted in Fig. 1.

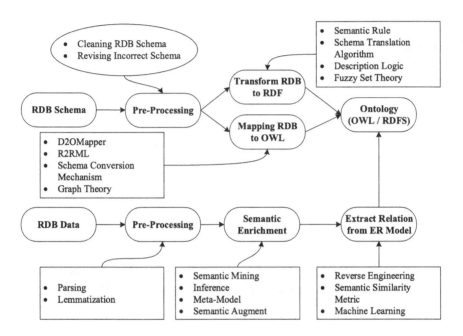

Fig. 1. Techniques of ontology learning from RDB.

The mainstream techniques of the OL from RDB could be classified into four categories: reverse engineering, schema mapping, data mining, and machine learning. The corresponding work could be illustrated as follows. Considering the richer semantic of the conceptual model (ER model), Sbai et al. [21] utilized reverse engineering to analyze and transform the relational model to the conceptual model for building ontology from RDB. This method could recover the lost semantic information and database table during the transformation.

There are two alternative solutions for constructing ontology from RDB schema: transform RDB to RDF and mapping RDB to OWL. To implement transforming from RDB to ontology, Dadjoo et al. [22] designed a transforming method. This method consists of three steps: extract information (Meta-data) from RDB, build graph middle conceptual model and create the final ontology. When it comes to the mapping method, Hazber et al. [23] proposed an approach for mapping the relational database into ontology-based on mapping rules. Moreover, there are several tools have been developed for supporting the mapping from RDB to ontology, e.g., DataMaster[3], KAON2[4] and RDBToOnto[5]. To improve the efficiency of the ontology construction, Aggoune [24] designed a semantic prototype based on the measurement of the similarity metric for automatic ontology learning from RDB. In this semantic prototype, the similarity measurement was employed to detect the synonymy relation based on Word-Net[6]. However, due to the RDB model does not store the semantic relationship among entities directly, there are some limitations of the automatic ontology learning from RDB, i.e., identify the incorrect semantic relationships between entities, ignore the implicit relations. To tackle the above issues, El Idrissi et al. [25] studied a novel approach of ontology learning from RDB based on semantic enrichment, in which the meta-model was introduced to augment the semantic of RDB model. The case study shows that this approach could deduce the relationship in various domains.

Given that not only the schema information is implied in RDB SQL, but also the data information is represented in RDB SQL. Hence, a new paradigm of ontology learning from SQL scripts was proposed in recent years. Hazber et al. [26] proposed a method for translating SQL algebra into SPARQL queries based on mapping rules. Initially, the RDB schema and data were transformed to the RDF triples, after that, the RDF triples were translated into OWL.

Generally, ontology learning from RDB SQL consists of three phases: pre-process, semantic enrichment, and transformation mapping. Before the transform and mapping, it is necessary to pre-process the RDB SQL. The majority of techniques of the pre-processing is parsing and lemmatization. To tackle the existing parsing methods that ignore the structure of database schema, there are two parsing methods of Text-to-SQL was proposed based on Graph Neural Network [27] and IRNet [28] respectively, which provide an essential theoretical foundation to construct ontology based on the approach of ontology learning from RDB SQL automatically.

4   Use of OL in Information System Integration

When it comes to information system integration, there is a consensus that ontology-based integration is a useful approach. However, there are some bottleneck problems that influence the performance of integration, while ontology learning provides a new perspective to tackle these bottlenecks.

4.1   Statement of the Existing Challenges

With the increasing volume of heterogeneous data from the various information systems, some bottleneck problems (BP) of the ontology-based information

---

[3] https://protegewiki.stanford.edu/wiki/DataMaster/, accessed on October 7, 2019.
[4] http://kaon2.semanticweb.org/, accessed on October 7, 2019.
[5] https://sourceforge.net/projects/rdbtoonto/, accessed on October 7, 2019.
[6] https://wordnet.princeton.edu/, accessed on October 7, 2019.

integration are emerging in recent years. The corresponding questions could be summarized as follows:

BP1: How to improve the efficiency and effectiveness of the ontology construction?

BP2: How to preserve the integrity of the semantic information and avoid the semantic loss in the construction of ontology?

BP3: How to access the data from various DBMS (database management system) of the different information systems efficiently?

BP4: How to learn and generate the domain-related knowledge from the increasing (semi-)structured data of the various information systems?

4.2 Mapping the Features of OL to Bottleneck Problems

According to the above investigation of the OL, the features and strengths of the OL could be formulated as follows:

(Semi-)automatic. In contrast to the traditional methods of ontology construction, the approach based on OL could construct domain-related ontologies (semi-)automatically by learning the knowledge from corresponding data. It could minimize the manpower and improve the efficiency and effectiveness of the generating ontology. Ontologies could be constructed based on the extraction of the entities and their relationships by using the techniques of machine learning and natural language processing.

Active Learning. OL is a paradigm of active learning, hence it is suitable for the large-scale data sets. In active learning, the model could select an unlabeled item from the dataset and present it to the user to obtain the label, which is beneficial to improve the efficiency of the learning [29]. Therefore, with the increasing volumes of the data, the accuracy and integrity of the semantic of the OL model will be improved. More importantly, it is unnecessary to label the data manually, which will create an opportunity to tackle the larger data sets.

Semantic Integrity. The methods of OL from RDB could maximize the preservation of semantic integrity because the RDB implicates strong semantic relationships among the original data. Especially, the RDB model could be converted into a conceptual model, which will enrich the semantic relation among entities to some extent. Therefore, the information integration based on OL could preserve the consistency and integrity of the semantics between original data and the corresponding ontology.

Information Accessibility. The main data sources of the OL is the RDB, while the RDB is easy to be accessed by the interface or the pipeline from the DBMS. Moreover, there is no requirement of the special interface, because the data could be access from the DBMS via the RDB scripts directly if the interface or the pipeline is unavailable for some legacy information system.

To investigate the opportunity of using OL in information integration, the bottleneck problems of the ontology-based information integration (OBII) and the features of the OL are mapped in the Table 2.

As shown in Table 2, the aforementioned features of the ontology learning are mapped with the bottleneck problems of the ontology-based information

Table 2. Mapping the features of OL to the bottleneck problems of OBII.

Bottleneck problems	Features of ontology learning (OL)			
	(Semi-) automatic	Active learning	Semantic integrity	Information accessibility
Improving the efficiency & Effectiveness	✓		✓	
Avoiding the semantic loss			✓	
Data access from the legacy system				✓
Scalability of large-scale data sets	✓	✓		

integration at many points. The result showed that ontology learning could provide an opportunity to tackle the above bottleneck problems.

5   Opportunity of Using OL in Information Integration

5.1   Summary of Existing Work

According to the results of the literature retrieval, there is a minority number of the existing works on the topic of information integration based on ontology learning. The corresponding works could be summarized as follows.

Initially, the techniques of using ontology learning to integrate data of the semantic web were analyzed and illustrated by Xu et al. [30]. And then, an approach of smart data integration based on goal-driven ontology learning was proposed by Chen et al. [31]. In this approach, the statistical method and NLP techniques were utilized to extract the relations of the entities, also, the prototype for ontology learning was developed. In our previous work [32], the framework of using ontology learning for integrating the legacy ERP system was proposed, and the key steps of ontology learning for system integration was described.

Therefore, the conclusion could be drawn that the existing research of the information integration based on ontology learning is in its early exploratory phase. In spite of the techniques and frameworks that were illustrated by some works, some specified works should be investigated further.

5.2   Directions of Using OL in Information System Integration

Based on the above summaries of existing works and mapping results, the possibility and directions of using OL in information system integration.

Ontology Learning from RDB SQL Scripts. SQL scripts of the RDB are kinds of text documents out of which all entities and their semantic relationships can be inferred. Moreover, SQL scripts can be accessed easily via the DBMS or database driver, especially, there is no requirement for a special interface. Hence, based on the ontology learning from SQL scripts, the heterogeneous information from various information systems could be accessed and integrated efficiently and effectively. Currently, there are some work [27,28] studied the algorithms of pre-processing the SQL scripts and transforming them to text, which provide the theoretical foundation for the ontology learning from SQL scripts. Hence, it is a meaningful work to investigate the algorithms, model, and tools for ontology learning from SQL scripts.

Ontology Learning from NoSQL Database. In several fields, an increasing number of NoSQL databases were built for storing the unstructured data and real-time data-driven by the business requirement. Consequently, there are some NoSQL databases, i.e., document database, graph database, object database, and so forth. Especially for the graph database, it is easy to extract the terms and relation because it already implies the potential relation between different objects. Moreover, there are some works have focused on the ontology learning from the NoSQL database [33,34], which will provide the possibility to integrate the unstructured information based on ontology learning from NoSQL database. Therefore, it is an interesting direction of integrating the unstructured information based on ontology learning from the NoSQL database.

6   Conclusion

This paper surveyed the latest developments of ontology learning for highlighting the possible applications in the scenario of information system integration. The existing surveys of ontology-based information integration and ontology learning were summarized, and the recent techniques and tools of the ontology learning from text and RDB were investigated respectively. Besides, the current challenges of ontology-based information integration were discussed, and the features and strengths of using ontology learning in information system integration were spotted. Also, the opportunity of using ontology learning in information integration were given by showing directions of investigating the ontology learning from RDB SQL scripts and the NoSQL database.

Acknowledgment. This work was supported by grants of the European Union co-financed by the European Social Fund (EFOP-3.6.3-VEKOP-16-2017-00002), by no. ED_18-1-2019-0030 (Application-specific highly reliable IT solutions) program of the National Research, Development, and Innovation Fund of Hungary, financed under the Thematic Excellence Programme funding scheme, and by the grant of China Scholarship Council (201808610145).

References

1. Wache, H., et al.: Ontology-based information integration–a survey of existing approaches. In: IJCAI 2001 Workshop on Ontologies and Information Sharing, IJCAI, pp. 108–117 (2001)
2. Nguyen, V.: Ontologies and information systems: a literature survey. Technical report, Defence science and technology organisation Edinburgh, Australia (2011)
3. Drumond, L., Girardi, R.: A survey of ontology learning procedures. In: 3rd Workshop on Ontologies and their Applications, pp. 1–13 (2008)

4. Buitelaar, P., Cimiano, P., Magnini, B.: Ontology learning from text: an overview. In: Buitelaar, P., Cimiano, P., Magnini, B. (eds.) Ontology Learning from Text: Methods, Evaluation and Applications, pp. 3–12. IOS Press, Amsterdam (2005)
5. Maedche, A., Staab, S.: Ontology learning for the semantic web. IEEE Intell. Syst. **16**(2), 72–79 (2001)
6. Asim, M.N., Wasim, M., Khan, M.U.G., Mahmood, W., Abbasi, H.M.: A survey of ontology learning techniques and applications. Database **2018**, 1–24 (2018)
7. Wong, W., Liu, W., Bennamoun, M.: Ontology learning from text: a look back and into the future. ACM Comput. Surv. (CSUR) **44**(4), 1–36 (2012)
8. Noy, N.F.: Semantic integration: a survey of ontology-based approaches. ACM SIGMOD Rec. **33**(4), 65–70 (2004)
9. Wimalasuriya, D.C., Dou, D.: Ontology-based information extraction: an introduction and a survey of current approaches. J. Inf. Sci. **36**(3), 306–323 (2010)
10. Hooi, Y.K., Hassan, M.F., Shariff, A.M.: A survey on ontology mapping techniques. In: Jeong, H.Y., S. Obaidat, M., Yen, N.Y., Park, J.J.J.H. (eds.) Advances in Computer Science and its Applications. LNEE, vol. 279, pp. 829–836. Springer, Heidelberg (2014). https://doi.org/10.1007/978-3-642-41674-3_118
11. Hazman, M., El-Beltagy, S.R., Rafea, A.: A survey of ontology learning approaches. Int. J. Comput. Appl. **22**(9), 36–43 (2011)
12. Biemann, C.: Ontology learning from text: a survey of methods. LDV Forum **20**(2), 75–93 (2005)
13. Venu, S.H., Mohan, V., Urkalan, K., T.V., G.: Unsupervised domain ontology learning from text. In: Prasath, R., Gelbukh, A. (eds.) MIKE 2016. LNCS (LNAI), vol. 10089, pp. 132–143. Springer, Cham (2017). https://doi.org/10.1007/978-3-319-58130-9_13
14. Petrucci, G., Ghidini, C., Rospocher, M.: Ontology learning in the deep. In: Blomqvist, E., Ciancarini, P., Poggi, F., Vitali, F. (eds.) EKAW 2016. LNCS (LNAI), vol. 10024, pp. 480–495. Springer, Cham (2016). https://doi.org/10.1007/978-3-319-49004-5_31
15. Petrucci, G., Rospocher, M., Ghidini, C.: Expressive ontology learning as neural machine translation. J. Web Semant. **52**, 66–82 (2018). https://doi.org/10.1016/j.websem.2018.10.002
16. Rani, M., Dhar, A.K., Vyas, O.: Semi-automatic terminology ontology learning based on topic modeling. Eng. Appl. Artif. Intell. **63**, 108–125 (2017). https://doi.org/10.1016/j.engappai.2017.05.006
17. Hong, W., Hao, Z., Shi, J.: Research and application on domain ontology learning method based on LDA. J. Softw. **12**(4), 265–273 (2017)
18. Dutkowski, J.J.: A method and system for ontology-based dynamic learning and knowledge integration from measurement data and text. USA Patent App. 16/060,400, 3 January 2019
19. Ghosh, M.E., Naja, H., Abdulrab, H., Khalil, M.: Ontology learning process as a bottom-up strategy for building domain-specific ontology from legal texts. In: 9th International Conference on Agents and Artificial Intelligence (ICAART 2017), pp. 473–480. INSTICC, SciTePress (2017). https://doi.org/10.5220/0006188004730480
20. Santoso, H.A., Haw, S.C., Abdul-Mehdi, Z.: Ontology extraction from relational database: concept hierarchy as background knowledge. Knowl. Based Syst. **24**(3), 457–464 (2011). https://doi.org/10.1016/j.knosys.2010.11.003
21. Sbai, S., Louhdi, M.R.C., Behja, H., Moukhtar Zemmouri, E., Rabab, C.: Using reverse engineering for building ontologies with deeper taxonomies from relational databases. J. Softw. **14**(3), 138–145 (2019). https://doi.org/10.17706/jsw.14.3.138-145

22. Dadjoo, M., Kheirkhah, E.: An approach for transforming of relational databases to OWL ontology. Int. J. Web Semant. Technol. **6**(1), 19–28 (2015)
23. Hazber, M.A., Li, R., Zhang, Y., Xu, G.: An approach for mapping relational database into ontology. In: 2015 12th Web Information System and Application Conference (WISA), pp. 120–125. IEEE (2015). https://doi.org/10.1109/WISA. 2015.25
24. Aggoune, A.: Automatic ontology learning from heterogeneous relational databases: application in alimentation risks field. In: Amine, A., Mouhoub, M., Ait Mohamed, O., Djebbar, B. (eds.) CIIA 2018. IAICT, vol. 522, pp. 199–210. Springer, Cham (2018). https://doi.org/10.1007/978-3-319-89743-1_18
25. El Idrissi, B., Baïna, S., Baïna, K.: Ontology learning from relational database: how to label the relationships between concepts? In: Kozielski, S., Mrozek, D., Kasprowski, P., Małysiak-Mrozek, B., Kostrzewa, D. (eds.) BDAS 2015. CCIS, vol. 521, pp. 235–244. Springer, Cham (2015). https://doi.org/10.1007/978-3-319-18422-7_21
26. Hazber, M.A., Li, B., Xu, G., Mosleh, M.A., Gu, X., Li, Y.: An approach for generation of SPARQL query from SQL algebra based transformation rules of RDB to ontology. J. Softw. **13**(11), 573–599 (2018). https://doi.org/10.17706/jsw. 13.11.573-599
27. Bogin, B., Gardner, M., Berant, J.: Representing schema structure with graph neural networks for Text-to-SQL parsing. In: 57th Annual Meeting of the Association for Computational Linguistics, pp. 4560–4565 (2019)
28. Guo, J., et al.: Towards complex Text-to-SQL in cross-domain database with intermediate representation. In: 57th Annual Meeting of the Association for Computational Linguistics, pp. 4524–4535 (2019)
29. Murugesan, K., Carbonell, J.: Active learning from peers. In: Guyon, I., et al. (eds.) Advances in Neural Information Processing Systems, vol. 30, pp. 7008–7017. Curran Associates Inc, New York (2017)
30. Xu, H., Zhang, R.: Research on data integration of the semantic web based on ontology learning technology. TELKOMNIKA Indones. J. Electr. Eng. **12**(1), 167–178 (2014)
31. Chen, J., Dosyn, D., Lytvyn, V., Sachenko, A.: Smart data integration by goal driven ontology learning. In: Angelov, P., Manolopoulos, Y., Iliadis, L., Roy, A., Vellasco, M. (eds.) INNS 2016. AISC, vol. 529, pp. 283–292. Springer, Cham (2017). https://doi.org/10.1007/978-3-319-47898-2_29
32. Ma, C., Molnár, B.: A legacy ERP system integration framework based on ontology learning. In: 21st International Conference on Enterprise Information Systems, (ICEIS 2019), pp. 231–237. INSTICC, SciTePress (2019). https://doi.org/10.5220/0007740602310237
33. Abbes, H., Boukettaya, S., Gargouri, F.: Learning ontology from big data through MongoDB database. In: 2015 IEEE/ACS 12th International Conference of Computer Systems and Applications (AICCSA), pp. 1–7 (2015). https://doi.org/10.1109/AICCSA.2015.7507166
34. Abbes, H., Gargouri, F.: M2Onto: an approach and a tool to learn OWL ontology from MongoDB database. In: Madureira, A.M., Abraham, A., Gamboa, D., Novais, P. (eds.) ISDA 2016. AISC, vol. 557, pp. 612–621. Springer, Cham (2017). https://doi.org/10.1007/978-3-319-53480-0_60

Mutation Operators for Google Query Language

Lorena Gutiérrez-Madroñal[1]([⊠]) [ID], Inmaculada Medina-Bulo[1] [ID],
and Mercedes G. Merayo[2] [ID]

[1] UCASE Research Group, University of Cádiz, Puerto Real, Spain
{lorena.gutierrez,inmaculada.medina}@uca.es
[2] Design and Testing of Reliable Systems Research Group,
Complutense University of Madrid, Madrid, Spain
mgmerayo@fdi.ucm.es

Abstract. Nowadays the technology is being created and adapted to
satisfy the user necessities. Among them, obtaining information as fast
as possible. Google knows how to meet this demand developing and offering new services that provide the requested information quickly. Google
technology can be used to develop products using the Google App Engine
(GAE). In order to manipulate the data, GAE uses the Google Query
Language (GQL), a SQL-like language, that has been designed to provide
a solution to the necessity of having super-fast access to data warehouses.
The quality of the developed products is essential and therefore, testing
them is mandatory. In this paper, we propose the use of mutation testing
to detect faults during the development of applications that use GQL.
With this goal, we introduce a set of specific mutation operators for
GQL.

Keywords: Google Query Language · Google App Engine · Mutation
testing

1 Introduction

Google has been investing, improving and creating new technologies during the
last decade. One of them, *Google Cloud Platform* (GCP), provides infrastructure
tools and services to build applications and websites, as well as store and analyse
data on Google's infrastructure [6]. These services have been adapted to novel
technologies and they can be applied not only to storage and web services, but
also to Internet of Things, Big Data and Machine Learning. GAE is one of the
services offered by GCP. GAE runs applications on a fully-managed Platform-
as-a-Service using built-in services. Its applications can be written in some of the
most popular programming languages: Python, Java, PHP and Go. However, the

Paper partially funded by the Spanish MINECO-FEDER (grant number DArDOS,
TIN2015-65845-C3-1-R, grant number FAME RTI2018-093608-B-C31 and RTI2018-
093608-B-C33); the Region of Madrid (grant number FORTE-CM, S2018/TCS-4314).

language that GAE uses to query, manage and offer the required data is GQL, a SQL-like language. The GAE data warehouses enable super-fast GQL queries that use the processing power of Google's infrastructure. Given that GAE is the base of the developed applications, testing the correct behaviour of the GQL sentences that manage the information is crucial.

Mutation testing [2] is a fault-based testing technique, which can be used to measure the effectiveness of a test suite in terms of its ability to detect faults. This technique introduces small syntactic changes in the program under test by applying *mutation operators* to generate faulty programs called *mutants*. Mutation testing has been applied to different query languages such as SQL [18], EPL [9–11], GraphQL [19] and SPARQL [13].

In this paper we propose the application of the mutation testing technique to GQL, which requires the definition of mutation operators. Taking into account that GQL is a subset of the SQL syntax, we need to determine if the mutation operators defined by Tuya et al. [18] are appropriate for being used in GQL syntax. Specifically, this work aims to reveal: *Is it necessary to define specific mutation operators for GQL?*

In order to answer this research question (RQ), several tasks have to be done. The mentioned tasks are summarised in the following contributions:

- **Definition of a set of mutation operators for GQL**; the analysis of the GQL syntax will let us know if specific mutation operators have to be defined for GQL.
- **GQLapp**, a tool implemented under GAE which helps us to compare the original and mutant results.
- **An analysis of the mutation operators**; the GQLapp outputs will help us to determine the killing criteria for the mutants generated by the GQL mutation operators.

The remainder of this paper is organised as follows. Section 2 looks in depth at the GQL and mutation testing. Section 3 explains not only the test suite used for the experiments but also its characteristics. Section 4 deals with the main contributions; the GQL mutation operators are defined and the GQL queries outputs are analysed. An analysis of SQL mutation operators and the answer to RQ appear in Sect. 4.1. Finally, in Sect. 5, we present the conclusions and propose new lines for future work.

2 Background

2.1 Google Query Language

GCP is a set of modular cloud-based services, that allows to create from simple websites to complex applications. GCP is offering hosting on the same supporting infrastructure that Google uses internally for end-user products like Google Search and YouTube [6].

In 2008 Google announced App Engine technology [1]. GAE not only lets run applications which are easy to built, maintain and scale, but also hosts sites and stores data. The scalability of the applications grows according to the traffic and the data storage. There are no servers to maintain because the application, at the moment that is uploaded, is ready to serve the users [4]. GAE applications are top-level containers that include the service, version, and instance resources that make up the applications; they are created under Cloud Platform projects.

Data objects in Cloud Datastore are know as *entities*. An entity has one or more named *properties*, each of which can have one or more *values*. In addition, every entity in Cloud Datastore has a *key* that uniquely identifies it. GQL is a SQL-like language for retrieving entities and keys [7]. Each entity is of a particular *kind*, which categorises the entity for the purpose of queries. In addition to a kind, each entity has an *identifier*, assigned when the entity is created. So, if we compare GQL with SQL we can say that GQL *kind* is similar to a SQL table, a GQL *entity* corresponds to a SQL row, and a GQL *property* can be compared with a SQL column. Nevertheless, a SQL row-column contains a single value, whereas in GQL a property value can be a list.

Entities in Cloud Datastore are hierarchically structured in a similar way to the directory structure of an operating system's file system. When you create an entity, you can optionally designate another entity as its parent; the new entity will be a child of the parent entity. An entity's parent, parent's parent, and so on, are its *ancestors*; its children, children's children, and so on, are its *descendants*.

The GQL queries retrieve entities from Cloud Datastore that meet a specific set of conditions. The GQL query structure includes the following:

- An entity kind to which the query applies.
- Optional filters based on the entities' property values, keys, and ancestors.
- Optional orders to sort the results.

The query retrieves the entities of the given kind that satisfy the filters, sorted in the specified order.

2.2 Mutation Testing

Mutation testing is a well-known fault-based technique that has been used to evaluate and improve the quality of the test suites to be applied to a system [2]. This technique injects small syntactic changes into the original program by applying *mutation operators* which generate syntactic variations called *mutants*. Each mutation operator represents common programming errors that developers make [12,15]. If a test case is able to distinguish between the original program and the mutant, i. e. their outputs are different, it is said that the test case kills the mutant. On the contrary, if no test case in the test suite is able to distinguish between the mutant and the original program, it is said that the mutant is *alive*. An *equivalent mutant* always produces the same output as the original program, hence it cannot be distinguished by any test case. At this point it is necessary to clarify that, program is used to denote the software under test, which could be a complete program or a smaller unit, such as a query.

3 Description of Test Suite for the Experiments

GAE provides high availability for reads and writes by storing data synchronously in multiple data centers. However, the delay from the instant a write is committed until it becomes visible in all data centers implies that queries across multiple entity groups (non-ancestor queries) can only guarantee *eventually consistent* results. Consequently, the results of such queries may sometimes fail to reflect recent changes to the underlying data [5]. It is needed to limit the results to a single entity group using an *ancestor query* to obtain *strongly consistent* query results. This works because entity groups are units of consistency as well as transactionality. All data operations are applied to the entire group; once this is up to date, its results will be returned by the ancestor query. So, based on their recommendations [8] the test suite for the experiment has been developed with ancestor queries in order to offer strongly consistent results [4].

The data model of the experiment presents three classes: *Tutor*, *Student* and *FinalProject* (see Fig. 1), whose definitions appear in the repository[1]. It is worth noting that a *Tutor* entity can have as ancestor another *Tutor* entity, a *Student* entity can have a *Tutor* entity as an ancestor and finally a *FinalProject* entity has as ancestor a *Student* entity, so the *FinalProject* entity has as ancestor the *Student*'s ancestor (an entity *Tutor*).

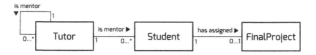

Fig. 1. Test suite entities

In GAE the data objects are known as *entities*, which have one or more named *properties*. Entities of the same kind do not need to have the same properties, and the entity's values for a given property need not be all of the same data type. The defined entities for this study are in the repository[2].

4 GQL Mutation Operators

Mutation operators are associated with frequent faults that are made by programmers when using a specific language. Some of them are common to many languages, but the features of each language make necessary a particular study. GQL is a SQL-like query language so it could be thought that most of the SQL mutation operators defined in the literature can be applied to this language. However, given that GQL features differ from those of a query language for

---

[1] https://github.com/lorgut/ACIIDS2020/tree/master/Classes.
[2] https://github.com/lorgut/ACIIDS2020/tree/master/Entities.

a traditional relational database and its syntax is very limited [7], a detailed analysis have to be done.

In this section, we review the SQL mutation operators proposed in [18] in order to determine which ones can be directly applied to the GQL language, which ones need to be adapted and the ones that cannot be applied. Later, we introduce a set of specific GQL mutation operators.

4.1 SQL Mutation Operators

In [18], with the goal of applying mutation testing to SQL code, 22 mutation operators are defined. They are classified in 4 categories:

1. SC - SQL clause mutation operators. Some of the operators included in this category, {JOI, SUB, GRU, AGR and UNI}, cannot be used in GQL code because the SQL operators to which they are applied are not considered in the GQL syntax. The only SQL mutation operator which can be applied without being modified is SEL; ORD mutation operator has been modified to be used as a GQL mutation operator.
2. OR - Operator replacement mutation operators: ROR and UOI can be applied without being modified, but {LCR, ABS, AOR, BTW and LKE} cannot be adapted because GQL syntax does not include the operators considered by these mutation operators.
3. NL - NULL mutation operators: The GQL syntax allows to include NULL values in queries. However, NUll represents a value, not the absence of value. Taking into account this fact, the only NULL mutation operator that can be applied without being modified is NLI. The rest of mutation operators considered in this category, {NLF, NLS and NLO}, are not applicable to GQL.
4. IR - Identifier replacement mutation operators: The mutation operators included in this category, {IRC, IRT, IRP and IRH}, can be adapted to GQL taking into account the fact that a GQL entity and a GQL property are similar to a SQL row and a SQL column, respectively. The only restriction we need to consider is the type compatibility of the objects to which the mutation operators are applied. The four mutation operators has been redefined to be used as GQL mutation operators.

The analysis of the SQL mutation operators carried out in this work help to answer the RQ. In spite of being a SQL language, and the fact that some SQL mutation operators can be adapted to be applied to GQL code, the GQL language contains several particularities which must be considered to define new mutation operators.

Following, we propose a collection of mutation operators and give examples of their use. The original and mutated GQL queries will be executed using GQLapp[3], a tool implemented under GAE Launcher. This is a Python SDK for GAE which allows to run projects locally [4]; the output is displayed in a

---

[3] https://github.com/lorgut/ACIIDS2020/tree/master/GQLapp.

browser at http://localhost:8080. The GQLapp outputs are used to determine if the original and mutant queries can be distinguishing. Experiment outputs can be found in the repository[4].

In next sections we explain new mutation operators that have been defined for applying to specific clauses, operators and values of GQL. Additionally, we also introduce the SQL operators that have been adapted to be used in GQL code.

4.2 GQL Clause Mutation Operators

FRM - From Clause: According to the GQL grammar [4], the `from` clause is optional. The optional `from` clause limits the result set to those entities of the given kind. This kind of queries, without `from`, are called *kindless queries*, and cannot include filters on properties. This GQL characteristic allows us to define a specific mutation operator for GQL, the FRM mutation operator. The mutation consists in removing the `from` clause, see Example 1.1. As a result a kindless query is obtained.

Example 1.1. Original and FRM mutated query example

```
select * from Student
where ancestor is key ('Tutor', 'Walter')

# Original results
Alanis Parket, Alex Kay, Denis Woodman, Robert Langdon
(all Student type)

select *
where ancestor is key ('Tutor', 'Walter')

# Mutant results
Walter White (Tutor), Alanis Parket (Student),
Alex Kay (Student), Alex Kay (FinalProject),
Denis Woodman (Student), Robert Langdon (Student),
Jessie Pickman (Tutor)
```

Under each query of the Example 1.1 the list of entities which meets the constrains is shown. The entities returned by the original query correspond to Student class, and the ones obtained from the mutant query belong to Student, Tutor and FinalProject classes. It is necessary to indicate that only the name and surname properties are shown in the results of the examples along the paper. Please, check the repository (see Sect. 4) for accessing all the values of the entities.

LIM - Limit Clause: The `limit` clause is used in the general form of `limit` `[offset,]` `count` where query results to a count or to results preceding an offset and a count. If the `limit` clause has two arguments the left one must be an offset and the right one must be an integer. In this case the mutation operator

---

[4] https://github.com/lorgut/ACIIDS2020/tree/master/Outputs.

perform different changes in the query: (1) the offset is removed leaving the count argument. The offset parameter is a integer that determine the number of results to skip before the query returns the first one. (2) The count argument is removed leaving the offset argument, which will be used as the count argument. (3) The `limit` clause and the two arguments are removed. (4) The two arguments are swapped. See an example of this specific GQL mutant operator in Example 1.2.

Example 1.2. Original and LIM mutated query example

```
select * from Student
where ancestor is key ('Tutor', 'Walter') limit 1, 2

# Original results
Alanis Parket, Alex Kay

select * from Student
where ancestor is key ('Tutor', 'Walter') limit 2

# Mutant results
Robert Langdon, Alanis Parket
```

This example shows how the offset parameter is removed from the query. If the `limit` clause of a query only presents one parameter, then it is considered as the count parameter. As a consequence of the application of this operator, the number of listed entities is the same, but the content is different.

In Example 1.3, another mutation is applied: offset and count parameters are swapped.

Example 1.3. Original and LIM mutated query example, swapping parameters

```
select * from Student
where ancestor is key ('Tutor', 'Walter') limit 1, 2

# Original results
Alanis Parket, Alex Kay

select * from Student
where ancestor is key ('Tutor', 'Walter') limit 2, 1

# Mutant results
Alex Kay
```

ORD - Order by Clause: The `order` by clause indicates that results should be returned sorted by the given properties, in either ascending (`ASC`) or descending (`DESC`) order. The `order` by clause can specify multiple sort orders as a comma-delimited list, evaluated from left to right. If the direction is not specified, it defaults to `ASC`. In this case we have adapted the ORD mutation operator defined in [18]; the mutation consists in replacing each keyword {`ASC`, `DESC`} by other, see Example 1.4.

Example 1.4. Original and ORD mutated query example

```
select * from FinalProject
where ancestor is key ('Tutor', 'Carol')
and pages >= 100 and pages < 300
order by name ASC, grade DESC

# Original results
Sheldom Cooper, Alicia Mant

select * from FinalProject
where ancestor is key ('Tutor', 'Carol')
and pages >= 100 and pages < 300
order by name ASC, grade ASC

# Mutant results
Alicia Mant, Sheldom Cooper
```

4.3   GQL Operator Mutation Operators

IN - in Operator: The in operator compares the value of a property with each item in a list. The in operator is equivalent to several = queries, one for each value. GAE interprets the in list (propA, propB, propC...) like an OR predicate (propA OR propB OR propC...). An entity whose value for the given property is equal to any of the values in the list can be returned by the query. The mutation consists in removing one item from the list, see Example 1.5.

Example 1.5. Original and IN mutated query example

```
select * from Student
where ancestor is key ('Tutor', 'Walter') and grade = 4
and name in ('Robert', 'Alex', 'Alanis', 'Denis')

# Original results
Alanis Parket, Alex Kay

select * from Student
where ancestor is key ('Tutor', 'Walter') and grade = 4
and name in ('Robert', 'Alanis', 'Denis')

# Mutant results
Alanis Parket
```

4.4   GQL Value Mutation Operators

IO - Integer Operator: An integer value is not equal to the equivalent float. This operator replaces an integer x by $x.0$ or vice-versa, see Example 1.6.

Example 1.6. Original and IO mutated query example

```
select * from FinalProject
where ancestor is key ('Tutor', 'Carol') and
mark <= 10.0 and mark > 9.0

# Original results
Sheldom Cooper

select * from FinalProject
where ancestor is key ('Tutor', 'Carol') and
mark <= 10.0 and mark > 9

# Mutant results
Aviva Webb, Alicia Mant, Sheldom Cooper
```

FDO - Format Date Operator: The date in the data types `date` and `datetime` must match the format `YYYY-MM-DD` and `YYYY-MM-DD HH:MM:SS`, respectively. This mutation operator is focused on the date part. The mutation consists in: (1) increasing one unit the year, (2) increasing one unit the month, (3) increasing one unit the day, (4) decreasing one unit the year, (5) decreasing one unit the month, (6) decreasing one unit the day and (7) swapping the day and the month if the day is less than 13. All these changes must generate valid dates in the Gregorian calendar, see Example 1.7.

Example 1.7. Original and FDO mutated query example

```
select * from Student
where ancestor is key ('Tutor', 'Helen')
and department = 'ComputerScience'
and date < datetime ('1982-12-15␣00:00:00')
and date > datetime ('1972-04-07␣00:00:00')

# Original results
Albert Lamb

select * from Student
where ancestor is key ('Tutor', 'Helen')
and department = 'ComputerScience'
and date < datetime ('1983-12-15␣00:00:00')
and date > datetime ('1972-04-07␣00:00:00')

# Mutant results
Albert Lamb, Litz Brown
```

BPO - Bound Parameter Operator: Argument binding provides a way for users to specify a value at runtime while, at the same time, preventing malicious behaviour, such as injection attacks. The query string uses binding sites to refer to the above bound argument values, using ":". The bound arguments can be numbered or named. In this case we will only use the numbered notation. The following query shows how to use argument binding with numbered arguments:

```
q = db.GqlQuery("select * from Student where name = :1 and average
          <= :2 order by average DESC", "Jaime", 6.5)
```

The arguments of the query are "Jaime" and 6.5. A query that contains a numbered argument binding site cannot skip any number. If appears the argument binding :3, it must also exist the argument bindings :1 and :2. If n bound arguments appear in the query the mutation involves changing the position of each bound argument generating $\binom{m}{2}$ mutants. See Example 1.8 where the actual values of the arguments bindings are 4 and 2; the mutated query does not return any entity.

Example 1.8. Original and BPO mutated query example

```
select * from Student
where ancestor is key ('Tutor', 'Walter')
and grade <= :1 and mingrade > :2

# Original results
Alex Kay, Alanis Parket

select * from Student
where ancestor is key ('Tutor', 'Walter')
and grade <= :2 and mingrade > :1
```

IR - Identifier Replacement Mutation Operators: These operators correspond to the adaptation of the IR mutation operators described in [18], taking into account the fact that a GQL property is similar to a SQL column.

- IRC - GQL property replacement: Each GQL property is replaced by each of the other GQL properties, constants and parameters that appear in the query and are type compatible.
- IRT - Constant replacement: Each constant is replaced by each of the other constants, GQL properties and parameters that appear in the query and are type compatible.
- IRP - Parameter replacement: Each parameter is replaced by each of the other parameters, GQL properties and constants that appear in the query and are type compatible.
- IRH - Hidden GQL property replacement: Each GQL property is replaced by each of the other GQL properties that are defined in the corresponding kind provided that they have not been the replacement in any of the other IR operators and are type compatible.

We show an example of an IR mutation operator in Example 1.9.

Example 1.9. Original and IR mutated query example

```
select * from Student
where ancestor is key ('Tutor', 'Walter')
and surname = 'Kay'

# Original results
```

Alex Kay

```
select * from Student
where ancestor is key ('Tutor', 'Kay')
and surname = 'Walter'
```

5   Conclusions and Future Work

Mutation testing has been applied to several languages of diverse nature. In this work we introduce a set of mutation operators for the GQL language. Most of them are specific of this language. However, due to the similarity of GQL and SQL syntaxes, we have also adapted those mutation operators defined for SQL that are compatible with the GQL language. The analysis of the SQL mutation operators reveals that 4 of them can be applied without modification {SEL, ROR, NLI and UOI}. The ORD and the ones from IR category must be adapted to be applied to GQL taking into account the particularities of this language. The rest of SQL mutation operators cannot being applied because GQL syntax does not include the clauses, values or operators to which them are applied.

As future work we plan to develop, using Wodel [3], a mutation tool for GQL queries. Thanks to Wodel characteristics, it can be used to generate mutants of models conforming to arbitrary metamodels. In addition, taking as initial step our previous work [14,16,17], we plan to extend our mutation testing framework to explicitly consider asynchronous communications.

References

1. Barry, P.: Doing IT the app engine way. Linux J. **2010**(197), 1 (2010). ISSN 1075–3583
2. DeMillo, R.A., Lipton, R.J., Sayward, F.G.: Hints on test data selection: help for the practicing programmer. Computer **11**(4), 34–41 (1978). ISSN 0018–9162
3. Gómez-Abajo, P., et al.: A tool for domain-independent model mutation. Sci. Comput. Program. **163**, 85–92 (2018)
4. Google: Google App Engine.. https://cloud.google.com/appengine/docs/. Accessed Oct 2019
5. Google. Google App Engine: Structuring Data for Strong consistency. https://cloud.google.com/appengine/docs/standard/java/datastore/structuring_for_strong_consistency. Accessed Oct 2019
6. Google. Google Cloud Patform. https://cloud.google.com/docs/. Accessed Oct 2019
7. Google. Google Query Language in Google App Engine. https://cloud.google.com/appengine/docs/standard/python/datastore/gqlreference. Accessed Oct 2019
8. Google. Pick strong consistency. https://cloud.google.com/blog/products/gcp/why-you-should-pick-strong-consistency-whenever-possible. Accessed Oct 2019
9. Gutiérrez-Madroñal, L., García-Domínguez, A., Medina-Bulo, I.: Evolutionary mutation testing for IoT with recorded and generated events. Softw. Pract. Exper. **49**(4), 640–672 (2019)

10. Gutiérrez-Madroñal, L., Medina-Bulo, I., Domínguez-Jiménez, J.J.: Evaluation of EPL mutation operators with the MuEPL mutation system. Expert Syst. Appl. **116**, 78–95 (2019). ISSN 0957–4174
11. Gutiérrez-Madroñal, L., et al.: Mutation testing of event processing queries. In: 2012 IEEE 23rd International Symposium on Software Reliability Engineering, pp. 21–30 (2012)
12. Hamlet, R.G.: Testing programs with the aid of a compiler. IEEE Trans. Software Eng. SE **3**(4), 279–290 (1977). ISSN 2326–3881
13. Hees, J., Bauer, R., Folz, J., Borth, D., Dengel, A.: An evolutionary algorithm to learn SPARQL queries for source-target-pairs. In: Blomqvist, E., Ciancarini, P., Poggi, F., Vitali, F. (eds.) EKAW 2016. LNCS (LNAI), vol. 10024, pp. 337–352. Springer, Cham (2016). https://doi.org/10.1007/978-3-319-49004-5_22
14. Hierons, R.M., Merayo, M.G., Núñez, M.: An extended framework for passive asynchronous testing. J. Log. Algebraic Methods Program. **86**(1), 408–424 (2017)
15. Jia, Y., Harman, M.: An analysis and survey of the development of mutation testing. IEEE Trans. Software Eng. **37**(5), 649–678 (2011). ISSN 2326–3881
16. Merayo, M.G., Hierons, R.M., Núñez, M.: A tool supported methodology to passively test asynchronous systems with multiple users. Inf. Softw. Technol. **104**, 162–178 (2018)
17. Merayo, M.G., Hierons, R.M., Núñez, M.: Passive testing with asynchronous communications and timestamps. Distrib. Comput. **31**(5), 327–342 (2018). ISSN 1432–0452
18. Tuya, J., Suárez-Cabal, M.J., la Riva, C.: Mutating database queries. Inf. Softw. Technol. **49**(4), 398–417 (2007). ISSN 0950–5849
19. Vázquez-Ingelmo, A., Cruz-Benito, J., García-Peñalvo, F.J.: Improving the OEEU's data-driven technological ecosystem's interoperability with GraphQL. In: Proceedings of the 5th International Conference on Technological Ecosystems for Enhancing Multiculturality, pp. 89:1–89:8. ACM, Cádiz (2017)

Combining Local Binary Pattern and Speeded-Up Robust Feature for Content-Based Image Retrieval

Prashant Srivastava[1(✉)], Manish Khare[2], and Ashish Khare[3]

[1] NIIT University, Neemrana, Rajasthan, India
prashant.jk087@gmail.com
[2] Dhirubhai Ambani Institute of Information and Communication Technology, Gandhinagar,
Gujarat, India
mkharejk@gmail.com
[3] Department of Electronics and Communication, University of Allahabad, Allahabad,
Uttar Pradesh, India
ashishkhare@hotmail.com

Abstract. Large number of digital image libraries containing huge amount of images have made the task of searching and retrieval tedious. Content-Based Image Retrieval (CBIR) is a field which finds solution to this problem. This paper proposes CBIR a technique which extracts interest points from texture feature at multiple resolutions of image. Local Binary Pattern (LBP) has been used to perform texture feature extraction and interest points are gathered through Speeded-Up Robust Feature (SURF) descriptors. The multiresolution decomposition of image is done using Discrete Wavelet Transform (DWT). DWT coefficients of gray scale image are computed followed by computation of LBP codes of resulting DWT coefficients. The interest points from texture image are then gathered by computing SURF descriptors of resulting LBP codes. Finally, feature vector for retrieval is constructed through Gray-Level Co-occurrence Matrix (GLCM) which is used to retrieve visually similar images. The performance of the proposed method has been tested on Corel-1 K dataset and measured in terms of precision and recall. The experimental results demonstrate that the proposed method performs better than some of the other state-of-the-art CBIR techniques in terms of precision and recall.

Keywords: Content-Based Image Retrieval · Local Binary Pattern · Speeded-Up Robust Feature · Gray-Level Co-occurrence matrix

1 Introduction

The process of image acquisition is no longer a difficult task due to the invention of low-cost image capturing devices. As a result, there are huge amount of different types of images. In order to have an easy access to these images, it is important that the images are properly organized. Image retrieval is a field which attempts to solve this problem. There are two types of image retrieval systems-text-based retrieval systems and content-based

P. Sitek et al. (Eds.): ACIIDS 2020, CCIS 1178, pp. 366–376, 2020.
https://doi.org/10.1007/978-981-15-3380-8_32

retrieval systems. Text-based retrieval systems perform searching and retrieval through keywords and text. Manual tagging of images is required in such systems and they fail to retrieve visually similar images. Content-Based Image Retrieval (CBIR) systems search and retrieve images based on the features present in the image. There is no need to manually annotate images and the images retrieved are visually similar [1].

Most of the early CBIR techniques exploited colour feature for constructing feature vector [2]. Later on, texture and shape features were also exploited for constructing feature vector for CBIR [3, 4]. The use of single feature, however proved to be insufficient because image consists of multiple objects and all objects may not be captured efficiently by single feature. These limitations are overcome by combining colour, texture, and shape features [5]. The combination of features not only extract more than one feature from an image but also overcome limitations of each other.

For extracting features from an image, most of the CBIR techniques exploit single resolution of image. However, single resolution processing of image may not construct efficient feature vector as an image consists of varying level of images. To overcome this limitation, multiresolution processing of images is performed. Extraction of features at multiple resolutions of image is advantageous as the features that are left undetected at one scale get detected at another scale. A number of CBIR techniques exploiting multiresolution techniques have been proposed [6, 7]. A novel CBIR technique has been proposed which extracts interest points from texture feature at multiple resolutions of image. Texture feature is computed using Local Binary Pattern (LBP) which has proved to be an efficient feature descriptor for object recognition. The interest points have been obtained through Speeded-Up Robust Feature (SURF) descriptor which efficiently extracts scale invariant features from an image and is faster to compute. Feature vector construction is done by combining LBP and SURF, and this combination is exploited at multiple resolutions of image. The multiresolution decomposition of image has been done through Discrete Wavelet Transform (DWT). The proposed method computes LBP codes of DWT coefficients followed by computation of SURF descriptors of resulting LBP codes. Finally, feature vector has been constructed using Gray-Level Co-occurrence Matrix (GLCM) which provides information about how frequently pixel pairs of specified value and in a specified direction occur in an image.

The rest of the paper is organized as follows- Sect. 2 discusses related work in the field of CBIR. Section 3 gives background concept of DWT, LBP and SURF. Section 4 discusses the proposed method. Section 5 discusses experiment and results and finally, Sect. 6 concludes the paper.

2 Related Work

The use of feature descriptors to construct feature vector for CBIR has been extensively used in the past few years. A number of feature descriptors exploiting multiple features of image have been proposed [8–10]. Liu et al. [11] proposed Multi-Texton Histogram (MTH) which exploits colour and texture feature for CBIR. Liu et al. [12] proposed Microstructure Descriptor (MSD) which combined colour, texture and shape features for CBIR. Most of the above descriptors perform single resolution processing of image for constructing feature vector. Single resolution processing of images may not be sufficient for extracting complex details from an image as an image consists of varying level of details. To overcome these limitations, a number of multiresolution descriptors have been proposed [13–15]. These descriptors decompose image into multiple resolutions and construct feature vector by extracting features at multiple scales of image. A principle advantage of these multiresolution feature descriptors is that the features that are left undetected at one scale get detected at another scale. This paper proposes a combination of feature descriptors which are exploited at multiple resolutions of image.

3 Discrete Wavelet Transform, Local Binary Pattern and Speeded-Up Robust Feature

3.1 Discrete Wavelet Transform

The wavelet series expansion of function $f(x) \in L^2(R)$ relative to the wavelet $\psi(x)$ and scaling function $\varphi(x)$ is defined as [16],

$$f(x) = \sum_k c_{j_0}(k)\varphi_{j_0 k}(x) + \sum_{j=j_0} d_j(k)\psi_{j,k}(x), \tag{1}$$

where j_0 is an arbitrary starting scale, $c_{j_0}(k)$ is approximation coefficients, $d_j(k)$ is detail coefficients.

The one-dimensional transform when extended to two-dimensional images yields a two-dimensional scaling function $\varphi(x, y)$ and three two-dimensional wavelets $\psi^H(x, y), \psi^V(x, y)$, and $\psi^D(x, y)$. These three wavelets perform measure of gray-level variations for images along different directions: ψ^H measures variations in horizontal direction, ψ^V measures variations in vertical direction and ψ^D measures variations in diagonal direction.

The DWT of function $f(x, y)$ of size $M \times N$ is given as

$$W_\varphi(j_0, m, n) = \frac{1}{\sqrt{MN}} \sum_{x=0}^{M-1} \sum_{y=0}^{N-1} f(x, y)\varphi_{j_0, m, n}(x, y), \tag{2}$$

$$W_\psi^i(j, m, n) = \frac{1}{\sqrt{MN}} \sum_{x=0}^{M-1} \sum_{y=0}^{N-1} f(x, y)\psi_{j, m, n}^i(x, y), \tag{3}$$

where j_0 is an arbitrary starting scale and the $W_\psi^i(j, m, n)$ coefficients define an approximation of $f(x, y)$ at scale j_0. The $W_\psi^i(j_0, m, n)$ coefficients add horizontal, vertical, and diagonal details for scales $j \geq j_0$.

3.2 Local Binary Pattern

Ojala et al. [17] originally proposed the concept of Local Binary Pattern (LBP) for texture analysis in an image. The original LBP operator is computed for a 3×3 pixel block of an image. The pixels in this block are thresholded by the centre pixel of the block. The LBP operator takes 3×3 surrounding of a pixel and

- generates a binary 1 if the neighbor is greater than or equal to the value of centre pixel.
- generates a binary 0 if the neighbor is less than the value of centre pixel.

The values in the thresholded neighbourhood are multiplied by the weights provided to the corresponding pixels. Some of the important properties of LBP which are useful for image retrieval are-

- It performs encoding of the relationship between gray value of centre pixel and neighbourhood pixels.
- It is an efficient feature descriptor to extract local features in an image.
- The structural arrangement of pixels in an image are efficiently represented by LBP.

3.3 Speeded-Up Robust Feature

The concept of SURF was first introduced by Bay et al. [18] in the year 2006. SURF is a local feature descriptor which is used for extracting interest points from an image. The concept of SURF is based on the principles of Scale Invariant Feature Transform (SIFT). However, as compared to SIFT, SURF is faster to compute and is invariant to certain image transformations such ad rotation, change in scale and illumination, and small change in viewpoint. SURF descriptors are extensively used in various Computer Vision applications such as object recognition, image classification, and image reconstruction. Following are important steps in SURF algorithm-

- Interest point detection using Hessian matrix.
- Orientation assignment to interest points.
- Feature matching between images to determine whether they have same contrast.

Following are some of the important properties of SURF which are useful for image retrieval-

1. It is an efficient feature descriptor to extract interest points in an image.
2. It covers the entire image for capturing interest points.
3. The distinct features in an image which are helpful in retrieving visually similar images are efficiently captured by SURF.
4. It is faster to compute than SIFT.

3.4 Gray-Level Co-occurrence Matrix

Haralick et al. [19] first proposed the concept of Gray Level Co-occurrence Matrix (GLCM). GLCM provides spatial information about intensity values. GLCM helps in determining how frequently adjacent pixel pairs of specified values and in specified directions occur in an image. This helps in getting information about spatial distribution of pixel values which other features such as histogram fail to provide. It also provides information about structural arrangement of pixels. GLCM helps in getting certain textural information of any surface such as smoothness, coarseness, and roughness etc.

4 The Proposed Method

The proposed method consists of the following steps-

1. Computation of DWT coefficients of gray scale image.
2. Computation of LBP codes of DWT coefficients.
3. Computation of SURF descriptors of resulting LBP codes.
4. Construction of GLCM for feature vector.
5. Similarity measurement.

4.1 Computation of DWT Coefficients

DWT coefficients of gray scale image are computed and stored in matrix. When DWT is applied on an image it produces three detail coefficient matrices which consists of coefficients computed in three directions- horizontal detail consisting of coefficients computed in horizontal direction, vertical detail consisting of coefficients computed in vertical direction, and diagonal detail consisting of coefficients computed in diagonal direction. These coefficients are stored in three separate matrices.

4.2 Computation of LBP Codes

LBP codes of resulting DWT coefficients are computed and stored in three separate matrices. LBP codes of directional DWT coefficients produce texture matrix from which the interest points are extracted using SURF.

4.3 Computation of SURF Descriptors

Interest points from texture image is obtained by computing SURF descriptors of resulting LBP codes. The resulting SURF descriptors are scale-invariant features which are used for constructing feature vector.

4.4 Construction of GLCM

The fourth step is computation of GLCM for constructing feature vector. GLCM determines co-occurrence of adjacent pixel pair values. This provides information about structural arrangement of pixel values which histogram fails to provide. GLCM of resulting three SURF descriptor matrices is computed and stored in separate matrices. Similarity measurement for each of these three matrices is done separately. GLCM is used as feature vector for retrieving visually similar images. In the proposed method, for the construction of feature vector, GLCM for $0°$ angle and distance 1 has been considered and rescaled to size 8×8.

4.5 Similarity Measurement

Similarity measurement is performed to retrieve visually similar images. Let $(f_{Q1}, f_{Q2}, \ldots f_{Qn})$ be the set of query images and let $(f_{DB1}, f_{DB2}, \ldots f_{DBn})$ be the set of database images. Then the similarity between query image and database image is computed using the following formula-

$$Similarity(S) = \sum_{i=1}^{n} \left| \frac{f_{DBi} - f_{Qi}}{1 + f_{DBi} + f_{Qi}} \right|, \quad i = 1, 2, \ldots, n \qquad (4)$$

4.6 Advantages of the Proposed Method

Following are the advantages of the proposed method-

- The proposed method attempts to extract interest points from texture image at multiple resolutions of image. Since texture represents structural arrangement of pixels, it can be used to extract scale invariant features if an efficient texture descriptor is used. LBP is an efficient local texture descriptor which effectively represents structural arrangement of pixels.
- LBP fails to extract directional information. However, its combination with DWT proves to be efficient as DWT computes coefficients in multiple directions and its combination with LBP extracts local information in multiple directions.
- The use of SURF descriptor for extracting interest points in an image proves to be efficient as SURF is an effective scale invariant descriptor which works faster than other scale invariant descriptors such as SIFT and extracts more distinct features than SIFT.
- The combination of LBP and SURF is exploited at multiple resolutions of image. The principle advantage of using multiresolution analysis of image is that features that are left undetected at one scale get detected at another scale.
- The use of GLCM for constructing feature vector proves to be advantageous as GLCM provides information about spatial distribution of intensity values which other features such as histogram fails to provide.

5 Experiment and Results

For performing experiment using the proposed method, images from Corel-1 K dataset [20] have been used. Corel-1 K dataset consists of 1000 natural images divided into ten different categories namely, Africans, Beaches, Buildings, Buses, Dinosaurs, Elephants, Flowers, Horses, Mountains, and Food. Each category consists of 100 images and each image is of size either 256×384 or 384×256.

Each image of the dataset is taken as query image. If the retrieved images belong to the same category as that of the query image, the retrieval is considered to be successful. Otherwise, the retrieval fails.

5.1 Performance Evaluation

The performance of the proposed method has been evaluated in terms of precision and recall. Precision refers to the ratio of total number of relevant images retrieved to the total number of images retrieved. Mathematically, precision can be represented as

$$P = \frac{I_R}{T_R} \tag{5}$$

where I_R denotes total number of relevant images retrieved and T_R denotes total number of images retrieved. Recall refers to the ratio of total number of relevant images retrieved to the total number of relevant images in the database. Mathematically, recall can be represented as

$$R = \frac{I_R}{C_R} \tag{6}$$

where I_R denotes total number of relevant images retrieved and C_R denotes total number of relevant images in the database. In this experiment, $T_R = 10$ and $C_R = 100$.

5.2 Retrieval Results

To perform the experiment, two-level DWT decomposition of 2-D gray scale image is done. DWT decomposition of image at each level produces three detail coefficient matrices- horizontal detail, vertical detail, and diagonal detail. LBP codes of each of these detail coefficient matrices are obtained separately and stored in separate matrices. SURF descriptors of resulting LBP codes are obtained to extract interest points from texture image. Finally, construction of feature vector is done by computing GLCM of SURF descriptor matrices. In the proposed method, 2-D gray scale image has been decomposed through DWT for two levels only because DWT decomposition of an image causes down sampling by a factor of 2. This reduces the size of image. For very small size image, SURF descriptors do not get computed. For computing SURF descriptors, the size of the image should be considerably large. Hence, only two levels of DWT decomposition are chosen for constructing feature vector.

When DWT is applied on 2-D gray scale image, it results in three detail coefficient matrices- horizontal detail, vertical detail, and diagonal detail. For performing similarity measurement, the feature vector for each of these matrices is constructed separately. This results in three sets of similar images. Final image set of similar images is obtained by taking union of these sets. Computation of recall is performed by counting total number of relevant image sets in the final image set. Computation of precision values is done by counting top n matches for each set. This results in final image set. The top n matches in the final set are considered for evaluating precision. Mathematically, this can be stated as follows. Let f_H be set of similar images obtained from horizontal detail feature vector, f_V be set of similar images obtained from vertical detail feature vector, and f_D be set of similar images obtained from diagonal detail feature vector. Then, the final set of similar images denoted by f_{RS} is given as

$$f_{RS} = f_H \cup f_V \cup f_D \tag{7}$$

Table 1. Average recall and precision values for two levels of resolution

Levels of Resolution	Recall (%)	Precision (%)
Level 1	37.71	54.68
Level 2	56.59	77.61

Similarly, let f_H^n be set of top n images obtained from horizontal detail feature vector, f_V^n be set of top n images obtained from vertical detail feature vector, and f_D^n be set of top n images obtained from diagonal detail feature vector. Then the final set of top n images denoted by f_{PS}^n is given as

$$f_{PS}^n = f_H^n \cup f_V^n \cup f_D^n \tag{8}$$

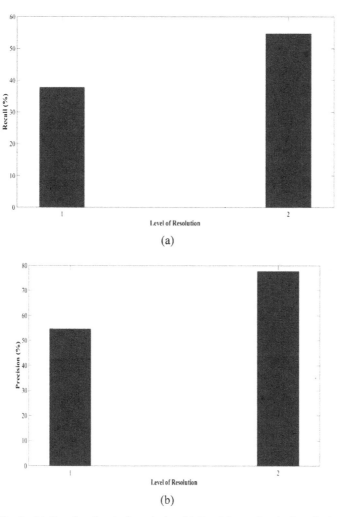

(a)

(b)

Fig. 1. (a) Recall vs level of resolution (b) Precision vs level of resolution

The above procedure is repeated for two levels of resolution. In each level the relevant image set of the previous level is also considered and is combined with current level to produce relevant image set for that level. If the values of precision and recall are high, the retrieval is considered to be good. The average values of precision and recall obtained for two levels of resolution of image are shown in Table 1. Figure 1b shows plot between average values of precision and level of resolution and Fig. 1a shows plot between average values of recall and level of resolution. From Table 1, Fig. 1a and b, it can be observed that the average values of precision and recall increase with the level of resolution.

5.3 Performance Comparison

The performance of the proposed descriptor is compared with other state-of-the-art CBIR techniques such as Structure Element Descriptor (SED) [10, 13], Multi-Texton Histogram (MTH) [11, 13], Microstructure Descriptor (MSD) [12], Colour Difference Histogram (CDH) [8, 13], Xia et al. [14] and Srivastava et al. [15]. These techniques combine multiple features for constructing feature vector and produce high retrieval accuracy. However, most of these techniques exploit single resolution of image for constructing feature vector. Single resolution of image proves to be insufficient to extract varying level of details. The proposed method extracts interest points from texture feature by computing SURF descriptor of LBP codes at multiple resolutions of image. Hence it produces high retrieval accuracy than other CBIR techniques. Table 2 shows the performance comparison of the proposed method with other CBIR techniques Structure Element Descriptor (SED) [10, 13], Multi-Texton Histogram (MTH) [11, 13], Microstructure Descriptor (MSD) [12], Colour Difference Histogram (CDH) [8, 13], Xia et al. [14] and Srivastava et al. [15] in terms of precision and recall. The proposed method performs better than other state-of-the-art CBIR methods in terms of precision and recall as can be observed from Table 2.

Table 2. Performance comparison of the proposed method with other state-of-the-art methods in terms of Recall (%) and Precision (%)

Method	Recall (%)	Precision (%)
SED [10, 13]	9.39	61.58
CDH [8, 13]	7.89	65.75
MSD [12]	9.07	75.67
MTH [11, 13]	10.40	69.32
Xia et al. [14]	45.81	75.39
Srivastava et al. [15]	46.98	76.46
Proposed method	**56.59**	**77.61**

6 Conclusion

The method proposed in this paper extracts interest points from texture feature at multiple resolutions of image. The texture feature was extracted using LBP and interest points were obtained through SURF. The multiresolution decomposition of image was done through DWT. The advantages of the proposed method can be summarized as follows-

1. Texture represents structural arrangement of pixels which can be used to extract interest points. LBP proves to be an efficient texture descriptor which supplies sufficient texture information for extracting interest points.
2. SURF is an efficient feature descriptor which efficiently extracts scale invariant interest points from texture image produced by LBP.
3. The use of multiresolution processing of image for feature extraction proves to be advantageous as features that are left undetected at one level get detected at another level.

Performance of the proposed method was measured in terms of precision and recall. The experimental results demonstrate that the proposed method performs better than other state-of-the-art CBIR techniques. The proposed method can be further improved by exploiting other local patterns such as Local Derivative Pattern and using other multiresolution techniques which is going to be our future work.

References

1. Dutta, R., Joshi, D., Li, J., Wang, J.Z.: Image retrieval: ideas influences and trends of the new age. ACM Comput. Surv. **40**(2), 1–60 (2008)
2. Smith, J.R., Chang, S.F.: Tools and Techniques for Color Image Retrieval. Electronic Imaging, Science and Technology. International Society for Optics and Photonics **2670**, 426–437 (1996)
3. Wang, X., Yu, Y., Yang, H.: An effective image retrieval scheme using color, texture and shape features. Comput. Stand. Interfaces **33**(1), 59–68 (2011)
4. Srivastava, P., Binh, N.T., Khare, A.: Content-based image retrieval using moments. In: Proceedings of Context-Aware Systems and Applications, Phu Quoc, Vietnam, pp. 228–237 (2013)
5. Srivastava, P., Binh, N.T., Khare, A.: Content-based image retrieval using moments of local ternary pattern. Mob. Netw. Appl. **19**, 618–625 (2014)
6. Youssef, S.M.: ICTEDCT-CBIR: integrating curvelet transform with enhanced dominant colors extraction and texture analysis for efficient content-based image retrieval. Comput. Electr. Eng. **38**, 1358–1376 (2012)
7. Srivastava, P., Khare, A.: Integration of wavelet transform, local binary pattern, and moments for content-based image retrieval. J. Vis. Commun. Image Represent. **42**(1), 78–103 (2017)
8. Liu, G.H., Yang, J.Y.: Content-based image retrieval using color difference histogram. Pattern Recogn. **46**(1), 188–198 (2013)
9. Zhang, M., Zhang, K., Feng, Q., Wang, J., Jun, K., Lu, Y.: A novel image retrieval method based on hybrid information descriptors. J. Vis. Commun. Image Represent. **25**(7), 1574–1587 (2014)
10. Wang, X., Wang, Z.: A novel method for image retrieval based on structure elements descriptor. J. Vis. Commun. Image Represent. **24**(1), 63–74 (2013)

11. Liu, G., Zhang, L., Hou, Y., Yang, J.: Image retrieval based on multi-texton histogram. Pattern Recogn. **43**(7), 2380–2389 (2008)
12. Liu, G., Li, Z., Zhang, L., Xu, Y.: Image retrieval based on microstructure descriptor. Pattern Recogn. **44**(9), 2123–2133 (2011)
13. Feng, L., Wu, J., Liu, S., Zhang, H.: Global correlation descriptor: a novel image representation for image retrieval. J. Vis. Commun. Image Represent. **33**, 104–114 (2015)
14. Xia, Yu., Wan, S., Jin, P., Yue, L.: Multi-scale local spatial binary patterns for content-based image retrieval. In: Yoshida, T., Kou, G., Skowron, A., Cao, J., Hacid, H., Zhong, N. (eds.) AMT 2013. LNCS, vol. 8210, pp. 423–432. Springer, Cham (2013). https://doi.org/10.1007/978-3-319-02750-0_45
15. Srivastava, P., Khare, A.: Content-based image retrieval using multiscale local spatial binary Gaussian co-occurrence pattern. In: Hu, Y.-C., Tiwari, S., Mishra, Krishn K., Trivedi, Munesh C. (eds.) Intelligent Communication and Computational Technologies. LNNS, vol. 19, pp. 85–95. Springer, Singapore (2018). https://doi.org/10.1007/978-981-10-5523-2_9
16. Gonzalez, R.C., Woods, R.E.: Digital Image Processing, 2nd edn. Prentice Hall Press, Upper Saddle River (2002)
17. Ojala, T., Pietikainen, M., Harwood, D.: A comparative study of texture measures with classification based on feature distributions. Pattern Recogn. **29**(1), 51–59 (1996)
18. Bay, H., Tuytelaars, T., Van Gool, L.: SURF: Speeded Up Robust Features. In: Leonardis, A., Bischof, H., Pinz, A. (eds.) ECCV 2006. LNCS, vol. 3951, pp. 404–417. Springer, Heidelberg (2006). https://doi.org/10.1007/11744023_32
19. Haralick, R.M., Shanmungam, K., Dinstein, I.: Textural features of image classification. IEEE Trans. Syst. Man Cybern. B Cybern. **3**, 610–621 (1973)
20. http://wang.ist.psu.edu/docs/related/. Accessed Oct 2017

Performance Analysis of Key-Value Stores with Consistent Replica Selection Approach

Thazin Nwe[✉], Tin Tin Yee[✉], and Ei Chaw Htoon[✉]

University of Information Technology, Yangon, Myanmar
{thazin.nwe,tintinyee,eichawhtoon}@uit.edu.mm

Abstract. A key-value store is the primary architecture of data centers. Most modern data stores tend to be distributed and to enable the scaling of the replicas and data across multiple instances of commodity hardware. Defining static replica placement mechanisms in different data centers lack the efficiency of the storage system. In the proposed system, dynamic scaling that changes the key/value store with replicas dynamically joining or leaving. To enhance the dynamic scaling of the replicas, the consistent hashing mechanism is enhanced in key-value stores due to the adaptability of node changes. This mechanism performs the eventual consistency services that offer quorum key-value store with increased consistency. According to the ordering of the hash values among the replicas in the ring, it could provide higher system throughput and reduce lower latency cost without using the random of the original consistent hashing method. An experimental result overwhelms the loss of original consistent hashing algorithms entirely and is proper for the distributed key-value store.

Keywords: Key-value store · Dynamic scaling · Consistent hashing · Eventual consistency · Quorum

1 Introduction

Replica and data management has become a challenge to support different performance such as consistency, fault tolerance, and scalability of large scale data centers. Consistency model such as causal consistency, eventual consistency, etc., has been applied broadly in distributed key-value store research [19]. Eventual consistency is weak consistency and returns the latest updated data with final accesses [4]. The probability of inconsistency depends on portions such as delay of the network communication, the workload of the system and the total replicas required in the replication method. For example, the only master to handle block position is applied in the Hadoop Distributed File System and Google File System. The main server optimizes the block placement but it may not have the scalability of the storage. Large block sizes are used in GFS to reduce the amount of metadata. Consistent hashing [3] is a different generally applied method for block placements to process many small data objects. Systems similar to Dynamo [12] or FDS (Flat Datacenter Storage) [13] all implement consistent hashing. One difficulty of consistent hashing is that the hash function defines the position of

© Springer Nature Singapore Pte Ltd. 2020
P. Sitek et al. (Eds.): ACIIDS 2020, CCIS 1178, pp. 377–387, 2020.
https://doi.org/10.1007/978-981-15-3380-8_33

the per block, and thus there is a problem in anywhere to place each block. In Apache Cassandra, the hash strategy uses with a random arrangement mechanism and defines the location of objects supported the hashing. It efficiently adjusts the load of the data within the system.

This article is constructed as follows. Section 2 performs related work. Section 3 defines the two replica placement strategies in the existing system. Section 4 represents the proposed architecture and algorithms. Section 5 outlines the implementation of the intended methods, and Section VI completes this paper.

2   Related Work

Several existing replica allocation methods for the consistency of distributed systems has been analyzed broadly and compared them in this section.

Suresh et al. presented a C3 algorithm as a replica selection method that chooses the servers according to the rank of the client with the scoring function. It could decrease the latency, but it does not work well in heterogeneous workloads [14]. Therefore, V. Jaiman et al. purposed Heron as a replica reading mechanism with the prediction of requests required important time by sustaining a record of keys according to large values [15]. This mechanism selected the replica that an incoming request more responsive than the separate replicas. Barroso et al. analyzed the problems of latency and presented a collection of tail latency tolerance methods performed in Google's massive scale systems [16]. Anti-entropy [17] method that started with the initiating replicas sending a vector of the latest local versions of all key. It optimized with Merkel or prefix trees to make comparisons faster. Experiments compared with uniform random peer selection with a greedy approach. It is efficient replication, faster visibility, and stronger eventual consistency while maintaining high availability and partition tolerance. J.P. Walters and V. Chaudhary et al. proposed to locate replica at some distant node with randomly rather than storing it near the significant place. The aim is to form replicas by node randomly, subject to specific restrictions [18].

P. Bailis et al. solved a stale read problem for eventual consistency. Probabilistically Bounded Staleness (PBS) is proposed to compute the inconsistency rate. The total replicas, replicas for a read request, replicas for the write request, timeSinceWrite, number versions, and read/ write latency are considered as an evaluation parameter. Although partial quorums were good enough for latency benefits, communicating some replicas for several requests typically decreases the guarantees on consistency [5].

Different from the above studies, the proposed system enhances the consistent hashing algorithm to improve the performance of quorum-based replication of key-value applications. By considering the location and read/write access time of replicas with adjusting the read/write consistency level [8], the proposed algorithms select the appropriate replicas for client access.

3   Background

In this section, the consistent hashing algorithm and Dynamic Snitching which is used in the proposed system is presented.

3.1 Replica Placement Strategy

This is correlated with the replica arrangement strategy for a data property. Cassandra uses the hashing way as placing randomly and decides the situation of objects with the hashing. It efficiently adjusts the amount on the system, nevertheless, it is not sufficient for transactional storage that demands co-located many data items. The method replicates a data object in the data nodes as the replicas (*R1, R2, R3*) which holds the most offers this data object. Although it lowers the transfer in the system, it is not suitable for a transactional store because the relevant data obtained with a transaction might be stored in separate areas.

3.2 Dynamic Snitching

Several Cassandra servers combine into a one-hop distributed hash table (DHT). A client will communicate either replica for the read offer. This replica then is a coordinator and inside retrieves the history of the replica holding the data. Coordinators choose the most reliable replica for the read request handling Dynamic Snitching. With Dynamic Snitching, every Cassandra replica rank and more lasting replicas by a factor of the read latencies to each of its peers, like I/O load information that each replica gives with the cluster into a gossip protocol [20].

3.3 Consistent Hashing

It is a key-value store type distributed data store technology. Servers and data are located on a circular space as a "Ring". Each datum has an ID as a point on the Ring. Each server manages data in the areas on the left side of the virtual nodes on the ring. To prevent data loss, each virtual node replicates its own data to the virtual node on the right. However, it lacks the performance of a heterogeneous environment where different storage devices such as hard disk drives. Various existing storage systems with hashing based distribution have a great role in a distributed system such as the Dynamo, DNS, P2P, Cassandra, Ceph, Sheepdon, and GlusterFS [3].

4   Architecture of Proposed System

Figure 1 presents the design of the proposed key/value store cluster. The proposed cluster model has two components of the read and writes for the client request. The requested data are distributed on different virtual nodes in the cluster as a ring. Every server has multiple virtual nodes. Loads of the servers are more balanced by "the law of massive numbers".

The procedures of the proposed system are mentioned as four steps. In the first step, the hash values of each replica are calculated with the MD5 algorithm. In the second step, the replicas are arranged in a cluster with the descending order of the PoR Algorithm. In the third step, the latency will be computed among various replicas with NR Algorithm. In the last step, the inconsistency rate is computed with CR Algorithm (Fig. 2).

And the proposed algorithms [6, 7] are used to retrieve the updated data associated with the request message. The description of algorithms is mentioned as follows.

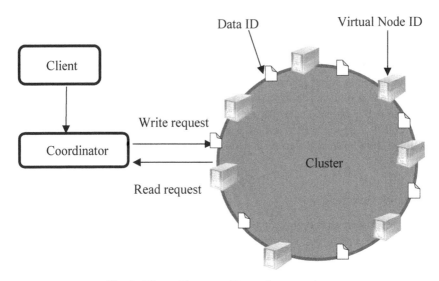

Fig. 1. The architecture of key-value store cluster

A write request is transferred to the PoR algorithm; the client picks the nearest node depends on the distance between neighboring cluster members in the ring. That nearest node is defined as a coordinator node and delivers the request to the adjacent data node. Each data node as a replica in the cluster architecture has a specific ID with the hashing an IP address to get value. Each ID is defined to a scale of a hash function as an output that is set as a circular area such as a ring. The hash values of replicas are sorted into the storage cluster. A key is defined on each data and also placed to the ring and moves clockwise around the ring from that position until finding the first node ID.

PoR Algorithm

Input: YCSB workloads, Data nodes
Begin
  Value = hash (DataNode$_1$_ID)
    for j ← 1 to N-1
    if hash (DataNode$_j$_ID) > Value **then**
        Replica$_j$ = DataNode$_j$
        Value= hash (DataNode$_j$)
    else Value= DataNode$_j$
        Ring. Append (Replica$_j$, data, timestamp, version)
    end if
  end for
End
Output: Replicas selected for data

This first node is responsible for the requested data. Thus, if the total request messages are larger than that of servers composing the cluster, the data keys are randomly chosen. Each node is needed to hold the equivalent amount of data to enhance the performance.

NR Algorithm

Input: Replicas in Ring
Begin
NearestReplica= DataNode$_j$
Value= hash (requestedID)
for j from 1◄— N **do**
  if the hash (DataNode) > Value **then**
    Sort the replicas in descending order of hash values
    ClosestReplica$_j$.add (j, DataNode$_i$)
    Value= DataNodej
    Compute the distance of DataNodej
  else
    Value= hash (DataNodej)
  end
end for
End
Output: The nearest replicas

In the architecture of a read request (NR Algorithm), a client assigns a read request to one of the replicas in the ring to get the value. And then the node sends these requests to other replicas. The coordinator chooses the nearest replicas of the sorted replica lists with ascending order until finding the first node ID.

CR Algorithm

Input: The closest replicas
Begin
for each NearestReplica$_j$
  while (consistentReplica <= RCL)
    if (inconsistencyRate<=maxStaleReadRate)
      then consistentReplica++
      NearestReplica$_j$. add (j, NearestReplica$_i$)
    end if
end for
return ConsistentReplica$_j$
End
Output: The number of replicas of consistency

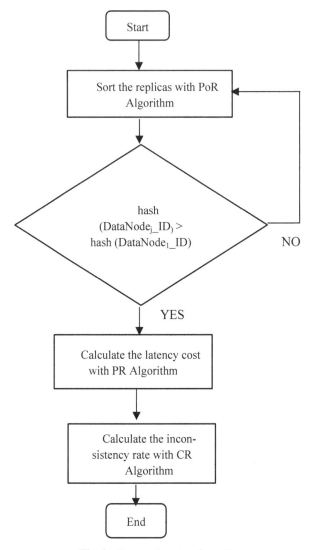

Fig. 2. Proposed system flow diagram

5   Evaluation

PoR Algorithm and NR Algorithm, and CR Algorithm are executed within the Apache Cassandra cluster 3.11.4. Apache Cassandra was designed to have the advantage of multiprocessor/multi-core machines and to work across many of these machines in various data centers. Especially it has been given to achieve the well supporting of the massive load. It consistently can show fast throughput for writes per second on basic commodity computers, whether physical hardware or virtual machines. It does a gossip protocol that implements each node to get the status of all the other replicas in which the nodes are not available. When the gossip shows the coordinator that the node has obtained, it gives the lost data. The Yahoo Cloud Serving Benchmark (YCSB) [1], a standardized benchmark, is applied to estimate the execution of these algorithms. YCSB generates different workloads such as read-heavy, read-only, and update-heavy. Seven servers are managed that provide an Intel ® Core™ i7-6700 CPU @3.40 GHz 3.41 GHz. The quorum consistency level is considered to achieve strong consistency.

5.1 Experimental Result

The set of measures proves the latency cost, the throughput, the probability of inconsistency rate, and the replicas to retrieve the consistent transaction.

Figure 3 indicates the 99th percentile latency among different workloads. The effects of latency are analyzed with varying different workloads. Each measurement includes ten million operations of the workload. In particular, the 99th percentile latencies are recorded wherein the difference between various workloads are up to five times.

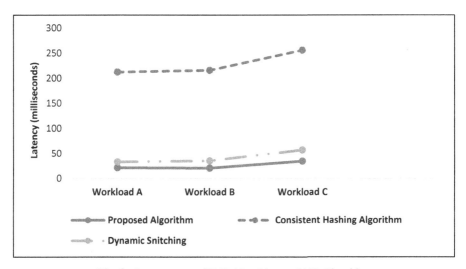

Fig. 3. Latency cost of PoR Algorithm and NR Algorithm

According to Fig. 3, the latency of the PoR Algorithm and NR Algorithm is lower than a consistent hashing algorithm in every different workload. As a reason, when a node joins a cluster with the consistent hashing method, it must perform to locate replicas randomly. To compare the consistent hashing algorithm and proposed an algorithm, the average distance between the node issuing a request and the replica serving it is computed. This increases the replicas, which makes it impossible to reduce the access time because it has to contact the replicas in the long distance. Thus the average distance is less than that allowed by the consistent hashing algorithm according to the descending order of hash values and total round trip time. This proposed replica placement strategy has an impact on the latency cost as well as in reducing resource cost. The proposed PoR

Algorithm and NR Algorithm are a broadly applied algorithm and a suitable method to the distributed key-value stores for load balancing and high reliability.

Figure 3 designates the read latency components of Cassandra crossed several workloads when using the proposed algorithms matched to Dynamic Snitching (DS). Regardless of the workload used, the proposed algorithms improve the latency across all the considered metrics, namely, 99th percentile latencies. With the read-heavy workload, the 99th percentile latency is 21 ms with the proposed algorithms, whereas, with DS, it is 33 ms. In the update heavy and read-only scenarios, the proposed algorithms improve the same difference by a factor of 20.4 ms and 30.4 ms. The proposed algorithms also improve the latency by between 12 ms and 15 ms, and 23 ms across all scenarios.

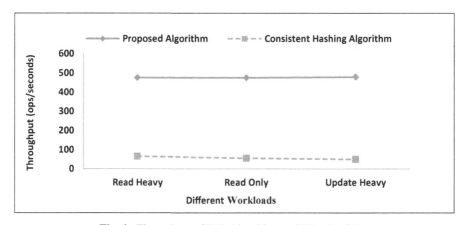

Fig. 4. Throughput of PoR Algorithm and NR Algorithm

In Fig. 4, the client uses a replica election approach to track the requests for a quorum of replicas. A request created at a client has an identical distribution delivered to other replicas. In particular, we recorded throughput between the proposed algorithm and the consistent hashing algorithm is up to five times. The proposed algorithm offers more useful the possible system space, appearing in an improvement in throughput across these workloads. In particular, the proposed algorithm enhances the throughput by roughly 75% across the considered workloads. This proposed replica placement strategy has an impact on the throughput in key-value data stores as the workload varies dynamically.

In the experiment of Fig. 5, 500 million 1 KB size records created by YCSB running in separate VMs are inserted, and the PoR Algorithm and NR Algorithm are analyzed for the impact of strong consistency for various workloads [9].

The read and update heavy workloads in distinct widespread over a description of Cassandra deployments [10, 11]. The staleness rate depends on increasing the consistency level or the read and write requests. The raised to read and write consistency level has a great possibility of an inconsistency rate because the further expecting time is required to obtain the read/write request. Nevertheless, the result proves that the inconsistency rate is not dramatically raising even the number of replicas and replicas for the read and write requests is large.

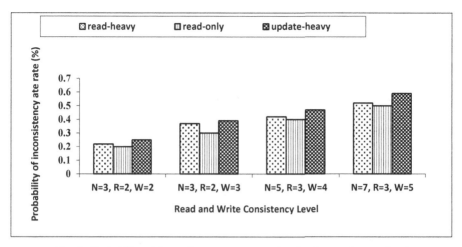

Fig. 5. Probability of inconsistency rate on read and write consistency level

From Fig. 6, CR Algorithm takes the fewest number of replicas for consistent data of each request related to a consistent hashing algorithm for quorum replication. NR Algorithm gets the closest replicas. Thus, the system does not require to obtain additional replicas for the choosing of consistent replicas.

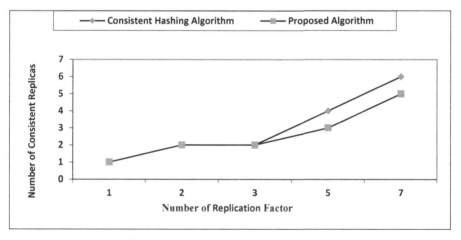

Fig. 6. Consistent replicas of CR Algorithm

The total consistent replicas of the CR algorithm are smaller than the consistent hashing algorithm when the replication factor is five and seven. Each node is needed to hold the equivalent amount of data to enhance the performance. When nodes randomly join the ring, each node is responsible for at most. This proposed idea can be reduced by holding each node run replicas in a cluster model.

6 Conclusion

In this research, we tend to address the issues of the static replication and intended the PoR Algorithm, NR Algorithm, and CR Algorithm for selecting the replica of consistency data in distributed key-value stores. The intended algorithms offer strong consistency which proposes the execution of the key-value stores with replica selection. The result is enhanced the overall achievement of the key-value store for a large-scale variance of different workloads. These algorithms compute the latency cost, throughput, inconsistency rate and choose the appropriate consistency level to take the least number of consistent replicas for increasing the read and write execution time in real-time. The tests prove that the purposed algorithms are adapted to define the minimum number of consistent replicas of key-value stores with the quorum replication.

As future work, YCSB workload D and workload E will be applied in the performance of the PoR Algorithm, NR Algorithm, and CR Algorithm. And, the throughput of the PoR Algorithm and NR Algorithm will be compared with the Dynamic Snitching algorithm.

Acknowledgement. I would also like to express my special thanks to Professor Junya Nakamura, Information and Media Center, the Toyohashi University, Japan for his valuable suggestions and guidelines.

References

1. Cooper, B.F., Silberstein, A., Tam, E., Ramakrishnan, R., Sears, R.: Benchmarking cloud serving systems with YCSB. In: Proceedings of the 1st ACM Symposium on Cloud computing, New York, pp. 143–154 (2010)
2. Malkhi, D., Reiter, M.K.: Byzantine quorum systems. In: Proceedings of the 29th Annual ACM Symposium on the Theory of Computing, STOC 1997, pp. 569–578, May 1997
3. Karger, D., Lehman, E., Leighton, T., Panigraphy, R., Levine, M., Lewin, D.: Consistent hashing and random trees: distributed caching protocols for relieving hot spots on the world wide web. STOC 1997 Proceedings of the Twenty-Ninth Annual ACM Symposium on Theory of Computing, pp. 654–663 (1997)
4. Diogo, M., Cabral, B., Bernardino, J.: Consistency models of NoSQL databases. Future Internet 11 (2019). https://doi.org/10.3390/fi11020043
5. Bailis, P., Venkataraman, S., Franklin, M.J., Hellerstein, J.M., Stoica, I.: Probabilistically bounded staleness for practical partial quorums. J. Proc. VLDB Endowment 5(8), 776–787 (2012). https://doi.org/10.14778/2212351.2212359
6. Nwe, T., Nakamura, J., Yee, T.T., Phyu, M.P., Htoon, E.C.: Automatic adjustment of read consistency level of distributed key-value storage by a replica selection approach. In: The 1st International Conference on Advanced Information Technologies, Yangon, Myanmar, pp. 151–156, November 2017
7. Nwe, T., Yee, T.T., Htoon, E.C.: Improving read/write performance for key-value storage system by automatic adjustment of consistency level. In: The 33rd International Technical Conference on Circuits/Systems, Computers and Communications, Bangkok, Thailand, pp. 357–360, July 2018
8. Nwe, T., Nakamura, J., Yee, T.T., Htoon, E.C.: Automatic adjustment of consistency level by predicting staleness rate for distributed key-value storage system. In: Proceedings of the 2nd International Conference on Advanced Information Technologies, Yangon, Myanmar, pp. 27–32, November 2018

9. Nwe, T., Nakamura, J., Yee, T.T., Htoon, E.C.: A consistent replica selection approach for distributed key-value storage. In: Proceedings of 2019 International Conference on Advanced Information Technologies, Yangon, Myanmar, pp. 114–119, November 2019

10. Rahman, M.R., Golab, W., AuYoung, A., Keeton, K., Wylie, J.J.: Toward a principled framework for benchmarking consistency. In: Proceedings of the Eighth USENIX Conference on Hot Topics in System Dependability, ser. HotDep 2012. USENIX Association, Berkeley, p. 8 (2012)

11. Lakshman, A., Malik, P.: Cassandra: a decentralized structured storage system. SIGOPS Oper. Syst. Rev. **44**(2), 35–40 (2010)

12. DeCandia, G., et al.: Dynamo: amazon's highly available keyvalue store. In: ACM SIGOPS Operating Systems Review, vol. 41, pp. 205–220. ACM (2007)

13. Nightingale, E.B., Elson, J., Fan, J., Hofmann, O.S., Howell, J., Suzue, Y.: Flat datacenter storage. In: OSDI, pp. 1–15 (2012)

14. Suresh, L., Canini, M., Schmid, S., Feldmann, A.: C3: cutting tail latency in cloud data stores via adaptive replica selection. In: 12th USENIX Symposium on Networked Systems Design and Implementation, NSDI 2015, 4–6 May 2015, Oakland, CA, USA (2015)

15. Jaiman, V., Mokhtar, S.B., Quema, V., Chen, L.Y., Riviere, E.: He'ron: taming tail latencies in key-value stores under heterogeneous workloads. In: 2018 IEEE 37th Symposium on Reliable Distributed Systems (SRDS), pp. 191–200 (2018)

16. Dean, J., Barroso, L.A.: The tail at scale. Commun. ACM **56**(2), 74–80 (2013)

17. Bengfort, B., Xirogiannopoulos, K., Keleher, P.: Anti-entropy bandits for geo-replicated consistency. In: 2018 IEEE 38th International Conference on Distributed Computing Systems (2018)

18. Walters, J.P., Chaudhary, V.: Replication-based fault tolerance for MPI applications. IEEE Trans. Parallel Distrib. Syst. **20**(7), 997–1010 (2009)

19. Davoudian, A., Chen, L., Liu, M.: A survey on NoSQL stores. ACM Comput. Surv. (CSUR) **51**, 1–43 (2018)

20. Williams, B.: Dynamic snitching in Cassandra: past, present, and future (2012). http://www.datastax.com/dev/blog/dynamic-snitching-in-cassandra-past-present-and-future

Intelligent Applications of Internet of Things

Development of IoT-Based Simply Constructed Mobile Biomedical Signals Extraction Device

Yu-Huei Cheng[1](✉) 🅾 and Che-Nan Kuo[2] 🅾

[1] Department of Information and Communication Engineering,
Chaoyang University of Technology, Taichung, Taiwan
yuhuei.cheng@gmail.com
[2] Department of Business Administration,
CTBC Financial Management College, Tainan, Taiwan
fkikimo@hotmail.com

Abstract. Medical care is no longer limited to specific times and places. Through the portable and wearable devices combined with the Internet of Things (IoT) technology, we can collect personal biomedical information, including heart rate, blood pressure, blood oxygen, respiratory rate, vital capacity and psychological index, anytime and anywhere, and transmit them to the cloud database and remote server through the network to store and analyze as future smart medical care applications. This not only eliminates the inconvenience of many measurement and record for patients and caregivers, but also ensures the correctness of the data. This study intends to use the IoT as the basis, applies communication technology, and combines with Arduino Pro Mini microcontroller and biomedical signal measurement sensors to complete the construction of a mobile biomedical measuring device for the measurement of blood oxygen, heart pulse and body temperature.

Keywords: Mobile medical care · Portable · Biomedical signals · Internet of things

1 Introduction

1.1 A Subsection Sample

The development of mobile technology and the advancement of mobile communication technology, along with the popularity of smart phones and tablets and the convenience and circulation of mobile applications (Apps), have completely changed people's lifestyles. With the advancement of information technology, the Internet of Things (IoT) [1–3] technology has been proposed and widely used, and medical care is no longer limited to specific times and places. Various mobile medical care devices have become the next trend in the Information and Communication Technologies (ICT) industry. The Food and Drug Administration (FDA) officially announced the final version of the Mobile Medical Application Final Guidance management guidelines in September 2013. The mobile medical app has also begun to have initial compliance standards, which is more conducive to the development of mobile medical care devices.

© Springer Nature Singapore Pte Ltd. 2020
P. Sitek et al. (Eds.): ACIIDS 2020, CCIS 1178, pp. 391–401, 2020.
https://doi.org/10.1007/978-981-15-3380-8_34

The concept of mobile medical care makes medical care easier and simpler. Medical care will no longer be limited to specific times and places. Through the portable and wearable devices combined with IoT technology, we can collect personal health information, including heart rate, blood pressure, blood oxygen, respiratory rate, vital capacity and psychological index, etc. This information is transmitted to the cloud database and remote server for storage and analysis through the network, which can be used as future smart care applications. This not only eliminates the inconvenience of many measurement and record for patients and caregivers, but also ensures the correctness of the data.

In the past, Fulford-Jones *et al.* proposed a portable, low-power, wireless EKG system in 2004 to expand the capabilities of medical care remotes [4]. In 2005, Bojovic and Bojic proposed a reference system for mobile availability analysis medical implementation and presented the implementation of mobilePDR. They evaluate similar tools with other aspects of mobilePDR, including key features, information, content, performance, and design issues, to learn from system development [5]. In 2006, Chakravorty proposed a proof-of-concept prototype MobiCare, a novel service architecture that provides a wide range of health-related services for efficient and mobile patient care [6]. In 2016, Kong *et al.* proposed combining wireless communication technology and medical sensor detection technology to realize remote medical monitoring of various physiological parameters [7]. In addition, Gatzoulis and Iakovidis outlined the latest technologies in wearable and portable electronic health systems for health monitoring and disease management in 2007, as well as new technologies that contribute to personalized care development [8]. In 2016, Dorosh *et al.* used Android Studio to easily develop mobile medical care applications that measure heart rate and blood pressure [9]. In 2017, Deng *et al.* proposed an improved integer coefficient infinite impulse response (IRR) filter for portable ECG monitors, which can meet the requirements of ECG instantaneous filtering and filtering performance [10].

Although there are many medical instruments, such as blood glucose measuring machine, blood pressure measuring meter, blood oxygen measuring machine, heart pulse measuring instrument, and thermometer, etc. on the market for measuring the basic physiological data, the functions of these medical instruments are mostly independent and do not have IoT functions. A small number of instruments have integrated measurement functions, such as the blood glucose and blood pressure machine, but most instruments are inconvenient to carry and must pass passive measurement to obtain physiological parameters. Therefore, it cannot be effectively utilized for the applications of mobile medical care. Lightweight mobile medical care devices Integrating IoT technology is a convenient platform for monitoring personal health-related parameters and providing and processing relevant information for users and medical professionals. It provides a solution for mobile medical care applications as a future direction for long-term care system integration. Lightweight mobile medical care devices can be implemented by sensing, processing, and communication devices integrated into body wear systems (e.g., wrist worn devices, patches, and even clothing [11]). This study uses the mobile medical care concept, combined with the IoT technologies and the applications of communication technology, using the Arduino Pro Mini microcontroller and the biomedical signals measuring sensors to complete the construction of a mobile biomedical signals measuring device for the measurement of blood oxygen, heart pulse, and body temperature.

2 Methods

In order to provide automated measurement and analysis of biomedical data for long-term care patients, this study uses Arduino Pro Mini microcontrollers to integrate various biomedical wireless sensors to develop a mobile medical care device for various physiological data measurements, such as blood oxygen, heart pulse and body temperature measurement, etc., to facilitate future patients to conduct physiological data measurement at anytime and anywhere, and caregivers and their families can also take care of long-term care at anytime and anywhere.

2.1 Blood Oxygen Sensing Device

The metabolic process of the human body is a biological oxidation process, and the oxygen required in the metabolic process enters the human blood through the respiratory system, and combines with hemoglobin (Hb) in the red blood cells of the blood to form oxyhemoglobin (HbO2), which is then transported to all parts of the tissue cells of the human body. Peripheral vascular oxygen saturation monitoring (SpO2) is generally considered to be no less than 94%, and below 94% is insufficient oxygen supply. Some scholars have set SpO2 < 90% as the standard for hypoxemia, and they believe that when SpO2 is higher than 70%, the accuracy can reach $\pm 2\%$, and when SpO2 is lower than 70%, there may be errors. Many clinical diseases will cause a lack of oxygen supply, which will directly affect the normal metabolism of cells, and will seriously threaten human life. Therefore, real-time monitoring of arterial oxygen concentration is very important in clinical rescue. In this part, the study uses the non-invasive module MAX30100 to complete the blood oxygen concentration measurement function. The circuit design and connection are shown in Fig. 1. The main application of optical measurement is based on the difference in oxygen concentration in the blood and the amount of light absorbed. Since oxygen is transported through the hemoglobin (Hb) in the blood, hemoglobin combines with oxygen molecules to form oxyhemoglobin (HbO2), and its absorption properties also change. The concentration of two heme (cHbO2 and cHb) in the blood indicates the blood oxygen concentration SpO2 = cHbO2/(cHbO2 + cHb).

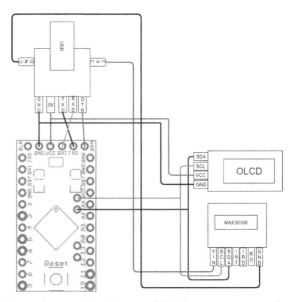

Fig. 1. Circuit design and connection diagram of blood oxygen concentration measurement by non-intrusive module MA30100.

2.2   Heart Pulse Sensing Device

Pulse refers to the contraction of the heart every time, after the blood is driven into the aorta, the fluctuations in the elastic arterial system can be seen in some parts of the body, or touched. In general, the pulse is the pulsation of the artery, and the cause of the pulsation comes from the heartbeat. Under normal conditions, the pulse rate is equal to the number of heartbeats. But sometimes the heartbeat is too small, the pulsation can't be detected, and the pulse rate is not equal to the number of heartbeats. Although the number of heartbeats and the pulse rate are sometimes different, the pulse value is still an important reference for the number of heartbeats. Table 1 shows the normal values of heartbeat for each age group.

Table 1.   Normal value of heartbeat for all ages.

Age group	Heartbeat (times/minutes)
Neonatal	130–150
Infancy	125–135
Childhood	65–105
Adolescent	65–100
Adulthood	65–100
Old age	65–100

The information that the pulse can reflect basically includes four aspects: pulse rate, rhythm, strength, and weakness. In terms of pulse rate, in most cases, the pulse rate is consistent with the heart rate, that is, the heart rate is reflected. Normal people are in the range of 60–100 beats per minute. Exceeding this range is called bradycardia or overspeed. In order to save costs, in this part, this study applies the same non-invasive module MAX30100 with blood oxygen concentration measurement to complete the heart pulse measurement function (circuit design and connection method is the same as Fig. 1 above). In addition, we also use the heart rate sensor (PulseSensor) to complete the independent heart rate measurement function, as shown in Fig. 2.

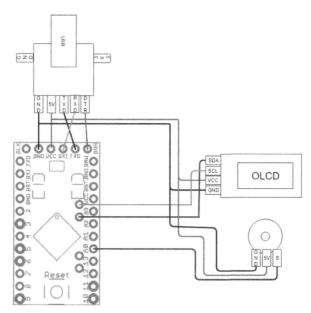

Fig. 2. Circuit design and connection diagram of heart rate sensor (PulseSensor) as independent heart rate measurement.

2.3 Body Temperature Sensing Device

Body temperature refers to the body temperature of the creature. Under normal circumstances, human body temperature is generally 37 °C. The body temperature measured by the oral cavity is generally 36.8 ± 0.7 °C, which is 36.1 °C to 37.5 °C. The body temperature reflects the metabolism of the body and is one of the necessary conditions for the body to perform various normal functions. In this part, the GY-906 module is used in this study to complete the function of body temperature measurement, as shown in Fig. 3. The GY-906 module has the advantages of small size and low cost. It uses MLX90614 chip, uses standard IIC communication protocol, power supply 3–5 V, and has internal low dropout voltage regulation. It is worth mentioning that the sensor temperature range (Ta) is $-40\,°C - +125\,°C$, the temperature range of the object to be tested (To) is $-70\,°C - +380\,°C$. Ta and To are accurate to $0.5\,°C$ (medical) with a precision of 0 to $+50\,°C$, and the measurement resolution is $0.02\,°C$.

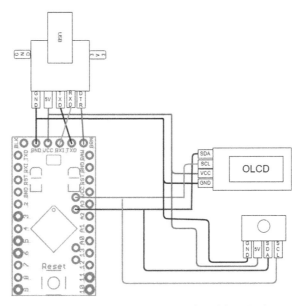

Fig. 3. Circuit design and connection diagram of GY-906 module as body temperature measurement.

2.4   Constructing a Simple Mobile Biomedical Signals Extraction Device

In order to construct the simple mobile biomedical signals extraction device, this study uses the Arduino Pro Mini as the main control board of the biomedical sensing module, which is responsible for controlling and receiving the data measured by all the expandable biomedical sensors. The Arduino Pro Mini is an Arduino-based microcontroller board (shown in Fig. 4) that has the advantage of miniaturization to meet the needs of the simple mobile biomedical signals extraction device that this study is intended to construct. The detailed specifications are shown in Table 2.

Fig. 4. Arduino Pro Mini microcontroller board.

Table 2. Arduino Pro Mini specifications.

Name	Specifications
Single-chip microcomputer	Atmel Atmega328P-AU
I/O port	14 digital I/O ports: RX, TX, D2–D13
Analog input port	8 analog input ports: A0–A7
Serial transmission and reception ports	1 pair of TTL level serial transmission and reception port: RX/TX
PWM ports	6 PWM ports: D3, D5, D6, D9, D10, and D11
Power supply	1. External 3.3 V–12 V DC power supply 2. 9 V battery powered
Clock frequency	16 MHz
Size	33.3 × 18.0 mm

3   Results and Discussion

This study has completed the simple mobile biomedical signals extraction device for the measurement of blood oxygen, heart pulse, and body temperature, described as follows:

Figure 5 shows the designed blood oxygen and heart pulse measurement circuit. Users can perform blood oxygen and heart pulse measurement through the optical sensing LEDs of the MAX30100.

Fig. 5. Blood oxygen and heart pulse measurement circuit.

Figure 6 shows an independent heart rate measurement circuit using a heart rate sensor (PulseSensor). Users can directly measure the heart rate through the optical sensing LEDs of the PulseSensor.

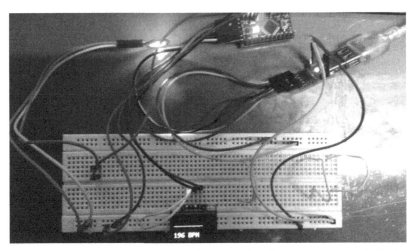

Fig. 6. Independent heart rate measurement circuit completed by heart rate sensor (PulseSensor).

Figure 7 is a body temperature measurement circuit. Users can directly measure the body temperature through the GY-906 module.

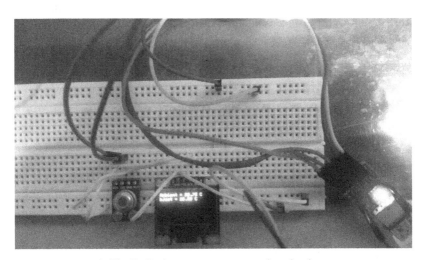

Fig. 7. Body temperature measuring circuit.

In order to facilitate user measurement, this study designed and built a prototype of the finger-type user operation interface model, and printed the model using a 3D printer as shown in Fig. 8. A user can measure the blood oxygen, heart pulse and body temperature by placing the finger into the prototype of user operation interface model.

| (A) | (B) | (C) |

Fig. 8. The prototype of the finger-type user operation interface model. (A) unequal view; (B) side view; (C) top view.

In addition, in order to make this model and circuit commercially available in the future, this study also continues to improve the design of the circuit and the design of the user interface model.

Figure 9 shows the improved blood oxygen and heart pulse measurement circuit, in which (A) is the state when the finger is not placed at the beginning, and the message "Waiting for your finger" is presented for waiting for the user to put the finger on the optical sensing LEDs. (B) After the finger is placed on the optical sensing LEDs, the measurement state is started. At this time, the "Measuring" message is displayed for indicating that the measurement is being performed. After the equivalent measurement is completed, (C) shows the measurement status.

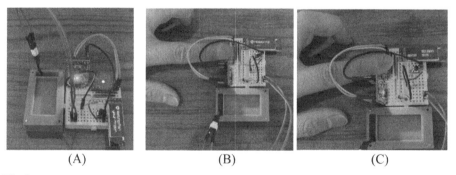

| (A) | (B) | (C) |

Fig. 9. Improved blood oxygen and heart pulse measurement circuit. (A) The state when the finger is not placed; (B) The measurement state is started after the finger is placed; (C) The state after the measurement is completed.

In addition, this study also improves the prototype of the finger-type user operation interface model, and completes the basic and available finger-type user operation interface model, as shown in Fig. 10.

Fig. 10. Basic and available finger-type user operation interface model.

Finally, in the simple mobile biomedical signals extraction device, we modularized the biomedical sensors, and each module is designed as a replaceable and expandable panel, as shown in Fig. 11.

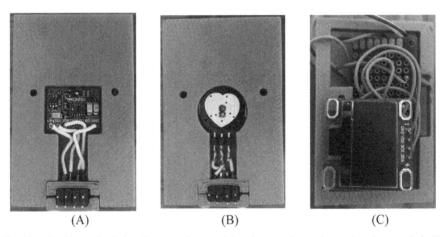

(A)   (B)   (C)

Fig. 11. The biomedical signals extraction modules that can be exchanged and expanded. (A) blood oxygen, heart pulse scalable measurement module; (B) heart rate measurement expandable module; (C) OLED panel display expandable module.

4   Conclusion

Based on the IoT, this study uses the information and communication technology, and combined the Arduino Pro Mini microcontroller with the biomedical signals measurement sensors to complete the construction of the simple mobile biomedical measuring device for the measurement of blood oxygen, heart pulse, and body temperature. We also designed and completed the basic and available finger-type user operation interface model. In the future, we will continue to address the long-term care needs, combined with the concept of mobile medical care applications, integrate portable mobile devices, and apply the information and communication technology to develop more accurate mobile medical signals extraction devices to enhance the quality of long-term care. It will be help to cope with the future global ageing services and addressing long-term care issues.

Acknowledgements. This work was supported in part by the Ministry of Science and Technology (MOST) in Taiwan under grant MOST108-2218-E-005-021, MOST108-2821-C-324-001-ES, and the Chaoyang University of Technology (CYUT) and Higher Education Sprout Project, Ministry of Education, Taiwan, under the project name: "The R&D and the cultivation of talent for Health-Enhancement Products."

References

1. Atzori, L., Iera, A., Morabito, G.: The internet of things: a survey. Comput. Netw. **54**(15), 2787–2805 (2010)
2. Gubbi, J., Buyya, R., Marusic, S., Palaniswami, M.: Internet of Things (IoT): a vision, architectural elements, and future directions. Future Gener. Comput. Syst. **29**(7), 1645–1660 (2013)
3. Zanella, A., Bui, N., Castellani, A., Vangelista, L., Zorzi, M.: Internet of Things for smart cities. IEEE Internet of Things J. **1**(1), 22–32 (2014)
4. Fulford-Jones, T.R., Wei, G.-Y., Welsh, M.: A portable, low-power, wireless two-lead EKG system. In: 26th Annual International Conference of the IEEE, IEMBS 2004 (2004). Paper presented at the Engineering in Medicine and Biology Society
5. Bojovic, M., Bojic, D.: MobilePDR: a mobile medical information system featuring update via internet. IEEE Trans. Inf Technol. Biomed. **9**(1), 1–3 (2005)
6. Chakravorty, R.: MobiCare: a programmable service architecture for mobile medical care. In: Proceedings of UbiCare, pp. 532–536 (2006)
7. Kong, X., Fan, B., Nie, W., Ding, Y.: Design on mobile health service system based on Android platform. In: 2016 IEEE Communicates, Electronic and Automation Control Conference (IMCEC) (2016). Paper presented at the Advanced Information Management
8. Gatzoulis, L., Iakovidis, I.: Wearable and portable eHealth systems. IEEE Eng. Med. Biol. Mag. **26**(5), 51–56 (2007)
9. Dorosh, N., Kuchmiy, H., Boyko, O., Dorosh, O., Stepanjuk, O., Maritz, N.: Development the software applications for mobile medical systems based on OS android. In: 2016 13th International Conference on Telecommunications and Computer Science (TCSET) (2016). Paper presented at the Modern Problems of Radio Engineering
10. Li, J., Deng, G., Wei, W., Wang, H., Ming, Z.: Design of a real-time ECG filter for portable mobile medical systems. IEEE Access **5**, 696–704 (2017)
11. Lymberis, A., Olsson, S.: Intelligent biomedical clothing for personal health and disease management: state of the art and future vision. Telemedicine J. e-health **9**(4), 379–386 (2003)

A Wearable Device for Monitoring Muscle Condition During Exercise

Shing-Hong Liu[1](✉), Jay Huang[2], Yung-Fa Huang[3], Tan-Hsu Tan[4], and Tai-Shen Huang[2]

[1] Department of Computer Science and Information Engineering, Chaoyang University of Technology, Taichung City 41349, Taiwan, R.O.C.
shliu@cyut.edu.tw
[2] Department of Industrial Design, Chaoyang University of Technology, Taichung City 41349, Taiwan, R.O.C.
[3] Department of Information and Communication Engineering, Chaoyang University of Technology, Taichung City 41349, Taiwan, R.O.C.
[4] Department of Electrical Engineering, National Taipei University of Technology, Taipei City 10608, Taiwan, R.O.C.

Abstract. In recent years, the wearable devices have been popularly applied in the health care field, which usually is worn on the wrist, like as a sport band, and an ECG patch. The common functions for these wearable devices are to display the body condition in real time, and have a small size. Therefore, two challenges in the development of the wearable device have to be overcome. First problem is the power consumption, and the second problem is the time of digital signal processing in the microcontroller system. The electromyogram (EMG) signal represents the condition of the muscle activity, which could be used to determine the degree of muscle fatigue. In this study, the goal is to develop an EMG patch which could be worn on any muscle to detect the muscle condition in real time when exercising. A Cortex-M4 microcontroller was used to calculate the median frequency of EMG which represents the muscle condition. In order to denoise the EMG signal, the empirical mode decomposition method was also used and run in this microcontroller. Two electrodes circuit was designed to measure the EMG which only used one instrument amplifier and two integrated circuits of operation amplifier. We compared the median frequency of EMG signal calculated by the microcontroller in the real time and personal computer in the off line, which different root mean square was only 3.72 Hz. Therefore, the EMG patch designed in this study could be applied to monitor the muscle condition when doing the exercise.

Keywords: Wearable device · EMG · Median frequency

1 Introduction

In recent years, People like to wear a wearable device to monitor their body condition during the exercising course. The wearable devices almost are the exercise watch or band to measure the heart rate or the steps. Some people will use sport equipment to

© Springer Nature Singapore Pte Ltd. 2020
P. Sitek et al. (Eds.): ACIIDS 2020, CCIS 1178, pp. 402–410, 2020.
https://doi.org/10.1007/978-981-15-3380-8_35

train their body for health improvement in the indoor activities. The sport's equipment includes the treadmill, elliptical trainer, and bike. Moreover, isokinetic exercise using the equipment has been widely applied for functional rehabilitation and assessment [1]. When people do the isokinetic tests, their low limb muscles have to do the isotonic contraction continuously [2]. If people do the over exercise, the muscle will be fatigue or injurious to health. However, how to exercise under an advantageous and healthy status is an important issue in healthy and pathological subjects.

Muscle fatigue is defined as a loss of the required or expected force from a muscle, and has been an attractive research issue for a long time. The nature of muscle fatigue and its relation to muscle activity have been studied [3]. It is well known that the power spectrum of the surface electromyography (sEMG) is toward the lower frequency during a sustained muscle contraction. At this time, the spectral parameters, such as the mean frequency (MNF) and the median frequency (MF), are the manifestation of localized muscle fatigue [4]. According to most reports that studied muscle fatigue, the changes in muscle fiber propagation velocity and the firing rate of muscle fibers could affect the sEMG power spectrum [4]. In an isometric and isotonic muscle contraction, the sEMG may be assumed as a wide-sense stationary signal, and thus, its power spectrum could be obtained using common spectral estimation techniques. Although the activity of isotonic muscle contraction is often satisfactory in rehabilitation medicine and ergonomics, the sEMG of the isotonic muscle contraction under the exercises is nonstationary and would couple a lot of noise. Therefore, appropriate spectral estimation techniques are required.

In many studies, the sEMG has been considered a realization of a nonstationary stochastic process, and the shift of the innervation zone always happens during a dynamic contraction [4]. Therefore, Molinari [5] proposed signal processing methods to assess the spectral changes of sEMG due to fatigue during the isometric contraction. Tscharner [6] used the wavelet analyses to estimate the sEMG parameters during a mildly fatiguing exercise on a cycle ergometer. In these research groups, they always used the measurement system of multiple channels and the complex analyzed method to quantify the electrical manifestations of muscle fatigue for the pathological subjects. However, these measurement system and analysis methods could not be easily applied in a wearable device for the exercise monitor.

Liu [7] designed a one channel sEMG patch that could measure the sEMG signal during the exercise with two electrodes. The sEMG signal was transmitted to the notebook by a Bluetooth 3.0 module. Liu [8] compared some decomposed methods for the sensitivity of estimating the degree of muscle fatigue, including wavelet transform, empirical mode decomposition (EMD) and ensemble empirical mode decomposition (EEMD). They found that the intrinsic component of muscle fatigue would occur on the high frequency of sEMG. The EEMD had the best sensitivity for detecting the muscle fatigue.

2   Method

Figure 1 shows the block diagram of EMG patch which includes analog circuit, MCU, BLE module, power circuit, and alarm parts. We use the wireless technique to charge the battery. The alarm parts have two LEDs to display the power and BLE conditions,

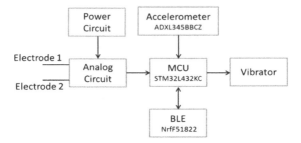

Fig. 1. Block diagram of EMG patch

and a vibrator to alarm the user. Because the hardware of EMG patch does not have any connector, like as USB, its ID shell must feet the IP 67 standard.

2.1 Hardware of EMG Patch

Figure 2 shows the analog circuit for the EMG patch. The raw sEMG signal is a low-amplitude signal. Therefore, it needs to be amplified. An instrument amplifier (AD8236, Analog Devices (AD) Company), with a gain of 10, is used to enhance the signal. Because a virtual-ground technique is used, there are only two electrodes used as the input of the instrument amplifier. Operational amplifiers (AD 8609, AD Company) are used in the design of a filter, amplifier, peak rectifier, and baseline offset circuit. A two-order Butterworth high-pass filter (cutoff frequency 30 Hz) is used to remove the direct current (DC) offset and baseline wandering, and a two-order Butterworth low-pass filter (cutoff frequency 500 k Hz) is used to reduce high frequency noise and to avoid aliasing. The gain of the non-inverting amplifier is 100. Finally, the baseline of sEMG signal was raised to 1 V by a baseline offset circuit.

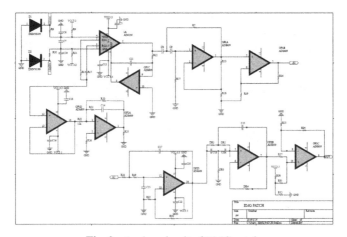

Fig. 2. Analog circuit of EMG patch.

In the power circuit, the Texas Instruments (TI) wireless receiver chip, BQ51003YFPR, is used to charge the battery. The IC (TPS78233, TI) is used to provide a voltage of 3.3 V, which is supplied from a lithium battery. The IC (TPS60400, TI) is used to provide a voltage of -3.3 V.

The BLE module is the NrfF51822 (Nordic Semiconductor, UAS). The STM32L432KC (STmicroelectronics, USA) is a 32 bits MCU which has 64 k bytes SRAM, and 256 k bytes flash memory. Its clock is 32 M Hz. The power consumption is 84uA/MHz at full run model. The sampling rate is 1000 Hz. The accelerometer is ADXL345BBCZ (AD Company). Moreover, a vibrator is used on the EMG patch to alarm the user when the degree of muscle fatigue exceeds the designed threshold. Figure 3 shows two views of the EMG patch, (a) from the top, (b) from the bottom. The size of main board is 30 mm, and the size of electrode's connector is 25 mm.

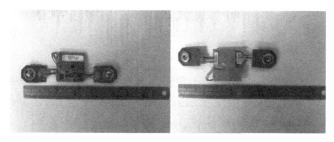

Fig. 3. Two views of the EMG patch, (a) top view, (b) bottom view.

2.2 Empirical Mode Decomposition

This subsection briefly reviews the EMD which will be applied to decompose an EMG signal to detect the muscle activity. For details, one may consult [8]. The EMD algorithm consists of the following steps.

Step 1. Find the local maxima and minima in x(k).
Step 2. Obtain the upper envelope by the local maxima and the lower envelope by local minima, respectively.
Step 3. Calculate the average of the upper and lower envelops, m(k).
Step 4. Acquire the difference signal d(k) = x(k)−m(k).
Step 5. Check if d(k) is a zero-average process. If yes, then stop and treat d(k) as the first-order IMF (IMF 1), denoted as $c_1(k)$; otherwise, replace x(k) with d(k) and go back to Step 1.
Step 6. Calculate the residual signal r(k) = x(k)−$c_1(k)$.
Step 7. Replace x(k) with r(k) and repeat Step 1 to Step 6 to find the second-order IMF (IMF 2), i.e., $c_2(k)$.
Step 8. Repeat Step 1 to Step 7 till $c_M(k)$ is obtained where M is the total number of IMFs.
Step 9. After the EMD, the original signal can be expressed as

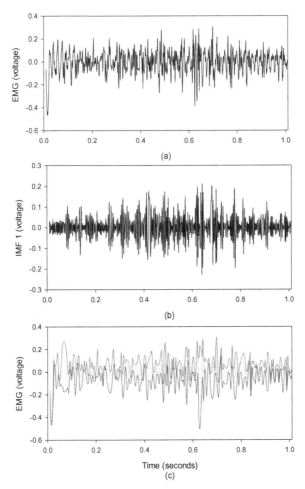

Fig. 4. The results of EMD by the C code running in the MCU, (a) the raw EMG, (b) IMF1 of EMG, (c) the upper (red) and lower (blue) envelops of EMG. (Color figure online)

$$x(k) = \sum_{i=1}^{M} c_i(k) + r(k), \tag{1}$$

where $r(k)$ is generally considered as cM + 1(k).

In this study, the size of data segment is 4096 points for each processing session, and the overlap points are 2048. According to the study of Liu [8], we only decomposed IMF 1 to do the MF calculation. Moreover, in order to run the EMD in an MCU system, we did the iteration ten times on Step 5.

The second order polynomial function is used to get the upper and lower envelops for Step 3. Figure 4 shows the results of EMD by the C code running in the MCU, (a) the raw EMG, (b) IMF1 of EMG, (c) the upper (red) and lower (blue) envelops of EMG.

2.3 Median Frequency

The IMF1 would do the fast Fourier Transform. The MF of each segment is extracted. MF is defined as the frequency where the accumulated spectrum energy is half of the total spectrum energy, as shown in Eq. (2). Where $p(f)$ is the power spectrum density of IMF 1

$$\int_0^{MF} p(f)df = \frac{1}{2}\int_0^\infty p(f)df \tag{2}$$

2.4 Experiment Protocol

There were two participators in this study. A bicycle trainer, Giant Taiwan, was used to do the exercise. The EMG patch was worn on the gastrocnemius, as shown in Fig. 5. A subject is required to wear the EMG patch. Alcohol is used to clean the surface, and electrolytic gel is smeared on the electrodes to decrease the contact impedance. There are three riding speeds in this experiment, 60 rpm (revolutions per minute), 80 rpm, and 100 rpm, with 60 rpm being light and 100 rpm being heavy. The bicycle trainer can detect the speed and display the rpm at a smart phone. A 10-min session is required for three different speeds. In the pre-experiment, the subjects tested the speed range and tried to keep these specific speeds at least 10 min.

Fig. 5. The experimental photo for EMG patch.

3   Results

Figure 6 shows the results of EMD by the Matlab code. The activities of the muscle isotonic contraction are clearly displayed in the IMF1 which is same to the study by Liu [8]. The other IMFs and the residual signal all do not have the clear activities of the muscle. The MF calculated by the C code running in the EMG patch was transmitted to the PC with the BLE. The EMG signal was recorded by our designed multi-channel physiological signal measurement system [9], synchronously. The MF of the measured EMG was calculated by the Matlab code running in the PC. Figure 7 shows the difference between the C code and Matlab code. The root mean square error is only 3.72 Hz.

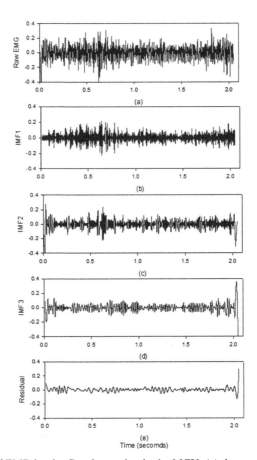

Fig. 6. The IMFs of EMD by the C code running in the MCU, (a) the raw EMG, (b) IMF1, (c) IMF2, (d) IMF3, (e) residual.

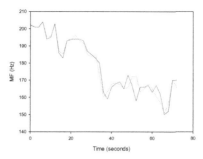

Fig. 7. The MF by the C code running in the MCU (red solid line) and the Matlab code in the PC (black dot line). (Color figure online)

4 Discussions and Conclusion

EMD method is a very complex algorithm which needs to do many times iterations for the different signal, d(k), and repeats the calculation of the different IMF components. Therefore, the running of EMD method needs much time. But, according to Liu study [8], the IMF1 has a highest sensitivity for the muscle fatigue than the other IMF components. We also found that the mean of the different signal was very close to zero when the iteration times of EMD is ten. Therefore, we can use a MCU system only to calculate the IMF1 of EMG.

The second problem is that there are more data to do the Fourier transform, the MF has the more high sensitivity for the muscle fatigue. However, the SRAM of MCU only has 64 k bytes. But, the Fourier transform represents a global energy spectrum. Thus, although we only did the Fourier transform of 2048 points, the MF is calculated with 4096 points. The overlap is 2048 points for each MF.

Finally, we designed an EMG patch to monitor the condition of the isotonic muscle contraction in this study. The Cotex-M4 MCU could do the EMD and MF calculations. A two electrodes circuit was used to measure the EMG signal. The results of this study show that the MF of this EMG patch is very close to the MF calculated by the Matlab code. Therefore, the EMG patch would be used to do the exercise experiment to evaluate its performance in the future.

Acknowledgment. This research was funded by the Ministry of Science and Technology in Taiwan under MOST 107-2221-E-324-001.

References

1. Kaikkonen, A., Natri, A., Pasanen, M., et al.: Isokinetic muscle performance after surgery of the lateral ligaments of the ankle. Int. J. Sports Med. **20**(03), 173–178 (1999)
2. Beelen, A., Sargeant, A.J.: Effect of fatigue on maximal power output at different contraction velocities in humans. J. Appl. Physiol. **71**, 2332–2337 (1991)
3. Morris, S.L., Allison, G.T.: Effects of abdominal muscle fatigue on anticipatory postural adjustments associated with arm raising. Gait Posture **24**, 342–348 (2006)

4. Merletti, R., Parker, P.: Electromyography: Physiology, Engineering, and Noninvasive Applications, IEEE/Wiley, Hoboken (2004)
5. Molinari, F., Knaflitz, M., Bonato, P., et al.: Electrical manifestations of muscle fatigue during concentric and eccentric isokinetic knee flexion-extension movements. IEEE Trans. Biomed. Eng. **53**, 1309–13016 (2006)
6. Tscharner, V.: Time-frequency and principal-component methods for the analysis of EMGs recorded during a mildly fatiguing exercise on a cycle ergometer. J. Electromyogr. Kinesiol. **12**, 479–492 (2002)
7. Chang, K.-M., Liu, S.-H., Wu, X.-H.: A wireless sEMG recording system and its application to muscle fatigue detection. Sensors **12**, 489–499 (2012)
8. Liu, S.-H., Chang, K.-M., Cheng, D.-C.: The progression of muscle fatigue during exercise estimation with the aid of high-frequency component parameters derived from ensemble empirical mode decomposition. IEEE J.Biomed. Health Inf. **18**, 1647–1658 (2014)
9. Liu, S-H., Lai, S-H., Huang, T.: A study on the development of portable wireless multi-channel physiological signal measurement system. In: IEEE 9th International Conference on Awareness Science and Technology, Kyushu University, Fukuoka, Japan, 19–21 September 2018

Towards Developing an IoT Based Gaming Application for Improving Cognitive Skills of Autistic Kids

Uzma Hasan$^{(\boxtimes)}$ ⓘ, Md. Fourkanul Islamⓘ, Muhammad Nazrul Islamⓘ,
Sifat Bin Zamanⓘ, Shaila Tajmim Anuva, Farhana Islam Emu,
and Tarannum Zaki

Department of Computer Science and Engineering, Military Institute of Science
and Technology (MIST), Mirpur Cantonment, Dhaka 1216, Bangladesh
uzmahasan041@gmail.com, fourkan246@gmail.com, nazrulturku@gmail.com

Abstract. With the advancement of technology, a wide range of automated tools are now used to teach children with autism. One of the
widely used therapies for children with Autism Spectrum Disorder (ASD)
is Applied Behaviour Analysis (ABA) training that focuses on improving
a wide range of behaviours like communication, adaptive learning skills,
social skills and a variety of motor skills. Thus, the objective of this article is to design and develop a gaming application for autistic children for
improving their cognitive skills. The Internet of Things (IoT) and ABA
techniques were adopted to develop the gaming application that consists
three games including a puzzle game, an object finding game and a road
crossing game. The cognitive development (in terms of gaming scores) of
a child over the time can be stored and analyzed using this application.
A light-weighted evaluation study was carried out; and found that the
proposed gaming application is usable, effective and useful for autistic
kids to improve their cognitive skills.

Keywords: Autism Spectrum Disorder · Applied Behaviour Analysis
(ABA) · Cognitive skill · Learning tool · Internet of Things · RFID ·
Sensors

1 Introduction

Cognitive skill development is an essential phase of any child's gradual growth
process which primarily involves building attention, memory and thinking. Children with autism are the ones who go through a different development cycle
than the ones who are normal by birth. Autism or Autism Spectrum Disorder
(ASD), refers to a broad range of conditions characterized by challenges with
social skills, repetitive behaviors, speech and nonverbal communication [1]. The
common thread are the differences in social skills, communication, and behavior compared with people who aren't on the spectrum [2]. Studies have shown

ⓒ Springer Nature Singapore Pte Ltd. 2020
P. Sitek et al. (Eds.): ACIIDS 2020, CCIS 1178, pp. 411–423, 2020.
https://doi.org/10.1007/978-981-15-3380-8_36

that they perceive the senses from the environment in a different way than any normal children. Thus, they are trained in some adaptive practical ways like Applied Behaviour Analysis (ABA) to develop normal senses correctly.

Statistics have proven that Autism Spectrum Disorders (ASD) are complex developmental disabilities affecting as many as 1 in 59 children [3]. In [4], Bakhtiari et al. mentioned that individuals with ASD are characterized by early onset impairments in communication and reciprocal social interaction as well as by the presence of repetitive and stereotyped behaviors. Again, greater autism symptomatology and lower intelligence were found among children who do not attain phrase/fluent speech, with nonverbal intelligence and social engagement emerging as the strongest predictors of outcome [5]. Often it becomes difficult for a teacher or parent to keep record of every such precise progress of the child. Thus if there is a system that can keep a regular track to analyze their development as well as be a good tool to keep them busy, then it may improve their development process.

Since technology these days have it's touch in almost every sphere of our lives, thus the application of technology for the development of autistic children is a matter of consideration. While various app based interfaces have been developed as their teaching tool, but survey says that they are better at learning if they have hands on experience of what is being aimed to teach them. Thus an interface incorporated with both hardware and software games would be a much more promising learning tool.

Considering this, the objective of this research is to develop a gaming application that will regularly track and record a child's gradual cognitive development according to their (autistic kids) gaming performance. The tool will be IoT based where both hardware and software games will be incorporated and individual's score will be stored and later presented graphically to analyze his/her mental progress and help in making recommendations for future improvement.

The organization of the paper is as follows: Sect. 2 highlights the related work to understand the background of the development. The conceptual framework highlights the overall idea of how different users interact with the device in Sect. 3. The actual implementation of the gaming system is discussed in Sect. 4 followed by discussing the evaluation of the prototype in Sect. 5. Finally, a brief concluding remark is presented in Sect. 6.

2   Literature Review

A significant number of children today are being affected due to autism spectrum disorder. Thus a number of studies have been conducted on the diverse applications of technology-based interventions in dealing with autism [6,7]. In this section we briefly present the related studies to this work.

First of all, a significant number of studies were conducted focusing on the development of assistive technologies for autistic children. Castillo et al. [8] developed an assistive tool for children with ASD in a web environment for teaching the basic emotions like anger, sadness, fear, joy, love and surprise.

Hwang et al. [9] reviewed sixteen empirical studies that investigated the effects of social interactive interventions designed to increase early social communicative skills of young children with autism. This study showed how the social interactive training could be a promising technique for promoting more advanced preverbal and verbal communication of children with autism in daily classroom activities. In [10], highlighted the relations between the assistive technologies and ASD and found that further research is required in developing assistive technologies for autism which focused on constructive skill.

With the ever-growing population of children with autism, research on their instructional aids is being conducted. Goldsmith et al. [11] reviewed five technologies that can be used as a temporary instructional aid for autism including: (a) tactile and auditory prompting devices, (b) video-based instruction and feedback, (c) computer-aided instruction, (d) virtual reality, and (e) robotics. This study also presented how technology based interventions are often useful for and appealing to children with autism. In [12], Parsons et al. reports and reflects their experiences of co-creating digital stories with school practitioners in a project named 'Shape' focusing on embedding innovative technologies for autistic children in classroom practice. The digital stories were short films or narrated sequences of slides and images to enhance children's social communication skills within the school environment. While Knight et al. [13] conducted a comprehensive review of articles published between 1993 and 2012 to determine the key concerns of using instructional technology to teach academic skills to students with autism and concluded that practitioners should use caution when teaching academic skills to individuals with ASD using technology-based interventions.

The study conducted by Bartoli et al. [14] showed that how autistic children behave when engaged in motion-based touchless gaming. In [15], a design of a novel collaborative virtual reality environment (CVE) for supporting communicative perspective-taking skills for high-functioning children with ASD is discussed. It concluded that CVE could form the basis for a useful technology-based educational intervention for autistic kids. Boucenna et al. [16] studied some of the interactive technologies for autistic children and found that robotic scenario is an excellent way to elicit behaviors of autistic children.

Children with autism have significant deficits in face recognition. Tanaka et al. [17] introduced the *Let's Face It!* program which is a practical intervention in face processing for children with ASD. They conducted a randomized clinical trial, where impaired face recognition was ameliorated through 20 h of computer based treatment. It has advantages of being cost-free, adaptable to the specific learning needs of the individual child and suitable for home and school applications. In [18], Zaki et al. introduced a cost-effective, portable and user-friendly interactive learning tool to provide autistic children with basic academics which consists of a pressure sensing keypad to provide an easy and flexible means of interaction for autistic kids.

As internet based support system for autism is the demand of the day for autistic children and their parents, Islam et al. [19] developed an online support system (Autism Sohayika) for autistic children and their parents in the context of Bangladesh. Silva et al. [20] developed a web-based application for individual interests of children with ASD. It allows the teachers and peers to prepare a unique setup whose layouts and contents are customizable as per the child's need.

A set of existing technologies are briefly presented in Table 1. The review showed that the existing technologies mainly focused to improving the communication skills, basic academic learning or emotion/facial recognition skills of an autistic child. A few of them also focused to developing the cognitive skills of autistic kids. But none of them are explicitly focused to improve the cognitive skills of autistic kids through an IoT based gaming tool. Thus this research focuses to the development of an interactive IoT based gaming tool for autistic children which will regularly track their cognitive skill development.

Table 1. Summary of the existing technologies

References	Technology	Objective
[8]	Web environment	Teaching and identification of basic emotions
[10]	Assistive technologies	A review of the mobile learning apps
[12]	Digital stories (Shape Project)	Explore creative ways in which children's social communication skills can be supported in schools
[14]	Motion-based touchless mini-games	Promote attention skills, positive emotions and stress relief
[15]	Collaborative virtual reality environment (CVE)	Supports communicative perspective-taking skills (teaching how to relate to other people)
[16]	Robotic environment	Improve motor skills and interactive behavior
[17]	Let's Face It	Improve facial recognition skills
[18]	Portable learning tool	Teach basic academics particularly English alphabets using a pressure sensing keypad
[19]	Autism Sohayika	An online support system for autistic kids and their parents
[20]	Web-based application	Communication Skills training based on multimedia content
[21]	Learning tool	Developed for vocally impaired people of Bangladesh to learn Bengali alphabet without any assistance or supervision of another person

3   Conceptual Framework

A conceptual framework has been proposed to develop an automated progress tracking gaming tool for autistic kids as shown in Fig. 1. The framework shows the interaction of the tool with it's primary users (autistic children, therapists and parents) and how the child's progress is recorded, stored and viewed. The gaming tool have two components basically: a hardware device and a mobile application. The tool consists of three games which were designed following the ABA concept. These games generally improve basic cognitive skills of the child like remembering, reasoning, learning and attention skills.

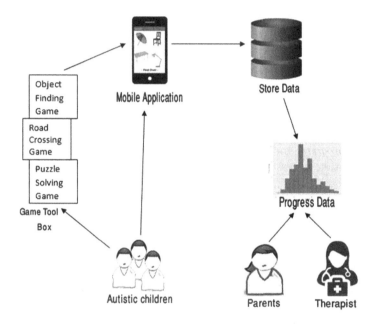

Fig. 1. Conceptual design of the proposed gaming tool

A detailed description of each of the games is discussed below:

(a) *Object finding game:* This game consists of some function cards each of which includes four images of similar type objects like animals, alphabets, fruits, etc. The child has to find the correct object as mentioned on the top of a card. It will also serve the purpose of teaching alphabets to the child. When an alphabet is pressed, an animation of the letter appears on the mobile screen. This game is designed with an aim to test the memory or remembering skills of the child and also aid alphabet learning purpose.

(b) *Puzzle game:* There are six cards which needs to be placed sequentially in order to either solve a puzzle or form the correct sequence of an event like brushing teeth, weather changing sequence, etc. The purpose of this game is to test the reasoning and learning capabilities of the child.

(c) *Road Crossing game:* This game is designed with a purpose to teach basic directions (left, right, top, down) and caution measures to the child to test his/her attention skills. It consists of an android game where the target is to cross a road safely avoiding the obstacles like car, objects, etc on the road and the movement of the person for crossing the road is controlled by a joystick.

Key features of the progress tracking gaming tool:

(1) *User account creation:* An user account will be created for individual kids to provide authorized access by therapists/guardians and maintaining privacy for the child.
(2) *Displaying result:* The success/failure of playing a game will be immediately shown through multimodal feedback like audio, animation and text or a combination of them.
(3) *Recording progress:* Data related to playing date, number of trials to accomplish the game, gaming results or scores will stored for each player which will be accessible only by the authorized person.
(4) *Generating progress charts:* The system will generate progress chart to show the individual's progress within a specific time period.
(5) *Viewing progress:* Individual's progress can be observed by any authorized person to take necessary actions for future improvement of a child.

4   Developing the Application

The gaming application was implemented considering the features stated in the above section and shown in Fig. 2. The entire development and implementation was carried out in an academic environment. The development tool consists of two parts: a hardware and a mobile application. The hardware is powered from a power source in order to activate the device. There are three switches corresponding to the three games on the device. When the respective switch is on, the connected devices get power. There are four piezo sensors fitted on the face of the game box in right side which is for the object finding game. It also has a slot for keeping the function cards there. In the left side of the tool, there are six RFID readers fitted on top which is basically the box for puzzle game. A joystick module is placed on the middle box which is for the road crossing game. It has an arrangement to keep the mobile phone standing while playing the game.

The main hardware component was the Arduino Mega that connected the other components or modules. Data from the piezo sensors, RFID, joystick modules are received in the Arduino. Then, this data is passed to the android application through the bluetooth module connected to Arduino where the results or animation can be viewed. In the object finding game (Fig. 3), when a card is placed on the corresponding position of the box, the RFID tag attached to the

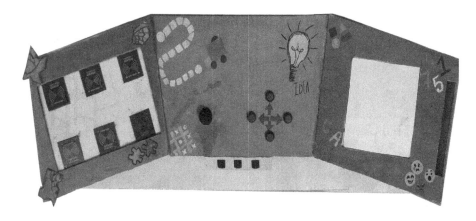

Fig. 2. The developed prototype

function card is read by the RFID reader on the box and this card is then shown on the mobile app. There is a piezo sensor under each of the object or character on the card. When an object is pressed on the card an animation of correct or wrong answer is shown on the app and the result is recorded in the database.

The puzzle game can be selected when the corresponding switch is on. The RFID readers on the game box in the left side read the tags on the back of the puzzle cards and then send the data to the mobile app where the puzzle parts are shown (in the similar way the players placed the cards on the game box) which is demonstrated in Fig. 4.

When the switch for the road crossing game is selected, a player can be seen on cross the road game on the android app. The player can be controlled by moving the joystick on the game box. User needs to make the player cross the road through zebra crossing by controlling him/her through the joystick/switch and the corresponding result is stored on the database. Game is won when successfully crossed the road avoiding any kind of obstacles (Fig. 5b).

An Android application was developed as software part of the proposed gaming system. The firebase authentication and database was used for account creation and result storage. Primary users of the app are autistic kids who will play the games and their parents/teachers/doctors to monitor or observe the progress of the kids. Guardians/teachers of the autistic child needs to open an account for a child to initiate game playing and to keep his/her progress through this application. Parents or authorized users can log in to the system with the mobile app, select the game that the child wants to play and also modify any kind of game settings from the *student/child view*. The parents/doctors can regularly check the progress of the child through a graphical view on the mobile app (Fig. 5a) and get a general overview of a child's gradual progress by selecting the *parents/doctor view* on the app. This progress is calculated from the results or performance of playing the games.

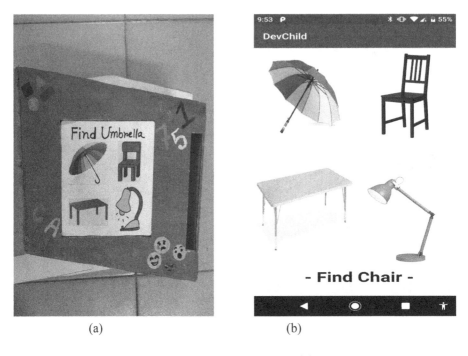

(a)   (b)

Fig. 3. Object finding game (a) tool box and (b) app user interface

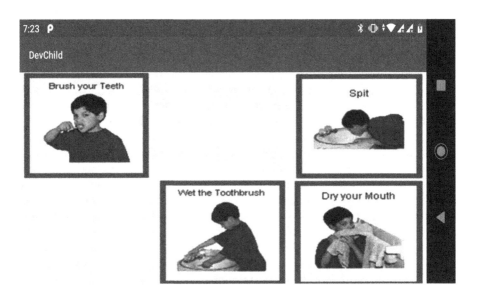

Fig. 4. App user interface of puzzle game

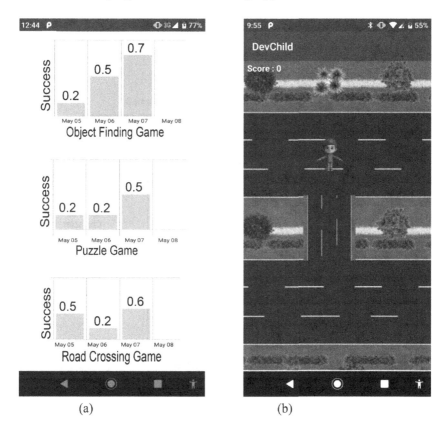

Fig. 5. App interface of (a) Progress chart and (b) Road cross game.

A flow diagram to show the working procedure of the proposed gaming application is shown in Fig. 6.

5   Evaluating the Application

A light weighted evaluation was carried out at the Software Engineering Laboratory of the authors' institute. Five faculty members who are familiar with autism related issues were invited as a test-subject. During the evaluation study, firstly a brief presentation about the objective of this study was given to the participants. Secondly, the proposed system was demonstrated to them and gave them the opportunity to explore and use the tool for around 5–10 min. Finally, participants were asked to play each of the game. Data related to the *number of trials* for success and *game completion time* in seconds were collected while they played the games. Finally they were asked to provide opinion about the usability and effectiveness of the proposed system and give any other related recommendations. A brief summary of the recorded data is given in Table 2.

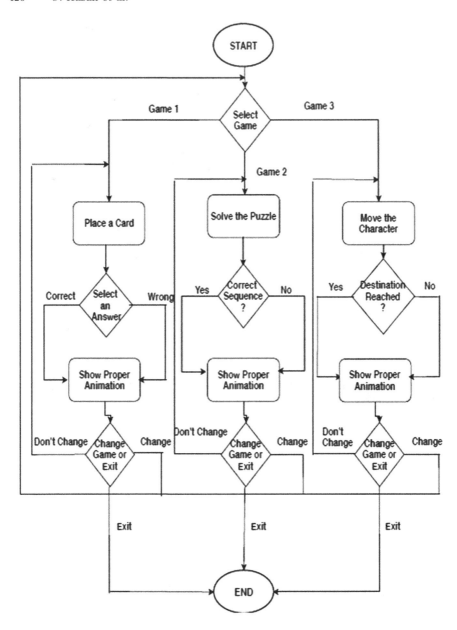

Fig. 6. Flow diagram of the developed games.

Table 2 showed that though the optimum number of trials for each game is 1, but the average number varies due to some reasons. For example, in the object finding game, the average number of trials required to successfully complete the game is 1.6 due to sometimes pressing outside the sensor's range. For the

Table 2. Summary results of the evaluation study

Object finding game		
Participant No.	Trials to success	Completion time (Sec)
1	2	14
2	1	11
3	1	8
4	3	13
5	1	9
Total = 5	$1.6 \pm .8$ (*Mean* $\pm$ SD)	11 ± 2.28 (*Mean* $\pm$ SD)
Puzzle game		
Participant No.	Trials to success	Completion time (Sec)
1	2	25
2	1	28
3	3	22
4	3	30
5	2	26
Total = 5	$2.2 \pm .75$ (*Mean* $\pm$ SD)	26.2 ± 2.7 (*Mean* $\pm$ SD)
Road crossing game		
Participant No.	Trials to success	Completion time (Sec)
1	1	17
2	3	13
3	2	18
4	2	12
5	1	15
Total = 5	$1.8 \pm .74$ (*Mean* $\pm$ SD)	15 ± 2.28 (*Mean* $\pm$ SD)

puzzle game, the average number of trials is 2.2 for not understanding the correct sequence initially. Finally in the road crossing game due to not being able to avoid the obstacles or cross the road safely, the average trials for success is deviated to 1.8. This result indicates that though the games can be played effectively but there are some difficulties. These issues were noted to improve it's effectiveness in the future.

The participants also viewed the graphical results generated by the tool and opined that it would be an efficient way for the therapists to view and maintain progress results of kids in the autism centres and similarly will be helpful for the doctors while giving recommendations for improvement.

6   Conclusions

In this research, an IoT based gaming application was developed for developing cognitive skills of autistic kids. This application can store and process player's gaming results to show (graphically) their progress within a specific time range. The proposed gaming application includes both hardware and software games which add a new dimension in the learning methods of autistic kids. A light-weighted evaluation study showed that each function or feature of the games is executed correctly. Moreover, the participants found the games interesting for autistic kids and useful for improving their cognitive skills. Some limitations of this research were that the proposed application was evaluated in an institutional environment with limited number of participants; and that the application was developed only for autistic children who are 3 years or above. In future, the proposed gaming application will be updated by addressing the minor problems found during the evaluation study. The updated application will be evaluated with real end users (autistic kids/therapists/guardians) through field study to show it's effectiveness and efficiency.

References

1. What is autism? https://www.autismspeaks.org/what-autism. Accessed 06 Aug 2019
2. Autism: Signs and symptoms. https://www.webmd.com/brain/autism/symptoms-of-autism#1. Accessed 01 Sept 2019
3. Data & Statistics on Autism Spectrum Disorder — CDC. https://www.cdc.gov/ncbddd/autism/data.html. Accessed 16 Aug 2019
4. Bakhtiari, R., et al.: Differences in white matter reflect atypical developmental trajectory in autism: a tract-based spatial statistics study. NeuroImage Clin. **1**(1), 48–56 (2012)
5. Wodka, E.L., Mathy, P., Kalb, L.: Predictors of phrase and fluent speech in children with autism and severe language delay. Pediatrics **131**(4), e1128–e1134 (2013)
6. Omar, K.S., Mondal, P., Khan, N.S., Rizvi, Md.R.K., Islam, M.N.: A machine learning approach to predict autism spectrum disorder. In: Proceedings of the International Conference on Electrical, Computer and Communication Engineering 2019, pp. 1–6. IEEE (2019)
7. Hasan, N., Islam, M.N.: Exploring the design considerations for developing an interactive tabletop learning tool for children with autism spectrum disorder. In: Proceedings of the International Conference on Computer Networks, Big Data and IoT – 2019, pp. 1–12. Springer (2019)
8. Castillo, T.A., et al.: Authic: computational tool for children with autistic spectrum disorder. In: 2016 International Symposium on Computers in Education (SIIE), pp. 1–6. IEEE (2016)
9. Hwang, B., Hughes, C.: The effects of social interactive training on early social communicative skills of children with autism. J. Autism Dev. Disord. **30**(4), 331–343 (2000)
10. Daud, S.N.S.C., Maria, M., Shahbodin, F., Ahmad, I.: Assistive technology for autism spectrum disorder: a review of literature, October 2018

11. Goldsmith, T.R., LeBlanc, L.A.: Use of technology in interventions for children with autism. J. Early Intensive Behav. Interv. **1**(2), 166 (2004)
12. Parsons, S., Guldberg, K., Porayska-Pomsta, K., Lee, R.: Digital stories as a method for evidence-based practice and knowledge co-creation in technology-enhanced learning for children with autism. Int. J. Res. Method Educ. **38**(3), 247–271 (2015)
13. Knight, V., McKissick, B.R., Saunders, A.: A review of technology-based interventions to teach academic skills to students with autism spectrum disorder. J. Autism Dev. Disord. **43**(11), 2628–2648 (2013)
14. Bartoli, L., Corradi, C., Garzotto, F., Valoriani, M.: Exploring motion-based touch-less games for autistic children's learning. In: Proceedings of the 12th International Conference on Interaction Design and Children, pp. 102–111. ACM (2013)
15. Parsons, S.: Learning to work together: designing a multi-user virtual reality game for social collaboration and perspective-taking for children with autism. Int. J. Child Comput. Interact. **6**, 28–38 (2015)
16. Boucenna, S., et al.: Interactive technologies for autistic children: a review. Cogn. Comput. **6**(4), 722–740 (2014)
17. Tanaka, J.W., et al.: Using computerized games to teach face recognition skills to children with autism spectrum disorder: the let's face it! program. J. Child Psychol. Psychiatry **51**(8), 944–952 (2010)
18. Zaki, T., et al.: Towards developing a learning tool for children with autism. In: 2017 6th International Conference on Informatics, Electronics and Vision & 2017 7th International Symposium in Computational Medical and Health Technology (ICIEV-ISCMHT), pp. 1–6. IEEE (2017)
19. Islam, M.N., et al.: Autism Sohayika: a web portal to provide services to autistic children. In: Younas, M., Awan, I., Ghinea, G., Catalan Cid, M. (eds.) MobiWIS 2018. LNCS, vol. 10995, pp. 181–192. Springer, Cham (2018). https://doi.org/10.1007/978-3-319-97163-6_15
20. Silva, M.L.D., Gonçalves, D., Guerreiro, T., Silva, H.: A web-based application to address individual interests of children with autism spectrum disorders. Procedia Comput. Sci. **14**, 20–27 (2012)
21. Islam, M.N., Hasan, A.M.S., Anannya, T.T., Hossain, T., Ema, M.B.I., Rashid, S.U.: An efficient tool for learning Bengali sign language for vocally impaired people. In: Awan, I., Younas, M., Ünal, P., Aleksy, M. (eds.) MobiWIS 2019. LNCS, vol. 11673, pp. 41–53. Springer, Cham (2019). https://doi.org/10.1007/978-3-030-27192-3_4

Continuous Improvement Process Model for Supporting the Construction of Internet of Things System Design Environments

Cezary Orłowski⑩, Dawid Cygert(✉), and Przemysław Nowak(✉)

WSB University in Gdańsk, Gdańsk, Poland
corlowski@wsb.gda.pl, dawidcygert@gmail.com,
pr.nowak@protonmail.com

Abstract. The aim of the article is to build a process model of Continuous Improvement for design support systems, the Internet of Things (IoT) and manufactured scalable systems. The developed model was based on the experience of the authors obtained during the design process of IoT nodes. That is why the article presents both the research experiment and the extent to which this experiment pointed to the need to design the manufacturing environment. To achieve this goal, the article is divided into four main parts.

In the beginning a project was presented, which goal was to create an IoT node. During its implementation, there were requirements for the system that would be used to monitor the status of IoT nodes and data flow. Therefore, the second chapter presents the functionalities of the manufacturing environment necessary for both designing the nodes and monitoring their condition. They were then referred to as Application Enablement Platform (AEP) functionalities used in IoT to assess their usefulness in improving the monitoring and maintenance processes of IoT nodes. This method shows how important it is to perceive the design process of IoT systems as a continuous process of incremental construction of the design environment for the implementation of the functionality of IoT systems.

Keywords: Internet of Things · Cloud · Microservices · Architecture · Patterns · Scaling · Information systems · Subdomains · API gateway · Access token · Serverless · Reverse proxy · High availability · Load balancing · Process manager · Connection pooling · Replication · Containers · Docker · Code generation · Queues · MQTT · SQL · NoSQL

1 Introduction (Purpose and Method of Implementation)

Creating IoT systems is a complex design process resulting from the need for constant changes that are a consequence of user requirements. Such a process creates to limit the ability of the available development environments. Therefore, the article focuses on the proposal to apply the Continuous improvement approach for continuous monitoring of the state of the design environment and to adapt it to the changing requirements of IoT systems.

© Springer Nature Singapore Pte Ltd. 2020
P. Sitek et al. (Eds.): ACIIDS 2020, CCIS 1178, pp. 424–435, 2020.
https://doi.org/10.1007/978-981-15-3380-8_37

Continuous Improvement is a programming practice that aims to ensure the efficient and effective implementation of the full software development cycle [1, 2]. This means that during the manufacturing process, the level of the design environment is adapted to the functionality of the IoT system expected by the customer. Achieving this state of affairs is possible by ensuring continuous integration of design environments with the IoT system being deployment. Such a state is possible thanks to the use of agile approach, use of the incremental approach in the production process, ensuring the work of programmers in closed workspaces, as well as the use of a common repository in the design process. Then, from the assault of continuous integration, they create conditions to control product development processes. To create such conditions, it is necessary to create a continuous integration environment, and to use feedback mechanisms that allow continuous construction of images with all incremental changes in implementation as well as their publication when certain criteria are met [17, 18].

The continuous integration process requires building an integration server. An example of such an integration process may be the use of the Analysis and Resolution process according to the maturity model of the CMMI-DEV v1.3 and Jenkins processes [4, 5]; Jenkins is treated as a tool for implementing Continuous improvement processes due to the possibility of including a wide range of available functionalities. Useful solutions in this case are, for example, version control, management and feedback, analytical and testing poles. Another mechanism necessary for the implementation of the continuous integration process is the feedback mechanism. It provides the ability to automate work in a situation, the emergence of problems with continuous integration. It is important to specify in this case the conditions in which the feedback process takes place, i.e. in such conditions in which changes in the functionality of the production environment occur.

Another of the processes important from the point of view of Continuous improvement is the compilation process, under which scripts are prepared for automating the compilation process. This means that the build processes are started automatically. This allows the team to collaborate easily when creating code and ensures that developers do not forget to install the necessary files. Another process is static analysis, which involves debugging a computer program. It is done by checking the program start code. Static analysis is designed to improve the quality of the code. The next stage is testing processes that are crucial for continuous integration. It is the results of these processes that indicate how much the next software version or the next added functionality can be implemented with the system. It is also a very important process to make sure that new functionalities of the production environment affect the improvement of the produced software. Then unit tests are used as well as automatic tests based on embedded scripts can be used [3].

The environmental management process improves continuous integration processes. An example would be using the Jira Project Management environment. It is an integrated system with which you can integrate tasks to Jenkins and direct information about them to the project team indicating the status of ongoing work. An example of continuous integration processes is shown in Fig. 1.

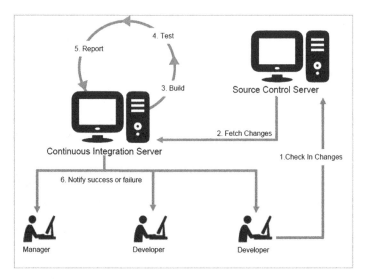

Fig. 1. Example of continuous integration processes [6]

2 Research Experiment

The research experiment was aimed at designing and implementing a system that would allow access to data on air pollution to users. It assumed the construction of a portable device that is capable of sending GPS data as well as receiving and displaying data on the built-in monitor. In addition, creation of a mobile and internet application that fulfils the function of displaying received data. It was also necessary to create a system capable of processing the data sent by the device and placing them in the database (Fig. 2).

The project group consisted of a dozen or so people—students carrying out the project, mainly outside the university, presenting only the results of the progress of work. The working time was to last about three months. The group has been divided into four teams dealing with: device, mobile and internet application, with backend application and database [7, 8]. Each team made autonomous decisions regarding the solutions used. Efforts were made to design according to Occam's razor principle, "The simplest solutions are usually the best."

In the construction of environmental architecture, the following solutions were decided:

- MQTT—data transmission protocol, popular and easy to use, M2M solution. It has a smaller overhead than the HTTP protocol. Due to the popularity of Mosquito, searching for information on, e.g. configuration of secure connections, was not difficult.
- PostgreSQL—is a relational database. The project assumed that the data processed by the system would largely be location data. It was decided to use the Postgres database with the PostGIS extension, which allows you to save geographical data directly to the database and use geospatial functions [9, 10].

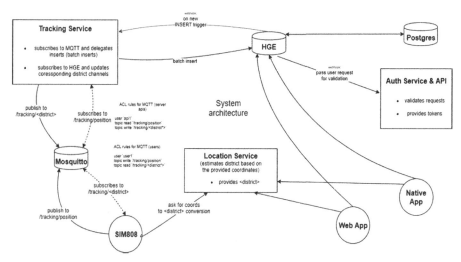

Fig. 2. Architecture of the environment for the production of mobile and internet applications and the system for processing data sent by the device and placing this data in the database [own source].

- Hasura—business layer application. Thanks to it, it was possible to connect to the database, generate a GraphQL schema and set data access permissions via a graphical interface. This solution allows for an integration with an existing database (postgres) and control of access to operations. When connected to the database, it enables the automatic generation of an API in GraphQL based on existing tables and relationships. An additional functionality offered by Hasura are subscriptions that allow notifying listening clients about changed data in real time. In case it is necessary to perform some procedure outside the database with some changes in the data—it is possible to use webhooks. Webhooks allow to send the data that has changed, with fixed headers to a certain address, which will get further treatment. In the event that the project would involve expanding the system in a different direction, this solution also acts as a data integrator for many sources (something like an API Gateway) with the use of Remote Schemas. Such an approach makes the integration of many GraphQL schemas easy to set up and allows for a modular schema stitching approach.
- The Arduino platform was used, using the Arduino UNO base with atmega328p clocked 16 MHz crystal. The device was compatible with the Sim808 overlay. Thanks to this, it was possible to communicate with satellites and send GPS data through the operator's network to the MQTT server.
- Applied fattening data for the quarter. Due to the possible increase in the number of users in the system, it was decided not to simplify the solutions used in connection with the small scale of the project, and to generate the map with air pollution data for districts in our city, instead of responding to each user separately—which would significantly increase the load server. The user, sending data to the MQTT server, had to previously specify through a micro-service dealing with the location—in which district it is. Now, sending his data to the appropriate channel, he informed about his

position and identifier, and wanting to download data on air pollution in the area, he chose the appropriate channel based on the district he had previously received.

- Data insertion. The MQTT server was able to handle a significant throughput of messages, but these also had to be sent to the database. We've set up a service that collected inserts, preparing them for a dispatch. After receiving a specific amount or meeting other criteria, we relayed a batch insert further, which translated into a slighter load of the SQL server.

During the implementation of the project, among other issues, the following problems have been discovered:

- Non-scalable MQTT broker—Mosquitto. In the later stages of the project, it turned out that the weakest element in the system was the service dealing with message ingestion—which could be easily improved with a replacement of the MQTT server, which did not allow for clustering and group subscriptions. The proposed solution was sufficient due to the very nature of the experiment, but it would be reasonable to use another broker, designed with scalability in mind e.g. VerneMQ.
- Problems with embedded libraries integration for a prototype device for the Arduino platform. The library used by the team was very extensive. It contained many supported devices on the list, which included the Sim808 module. Unfortunately, after research, it turned out that many people speaking on the Internet had problems similar to those faced by the team when establishing a secure and stable connection through the HTTP client embedded in the standard library of the Arduino platform. Ultimately, the project used manually entered AT commands and a fully unused library.

3 Possibilities of Extending the Existing Design Environment

The analysis of the research experiment carried out, as well as the conclusions resulting therefrom, pointed to the need to expand the existing design environment. Attention was paid to problems with the use of the MQTT broker, integration of libraries, and the need to look differently than in a situation in which a small, non- scalable IoT system is designed.

Therefore, below, based on the experiment carried out, the possibilities and needs of such development of the design environment are shown. The authors of the article wanted to remove the problems encountered on the one hand, but on the other hand try to create a design environment that would allow designing any number of IT devices, and thus a system that would create conditions for obtaining data from any number of devices.

This chapter indicates the functionality of design environments showing the types of architectures that can be used for designing information systems. This diverse approach to design can be based on docker and containers, and also enable the integration of services if you choose a microservice-based approach. The information contained in this chapter creates the conditions for extending the existing design environment to be open to any challenges posed by IoT systems [11, 12].

Before presenting the possibilities of developing the design environment, it is necessary to answer the question about the architecture type of the proposed IoT system. There are three patterns with different assumptions: monolithic, assuming the existence of a single server serving client requests, distributed, in which the server is replaced by cooperating, autonomous micro-services and PaaS (*Platform as a Service*), where services related to virtualization, server and data warehouse support others with a vendor such as Amazon AWS or Microsoft Azure, leaving the developer control over applications and data.

- **Load Balancing**—is used for dispersing requests between many instances that provide the same functionality, while leveraging the resources. Load Balancing is most often software, implemented on the application layer, DNS servers or even hardware, e.g. a multi-layer switch. Load Balancer can operate on different layers of the OSI (*ISO Open Systems Interconnection Reference Model*) [19]. Distribute traffic: by exchanging frames in layer 2, with the use of special commodity hardware or software, programmatically on ports in layer 4 and based on established rules for HTTP headers in layer 7. Processes related to responding to requests are transferred to multiple servers, which should have their own dedicated network interfaces. Thanks to this solution, we increase the throughput of the entire system in a controlled manner.

In case of an event, when the service must be available worldwide, it is worth to consider the usage of DNS-based load balancing. This will reduce access time, which is critical for many applications displayed globally.

- **Process Manager**—The designer must secure his system from the side of service failure. In the event that the program encounters a problem and an unplanned shutdown occurs, without using the appropriate tools, it will not be able to restart the process automatically. The designer can set a service program (daemon), executed without having to interact with the user that will restart it. For the runtime environment Node.js there are e.g. PM2, StrongLoop—process managers, which allow you to easily run subsequent instances of our process on each machine core, which also allows for a huge increase in application performance without the need for manual use of the cluster module. It is also possible to use systemd and create a unix service that will restart when an error occurs, and start the code itself, using a different library on many cores, if that has not already happened.
- **Server-side preprocessing**—Sometimes, the project team is not able to predict all the functionalities needed to be implemented in the system. The need to add new elements or the possibility of simplification may occur as the project develops. It is often the case that the collected data can be generalized or processed for a wider audience. A good example for this case is the application that gives users the option of receiving back-weather forecasts. If they have access to the base records and would like to retrieve data on the average temperature at the turn of the month, regarding the city of Warsaw, they will have to download a lot of data related to temperatures, and then process them, resulting in the desired effect [15, 16]. If there are many users interested in the average temperature for Warsaw, it is worth considering creating a service that will have processed data on this type of query and will only make it

available to interested parties. This will reduce the load on the client and server that performs the operations for each user [14].

- **Containerization of solutions**—A container is a standardized software unit. It stores the code and all its dependencies. It is created on the basis of configuration files describing your template, i.e. the image it should use, which ports it must display, and other configuration parameters. By using containerization, designers get rid of the problems associated with basic manual installation and configuration of systems, and simplify processes for other teams that use their components when developing software. The idea is very similar to virtual machines. The most popular container types are LXC (Linux Containers) and Docker.

It is worth noting that there is a wide range of images, e.g. for an application written for the node runtime. Is image can weigh up to 670 MB, but you can also use an Alpine image weighing about 60 MB. Thanks to this, it is possible to eliminate many possible security holes in the components installed on the system, because they are less extensive. You can also use the docker-slim tool, which will try to slim the distribution further down.

- **Code Generation**—There are several main reasons for using code generation. Productivity is one of those aspects. Well, repeating the same steps with other elements or even other projects will save a lot of time and we will be able to devote to other important aspects.

Code generation can be performed, among others, from the level of UML (Unified Modeling Language) or class schemes. It significantly accelerates the process of software development, organizes it, which also translates into faster TTM (Time to Market) and thus reduces costs. It is also easier to find inconsistencies in naming or action. The generator that we write can use many parsers, e.g. we can design a REST API generator for C# at the beginning, and then add a parser for C which will allow us to change the target language or framework or the library we want to use. A good example is database schemas with which we can generate DAO (Data Access Object) which allows us to easily map objects on elements in the system, and sometimes even entire generation CRUD (Create, Read, Update, Delete) [13, 15].

4 Directions of Project Development

On the basis of observations from the implementation of the project and analysis of possible functionalities from the third chapter, which could be used in the design of the production environment, directions of project development were proposed. On the one hand, they are an example of activities in which the state of the existing manufacturing environment and the possibility of implementing new functionalities should be considered. On the other hand, they show how it is possible to use Continuous Improvement processes in which the functions presented in chapter three could be included.

The summary of chapter four is the new architecture of the solution developed as part of the research experiment. It took into account both the state of functionality of the environment proposed in the third chapter, but also a certain vision of project development under which the various functionalities discussed in the third chapter can be attached. Below are indicated two areas necessary for the development of the system proposed as part of the experiment.

- **Data storage**—Data sets that are not strictly relational and can be easily presented in the form of documents are in many cases better and more convenient to process and handle. However, there are cases where relational data will be more appropriate, and where standard key-value storage is sufficient. In the conducted experiment, the use of a combination of many such technologies would be the most optimal and would allow the use of OLAP databases, paying special attention to the reporting possibilities in the form of cubes.
- **MQTT broker scalability**—Replacement of the MQTT broker with Mosquitto for solutions such as: VerneMQ, HiveMQ, RabbitMQ due to easier clustering at the time of further development of the project.
- **RDBS records scaling**—Due to the small scale of the experiment and the fixed geographical position, no available solutions for database clustering or geographical multi-sharing were used. Nevertheless, due to the limit of data writing speed, when there is only one instance of the master type, data such as user position or pollen concentration should be stored in a no relational database. It will definitely simplify the process of implementing BigData solutions in the future.
- **Message queues**—Most tasks that perform services should be performed asynchronously at a particular point in time. It would be reasonable to use a queue system connected e.g. to Redis to process data and perform operations such as sending emails during registration, or total calculations for a given area during the day. These tasks can be commissioned to be completed at a specific time. When you have the queue

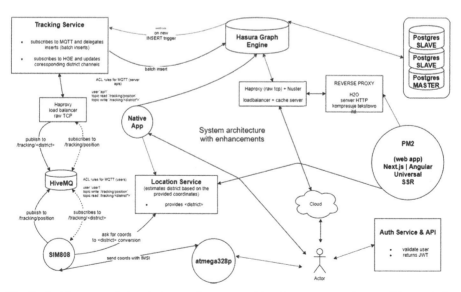

Fig. 3. Architecture of the design environment taking into account the conditions of the experiment as well as functionaries of the design environment [own source].

and the correct configuration, data about the tasks ordered to be performed will not be lost in case of failure of some elements. In addition, thanks to this, the system will be able to delegate some of the work to be carried out, at moments of excessive movement, later. Performing tasks with a higher and lower priority will allow the use of real asynchronous programming methodologies, which will have greater potential for task handling.

On Fig. 3 shows a highly-abstract look at the flow of data and the system itself, which was created as an experiment, with minor amendments, which should be included in the next iteration.

5   Application Enablement Platform Systems

Considering the issues presented in the third chapter, as well as analyzing the presented architecture (Fig. 5) after considering the case study and the functionalities proposed in the third chapter, the architecture and description of the Application Enablement Platform (AEP) systems was presented. The presentation of these systems is intended to show what the architecture of the systems used to design and monitor the state of IoT systems should look like. The presentation of these systems here is intended to present the final version of the system used for IoT management. With such architecture, we are able to show how much the design environment we design is adequate to create and design such a system. It also creates conditions for us to have a design environment on the one hand and an existing application on the other. That we also answer the question to what extent it is possible to build Continuous improvement processes supplementing the conditions of the design environment and the requirements used for IoT systems.

The AEP system, thanks to the Software Development Kit creates conditions for managing any IoT services. It should be assumed when building such a system that it is possible to monitor the status of individual devices and treat it as support for initiatives aimed at improving the operation of the IoT system. To build an AEP, comprehensive knowledge is needed to demonstrate their potential for use. Because we do not have such knowledge, hence a solution based on the incremental structure of such a system is proposed. The AEP system integrates three groups of processes: system production, maintenance and management. It also creates conditions to ensure the scalability of designed services based on IoT system architects. This approach is extremely important from the point of view of designing the user interface relevant to the user's use. Figure 5 shows an example of such a system integrating three layers constituting a set of functionalities discussed in chapter three.

Their use in the processes of designing processing processes as well as device design and data visualization depends on the type of system. It should be assumed that before proceeding with the Continuous Improvement process, various types of AEP systems will be evaluated in order to choose the one that will constitute the set of functionalities appropriate to the class of the system being designed. There are currently about 300 such systems available.

6   Continuous Improvement Process Model

The Continuous Improvement process model was developed based on the research experiment carried out as well as on the basis of the analysis of functionalities necessary for the design of IoT systems. This model takes into account two areas (Fig. 4): the area of design environment and the area of functionality of IoT systems. It is between these areas that there should be cooperation analyzed from the point of view of feedback processes, in which the analysis of functionality indicates the possibility of their design using the design environment. You should consider how the support will look for both the design environment (infrastructure and tool support) and how the support for changes in the functionality of the IoT system will look. Nevertheless, the experience gained regarding both the single node design process and the analysis of the functionality of AEP systems indicate that there is a need to treat the IoT system production process as a process in which Continuous Improvement processes will be essential. It is thanks to these processes that it will be possible to iteratively supplement the functionality of the design environment for the needs of designing the IoT system.

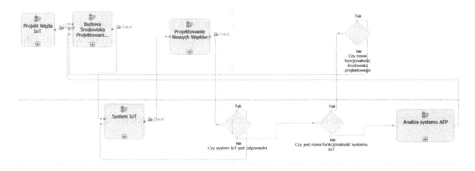

Fig. 4.   Continuous Improvement process model for IoT system design [own source]

7   Conclusions

The paper presents a model of continuous improvement processes to support the construction of Internet of Things systems design environments. The prepared article is a response to the problems of designing environments for the production of IoT systems. Current systems are becoming increasingly complex, and for this complexity it is necessary to design appropriate environments that allow the production of these systems. Therefore, the authors of the work proposed a solution in which a simple research experiment consisting in the construction of one IoT node was carried out. Then, a suitable system was designed for this node using a simple design environment. They have subsequently carried out an analysis of the functionality of design environments for the production of IoT systems seeing for functionality for these environments.

Existing AEP systems were also analyzed as the most complex IoT management systems. Based on these analyses, a process model in continuous integration was developed.

This model is the answer to the problem of holistic vision of IoT systems. A bottom-up approach was proposed in the article, which first designs the node and then builds, which is why the node has the appropriate system. Next, further nodes are added and the existing system is checked for suitability. Subsequently, processes of analyzing the existing system functionalities in the design are carried out to determine which of them will be suitable for the increased number of nodes. In the absence of such functionalities, AEP systems are tested as the most complex and most useful for visualizing the complexity of IoT systems. Then, on the one hand, we have a design environment and, on the other, a complex IoT system.

Linking the design environment to a complex IoT system using a process model in Continuous Improvement streamlines the process of building such environments suitable for the complexity of the system. The word appropriate is deliberately given here, which is why the design environment cannot be too complex or too simplified. Its structure from the point of view of individual nodes is not important and problems with the use of these environments appear when increasing the number of nodes. For this reason, the developed model may be useful in software development processes and is an example of how you can manage these processes so that you can design IoT systems using appropriate design environments for this complexity.

Our experience to date shows that the creation of a perfectly designed system the first time is unlikely, and the selected solutions and technologies should be well thought out before their implementation due to further possible complications and technical support. Premature optimization can be a loss in which we can easily lose ourselves at the expense of other important elements of the operating system. The solutions used should be designed and applied in a reasonable manner that allows for easy expansion and expansion of the scale to avoid bottlenecks limiting the capacity in the system.

References

1. Burns, B., Lachowski, L.: Projektowanie systemów rozproszonych. Helion SA (2018)
2. Kurose, J., Ross, K., Walczak, T.: Sieci komputerowe. Helion SA (2019)
3. Ncoder. https://ncoder.pl/docker-podstawowa-idea-wirtualizacja-vs-konteneryzacja. Accessed 10 July 2019
4. Blog-i-systems. https://blog.i-systems.pl/json-web-tokens-jwt/. Accessed 22 July 2019
5. Computerworld. https://www.computerworld.pl/news/System-monolityczny-czy-rozwiazania-komponentowe,407905.html. Accessed 1 July 2019
6. Itwiz. https://itwiz.pl/czym-jest-nosql-jak-wykorzystac-nierelacyjnebazy-danych. Accessed 5 July 2019
7. Docker. https://docs.docker.com/engine/swarm/. Accessed 7 July 2019
8. Bulldogjob. https://bulldogjob.pl/news/611-kubernetes-vs-docker-swarm-ktorywybrac. Accessed 7 July 2019
9. Bulldogjob. https://bulldogjob.pl/articles/1047-serverless-czym-jest-i-jak-dziala. Accessed 10 July 2019
10. Cloudflare. https://www.cloudflare.com/learning/serverless/glossary/serverless-microservice. Accessed 10 July 2019
11. Microsoft. https://docs.microsoft.com/plpl/dotnet/standard/microservices-architecture/architect-microservice-container-applications/direct-client-to-microservice-communication-versus-the-api-gateway-pattern. Accessed 10 July 2019

12. Traefik. https://docs.traefik.io/. Accessed 10 July 2019
13. Fowler, S.: Production-Ready Microservices. O'Reilly Media, Inc., Sebastopol (2016)
14. Gonzalez, D.: Developing Microservices with Node.js. Packt Publishing, Birmingham (2016)
15. Hasura.   https://blog.hasura.io/the-ultimate-guide-to-writing-dockerfiles-for-go-web-apps-336efad7012c/. Accessed 10 July 2019
16. Microservices.   https://microservices.io/patterns/decomposition/decompose-bysubdomain.html. Accessed 10 July 2019
17. Microservices. https://microservices.io/platform/microservice-architecture-assessment.html. Accessed 10 July 2019
18. Newman, S.: Building Microservices. O'Reilly, Sebastopol (2015)
19. Swersky, D. https://thenewstack.io/thehows-whys-and-whats-of-monitoring-microservices/. Accessed 10 July 2019

Estimation of PM_{10} Concentration with Features Extraction by Digital Image Processing

Jiun-Jian Liaw[1], Cheng-Xin Hong[1], Cheng-Hsiung Hsieh[2], Chuan-Bi Lin[1(✉)], and Dung-Ching Lin[1]

[1] Department of Information and Communication Engineering,
Chaoyang University of Technology, 168, Jifong E. Rd., Taichung, Taiwan, ROC
{jjliaw,s10830602,cblin,s10630605}@cyut.edu.tw
[2] Department of Computer Science and Information Engineering,
Chaoyang University of Technology, 168, Jifong E. Rd., Taichung, Taiwan, ROC
chhsieh@cyut.edu.tw

Abstract. Since the city's air quality has declined, developing an efficient and convenient method to measure PM_{10} concentration has become an interesting research topic. There is a correlation between the characteristics of air pollution and the reducing in visibility which can be estimated by image processing methods. To estimate the concentration of PM_{10} by image processing is the main purpose of this paper. The automatically selecting RoI is applied for extracting the features from the image. The high frequency information, portion of the non-scattered light, relative humidity and PM_{10} concentration are regressed by Support Vector Regression. The real images and two indices are used to show the performance of the estimation. According to the experimental results, R^2 is obtained greater than 0.71 and the RMSE is less than 16.1.

Keywords: PM_{10} concentration · Region of interest · High frequency information · Support Vector Regression

1 Introduction

As a result of industrial advances that have caused air pollution, the city's air quality has declined. It is also causing public health and socio-economic problems [1]. Since we want to know the ingredients of air pollution, the establishment of a particulate matter (PM_{10}) monitoring system has become a research topic [2]. Among the known air contaminants, PM_{10} is directly associated with a variety of serious health problems such as asthma, cardiovascular disease, respiratory disease, lung cancer and premature death [3]. The outdoor PM_{10} concentration measurement currently in use are usually installed in various professional air quality monitoring stations [4, 5]. These instruments placed on the monitoring station are expensive and they are not easy to use in high density human activity areas. Some studies have used air pollution diffusion models to estimate PM_{10} concentrations between different monitoring stations [6]. However, the accuracy of the estimate depends on the direction, topography and distance of the airflow. In addition, the measurement results are only effective for air pollution with

© Springer Nature Singapore Pte Ltd. 2020
P. Sitek et al. (Eds.): ACIIDS 2020, CCIS 1178, pp. 436–443, 2020.
https://doi.org/10.1007/978-981-15-3380-8_38

uniform atmospheric distribution, and it is impossible to instantly display the air quality in our living environment [7]. Developing an efficient and convenient method to measure PM$_{10}$ concentration has become an interesting research topic. The easy technology to estimate PM$_{10}$ can be easily placed in the city to provide real-time information on PM$_{10}$ concentrations.

The traditional measurement of PM$_{10}$ technology focuses on the chemical scheme [8]. We know that pollutants in the air reduce the light intensity, and the most direct effect is to reduce the visibility. There is a correlation between the characteristics of air pollution and the reducing visibility [9]. Previous research has pointed out that the high-frequency information of the image can be used to estimate the visibility and has good performance [10]. Based on these concepts, estimating the concentration of PM$_{10}$ by image processing is the primary purpose of this paper.

The situation we set is to shoot urban images in a fixed direction at the heights of the city. The obtained image contains a number of distant urban buildings. Under the pollution of PM$_{10}$ concentration, the images of the same building will have different levels of high frequency information. The concept of this part is the technique of estimating the visibility using high frequency information [11]. Buildings in the same image have different levels of high frequency information because of different distances. Therefore, the estimation of air pollution in which building or image area has become one of the main problems. Some scholars have mentioned that the selection of the region of interest (RoI) from the image can be improved the efficiency of air pollution estimation [12]. Lin has also proposed a method for automatically selecting RoI, which is applied to the estimation of PM$_{2.5}$ [13]. However, Lin did not study the effect of the proposed method on PM$_{10}$.

In this paper, the automatically selecting RoI is applied and used to estimate the PM$_{10}$ concentration in the urban images. We collected urban images taken from the top floor of the Renwu Environmental Monitoring Station, Kaohsiung. The PM$_{10}$ concentration and relative humidity are also recorded by the station at the same time. We apply automated methods to select RoI and features in the RoI. The high frequency information, portion of the non-scattered light, relative humidity and PM$_{10}$ concentration are regressed by SVR (Support Vector Regression) to obtain the relationship with each other [14]. The relationship can be used to estimate the PM$_{10}$ concentration. In order to show the performance of the proposed method, the data collected from May to October 2016 are used for experiments.

2 Selecting the RoI for PM$_{10}$

A consumer camera was set at the top of Renwu Environmental Monitoring Station. It took one image every ten minutes in the period of 7:00 to 17:00 from May to October 2016. The data from the first month, May, are used to select RoI. We separate images taken at high PM$_{10}$ concentrations ($>125\ \mu g/m^3$) and images taken at low PM$_{10}$ concentrations ($<20\ \mu g/m^3$). We obtained 30 images with high concentration and 120 images with low concentration. Each high and low concentration images are used to calculate three RoI candidates. The steps of the calculation are as follows.

Step 1: Two images (high and low PM_{10} concentration) are converted to binary im ages by Sobel operation [11] and Otsu thresholding [15], respectively.

Step 2: To execute dilation operation for each of two binary images. The outputs of this step are also two binary images.

Step 3: Subtract two binary images to obtain a binary image. The information left in this image is the common area of high and low concentration images.

Step 4: Labeling is applied to the binary image to indicate the area with connected white pixels [16]. The three RoI candidates can be selected as three largest areas.

Since we have 30 images with high concentration and 120 images with low concentration, we can obtain 3600 results and each result with 3 RoI candidates. We overlap all the selected candidates and then select the three RoIs with the highest overlap. An example of obtained subtracted image is shown in Fig. 1(a) and selected three RoIs are shown in Fig. 1(b). The selected three RoIs are applied to all images from May 2016. The high frequency energy of areas in RoIs are extracted and gathered statistics. The RoI with the highest average value of high frequency energy is selected as RoI for PM_{10}. In our data from May 2016, the statistics for three RoIs are shown in Fig. 2. According to the statistics results, R_1 is the selected RoI.

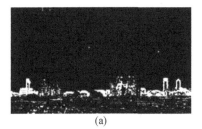 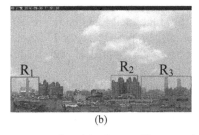

(a)   (b)

Fig. 1. The examples of the RoI selection for PM_{10} concentration. (a) subtracted image and (b) selected three RoIs

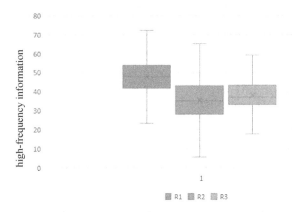

Fig. 2. The boxplots for three RoIs.

3 Features Extraction from Digital Image

Since the selected RoI may contain the sky, the area of sky should be removed before we extract the features. The sky area of our images is the same because the images are taken by the same camera with the same position and direction. Since the boundaries of the sky area are less than the area of buildings, it is easy to separate the sky area by the boundary. The flowchart of the sky area classification is shown in Fig. 3. The input image is processed to two ways, one is processed by edge detection and Otsu thresholding and one is processed by only Otsu thresholding. The processing with edge extraction obtains the binary data with edge and the processing without edge extraction obtains the binary data with brightness. The OR operator is used to compose two binary data to obtain the intersection of the buildings with edge and brightness. We apply dilation and labeling to the obtained data, and the sky area can be classified by the label with the largest number of pixels. The labeled result and the sky area remove result are shown in Fig. 4(a) and (b), respectively.

High frequency is extracted from the RoI without sky area. Since the RoI is selected by Sect. 2, the RoI without sky area is the intersection with removed sky area and RoI.

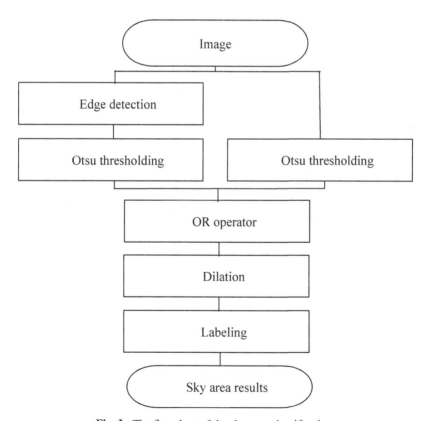

Fig. 3. The flowchart of the sky area classification.

(a)   (b)

Fig. 4. The result of sky removal. (a) labeled data and (b) removed sky area

We set the pixels excluded sky area in RoI are belonged to N and the number of N is $n(N)$. The high frequency can be extracted by

$$HF = \frac{1}{n(N)} \sum\nolimits_{(x,y)\in N} G(x, y) \tag{1}$$

where $G(x, y)$ is the results of Sobel operation. Portion of the non-scattered light is also calculated by

$$PL = \frac{1}{n(N)} \sum\nolimits_{(x,y)\in N} t(x, y) \tag{2}$$

where $t(x, y)$ is the portion of the non-scattered light at (x, y) [17].

4   Experiments and Results

We set a consumer camera to take one image every ten minutes but the air factors, such as PM_{10} concentration and relative humidity, are recorded hourly. In other words, six images are related to only one PM_{10} concentration and one relative humidity value for each hour. The variance of six images taken in the same hour is calculated. If the variance is greater than 1, the images are considered as void data and discarded. The remaining images are divided into training data and test data. The training data are used to find the regression model by SVR [14]. The extracted features (HF and RL), measured factors (PM_{10} concentration and relative humidity) are the input of SVR. The testing data are used to estimate PM_{10} concentration by the obtained regression model.

4.1   Evaluation Indices

In order to evaluate the performance of the proposed estimation method, three indices, RMSE (root mean square error) and R^2 are calculated by estimated values and recorded values of PM_{10} concentration. RMSE and R^2 can be described as

$$RMSE = \sqrt{\frac{1}{N} \sum\nolimits_{i=1}^{N} \left(y_i - \hat{y}_i\right)^2}, and \tag{3}$$

$$R^2 = 1 - \frac{\sum_{i=1}^{N}(y_i - \hat{y}_i)^2}{\sum_{i=1}^{N}(y_i - \bar{y})^2},$$ (4)

respectively. Where $\hat{y}_i$ is the estimated values, y_i is the recorded value and $\bar{y}$ is the mean of y_i.

We can see that the smaller RMSE is shown the smaller error between the estimated and recorded values. The value of R^2 is between 0 and 1. It means that the estimated value is in perfect agreement with the recorded value while $R^2 = 1$.

4.2 Experimental Results

The training data and test data are randomly selected. The ratios of training data and test data are set as 1:9, 2:8, 3:7, ... , 8:2, and 9:1, respectively. In each ratio, we randomly selected ten samples in proportion and experimented separately. The results are shown in Table 1.

Table 1. The results of PM$_{10}$ estimation.

Ratio	Indices	Ten times of randomly selected samples									
		#1	#2	#3	#4	#5	#6	#7	#8	#9	#10
1:9	RMSE	21.60	22.66	23.22	25.88	22.41	22.08	24.08	22.33	23.63	23.67
	R^2	0.47	0.43	0.38	0.34	0.42	0.44	0.37	0.43	0.36	0.37
2:8	RMSE	19.48	20.53	20.01	20.65	19.77	20.07	21.01	21.14	20.73	20.76
	R^2	0.55	0.51	0.55	0.52	0.56	0.55	0.5	0.49	0.52	0.51
3:7	RMSE	19.24	18.43	22.34	19.5	18.23	19.58	18.19	17.76	19.54	18.54
	R^2	0.58	0.6	0.47	0.55	0.61	0.6	0.61	0.62	0.56	0.6
4:6	RMSE	16.15	19.02	17.7	17.67	16.93	17.37	18.67	19.17	17.45	17.63
	R^2	0.68	0.6	0.63	0.63	0.67	0.63	0.6	0.57	0.64	0.63
5:5	RMSE	15.99	16.05	17.52	15.84	17.27	17.98	18.14	16.78	16.32	16.24
	R^2	0.7	0.7	0.65	0.71	0.67	0.62	0.63	0.68	0.69	0.68
6:4	RMSE	15.48	15.55	15.76	16.61	15.86	15.16	16.41	16.21	15.7	15.7
	R^2	0.71	0.72	0.69	0.69	0.68	0.72	0.68	0.7	0.7	0.69
7:3	RMSE	14.81	16.83	15.83	14.0	15.47	15.87	15.69	16.66	14.74	15.17
	R^2	0.74	0.68	0.73	0.76	0.72	0.67	0.71	0.66	0.72	0.73
8:2	RMSE	14.93	15.76	14.34	14.3	16.58	13.94	16.97	15.69	13.9	14.53
	R^2	0.73	0.72	0.75	0.75	0.68	0.78	0.69	0.69	0.77	0.78
9:1	RMSE	15.69	15.47	12.83	11.45	16.1	13.27	15.44	13.59	13.14	11.21
	R^2	0.77	0.74	0.83	0.82	0.71	0.8	0.77	0.83	0.78	0.84

From the results, we can see that the performance of estimation increases with the increase of training data rate. When the training data reaches 90%, the best PM$_{10}$ concentration can be estimated. The best results of RMSE and R^2 are between 11.21–16.10 and 0.71–0.84, respectively.

5 Conclusion

In this study, a method is proposed for estimating the concentration of PM_{10}. Unlike traditional chemical detection, this method uses digital image processing techniques to estimate. We first determine RoI from the known PM_{10} high and low concentration images. This area obtained by the automatic selected of RoI has higher response to PM_{10} changes. The features are extracted from the RoI with the training images, including high frequency information and transmittance. The obtained features were correlated with known air parameters for SVR to obtain a regression model. The test image was estimated by the regression model for PM_{10} concentration. According to the experimental results, R^2 is obtained greater than 0.71 and the RMSE is less than 16.1.

Acknowledgments. This research is partially sponsored by Chaoyang University of Technology (CYUT) and Higher Education Sprout Project, Ministry of Education (MOE), Taiwan, under the project name: "The R&D and the cultivation of talent for health-enhancement products."

References

1. Tang, X.: An overview of air pollution problem in megacities and city clusters in China. American Geophysical Union (2007)
2. US EPA Smart City Air Challenge. https://developer.epa.gov/smart-city-air-challenge. Accessed 01 Oct 2019
3. Ostro, B.: Outdoor Air Pollution: Assessing the Environmental Burden of Disease at National and Local Levels.: WHO environmental burden of disease series. World Health Org, Geneva, Switzerland (2004)
4. Air Quality Data—Central Pollution Control Board. https://cpcb.nic.in/real-time-air-qulity-data. Accessed 01 Oct 2019
5. Air Pollution—European Environment Agency. https://www.eea.europa.eu/themes/air/intro. Accessed 01 Oct 2019
6. Lung, S.C.C., Maod, I.F., Liu, L.J.S.: Residents' particle exposures in six different communities in Taiwan. Sci. Total Environ. **377**(1), 81–92 (2007)
7. Lung, S.C.C., Hsiao, P.K., Wen, T.Y., Liu, C.H., Fu, C.B., Cheng, Y.T.: Variability of intra-urban exposure to particulate matter and CO from Asian-type community pollution sources. Atmos. Environ. **83**, 6–13 (2014)
8. Samara, C., et al.: Chemical characterization and receptor modeling of PM10 in the surroundings of the opencast lignite mines of Western Macedoina, Greece. Environ. Sci. Pollut. Res. **25**(13), 12206–12221 (2018)
9. Shih, W.Y.: Variations of urban fine suspended particulate matter (PM2.5) from various environmental factors and sources and its role on atmospheric visibility in Taiwan, Master Thesis, National Central University, Taiwan (2013)
10. Liaw, J.J., Lian, S.B., Huang, Y.F., Chen, R.C.: Using sharpness image with haar function for urban atmospheric visibility measurement. Aerosol Air Qual. Res. **10**(4), 323–330 (2010)
11. Jin, S., Kim, W., Jeong, J.: Fine directional de-interlacing algorithm using modified Sobel operation. IEEE Trans. Consum. Electron. **54**(2), 587–862 (2008)
12. Liu, C., Tsow, F., Zou, Y., Tao, N.: Particle pollution estimation based on image analysis. Plos One **11**, e0145955 (2016)
13. Lin, D.-C.: Estimation of urban PM2.5 concentration based on digital image processing technology, Thesis for the Master Degree, Chaoyang University of Technology, Taiwan (2019)

14. Wu, C.H., Ho, J.M., Lee, D.T.: Travel-time prediction with support vector regression. IEEE Trans. Intell. Transp. Syst. **5**(4), 276–281 (2004)
15. Goh, T.Y., Basah, S.N., Yazid, H., Safar, M.J.A., Saad, F.S.A.: Performance analysis of image thresholding: Otsu technique. Measurement **114**, 298–307 (2018)
16. Dougherty, E.R., Lotufo, R.A.: Hands-on Morphological Image Processing, 1st edn. SPIE Press, Bellingham (2003)
17. Hsieh, C., Chen, J., Zhao, Q.: A modified DCP based dehazing algorithm. In: IEEE International Conference on Systems, Man, and Cybernetics 2018, pp. 1779–1784 (2018)

Vision System for a Cell with a KUKA Robot

Szymon Głębocki and Artur Babiarz[(✉)] [iD]

Silesian University of Technology, Akademicka 2A, 44-100 Gliwice, Poland
szymgle466@student.polsl.pl, artur.babiarz@polsl.pl

Abstract. The following article presents the designing process of vision system for cell with KUKA robot. We describe each of part of designed system: hardware, software and final application. The main idea is to plan and implement the vision system which allows grab an arbitrary objects. The process is controlled by external computer. The operator of system should be able to expand the application. At the end, the illustrative example is shown.

Keywords: Vision system · KUKA robot · Path planning

1 Introduction

Nowadays manipulators are widely used for robotic manufacturing processes such as welding, painting, molding, handling press, assembly etc., concentrating on those that require heavy lifting capabilities or are hazardous to human health [14]. The integration of robots with vision systems can extend the functionality of inspection, selection and quality control applications in automated industrial processes [5,12,15].

The idea behind this work is to design and implement such automated process using industrial grade equipment used in real manufactories, as well as to create a visualization allowing for the process supervision. The vision systems for KUKA robots are presented, for example, in [18,19] where authors use the dedicated vision systems for KUKA robots and solve different problems.

The process which will be presented in this paper is identification of color objects on a worktable and sorting them by colors using a KUKA robot arm. The solved problem is similar to main topic of the article [13]. But in below presented problem the most important fact is integration of all industrial parts of the robot cell (for details, see [4]). In order to accomplish this objective, the robot is to be equipped with a camera which will classify the objects, and a gripper allowing the robot to translocate the objects. Then, several programs

The research presented here was done by authors as parts of the projects funded by the National Science Centre in Poland granted according to decision DEC-2017/25/B/ST7/02888 and Polish Ministry for Science and Higher Education funding for statutory activities 02/010/BK_19/0143.

P. Sitek et al. (Eds.): ACIIDS 2020, CCIS 1178, pp. 444–455, 2020.
https://doi.org/10.1007/978-981-15-3380-8_39

are to be created: computer program for object recognition using the camera feed, together with a visualization of the necessary data, programmable logic controller (PLC) program for communication between a computer and the robot via PROFINET and KUKA robot program for transporting the objects. Having constructed the additional hardware, equipped the robot with it, and created the programs, it was able to perform tests on the real environment. The main concept of the system is presented on Fig. 1.

The robot itself is a base without a specific purpose. It can perform a wide variety of tasks if it is equipped with appropriate tools for these tasks and programmed. The cell provided for the work is shown on Fig. 2. The task was to figure out such a process that would both use the whole range of the cell's possibilities as well as portray something useful in the industry. The process that has been chosen was sorting of color objects, which additionally puts emphasis on robot vision systems, which undeniably broaden the capabilities of a robot. The second part of the task was to resolve how to expand the cell with tools necessary for the process and create systems which will manage it. First problems in design were hardware implementations of the camera which will be used in object recognition and color classification. Some existing solutions include usage of a single camera providing vision of two dimensional field and some way of determining the depth, or two cameras providing stereo vision, which allows for extracting three dimensional information of an object. The camera could be stationary in the cell, or mounted to the robot. Secondly, there was a need for a tool for the robot which will allow it to transport those objects to their color distinguished destinations. This could be accomplished with the use of either a robot servo gripper, a pneumatic vacuum gripper or an electromagnet. The next and most extensive problem was to create a robot vision system which will analyze and process the camera feed in order to extract information about the objects placed on the worktable. Communication between the robot and camera image acquisition is discussed as well as transformation of visual information of the robot position and orientation [1,2]. The most important information will be the position in space and the color of an object. There are many algorithms used in the vision systems that allow for object and color recognition in an image such as segmentation and clustering methods. To accomplish this task, literature describing machine vision [3,8,17] was referred to, as well as image processing manuals for National Instruments (NI) LabVIEW [6,7,9]. Creation of an HMI was also necessary for displaying of information which is used for supervision of the process. Both the robot vision system and an HMI can be created in various software, such NI Instruments LabView, MathWorks MATLAB or Microsoft Visual Studio. A subsequent problem was to establish communication between the KUKA robot and PLC via PROFINET, which will allow the robot to perform actions autonomously, being managed by a higher-level controller, instead of manually by a human. For this to be possible, it is necessary to properly configure and program both devices, thus the guidelines from the KUKA and SIEMENS manuals [10,11,16] were used.

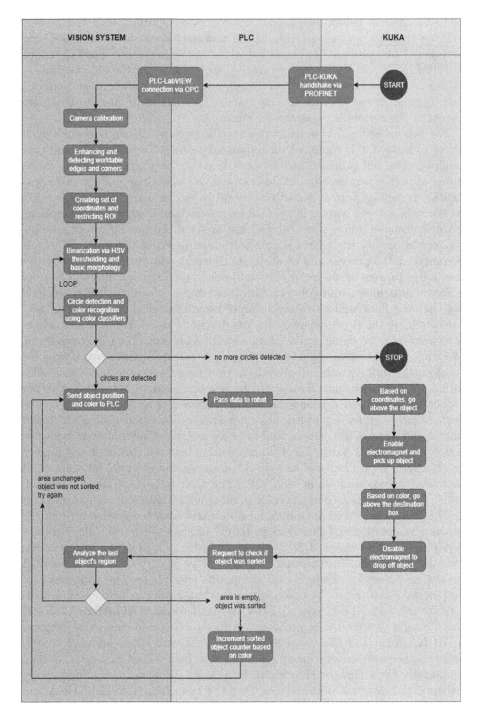

Fig. 1. The main idea of vision system

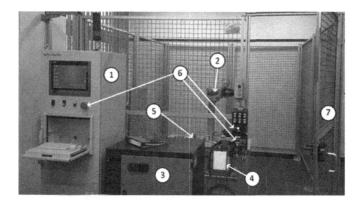

Fig. 2. A cell with a KUKA robot: 1. The electrical cabinet with Siemens S7-1500 PLC and a Siemens computer serving as a Human Machine Interface (HMI). 2. KUKA robot KR20 R1810. 3. KUKA robot controller KRC4. 4. KUKA robot teach pendant (TP). 5. Worktable. 6. Safety switches and mechanisms. 7. Safety door.

In order to convey the information gathered by the vision system to the robot, it is necessary to extend the PLC program. Achieving this was made easier with SIEMENS PLC programming manuals and tutorials. And finally, for the robot to react to acquired data and perform the sorting itself, it was required to program the robot itself using the teach pendant. For this, the KUKA robot programming manuals [10,11] proved to be helpful.

2   Requirements and Tools

The first choice to be made was of the objects to be sorted. As the process includes sorting of color objects, it was needed for them to be of very distinguishable colors, and of size big enough to easily be visible in the camera image, but small enough to be easy to pick up by the robot. The shape also plays a huge role in recognizing the objects, so it should be uniform. The objects were chosen to be round, colourful fridge magnets, as they fit the requirements and their shape makes it so their rotation will not influence the recognition algorithm in any way. Four of the colors were chosen: red, green, blue and yellow. As the objects needed to have a destination point while being sorted, small boxes were used with colors corresponding to the objects. The containers were attached to the side of the worktable for easy deployment. The implementation of destination boxes and objects themselves is presented on Fig. 3.

For the vision acquisition system, a single camera has been chosen to provide the view of the worktable and objects to be recognized. The requirement for this camera is such, that it provides view of the whole worktable, does not obstruct the robot pathing, and does not introduce image distortions due to lens or camera angle. A phone camera was used for the purpose of this paper. The camera was set to be stationary, mounted on the cell. Its position is such, that its lens is

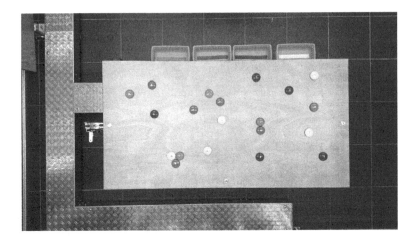

Fig. 3. Objects

parallel to the worktable and pointing towards its center. This way it fulfils the requirements – there is no camera angle distortion, and the distortion at the lens edges is equally spread around the worktable's center.

In order to get rid of the camera lens distortion, calibration techniques using calibration grids could have been used, although it was decided against using those techniques, as the error was acceptable and did not influence the process. Positioning of the worktable towards the center of the image, instead of covering it entirely helped reduce the distortions around the worktable.

A robot tool was to be designed for the purpose of picking up and transporting the objects. From the many solutions, the simplest one to implement was the electromagnetic gripper (Fig. 4).

Fig. 4. The electromagnetic gripper

3   Software

The cell PC was already equipped with programs necessary for programming of PLCs, namely Siemens Totally Integrated Automation (TIA) Portal V14. Software in which the robot vision system and the visualization system was created, was the NI LabVIEW (Fig. 5). The application provides various vision acquisition, processing and development functions to be used in creation of the system for the process. In order to exchange data between the LabVIEW application and the PLC, an additional client-server software had to be implemented. For this task, the NI Open Platform Communications (OPC) server was used which allows a PC to communicate with hardware industrial devices, and is natively compatible with LabVIEW. The most important part of the HMI is the camera video in the middle. The area consists of 5 tabs which show different parts of object detection algorithms:

- Camera View – shows direct camera feed,
- ROI Preview – allows to check if the program properly restricted the region of interest (ROI) to the worktable, based on the coordinate set origin and the table physical parameters,
- Detected Edges – presents an image with enhanced and detected edges of the worktable, allowing to check if the edges and origin of set of coordinates have been found correctly,
- Detected Circles – shows a binary image of circles detected within the ROI, allowing to observe if the detection algorithm works correctly,
- Main Screen – similar to camera view tab, but additionally shows a Ferret box around each object, its number and detected color.

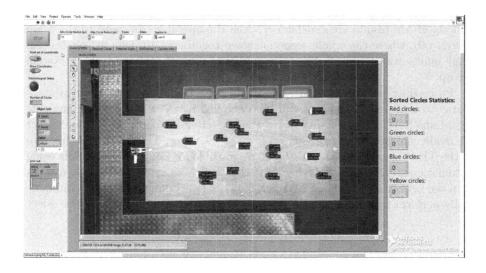

Fig. 5. Labview application

On the left-hand side, there are controls allowing to do such actions as stopping the application, resetting the detected origin of set of coordinates and showing an overlay of coordinates on the image. There is also information about the status of electromagnet, the number of detected objects and their parameters, as well as error feed coming from the program. At the top, a few controls are placed allowing to change parameters of the algorithm, in case of unsatisfactory object recognition. Finally, to the right there are sorted circles statistics for supervising the process when it is activated. Values are reset whenever the program is launched anew.

The vision system should be set up correctly by default, but it is important to analyze the algorithm's work in the different image tabs. Firstly, to ensure correctly chosen origin of set of coordinates, which should be at the bottom left corner of the worktable, the operator should head over to the Detected Edges tab as shown on Fig. 6. The green rectangles show areas where left and bottom edge of the worktable are sought, and red lines are the detected edges. Their crossing point is the coordinate set origin. By clicking the Reset set of coordinates button, the algorithm will run once more. It can be repeated until results are satisfactory. The next step is to observe if the ROI for object detection is correctly set to enclose the worktable alone. This is done in the ROI Preview tab and should look like on Fig. 7. This makes it so the algorithm does not search for objects beyond the worktable. A few degrees of rotation in the image are allowed for correct ROI description. Second to last step is to review the Detected Circles tab and analyze the object detection algorithm. The red color on the image signifies the detected circles. The visible overlay shows the information about each circle, it can be toggled off and on using the Show Coordinates button to the left. If nothing appears on this tab, one may experiment with controls at the top of the application to change the circle detection radius, erosion and dilatation kernel sizes. Correct set up is shown on Fig. 8. If the set up is complete and algorithm results are satisfactory, then the operator can move to the Main Screen tab, where the whole scene is shown together with detected circles and their information (Fig. 5). This concludes the part of HMI and vision system set up.

Proceeding to the next part, the robot must be prepared to work in automatic external mode, where it will be controlled by the PLC and communicate with LabVIEW. First step is to turn the keyswitch at top of the TP and select T1 mode, which allows for manual control of the robot. Then, a special program in the TP is to be selected. This file is responsible for launching programs using automatic external mode. Having done that, all there is left to do is once again turn the keyswitch and select AUT EXT mode. Everything is set up to automatically perform the object sorting process. Button labelled START on the safety

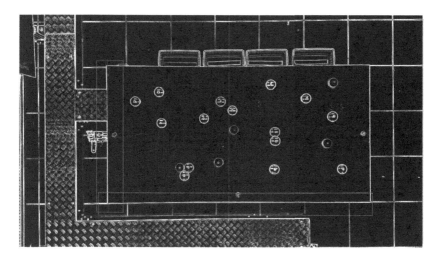

Fig. 6. Detected edges

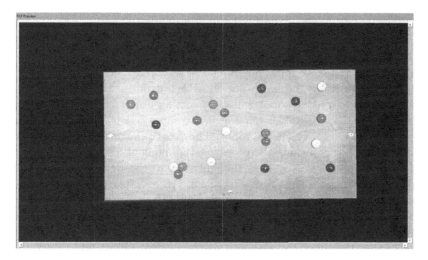

Fig. 7. ROI preview tab

door is used to starting the process, and the non-safety button labelled STOP pauses the process. At this moment, robot will start sorting objects with number 0, which will always be the one closest to it. After the process is done, the boxes will be filled with objects of corresponding color, and the robot will return to the home position and wait for another round of sorting.

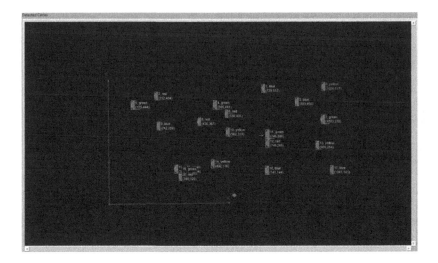

Fig. 8. Correct set up

4   Usage Examples

When both the vision system and robot are set up according to the previous remarks, when pressing the hardware START button on the keyboard to the left of the safety door, the robot will start sorting objects by color if there are any present on the worktable. On Fig. 9 a comparison is shown of what the HMI shows and a sideview of the robot. The Electromagnet Status lamp is lit, meaning that robot is picking the object at the moment. A few objects already sorted can be observed, as well as the statistics to the right. In this example, 20 objects were to be sorted, 5 of each color. An exemplary view of a finished process is shown on Fig. 10, where a side view of the destination containers is shown, each filled with corresponding objects, as well as the mentioned statistics. At any point during the process, the non-safety STOP button can be pressed. This will cause the robot to finish sorting the current object and return to the home position. Resuming the process is done via pushing the START button.

In creation of the LabVIEW application for the robot vision system, built-in image processing algorithms are applied. The algorithm works as follows:

1. From the original image the luminance plane is extracted to convert the image to grayscale and then filtered using Prewitt operator. This emphasizes all horizontal and vertical edges, and to further enhance them, brightness and contrast are tweaked.
2. Left edge of the worktable is sought with an algorithm projecting straight horizontal lines and a straight line with most perpendicular results is chosen, job is done easier thanks to previous transformations.
3. Similarly, the bottom edge of the worktable is searched for.

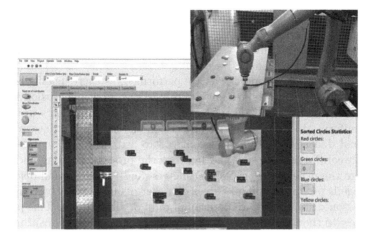

Fig. 9. An example

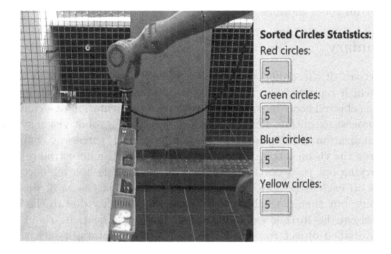

Fig. 10. Statistics

4. Using the caliper function, crossing point of both edges is found, which is the bottom left corner of the worktable. The transformed image is displayed in the HMI.
5. Using the information about the crossing point, an origin of the set of coordinates is created.

The region of interest is restricted to the worktable by using the previously found bottom left corner of the worktable and the upper right corner, retrieved based on the known worktable dimensions. Having the worktable extracted, the next step is to detect the circular objects. For this, algorithm is as follows:

1. The image is converted into binary using HSV plane thresholding. Only the hue value was restricted, and its values was chosen specifically to reject the worktable, and works under varied lighting. After this procedure, only the objects are present as binary 1 s.
2. Additional morphology operations are performed, as there usually is noise in the image and the objects are not uniform. Thus, multiple erosion functions are used to remove small particles, holes in remaining objects are filled to create uniform objects and finally objects on the border are rejected.
3. Additional dilatation and erosion controls are extracted to the HMI for the user to tweak, in order to try and improve the process. Eroding and dilating the image smoothens the circles' perimeters, and removes small defects.
4. The image is processed to find circles of a user-defined radius by constructing a Danielsson distance map to determine radii of all particles. This procedure provides with the number of detected circles, their calibrated position relative to the previously created set of coordinates, and the radius.

Next, we use algorithm which allows exchanging data with the PLC and it is responsible for robot motions.

5   Summary

The objectives of the paper and its requirements have been met in the final product, which represents an automated process with the use of an industrial robot. The achieved goals include the hardware implementation of a camera and tools for process execution, software implementation of a robot vision system fit with a visualization of the process presented in an HMI, three-way communication between the vision system, high-level controller and an industrial robot, and finally carrying out tests on the real object, while troubleshooting encountered difficulties on each step. The exemplary process used in the work was simple conceptually, but thanks to the added vision functionality due to the camera, the process can be further expanded. Exemplary modifications could include a more diversified object recognition regardless of its rotation, such as letter-shaped objects which the robot could arrange to reflect a user-defined keyword. Other changes would consist of improving the camera and the electromagnet, or transitioning to the use of a gripper. Achieving the goals of this paper involving the educational cell were a great introduction to industrial grade automated process design, and can be a subject for further development.

References

1. Bonilla, I., et al.: A vision-based, impedance control strategy for industrial robot manipulators. In: IEEE Conference on Automation Science and Engineering (CASE), pp. 216–221 (2010)
2. Bonilla, I., Mendoza, M., Gonzalez-Galván, E., Chavez-Olivares, C., Loredo-Flores, A., Reyes, F.: Path-tracking maneuvers with industrial robot manipulators using uncalibrated vision and impedance control. IEEE Trans. Syst., Man, Cybern., Part C Appl. Rev. **42**(6), 1716–1729 (2012)

3. Davies, E.R.: Machine Vision: Theory, Algorithms, Practicalities. Elsevier, Amsterdam (2004)
4. Glebocki, S.: Implementation and visualization of an exemplary process in a cell with a KUKA robot, Bachelor's Thesis, Silesian University of Technology (2019)
5. Guo, D., Ju, H., Yao, Y.: Research of manipulator motion planning algorithm based on vision. In: Sixth International Conference on Fuzzy Systems and Knowledge Discovery, 2009. FSKD 2009, vol. 5, pp. 420–425 (2009)
6. National Instruments: IMAQ image processing manual. http://www.ni.com/pdf/manuals/372320a. Accessed 09 Jan 2010
7. National Instruments: IMAQ vision for LabVIEW manual. http://www.ni.com/pdf/manuals/371007a. Accessed 09 Jan 2010
8. Jain, R., Kasturi, R., Schunck, B.: Machine Vision. McGraw-Hill, New York (1995)
9. Klinger, T.: Image Processing with LabVIEW and IMAQ Vision. Prentice Hall Professional, Upper Saddle River (2003)
10. KUKA Roboter GmbH: Operating and programming instructions for end users (2013)
11. KUKA Roboter GmbH: Operating and programming instructions for system integrators (2013)
12. Liu, Y., Hoover, A., Walker, I.: A timing model for vision-based control of industrial robot manipulators. IEEE Trans. Robot. **20**(5), 891–898 (2004)
13. Palenta, K., Babiarz, A.: Kuka robot motion planning using the 1742 NI smart camera. In: Gruca, D.A., Czachórski, T., Kozielski, S. (eds.) Man-Machine Interactions 3, pp. 115–122. Springer, Cham (2014). https://doi.org/10.1007/978-3-319-02309-0_12
14. Ren, L., Wang, L., Mills, J., Sun, D.: Vision-based 2-D automatic micrograsping using coarse-to-fine grasping strategy. IEEE Trans. Ind. Electron. **55**(9), 3324–3331 (2008)
15. Rendón-Mancha, J., Cárdenas, A., García, M., González-Galván, E., Lara, B.: Robot positioning using camera-space manipulation with a linear camera model. IEEE Trans. Robot. **26**(4), 726–733 (2010)
16. Siemens, A.G.: Programming guideline for S7–1200/S7-1500. http://www.siemens.com/simatic-programming-guideline. Accessed 09 Jan 2019
17. Sonka, M., Hlavac, V., Boyle, R.: Image Processing, Analysis, and Machine Vision. Cengage Learning, Boston (2014)
18. Svaco, M., Sekoranja, B., Suligoj, F., Jerbic, B.: Calibration of an industrial robot using a stereo vision system. Procedia Eng. **69**, 459–463 (2014). https://doi.org/10.1016/j.proeng.2014.03.012. http://www.sciencedirect.com/science/article/pii/S1877705814002586
19. Zyzak, P., Zeglen, D.: Zastosowanie systemu wizyjnego KUKA. VisionTech 3.0 zintegrowanego z robotem przemyslowym KUKA KR AGILUS do wyszukiwania pionkow na planszy szachowej. Przeglad Mechaniczny **11**, 32–39 (2015)

Rise and Rise of Blockchain: A Patent Statistics Approach to Identify the Underlying Technologies

Priyanka C. Bhatt[1], Vimal Kumar[1(✉)], Tzu-Chuen Lu[1(✉)], Rico Lee-Ting Cho[2], and Kuei Kuei Lai[3]

[1] Department of Information Management, Chaoyang University of Technology, Taichung City 413, Taiwan, Republic of China
bhattpriyanka88@gmail.com, {vimalkr,tclu}@cyut.edu.tw
[2] Wispro Technology Consulting Corporation, Taipei, Taiwan, Republic of China
ricocho@wispro.com
[3] Department of Business Administration, Chaoyang University of Technology, Taichung City 413, Taiwan, Republic of China
laikk@cyut.edu.tw

Abstract. Researchers have always tried to identify the technological evolution of any particular technology with the help of patent statistics. Blockchain is one such technology which, although emerged more than a decade ago, but has been aggressively applied and studied within the past five years only. Therefore, this study is an attempt to identify the underlying technologies that eventually constitute the Blockchain technology. This paper identifies the literature related to the primary Blockchain technologies and then tries to perform basic patent statistics to identify the earliest innovation that conforms to the idea of blockchain that we know today. Critical Cooperative Patent Classification (CPCs) codes to analyze Blockchain patents in the future are identified. Specific and detailed analysis methods are suggested for the future Blockchain patent research.

Keywords: Blockchain · Private-key cryptography · Distributed network · Patent statistics · Patent analysis

1 Introduction

Emerging technologies and innovation have come together as consociates in Industry 4.0. The swiftly changing digital technologies have affected all business operations and therefore there is need to understand the emerging landscape of technologies such as, Artificial Intelligence (AI), Internet of Things (IoT), Could Computing, and newest one Blockchain; and how these technologies affect the existing business models or operations. Blockchain has been termed as the most revolutionary and disruptive technology within past decade [1]. Blockchain was first introduced as the backstage technology for the cryptocurrency, Bitcoin. However, Blockchain technology as a whole provides

© Springer Nature Singapore Pte Ltd. 2020
P. Sitek et al. (Eds.): ACIIDS 2020, CCIS 1178, pp. 456–466, 2020.
https://doi.org/10.1007/978-981-15-3380-8_40

wider opportunities for any transactions that require authentication, which can be useful in sectors like supply chain, real estate, fintech, or public administration, particularly in organizations involved in valuable and sensible products. Various generations or phases of the Blockchain have been discussed by various researchers since 2008. Usually researchers classify Blockchain into three generations, however varying in their taxonomy. For instance, three generations, which are quite the basic classifications for Blockchain development are given by researchers [2, 3], where first generation refers to "Digital Currency", second generation as "digital economy or finance" and third one as "digital society". However, Yang et al. [4] highlight four Blockchain generations, where addition of fourth generation includes even more wider industrial applications of Blockchain using AI mechanisms, such as Neural Networks. Furthermore, Luthra [5] introduces fifth generation, which promises much smaller block-sizes and more than million transactions per second, e.g., Relictum Pro. In general, the major application of Blockchain technology has been centered around financial technology (Fintech), due to its ability to enable transparent, efficient and cost effective services in the domain [6].

Even though Bitcoin, the first product of Blockchain technology was introduced in 2008, the focus of academic research on this technology has reverberated only within past five years, showcasing the application trends of this technology on an increasing curve with varied domains. Therefore, it is also of much importance to understand the evolution of this technology within last decade. Patent analysis is the one major approach to understand the technological progress in any industry or domain by identifying the technology trends over the defined period of time. Patent analysis enables us to understand the innovation of a technology in addition to the academic research [7]. Patents usually represent the inventive capability as well as outputs of industries or organizations in different domains, times periods as well as countries. Various researchers [7–12] have tried to use different patent analysis techniques to identify technology trends, or technology forecasting in various domains for varying products or technology innovation and in different industries or organizations. Therefore, this paper aims to answer the research question: What has been the global development path of Blockchain technology?

2 Literature Review

Plethora of literature has emerged since past five years related to the concepts of Blockchain technology. A mere search of "Blockchain" on Scopus shows 7000 + results, tabulated in Table 1 below, where rise in publications can be seen from 10 in 2014 to more than 13% increase from year 2018, having more than 2800 results, and more than 4000 publications in 2019. Therefore, the popularity of the technology is certainly on a rising path. However, it does not imply that the technology was not at all present before the said period. Before Bitcoin, the concepts of Blockchain technology were present in fragmented form with diverse applications. It was in 2008 [13] when Bitcoin was introduced, which was built (or enhanced) upon three significant terminologies, namely, "private key cryptography, distributed network with shared ledger, and an incentive to service the networks' transactions, record keeping and security, eventually leading to Blockchain technology" [14–18].

It is thus important to understand the connectivity among these technologies to understand the rise of Blockchain as a whole. The basic idea of Blockchain is to add a

Table 1. Rise in number of academic publications on Blockchain

Year	No. of publications
2014	10
2015	37
2016	180
2017	804
2018	2820
2019	4040

transparency to any process without the intermediate authority. Moore and Tavares [19] proposed a private key cryptography algorithm, which had a 'transparency' property between the operation layers. McInnes and Pinkas [20] attempted a secure technique of secret information broadcast via communication lines using a secure cryptosystem. Beller et al. [21] tried to compare the public- and private- key cryptography to develop private and accurate Personal Communication Services (PCS). One important use of private key cryptography arose as in the digital signature systems since the early 90 s [22–24]. And with the rise of internet in 1998, and the enormous future possibilities that it brought, a rise in the concepts of e-commerce and web security provided a scope for further improvement in cryptography techniques. Previous researchers emphasized on the secure online transactions and the factor of trust among buyers and sellers for electronic trade [23, 25–28]. And intermittently, as the acceptance to e-commerce rose, the methods for secure e-payment [29] and record keeping started to emerge [30, 31], including the identity [32] as well as transaction [13] management.

Distributed networks and shared ledger have also existed over a significant period of time. Good [33] gave an introduction of distributed computing facility (DCF) which automated the process of teller function as well as the ledger updates. Duffy et al. [34] introduced the concept of a "general ledger" based on a distributed component, transaction-based architecture to support operations related to the transactions, inventory or workflow functions. And therefore, when the private key cryptography and a distributed network are executed together, in a Blockchain system, it signifies the proof of a transaction [18].

Incentive mechanism for the proof-of-work was first introduced by Back [35], upon which Nakamoto [13] built the Bitcoin functionality. This mechanism refers to solving a problem using computational power and energy, and once approved the transaction by the candidate (or miner) can be added or modified in the block [36–40].

These three technologies together, thus enable Blockchain technology to rule over the existing traditional, centralized ledgers or authoritative intermediaries in a transaction by enabling immutable as well as indestructible records of transactions verified by a shared system of global candidates or computers. And since the first concept of cryptocurrency, Bitcoin, in 2008, various applications have emerged of the underlying technology, i.e., Blockchain. Just as the academic literature, it is also important to understand the connecting thread between the underlying technologies in terms of invention and innovation over the years leading to the technology in subject, Blockchain. Therefore, this research tries to identify the technological innovation in Blockchain technology by analyzing the patents.

Patent statistics has been used over an extended period of time to understand the technology development or evolution [11, 41–44], important patents in an innovation [7, 45–48], as well as to predict the emerging technologies [11, 49, 50]. Although many studies have emerged regarding the analysis of patents in various domains, viz. fintech [44], artificial intelligence and machine learning [7], solar cells and energy [11, 43], to name a few. However, no study identifies the emergence of Blockchain through patent analysis.

This study, therefore, is an attempt to initiate the Blockchain patent statistic approach to understand the beginning of the technology as well as a way forward for future Blockchain patent research.

3   Research Process

This research identifies the patents from Derwent's Worldwide Patent Index (DWPI), specifically US patents based on Blockchain and its underlying technologies. First a search strategy is formulated to obtain the data. Data is then classified in excel and data cleanup is performed to obtain the relevant patents. A patent dataset is thus created for the analysis. Cooperative Patent Classification (CPC) codes, Yearly distribution of patents, and Assignee classification is analyzed to understand the evolution of Blockchain technology. The following sections provide detailed steps of the research process performed.

3.1   Data Collection

Step 1: Search Strategy – Keyword(s) selection and Search Strategy
The literature on Blockchain technology with respect to private key cryptography, distributed network and shared ledgers, helps to identify the accurate search keywords for the analysis. Therefore, the variation of keywords here are three principal technologies that combine to create a Blockchain. None of them are new, rather, it is their adaptation and application that is new. These technologies, as discussed in previous section are: (1) private key cryptography, (2) a distributed network with a shared ledger and (3) an incentive to service the network's transactions, record-keeping and security. Therefore, the search term for the data collection is constituted as follows".

ALL = ((blockchain* or "block-chain" or "block chain*") or (cryptograph* and "distributed network" and transaction*) or (cryptograph* and ledger* and transaction*));

The components included for the data retrieval from DWPI database are: Publication Number, Title, Title – DWPI, Application Number, Application Date, Publication Date, IPC – Current, IPC – Current – DWPI, Assignee/Applicant, Assignee – Current US, Inventor Count of Citing Patents, Count of Cited Refs – Patent, Citing Patents, Citing References Details – Patents, US Class, Abstract – DWPI, Assignee – Original w/address, CPC – Current, CPC – Current – DWPI.

This research used US patent data to conduct the patent analysis with two main reasons. First, the US is usually considered as an important market to patent owners so that patent owners may file patents with important inventions in US. Second, US may offer more complete patent systems, cases and resources from prosecutions to litigations. Patent owners may enforce their patent rights in the US against their competitors. For example, they may file lawsuit to those who may infringe their patents or may try to invalid competitors' patents to ensure freedom to operate business.

Step 2: Data Cleanup
After performing the search, a total of 3230 records were extracted. Data was cleaned up to exclude the records from chemistry or bio-chemistry domain. And after cleaning up the data for relevant records, a dataset of 2479 patents were finalized.

3.2   Analysis and Results

The dataset consisting of the underlying technologies that form Blockchain can be examined to consist of patents beginning from 1992. Thus, even though, Bitcoin was introduced in 2008, the underlying technologies had existed since a long time. Figure 1 showcases the yearly distribution of patents extracted from 1992 to 2019.

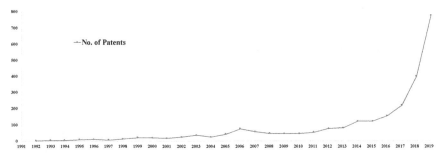

Fig. 1.   Yearly distribution of patents published for Blockchain and underlying technologies.

As observed in Fig. 1, compared to one patent application in 1992, patent no. US5121390A, to a rising graph around 2006–2008, where it is observed that 74, 56 and 46 patents were published respectively. And the number of applications goes on increasing to more than 100 patents since 2014, and a huge number of 774 published patents in 2019. This result conforms with the increasing popularity or period of growth of Blockchain after 2014–1205.

Another important factor to be analyzed from the dataset is that of Cooperative Patent Classification (CPC) code, which signifies the general classification of patent domain. Sometimes, a single patent publication is given more than one CPCs, depending upon the technology or domains used in the innovation. From the dataset of extracted patents, we were able to identify most prominent CPC codes, as shown in Fig. 2 below.

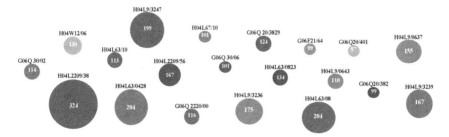

Fig. 2. Top current CPCs

Figure 2 illustrates the distribution of the CPCs based on our patent dataset. The circles with bigger size define more patents in a specific CPC. The top class is H04L, about transmission of digital information. H04L can be divided into further main sub-classes. For instance, the H04L 2209/38, with the most patents, is related to chaining technologies (e.g., hash chain or certificate chain). The H04L 63/08 is focusing on cryptographic mechanisms or cryptographic arrangements of authentication in a network, and the H04L 63/0428 is addressing encrypting or encapsulating in a network.

Another significant class of CPC is G06Q 20, which presents technologies associated with payment architectures, schemes or protocols. For example, G06Q 2220/00 demonstrates technologies about business processing using cryptography (e.g., use of third party for collecting or distributing payments). G06Q 20/4 shows authentication in payment process (e.g. identification of users, verification of customer or shop credentials) and review and approval of payers (e.g., check credit lines or negative lists). G06Q 30/06 corresponds to transaction process (e.g., buying, selling or leasing transactions during electronic shopping), and the most significant one that establishes connection with the Blockchain technology is that of G06F, which is related to the e-data processing and more specifically that of 'G06F 21/', which demonstrates technologies related to security and protection against unauthorized activity. Since, the rise of Blockchain technology can be observed from 2014, it is important to consider all these classes when analyzing the technological innovation in this domain.

Another substantial factor, while performing the patent analysis is the inventor or innovator. It is essential to understand the position of companies or organizations in the path of a particular technology evolution, as illustrated in Fig. 3. Hence, from the extracted dataset it is observed that International Business Machines (IBM) Corporation dominates the trend with a total of 128 published patents, followed by Accenture and Dell with 74 and 64 patents respectively. However, it should be noted that these patents do not necessarily comprise of Blockchain technology as a whole and may be of the underlying technologies as mentioned earlier. Although, some important mentions, related to the Blockchain technology are the assignee Hewlett Packard (HP) and Google Technology Holdings, with Publication number US5802497A and US6061449A respectively. These two could be considered as the earliest innovations leading to the concept of Blockchain being published in 1998 and 2000 respectively.

Patent publication number US5802497A describes a "Computerized commerce method for use in computer networks involves broker, vendor and customer systems

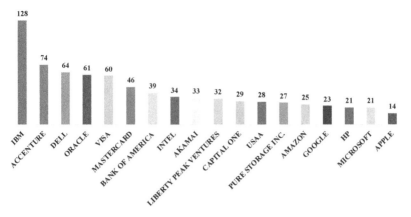

Fig. 3. Optimized patent assignees based on the number of published patents

exchanging broker and vendor scripts allowing purchase of vendor products" and publication number US6061449A describes "Descrambling receiver and cryptographic key generator for pay television applications and software copyright protection". These again conform to the underlying technologies of Blockchain. However, a more direct innovation, can be seen that of digital/virtual currency in the gaming platforms, most earliest application of Bitcoin, US8210934B2 which includes "Method of determining dynamic conversion rate between payment and requested virtual currency types used while playing online games, involves adjusting base conversion rate with game progression adjustment to determine conversion rate" with application date of year 2010 filed by assignee Zynga Inc.

4   Conclusion and Future Scope

Blockchain technology is still emerging and more recently, there has been a rigorous approach towards understanding and implementing this disruptive technology. Researchers and innovators are actively participating in identifying the capabilities of this technology. This study attempted to identify the existing literature on the underlying technologies of Blockchain and tried to find the innovations using patent data related to the same. It is an attempt to understand the beginning and to follow a direction for the Blockchain research. Based on the analysis of CPCs in previous section, it can be concluded that to perform the patent analysis for Blockchain, it is important to consider the classifications, such as, H04L, G06Q and, G06F. It is interesting to identify the earlier applications corresponding to the base technologies of Blockchain as discussed in previous section. The trend could be seen going from application of e-commerce (US5802497A) to digital currency for gaming platforms (US8210934B2), eventually rising to virtual payment sector and finally predominantly capturing the banking and transactions. After 2008, more increasing trend can be seen in the dataset towards patent applications related to secure and trusted virtual transactions, user authentication and identity management, secure electronic document revisions, dynamic transaction cards, internet of things (IoT) applications, biometric electronic signatures; all these applications consisting of underlying structure of private key cryptography or distributed networking. The market of

Blockchain, however is moving into a very diverse direction. From researchers [51–60] studying its amalgamation with other technologies such as Industry 4.0 technologies (Internet of Things, Cloud Computing, Cyber Physical Systems, Artificial Intelligence, Enterprise Architectures, etc.), to government bodies investing in research on Blockchain [17, 61–63], to various industries realizing the potential of this technology and thriving to introduce business models based on this technology [64–66]. Once, just a virtual currency technology, Blockchain is now being researched to be applied into almost every industrial application. Advances in other technologies also aid in more advanced application of Blockchain technology. For instance, penetration of 5G networking speeds in the market will certainly aid faster and more efficient Blockchain applications in all domains.

This research however had some limitations, even though a dataset of 2479 patents is formed, it is not sufficient to perform the patent analysis techniques to clearly identify the technology parameters. Further research should enclose patents from the other significant players (e.g., Chinese patents, European patents, etc.), so that we may expand technology development, business strategy and entrepreneurial activities to different areas to have clearer view on Blockchain industry. Also, this research is the first to consider Blockchain patent statistics and provides a way forward for detailed patent analysis and its need in the purview of Blockchain technology. Future direction of this research includes identifying the patent families to distinctly understand the earliest source of Blockchain technology with further applied domains and applications, such as healthcare, real-estate, e-commerce or fintech, etc. and, to expand further the research implications of Blockchain technology, using the patent analysis including main-path analysis as well as forecasting of the emerging trends based on Blockchain patent data. Blockchain as a technology has come a long-way than being identified as a pseudonym for Bitcoin and its applications are estimated to grow exponentially in next few years to come.

References

1. Fisch, C.: Initial coin offerings (ICOs) to finance new ventures: an exploratory study. J. Bus. Ventur. **34**, 1–22 (2019)
2. Efanov, D., Roschin, P.: The All-pervasiveness of the blockchain technology. Procedia Comput. Sci. **123**, 116–121 (2018)
3. Nowiński, W., Kozma, M.: How can blockchain technology disrupt the existing business models? Entrep. Bus. Econ. Rev. **5**, 173–188 (2017)
4. Yang, W., Garg, S., Raza, A., Herbert, D., Kang, B.: Knowledge management and acquisition for intelligent systems. In: 15th Pacific Rim Knowledge Acquisition Workshop, pp. 201–210. Springer, Cuvu (2019). https://doi.org/10.1007/978-3-319-97289-3
5. Luthra, E.S.: What the Emergence of Blockchain 5.0 Means for Business Managers and Entrepreneurs (2019). https://www.forbes.com/sites/forbestechcouncil/2019/11/14/what-the-emergence-of-blockchain-5-0-means-for-business-managers-and-entrepreneurs/#1ab69b135d47
6. Zavolokina, L., Dolata, M., Schwabe, G.: Enterprise applications, markets and services in the finance industry. In: Feuerriegel, S., Neumann, D. (eds.) 8th International Workshop, FinanceCom 2016. pp. 75–88. Springer, Frankfurt (2017). https://doi.org/10.1007/978-3-319-52764-2

7. Zambetti, M., Sala, R., Russo, D., Pezzotta, G., Pinto, R.: A patent review on machine learning techniques and applications: depicting main players, relations and technology landscapes. Proc. Summer Sch. Fr. Turco. **2018**, 115–128 (2018)

8. Mariani, M.S., Medo, M., Lafond, F.: Early identification of important patents: design and validation of citation network metrics. Technol. Forecast. Soc. Change. **146**, 644–654 (2019)

9. Choi, D., Song, B.: Exploring technological trends in logistics: topic modeling-based patent analysis. Sustainability **10**, 15–17 (2018)

10. Kim, D.H., Lee, B.K., Sohn, S.Y.: Quantifying Technology-Industry Spillover Effects Based on Patent Citation Network Analysis of Unmanned Aerial Vehicle (UAV). Technol. Forecast. Soc. Change. **105**, 140–157 (2016)

11. Huang, Y., Zhu, F., Guo, Y., Porter, A.L., Zhang, Y., Zhu, D.: Exploring technology evolution pathways to facilitate technology management: a study of dye-sensitized solar cells (DSSCs). In: PICMET 2016 - Portland International Conference on Management of Engineering and Technology: Technology Management For Social Innovation, Proceedings. pp. 764–776. Portland (2017)

12. Abraham, B.P., Moitra, S.D.: Innovation Assessment through Patent Analysis. Technovation **21**, 245–252 (2001)

13. Nakamoto, S.: Bitcoin: A Peer-to-Peer Electronic Cash System (2008)

14. Krylov, A.V., Gritsai, I.P.: Blockchain and cryptocurrency. Sci. Educ. Today **5**, 28–30 (2018)

15. Drescher, D.: Blockchain Basics: A Non-technical Introduction in 25 Steps (2017)

16. Sun, J., Yan, J., Zhang, K.Z.K.: Blockchain-based Sharing Services: what blockchain technology can contribute to smart cities. Financ. Innov. **2**, 26 (2016)

17. Berryhill, J., Bourgery, T., Hanson, A.: Blockchains Unchained: Blockcahin Technology and its Use in the Public Sector. OECD Working Papers on Public Governance, Paris (2018)

18. Rust II, R.W.: Banking on blockchains: a transformative technology reshaping latin american and caribbean economies. Univ. Miami Inter-American Law Rev. **50**, 185–211 (2019)

19. Moore, T.E., Tavares, S.E.: A layered approach to the design of private key cryptosystems. In: Williams, H.C. (ed.) Advances in Cryptology — CRYPTO 1985 Proceedings, pp. 227–245. Springer, Heidelberg (1986). https://doi.org/10.1007/3-540-39799-X_18

20. McInnes, J.L., Pinkas, B.: On the Impossibility of Private Key Cryptography with Weakly Random Keys. In: Menezes, A.J., Vanstone, S.A. (eds.) Advances in Cryptology-CRYPT0 1990, pp. 421–435. Springer, Heidelberg (1991). https://doi.org/10.1007/3-540-38424-3_31

21. Beller, M.J., Chang, L., Yacobi, Y.: Security for personal communications services: public-key vs. private key approaches. In: 1992 Proceedings on the Third IEEE International Symposium on Personal, Indoor and Mobile Radio Communications, pp. 26–31. IEEE (1992)

22. Adam, J.A.: Data security-cryptography = privacy? IEEE Spectr. **29**, 29–35 (1992)

23. Menascé, D.A.: Security performance. IEEE Internet Comput. **7**, 84–87 (2003)

24. Lorencs, A.A.: A problem of digital signature implementation based on the El gamal scheme. Autom. Control Comput. Sci. **37**, 56–61 (2003)

25. Skevington, P.J.: From security to trust - creating confidence to trade electronically. In: IEE Colloquium on eCommerce - Trading But Not As We Know It (Ref. No. 1998/460). pp. 6/1-6/6. IEE, London, UK (1998)

26. Khalifa, O.O., Islam, M.D.R., Khan, S., Shebani, M.S.: Communications cryptography. In: Ghodgaonkar, D.K., Esa, M., Lin, A., Awang, Z., Habash, R.W. (eds.) 2004 RF and Microwave Conference, RFM 2004. pp. 220–223. Selangor (2004)

27. Camp, L.J.: Web security and privacy: an american perspective. Inf. Soc. **15**, 249–256 (1999)

28. Vlachos, I., Kalivas, D., Panou-Diamandi, O.: An electronic post market surveillance system for medical devices. Comput. Meth. Programs Biomed. **71**, 129–140 (2003)

29. Nguyen, T.N.T., Shum, P., Chua, E.H.: Secure end-to-end mobile payment system. In: 2005 2nd Asia Pacific Conference on Mobile Technology, Applications and Systems. IEEE, Guangzhou (2005)

30. Bansal, A.: Mobile e-health for developing countries. In: HEALTHCOM 2006 8th International Conference on e-Health Networking, Applications and Services, pp. 224–227. IEEE, New Delhi (2006)

31. Boyen, X., Shacham, H., Shen, E., Waters, B.: Forward-secure Signatures with untrusted update. In: CCS 2006: 13th ACM Conference on Computer and Communications Security. pp. 191–200. Alexandria, VA (2006)

32. Chow, S.S.M.: Verifiable pairing and its applications. In: Lim, C.H., Yung, M. (eds.) WISA 2004. LNCS, vol. 3325, pp. 170–187. Springer, Heidelberg (2005). https://doi.org/10.1007/978-3-540-31815-6_15

33. Good, J.R.: Experience with a large distributed banking system. Database Eng. **6**, 50–56 (1983)

34. Duffy, M., Haren, P., Schenck, J.: A distributed object framework for financial applications. In: 2nd International Enterprise Distributed Object Computing Workshop, EDOC 1998. pp. 148–154 (1998)

35. Back, A.: Hashcash - A Denial of Service Counter-Measure (2002). http://www.hashcash.org/papers/Hashcash.Pdf

36. Singh, S., Singh, N.: Blockchain: future of financial and cyber security. In: 2nd International Conference on Contemporary Computing and Informatics, IC3I 2016, pp. 463–467. Institute of Electrical and Electronics Engineers Inc. (2016)

37. Tang, S., Chow, S.S.M., Liu, Z., Liu, J.K.: Fast-to-finalize nakamoto-like consensus. In: Jang-Jaccard, J., Guo, F. (eds.) ACISP 2019. LNCS, vol. 11547, pp. 271–288. Springer, Cham (2019). https://doi.org/10.1007/978-3-030-21548-4_15

38. Lo, Y.C., Medda, F.: Bitcoin mining: converting computing power into cash flow. Appl. Econ. Lett. **26**, 1171–1176 (2019)

39. Gramoli, V.: From blockchain consensus back to byzantine consensus. Futur. Gener. Comput. Syst. (2017)

40. He, Y., Li, H., Cheng, X., Liu, Y., Yang, C., Sun, L.: A blockchain based truthful incentive mechanism for distributed P2P applications. IEEE Access **6**, 27324–27335 (2018)

41. Ho, M.H.-C., Lin, V.H., Liu, J.S.: Exploring knowledge diffusion among nations: a study of core technologies in fuel cells. Scientometrics **100**, 149–171 (2014)

42. Rosenkopf, L., Nerkar, A.: Beyond local search: boundary-spanning, exploration, and impact in the optical disk industry. Strateg. Manage. J. **22**, 287–306 (2001)

43. Kumar, V., Chen, H.C., Lin, C.Y., Lai, K.K., Chang, Y.H.: Technological evolution of thin-film solar cells through main path analysis. In: ACM International Conference Proceeding Series. pp. 160–164 (2018)

44. Lin, C.Y., Su, F.P., Lai, K.K., Shih, H.C., Liu, C.C.: Research and development portfolio for the payment fintech company: the perspectives of patent statistics. In: ACM International Conference Proceeding Series. pp. 98–102 (2018)

45. Park, H., Magee, C.L.: Tracing technological development trajectories: a genetic knowledge persistence-based main path approach. PLoS ONE **12**, e0170895 (2017)

46. Verspagen, B.: Mapping technological trajectories as patent citation networks: a study on the history of fuel cell research. Adv. Complex Syst. **10**, 93–115 (2007)

47. Su, F.P., Lai, K.K., Yang, W.G., Sharma, R.R.K.: A heuristic procedure to identify most valuable chain of patents in a given technology. In: PICMET: Portland International Center for Management of Engineering and Technology, Proceedings, pp. 1959–1965 (2009)

48. Chang, S.B., Lai, K.K., Chang, S.M.: Exploring technology diffusion and classification of business methods: using the patent citation network. Technol. Forecast. Soc. Change **76**, 107–117 (2009)

49. Érdi, P., et al.: Prediction of emerging technologies based on analysis of the US patent citation network. Scientometrics **95**, 225–242 (2013)

50. Breitzman, A., Thomas, P.: The emerging clusters model: a tool for identifying emerging technologies across multiple patent systems. Res. Policy **44**, 195–205 (2015)
51. Kak, E., Orji, R., Pry, J., Sofranko, K., Lomotey, R., Deters, R.: Privacy improvement architecture for IoT. In: 2018 IEEE International Congress on Internet of Things (ICIOT), pp. 148–155. IEEE (2018)
52. Arutyunov, R.: The next generation of cybersecurity in oil and gas. Pipeline Gas J., **245** (2018)
53. Rawat, D.B., Parwez, M.S., Alshammari, A.: Edge computing enabled resilient wireless network virtualization for internet of things. In: Proceedings - 2017 IEEE 3rd International Conference on Collaboration and Internet Computing, CIC 2017, pp. 155–162. Institute of Electrical and Electronics Engineers Inc. (2017)
54. Agbo, B., Qin, Y., Hill, R.: Research directions on big IoT data processing using distributed ledger technology: a position paper. In: Chang, V., Ramachandran, M., Walters, R., Muñoz, V.M., Wills, G. (eds.) 4th International Conference on Internet of Things, Big Data and Security, IoTBDS 2019, pp. 385–391 (2019)
55. Shyamala Devi, M., Suguna, R., Joshi, A.S., Bagate, R.A.: Design of IoT blockchain based smart agriculture for enlightening safety and security. In: Somani, A.K., Ramakrishna, S., Chaudhary, A, Choudhary, C., Agarwal, B. (eds.) ICETCE 2019. CCIS, vol. 985, pp. 7–19. Springer, Singapore (2019). https://doi.org/10.1007/978-981-13-8300-7_2
56. Tosh, D.K., Shetty, S., Liang, X., Kamhoua, C.A., Kwiat, K.A., Njilla, L.: Security implications of blockchain cloud with analysis of block withholding attack. In: 2017 17th IEEE/ACM International Symposium on Cluster, Cloud and Grid Computing (CCGRID), pp. 458–467. IEEE (2017)
57. Singh, J., Michels, J.D.: Blockchain as a service (BaaS): providers and trust. In: 2018 IEEE European Symposium on Security and Privacy Workshops (EuroS&PW), pp. 67–74. IEEE (2018)
58. Kirillov, D., Iakushkin, O., Korkhov, V., Petrunin, V.: Evaluation of tools for analyzing smart contracts in distributed ledger technologies. In: 19th International Conference on Computational Science and its Applications, ICCSA 2019, pp. 522–536 (2019)
59. Mendes, D., Rodrigues, I.P., Fonseca, C., Lopes, M.J., García-Alonso, J.M., Berrocal, J.: Anonymized distributed PHR using blockchain for openness and non-repudiation guarantee. Stud. Health Technol. Inform. **255**, 170–174 (2018)
60. Ince, P., Liu, J.K., Zhang, P.: Adding confidential transactions to cryptocurrency IOTA with bulletproofs. In: Au, M.H., Yiu, S.M., Li, J., Luo, X., Wang, C., Castiglione, A., Kluczniak, K. (eds.) NSS 2018. LNCS, vol. 11058, pp. 32–45. Springer, Cham (2018). https://doi.org/10.1007/978-3-030-02744-5_3
61. Grody, A.D.: Rebuilding financial industry infrastructure. J. Risk Manage. Financ. Inst. **11**, 34–46 (2018)
62. Batubara, F.R., Ubacht, J., Janssen, M.: Challenges of blockchain technology adoption for e-Government: a systematic literature review. In: C.C., H. and A., Z. (eds.) 19th Annual International Conference on Digital Government Research: Governance in the Data Age, DG.O 2018 (2018)
63. Wijaya, D.A., Liu, J.K., Suwarsono, D.A., Zhang, P.: A new blockchain-based value-added tax system. In: Okamoto, T., Yu, Y., Au, M.H., Li, Y. (eds.) ProvSec 2017. LNCS, vol. 10592, pp. 471–486. Springer, Cham (2017). https://doi.org/10.1007/978-3-319-68637-0_28
64. Carson, B., Romanelli, G., Walsh, P., Zhumaev, A.: Blockchain Beyond the Hype: What is the Strategic Business Value? McKinsey Co. (2018)
65. Heutger, M.: Blockchain in Logistics: Perspectives on the Upcoming Impact of Blockchain Technology. Dtsch. Post DHL Gr. Accent. pp. 1–28 (2018)
66. Benhamouda, F., Halevi, S., Halevi, T.: Supporting private data on hyperledger fabric with secure multiparty computation. In: 2018 IEEE International Conference on Cloud Engineering (IC2E), pp. 357–363. IEEE (2018)

Recommendation and User Centric Applications of Intelligent Systems

Person Search by Queried Description in Vietnamese Natural Language

Thi Thanh Thuy Pham[1], Dinh-Duc Nguyen[2], Ba Hoang Phuc Ta[1],
Thuy-Binh Nguyen[2,3], Thi-Ngoc-Diep Do[2], and Thi-Lan Le[2(✉)]

[1] Academy of People Security, Hanoi, Vietnam
[2] International Research Institute MICA,
Hanoi University of Science and Technology, Hanoi, Vietnam
`Thi-Lan.Le@mica.edu.vn`
[3] University of Transport and Communications, Hanoi, Vietnam

Abstract. Nowadays, surveillance camera systems are widely deployed today from public places to private houses. This leads to huge image databases. Recent years have witnessed a significant improvement of surveillance video analysis, especially for person detection and tracking. However, finding the interested person in these databases is still very challenging issue. A majority of the existing person search methods bases on the assumption that the example image of the person of interest is available. This assumption is however not always satisfied in practical situations. Therefore, recently, person search by using query of natural language description has attracted the attention of researchers. However, they mainly dedicate to queried descriptions in English. In this paper, we propose a person search method with query of Vietnamese natural language. For this, Gated Neural Attention - Recurrent Neural Network (GNA-RNN) is employed to learn the affinity from pairs of description and image and then to estimate the similarity between query and images in the database. To evaluate the effectiveness of the proposed method, extensive experiments have performed in two datasets: CUHK-PEDES with description translated in Vietnamese and our own collected dataset named VnPersonSearch. The promising experimental results show the great potential of the proposed method.

Keywords: Person search · Natural language · Vietnamese query · Deep learning

1 Introduction

Person searching is a crucial problem in many applications such as automatic surveillance, digital forensics for criminal investigation or action analysis. Surveillance camera systems are widely deployed today from public and crowded places to private houses. This leads to huge image databases. Recent years have witnessed a significant improvement of surveillance video analysis, especially for person detection and tracking. However, finding the interested person in these

© Springer Nature Singapore Pte Ltd. 2020
P. Sitek et al. (Eds.): ACIIDS 2020, CCIS 1178, pp. 469–480, 2020.
https://doi.org/10.1007/978-981-15-3380-8_41

databases is still very challenging issue. Figure 1 shows the position of person search in a camera-based surveillance system. There are two approaches for person searching. The first one is based on the available images of a person. The searching system will automatically find the corresponding targets by matching the queried images with the collected images from different surveillance cameras. This is a well-known problem of person ReID (re-identification) in computer vision [1]. In the second approach, a person is found out by matching the descriptive sentences about her/him with the collected person images. This relates to solve both problems of natural language processing and image processing. Basing on the input of text sequences about a person, the system will give the visual output of related ones. This is an emerging problem that has been studying in recent years with many open issues needed to be considered. In comparison with the first approach of person ReID by visual attributes, person search by language descriptions brings a more flexible and effective way in describing interested people [2]. In fact, in some situations, criminal investigation for example, it is often that the sample image of person of interest is unavailable. Meanwhile a lot of evidence is gathered from the initial testimony of witnesses or related subjects in the cases. The problem is how to get from this initial testimony, the system can automatically find corresponding images from a huge amount of visual data captured by surveillance cameras. Although the potential of the problem is high, due to its challenging, few works have been proposed for person search through natural language [2–4]. Moreover, these works are totally dedicated to English language.

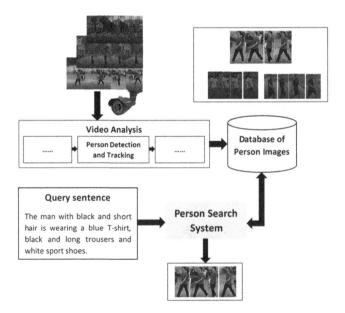

Fig. 1. The position of person search in a camera-based surveillance system.

In this paper, we propose for the first time a person search method by using Vietnamese language description. The proposed method bases on the Gated Neural Attention - Recurrent Neural Network (GNA-RNN) that is proposed for English query-based person search. In order to evaluate the effectiveness of the proposed approach, two main works are conducted: (1) experiments are carried out on the existing database of pairs of person image-English language description. However, these English sentences are translated into Vietnamese and pre-processed before putting into the training model; (2) Expanding the experimental database by building another database of 72 Vietnamese people, with the Vietnamese descriptive sentences for the person images. The experimental results are quite satisfactory for the first time to apply deep learning models for person image query problem based on the description of natural language in Vietnamese.

2   Related Work

Person searching based on natural language description is a new problem that has been researched in recent years. It is the inverse case of popular problem of image caption, in which the description sentences are given out from the corresponding images. The person searching problem has to tackle one main issue: How to find out the correspondence/affinity between image attributes and words and sentences. In order to solve this problem, the current approach mainly uses deep learning neural networks. However, in order to effectively apply these networks, it is necessary to solve two main issues. The first one is preparing the database for model training. The second issue is building a model that can well describe the relationship between the word/sentence description and the related image attributes.

There are a few databases of description sentences and related images, currently. The research given in [3] uses 5 descriptive sentences for each person, each description must have at least 8 words and the description must contain all the important components of people like clothes, their actions. In [2], the authors proposed two sentences for each image in the ReID database. The descriptive sentences contain rich vocabulary, phrases, structures and sentence components. The descriptors do not have any language constraints to describe. Another type of description is given in [4], in which the authors have a built-in interface that guides the descriptors to use 5–20 words depending on the complexity of the scene. In this report, a total of 25 attributes are divided into 8 classes. In general, the above mentioned datasets are all devoted for English descriptions and person images are mainly European and American. The descriptive style as well as perspective on the described objects also bring cultural characteristics of foreigners. Therefore it will not be suitable for the Vietnamese culture which is expressed through the Vietnamese language.

The deep learning models that present the relation between sentence/word description are proposed in some resent studies. The methods for embedding images-visual semantics are proposed in [5–7] to learn to embed language and images into a common space to classify and search images. In [8], a CNN-RNN (Convolution Neuron Network - Recurrent Neural Network) model was trained to embed images and descriptions simultaneously into the same feature space for zero-shot learning. Based on this, searching from text to image is possible by calculating the distances in the embedded space. In [9], the authors have linked semantic knowledge of text objects to image objects by building a deep image-visual semantics model which can simultaneously train the neural-network-based language and the image object recognition models. The research in [2] used GNA-RNN (Gated Neural Attention - Recurrent Neural Network) network to search for people in the images based on descriptive sentences. In this model, a text description and the corresponding image of a person will be the input, and the output is the relationship between them.

In short, the experimental results in the recent announcements of deep learning networks for the problem of person search by natural language description are still modest. This shows the challenge of the problem and it still requires new researches, especially for Vietnamese language used for description of Vietnamese person images. In this work, GNA-RNN model in [2] is applied for the first time for person search by Vietnamese query sequences. The model is trained on the Vietnamese database of descriptions. In addition, a new Vietnamese person dataset and the corresponding language descriptions in Vietnamese style is built for experimental evaluation.

3   Proposed Method

The overall framework of person searching based on Vietnamese natural language descriptions is presented in Fig. 2. The proposed framework consists of two phases: training phase and retrieval phase. In the training phase, Gated Neural Attention (GNA-RNN) network [2] is employed to train the language-vision model from sentence-image pairs. Then, in the retrieval phase, given a Vietnamese language query, the affinity between the query and the images in the database is estimated. In the following section, we will describe in detail how to learn sentence-image affinity and how to estimate the affinity of the query with the images in the database.

3.1   Learning Sentence-Image Affinity by GNA-RNN

In order to learn the affinity between sentence and image, in [2], the author proposed GNA-RNN network. The network consists of two sub networks: visual-sub network and language-sub network. The main goal of the visual-sub network is to capture the human appearance attributes such as yellow T-shirt, black hair, ... while the language-sub network aims at learning the importance of the visual neurons through attention network and the role of different words in a sentence through LSTM network (Fig. 3).

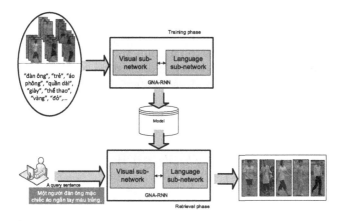

Fig. 2. The proposed framework for person retrieval based on Vietnamese language.

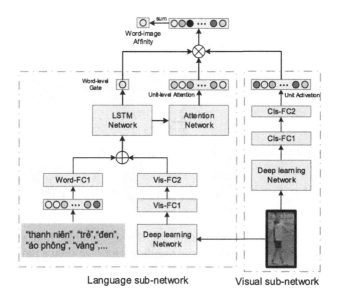

Fig. 3. A Recurrent Neural Network with Gated Neural Attention mechanism adapted from [2]

Visual Sub-network. Given a person image, the visual sub-network computes visual neurons $\mathbf{v}$ that allows to capture human appearance. In the original work, 512 visual neurons denoted by $\mathbf{v} = [v_1, ..., v_{512}]^T$ are generated based on VGG-16 with two added fully connected layers. It is worth to note that other networks such as ResNet [10] can be used in the visual sub-network.

Language Sub-network. In the language sub-network, given a pair of sentence-image, the network computes embedding word feature x_t^w and image feature x^v, then concatenate them to an input vector $x_t = [x_t^w, x_v]^T$ for LSTM network. LSTM with a memory cell c_t, hidden state h_t and three controlling gates: input gate i_t, output gate o_t, forget gate f_t is defined as follows:

$$
\begin{aligned}
i_t &= \sigma \left(W_{x_i} x_t + W_{h_i} h_{t-1} + b_i \right), \\
f_t &= \sigma \left(W_{x_f} x_t + W_{h_f} h_{t-1} + b_f \right), \\
o_t &= \sigma \left(W_{x_o} x_t + W_{h_o} h_{t-1} + b_o \right), \\
c_t &= f_t \odot c_{t-1} + i_t \odot h \left(W_{x_c} x_t + W_{h_c} h_{t-1} + b_c \right), \\
h_t &= o_t \odot h \left(c_t \right),
\end{aligned}
\tag{1}
$$

The hidden state of LSTM for each word h_t is fed into attention network in order to result attention value $A_t(n)$ for this word. As different words carry significantly different amount of information for obtaining language-image affinity, the word-level gate tries to compute words's weight. For this, the hidden state of LSTM h_t will be mapped via a fully-connected layer with sigmoid non-linearity function.

$$
g_t = \sigma(W_g h_t + b_g)
\tag{2}
$$

The affinity between word t^{th} and person image is defined as follows:

$$
a_t = g_t \sum_{n=1}^{512} A_t(n) v_n
\tag{3}
$$

Then the network is trained by using the cross entropy loss:

$$
E = -\frac{1}{N} \sum_{i=1}^{N} \left[y^i \log a^i + (1 - y^i) \log \left(1 - a^i \right) \right]
\tag{4}
$$

where a^i denotes the predicted affinity for the ith sample, and y^i denotes its ground truth label: $y^i = 1$ for the corresponding sentence-image pairs and $y^i = 0$ means non-corresponding ones.

3.2   Person Search Through Vietnamese Query

Once the GNA-RNN network is trained by using image-sentence pairs, in the retrieval phase, given a sentence query, the affinity of each word in the query with the images in the database is computed using Eq. 3. Then the affinity between a query sentence and each image in the database is computed as follows: $a = \sum_{t=1}^{T} a_t$, where T is the number of words in sentence query. A list of images ranked by its affinity with the query sentence is returned to the users.

4 Building Dataset of Vietnamese Descriptive Sentence-Image

Since there is no person dataset with textual description in Vietnamese available, to evaluate the proposed method, we prepare two datasets. The first one is taken from the database of CUHK-PEDES [2] in which the English descriptive sentences are translated to Vietnamese and pre-processed. The second one is our dataset named VnPersonSearch. It contains Vietnamese person images and the corresponding descriptive sentences in Vietnamese.

4.1 CUHK-PEDES Dataset

CUHK-PEDES is a large-scale language dataset which contains 40.206 images of 13,003 persons from five existing person ReID datasets (CUHK03, Market-1501, SSM, VIPER, CUHK01) [2]. Each person image is described with English descriptions written by two independent workers on Amazon Mechanical Turk (AMT) (each description can contain one or more sentences). There are 80,412 descriptions, containing abundant vocabularies, phrases, and sentence patterns and structures in English. The descriptions are generally long, and has abundant vocabulary and little repetitive information. In comparison with other image caption datasets such as MS-COCO or Visual Genome, the description length is significantly longer, and most descriptions have 20 to 40 words. There are a total of 1,893,118 words and 9,408 unique words in the dataset. The longest description has 96 words and the average description length is 23.5 words.

In order to use this dataset for our work, the English sentences are translated to Vietnamese by Google Translate API[1]. These results are then processed by a step of word/token segmentation for Vietnamese. It is an important step to keep the right semantic in Vietnamese language processing.

Vietnamese is an isolating language in which the basic unit is syllable. In writing, syllables are separated by a white space. One word corresponds to one or more syllables. Almost vocabulary is created by two or more syllables (80% of words are bi-syllable). For example a Vietnamese sentence "Một người đàn ông mặc áo khoác màu đen" (in English: a man wears a black coat) containing 9 syllables is segmented into 5 words as follows "một(one) người_đàn_ông(man) mặc(wear) áo_khoác(a coat) màu_đen(black)". These segmented units are words and also called tokens. We use the underscore symbol '_' to concatenate syllables into a word. Therefore we can keep the space as the separator for word/token. There are several popular word segmentation tools for Vietnamese such as JVnSegmenter, vnTokenizer, UETsegmenter. In this paper, we use RDRsegmenter tool which is reported to be outperformed other tools at this moment in both accuracy and performance speed. The current accuracy of the RDRsegmenter is reported on a two thousand sentence testing set is about 97.90% F1 score [11]. The main error of word segmentation is ambiguity error, for example: the sequence of word "tổ hợp âm" can

---

[1] https://cloud.google.com/translate/docs/ Cloud Translation documentation.

Frequence of sentence length
Number of sentences=80440
μ=26.10, std=9.83
max=115, min=9
Frequence
Sentence length
Frequence of sentence length
Number of sentences=890
μ=31.74, std=11.06
max=80, min=10
Frequence
Sentence length

(a) (b)

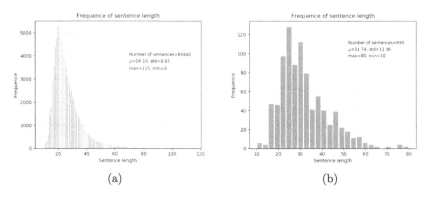

Fig. 4. Frequency of Vietnamese sentence length in (a) CUHK-PEDES dataset and (b) VnPersonSearch dataset.

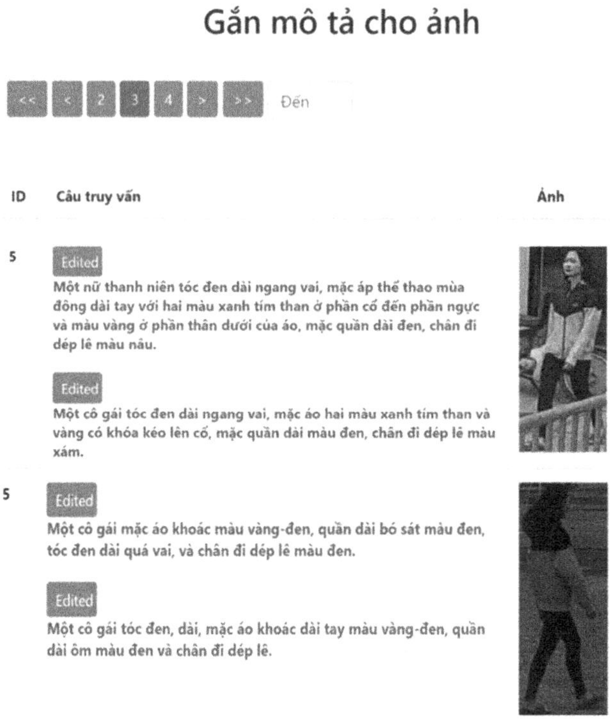

Gắn mô tả cho ảnh
<< < 2 3 4 > >> Đến
ID
Câu truy vấn
Ảnh
5
Edited
Một nữ thanh niên tóc đen dài ngang vai, mặc áp thể thao mùa đông dài tay với hai màu xanh tím than ở phần cổ đến phần ngực và màu vàng ở phần thân dưới của áo, mặc quần dài đen, chân đi dép lê màu nâu.
Edited
Một cô gái tóc đen dài ngang vai, mặc áo hai màu xanh tím than và vàng có khóa kéo lên cổ, mặc quần dài màu đen, chân đi dép lê màu xám.
5
Edited
Một cô gái mặc áo khoác màu vàng-đen, quần dài bó sát màu đen, tóc đen dài quá vai, và chân đi dép lê màu đen.
Edited
Một cô gái tóc đen, dài, mặc áo khoác dài tay màu vàng-đen, quần dài ôm màu đen và chân đi dép lê.

Fig. 5. Web-based interface for editing Vietnamese descriptions of person images.

be segmented as "tổ_hợp âm" (combination of sound) or "tổ hợp_âm" (group of chords). Figure 4a shows the histogram of Vietnamese description length in word/token of the CUHK-PEDES dataset. It can be seen from this chart that most descriptions have 17 to 29 words in length, the longest one has 115 words, the shortest is 9 words. And the average length is 26.10 words. There are a total of 2.099.259 words and 4.872 unique words. Vocabulary is built for CUHK-PEDES with Vietnamese descriptions based on the rules in [2]. Each work/token appearing less than five times in the database will be removed from the vocabulary (considered as UNK words). The number of these unknown words is 2.836 words (0.14% of the total words). Therefore, the vocabulary size for this dataset is 2.096.423 words.

4.2 VnPersonSearch Dataset

VnPersonSearch dataset includes person images of 72 people. Each person has around 6 images which are taken from manual bounding boxes on the frames captured from different cameras with different field of views. Each image has two descriptions that made by different subjects. To facilitate the description process, a web-based interface is developed for the descriptors to give the sentences for the relating person images (see Fig. 5). There are a total of 445 person images with 890 descriptions. Average length of the descriptions is 31.74 words, the longest one contains 80 words and the shortest one has 10 words (see Fig. 4b). There are 494 unique words with a total of 28.251 occurrences in the dataset.

5 Experimental Results

In this section, we show the evaluation metrics and the experimental results on two above-mentioned datasets of CUHK-PEDES with Vietnamese descriptive sentences and VnPersonSearch.

5.1 Evaluation Measures

In this work, top-k ranking is used to evaluate the performance of Vietnamese descriptive sentence-based person search. The system calculates the similarity of a query sentence with all testing images and ranks these images according to their affinities with the query. A successful person ID retrieval is achieved if the images of the corresponding person ID is among the top-k images. In our experiments, the accuracy of top-1, top-5 and top-10 accuracy are reported.

5.2 Experimental Results on CUHK-PEDES

Table 1 shows the obtained results of person search using queried description in English and in Vietnamese. For both English and Vietnamese, we perform the experiment as described in [2]: the descriptions that are longer than 50 words/tokens will be cut down to 50 and the shorter ones of 50 will remain the same. The CUHK-PEDES dataset is split into three subsets for training, validation and test without having person identity overlaps. The training set contains 11.003 persons, with 34.054 images and 68.108 Vietnamese descriptions. The validation set includes 3.078 images for 1000 persons, with 6.156 Vietnamese descriptions, The test set consists of 3.074 images with 6.148 descriptions for 1000 persons. It can be seen from the Table 1 that top-1, top-5, and top-10 accuracies when using Vietnamese query are a little bit smaller than those obtained with English query [2]. The difference of accuracy at top-1 is only 1.31%. This shows the effectiveness of the pre-processing tool and proposed method. The decrease of accuracy can be caused by the quality of the automatic translation tool.

Table 1. Top-k accuracy for CUHK-PEDES dataset with Vietnamese descriptive sentences.

Ranking	Using English sentences [2]	Using Vietnamese sentences
Top-1	19.71%	18.40%
Top-5	43.20%	39.87%
Top-10	55.24%	52.34%

5.3   Experimental Results on VnPersonSearch

For VnPersonSearch, we perform two cross-dataset evaluations. This means we do not retrain the network on VnPersonSearch dataset. The pre-trained model on CUHK-PEDES dataset in Vietnamese is used. In the first evaluation, all 890 descriptions for 445 images of 72 people are used as query. For each description, only one person that corresponds to the description in the dataset is considered as relevant. This evaluation is similar to the evaluation in CUHK-PEDES dataset [2]. In the second evaluation, we ask a subject to express his/her own new queries. These queries does not need to be similar to the descriptions in the database. For each query, a list of retrieved persons will be returned by the method. The relevant persons will be manually marked in order to compute the accuracy of the system. In this evaluation, one female subject has given 28 queries in Vietnamese natural language. To show the search result, we have developed an web interface that allows users to express their query and see the list of retrieved persons ranked by the affinity between the query and person image. Figure 6 shows a snapshot of our web interface. The Vietnamese query is "Một cô gái tóc đen, mặc áo cộc tay màu trắng, mặc quần sẫm màu" (in English: A girl with black hair wears a white T-shirt and a dark color trouser). The relevant persons are returned as shown in the Figure. Among retrieved persons, the persons with the IDs 25, 56, 68 and 71 are relevant while those with IDs 9, 10, 49 are mismatched.

Table 2 shows the accuracy for Top-1, Top-5, Top-10 of the two evaluations. These results are higher than the ones in Table 1 for Vietnamese queried description. This shows that on the same trained model, the testing data of pure Vietnamese style including sentences described in Vietnamese language and the

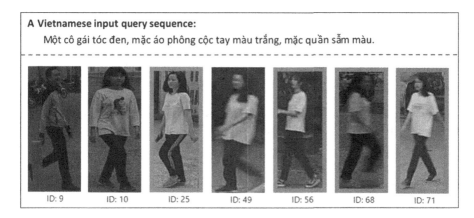

A Vietnamese input query sequence:
Một cô gái tóc đen, mặc áo phông cộc tay màu trắng, mặc quần sẫm màu.

ID: 9   ID: 10   ID: 25   ID: 49   ID: 56   ID: 68   ID: 71

Fig. 6. An example of retrieval result with a Vietnamese query sequence.

corresponding Vietnamese person images gives better results than the automatically translated Vietnamese sentences as in Table 1. It is also depicted in the Table 2 that the accuracy for two evaluations are relatively similar. The accuracy at top-1 of the second evaluation is lower than that of the first evaluation. However, those for top-5 and top-10 are higher. The results can be explained by the fact that the first evaluation employs a stricter rule: one relevant person for one query. However, in reality, there are several persons that are relevant to the same query. The results of the two evaluations also show that the performance of the Vietnamese-query based person search method is quite promising. The method can return the relevant person in the ten first results with approximately 70% of probability (66.4% in evaluation 1 and 71.4% in evaluation 2).

Table 2. Results obtained on VnPersonSearch with two evaluations. The best result is in bold.

Ranking	Results of evaluation 1	Results of evaluation 2
Top-1	**26.85%**	25.00%
Top-5	52.47%	**53.57%**
Top-10	66.40%	**71.4%**

6   Conclusion

In this paper, for the first time, a person search method with Vietnamese language description based on the Gated Neural Attention - Recurrent Neural Network (GNA-RNN) is proposed. To evaluate the effectiveness of the proposed approach, two datasets are prepared: CUHK-PEDES with description translated in Vietnamese and our own collected dataset named VnPersonSearch.

Extensive experiments have been performed on these two datasets. The obtained experimental results show that the performance of the Vietnamese-query based person search method is quite promising. However, the collected Vietnamese description-image pair dataset is relatively small and the obtained accuracy is still needed to be improved in order to deploy in real applications.

Acknowledgement. This research is funded by Vietnam National Foundation for Science and Technology Development (NAFOSTED) under grant number 102.01-2017.315.

References

1. Nguyen, T.B., Le, T.L., Devilliane, L., Pham, T.T.T., Pham, N.N.: Effective multi-shot person re-identification through representative frames selection and temporal feature pooling. Multimedia Tools Appl. **78**(23), 33636–33967 (2019)
2. Li, S., Xiao, T., Li, H., Zhou, B., Yue, D., Wang, X.: Person search with natural language description. In: Proceedings of the IEEE Conference on Computer Vision and Pattern Recognition, pp. 1970–1979 (2017)
3. Yamaguchi, M., Saito, K., Ushiku, Y., Harada, T.: Spatio-temporal person retrieval via natural language queries. In: Proceedings of the IEEE International Conference on Computer Vision, pp. 1453–1462 (2017)
4. Zhou, T., Chen, M., Yu, J., Terzopoulos, D.: Attention-based natural language person retrieval. In: Proceedings of the IEEE Conference on Computer Vision and Pattern Recognition Workshops, pp. 27–34 (2017)
5. Gkioxari, G., Malik, J.: Finding action tubes. In: Proceedings of the IEEE conference on computer vision and pattern recognition, pp. 759–768 (2015)
6. Nagaraja, V.K., Morariu, V.I., Davis, L.S.: Modeling context between objects for referring expression understanding. In: Leibe, B., Matas, J., Sebe, N., Welling, M. (eds.) ECCV 2016. LNCS, vol. 9908, pp. 792–807. Springer, Cham (2016). https://doi.org/10.1007/978-3-319-46493-0_48
7. Soomro, K., Idrees, H., Shah, M.: Action localization in videos through context walk. In: Proceedings of the IEEE international conference on computer vision, pp. 3280–3288 (2015)
8. Reed, S., Akata, Z., Lee, H., Schiele, B.: Learning deep representations of fine-grained visual descriptions. In: Proceedings of the IEEE Conference on Computer Vision and Pattern Recognition, pp. 49–58 (2016)
9. Frome, A., Corrado, G.S., Shlens, J., Bengio, S., Dean, J., Mikolov, T., et al.: Devise: A deep visual-semantic embedding model. In: Advances in Neural Information Processing Systems, pp. 2121–2129 (2013)
10. He, K., Zhang, X., Ren, S., Sun, J.: Deep residual learning for image recognition. CoRR abs/1512.03385 (2015)
11. Nguyen, D.Q., Nguyen, D.Q., Vu, T., Dras, M., Johnson, M.: A fast and accurate Vietnamese word segmenter. In: Proceedings of the Eleventh International Conference on Language Resources and Evaluation (LREC-2018), Miyazaki, Japan, European Languages Resources Association (ELRA), May 2018

A Proposal of Personalized Information Distribution System Using Smart Watch and Wireless Headphones

Takuya Ogawa[1]([envelope]), Takuya Fujihashi[2], Keiichi Endo[1], and Shinya Kobayashi[1]

[1] Graduate School of Science and Engineering, Ehime University, Matsuyama, Japan
ogawa@koblab.cs.ehime-u.ac.jp
[2] Graduate School of Information Science and Technology, Osaka University,
Osaka, Japan

Abstract. There is a huge amount of news information on the Internet
while the Internet user is interested in a part of the news information. It
takes a cost to find the user's interest news from a huge amount of news
information. In this paper, we propose NEAR, which is a smartphone
application that learns the user's interest and provides a limited amount
of news information based on the learned interest. By using NEAR, users
do not need to search for his/her preferred news information. In addition, NEAR can provide the preferred information by voice to know the
information without looking at the smartphone's display. In this case,
the proposed NEAR can provide voice-based information from the user's
smart watch in addition to his/her smartphone. This is for a situation
where each user does not use his/her own smartphone such as the congestion on the train. Evaluation results show that NEAR can provide many
amounts of user's preferred news information compared with the text-
based conventional application. This is because the users browse many
amounts of news information from the proposed NEAR and the proposed
NEAR learns his/her interest from many times of past browsing.

Keywords: Information distribution system · User-aware · Smart
watch · Wireless headphone

1 Introduction

Many people use the Internet to obtain news information. Figure 1 shows changes
in the Internet usage rate [1]. This figure shows the percentage of households
using the Internet over the past year. From this figure, you can see that so many
people use the Internet. The purpose of using the Internet is shown in Fig. 2 [1].
This figure shows the percentage of Internet services used over the past year.
From this figure, it can be seen that many people acquire news information from
the Internet.

However, news delivered via the Internet does not take into consideration
individual interests. Therefore, when a user reads Internet news, they need to

P. Sitek et al. (Eds.): ACIIDS 2020, CCIS 1178, pp. 481–492, 2020.
https://doi.org/10.1007/978-981-15-3380-8_42

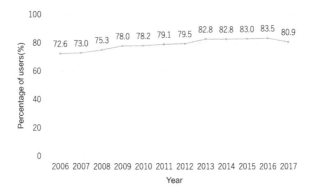

Fig. 1. Internet usage rate

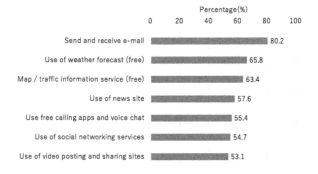

Fig. 2. Purpose of using the Internet

find interesting news from a huge amount of news. It is said information overload that makes it difficult for users to select useful information due to an increase in information. In order to solve the information overload in Internet news, individual information development system "PINOT" (Personalized INformation On Television screen) which displays news information on the TV screen in consideration of the user's interest was developed in previous research [2].

Next, the devices used when using the Internet are shown in Fig. 3 [1]. From this figure, it can be seen that the Internet is often used from smartphones. From this data and the purpose of using the Internet, it can be expected that many people obtain news information using smartphones. However, many news applications provide the user with all of the distributed information, and users need to find the information they want to read. In order to solve information overload in news applications for smartphones, smartphone applications using PINOT were developed in previous research [3].

However, the developed app could not provide news unless the user spontaneously launched the app. Therefore, even if the news of interest is distributed, the news may not be provided to the user, and the learning opportunity of

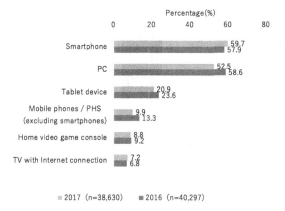

Fig. 3. Types of internet devices

interest has been lost. In order to obtain the user's interest more accurately and to provide only the news of interest to the user, it is necessary to prevent the loss of the learning machine. Therefore, we proposed an application in which a news headline display function on a wristwatch-type wearable device was added to a smartphone application that applied PINOT. However, there was no increase in the number of learnings.

2   Previous Researches

2.1   Smartphone Version PINOT

Introduction. Given the fact that the Internet is widely used on smartphones, we thought that there were problems of information overload in acquiring news information on smartphones. To solve the problem of information overload, the smartphone version PINOT was developed. The smartphone version PINOT is a smartphone application having the PINOT function.

Overview. An overview of smartphone version PINOT is shown in Fig. 4. The smartphone version PINOT consists of an information distribution server that distributes news and a smartphone that the user uses. When the user activates the PINOT application on the smartphone, the smartphone acquires the news information from the information distribution server. Information filtering based on the interests of the user is performed on the acquired news information so that only news that the user is interested in is provided to the user.

Learning User Interests. Smartphone version PINOT provides news information that users are interested in. The procedure for determining the interest in news headlines is as follows.

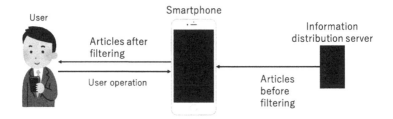

Fig. 4. Overall image of smartphone version PINOT

1. Acquire the degree of interest for each word

   For each word $w_n(n = 1, 2, ..., N)$ extracted in Step 2, refer to the user profile and calculate the degree of interest of each word $i(w_n)(0 \leq i(w_n) \leq 1)$. Where N is the total number of extracted words. If the extracted word is a new word that is not included in the user profile, $i(w_n) = 1$.

2. Calculate the degree of interest in character information

   Use the following expression(1) to calculate the degree of interest $I(W)$ for the article header text W. This $I(W)$ is the average value of the degree of interest $i(w_n)$ of each extracted word.

$$I(W) = \frac{\sum_{n=1}^{N} i(w_n)}{N} \tag{1}$$

Smartphone version PINOT analogizes and learns the user's interest from the behavior of the user's application.

– Estimate of the interest in the displayed article headline

   If the degree of interest in the article headline exceeds the threshold, it will be displayed on the smartphone. The user's interest is estimated by the tap operation performed by the user on the displayed article headline.

   In the article headline sentence that the tapped article headline sentence is "interested", the headline sentence not tapped is judged as "not interested", and estimate the interest of the article headline.

– Update user profile

   Updating the user profile means that the degree of new interest of each word w_n extracted from the article headline text W based on the result of estimating interest in the article headline text W (iw_n), and rewrite them to new ones. The degree of interest is calculated for each word $w_n(n = 1, 2, ...N)$ using the following expression (2).

$$i(w_n) := \alpha \cdot i(w_n) + (1 - \alpha) \cdot J \tag{2}$$

Here, J takes a value of 1 if it is judged as "interested" in the estimate of the interest in the headline sentence and takes a value of 0 if it is judged as "not interested". The amount of change in the degree of interest of the word is adjusted by the threshold α. If the value of α is small, when updating the degree of interest of a word, the proportion of the degree of new interest increases, and conversely, if α is large, the proportion of the degree of old interest increases.

By repeatedly updating the user profile, the numerical value of the degree of interest of the word frequently appearing in the character information of interest increases, and the numerical value of the degree of interest of the word frequently appearing in the character information not interested Is low. As a result, user profiles matching the user's interests are created.

Problem of Smartphone Version PINOT. The articles provided to users by PINOT are limited to those distributed when the user launches the PINOT application. Articles distributed during a period when the user has not used the application are not provided to the user even if the content is in accordance with the user's interest. PINOT cannot learn the user's interest in those news articles. As the learning opportunities decrease, it is possible that articles provided to the user may not be accurately considering the user's interests. In order to reduce the necessity of sorting out information by the user, it is required to prevent the loss of learning opportunities.

2.2   Smart Watch Cooperation PINOT

Introduction. The problem with the smartphone version PINOT was that the user's interest in news delivered during the period when the user did not launch the app could not be learned. The reason why the user did not start the application is that the user could not start the application. An example of a situation where an app cannot be started is when a car is driving. Under these situations, it is difficult to use a smartphone and the user cannot use the application. Therefore, we thought that it was possible to prevent loss of learning opportunities of interest by providing information to users from devices other than smartphones.

Therefore, we proposed a smart watch cooperation PINOT that adds a smart watch news provision function to the smartphone version PINOT [4]. By providing news using a smart watch, the user can obtain the news without operating the smartphone. In addition, with the smartphone version PINOT, news that was delivered during the period when the user did not launch the app was not provided to the user even if they encountered interesting content. However, smart watch cooperation PINOT automatically acquires news information and provides news on the smart watch in consideration of the user's interest. Users can get news on smart watch, reducing the chances that they will miss news that interests them.

Overview. An overview of the smart watch cooperation PINOT is shown in Fig. 5. This system consists of a server that sends a silent notification, a server of a news site, an iPhone that the user uses, and an Apple Watch. The server of the news site provides news information to the iPhone. The iPhone automatically gets news when it receives a silent notification. The iPhone provides news information to the user, and learns the user's interest from the user's behavior on the provided news information. Through learning, articles that are determined to be interested are sent by Apple Watch. Articles sent from iPhone are displayed on Apple Watch, and those that the user wanted to read are designated as "Articles read later".

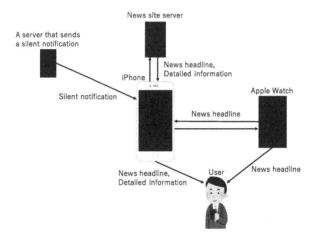

Fig. 5. Overview of Smart Watch Cooperation PINOT

Idea to Encourage Users to Launch Applications. Apple Watch displays only the news articles that are judged to be of interest to users from the news articles that are distributed. When user tap the headline sentence displayed on Apple Watch, the article is saved on your iPhone as an "Articles read later". "Articles read later" is displayed when the iPhone application is launched by the user. By tapping "Articles read later" on iPhone, the user can obtain the detailed information of the article. In order to know the details of "Articles read later", the user needs to use the application of the iPhone, which allows the user to launch the application.

Users can also see other news by launching the application. If there is content of interest among them, the user is expected to read the news, which leads to an increase in the number of times of learning.

Problems of Smart Watch Cooperation PINOT. As a result of the evaluation experiment of the smart watch cooperation PINOT, there was no change in the number of learning of the user's interest. One reason is that the information provided on Apple Watch was limited. In smart watch cooperation PINOT, the information provided to users from Apple Watch was limited to news headlines in consideration of the screen size of Apple Watch. However, for news that the user is interested in, the information that the user wants is detailed information, not a headline. The use of the iPhone was indispensable for users to obtain the information they wanted with the smart watch cooperation PINOT. As a result, users were not given the benefit of using Apple Watch. Therefore, we thought that there was a need for an app that could provide users with detailed news information without using a smartphone.

3   Proposed System

3.1   NEAR

We propose "NEAR" (News EAR), which adds a function to provide information by voice to the smartphone version PINOT so that users can obtain detailed information without operating the smartphone [6]. In recent years, with the widespread use of wireless headphones, it is considered that there are many opportunities for users to obtain voice information. The provision of information by voice in contrast to the provision of information by text eliminates the need for the user to visually recognize the device, so the usage scene of the application can be expected to expand. In addition, since it is not necessary to consider the screen size, there is no need to limit the information to be provided. Therefore, the information that the user wants can be acquired without using a smartphone. A radio news program is one way to obtain news information while driving a car. However, radio programs cannot provide news considering personal interests. By using this system, it is possible to get news taking into account individual interests while driving.

3.2   Related Research

There are many applications for smartphones that learn user's interest and provide information according to the user's interest. One example of such an application is "NCRRA" (News Curation and RSS Reader Application) [5]. NCRRA learns the user's interests and provides information according to the learned user's interests. And by adding an RSS reader function, it is possible to collect information specialized to the user's interest. As described above, many news applications including NCRRA have a mechanism for preferentially providing news that the user likes. On the other hand, the information provided to the user is often text information, and there are few ideas about the providing method. NEAR aims to create an app that learns more about the user's interests by devising a new way of providing news to the user.

3.3   Overview

An overview of the NEAR is shown in Fig. 6. In this system, the user can makes requests from the smart watch to skip and previous the spoken news information and to play detailed information. From these operations, the application analogizes the user's interest. By providing the news that the user is interested in by voice, the user can obtain the news information of interest without operating the smartphone.

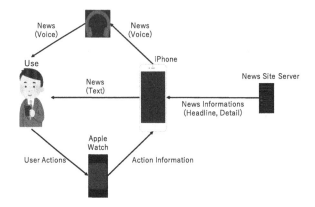

Fig. 6. Overview of NEAR

3.4   Operation for Voice Information

The operations related to voice information are as follows.

- Play
  Start speaking news.
- Pause
  Stop speaking news.
- Skip
  Skip the current news and speak the next news.
- Previous
  Speak the previous news.
- Rewind
  Speak the current news from the beginning again.
- Play Detailed Information
  Speak the detailed information of the current news.
- Update
  Update news information.

Among these operations, the operations that are determined to be of interest are the previous, rewind, and play detailed information operation. Also, the operation to determine that there is no interest is Skip.

User can operate these operations not only from iPhone but also from Apple Watch. By enabling operation from Apple Watch, users can obtain detailed information on news of interest without touching the iPhone at all.

3.5   Speaking Speed

When providing information by voice, the playback speed of voice is one of the important factors. If the user cannot hear the voice, it will be difficult to obtain the news information accurately. Because it has the property of providing information only by voice, a news program on radio was used as a reference, and a standard speed for speaking news was set. And by making it possible to set the speed from the standard speed in 5 steps from 0.8 times to 1.2 times, it is possible to provide information at a speed that is easy for the user to hear.

4 Experimental Results and Discussion

By using NEAR, we investigate how the number of times the app learns the user's interest changes. smart watch cooperation PINOT is used as a comparison target of NEAR. In the evaluation experiment, the application is used by multiple users, and the number of times the application is activated, the number of displayed news articles, and the number of times it is determined to be interesting are recorded. When using NEAR, record the number of times information was provided by voice and the number of times learning of interest was performed by the user's operation on the information provided by voice. In this experiment, applications were used for 7 users. 4 out of 7 people use Apple Watch. Evaluate whether setting the user who uses Apple Watch and the user who doesn't use it will affect the presence or absence of Apple Watch.

The records when using smart watch cooperation PINOT and NEAR are shown in Table 1. For each count, the average per activation of the application is described. The average number of displayed news articles and the number of times it is determined to be interesting in the proposed system in the Table 1 do not include information provided by voice and learning of interest by user operation on them. By omitting the provision of information by voice, we evaluate how much each application was able to provide news and learn to users in situations where smartphones can be used. In addition, the average number of displayed news articles and the average number of times it is determined to be interesting when the user who uses Apple Watch and the user who did not use Apple Watch are divided are also described.

From the Table 1, 5 out of 7 users increased the number of displayed news articles and the number of times it is determined to be insteresting by using NEAR. In addition, the average number of displayed news articles and the number of times it is determined to be insterestings of all users are more when the proposed system is used.

Next, we focus on the difference between users who used Apple Watch and those who did not. Although the number of displayed news articles increased regardless of whether or not Apple Watch was used, it can be seen that the number changed significantly when Apple Watch was used. In addition, as for the number of times it is determined to be insterestings, it can be seen that only the average of users using Apple Watch is increasing.

Next, the Table 2 shows the number of times information is provided by voice and the number of times learning of interest was performed by the user's operation on the information provided by voice in the proposed system. From the Table 2, we evaluate the number of times we were able to provide information to users without using a smartphone display.

Table 1. Providing information when smartphones can be used

Smart Watch Cooperation PINOT

Apple Watch	User	Average number of displayed news articles	Average	Average number of times it is determined to be interesting	Average
Available	User A	11.2	20.5	0.0	0.5
	User B	28.4		0.6	
	User C	16.0		0.9	
	User D	26.6		0.4	
Unavailable	User E	14.0	23.5	0.3	0.4
	User F	46.8		0.8	
	User G	9.8		0.1	
	Average	21.8		0.4	

NEAR

Available	User A	16.8	30.6	0.4	1.0
	User B	26.8		2.2	
	User C	18.3		0.3	
	User D	60.6		1.0	
Unavailable	User E	19.0	24.5	0.4	0.4
	User F	38.5		0.5	
	User G	16.0		0.4	
	Average	28.0		0.7	

Table 2. Providing information by voice

Apple Watch	User	Number of times of speaking news	Number of times it is determined to be interesting	Average number of times of speaking news	Average number of times it is determined to be interesting
Available	User A	23	10	30.2	22.7
	User B	124	78		
	User C	9	1		
	User D	29	2		
Unavailable	User E	39	2	17.0	1.0
	Uscr F	7	1		
	User G	5	0		

Table 3. Providing information by NEAR

Apple Watch	User	Average number of displayed news articles	Average number of times it is determined to be interesting	Average	Average
Available	User A	16.8	1.6	30.6	2.1
	User B	26.8	5.2		
	User C	18.3	0.5		
	User D	60.6	1.1		
Unavailable	User E	19.0	0.4	24.5	0.5
	User F	38.5	0.8		
	User G	16.0	0.4		
	Average	28	1.4		

From the Table 2, it can be seen that the users that use Apple Watch acquire more news information by voice and learn more interests by voice than users that not use Apple Watch. Users who do not use Apple Watch need to use iPhone when user want to obtain news information by voice. However, users who use Apple Watch can obtain information without having to operate the iPhone by using Apple Watch. From this result, it can be said that providing information by voice is useful as a method of providing news information in situations where a smartphone cannot be used.

Lastly, the Table 3 shows the number of displayed news articles and the number of times it is determined to be insterestings, including provided news information by voice in NEAR.

From these results, it can be said that the number of learning of the user's interest is increased by using NEAR.

5   Summary and Future Challenges

We proposed NEAR, a smartphone application that provides news information to users by voice. By providing information by voice, it is possible to obtain information in situations where the smartphone cannot be operated, such as when driving a car. In this paper, the evaluation of NEAR was described. As a result of the evaluation, we were able to provide more information than conventional apps. Therefore, NEAR can learn the user's interest in more news articles, and can provide the user with news information that reflects the user's preference.

Since this evaluation experiment was conducted with a small number of people, the data is not sufficient. Therefore, in the future, we will ask further users to use NEAR, and investigate how the provision of information by voice has brought about changes to users.

References

1. Ministry of Internal Affairs and Communications, Japan: "2018 White Paper on Information and Communications in Japan"
2. Personal information distribution system "PINOT". http://koblab.cs.ehime-u.ac.jp/misc/pinot/intro.html. Accessed 15 Oct 2019
3. Ono, S., Inamoto, T., Higami, Y., Kobayashi, S.: Development of the smartphone application to choose and display news for individuals based on an operation history. In: Multimedia, Distributed, Cooperative and Mobile Symposium 2016 Proceedings in Japanese (2016)
4. Ogawa, T., Fujihashi, T., Endo, K., Kobayashi, S.: Increasing the chance of interest learning in the user-aware information distribution system using a smart watch. In: The 5th International Symposium on Affective Science and Engineering (2019)
5. Yanagisawa, N., Terasawa, T.: A proposal and implementation of news curation application using RSS. In: Proceedings of the 79th National Convention of IPSJ in Japanese, vol. 2017, no. 1, pp. 565–566 (2017)
6. Ogawa, T., Fujihashi, T., Endo, K., Kobayashi, S.: Personalized Information Distribution System Using Smart Watch and Wireless Headphones. In: Multimedia, Distributed, Cooperative and Mobile Symposium 2019 Proceedings in Japanese (2019)

A Recommender System for Trip Planners

Rathachai Chawuthai$^{(\boxtimes)}$ ⓘ, Prodpran Omarak, and Vitchaya Thaiyingsombat

Department of Computer Engineering, Faculty of Engineering,
King Mongkut's Institute of Technology Ladkrabang, Bangkok, Thailand
{rathachai.ch,58010804,58011148}@kmitl.ac.th

Abstract. Making a trip plan is a key activity for having a satisfying trip for tourists. However, as we survey, there are many users do not need to spend a lot of time to write the plan, and it becomes a pain point for users. The users prefer to have a simple way to create a whole trip plan from a few users' constraints, and the users just customize some items for their satisfaction. Thus, this work introduces a recommender system that mainly employs the genetic algorithm for generating a trip plan. The approach accepts a few roughly input requirements from users, and then it creates a whole trip schedule and allows users to modify. To have a quality trip plan, any places and times in the plan have to correspond to places' categories, open weekdays, times to spend, favorite daytimes and months, and possible routes. A web application for trip planner is developed to demonstrate the suitability and feasibility of the proposed recommender system. After that, the user feedback and usage statistic present the high degree of user satisfaction and opportunity to improve tourism of any city.

Keywords: Genetic algorithm · Recommender system · Travel itinerary · Trip planner

1 Introduction

It is known that travelling is one of the most popular activities for enhancing living standards [1]. In general, before travelling, users search information about the destination via any travel websites such as Google Travel [2], Expedia [3], Kayak [4], TripAdvisor [5], etc. for finding some popular travel attractions to make an own travel itinerary plan. As discussions with users, searching for travel information and making a satisfying plan took a long time especially in locations that they do not know before. As we provide a questionnaire to 473 people whose age above 20 years old, we found that 30.6% of samples do not like to do a trip plan, 26.3% of samples spend 2 days, 25.2% of samples spend 3 days for making a 3-day trip plan, 36.1% of samples use to have no idea when arriving the target place, and 83.4% of samples prefer to have an application to make a trip plan. Based on our discussion and questionnaire, we would like to introduce a persona of Mr. Dan in order to give a simple explanation about a pain point of users to demonstrate our research problem.

Persona: Dan is a senior salesman working in a company in Europe. He has to go to Chonburi province in Thailand for visiting one customer on Friday and the other

© Springer Nature Singapore Pte Ltd. 2020
P. Sitek et al. (Eds.): ACIIDS 2020, CCIS 1178, pp. 493–504, 2020.
https://doi.org/10.1007/978-981-15-3380-8_43

customer on Monday, so he has free days on Saturday and Sunday. He personally plans to attend the Loi Krathong festival at Pattaya floating market in the evening of that Saturday, and he prefer to go to any temples and beaches anytime. Since he is very busy due to his job, he does not have time to find information for making his trip plan on that weekend. He needs a trip plan that contains a few places from his conditions, and the trip plan must be filled by other possible places in a suitable time and routes.

The scenario of this persona is commonly found in real life when users do not have much time to do a trip plan. For this reason, this paper aims to introduce a recommender system that recommends a trip plan from a few constraints from users. The generated plan is also targeted to satisfy suitable places, categories, times, and routes.

In this paper, the data modelling was designed, the recommendation model was proposed by employing the power of the generic algorithm [6], and a trip planner application was implemented in order to demonstrate the suitability and feasibility of our approach. The evaluation against real users showed the high degree of user satisfaction and opportunity to improve city tourisms.

To this end, the overall of our research is explained in Sect. 1, relate work and computational methods are reviewed in Sect. 2, our recommender system and the application are proposed in the Sect. 3, the results are described and discussed in Sect. 4, and conclusion and future work are drawn in Sect. 5.

2 Literature Review

In this section, related work and the artificial intelligent that benefits to our work are studied.

2.1 Related Work

As we studied the state of the art of research about trip planning [7], some key criteria of the trip planner are emphasized, such as mandatory places (must see), multiple days support, possible routing, and opening times. There are many pieces of research aims to do trip planning in various perspectives. Vansteenwegen et al. estimated user preference through a questionnaire in order to create a city trip plan [8]. Yoon et al. used the statistical analysis on social information including user-generated GPS trajectories to recommend a trip plan [9]. Zeng introduced the trajectory mining for trip recommendation [10]. Lu et al. recommended a trip plan based on trip packages and budgets of tourists, and emphasized on user preferences and temporal aspects [1].

In addition, some applications about trip planning are reviewed. We first studied Google Travel [2]. Due to a very big data held by Google, Google Travel analyzed travel data from many users at the tourist destinations to generate a list of things to do and suggested day plans. For the latter feature, the suggested day plans are itineraries that users commonly traveled. The plans are categorized into interesting groups for users to choose, for example, markets, inside the city, old towns, temples, natures, etc. Second, we study Inspirock [11]. This application provides a simple user scenario to create a trip plan. Users are allowed to create a personal plan based on a day-by-day trip, book some hotels and restaurants nearby the tourist place, and manage the plan by editing them in a timeline and calendar. Third, we reviewed Roadtrippers [12]. This application is created for travel along a roadside. It also recommends some interesting places nearby users in order to let users have a convenient trip plan.

2.2 Artificial Intelligence

A closer look at our challenge indicates that our research problem is similar to a task scheduling problem and a vehicle routing problem. Both problems are commonly solved by the Genetic Algorithm (GA) [13, 14]. GA is a well-known technique of Artificial Intelligence (AI) [6]. It is a search heuristic that finds an optimal answer using the process of natural selection inspired by the theory of natural evolution of Charles Darwin. There are 4 main steps.

1. **Chromosome Encoding** is a step to transform any features of a solution into a sequence of genes in a chromosome.
2. **Initial Population** is to randomly create the population of candidate chromosomes or candidate solutions.
3. **Fitness Function** is a defined function to value the quality of chromosomes.
4. **Genetic Operator** is an activity to create a new solution from existing ones. There are selection, crossover, and mutation. First, selection is to select high qualitied chromosomes determined by the fitness function. Second, crossover is to exchange some parts of two chromosomes to be new solutions. Last, mutation is to randomly change some genes to other ones.

3 Method

To demonstrate how the proposed method works, this section describes an approach to the trip planner application. Contents includes definitions, key user scenario, system design, data modeling, and a proposed technique.

3.1 Definitions

First, this part expresses some definitions used by our recommender system and application. The terms are formally explained as follows:

poi. The point of interest (poi) is expressed by the relation *(name, loc, avg_visit_hrs, fav_daytimes, fav_months, open_weekdays)*, where *name* is the name of that *poi*; *loc* is a location including the latitude and the longitude of the *poi*; *avg_vist_hrs* is an average hours that most tourists visit that *poi*; *fav_daytimes* is a set of favorite periods in a day for tourist including morning, noon, afternoon, evening, night; *fav_months* is a set of favorite months of the *poi*; and *open_weekdays* is a set of week days that tourists can visit that place including sun to sat (Sunday to Saturday). For example, going to a temple in the morning is more attractive than another time, going to a bazaar at nighttime is better, etc.

cat. Due to requirements from users, users can choose a category of tourist attractions such as nature, building, sport, temple, market, etc. The category is a named category of *pois*.

pcat. The *pcat* is the function mapping between a *poi* and a *category*. The function is denoted by $pcat: POIS \times CATS \rightarrow VAL$; where *POIS* is a set of *pois*, *CATS* is a set of named categories, and *VAL* is a set of real number between 0 and 1 for representing the possibility of a *poi* under that category. For example, in case a place *p* has a 70% possibility to belong to a category *c*, it can be expressed by *pcat(p, c) = 0.7*. The relationship between *pois* and *cats* is many-to-many. For example, some beaches can be categorized as natural places 100% and can be markets 50%.

travel_time. The *travel_time* shows the travel time in minutes between 2 pois within a 50-km radius. It is formulated by $travel\_time: POIS \times POIS \rightarrow VAL$, where *VAL* is a set of real number representing minutes between both *pois*.

trip_event. The *trip_event* is a relation (*poi, begin_datetime, end_datetime*) where *poi* is a previously described *poi*, *begin_datetime* is a beginning date time of the event, and *end_datetime* is the end of date time of the event.

trip_plan. The *trip_plan* is a sequence of none-overlapped *trip_event*.

pref_event. The *pref_event* is a preferent event that users give a condition to be an input of the recommender system. It is represented by a relation (*POIS, CATS, begin_datetime, end_datetime*), where *POIS* is a set of *pois*, and *CATS* is a set of categories. Users do not need to give all parameters to *pref_event*, because it is used to be a sketchy event to generate possible *trip_event* for the recommender system. For example, *(any, {nature}, any, any)* means users prefer to go to any natural places at any time in a trip plan.

3.2 Key User Scenario

As the goal of the trip planner, the application allows users to create a complete trip schedule by oneself quickly. Thus, some key requirements are demonstrated by user scenario including the following steps

1. Users enter a start date, duration, and a target city or town.
2. Users add some specific places and specific time periods (input *trip_event*), for example, going to the national museum at 13:00 of the first day.
3. Users give some categories of tourist places with or without specific time periods (input *pref_event*), for instance, going to any market in the morning of the second day.
4. Users get a whole trip schedule (*trip_plan*) generated by the trip planner.
5. Users can ask for regenerating the whole trip schedule; they can fix some trip events and regenerate the other unfix events; and they can ask for regenerating some events directly but not the whole plan.
6. Users can save the final trip plan.

3.3 System Design

To build the trip planner to serve the according scenario, the system is designed and demonstrated through the system architecture diagram as shown in Fig. 1. The system architecture has 5 components that are located in 3 tires: an application tier, a service tier, and a data tier; and all components are described as follows.

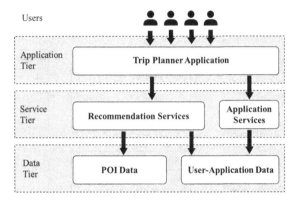

Fig. 1. The system architecture of the trip planner system

Trip Planner Application. A web application that allows users to register, login, logout, specify some requirements, get the whole trip plan, edit the plan, and save. The application has been implemented using HTML and JavaScript that access information from the service tier. Users can input *trip_event* and *pref_event*, and they finally view a *trip_plan* at this application.

Recommendation Services. This service is written using Python for providing core functions of the recommender system. It generates a *trip_plan* from input *trip_events* and *pref_events*. The technical detail of this module is described in hereafter part.

Application Services. This module provides other helpful functions for supporting the trip planner application, for example, register, login, logout, forgot password, edit user profile, etc.

POI Data. The POI Data is a database containing data about trips and places. It covers poi, cat, pcat, travel_time, trip_event and saved trip_plan.

User-Application Data. This module stores other data that used by users and applications, for example, data about user profiles and application configurations.

3.4 Data Modeling

According to the definitions, the database is modeled as shown in Fig. 2. There are 4 main tables for building a trip plan that are POIS, CATS, PCAT, TRAVEL_TIME,

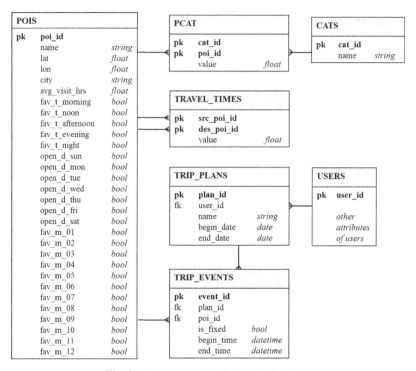

Fig. 2. The data model of the POI database

TRIP_PLANS, and TRIP_EVENTS, and the other tables including USERS to fulfill the application. The table POIS, CATS, PCAT, TRAVEL_TIME, TRIP_PLANS,
and TRIP_EVENTS represents the definitions *poi*, *cat*, *pcat*, *travel_time*, *trip_plan*,
trip_event respectively. In the table POIS, there are many Boolean attributes that correspond to favorite daytimes (*fav_t_* ~), open weekdays (*open_d_* ~), and favorite months
(*fav_m_* ~). For the table PCAT, it shows the many-to-many relations between *pois* and
categories with a possibility value as described in the definition. In addition, the table
TRIP_EVENTS represents the relation between a *poi* and a time period. It also has an
attribute "is_fixed" in case the user is satisfied that *trip_event* and informs the recommender system not to change the *poi* and the period after regenerating a new trip plan.

3.5   Trip Planner Technique

To generate a trip plan, the recommender system employs the genetic algorithm to
be a key component of our recommendation model. Our recommendation model is
demonstrated in a flow as shown in Fig. 3. There are 8 activities in the flow that are
described in the following steps.

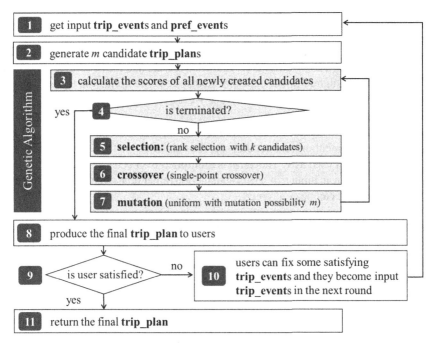

Fig. 3. Trip Planner Recommender System Flow

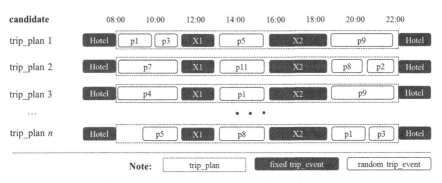

Fig. 4. The idea of generated candidate trip_plans

1. First, the recommender system get data about the user plan including city, start date, and end date. The application also submits *trip_events* and *pref_events* to be key conditions of the plan.

2. Second, the recommender system generates possible *m trip_plans* or candidates as depicted in Fig. 4. It is noted that the *m* is a configured number of candidate *trip_plans*. This work uses *m* being 1,000. The rule is that all *trip_plans* must include all input *trip_events* or fix *trip_events* by assigning the specific *pois* at the specific time periods. After that, the system randomly fills any *pois* at any available spaces. The time period of a random *trip_event* corresponds to the attribute avg_visit_hrs

of that *poi*. There is no *poi* presented more than 1 time in a candidate chromosome. Moreover, any random *pois* must open in the day of the *trip_plans*.

3. Third, the system calculates the score of each candidate trip_plan. The idea is that if many trip_events satisfy cover constraints from users and the condition of *pois*, the score becomes higher. In our experimented system, we define the fitness function to calculate the score $score = 5 \, \Sigma \, a_i + b + c + d$.

   a_i is a weight when a random *trip_event* satisfying an input *pref_event*, if the *pref_event* mentions about category; the value of a_i is from the function *pcat*; otherwise, it used as 1. This term is multiplied by 5 because we prefer to place important on an input *trip_event* satisfaction rather than other criteria. However, this number can be configured.

   b is the number of random *trip_events* having a *poi* in a favorite daytime.

   c is the number of random *trip_events* having a *poi* in a favorite month.

   d is the number of random *trip_events* having distances between connected places not more than 30 driving minutes

4. Next, the top-score *trip_plan* is evaluated. If all *trip_events* satisfy all conditions from the user, pois, and time; it becomes a perfect plan. In case the perfect one found; the algorithm is terminated and produces the final *trip_plan* to the 8th step; otherwise, the genetic operations which are selection, crossover, and mutation are performed in the next steps until t times to terminate. The t is configurable in our application. We use the t as 50.

5. The selection operation using the technique of rank selection is firstly done by selecting top k plans having high scores. The k is a configurable parameter in the application, our work uses it k as 100.

6. Next, the crossover operation using the single-point crossover technique is operated. All selected candidates are paired. In each pair, a fix *trip_event* from ones in the middle is randomly selected to be a crossover point, and then exchange the parts of both plans based on that point. In this case, two child *trip_plans* are newly created.

7. After that, the mutation operation using the uniform mutation method is run. The mutation probability m is configured as 0.1 (or 10%). For doing mutation, a random *trip_event* is replaced by another random *trip_event* in the range of *trip_events* that satisfy the user conditions to be a new *trip_plan*.

8. In this step, the final *trip_plan* is provided to the user.

9. After that, the user can decide to choose the generated *trip_plan*.

10. If the generated *trip_plan* is not satisfying, the user will ask to regenerate the *trip_plan* again. In case the user is satisfied some *trip_events*, he or she can fix those *trip_events* to be input *trip_events* for the next round. After that, the algorithm moves to the first activity. In addition, the users can ask for randomly changing an output *trip_event* directly.

11. At last, when the user is satisfied the generated *trip_plan* from the sixth activity, the final *trip_plan* is saved.

4 Result and Discussion

The recommender system and the trip planner application are implemented to testify the possibility and practicability of our approach. In this section, the application, evaluation, and the discussion are described.

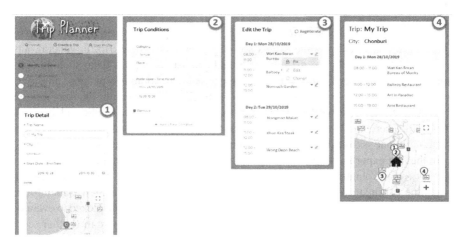

Fig. 5. The captured screens of the trip planner application

4.1 Application

The prototype of the trip planner application is developed based on the design and method in the third section. It is a mobile-friendly web-based application. In the application, there are 3 main menu items: Home, Create a Trip Plan, and User Profile. The key feature is to Create a Trip Plan as shown in Fig. 5. In this feature, there are 4 steps as follows:

1. First, to identify a trip detail as shown in Fig. 5 (1), a user gives information about trip name, city, start date, end date, and pins the location of the hotel.
2. Second, to add trip conditions as depicted in Fig. 5 (2), the user adds input *trip_events* and *pref_events* in this step. The user interface provides input boxes of *pois'* categories, *pois*, date, and time period. In case of adding a *pref_event*, the user does not need to give all inputs, for example, giving only a category and leave the date and time period blank. After submitting this form, the recommender system executes the algorithm and generates a *trip_plan* that is displayed in the next step.
3. Third, the step to edit the trip is demonstrated in Fig. 5 (3). In this step, the user can get the generated *trip_plan* and the plan can be edited. There are 2 ways to edit the plan: (1) to regenerate the whole plan, and (2) to rechange a *trip_event* directly. If some generated *trip_events* are satisfying, the user can mark to fix them in the schedule. In this case, when the user asks to regenerate the whole trip plan, the *trip_plan* is altered while all fixed *trip_events* are unchanged.

4. The last step, to display the final *trip_plan* as displayed in Fig. 5 (4), the user can access the full trip plan including trip schedule of each date together with a map having pins of the hotel and the running number of all *poi*.

4.2 Evaluation

The application provides a feature to recommend a trip plan based on user criteria. It also allows users to fix some events and regenerate the whole trip. In general, any recommendation models are directly evaluated against supervised data, such as user-item datasets. However, in this work, the supervised data about trip plans of any users are hardly gathered. Thus, the evaluation in this work has to be mainly focusing on user satisfaction. In this case, we delivered the application to real users and collected feedback from them. There are 2 experiments: (1) one is to get feedback from users directly, and (2) the other one is to check the behavior when they use the application.

In the first experiment, the evaluation was done by using our application and filling a survey form. Volunteers were firstly screened by choosing ones who did not like to waste time writing travel plans. This is the target group for our application as mentioned in the introduction. Therefore, there were 40 potential users who were picked to evaluate our approach. The form asks about user satisfaction from 0 to 5 where the higher score means higher satisfaction. As the feedback was summarized, the average score all users are 4.25 of 5.00. It is resulted in the high ranking of user satisfaction.

In the second experiment, we analyzed the behavior from the usage of the application. According to the application, users can save the final trip plan. In this case, we assume that users ask for regenerating the plan until they satisfy and save the final trip plan. Thus, we evaluate this behavior by counting the number of times the button "Regenerate" or "Change" is clicked until the final plan is saved. The experiment was conducted with the same group of users. In this experiment, we analyzed only 31 of 40 users who gave 4–5 mark in the previous survey. It is found that the average times of regenerating the whole trip per one user is 0.714, and the average times of regenerating some part of the trip plan is 1.142. It can be interpreted that users regenerated the trip plan not more than 3 times until they were satisfied and saved the plan.

4.3 Discussion

Our recommender system and application provide a key feature to produce a trip plan based on a few user criteria. Some criteria are clearly defined (input *trip_event*), and some are flexible (input *pref_event*). This feature is suitable for users who do not have time to make a trip plan as mentioned by the persona in the introduction section. Users sometime need a complete trip schedule, but they do not need a really perfect trip plan, because they prefer to spend the any free time for traveling activities. Thus, this application can support their requirement. As we mentioned about the result of our survey in the introduction section, there are 30.6% of users who do not prefer to do a trip plan. It is because they do not need to spend a lot of time to do the plan, and 83.4% of samples need recommended trip plans that allow them to customize easily.

As the process of our recommendation model, the trip plan is corresponding to the features of attractions such as open weekdays, times to spend, favorite times and months, and feasible routes. As we reviewed, most related work [1, 8–10] placed important to the technique of trip pattern recognition and trajectory mining. They did not much mention about the aspects of *pois*. In addition, As comparing to related applications, Google Travel [2], Inspirelock [11], and Roadtrippers [12] provide information and ready recommend plans, but they do not have a flexible way to customize the trip based on user constraints and features of tourist places. Since the mentioned constrains are the key features of our trip planner application, the consensus view seems to be that it can demonstrate the novelty of our recommendation system.

Since our recommender system produces a trip plan from a few flexible user criteria, our work is directly evaluated from user feedback directly. According to the result of evaluation in the previous part, users are highly satisfied this trip planner application. As they occasionally regenerated the plan, it shows that users are pleased with the result generated from our recommender system.

Overall, this study focuses on the problem representation of trip planner using the data model and the fitness function, and the model through the computing process together with the system architecture and the user flow. The data model mentions about the schema and the description of pois, categories, trip plans, and trip events. Some aspects such as multiple-possible categories, recommended visit times, and times spent visiting are introduced in this data model to fulfill requirements from users. Besides, the computing process takes advantage of the genetic algorithm to find an appropriate solution. The formation of a chromosome and a fitness function are also proposed to respect the conditions from the tourism domain and the traveler domain. The suitability and feasibility of this work are demonstrated by the prototype.

In addition, some discussions with smart city experts found that our approach are benefits to tourism development in each city. Since the favorite time periods and months are mentioned in the model, they can be adapted to be some special events and festivals. The model should take advantage of social media in order to improve the precision of open time, close time, suggested visit time, recommended time spent visiting, and festivals as well.

5 Conclusion and Future Work

This paper introduced a recommender system for trip planners. In our research methodology, we firstly surveyed the needs of users, and found that users prefer to have an application to recommend a trip plan from a few constrains and they can modify the generated plan according to their satisfaction. We formulate the research requirements into a fitness function to measure the quality of any generated trip plan. This function gives a high score if a plan and tourist attractions in the plan correspond to specific place, places' categories, open weekdays, times to visit, favorite daytimes, favorite months, and feasible routes. These features are designed in the proposed data model. To execute the recommender system, users just input a few criteria such as some places, places' categories, and some specific time periods; and then the recommender system employed the genetic algorithm to produce the final trip plan having the highest score. To demonstrate the suitability and feasibility of the model, a trip planner prototype, which is a mobile-friendly web application, has been developed. Lastly, our work is evaluated using the prototype. It has been found that users appreciate the application and they are satisfied most of initially generated plans, because they spend a few times to regenerate the plans until they are satisfied. It is also discussed that our work can be enhanced to improve tourism development of any cities.

In order to increase the capability of our work, the user interface and user experience should be considered. In addition, social media should be studied and utilized to improve the precision of tourist attractions' aspects and recommended trip plans.

References

1. Lu, E.H., Fang, S.H., Tseng, V.S.: Integrating tourist packages and tourist attractions for personalized trip planning based on travel constraints. GeoInformatica **20**(4), 741–763 (2016)
2. Google Travel. https://www.google.com/travel. Accessed 10 Oct 2019
3. Expedia. https://www.expedia.com. Accessed 10 Oct 2019
4. Kayak. https://www.kayak.com. Accessed 10 Oct 2019
5. TripAdvisor Homepage, https://www.tripadvisor.com. Accessed 10 Oct 2019
6. Eiben, A.E., Smith, J.E.: Introduction to Evolutionary Computing. Springer, Heidelberg (2003). https://doi.org/10.1007/978-3-662-05094-1
7. Souffriau, W., Vansteenwegen, P.: Tourist trip planning functionalities: state–of–the–art and future. In: Daniel, F., Facca, F.M. (eds.) ICWE 2010. LNCS, vol. 6385, pp. 474–485. Springer, Heidelberg (2010). https://doi.org/10.1007/978-3-642-16985-4_46
8. Vansteenwegen, P., Souffriau, W., Berghe, G.V., Oudheusden, D.V.: The city trip planner: an expert system for tourists. Expert Syst. Appl. **38**(6), 6540–6546 (2011)
9. Yoon, H., Zheng, Y., Xie, X., Woo, W.: Social itinerary recommendation from user-generated digital trails. J. Pers. Ubiquit. Comput. **16**(5), 469–484 (2012)
10. Zheng, Y.: Trajectory data mining: an overview. ACM Trans. Intell. Syst. Technol. (TIST) **6**(3), 1–41 (2015)
11. Inspirock. https://www.inspirock.com. Accessed 10 Oct 2019
12. Roadtrippers. https://roadtrippers.com. Accessed 10 Oct 2019
13. Omara, F.A., Arafa, M.M.: Genetic algorithms for task scheduling problem. In: Abraham, A., Hassanien, A.E., Siarry, P., Engelbrecht, A. (eds.) Foundations of Computational Intelligence, vol. 3, pp. 479–507. Springer, Heidelberg (2009). https://doi.org/10.1007/978-3-642-01085-9_16
14. Mohammed, M.A., Ghani, M.K.A., Hamed, R.I., et al.: Solving vehicle routing problem by using improved genetic algorithm for optimal solution. J. Comput. Sci. **21**, 255–262 (2017)

Interactive Skill Based Labor Market Mechanics and Dynamics Analysis System Using Machine Learning and Big Data

Leo Mrsic[✉] [iD], Hrvoje Jerkovic, and Mislav Balkovic [iD]

Algebra University College, Ilica 242, 10000 Zagreb, Croatia
{leo.mrsic,hrvoje.jerkovic,mislav.balkovic}@algebra.hr

Abstract. Interest in talent recognition, talent recruitment, education and labor mobility has been on the rise in last years. Business sector is changing its human resources (HR) policies globally, changing ways in policies and practices related to employee management and employer branding. The process of talent recognition and/or search was mostly manual work, often carried by professional agencies or HR officer in organization. In today's challenging labor market environment, this process is inefficient and slow with and often limited in success. In this paper we are focused on skills, education and lifelong learning domain which has an important role in the 10 priorities of the European Commission (EC) 2014–2019. Our starting point was to look for machine learning and big data techniques to support the policy makers and analysts in reducing mismatch between jobs and skills at regional level in the European Union (EU) through the use of data. Our research includes massive semi structured resume dataset (50+ million documents) combined with several official statistical surveys. We were able to leverage the advances in machine learning and big data to automate resume/skill classification and to improve productivity in skill-based labor market mechanics and dynamics analysis. This paper proposes a model of extracting important information after resumes are being partially classified, classify skills using European multilingual classification of Skills, Competences, Qualifications and Occupations (ESCO) by skill pillar matching and use modern interactive visualization tools to gain smart insights powered by geospatial and time-series analysis. Research goals are to point attention towards data science and machine learning and its usage in labor and educational market mechanics and dynamics.

Keywords: Resume analytics · Skill recognition · Labor market dynamics and mechanics · Interactive labor market visualization · Talent management · ESCO · European Union labor market analytics · Machine learning · Big data · Data science

1 Introduction

In the context of digital transformation, there is a big pressure on agility of the governments. Digital solutions for government need to be proven and efficient while rapidly changing technological environment request significant resources both in terms of money

© Springer Nature Singapore Pte Ltd. 2020
P. Sitek et al. (Eds.): ACIIDS 2020, CCIS 1178, pp. 505–516, 2020.
https://doi.org/10.1007/978-981-15-3380-8_44

and intellectual capital. Industry is facing similar pressure however their efficiency is measured by profitability of ability to produce solutions that are sellable. For mentioned stakeholders, it is not easy to maintain interdisciplinary ad focused research and development teams with ability to iterate and deliver in short period of time. This situation opens opportunity to educational sector, sector which is by default oriented on talent capacity building which can adopt some practices from industry and fill in market gap with prototypes using available technology, moving attention towards research outsourcing supporting triple helix teams on society/industry important tasks [1–5].

1.1 Government Role: A New Way of Collaborating in the Digital Ecosystem

We started our research with simple goal: we want to harness the potential of big data for producing insights faster and at lower cost for society. Public organizations, like education organizations or labor market support institutions, face pressure to fill the skill gaps and do not always have the right level of flexibility. Industry is under pressure looking for ways how to find best candidates for various positions, especially those related to digital disruptive skills (in both ways). This is why market in general need to rely on broader communities and collaborative environments as an example of a more permanent change in our working methods: (i) work in small iterations (trial and error/learning by doing), (ii) sustained collaboration with private sector and academia, needs follow up; moving into a permanent iteration spirit [6–8]. Data is most important asset company can have in modern economy. Being able to understand how data can be used is based both on experience in data management and industry expertise. Machine learning and big data concepts are important because researchers can use real data sets to test their ideas in analysis and advanced visualization which can be further improved into products [9].

2 Related Work

Resumes are a great source of data which can be usefully analyzed to gain powerful insights. There are several companies working on resume semantics for years now and, due to limitation of public portals and variety of private ones, they are forced to scrape data while making their own classifications as part of that process. Importance and complexity of the process of finding the right candidate for a particular job increased while candidates as well expect to find more information about labor market and service that will support their needs like: looking for best country for their specific skills or looking for environment suitable for their research to be supported. Analyzing millions of resumes is complex and sensitive task and results can vary from shortlisting of wrong skills, rejection of a right candidate or supporting obsolete skills through education: all may result in significant cost of time and other resources [10]. Many authors were looking to simplify process, mostly in segment of resume description phase. Using techniques from text analytics to judge resumes on the basis of their content, sentiment analysis approach to look for proof based on description he or she provides. Recruitment has also experienced exponential increase in recent time and are moving towards selection in very early stage. Around the globe, more than 5.0 million students are being mobile as part of education process which increase competitivity level among labor market actors as well as make additional pressure on candidates, being in situation to make decision very early. All actors would like to be treated individually, having specific background, would like their skill sets to be considered, interests and work experience to be mentioned in the process. The world of artificial intelligence (AI) and machine learning (ML) push expectations to all new level, where availability of large amounts of data brought about by advancements in technology made systems to become widely accessible [11–16]. With growing demand on public stakeholders to better support growing labor market dynamic, ESCO was developed as the European multilingual classification of Skills, Competences, Qualifications and Occupations. ESCO works as a dictionary, describing, identifying and classifying professional occupations, skills, and qualifications relevant for the EU labour market and education and training. Those concepts and the relationships between them can be understood by electronic systems, which allows different online platforms to use ESCO for services like matching jobseekers to jobs on the basis of their skills, suggesting trainings to people who want to reskill or upskill. The aim of ESCO is to support job mobility across Europe and therefore a more integrated and efficient labour market, by offering a "common language" on occupations and skills that can be used by different stakeholders on employment and education and training topics [20]. Our research was based on winning solution developed for First EU Big Data Hackathon take place in Brussels in 2017 and on-going project making national Labour market data portal for Employment Bureau at Ministry of Labor, Republic of Croatia.

3   Background

3.1   Data Sources

Acknowledgement: Data sources were provided by official institutions and were anonymized using primary and secondary anonymization process, no individual data was captured, stored or processed during research process at any time. During preparation process for prototyping, we used 4.7 million European Job Mobility portal (EURES) resume documents, 35.0 million EURES employer job ads, 7.4 million web scraped job ads (various data from different countries), 1.0 million records from EU Statistics on Income and Living Conditions Survey (SILC), 0.2 million records from OECD Programme for the International Assessment of Adult Competences Survey (PIAAC and 1.4 mil records from EU Labour Force Survey (LFS). In total we used more than 50.000.000 documents. For matching, we used ESCO and International Standard Classification of Occupations (ISCO) classification to provide a common taxonomy to which all data sources are mapped to. Additionally, we used European Centre for the Development of Vocational Training, (Cedefop) European skills and jobs (ESJ) survey and various European Statistical Office (Eurostat) datasets at regional level: macroeconomic indicators, social indicators, shape files for Nomenclature of Territorial Units for Statistics (NUTS) regions [31–34].

3.2 Machine Learning and Big Data Environment for Resume Analysis

Entire prototype system is running on Google Cloud Platform. Raw data was loaded to Google Cloud Storage using data lake. After some initial data preparation, we load all data sets in Google BigQuery, which is an analytical database able to scale to billions of rows with extreme query performance on reasonable budget for prototyping. For most data preparation, processing and modelling we use a Google Compute Engine instance with 64 CPUs and 240 GB of RAM with the following software: Debian OS, Anaconda distribution of Python 3.6, Jupyter with python, R and Octave kernels, JupyterHub for multi-user collaboration, various python packages (numpy, pandas), R language and R Studio Server for multi-user collaboration. For very large data processing we use Google Dataflow next generation distributed processing system (Apache Beam). For front-end we use web technologies such as Tableau, javascript, API, D3.js and Google Search trends. All code is kept under distributed version control system: Git (Google Source Repositories) while all documentation is done using Google Docs.

Fig. 1. Machine learning and big data platform setup

For production system we are using Microsoft SQL Server on Windows platform and on-premise Tableau Server followed by responsive design for client front end as explained in Fig. 1.

3.3 Value Proposition

Aim of the prototype was to developed a fully functional web application prototype consisting of several visual, interactive dashboards. Prototype portal was structured the main policy question into 4 parts as explained in Table 1.

Table 1. Value proposition structure

Group	Proposition question	Solution
1. Skill supply	Which skills are in supply across regions?	1.1. We measured the supply side using EURES CV data, identifying top skills in supply for each region at all NUTS levels and across all 4 ESCO skill levels 1.2. We analyzed how the skills are clustered or related, we did this by looking at which skills are often found together in a CV or a job ad 1.3. We identified obsolete skills by using LFS and SILC data to find differences in skills between the working and the unemployed or inactive population
2. Skill demand	Which skills are in demand across regions?	2.1. We measured the demand side using Cedefop scraped data and EURES job vacancies, calculated several demand measures such as: number of job ads demanding a particular skill, median time between CV publication and deactivation, etc 2.2. We identified top skills in demand for each region at all NUTS levels and across all 4 ESCO skill levels 2.3. We build simple prediction model, forecasting skill demand for several years in advance across regions We identified which occupations are changing the most in terms of skills required
3. Skill mismatch	Where is the biggest mismatch in skill demand and supply?	3.1. We measured mismatch by mismatch indicator which is equal to number of job ads requiring a particular skill over number of CVs with a particular skill, for all regions at all NUTS levels and across all skills at all ESCO levels
4. Policy action	How can the mismatch (skill gap) be closed? (e focused on two areas: educational system and workforce migration)	4.1. For educational system we identified the gap between skills and qualifications 4.2. Using LFS, SILC and PIAAC data we are measuring the proportion of population taking part in education, trying to improve their skills 4.3. We measured which regions offer which type of education for a particular skill 4.4. We measured workforce migrations by taking current region of job seekers and desired region 4.5. We measured the attractiveness of skills by looking at which skills are mentioned in CV-s which are quickly deactivated assuming that the job seeker found a job and so his skills are attractive in the labor market 4.6. We correlated various macroeconomic, socio-demographics and other indicators with skills mismatch indicator across regions and skills

3.4 Skills Recognition and Matching Process

In order to achieve the desired goal during the matching process, the entire process has been divided into several basic steps. The first step consists of segmenting the entire resume based on the topic of each part, the second step consists of extracting data in structured form from the unstructured data, the third step include matching process (we used ESCO classification as standard), the fourth segment include machine learning models for clustering, trend analysis, forecasting and matrix data preparation, and the final segment consists of visualizing data on cloud portal [17–19, 21–25]. As key research finding, we will focus here on matching process between resume input (often plain text, explained by candidate). After detection of resume part which include skills, matching process was done in two phases. In first phase we used composite index combining Levenshtein string distance and Metaphone distance to measure similarity between text as explained in Table 2.

Table 2. Content matching rules

Phrase A	Phrase B	String distance	Metaphone distance	Confidence
Natural passion for data analytics	Knowledge of web technologies	25	10	86,53%
Natural passion for data analytics	Exposure to data management	22	12	85,78%
Accuracy and attention to detail	Exposure to data management	27	10	85,45%
Accuracy and attention to detail	Ability to work as part of a team	26	12	83,19%
Natural passion for data analytics	Knowledge of web technologies	25	10	86,53%
…	…	…	…	…
A high level of mathematical ability	Work in a cross function agile team to identify and deliver business outcomes	63	28	4,96%

During second phase we use similar technique to measure similarity with ESCO skill pillar, dividing results into three categories: (i) matched inside threshold criteria, (ii) not matched but relevant to be evaluated and included in ESCO (as meta classification) and (iii) other [26]. Levenshtein distance is a string metric for measuring the difference between two sequences. In our solution we measured distance between two words as the minimum number of single-character edits (i.e. insertions, deletions, or substitutions) required to change one word into the other [29, 30]. Mathematically, the Levenshtein distance between two strings, a and b (of length |a| and |b| respectively), is given by lev a, b(|a|, |b|) where:

$$
lev_{a,b}(i, j) = \begin{cases} \max(i, j) \\ \min \begin{cases} lev_{a,b}(i - 1, j) + 1 \\ lev_{a,b}(i, j - 1) + 1 \\ lev_{a,b}(i - 1, j - 1) + 1_{(a_i \neq b_j)} \end{cases} \end{cases} \tag{1}
$$

Here, 1(ai ≠ bi) is the indicator function equal to 0 when ai ≠ bi and equal to 1 otherwise, and leva, b(i, j) is the distance between the first i characters of a and the first j characters of b.

Metaphone is a phonetic algorithm used for indexing words by their English pronunciation. It fundamentally improves on the Soundex algorithm by using information about variations and inconsistencies in English spelling and pronunciation to produce a more accurate encoding, which does a better job of matching words and names which sound similar. As with Soundex, similar-sounding words should share the same keys. Original Metaphone codes use the 16 consonant symbols "0BFHJKLMNPRSTWXY". The '0' represents "th" (as an ASCII approximation of Θ), 'X' represents "sh" or "ch", and the others represent their usual English pronunciations. The vowels AEIOU are also used, but only at the beginning of the code [27, 28]. Once matching with ESCO was done, we have powerful standard and automatic support for 26 languages.

4 Results

4.1 Matching Process Confidence

We divided confident factor in quartiles to group matching process confidence. Target data tables were created using prepared data sample with up to 1.0 billion records for large one (skill demand) based on resume data available as explained in Table 3.

Table 3. Confidence matching statistics

Confidence quartile	Percentage of records in matching quartile
Q1 (highest match confidence)	41%
Q2	37%
Q3	17%
Q4 (lowest match confidence)	5%

Following results shown, 85%+ matches fits above threshold of 0.5 confidence score. Total computing power cost was given in Fig. 2 (peak selected).

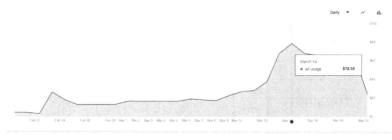

Fig. 2. Computing architecture resource total cost (peak time selected, measurement in cost per US$)

4.2 Interactive Visualization

By combining number of skills (count per attributes) we were able to deliver functional map for skill supply and demand among regions. Interactive map is available for filtering on geolocation (NUTS) and ESCO levels for better insight management and understanding dynamics on labor market as explained in Fig. 3.

Fig. 3. Skill supply analysis map

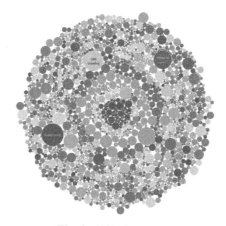

Fig. 4. Skill cluster map

By combining various skills in clusters, we show it is possible to analyze representation of groups as part of sample. By using this information, it is possible to track down most popular skills grouped among occupations, helping education and policy stakeholders to understand mechanics on labor market as explained in Fig. 4.

Among most interesting insights time matrix on occupation change was provided. Many countries these days have pressure in understanding how to efficiently motivate candidates to change between their current sectors and move into more lucrative ones or just look for analysis of resources spent for reskill as explained in Fig. 5.

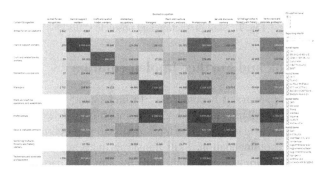

Fig. 5. Occupation migration time matrix

By collecting data on talent affinity to work in specific industry, providing their skills but willing to relocate, we shown possible to create geospatial map showing affinity of Croatian records to work among Europe. Filtering deeper into occupation we can analyze various industries and calculate trends among regions as explained in Fig. 6.

Fig. 6. Talent migration affinity

Finally, using skills it is possible not only to calculate gap for a certain region but also to analyze trend also to calculate most popular (or new) skill trend or, using it backwards, to understand which skills are becoming obsolete as explained in Fig. 7.

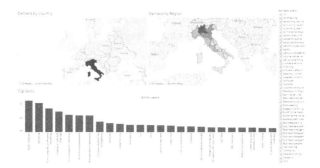

Fig. 7. Skill prediction and obsolete skills

5 Future Outlook and Further Implementation

Utilizing technology in ways it become easy to understand we are able to develop further features like: (i) skill transition index, (ii) competitivity index, (iii) employability index, (iv) career path navigator, (v) location-based skill gap optimization or (vi) next most valuable skill recommendation. Skill transition index represents index of skills transition over time, creating insights into skill dynamics as part of overall market, education or specific industry changes. For example, by looking into analyst skills few years ago we will find skills like accounting or mathematics wile today those skills become usual while technology related ones like analytics tools experience are more likely to be pointed out. Competitivity index represents comparation between person and average profile of employees in same industry with similar skills. This index can be more expanded towards recommendation of just be used to monitor competitivity of students entering labor market. Employability index represent ability for person with certain level of education and skills to be hired in certain region where talent shortage is detected. Career path navigator can help persons in different life stages to understand their options od labor market in order to make better decision about their career. Location-based skill gap optimization can help policy makers to identify and proactively react to skill gaps on regional level. Next most valuable skill recommendation can be support tool for education sector to improve and align educational programs towards future efficiency once person enter labor market.

6 Conclusion

Only in 2018. EU budget for "Competitiveness for growth and jobs" was more than 62 billion EUR (55+ billion EUR annual average from 2014, 2017) showing how important these activities are. In 2018. It represents 48% of total EU budget for that year. Understanding mechanics and dynamics of labor market, similarities and trend is one of the problems faced by the labor market stakeholders today in most of the countries. We have extended the notion of special features to extract and categorize skills from given set of resumes making them available in ESCO notation for analysis. We have proposed an approach to match skills analyzing "skill" related information. The proposed approach has the potential to improve the performance of policy makers (at least in measuring results of government support), understanding of market for general public and also to improve market overview for educational institutions, looking to compete on modern labor market. With the help of the experimental results we have shown that there is a significant potential in simplifying approach while different NLP and machine learning techniques for text parsing are developed and can be used as commodity these days creating foundation for more industry related research topic to be made on top of that. Monitoring skill selection process is a more complex problem as resume contains freeform texts which are difficult to compare and also has a hierarchical structure containing different sections. As each resume contains different sections with each section containing different types of text, an integrated approach has to be developed by considering information in each section. In this paper, we used semi structured data sources and focused on usage of that data to create efficient system that can be refreshed on short time interval and provide valuable insight into mechanics and dynamics of labor market. As a part of future work, we are developing national platform starting with basic information with aim to continue our research and make most of value proposition points available as part of society shift towards digital economy. Research goals are to point attention towards data science and machine learning and its usage in labor and educational market mechanics and dynamics.

References

1. Smedt, J.D., Le Vrang, M., Papantoniou, A.: ESCO: Towards a Semantic Web for the European Labor Market (2015)
2. European Commission: ESCO, European classification of skills: The first public release. Publications Office of the European Union, Luxembourg (2013)
3. Piatetsky, G.: Top methodologies for Analytics, 25 July 2017. http://www.kdnuggets.com/2014/10/crisp-dm-top-methodology-analytics-data-mining-data-science-projects.html
4. Abbott, D.: Applied Predictive Analytics: Principles and Techniques for the Professional Data Analyst. Wiley, Indianapolis (2014)
5. Lin, N.: Applied Business Analytics: Integrating Business Process, Big Data, and Advanced Analytics. Pearson, Upper Saddle River (2015)
6. Putler, D.S., Krider, R.E.: Customer and Business Analytics: Applied Data Mining for Business Decision Making Using R. CRC Press, Boca Raton (2012)
7. Otte, E., Rousseau, R.: Social network analysis: a powerful strategy, also for the information sciences. J. Inf. Sci. **28**(6), 441–453 (2016)
8. Wernicke, S., Rasche, F.: FANMOD: a tool for fast network motif detection. Bioinformatics **22**(9), 1152–1153 (2006)
9. European Commission: European Classification of Skills/Competences, Qualifications and Occupations. Booklet, Publications Office of the European Union, Luxembourg (2013)
10. Kofler, A., Prast, M.: OpenSKIMR A Job and Learning Platform. CS & IT-CSCP, pp. 95–106, January 2017
11. European Commission: ESCO Strategic framework - European Skills, Competences, Qualifications and Occupations, July 2017 (2017)
12. Cormen, T.H., Leiserson, C.E., Rivest, R.L., Stein, C.: Dijkstra's algorithm. In: Introduction to Algorithms, 2nd edn, Chap. 24, pp. 595–599. MIT Press (2009)
13. Guyon, I., Elisseeff, A.: An introduction to variable and feature selection. J. Mach. Learn. Res. **3**, 1157–1182 (2003)
14. Blum, A.L., Langley, P.: Selection of relevant features and examples in machine learning. Artif. Intell. **97**(1–2), 245–271 (1997)

15. Shankar, S., Karypis, G.: A feature weight adjustment algorithm for document categorization. In: KDD-2000 Workshop on Text Mining, Boston, USA (2000)
16. Breiman, L., Friedman, J.H., Olshen, R.A., Stone, C.J.: Classification and Regression Trees. Wadsworth, Belmont (1984)
17. Almuallim, H., Dietterich, T.G.: Efficient algorithms for identifying relevant features. Oregon (2014)
18. Yu, L., Liu, H.: Efficient feature selection via analysis of relevance and redundancy. J. Mach. Learn. Res. **5**, 1205–1224 (2004)
19. Fu, S., Desmarais, M., Chen, W.: Reliability analysis of Markov blanket learning algorithms. IEEE (2010)
20. Sovren Group: Overview of the Sovren Semantic Matching Engine and Comparison to Traditional Keyword Search Engines. Sovren Group, Inc. (2006)
21. Rafter, R., Bradley, K., Smyth, B.: Automated collaborative filtering applications for online recruitment services. In: Brusilovsky, P., Stock, O., Strapparava, C. (eds.) AH 2000. LNCS, vol. 1892, pp. 363–368. Springer, Heidelberg (2000). https://doi.org/10.1007/3-540-44595-1_48
22. Malinowski, J., Keim, T., Wendt, O., Weitzel, T.: Matching people and jobs: a bilateral recommendation approach. In: Proceedings of the 39th Annual Hawaii International Conference on System Sciences, HICSS 2006, Hawaii, USA, 4–7 January 2006 (2006). 137c
23. Guo, X., Jerbi, H., O'Mahony, M.P.: An analysis framework for content-based job recommendation. Insight Centre for Data Analytics, Dublin (2014). https://doi.org/10.13140/2.1.1090.4328
24. Al-Otaibi1, S.T., Ykhlef, M.: A survey of job recommender systems. Int. J. Phys. Sci. **7**(29), 5127–5142 (2012)
25. Kotthoff, L., Gent, I.P., Miguel, I.: An evaluation of machine learning in algorithm selection for search problems. AI Commun. **25**(3), 257–270 (2011)
26. Bojars, U., Breslin, J.G.: ResumeRDF: expressing skill information on the semantic web (2007)
27. Turney, P.D., Littman, M.: Unsupervised learning of semantic orientation from a hundred billion-word corpus. Technical report ERC-1094 (NRC 44929), National Research Council of Canada (2002)
28. Marjit, U., Sharma, K., Biswas, U.: Discovering resume information using linked data. Int. J. Web Semant. Technol. (IJWesT) **3**(2), 51–61 (2012)
29. Fazel-Zarandi1, M., Mark, S.: Fox2, semantic matchmaking for job recruitment: an ontology-based hybrid approach. In: IJCA Proceedings of the 3rd International SMR2 2009 Workshop on Service Matchmaking and Resource Retrieval in the Semantic Web (2013)
30. Kopparapu, S.K.: Automatic extraction of usable information from unstructured resumes to aid search. In: IEEE International Conference on Progress in Informatics and Computing (PIC) (2010)
31. Jiang, Z.X., Zhang, C., Xiao, B., Lin, Z.: Research and implementation of intelligent Chinese resume parsing. In: WRI International Conference on Communications and Mobile Computing (2009)
32. Chuang, Z., Ming, W., Guang, L.C., Bo, X.: Resume parser: semi-structured Chinese document analysis. In: WRI World Congress on Computer Science and Information Engineering (2009)
33. Celik, D., Karakas, A., Bal, G., Gultunca, C.: Towards an information extraction system based on ontology to match resumes and jobs. In: IEEE 37th Annual Workshops on Computer Software and Applications Conference Workshops (2013)
34. Wu, D., Wu, L., Sun, T., Jiang, Y.: Ontology based information extraction technology. In: International Conference on Internet Technology and Applications (iTAP) (2011)

Personalised English Language Education Through an E-learning Platform

Vladimír Bradáč$^{(\boxtimes)}$ and Pavel Smolka

University of Ostrava, 30.dubna 22, Ostrava, Czech Republic
{vladimir.bradac,pavel.smolka}@osu.cz

Abstract. The article aims at modern processes in order to get most out of student's progress in an e-learning course. This desired progress is achieved by adopting a new methodology, which incorporated innovative features to enable the creation of a personalised study plan for students in a given course (in our case it means a course of the English language). The new features include two blocks. A block integrating a questionnaire to find out student's sensory preferences and a block of student's knowledge. Such blocks served as input values and information to create and verify the tested e-learning course. The suggested methodology made use of exiting capabilities of an e-learning platform Moodle, namely conditioned progress though a course. It also integrated new elements so that a new individual study plan would be created *in an automated way*. Such a complex system served as a testing unit to verify its functionality. We use a group of bachelor students studying at our institution.

Keywords: Intelligent tutoring systems · Distance education · Adaptive systems · e-learning · Language education

1 Introduction

Language education through a computer-based form has been gradually rising in popularity among the end-users [1]. [2] proves that languages can be mastered using e-learning, although with certain limitations. The outcomes of learning a foreign language through e-learning lags behind in feature such as personalised approach and flexible feedback [3]. Therefore, such efforts have resulted in numerous systems to get over this insufficiency. Being able to provide a personalised focus on students bring up a demanding challenge requiring a different concept of an e-learning system as a whole. A solution might be provided by systems enabling work with inaccurate information.

Even inaccuracy, or poor description of such processes, can be structured. This fact makes it possible to engage suitable tools to work with a specific kind if incompleteness. An analysis of inaccuracies presented in solutions of given decision-making processes reveals that the given inaccuracy is often perceived as insufficient information as well. Therefore, its root can stem from student's incapability to describe their knowledge. Nevertheless, testing a student does not imply that we will get all information on student's knowledge. A problem arises when we want to describe student's knowledge in all parts

© Springer Nature Singapore Pte Ltd. 2020
P. Sitek et al. (Eds.): ACIIDS 2020, CCIS 1178, pp. 517–526, 2020.
https://doi.org/10.1007/978-981-15-3380-8_45

of a foreign language in a single test – e.g. if a student is able to use the zero and the first conditional clause, does it imply that the knowledge of conditional clauses is sufficient, good or bad? Next kind of insufficiency arises from the use of a natural language. This insufficiency lies in the fact that a human can use only a finite set of words to describe an endless variety of situations. This undoubtedly results in state when verbal expression has a wide range of significance and relevance to the given situation. Each word has a different semantic meaning in various contexts, thus the meaning causes certain blurriness (fuzziness). The mathematical science is not able to appropriately deal with such fuzziness of linguistically described states. Our approach must use a bit different approach, i.e. a tool which effectively enables to work with uncertain information. This tool is called fuzzy logic.

2   Adaptivity

In order that a system could be called adaptive, it has to be able to adapt to changes in the system that is being controlled (e.g. a student). The system, then responds with an appropriate action. Contemporary LMS systems, as such, do not provide many possibilities how to accommodate to users' needs.

Research into adaptive systems can be divided into more specialised areas. One of the most frequently researched field are learning styles, their classification and further use in an educational process, e.g. in [4] or [5] and their computer-based testing of learning styles. Nevertheless, such efforts do not result in adaptivity as defined above because most of them only use predefined "model" groups of students where reals students are classified and study in groups of their learning-style-similar classmates.

In [6], the authors presented an example of a more sophisticated adaptive system focused on adaptable content which can be used again, named as KOD (Knowledge on Demand).

Our research is rather oriented on personalisation, i.e. changing the educational subject matter for each student on the basis of information provided before the start of an educational process combined with information gathered during student's studies.

3   Proposed Model

The authors of this paper have been carrying research in the area of proposing an adaptive model that would be applicable in foreign language learning in an e-learning environment. LMS Moodle served as the verification tool. The model can be divided into two threads (levels) providing the grounds for further processes. The first thread orients on a pedagogical area targeting at a student, i.e. acquisition of information on their learning and the style of perceiving information (so-called learning preferences) together with their level of their knowledge of the language. Research providing a more detailed study in this area is described in [7]. The second thread targets at applying a fuzzy logic expert system LFLC 2000 [8] to evaluate a didactic test on student's language proficiency. The advantages of applying this an approach were described in [9].

This paper closely relates to the stage after relevant student's information is acquired and kept in a student's database, which is composed of 2 subordinate databases, see Fig. 1.

Our approach does not aim at creating a model of students in a universal way where individual real studying students would be grouped in. Our idea is that each student has their own portfolio containing their personal information.

There are three modules M1–M3 in our proposed model. The first module, M1, focuses on creating student's portfolio. Module M1 comprises two sub-processes M1A and M1B. In process M1A, current student's language proficiency is acquired and evaluated, which means that we know what is student's input knowledge of the language at the beginning of the learning process. The data from M1A is kept in Base 1, named as B1. In process M1B, study preferences of each student are mapped. M1B focuses on gathering information on learning preferences from the view of point as they absorb external perceptions. The data from M1B is kept in Base 2, named as B2.

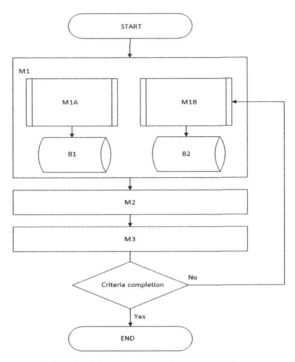

Fig. 1. Adaptation of student's study plan

Module M2 constitutes a procedure to control the learning. It mainly targets at adaptation of the content included in an e-learning course so that it meets the student's needs identified in M1A and M1B. The learning materials are adapted in their form and content. In order to perform the adaptation in M2 at a deeper level, the learning content must be divided into specific learning segments corresponding with thematic areas studied in a given course. Having completed the M2 module, module M3 is initialised.

Module M3 targets at the final diagnostics, which lies in adapting the form of the learning content. Such diagnostics is rather normative and can be carried out repeatedly, although the number of diagnostic iterations is limited. Once the required normative of knowledge has been achieved, the learning process is regarded successfully completed. On the contrary, a failure in the learning achievements would imply to redefine the B2 database in order to find out a more appropriate form of the learning content for a given student.

3.1 Application of Module M1

In order to apply the proposed e-learning model adaptivity, we have used e-learning environment of the LMS Moodle. The distinctiveness of each student was in the basis of the approach. Such a thought thus corresponded with students' profile, mainly in optional areas in users' profile. These areas were represented by twenty-five new attributes. The enlargement was composed of two parts.

The first part of user's profile area acted as a definition of study materials preferences. Those areas were denoted as VARK. This part agrees with the B2 base. The areas include values *yes* and *no*, which were received from a questionnaire filled-in by a student. VARK preferences is a methodology designed by Neil Fleming (VARK homepage), later further developed by Leite in work [10]. VARK shows the way people optimally absorb what they see, read or hear and how they process it and remember it. VARK preferences are sorted as: **V**isual – pictures, drawings, designs, tables, maps; **A**ural – audio files of any type; **R**ead/write – texts of any type; **K**inaesthetic – active practicing, experiencing by own work.

Verification of this approach was described in more detail in [11]. Having processed a questionnaire of VARK preferences, the results are then stored in the database of students. Although each person possesses a certain mixture of VARK preferences, none of us is ultimately reduced to a single preference (see Table 1 for the verification results).

Table 1. VARK preferences in students' profiles in course XANG3

First name	Last name	Profile_Field_V	Profile_Field_A	Profile_Field_R	Profile_Field_K
StudentA	StudentA	YES (21.7)	YES (30.4)	YES (34.8)	NO (13.1)
StudentB	StudentB	NO (15.2)	YES (30.4)	YES (27.2)	YES (27.2)
StudentC	StudentC	YES (21.4)	YES (35.7)	NO (14.3)	YES (27.6)
StudentD	StudentD	NO (12.8)	YES (38.4)	YES (23.2)	YES (25.6)
StudentE	StudentE	YES (33.3)	NO (16.6)	YES (30.1)	YES (20)
StudentF	StudentF	NO (16.6)	YES (29.2)	YES (29.2)	YES (25)
StudentG	StudentG	YES (29.7)	YES (21.6)	YES (21.6)	YES (27.1)
StudentH	StudentH	YES (20.7)	YES (24.4)	YES (24.1)	YES (31.1)
StudentI	StudentI	NO (13.8)	YES (31)	YES (41.4)	NO (13.8)
StudentJ	StudentJ	NO (11.8)	YES (41.2)	NO (5.8)	YES (41.2)
StudentK	StudentK	YES (20.3)	YES (33.3)	NO (11.1)	YES (30.3)
StudentL	StudentL	NO (11.1)	YES (29.6)	YES (37)	YES (22.3)

The second group of profile fields was focused on thematic groups and corresponds to the base B1. The process of analysing individual categories considers the following input variables for each individual category (the list also includes linguistic expressions for the variables):

- Knowledge of the given category (V1) – *low, medium, high*
- Weight of correctly answered questions (V2) – *low, medium, high*
- Importance for further study (V3) – *very low, low, medium, high, very high*
- Time required to answer (V4) – *low, medium, high*

Knowledge of the Given Category (V1)
How many correct answers the student has scored. The less correct answers, the lower the knowledge is.

Weight of Correctly Answered Questions (V2)
Questions within the category are of higher or lower difficulty. For example, Conditional clauses include the 1st, 2nd and 3rd conditional. Knowledge of the 3rd conditional clause is a sign of higher knowledge, thus this correct answer has a bigger weight.

Importance of the Category for Further Study (V3)
How the student should be already know the given category – very well, partially or no knowledge is required before the start of the studies. For example, the need to know the Present Continuous tense for students of XANG3 is very big. When assessing the same category for students of XANG1 (a course two level lower to XANG3), the need to know the Present Continuous is assessed as only small. However, if the student proves to know the past Perfect, the system assesses it as completed category and the student can focus on other "trouble-making" categories.

Time Spent on Questions of the Given Category (V4)
The time needed to answer individual questions is recorded. The times are then summed up for the given category and the system assesses if it took long or short time to answer. As the whole test is designed for 40 min, an average time spent on one question is 20 s, which is considered sufficient. If the student answer more quickly, it influences the result for the given category more positively and vice versa.

Output Variable (V5)
Necessity to study the category (V5): *extremely small, very small, small, more or less medium, medium, big, very big, extremely big.*
It means how intensively the student should study the given category in order to successfully achieve study objectives. The output variable reflects a real state of student's knowledge and sets the need/importance of studies for the given course.

Didactic Test Assessment Using LFLC 2000
The last step consists in assessing the didactic test. Before describing the assessment itself, let's describe the knowledge base stored, which is stored in the ES. The ES has a knowledge base made up of 135 IF-THEN linguistic rules. Figure 2 shows a sample screenshot of the IF-THEN rules in tool LFLC 2000, where the rules were created:

V1 & V2 & V3 & V4 --> V5

		V1	V2	V3	V4	V5
2.	☑	me	sm	vesm	sm	vesm
3.	☑	bi	sm	vesm	sm	exsm
4.	☑	sm	me	vesm	sm	sm
5.	☑	me	me	vesm	sm	vesm
6.	☑	bi	me	vesm	sm	exsm
7.	☑	sm	bi	vesm	sm	sm
8.	☑	me	bi	vesm	sm	vesm

Fig. 2. A screenshot of user interface in LFLC 2000

When assessing the test, student's answers are grouped into categories (topic respectively). For each category, the values of all input variables (V1–V4) are counted. The results from LFLC 2000 are stored in base B1.

Implementation of Module M2
We do not create a universal model of a student because each student is unique, thus we do not use several pre-set models of students to which a student would be assigned and thus more student would have the same study plan. Our concept considers own database for each student, which is shaped by the results of the didactic test and questionnaire of sensory preferences.

Each course has its electronic version, but electronic versions are not interconnected. Therefore, it was needed to include all the data from the previous courses. After the upload was done, we had to set how to guide the student in the course.

Methodology of Guiding a Student in an E-course
Guiding a student in an e-course was based on a methodology which had to ensure to correspond with the results of the initial didactic test and the questionnaire as well as to enable to react to student's progress during his study (if possible with no manual interference from teacher's side).

In a regular e-course, the students has the same study materials and all lessons available. But having gathered all necessary information about students, we can proceed to adapting the e-course to them. LMS Moodle enables to work with Access restriction possibilities, as shown in Fig. 3.

Figure 4 shows how to restrict access to a whole lesson on the basis of the results from the didactic test. Figure 4 shows how a student sees it in Moodle.

However, a complication might arise in a moment when the student could avoid a lesson due to the initial didactic test result (V5 = *extremely small, very small or small*), i.e. access is restricted, but the student must pass a revision lesson = Cumulative test. A Cumulative test checks if the student were not lucky during the initial didactic test or whether he has done a good job during studying the corresponding lesson, i.e. if

Access restrictions ☑ Student must ▾ match any ▾ of the following

User profile field Present simple ▾ contains ▾ velká ✕

or

User profile field Present simple ▾ is equal to ▾ střední ✕

or

Grade CUMULATIVE TEST - PRESENT TENSES ▾ ☐ must be ≥ % ☑ must be < 70 % ✕

Add restriction...

Fig. 3. Restricting access to a whole lesson

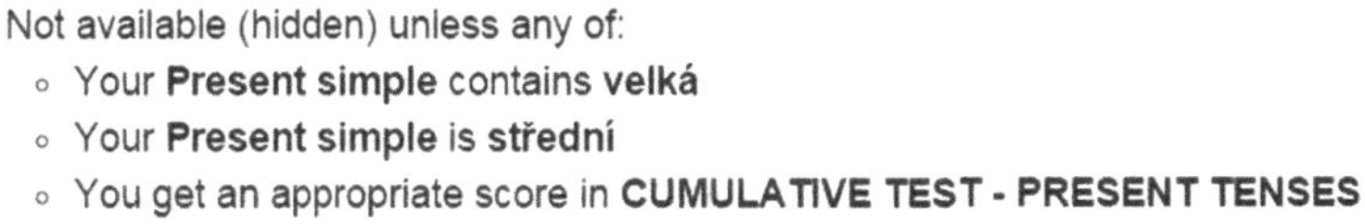

Not available (hidden) unless any of:
 ◦ Your **Present simple** contains **velká**
 ◦ Your **Present simple** is **střední**
 ◦ You get an appropriate score in **CUMULATIVE TEST - PRESENT TENSES**

Fig. 4. Access restriction from student's point of view

student's knowledge is consistent. If the student fails the Cumulative test, the lesson is retroactively opened, which is ensured by conditional access restriction by Cumulative test – Present tenses grade. If the grade is lower than 70%, the lesson is opened. Thus, the student has a possibility to come back to the given Category and subsequently to attempt the Cumulative test two more times. Three attempts are the limit for all tests in the course.

Setting restrictions for Cumulative tests is more complicated. There are more Cumulative tests as each test checks knowledge of the preceding lessons (Present tenses, Past tenses, Future tenses, Perfect tenses, etc.).

The initial didactic test has not assessed V5 of both categories (Present tenses) as *extremely big, very big* or *big*. Both categories are closed and the student can proceed directly to the Cumulative test.

The initial didactic test has not assessed V5 of one Category as *extremely big, very big* or *big*, but the other one yes. Prior to proceeding to the Cumulative test, the student must pass the Progress test of the open category.

The initial didactic test has assessed V5 both categories (Present tenses) as *extremely big, very big* or *big*. Both categories are open and prior to proceeding to the Cumulative test, the student must pass the Progress test in each open Category.

Having successfully passed the Cumulative test, the student is able to go to the following part in their study plan, which means to another open lesson or Cumulative test. This procedure is repeated until a successful end. Individual setting of the studied subject matter is based on student's results from the initial didactic test as well as on his progress through the course.

Applying Module M3
Diagnostics in this module is changed in the form presented to the student. This process is normative. This stage can be applied more times, even it is limited by the number of

repetitions. If the expected amount of knowledge is acquired, the student has successfully finished the course. If it is on the contrary, B1 must be changed so the a different way of study materials are found.

4   Verification

4.1   Target Group of the Experiment

The reasons to verify the proposed model on the XANG3 students were as follows:

It was necessary to select a course taught in the winter term (XANG2 is taught in the summer term).

Students of higher grades are familiar with LMS Moodle.

Students entering XANG3 are expected to have knowledge of XANG1 and XANG2.

Thus we can use testing of a wide range of categories which have different weights of importance for further studies.

Students are expected to finish; the first grade students have a high drop-out ratio.

The number of XANG3 students is not lower than in XANG1 (XANG1 = 207; XANG3 = 212 in a demonstration period of 2008–2014), see Fig. 5 (newer data is not needed as it only serves for a demonstration purpose).

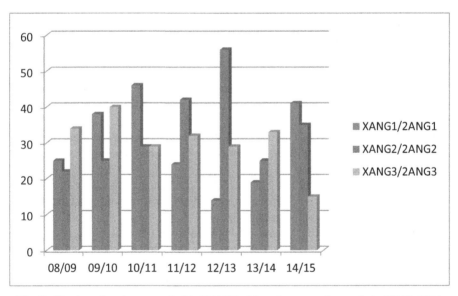

Fig. 5. Number of students enrolled in XANG1–3 in a demonstration period of 2008–2014

Students entering this course should already have knowledge of XANG1 and XANG2 grammar:

Present tenses (XANG1), Past tenses (XANG1), Numerals (XANG1), Present perfect tenses (XANG2), Passive voice (XANG2), Adjectives (XANG2), Modal verbs (XANG2), Verb patterns (XANG2).

XANG3 follows with: (a) Grammar: Past perfect tenses, Future tenses and conditionals, Countable nouns, Phrasal verbs and idioms. (b) Topics: Databases, Computer security, Networking, Network topologies, Giving talks.

4.2 Evaluation of the Structure and Setting of the E-learning Course

The structure of XANG3 e-learning course was designed in order that the student had a possibility to successfully pass it without the need to enter XANG1 or XANG2.

Each lesson contained study materials for each VARK modality. In addition, it contained auto-tests to student's self-revision before taking the Progress or Cumulative tests. As mentioned above, no student had only one VARK type of study materials available, but rather two or three types. Similarly, no student had all four types available.

A combination of lessons that were recommended for a student was also varying. In the case of an advanced student, the study plan would "narrow" to a mere 6 Cumulative tests, which would allow the student to use the saved time for studies of other, less mastered, courses. In opposite, extreme case, the student would have to take all 21 compulsory tests, which would indicate very low level of knowledge.

The setting of student's progress through the course proved to be satisfactory. The created and implemented methodology, i.e. a system of conditions, enabled the system to react to student's results and considered them in further planning. The verification has not been carried out on a sample of students divided into an experimental and verification group due to a low number of students enrolled in the given semester (only 14 students). The results would not lead then to statistically representative conclusions.

5 Conclusion

In this paper, the authors have presented their approach to new processes how to deal with an e-learning course. In the introductory part, the approach was compared with other approaches used in e-learning, primarily in the area of learning styles. Next part introduces necessary changes to the e-learning platform. The proposed approach follows the contemporary challenges in e-learning.

A great advantage of the proposed methodology is that it takes advantage of a conditional progress in the course as well as it integrates new parts in student's portfolio, which enables to develop a personalised study plan automatically, i.e. without any manual interference.

Our future research should be oriented on creating a student's plan of studies while taking into consideration time requirements of each study object and the e-course as a whole.

Acknowledgements. This paper was supported by the internal grant SGS05/PRF/2019.

References

1. Bos, E., van de Plassche, J.: A knowledge-based, English verb-form tutor. J. Artif. Intell. Educ. **5**, 107–129 (1994)

2. Rudak, L.: Susceptibility to e-teaching. In: ICT for Competitiveness, Karviná, pp. 10–16 (2012)
3. Murphy, M., McTear, M.: Learner modelling for intelligent CALL. In: Jameson, A., Paris, C., Tasso, C. (eds.) User Modeling. ICMS, vol. 383, pp. 301–312. Springer, Vienna (1997). https://doi.org/10.1007/978-3-7091-2670-7_31
4. El Hmoudová, D., Milková, E.: Computer-based testing in the field of foreign language assessment. In: Efficiency and Responsibility in Education, Czech University of Life Sciences, Prague (2012)
5. Kostolanyová, K.: Teorie adaptivního e-learningu. Ostravská univerzita, Ostrava (2012)
6. Samson, D.: An architecture for web-based e-learning promoting re-usable adaptive educational e-content. Educ. Tech. Soc. **5**, 27–37 (2002)
7. Bradáč, V.: Adaptive model to support decision-making in language e-learning. In: International Conference on Education and New Learning Technologies - Proceedings, Barcelona, pp. 4036–4045 (2013)
8. Habiballa, H.: Using software package LFLC 2000. In: 2nd International Conference Aplimat 2003, Bratislava, pp. 355–358 (2003)
9. Bradáč, V.: Enhacing assessment of students' knowledge using fuzzy logic in e-learning. In: 10th International Scientific Conference on Distance Learning in Applied Informatics, pp. 251–262. Wolters Kluwer, Štúrovo (2014)
10. VARK (n.d.). http://vark-learn.com/home/
11. Leite, W.L.: Attempted validation of the scores of the VARK: learning styles inventory with multitrait-multimethod confirmatory factor analysis models. Educ. Psychol. Measur. **70**(2), 323–339 (2009)

Social Role in Organizational Management Understanding People Behavior and Motivation

Nuno Maia[1] , Mariana Neves[2] , Agostinho Barbosa[3] , Bruno Carrulo[4] ,
Nuno Araújo[5] , Ana Fernandes[6] , Dinis Vicente[7] , Jorge Ribeiro[8] ,
Henrique Vicente[1,6] , and José Neves[1,5(✉)]

[1] Centro Algoritmi, Universidade do Minho, Braga, Portugal
nuno.maia@mundiservicos.pt, jneves@di.uminho.pt
[2] Deloitte, London, UK
maneves@deloitte.co.uk
[3] CHTS, EPE, Penafiel, Portugal
agostinhobarbosa@hotmail.com
[4] Unidade Local de Saúde de Castelo Branco, Castelo Branco, Portugal
bruno@carrulo.me
[5] Instituto Politécnico de Saúde do Norte, CESPU, Gandra, Portugal
nuno.araujo@ipsn.cespu.pt
[6] Departamento de Química, Escola de Ciências e Tecnologia, REQUIMTE/LAQV,
Universidade de Évora, Évora, Portugal
anavilafernandes@gmail.com, hvicente@uevora.pt
[7] Escola Superior de Tecnologia e Gestão de Leiria,
Instituto Politécnico de Leiria, Leiria, Portugal
dinisvicente98@gmail.com
[8] Escola Superior de Tecnologia e Gestão, ARC4DigiT – Applied Research Center for Digital
Transformation, Instituto Politécnico de Viana do Castelo, Viana do Castelo, Portugal
jribeiro@estg.ipvc.pt

Abstract. The aim of this work is to respond to the need to rethink the behavior and motivation of employees in their relationship with managers and social groups, i.e., one's main goal is based on increasing engagement in order to reach organizational goals and job workers satisfaction, a complex concept that is influenced by different causes. Indeed, in this work it is analyzed the impact of working conditions on job satisfaction. This is where attention is drawn to the concept of entropy, since we are not focusing on the value a variable can take, but on the effort that has been expended to obtain it. The idea of entropy comes from a principle of thermodynamics dealing with energy. It usually refers to the idea that everything in the universe eventually moves from order to disorder, and entropy is the measurement of that change, that is used here to understand and assess the workers behavior and motivation. The subsequent formal model is based on a set of logical structures for knowledge representation and reasoning that conform to the above entropic view, then leading to an Artificial Neural Network approach to computation, an archetypal that considers the motive behind the action.

Keywords: Motivation and Behavior · Job Satisfaction · Entropy · Logic Programming · Knowledge Representation and Reasoning · Artificial Neural Networks

© Springer Nature Singapore Pte Ltd. 2020
P. Sitek et al. (Eds.): ACIIDS 2020, CCIS 1178, pp. 527–536, 2020.
https://doi.org/10.1007/978-981-15-3380-8_46

1   Introduction

Motivation and *Behavior* issues are intertwined; unmotivated workers normally mis-behave and workers who misbehave do not care about corporate aims. Motivational qualities are associated with poorer to better persistence of behavior and with worse to better psychological outcomes such as well-being and personal satisfaction [1]. Motiva-tion is to be seen as the energy that self-controls our behavior that, in turn, may emerge from different sources. From the point of view of self-determination, both the expanse of motivation one has and the quality of that motivation are important. One's interest is in the quality of motivation that may show the way to perseverance. These are the causes expected to be associated with positive outcomes, like better persistence and feelings of personal satisfaction [2]. This meta-framework has also yielded new theo-ries and research aimed at more accurate measurement and understanding of personal, social, and contextual influences on target selection, target construction, and behavioral intentions. The article is divided into four sections. Following the introduction, a new section is presented which explores the fundamentals adopted in this work, namely the concept of Entropy and the use of Logic Programming for Knowledge Representation and Reasoning [3, 4], consistent with an *Artificial Neural Network* approach to compu-tation [5, 6], where data is worked out in terms of energy transfer operations [7]. Then conclusions are drawn and future work is outlined.

2   Fundamentals

Knowledge Representation and Reasoning (*KRR*) practices may be understood as a process of energy devaluation [7], i.e., according to the *First Law of Thermodynamics* is a quantity well-preserved that cannot be consumed in the sense of destruction, but may be consumed in the sense of devaluation. It is this facet of the thermodynamic concept that will be dissected here so as to understand this revolutionary turn in terms of the representation of information and knowledge [8, 9]. Consider, for example, a collective of workers who want to estimate their health literacy. To fulfil this goal it will be used a questionnaire with four (4) entries, *R1*, *R2*, *R3*, and *R4,* and entitled *Collective Workers Questionnaires-Four-Item* (*CWQ – 4*), to which is associated an extended version of a Likert-type scale, viz.

Very Good (4), Good (3), Fair (2), Poor (1), Fair (2), Good (3), Very Good (4)
and a question stated in the terms, viz.

How do you evaluate the health knowledge of the workers' group referred to above?

The answers, illustrated in Table 1, seek to enable the energy expended by each worker (*EXergy*) to achieve a certain level of literacy (Fig. 1). In general terms, the total amount of energy it is represented by a circle with area 1 (one), divided into four slots, once we are considering four issues (i.e., *R1*, *R2*, *R3* and *R4*). An analysis of Table 1 shows that the answer for *R1* was *Very Good (4)* → *Fair (2)*, reflecting the fact that literacy levels are in principle considered *Very Good (4)* (the symbol → indicates a tendency towards energy consumption). However, signs of deterioration can lead to a *Fair (2)* answer. For *R2* the answer was *Fair (2)* → *Very Good (4),* indicating that while the rating is *Fair (2)* overall, there is an uptrend that can lead to a *Very Good (4)* answer.

Table 1. *CWQ – 4* worker answer.

Questions	Scale							vagueness
	(4)	(3)	(2)	(1)	(2)	(3)	(4)	
R1	×		×					
R2					×		×	
R3						×		
R4								×

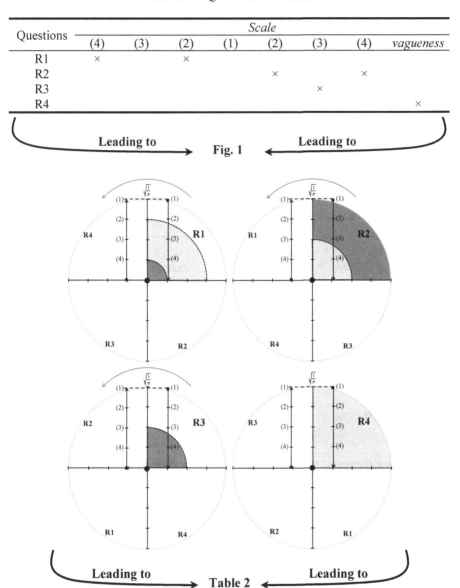

Leading to **Fig. 1** ← Leading to

Leading to **Table 2** ← Leading to

Fig. 1. A graphical representation of a worker answer to *CWQ – 4* questionnaire for the *Best-case scenario*.

For *R3*, the answer was *Good (3)*, a fact that speaks for itself. For *R4*, the answer is *I do not know* what causes us to believe that the energy consumed ranges in the interval *0…1* (indicating *VAgueness*). The remain energy, i.e., the energy not yet consumed is named *ANergy*. These terms designate all possible energy operations as pure energy transfer

Table 2. *Best* and *worst-case's scenarios* evaluation.

Questions	Best Case Scenario	Worst Case Scenario
R1	$exergy_{R1} = \frac{1}{4}\pi r^2 \Big]_0^{\frac{1}{4}\sqrt{\frac{1}{\pi}}} =$ $= \frac{1}{4}\pi \left(\frac{1}{4}\sqrt{\frac{1}{\pi}}\right)^2 - 0 = 0.02$ $vagueness_{R1} = \frac{1}{4}\pi r^2 \Big]_{\frac{1}{4}\sqrt{\frac{1}{\pi}}}^{\frac{3}{4}\sqrt{\frac{1}{\pi}}} = 0.12$ $anergy_{R1} = \frac{1}{4}\pi r^2 \Big]_{\frac{1}{4}\sqrt{\frac{1}{\pi}}}^{\sqrt{\frac{1}{\pi}}} = 0.23$	$exergy_{R1} = \frac{1}{4}\pi r^2 \Big]_0^{\frac{3}{4}\sqrt{\frac{1}{\pi}}} = 0.14$ $vagueness_{R1} = \frac{1}{4}\pi r^2 \Big]_{\frac{3}{4}\sqrt{\frac{1}{\pi}}}^{\frac{3}{4}\sqrt{\frac{1}{\pi}}} = 0$ $anergy_{R1} = \frac{1}{4}\pi r^2 \Big]_{\frac{3}{4}\sqrt{\frac{1}{\pi}}}^{\sqrt{\frac{1}{\pi}}} = 0.11$
R2	$exergy_{R_2} = \frac{1}{4}\pi r^2 \Big]_{0\sqrt{\frac{1}{\pi}}}^{\frac{2}{4}\sqrt{\frac{1}{\pi}}} = 0.06$ $vagueness_{R_2} = \frac{1}{4}\pi r^2 \Big]_0^{\frac{2}{4}\sqrt{\frac{1}{\pi}}} = 0.06$ $anergy_{R_2} = \frac{1}{4}\pi r^2 \Big]_{2\sqrt{\frac{1}{\pi}}}^{\sqrt{\frac{1}{\pi}}} = 0.19$	$exergy_{R_2} = \frac{1}{4}\pi r^2 \Big]_0^{\sqrt{\frac{1}{\pi}}} = 0.25$ $vagueness_{R_2} = \frac{1}{4}\pi r^2 \Big]_{\sqrt{\frac{1}{\pi}}}^{\sqrt{\frac{1}{\pi}}} = 0$ $anergy_{R_2} = \frac{1}{4}\pi r^2 \Big]_{\sqrt{\frac{1}{\pi}}}^{\sqrt{\frac{1}{\pi}}} = 0$
R3	$exergy_{R_3} = \frac{1}{4}\pi r^2 \Big]_{0\sqrt{\frac{1}{\pi}}}^{\frac{2}{4}\sqrt{\frac{1}{\pi}}} = 0.06$ $vagueness_{R_3} = \frac{1}{4}\pi r^2 \Big]_{\frac{2}{4}\sqrt{\frac{1}{\pi}}}^{\frac{2}{4}\sqrt{\frac{1}{\pi}}} = 0$ $anergy_{R_3} = \frac{1}{4}\pi r^2 \Big]_{\frac{2}{4}\sqrt{\frac{1}{\pi}}}^{\sqrt{\frac{1}{\pi}}} = 0.19$	$exergy_{R_3} = \frac{1}{4}\pi r^2 \Big]_0^{\frac{2}{4}\sqrt{\frac{1}{\pi}}} = 0.06$ $vagueness_{R_3} = \frac{1}{4}\pi r^2 \Big]_{\frac{2}{4}\sqrt{\frac{1}{\pi}}}^{\frac{2}{4}\sqrt{\frac{1}{\pi}}} = 0$ $anergy_{R_3} = \frac{1}{4}\pi r^2 \Big]_{\frac{2}{4}\sqrt{\frac{1}{\pi}}}^{\sqrt{\frac{1}{\pi}}} = 0.19$
R4	$exergy_{R_4} = \frac{1}{4}\pi r^2 \Big]_0^0 = 0$ $vagueness_{R_4} = \frac{1}{4}\pi r^2 \Big]_0^{\sqrt{\frac{1}{\pi}}} = 0.25$ $anergy_{R_4} = \frac{1}{4}\pi r^2 \Big]_0^{\sqrt{\frac{1}{\pi}}} = 0.25$	$exergy_{R_4} = \frac{1}{4}\pi r^2 \Big]_0^{\sqrt{\frac{1}{\pi}}} = 0.25$ $vagueness_{R_4} = \frac{1}{4}\pi r^2 \Big]_{\sqrt{\frac{1}{\pi}}}^{\sqrt{\frac{1}{\pi}}} = 0$ $anergy_{R_4} = \frac{1}{4}\pi r^2 \Big]_{\sqrt{\frac{1}{\pi}}}^{\sqrt{\frac{1}{\pi}}} = 0$

Leading to → **Table 3** ← Leading to

and consumption practices, in an open system, where the evaluation of *Job* Satisfaction (*JS*) and the *Quality-of-Information* (*QoI*) for the various elements that make up the *CWQ-4* follow the practice presented in [8, 9] (Tables 2 and 3).

Table 3. The *collective workers* (*cw*) predicate's extent obtained according to the answer of a worker to the *CWQ – 4* questionnaire.

EX BCS	VA BCS	AN BCS	JS BCS	QoI BCS	EX WCS	VA WCS	AN WCS	JS WCS	QoI WCS
0.14	0.43	0.86	0.90	0.43	0.70	0	0.30	0.95	0.30

where *BCS* and *WCS* stand for the *Best Case Scenario* and *Worst Case Scenario*, respectively.

3   Organizational Behavior – The Leadership Dimension

Organizational behavior relies on the notion that managers must understand the workers' aspects and treat them as key assets to achieve their aims. Management taking a special interest in workers that make them feel like part of a special group, i.e., to be part of a special culture that makes possible the identification of their members in an immaterial dimension based on the inter-relationship among individuals in an organizational setting. The management as a way to achieve organizational goals (results) [10] must see persons as an asset towards group performance. This process is associated to the leadership's course of action where the variables *Power* and *Justice* are paramount. Indeed, the leader must be in charge of people's behavior and attitudes that, in turn, are the back bone of social skills [11, 12]. One may look to its complexity in terms of the questionnaires, viz.

- *The use of Power, i.e., those at the metalevel have to involve those at the object one*
- *The evaluation of Justice, where rewards and merit or value are central issues and have a positive effect on group's cooperation; and*
- *The Leadership process that shapes up the involvement and participation of all actors, where persons in charge have to be involved and be in the lead.*

The purpose of the operandi leadership mode is to encourage people to create uniqueness with the organization/institution, therefore enabling the involvement and participation of individuals/groups. Indeed, the leader is the aggregating element that builds the organization's image as the organizer of the management course of action. This process is associated with the development of the *affective* dimension where the *emotions* and *feelings* that develop in the inter-relational proceedings structure the forms of identification and involvement of the people that interact within the system [13]. The leader has the challenge of being an empathic person. *Empathy* is the aggregate force that enables the development of identity between people and the people inside the group. Indeed, the process of regulating people's identification is based on values, i.e., on the organizational principles of an inter-relational activity, values that weigh in the shaping of the

Leadership Dimension, given here in terms of the extensions of the relations or predicates *working environment* (*we*) and *communication* (*com*). To the *Working Environment Questionnaires-Four-Item* (*WEQ – 4*) one may have, viz.

R1 – Creates a good working environment where people feel good;
R2 – Accepts criticism with openness;
R3 – Articulate ideas, know how to argue and express his/her disagreement; and
R4 – Gives clear directives and sets priorities for the team.

For the *Communication Questionnaires-Five-Item* (*CQ – 5*) one may have, viz.

R1 – Form effective teams considering the complementarities of their members;
R2 – Search, integrate and evaluate the information needed before making decisions;
R3 – Inspire confidence;
R4 – May listen and facilitates dialogue; and
R5 – Facilitates and promotes access to information.

Understanding Others is one of the vectors of involvement and participation of subordinates. In order to evaluate this factor, it was used the *Understanding Others Questionnaires-Four-Item* (*UOQ – 4*), viz.

R1 – The leader knows how to end a discussion;
R2 – The leader knows when to support and advise or give autonomy;
R3 – The leader knows how to manage a debate, clarifying and questioning others to achieve a deeper understanding of the situations; and
R4 – The leader always imposes his/her will.

These three questionnaires are now judged on the basis of the scale, viz.
    Yes, definitely (4), Yes, to some extent (3), No (2), I do not Know (1), No (2), Yes, to some extent (3), Yes, definitely (4)
    and the query, viz.
    As a member of the organization, *how much would you agree with each one of the questionnaires referred to above?*
    Table 4 shows an employee' responses to questionnaires *WEQ-4*, *CQ-5* and *UOQ-4*. The evaluation process for each questionnaire is the same as for *CSEQ-4*. Table 5 describes the scope of the predicates that were determined for each questionnaire.

4   Computational Thinking

Context-oriented programming is not new, but an out of the ordinary field that can help us to figure out or work out data. On the other hand, as much as Artificial Intelligence or Machine Learning is presently exercised, we have not found a way to ask the computer why did he do it? We know how to teach an algorithm to identify a cat in a photo, but we cannot ask why it is a cat. This was the main reason why we changed the system of

Table 4. A worker answers to the *WEQ* – *4*, *CQ* – *5* and *UOQ* – *4* questionnaires

Questionnaire	Questions	Scale							vagueness
		(4)	(3)	(2)	(1)	(2)	(3)	(4)	
WEQ – 4	R1		×						
	R2		×		×				
	R3						×		
	R4								×
CQ – 5	R1								×
	R2			×					
	R3						×	×	
	R4	×			×				
	R5								×
UOQ – 4	R1								
	R2								×
	R3						×		
	R4						×	×	

Leading to	**Leading to**
→**Table 5** ←	

information or knowledge representation. Here we are not concerned with knowing the absolute value that a variable assumes, but with quantifying the evolutionary process associated with it, i.e., which has led this variable to take on a certain value.

Program 1. The *we*, *com* and *uo* predicates' scopes for the *Best-case scenario*.

```
{
/* The sentence below states that the extent of predicate we are made on the clauses that are
explicitly stated plus the ones that cannot be discarded */
    ¬ we (EX, VA, AN, JS, QoI) ← not we (EX, VA, AN, JS, QoI),
                    not exception_we (EX, VA, AN, JS, QoI).
/* The sentence below denotes a we axiom*/
    we (0.28, 0.42, 0.67, 0.71, 0.30).
/*The sentence below states that the extent of predicate com is made on the clauses that are
explicitly stated plus the ones that cannot be discarded*/
    ¬ com (EX, VA, AN, JS, QoI) ← not com (EX, VA, AN, JS, QoI),
                    not exception_com (EX, VA, AN, JS, QoI).
/* The sentence below denotes a com axiom*/
    com (0.24, 0.59, 0.65, 0.56, 0.17).
/*The sentence below states that the extent of predicate uo is made on the clauses that are
explicitly stated plus the ones that cannot be discarded*/
    ¬ uo (EX, VA, AN, JS, QoI) ← not uo (EX, VA, AN, JS, QoI),
                    not exception_uo (EX, VA, AN, JS, QoI).
/* The sentence below denotes a uo axiom*/
    uo (0.34, 0.36, 0.52, 0.71, 0.30)
```

Table 5. The *working environment* (*we*), *communication* (*com*) and *understanding others* (*uo*) predicates' scopes obtained according to an employee's answers to the *WEQ − 4, CQ − 5* and *UOQ − 4* questionnaires.

Questionnaire	EX BCS	VA BCS	AN BCS	JS BCS	QoI BCS	EX WCS	VA WCS	AN WCS	JS WCS	QoI WCS
WEQ − 4	0.28	0.42	0.67	0.71	0.30	0.75	0	0.27	0.66	0.25
CQ − 5	0.24	0.59	0.65	0.56	0.17	0.88	0	0.24	0.47	0.12
UOQ − 4	0.34	0.36	0.52	0.71	0.30	0.73	0	0.30	0.68	0.27

Leading to $\longrightarrow$ **Program 1** $\longleftarrow$ **Leading to**

where $\neg$ denotes *strong negation* and not stands for *negation-by-failure*. Based on these data, an *Artificial Neural Network (ANN)* [5, 6] (Fig. 2) can now be trained to assess the social role of workers in organizational management and a measure of its sustainability. To an enterprise with 30 (thirty) employees, the training sets may be gotten by making obvious the theorem, viz.

$$\forall\, (EX_1, VA_1, AN_1, JS_1, QoI_1, \cdots, EX_3, VA_3, AN_3, JS_3, QoI_3),$$
$$(we(EX_1, VA_1, AN_1, JS_1, QoI_1\,), \cdots, uo(EX_3, VA_3, AN_3, JS_3, QoI_3))$$

in every way possible, i.e., generating all the different possible sequences that combine the extents of the predicates *we, com* and *uo*. It amounts to 27405 sets (75% for training, 25% for tests) that are given in the form, viz.

$$\{\{we(EX_1, VA_1, AN_1, JS_1, QoI_1),$$
$$com(EX_2, VA_2, AN_2, JS_2, QoI_2), uo(EX_3, VA_3, AN_3, JS_3, QoI_3)\}, \cdots\} \approx$$
$$\approx \{\{we(0.28, 0.42, 0.67, 0.71, 0.30),$$
$$com(0.24, 0.59, 0.65, 0.56, 0.17), uo(0.34, 0.36, 0.52, 0.71, 0.30)\}, \cdots\}$$

In terms of the output of the *ANN*, it is considered the evaluation of the workers *Job Satisfaction (JS)*, which may be weigh up in the form (Fig. 2), viz.

$$\{\{(JS_{we} + JS_{com} + JS_{uo})/3\}, \cdots\} \approx$$
$$\approx \{\{(0.71 + 0.56 + 0.71)/3 = 0.66\}, \cdots\}$$

and, viz.

$$\{\{(QoI_{we} + QoI_{com} + QoI_{uo})/3\}, \cdots\} \approx$$
$$\approx \{\{(0.30 + 0.17 + 0.30)/3 = 0.26\}, \cdots\}$$

In fact, there are many definitions of organizational culture, but the basic idea to which it refers is a set of values, beliefs, and behaviors created and maintained by the organization's executives and carried out by employees, leading to a sense of responsibility, in terms of an assessment of the employee's degree of *Job Satisfaction* and its level of *Sustainability*, which is done either using the logical program outlined above or the ANN agency shown in Fig. 2.

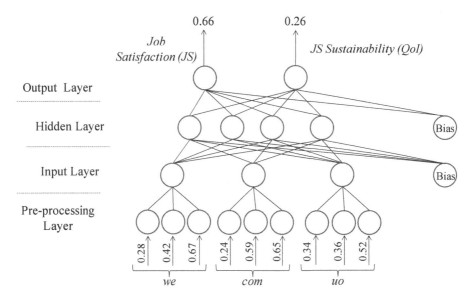

Fig. 2. An abstract view of the *ANN* topology and their training and test processes.

5   Conclusions and Future Work

Motivation can be described as the inner force that influences the direction, intensity and endurance of the voluntary choice of a person's behavior. Motivation is an inner feeling, it defines the psychological state of a person. We have all heard that man is a social animal, and we want to be accepted as we are. This principle helps managers think about encouraging their workforces by identifying their needs. In short, it represents motivation as an ever-changing force and expresses the constant need to satisfy new and higher employee's needs. The approach here proposed potentiate self-actualization, which means realizing one's full potential. This was delivered as a computational agency that integrates the phases of data gathering, foreseeing a logic representation of uncertainty and vagueness, as well as the phases of data processing and results analysis. As future work, and considering how social factors may shape the individual perception of the environment, it is intended to look at ways to figure out the milieu according to the individuals or groups labor's modes.

Acknowledgments. This work has been supported by national funds through FCT – Fundação para a Ciência e Tecnologia within the Project Scope UID/CEC/00319/2019 and UID/QUI/0619/2019.

References

1. Alavi, H.R., Askaripur, M.R.: The relationship between self-esteem and job satisfaction of personnel in government organizations. Public Pers. Manag. **32**(4), 591–600 (2003)
2. Kumar, N., Singh, V.: Job satisfaction and its correlates. Int. J. Res. Econ. Soc. Sci. **1**(2), 11–24 (2011)
3. Neves, J.: A logic interpreter to handle time and negation in logic databases. In: Muller, R., Pottmyer, J. (eds.) Proceedings of the 1984 Annual Conference of the ACM on the 5th Generation Challenge, pp. 50–54. ACM, New York (1984)
4. Ferraz, F., Vicente, H., Costa, A., Neves, J.: Analysis of dyscalculia evidences through artificial intelligence systems. J. Softw. Netw. **2016**, 53–78 (2016)
5. Cortez, P., Rocha, M., Neves, J.: Evolving time series forecasting ARMA models. J. Heuristics **10**, 415–429 (2004)
6. Fernández-Delgado, M., Cernadas, E., Barro, S., Ribeiro, J., Neves, J.: Direct kernel perceptron (DKP): ultra-fast kernel ELM-based classification with non-iterative closed-form weight calculation. J. Neural Netw. **50**, 60–71 (2014)
7. Wenterodt, T., Herwig, H.: The entropic potential concept: a new way to look at energy transfer operations. Entropy **16**, 2071–2084 (2014)
8. Neves, J., et al.: Entropy and organizational performance. In: Pérez García, H., Sánchez González, L., Castejón Limas, M., Quintián Pardo, H., Corchado Rodríguez, E. (eds.) HAIS 2019. LNCS (LNAI), vol. 11734, pp. 206–217. Springer, Cham (2019). https://doi.org/10.1007/978-3-030-29859-3_18
9. Fernandes, B., Vicente, H., Ribeiro, J., Capita, A., Analide, C., Neves, J.: Fully informed vulnerable road users – simpler, maybe better. In: Proceedings of the 21st International Conference on Information Integration and Web-Based Applications & Services (iiWAS 2019), pp 600–604. ACM, New York (2019)
10. Goleman, D.: Working with Emotional Intelligence. Bantam Book, New York (1998)
11. Damásio, A.: Looking for Spinoza – Joy, Sorrow and the Feeling Brain. A Harvest Book Harcourt Inc., London (2003)
12. Luhtanen, R., Crocker, J.: A collective self-esteem scale: self-evaluation of one's social identity. Pers. Soc. Psychol. Bull. **18**, 302–318 (1992)
13. Drucker, P.: Management Challenges for the 21 Century. HarperCollins Publishers, New York (1999)

Development of Southern Research Recommendation System

Nawapon Kewsuwun[1][(✉)], Kanyarat Kwiecien[1], and Chumchit Sae-Chan[2]

[1] Department of Information Science, Faculty of Humanities and Social Sciences,
Khon Kaen University, Khon Kaen 40002, Thailand
tn.kewsuwun@hotmail.com
[2] Department of Library and Information Science, Faculty of Humanities and Social Sciences,
Prince of Songkla University, Pattani 94000, Thailand

Abstract. The research was to identify needs on design and development of a research recommendation system for southern province groups in Thailand. The system employs semantic search function, research system structure and scope of knowledge during January 2008 to December 2017. 3,873 entries had been gathered from ThaiLIS, TNRR, and Southern universities research database by employing textual analysis and knowledge organization focusing on Classification Approach and categorization which main topics are sorted and categorized. To develop ontology, it applies knowledge engineering concept and using Protégé Ontology Editor version 5.5 beta to process the data for the accurate system development according to user-centered design concept. The study findings were the developed system is able to support information exchange, information retrieval, and research search and to decrease research redundancy and unnecessary budgeting. Moreover, the system could possible enhance conducting more innovations, confirming experts in the area, showing research trends, and showing research results on related fields, strategies, and problems which leads to the Southern developments extensively. After the implementation, the users' overall opinions and satisfaction was at a high level and information retrieval efficiency of system was at a good level with 0.70 accuracy, 0.78 recall, 0.88 precision, and 0.82 F-measure.

Keywords: Southern research recommendation · Southern Thailand · Research for development · Information and knowledge management · Ontology

1 Introduction

South of Thailand is coastal areas along Thai Gulf and Andaman Sea also it is closed to Malaysia border. Therefore, there are advantages on border trade and tourism [1]. Most of the South are forests and wetlands which is valuable for planting and eco-tourism [2]. Besides, the Southern economic structure consists of agriculture, industry, trade, and tourism, moreover, Southern culture portrays its own identity as uniqueness and diversity which could be conveyed as multiculturalism. In accordance to multiculturalism, the South welcomes all tourists as a hub of diversity [3]. These factors are strengths of the

© Springer Nature Singapore Pte Ltd. 2020
P. Sitek et al. (Eds.): ACIIDS 2020, CCIS 1178, pp. 537–549, 2020.
https://doi.org/10.1007/978-981-15-3380-8_47

South also relate to Thailand 4.0 concept in which the government encourages the people to have outstanding innovations along with creative culture, and to create services which lead to effective product development and tourism services [4].

Southern development policy and strategic plan and the Office of Strategy Management, Southern province group focuses on setting up Thailand stability and sustainable development framework under the sufficient economy concept. Moreover, international network has been brought to help on agriculture, food processing industry, and tourism development which based on economic expansions as increasing various types of business and employment rate also enhancing competitive man-power as to be ready for industry investment and marine transportation development like Joint Development Strategic for Border Area or JDS and Indonesia - Malaysia - Thailand Growth Triangle or IMT – GT [4].

Process on employing strategies into practice and driving the region is based on participation among the people, organizations, and departments in province group for the utmost development [5]. This drive and development pay attention to fundamentals, in other words, the developments on basic structures of economy, society, and community along with research and development on inventing innovations, gaining new knowledge, and solving problems systematically. In terms of development process and problem-solving, it employs needs and problem analysis as to gain findings which lead to practical research methodology [6]. Further research has been used as tools to reach body of knowledge, answers, explanations and systematic development, to reconfirm whether the knowledge is existing, and to see if the knowledge can be applied or solved problems [1].

Conducting research leads to freshly effective innovations which used for further development and precise solutions to strengthen the region and the nation. To conduct research for development in the South becomes an essential tool in constructing new knowledge which could lead to innovations especially agriculture and fisheries also research on multiculturalism. These 2 research topics included 5 targets which are encouraged and launched by the government [7]. Research procedure includes research problem, research statement, literature review, research framework, population and target group, research design, research tools, data analysis, research findings, and implement [8]. Each step needs information to be part of literature review and to support the ongoing research [9]. Gathering related information expands the area of knowledge to be multidisciplinary, yet due to information overload, it causes unreliability and unclear scope of knowledge.

To ease data search, confirmation, and support research in the South there should be a systematic knowledge management as categorizing and classifying data [10] which is easy to access. The knowledge has been categorized into tree structure according to the relationship of each concept [11] in accordance to policies, plans, strategies, problems context. These relationships are combined into the structure of information systems that the semantic web technology uses to search or recommendation system can understand, therefore, it helps on showing clear causes and effects also differentiating relationship in scope of related knowledge in the form of ontology [12] will serve to support the separation relationship process of knowledge scope relevant and not related to each other. Moreover, it helps users making decisions, gathering information, or continuing further research for development in the South. Previous studies regarding recommendation system in Thailand show that there were systems developed for particular topics or areas, for example, a recommendation system for North Eastern Thailand, a system on collecting autobiography, a knowledge database on enhancing services for diabetic patient or a research database on rice. Yet the researchers did not find any research recommendation system for Southern part of Thailand even it is one of the main resources on economic and education in Thailand [1]. Consequently, 14 provinces of the South could not confirm or manage existing knowledge effectively [3]. Besides, the knowledge was scattered; it might need to be managed and shared systematically.

Therefore, this research aims to identify needs on design and development of a research recommendation system for 14 southern province Thailand development. The findings in this research will show the relationships and trends of knowledge based on research of Southern Thailand from the synthesized fixed data, additionally, it is beneficial to reflect gaps on some research points which can be resolved or reused. Identifying research knowledge relationships is to point out relationships between research and strategies, policies and needs which relate to problems. To resolve problems effectively a systematically research should be conducted according to existing research knowledge and grant. Further, this could explain more on relationships of information clearly, similarly, the system will help researchers scoping area of study, searching for information, reducing research redundancy, reducing costs on research redundancy and reconfirming existing knowledge, and creating innovations.

2 Research Objective

To identify needs on design and development of southern research recommendation system for southern province groups in Thailand.

3 Materials and Methodology

The search system development focuses on research and development methodology for innovation, new technology, and new knowledge [13] employing research-based development to be a framework for systematic research process as three phase as follows

3.1 To Scope and Categorize Knowledge Found on Research for Southern Development (Phase 1)

3.1.1 Underlying Concepts
Textual analysis and knowledge organization focusing on classification approach have been applied to sort main topics into tree structure. Approach and theoretical framework applied to this system development are based on classification theory or semantic relationship. To categorize knowledge is to sort and group similar content according to subclasses, meanings, purposes, durations, or locations for gathering proper amount of knowledge structure elements on developing the system [14–17].

3.1.2 Methodology

Mix method research has been brought to manage knowledge structure as using content synthesis to generate research contents and relationships, also using classification approach to classify data concerning meaning and content and then to synthesize research key points systematically.

(1.) The researchers to scope the knowledge 5 references had been used as follows;

1.1 7 strategies from the Ninth National Research Policy and Strategy (2017–2021) formulated by the National Research Council of Thailand.

1.2 10 strategies from the Twelfth National Economic and Social Development Plan (2017–2021) and the 20-year National Strategy framework (2017–2036) formulated by the office of the National Economic and Social Development Board.

1.3 11 strategies from 3 departments of administration and strategy planning of Southern province group development framework (2018–2021).

1.4 Synthesis on problems and needs of people in the Southern province group by the Office of Strategy Management.

1.5 Related research on TNRR, ThaiLIS and southern universities research database in the past 10 years from 2008–2017 then synthesizing the data according to 3 aspects of research knowledge structure: research documents, research basic information, and other related research information. Those research were carefully selected in terms of correctness, completeness, and conciseness, as a result, there were 3,873 entries from 78 departments.

(2.) Textual analysis and knowledge organization had been used to develop the system also focused on classification approach to categorize by analyzing contents to get concepts, relationships, and semantic groups of research data [18–20]. After analyzing the structure was developed based on *(1.)*. The structure had been evaluated by 7 experts (cover expert of policies and plan, information and knowledge management expert and research expert) using Index of item Objective Congruence. Lastly, the system had been fixed according to the experts' feedback and suggestions.

3.1.3 Result

After classifying and categorizing research for southern Thailand development, according to policy and strategy, problem and needs of community: the knowledge structure had been revised according to experts' suggestions in index, domain, concept issues and scope. The results of the knowledge structure had the concept, sub-concept and knowledge scope are as follows [21]:

(1) The overview on scopes of knowledge on Southern development research are as follows;

(1.1) Knowledge Structure consists of 2 domain; each domain consists of 20 class; each class consists of 139 concept; each concept consists of 327 Sub-concept.

(1.2) 2 domains consists of research aspects domain and research work domain.

(1.3) Research aspects domain refers to knowledge related to the research for development of Southern Thailand which consists of 3 knowledge sets: (1) research knowledge on policy, strategy, and management of Southern province group, and (2) research knowledge on problems and needs of Southern province people, consist of 17 class; each class consists of 113 concept; each concept consists of 215 sub-concept.

(1.4) Research work domain refers to knowledge related to the scopes of the research for development of Southern Thailand which consists of 3 classes such as: (1) research documents, (2) basic information and (3) other related information, each class consists of 26 concepts and each concept consists of 112 sub-concepts.

(2) Research synthesis on the Ninth National Research Policy and Strategy, the Twelfth National Economic and Social Development Plan and the 20-year National Strategy framework, administration and strategy planning of Southern province group development framework is classified into 6 classes, 31 concepts, and 95 sub-concepts on research aspects domain: such as research and development, infrastructure development, social development, economic empowerment, sustainable development, and production development.

(3) Research synthesis on the problems and needs of people in Southern province groups in (1) the Office of Strategy Management of Southern border provinces, (2) the Office of Strategy Management of Thai Gulf coast provinces, and (3) the Office of Strategy Management of Andaman coast provinces is classified into 11 classes, 82 concepts, and 120 sub-concepts on research aspects domain: such as safety system and welfare development, education development, career development, business development, tourism development, natural and environmental resources development, public health development, family unit development, agricultural area and innovation system development, transportation development, and solutions on immigrant worker.

(4) Research synthesis on the Southern university research database system, TNRR and ThaiLIS is classified into 3 classes, 26 concepts and 112 sub-concepts on research works domain:

(4.1) Research document – refer to the research documents, article and proceedings on southern development, consist of 2 concepts and 7 sub-concepts

(4.2) Basic research information – refer to Academic positions, qualification, researchers status, tools, population and research target, statistics, researchers contact information and research areas, consist of 8 concepts and 35 sub-concepts

(4.3) Related information – refer to affiliation of researchers, research type, research type divided by subject science and provincial group strategy, researcher region/ province, research area divided by province group, southern regional development strategy office, research funding source, distribution model, source of research, research copyright and data source, data collection method, consist of 16 concepts and 70 sub-concepts.

3.2 System Needs of Researchers' on Southern Development Research (Phase 2)

3.2.1 Underlying Concepts

Quantitative research and user-centered design had been adopted to explore researchers' needs as follows;

Quantitative research and user-centered design had been brought to study the needs focusing on importance, needs, and satisfaction of users. The findings of this assessment are used in the system development process [22]. Moreover, the development uses system approach to construct an effective recommendation system in accordance with the needs and the Southern development strategies. The needs were from 327 researchers of 78 organizations who conducted research regarding Southern Thailand during January 2008 to December 2017. Those 10-year entries had been gathered from ThaiLIS, TNRR, and Southern universities research database which the researchers were able to access. The researchers employed rule of three to get 327 researchers of 78 organizations from the population. After that the researchers used simple random sample method as to get numbers of researchers from each organizations, then collected data from data based. The researchers were able to utilize needs of basic research data, related research data, and suggestions and recommendations on the next phase.

3.2.2 Methodology

(1.) Related data had been collected by reviewing literature focusing on online research database, research search, and research retrievals to compare and contrast the information for reinventing a needs assessment form. Consequently, the form was a 5-rating scale which divided into 3 parts; 7 items on background information, 40 items on needs in design and system development, and open-ended question on needs, opinions, and suggestions. The needs assessment had been sent by post and personally delivered to 327 researchers from 78 organizations to assess.

(2.) The quantitative data had been collected from June–August 2018 and analyzed quantitatively in terms of frequency, percentage, average, and standard deviation to set system development criteria according to the needs. Further, the research proposal and the collected data by quantitative process was confidential and approved by the Center for Ethics in Human Research, Khon Kaen University following the Declaration of Helsinki and ICH GCP.

3.2.3 Findings

Synthesized result of researchers' needs on research for Southern development, collected the data from the needs assessment form (quantitative), the results were the overall of system needs on the system design and development was at a high level as ($\overline{X} = 4.11$), additionally, each needs item portrays the same result as it is at the high level. The first two highest needs item were related research information and basic research information, on the basic research information aspect, it was found that overall needs on system design and development was at a high level ($\overline{X} = 4.07$), further, there were 3 highest needs items as a research area search function, a research population search function, and a search function on research statement or research problem. And the related research information aspect, it was found that overall needs on system design and development was at a high level ($\overline{X}$ = 4.15), further, there were 3 highest needs items as a search function showing research area regarding the Southern province group, a search function showing related research regarding research references, and a search function showing research related to its area and a search function showing research summary.

3.3 Developing the Research Recommendation System for Southern Thailand Development (Phase 3)

Phase 1 (3.1) and Phase 2 (3.2) findings had been brought to conduct in phase 3 (3.3) which are (1.) Ontology development base on knowledge engineering to gather basic knowledge structures (2.) system development to construct the system according to the needs and concepts on user-centered design and system approach.

(1.) Ontology development base on knowledge engineering

(1.1) Underlying concepts: To develop ontology for the system it was designed as a knowledge structure. This development is from 2 domains; research aspects domain referring to knowledge related to the research for development of Southern Thailand and research work domain referring to knowledge related to the scope of the research for development of Southern Thailand into concepts, classes, sub-classes, also systematically categorizing hierarchy of classes and sub-classes. Protégé Ontology Editor version 5.5 beta had been used to develop the ontology.

(1.2) Ontology development procedure: Protégé Ontology Editor Software had been selected as a tool to transfer and store knowledge in terms of ontology and to effectively support semantic search system in terms of knowledge sharing and reusing. The procedure is as follows;

(1.2.1) Developing ontology; related research knowledge had been analyzed and studied for gathering structures and relationships in detail and getting some as representatives and defining clear scopes of the study and setting the node Is-a relationships; labeling nodes based on the multiple levels of a hierarchy after that considering the relationships which reconfirmed by cross-checking sided and top levels of the instance.

(1.2.2) Considering Role Part-of (p/o) relationships; they should be changeable in terms of property, objection, core, and sibling. And considering Role Attribute-of (a/o); they should be filled or uncountable. Reconfirming every concept; having role physical and object containing Role (Part-of). Defining each concept before relating to others, p/o (Object property) refers to concept on ontology and a/o (Instance) refers to Data on Database or Data type Property and Categorizing semantic group and concept group search.

(1.3) Ontology of the recommender system: The designed ontology had been exported as Ontology Web Language or OWL. The ontology design and development of the recommender system consist of 2 domains, 5 concepts, 42 classes, 214 sub-classes, and 54 properties.

(1.4) Ontology evaluation: Ontology evaluation is one of ontology development procedures since it helps tracking the process also reconfirming its reliability, validity, and accuracy. The concepts on scope determining, class, sub-class, concept defining, properties defining, instance defining, application, and future trends on ontology development were used to generate 5-rating scale ontology development evaluation form. The ontology had been evaluated by 5 experts in the following fields; knowledge engineering, computer science, and information technology, the findings it was found that; the overall ontology was at a high level ($\overline{X} = 4.21$), yet there were 4 high level items as Determining Scope), Application and future trends on ontology development, Defining Properties, and Defining Classes, Sub-class, Concept. There was only 1 highest level as Defining Instance ($\overline{X} = 4.60$).

(2.) Developing the recommendation system

The system and a part of knowledge base system was developed based on the findings from Phase 1 (3.1), Phase 2 (3.2) and phase 3 (from ontology development base on knowledge engineering step)

(2.1) Underlying theories

2 theories were adopted to develop the system as (1) System Approach: using a system to manage information as scoping problems or suggesting solutions. (2) User-Centered Design: exploring problems and user's needs and interests [22]. Moreover, phase 2 findings were used to design user interface. The steps on developing are as follows;

Step (1) Designing database: MySql was used to design a server and database and PHP was used to design the system interface.

Step (2) Mapping Database to Ontology: To enhance search ability Apache Jena API which is an open source map tool framework for semantic search was used to get information from database and create Resource Description Framework or RDF. Then, SPARQL (SPARQL Protocol and RDF Query Language) was used to search for information through the designed ontology and show search results on the system.

Step (3) User Interface: JavaScript, PHP, and CSS were combined to design a beautiful friendly-user interface.

Role of the recommendation system is to suggesting useful research information to users as analyzing then selecting the information systematically.

(2.2) The system functions

(2.2.1) Storing aspect; the system could store the following items;

(1) Research information (2) Researcher information (3) Research category, (4) Related research primary and secondary policies (5) Related research primary and secondary problems (6) Research related to Southern province groups.

(2.2.2) Processing aspect

(1) It is a combined system of relational database and ontology.
(2) To search for information it is convenient to choose primary and secondary requirements as discipline, policy, problems, statistics used, or research area.
(3) Processing data with relational database and ontology leads to effective search and shows semantic search results according to the design ontology.
(4) Systematic processing leads to fast semantic search.

(2.3) The system development procedure

(2.3.1) Transcribing ontology data into Ontology Web Language or OWL by Protégé Ontology Editor Version 5.5 beta.
(2.3.2) Creating a database to store all the collected data by using MySql Database. There were 38 tables created according to data relationships and relational database system.
(2.3.3) Mapping Database to Ontology in OWL by using Apache Jena API to draft RDF (Resource Description Framework). Then, SPARQL was used to search for information through the designed ontology and show accurate results. After connecting the database and ontology further steps were continued as follows (1.) Mapping Class Table (2.) Mapping Property Column; Data type Property and Object Property and (3.) Mapping Vocabulary between words of data in data table to class inside ontology knowledge base.

(2.4) The system evaluation findings.

The result was the system shows search result according to keyword and/or other conditions. Then, the system recommends related research regarding the keyword and/or conditions and the search results also show relate the policies, strategies, problems, needs of community, basic information, and relate research information. The system had been developed in accordance with users' needs and it was evaluated and used by 28 experts in various academic fields were asked to evaluate the system regarding (1) information presentation and report (2) user support (3) information search (4) support system (5) overall system and (6) the usefulness of the system. The 5-rating scale on satisfaction survey was delivered to the experts along with the system link. Moreover, the search effectiveness was measured by studying all keyword searches in accuracy, recall, precision, and F-measure to study practical solutions for the system.

The results on Accuracy, Recall, Precision, and F-measure of the system was found at a good level (0.70–0.88); Accuracy is 0.70, Recall is 0.78, Precision is 0.88, and F-measure is 0.82 respectively. And The user's overall opinions and satisfaction from evaluated form it was found at a high level ($\overline{X} = 4.14$), further, 2 items are at a high level; support system and information search. The least preferred items are user support and overall system.

4 Results and Discussion

(4.1) Needs analysis on the research recommendation system's design and development

It was found that 327 users who were researchers, scholars, administrators of 78 organizations shared 2 system needs aspects as basic research information and related research information. These needs were considered as basic data which users are able to collect, refer, summarize, and apply to their further studies as follows:

Needs on basic research information is at a high level since researchers could use this data on stating the problems. Moreover, researchers could make research plans more effective as setting goals, exploring population and research area. The data is crucial for budgeting and time frame. Therefore, it is better if users could gather basic research information in advance.

Related research information is at a high level as same as needs on basic research information. Users need more information, for instance, specific research areas in the Southern border Thai gulf or Andaman Sea, references, or abstracts. Once users could access to secondary or tertiary sources, it is possible for users to conduct more productive research also create research network and community for future development [24, 25]. Besides, gathering references and abstracts is value-added to research [23].

(4.2) Scope of knowledge on research for Southern development

The scope consists of systematic knowledge structure, knowledge sets, categories, concepts and classes related to Southern research, strategies, guidelines, and management policies. The knowledge structure will be applied to use as a framework on setting Southern research or relate research topics, trends, grants, information system development or database, other further studies [11]. It could be used to setting subject, phrase, or keyword in categorizing information [9, 16] also the system keywords could be used with other databases or search engines. And the ontology could be further developed as a tool on semantic search system which could relate various aspects [12] and show the result in one search, for example, primary and secondary research topics, disciplines, strategies, problems, and needs. Besides, the system is able to show search results on research methodology, data collection, population and target groups, research area, and research province group area.

(4.3) Research recommender ontology for Southern development

The ontology was developed according to research knowledge structure for Southern development and it covered all important research knowledge related to the Ninth National Research Policy and Strategy, the Twelfth National Economic and Social Development Plan and the 20-year National Strategy framework, and 3 departments of administration and strategy planning of Southern province group development framework. Underlying concepts of the ontology are in hierarchy shown as primary and secondary relationships [18–20]. Therefore, the structure is new and could be used as follows;

(1) It is reusable by adding classes, for instance, disciplines, strategies, policies, problems, or needs and (2) It is a prototype of ontology development in region or province level.

(4.4) The research recommender system for Southern development

The final version of the system is similar to semantic web which stores data, runs by ontology, shows search results as relationship sets of information [11, 12] for example, shows research that relate to problems and strategies, research data collection area, population and target groups, or research tools.

The highlight aspect of this research is not only scopes and body of knowledge regarding situations, needs, strategies, and policies of the South which reflect gaps and lead researchers to acquire systematic plans and solutions but also it is able to disseminate on further effective recommender system developments as reducing search procedures, redundancy, and costs.

Additionally, the research findings could be applied in terms of policy area and national strategies, for example, the body of research knowledge on tourism and agricultural development which is crucial for national economic and resource. The government could take the knowledge into account the research or tourism policies, agricultural production as Start-up: Smart tourism and smart agro technology that supports production capacity and business value of products and services, responds to needs and expectations of customers, enhances competition capacity in nation level, or applies as a part of solutions. Further, it could also enhance long-term learning community.

5   Conclusions

The findings on identifying needs phase helps researchers to develop the system accurately and flexibly according to the needs and user center design, therefore, the system could be a prototype for students, researchers, administrators, or interested users to access and study the system structure individually. This system was developed from systematic ontology which could distinguish relevant or irrelevant data, therefore, this leads to research effectiveness as decreasing research topic and budgeting redundancy, saving search time, suggesting relevant research information or trends, and enhancing further studies. The knowledge structure inside the system allows us to see relationships among research, policies, strategies, disciplines, and problems and needs of Southern people so that researchers or interested people could use this structure to explore future research trends or use it as a resource for current studies. And the system is practical since it stores research data, saves time, and is easy access. On the contrary, there are 3 limitations on this development. First, diffusion of the model in the future in changing regarding needs, strategies, policies, or plans. Second, dissemination of the system within government sections might take time. Finally, distribution platforms could be more various for users as phone application.

Acknowledgments. With this research article the researcher would like to thank you the Office of Higher Education Commission on kindly provided research grant also thank you Prince of Songkla University and Khon Kaen University for support.

References

1. Office of Southern Border Administration Management. http://osmsouth-border.go.th/news_strategy. Accessed 9 Aug 2019
2. Bureau of Land Survey and Land Use Planning. http://www.tnmc-is.org/wp-content/uploads/2018/07/8_Lanuse-Planning-and-LanuseChangeLDD2561_Direk.pdf. Accessed 09 Aug 2019
3. Office of the National Economics and Social Development Board. https://www.nesdb.go.th/ewt_news.php?nid=5748. Accessed 09 Aug 2019
4. Kewsuwun, N.: The synthesis of problem needs and strategies of 14 southern provinces group administrative offices with correspondence of academic branches from national research council. Parichart J. **32**(1), 389–423 (2019)
5. Office of Southern Andaman Administration Management. http://www.osmsouth-w.moi.go.th/submenu.php?page=163&l=th. Accessed 09 Aug 2019
6. Podhisita, C.: The Science and Art of Quality Research, 8th edn. Institute for Population and Social Research, Mahidol University, Bangkok, Thailand (2019)
7. Chan-o-cha, P. http://www.thaigov.go.th/news/contents/details/3981. Accessed 09 Aug 2019
8. Prasitrathasin, S.: Research Method in Social Sciences, 15th edn. Chulalongkorn University Press, Bangkok (2012)
9. Mueanrit, N.: The information architecture for research information storage and retrieval. Ph.D. thesis, Department of Information Science, Khon Kaen University, Khon Kaen, Thailand (2013)
10. Chan, L.M.: Cataloging and Classification: Intro. McGraw-Hill Book, New York (1985)
11. Panawong, J.: Development of knowledge base system for Northeastern Thailand. Ph.D. thesis, Department of Information Science, Khon Kaen University, Khon Kaen, Thailand (2015)
12. Archint, N.: Semantic Web Technologies. Klangnanawitaya, Khon Kaen (2014)
13. Boonprasaert, U.: Action research. Office of the Education Council, Bangkok, Thailand (2012)
14. Tripathy, B.K., Acharjya, D.P.: Global Trends in Intelligent Computing Research and Development. PA of IGI Global, Hershey (2014)
15. Vu, B., Mertens, J., Gaisbachgrabner, K., Fuchs, M., Hemmje, M.: Supporting taxonomy management and evolution in a web-based knowledge management system. In: Proceeding of HCI, 2018 Proceedings of the 32nd International BCS Human Computer Interaction Conference, pp. 1–11 (2018)
16. Hodge, G.: Systems of Knowledge Organization of Digital Libraries: Beyond Traditional Authority Files. Digital Library Federation, Washington (2000)
17. Hjorland, B.: Nine principles of knowledge organization. The royal school of Library and Information Science, DK-2300, Copenhagen (2015)
18. Taylor, A.G., Joudrey, D.N.: The Organization of Information. Libraries Unlimited, Wesport (2009)
19. Rowley, J.: Organizing knowledge: Intro Information Retrieval, 2nd edn. Ashgate Publishing, London, Hampshire (1992)
20. Fricke, M.: Logic and the Organization of Information. Springer, New York (2012). https://doi.org/10.1007/978-1-4614-3088-9_9
21. Kewsuwun, N.: Knowledge Structure of research for the Southern of Thailand development. In: The LISSASPAC: The 1st International Conference on Library and Information Science: From Open Library to Open Society on Proceedings, pp. 332–345 (2018). Sukhothai Thammathirat Open University, Nonthaburi, Thailand
22. Norman, D.: Administrative Office Management: AOM, 11th edn. South-Western Education Publishing, Cincinnati (1996)

23. Wipawin, N.: Digital data management process and research data management standards in digital data warehouses: research information warehouse. Sirindhorn Anthropology Center (Public organization), Bangkok (2016)
24. Davenport, T., Prusak, L.: Working Knowledge. Harvard Business School Press, Boston (1998)
25. Houda, S., Naila, A., Samir, B. https://doi.org/10.3991/ijet.v14i16.10588. Accessed 15 Aug 2019

A Modular Diversity Based Reviewer Recommendation System

Marcin Maleszka[1]([envelope]) [ID], Bernadetta Maleszka[1] [ID], Dariusz Król[1] [ID],
Marcin Hernes[2], Denis Mayr Lima Martins[3], Leschek Homann[3],
and Gottfried Vossen[3]

[1] Wroclaw University of Science and Technology, 50-370 Wroclaw, Poland
{marcin.maleszka,bernadetta.maleszka,dariusz.krol}@pwr.edu.pl
[2] Wroclaw University of Economics, Wroclaw, Poland
marcin.hernes@ue.wroc.pl
[3] WWU Munster, Munster, Germany
{denis.martins,leschek.homann,vossen}@wi.uni-muenster.de

Abstract. A new approach for solving the problem of reviewer recommendation for conference or journal submissions is proposed. Instead of assigning one best reviewer and then looking for a second-best match, we want to start from a single reviewer and look for a diverse group of other possible candidates, that would complement the first one in order to cover multiple areas of the review. We present the idea of an overall modular system for determining a *grouping* of reviewers, as well as three modules for such a system: a keyword-based module, a social graph module, and a linguistic module. The added value of modular diversity is seen primarily for larger groups of reviewers. The paper also contains a proof of concept of the method.

Keywords: Recommender system · reviewer recommendation · Social recommendation · linguistic recommendation · Paper-reviewer assignment problem

1 Introduction

The assignment of scientific papers to the most suitable reviewers is an essential and crucial aspect of accepting papers to a scientific journal or conference. Each paper should be reviewed by a few experts in the scientific fields of the paper. In case of a very specialized or narrow range of topics of the conference or journal, the best experts are authors of the other submitted papers (peer review). Based on the reviewers' opinions, it is decided whether a paper is accepted or rejected. Only the high quality of the review process allows keeping the highest scientific level of the conference or journal. The (ideally automatic) recommendation of appropriate reviewers is the subject of this paper.

In the literature, one can find a few approaches to the review process organization. The most popular is a manual process where each reviewer has access

© Springer Nature Singapore Pte Ltd. 2020
P. Sitek et al. (Eds.): ACIIDS 2020, CCIS 1178, pp. 550–561, 2020.
https://doi.org/10.1007/978-981-15-3380-8_48

to the list of all papers, and he or she has to select a subset of papers to review. It is also possible to mark papers with a conflict of interest [1].

More advanced systems gather information about reviewers' interests and compare them with keywords of papers, using statistical approaches, e.g., based on similarity, to select the most suitable reviewer [2] or more sophisticated methods from artificial intelligence [3], [7], [18], and [21].

Many systems try to balance the number of papers to review, and the topic of the paper is frequently overlooked. In this paper, we focus mostly on the paper point of view — the aim is to select the most suitable group of reviewers in terms of topic compatibility and heterogeneity of reviewer approaches. The Recommender System we propose in this paper is based on using multiple diversity measures that are then averaged into a single one, in order to create a list of recommended reviewers that will cover different aspects of the reviewing process. This allows us to determine a group of reviewers for a paper in a step-by-step process. We consider interest diversity (based on reviewer's keywords), social diversity (based on co-authorship graph) and style diversity (based on differences in text style of reviews).

We want to verify the proposed method in an experiment using real conference data with anonymized papers. We will use review texts from a 2018 conference to train the style module and a co-authorship graph from 2018 for the social module. We will then test the recommended reviewers against data from a 2019 conference from the same series. Due to privacy reasons, this evaluation will be done as part of our future work. In this paper we instead present a short description of the process on simulated data.

The remainder of this paper is organized as follows: in Sect. 2 we discuss related research in the area of reviewer recommendation; in Sect. 3 we provide details on the system as a whole and the inner workings of each module; in Sect. 4 we present details on the planned experimental evaluation of the system, as well as include a proof of concept of the method and we conclude the paper in Sect. 5 with some final remarks on future works and applicability.

2   Related Work

There are different approaches to reviewer recommendation. The work [5] presents the Word Mover's Distance – Constructive Covering Algorithm. The authors transform the reviewer recommendation problem into a classification problem by integration the research field information of a submission. Based on information about reviewer candidates and a newly submitted paper, the research field labels for reviewers are predicted and assigned one to the submission characterized by the same label issue.

[6] proposes the recommendation of reviewers based on a *conflict of interest* between authors of submitted papers and reviewers. On the basis of institution-to-institution relationships (extracted from academic activity records), the distance between authors and reviewers is measured. The measure of distance is based on the similarity between the content of submitted papers and publications

of reviewers. The assignment of a paper to a reviewer is based on maximizing the topic relevance and minimizing the *conflict of interests*.

Paper [7] presents a two-layers method for reviewer recommendation. In the first layer, a cluster-based model for representing the research interests of experts is developed. In the second layer, a similarity computation method between the paper and the expert's research interests is applied. Based on the similarity, reviewers get recommended.

There are many papers related to reviewers recommendation of software code recommendation. A reviewer recommendation approach based on Latent Dirichlet Allocation (LDA) is proposed in [8]. First, the review expertise for topics of the source document from the review history is extracted. Then review scores are calculated on the basis of the topic of the source document and the review expertise.

[9] presents a recommendation model to recommend reviewers for GitHub projects. The developers to review the target projects based on a hybrid recommendation method are proposed in the first layer of the model. The second layer aims to specify whether the target developer will participate in the reviewing process.

Paper [10] proposes a code reviewer recommendation technique. It takes into consideration the relevant cross-project work history and, in addition, the experience of a developer in certain specialized technologies.

A two-layer reviewer recommendation model to recommend reviewers for Pull-Requests in GitHub projects is developed in [9]. The hybrid recommendation method for developers to review the project is developed in the first layer. On the basis of the recommendation results from the first layer, the specification of whether the target developer will technically or managerially participate in the reviewing process is performed in the second layer.

Taking graph-based recommendation into consideration, the work [11] presents a generic graph-based embedding model. Embedding learning techniques are used to this end. The model captures the sequential effect, geographical influence, temporal cyclic effect, and semantic effect in a unified way by embedding the four corresponding relational graphs into a shared low dimensional space. The recommendation is based on the time-decay method for performing dynamical computation the user's latest preferences.

Paper [12] presents the meta-graph to HIN-based recommendation. A matrix factorization and factorization machine are used in this purpose. A general graph-based model to recommendation problems related to event-based social networks is presented in [13]. The recommendation problem is transformed into a query-dependent node proximity problem. A learning scheme to set the influence weights between different types of entities has been developed.

Paper [14] presents a collaborative filtering method for the recommendation problem resolution. A novel graph clustering algorithm has been developed to obtain the appropriate clusters of users on top of which the recommendation process is leveraged.

Additionally, the problem of social recommendation is considered in the literature. For example, paper [15] analyzes a CROKODIL's folksonomy, mainly its hierarchical activity structure. Scoring approaches are proposed for recommending learning resources. Additional semantic information gained from activity structures is used.

In [16], tags and friendship links are analyzed to determine the accuracy of a graph-based recommender. The impact the features extracted from this data on the recommendations is measured.

The authors of [17] develop three taxonomies that partition recommender systems according to the properties of social media data. The following categorization criteria are taken into consideration: the objective of the recommendation (locations, users, activities, or social media), the methodologies (content-based, link analysis-based, and collaborative filtering-based methodologies), the data sources used (user profiles, user online histories, and user location histories).

Paper [18] presents several deep learning models for a recommendation based on users' needs. Large scale graph partitioning is used for improving the accuracy of models. An approach for automatically recommending a sub-type of evolution, evolutionary growth is presented in [19]. The groups are extracted from the social graph.

To sum up, there are many solutions related to the recommendation of software code reviewers. However, they cannot be indirectly used for recommending reviewers of scientific papers, because, in the case of scientific articles, the thematic scope is much broader than in the case of source code. There is also no system based on a reviewer's keywords, co-authorship graph, and differences in text style of reviews at the same time.

3   Recommender System Overview

The aim of our system is to recommend a list of the most suitable reviewers for a given paper. The reviewers should be experts in the field of the paper, but simultaneously they should have a broader area of interests and take different aspects of paper content into account to obtain less overlap in their reviews of the same papers.

The general idea of the proposed recommendation system may be described as follows: We start with a single reviewer determined by some other method (in this paper we choose one reviewer randomly, based on fitting keywords). Each module of the system is provided with this reviewer and the details of the paper as input. It will produce an output consisting of a list of potential other reviewers, ordered based on some diversity measure from best to worst fitting. Currently, we consider three such modules: interest (reviewer keywords, besides those fitting the paper, are most different), social (the reviewers are most distant in a co-authorship graph) and style (the reviewers focus on different elements in their reviews). The system averages those ordered lists into a single one, which presents potential reviewers ordered from most different to most similar from the current one. The most diverse reviewer is then selected and added to the pool of accepted reviewers. If we need more than those two reviewers, we repeat the procedure, providing the modules not with a single reviewer as input, but with the list of already accepted ones. We repeat this until the number of accepted reviewers is as desired.

One may note that this approach works better when selecting larger numbers of reviewers (scientific papers usually need only two to four), thus it may also be used to determine reviewers for a special session during a conference (e.g., out of 200 total reviewers for the conference, select 10 for the special session).

In the following sections, we present the details of all three modules: The Interest, Social, and Style Diversity Modules.

3.1   The Interest Diversity Module

The recommendation provided by the Interest Diversity Module is based on the assumption that reviewers with different research interests will focus on different aspects during the review process. In this sense, this module searches for reviewers whose research interests have a large intersection with the seed paper (i.e., paper to be reviewed), while maintaining the diversity of such interests.

To achieve this, we create a database containing reviewer candidates and their research interests in the form of a vector of keywords. Each reviewer is described by a tuple $< s, k_1, k_2, \ldots, k_{n_s} >$, where s is the name of the reviewer and $k_1, k_2, \ldots, k_{n_s}$ are the keywords representing his or her interests, and n_s denotes the number of keywords for each reviewer candidate s. Additionally, we precompute the Jaccard index between all vectors. In this approach, even if two reviewers have identical interests, the Jaccard index between them will not be 1, due to the assumption that some interests are not stated in the form of keywords.

Upon receiving the input in the form of one or more reviewer names and the keyword(s) for the reviewed paper, a temporary list of reviewers is created by selecting from the database those reviewer candidates for which at least one keyword intersects with the paper. Then the list is ordered by increasing the distance with the input reviewer(s). In case of multiple input reviewers, the distances are added before sorting the list. Thus the output of the module is a list of pairs $< s, d >$ where s is the reviewer name and d is the distance.

3.2   The Social Diversity Module

The Social Diversity module aims to find a list of reviewers that are weakly connected in a co-authorship graph. The assumption behind this module is that reviewer candidates that do not collaborate with each other in the past are likely to focus on diverse aspects of the paper review process, and, therefore, may contribute to producing a richer review.

In this context, recommending reviewers to a seed paper involves the following task: Given a co-authorship graph G and a reviewer r (e.g., one discovered by one of the methods mentioned previously in this work) as input, find a list of recommended reviewers R such that the distance between r and each reviewer candidate $r' \in R$ w.r.t. G is maximized. Hence, the module outputs a list of reviewers ordered by the most distant to the nearest ones in the co-authorship graph G.

In order to create a co-authorship graph G the Social Diversity module uses two data sources. The primary data source, as described in Sect. 4, is the database of the Digital Bibliography and Library Project (DBLP), which contains information about scientific articles and their authors, and is updated regularly. As a second data source, a list L of potential reviewers for the considered conference is used. Such a list is frequently available since the conference organizers are likely to define a potential review board composed by scholars that are familiar with the conference topic.

With these data sources, the co-authorship graph is constructed by first filtering the DBLP dataset[1] to consider publications where at least one reviewer in the reviewer list L participated in. Then, for every selected publication P, a set of nodes $a_1, a_2, \ldots, a_n$ is added in the graph G, where each a_i corresponds to one of the authors of P. Likewise, an edge (a_i, a_j) is created between authors of the same publication, that is, an edge (a_i, a_j) in G represents a co-authorship relation between authors a_i and a_j. As a result, a co-authorship graph has been created, which can be used to determine the diversity between two authors by determining their distance in the graph.

To illustrate the construction of the graph, consider the following example: Let a_1, a_2 and a_3 be authors of the paper p_1, but only a_1 and a_2 are the potential reviewers, that is, both a_1 and a_2 are in the provided list L. Furthermore, let a_3 and a_4 be authors of the paper p_2 with only a_4 being a potential reviewer. By adding a node for a_3, although not part of the potential reviewer, a connection between a_1 and a_4, respectively, and another one between a_2 and a_4 over a_3 is visible. In this case, the distance between a_1 and a_4 is one. The resulting graph of the example is depicted in Fig. 1.

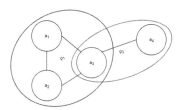

Fig. 1. The authors a_1, a_2 and a_4 are potential reviewers. a_1, a_2 and a_3 are authors of the paper p_1 indicated by the green ellipse and the authors a_3 and a_4 of the paper p_2 as indicated by the blue ellipse. The author a_3 is not part of the potential reviewer but creates a connection among the other authors.

---

[1] https://dblp.uni-trier.de/xml.

3.3   The Style Diversity Module

The Style Diversity Module is based on distinguishing reviewers by the aspects of the review they focus on. Some reviewers look more into language problems than others; some focus on the experimental part of papers, and some on literature review. Additionally, the language used may differ, for some reviewers positive terminology in the text may be common while the numerical grading of the review is low, while other reviewers do not write any praise but grade papers highly.

For considering the reviewer's style in the recommendation process, this module employs a deep learning method based on the research conducted by [20]. We call this approach *deep recommendation*.

The method is based on processing text reviews and ratings given to papers from previous conference editions, which may later be used to distinguish reviewers by the so-called user-word composition vector model (UWCVM). Each word w_i from a review is represented by a continuous vector $e_i \in R^d$ and each user (i.e., a reviewer) u_k by a matrix $U_k \in R^{d \times d}$, where d is the dimension of continuous vector. Due to large size of such matrix, it is reduced by approximation $U_k = U_{k1} \times U_{k2} + diag(u')$ where $U_{k1} \in R^{d \times r}$, $U_{k2} \in R^{r \times d}$ and $u' \in R^d$ is the shared background (e.g., keyword, reviewed paper, etc.). Each word is then transformed to a modified vector $p_i = tanh(e_{ik}) = tank(U_k \times e_i) = tanh((U_{k1} \times U_{k2} + diag(u')) \times e_i)$. Thus, the same words have different values for different reviewers, which appropriately captures the style of a reviewer.

In next step, a predictor is trained for ratings given, as $softmax_i = \frac{exp(z_i)}{\sum_{i'} exp(z_{i'})}$, where $z \in R^C$ is a linear vector based on the review representation $vec(doc)$: $z = W \times vec(doc) + b$, $W \in R^{C \times d}$ and $b \in R^C$ are parameters and C is the number of possible ratings. Using $f(r, l)$ as the probability of predicting review r with rating l we can train the predictor with $L(r) = \sum_{l \in C} f^g(r, l) \cdot log(f(r, l)) + \lambda_\theta \cdot |\theta|^2_F$ where f^g is a normal distribution of ratings (in original word, gold distribution; but for papers we assume that the normal distribution is proper), $|\theta|^2_F$ is a Frobenius norm regularization term and θ represents the parameters.

Finally, the distance between reviewers may be measured as a sum or average of distances between their reviews, which is calculated by using cosine similarity between vectors. This allows not only distinguishing the reviewers by their style but maintains the *normal* distribution of the reviews (with only a small number of reviewers assigned to a single paper this distribution will not be visible, but maybe crucial in case of selecting a pool of reviewers for a special session, out of a larger number of reviewers). As with previous modules, we use this distance to create a list of most diverse reviewers.

3.4   Result Integration

The output of all the diversity modules in the system is a list containing reviewer candidates and their distance from previously selected reviewers. More modules may be added as necessary, or the system may be reduced to a single diversity module, depending on the application requirements and system evaluation. The case of multiple modules requires some method of integrating multiple results into a single list of recommended reviewers. Different use cases may also require different integration methods; thus we present several simple methods that we intend to evaluate further:

- Average ranking
- Weighted and non-weighted average distance
- Weighted and non-weighted median distance

4 Evaluation of the Recommendation System

The presented system is currently being finalized, with different datasets being prepared for testing. Due to privacy reasons, much of this process is internal and cannot be presented in this paper. Due to this in this section we discuss only the three datasets used and provide a proof of concept for the proposed method with generalized data.

4.1 Dataset Description

We consider three primary datasets for the purposes of experimental evaluation of the proposed system, two for learning in different modules, and one for testing.

The DBLP [4] database provides information about scientific publications and is publicly available in the form of a downloadable XML file. According to the published statistics on the official web site [4], the database contains about 4.7 million publications, 2.3 million authors, 5,700 conferences, and 1,600 journals. The structure of the XML file is described by a Document Type Definition (DTD)[2], with basic elements being articles, proceedings, books, collections, master theses, Ph.D. theses, Web sites, and persons. In particular, the proposed system focuses on exploiting article elements, which contain information like the title, the participating authors, the journal, the publisher, or the publication date.

For the Style Diversity Module and Interest Diversity Module, we obtained data on reviews from a conference taking place in 2018. The keywords for Interest Diversity are from both input by the reviewer and extraction of keywords from the paper they wanted to review (but were not necessarily assigned to). There are a total of 216 reviewers with keyword data and 330 text reviews in this dataset.

For testing of the proposed system, we intend to use data on reviews from a conference taking place in 2019 (the next edition of the conference considered previously). There are a total of 337 reviewers in this dataset, but only 172 are present in both 2018 and 2019 data. It was possible to extract 69 groups of reviewers (2 to 4 reviewers assigned to the same paper) out of those, that are common to both sets. This will be the basis for testing the proposed approach.

---

[2] https://dblp.uni-trier.de/xml/dblp.dtd.

The evaluation of experimental results will require input from conference chairs responsible for assigning the reviewers. While the 2019 conference dataset contains groupings of reviewers (2 to 4 reviewers assigned to the same paper), these were not necessarily done with diversity in mind. For this reason, the simple comparison of existing groupings with system output will probably be insufficient, and conference chairs' comments will be required to evaluate the results correctly. The chairs will be presented with a table with several groupings in a row: Dataset, only Social module, only Style module, only Keyword module, and one or more Integrated groupings. They will be then asked to point the best and worst grouping in their opinion, as well as present general comments on the results.

4.2   Proof of Concept

As proof of concept we have performed evaluation based on simulated data of ten potential reviewers $(A0, \ldots, A9)$ that previously wrote reviews using 10 distinct words $(w_0, \ldots, w_9)$ and have selected three keywords each out of the set of 10 distinct ones $(k_0, \ldots, k_9)$. Instead of full DBLP database, we use a social graph presented in Fig. 2. The keyword and review words combinations are shown in Table 1. Note that all reviewers have one keyword in common (k_0), as it represents the keyword of the reviewed paper.

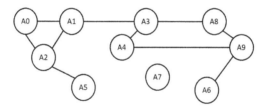

Fig. 2. The simplified social graph used for the proof of concept.

Out of the group of ten potential reviewers, the aim is to select a group of 3 most diverse ones (covering multiple aspects of the review). The proposed method requires the first reviewer to be selected by some other algorithm. Here, we use reviewer A0 for simplicity. The proposed method will need to be used twice, first to determine the second reviewer – most different from the first; then to determine the third reviewer – most different from both previously selected. Such group should be most diverse. For result integration we used average approach, as most suited to this type of data.

The approach requires first for each module to calculate the distance from each already added reviewer, using the specific method for each module. These distances are then used to rank the reviewers from most distant (most different) to closest (most similar). For the considered case, these ranks are presented in Table 2 in columns "S1: Style", "S1: Key" and "S1: Social" representing the

Table 1. Review data used for proof of concept. Three keywords and a combination of words used in reviews are given for all ten reviewers.

Reviewer	Words in reviews	Keywords
A0	w0, w1, w2	k0, k1, k2
A1	w4, w5	k0, k2, k9
A2	w4, w6, w7, w9	k0, k3, k4
A3	w2, w3, w8, w9	k0, k5, k6
A4	w0, w1, w4, w8	k0, k1, k4
A5	w1, w5, w6, w7	k0, k4, k8
A6	w0, w1, w8	k0, k5, k7
A7	w4, w5, w8	k0, k6, k7
A8	w4, w7, w9	k0, k2, k8
A9	w0, w2, w3, w4, w5, w9	k0, k3, k5

results of the style diversity module, keyword diversity module and social diversity module, respectively. Next, we calculate the average of those ranks, which allows us to determine that the most different reviewer is $A7$. Thus, after the first step the new set of reviewers is $\{A0, A7\}$.

In the next step we repeat the procedure, this time calculating the combined distance from both already selected reviewers. The results for specific modules are presented in Table 2 in columns "S1: Style", "S1: Key" and "S1: Social". With these results we calculate the average of those ranks, this time determining the most different reviewer to be $A9$. Thus the final set of reviewers selected is $\{A0, A7, A9\}$.

Table 2. Double application of the method. Determining the second reviewer based on difference from the first. Determining the first reviewer based on difference from previous two. Only ranks of distance shown, from farthest (rank 1) to closest.

Reviewer	S1: Style	S1: Key	S1: Social	S1: Total	S2: Style	S2: Key	S2: Social	S2: Total
A1	1	2	6	3	4	2	5	3,6
A2	1	1	6	2,6	1	1	5	2,3
A3	3	1	5	3	2	2	4	2,6
A4	4	2	4	3,3	4	2	3	3
A5	3	1	5	3	2	1	4	2,3
A6	5	1	2	2,6	4	2	1	2,3
A7	1	1	1	1	–	–	–	–
A8	1	2	4	2,3	2	2	3	2,3
A9	2	1	3	2	3	1	2	**2**

5   Conclusions

In this paper, we propose a modular recommender system for reviewer recommendation. Unlike other previous approaches, our system focus on determining a diverse group of reviewers instead of independently searching for the best fitting reviewers. In fact, other reviewer recommendation methods may be used to find the first reviewer, who will then be used as a *seed* for our proposed approach.

This paper also describes a structured plan for evaluating the proposed system, which includes a description of the real conference data sets to be employed as well as a user study to be conducted in order to obtain feedback from conference chairs. Due to privacy reasons and ongoing conference-related tasks, this data could not be used in this paper. It will also not be possible to put this data to any open repository, but we will also use it in some follow-up publications.

As noted previously, the proposed approach works better for larger groups of reviewers. Thus it may be applied even better to determining reviewers for a special session, out of a larger pool of reviewers for a conference.

Acknowledgments. This research within Polish-German cooperation program is financially supported by the German Academic Exchange Service (DAAD) under grant PPP 57391625 and by the Wrocław University of Science and Technology under project 0401/0221/18. This research was also financially supported by the Brazilian National Council for Scientific and Technological Development (CNPq) – Science without Borders Program.

References

1. Charlin, L., Zemel, R.S., Boutilier, C.: A framework for optimizing paper matching (2012). CoRR. http://arxiv.org/abs/1202.3706. Accessed 25 Sept 2019
2. Mimno, D., McCallum, A.: Expertise modeling for matching papers with reviewers. Computer Science Department Faculty Publication. Series 73 (2007)
3. Li, X., Watanabe, T.: Automatic paper-to-reviewer assignment, based on the matching degree of the reviewers. Procedia Comput. Sci. **22**, 633–642 (2013)
4. DBLP Computer Science Bibliography. https://dblp.uni-trier.de/. Accessed 25 Sept 2019
5. Zhao, S., Zhang, D., Duan, Z., Chen, J., Zhang, Y.P., Tang, J.: A novel classification method for paper-reviewer recommendation. Scientometrics **115**(3), 1293–1313 (2018)
6. Yan, S., Jin, J., Geng, Q., Zhao, Y., Huang, X.: Utilizing academic-network-based conflict of interests for paper reviewer assignment. Int. J. Knowl. Eng. **3**, 65–73 (2017)
7. Rahman, M.M., Roy, C.K., Collins, J.A.: Correct: code reviewer recommendation in GitHub based on cross-project and technology experience. In: 2016 IEEE/ACM 38th International Conference on Software Engineering Companion (ICSE-C), pp. 222–231. IEEE, May 2016
8. Kim, J., Lee, E.: Understanding review expertise of developers: a reviewer recommendation approach based on latent dirichlet allocation. Symmetry **10**(4), 114 (2018)

9. Yang, C., et al.: RevRec: a two-layer reviewer recommendation algorithm in pull-based development model. J. Cent. South Univ. **25**(5), 1129–1143 (2018). https://doi.org/10.1007/s11771-018-3812-x

10. Zhao, H., Tao, W., Zou, R., Xu, C.: Construction and application of diversified knowledge model for paper reviewers recommendation. In: Zhou, Q., Miao, Q., Wang, H., Xie, W., Wang, Y., Lu, Z. (eds.) ICPCSEE 2018. CCIS, vol. 902, pp. 120–127. Springer, Singapore (2018). https://doi.org/10.1007/978-981-13-2206-8_11

11. Xie, M., Yin, H., Wang, H., Xu, F., Chen, W., Wang, S.: Learning graph-based POI embedding for location-based recommendation. In: Proceedings of the 25th ACM International on Conference on Information and Knowledge Management, pp. 15–24. ACM, October 2016

12. Zhao, H., Yao, Q., Li, J., Song, Y., Lee, D.L.: Meta-graph based recommendation fusion over heterogeneous information networks. In: Proceedings of the 23rd ACM SIGKDD International Conference on Knowledge Discovery and Data Mining, pp. 635–644. ACM, August 2017

13. Pham, T.A.N., Li, X., Cong, G., Zhang, Z.: A general graph-based model for recommendation in event-based social networks. In: 2015 IEEE 31st International Conference on Data Engineering, pp. 567–578. IEEE, April 2015

14. Moradi, P., Ahmadian, S., Akhlaghian, F.: An effective trust-based recommendation method using a novel graph clustering algorithm. Physica A **436**, 462–481 (2015)

15. Anjorin, M., Rodenhausen, T., Domínguez García, R., Rensing, C.: Exploiting semantic information for graph-based recommendations of learning resources. In: Ravenscroft, A., Lindstaedt, S., Kloos, C.D., Hernández-Leo, D. (eds.) EC-TEL 2012. LNCS, vol. 7563, pp. 9–22. Springer, Heidelberg (2012). https://doi.org/10.1007/978-3-642-33263-0_2

16. Tiroshi, A., Berkovsky, S., Kaafar, M.A., Vallet, D., Kuflik, T.: Graph-based recommendations: make the most out of social data. In: Dimitrova, V., Kuflik, T., Chin, D., Ricci, F., Dolog, P., Houben, G.-J. (eds.) UMAP 2014. LNCS, vol. 8538, pp. 447–458. Springer, Cham (2014). https://doi.org/10.1007/978-3-319-08786-3_40

17. Bao, J., Zheng, Y., Wilkie, D., Mokbel, M.: Recommendations in location-based social networks: a survey. GeoInformatica **19**(3), 525–565 (2015)

18. Bathla, G., Aggarwal, H., Rani, R.: Improving Recommendation Techniques by Deep Learning and Large Scale Graph Partitioning. Int. J. Adv. Comput. Sci. Appl. **9**(10), 403–409 (2018)

19. Bartel, J.W., Dewan, P.: Towards evolutionary named group recommendations. Comput. Support. Coop. Work, 27, 3-6 (December 2018), 983-1018 2018. https://doi.org/10.1007/s10606-018-9321-5

20. Tang, D., Qin, B., Liu, T., Yang, Y.: User modeling with neural network for review rating prediction. In: Proceedings of the Twenty-Fourth International Joint Conference on Artificial Intelligence (IJCAI 2015) (2015)

21. Kolasa, T., Król, D.: A survey of algorithms for paper-reviewer assignment problem. IETE Tech. Rev. **28**(2), 123–134 (2011). https://doi.org/10.4103/0256-4602.78092

Fake News Types and Detection Models on Social Media A State-of-the-Art Survey

Botambu Collins[1], Dinh Tuyen Hoang[1,3], Ngoc Thanh Nguyen[2], and Dosam Hwang[1(✉)]

[1] Department of Computer Engineering, Yeungnam University, Gyeongsan-si, South Korea
botambucollins@gmail.com, hoangdinhtuyen@gmail.com,
dosamhwang@gmail.com
[2] Faculty of Computer Science and Management,
Wroclaw University of Science and Technology, Wroclaw, Poland
Ngoc-Thanh.Nguyen@pwr.edu.pl
[3] Faculty of Engineering and Information Technology, Quang Binh University, Đồng Hới,
Vietnam

Abstract. Fake news has gained prominence since the 2016 US presidential election as well as the Brexit referendum. Fake news has abused not only the press but also the democratic rules. Therefore, the need to restrict and eliminate it becomes inevitable. The popularity of fake news on social media has made people unwilling to engage in sharing positive news for fear that the information is false. The main problem with fake news is how quickly it spreads to social media.

In this paper, we introduced an overview of the various models in detecting fake news such as Machine learning, Natural Language Processing, Crowdsourced techniques, Expert fact-checker, as well as Hybrid Expert-Machine. We also do reviews of different types of fake news, which is an essential criterion for detecting fake news. Our findings show that detecting fake news is a challenging but workable task. The techniques that combine people and machines bring very satisfactory results. We also study about open issues of fake news, then propose some potential research tasks for future works.

Keywords: Fake news · Fake news detection · Deception detection

1 Introduction and Background

The growth and advancement of information and communication system have made news content easily available for consumption especially with the use of social media [1]. Although the development of the internet is a blessing to mankind, on the contrary, it has certain negative effects. Unlike the traditional media (newspaper, TV, and Radio) Social media has ushered in a new trend in news known as "fake news" where malicious or misleading information is rapidly spread [2].

Although social media was created to enhance communication, it has almost replaced mainstream media. A vast majority of people no longer watch television or listen to the radio, even if they listen to it, it will be done on social media. Fake news can be traced

© Springer Nature Singapore Pte Ltd. 2020
P. Sitek et al. (Eds.): ACIIDS 2020, CCIS 1178, pp. 562–573, 2020.
https://doi.org/10.1007/978-981-15-3380-8_49

as far back as in 1439 when the printing press was invented [3], however, the discourse on fake news gained prominence especially during the 2016 US presidential election [4, 5]. With the growing popularity of social media, we are increasingly being exposed to a plethora of fake news. Fake news has caused enormous damage to our society and hence emerged as a potential threat not only to press freedom but to democracy as well [1, 3, 4]. There has not been any clear definition or acceptance of the concept of fake news [1, 3, 4]. Therefore, for us to accept what is considered to be fake news, one must first understand what news is, authentic or real news.

Based on Jack Fuller (1996) in [6] "News is a report of what a news organization has recently learned about matters of some significance or interest to the specific community that news organization serves" [6]. Gans [7] gave a precise and widely acceptable definition of news, he contended that news is "information which is transmitted from the source to recipients by journalists who are both - employees of bureaucratic, commercial organizations and also members of a professional group" [7]. This definition makes us understand that news has an author i.e.; journalist to give concrete news to its followers. This gives us an insight into why fake news is spreading so fast, fake news has no author, journalists are licensed to give news [9] or work for a news organization, those on social media works for themselves and propagate fake news for financial gains such as the Macedonia teenage group. Revealed by [8] regardless of potential benefit, the proliferation of fake news is further exacerbated by the social media outlet.

In order to attempt a true meaning of fake news, we borrow the definition from [10] who alluded that "fake news is fabricated information that mimics news media content in form but not in organizational process or intent. Fake-news outlets, in turn, lack the news media's editorial norms and processes for ensuring the accuracy and credibility of information". Brummet and Colleagues [8] coined the term "ideologically motivate fake news" to resemble those who are not driven by financial benefit in participating in fake news but are fabricated to enhance uniques principles as well as beliefs, this will lead to smearing misinformation which is contrary to other people's belief and principles [8].

Prior surveys to fake news detection strategies have been a useful guide to this study given the fact that fake news is a hot issue nowadays. Review by [11] focus on social bots detection model on three social networks platforms namely; Facebook, Twitter, and

Fig. 1. Showing sample of social bots account

LinkedIn and posit that some bots are of good nature in the sense that they automatically respond to customers' need faster than real humans and could attend to many customers within a short period, weather updates and news pushing are essential elements of social bots. However, nowadays, social bots have been created for malicious functions such as spreading false information. This survey is different in ours in that it focuses on social bots detection, which is just a tool used in spreading fake news, instead our work focus on detecting fake news irrespective of which particular tools are used to spread it. Zhou and Zafarani [4] surveyed fake news detection methods and opportunities. They classified fake news into four distinct categories. Knowledge-based, style-based, user-based, propagation-based study. Our work is different in that we did an in-depth overview of various detection models and select only those models which have a high accuracy rate as compare to the previous author who did a general review. We further classified the different types of fake news and the motives which is an essential criterion in detecting fake news. The work of [12] centers on data mining perspective on fake news characterization and detection. In characterization, the author classified fake news in two features, such as on traditional media as well as on social media. The detection models were based on news content and social content while giving a narrative approach to those models.

A study closer to this is that of Klyuev [2] who did an overview of various semantic approaches in filtering fake news, he focused on natural language processing (NLP), mining of text to verify their authenticity. Machine Learning (ML) including to detect social bots. His approach differs from ours in the sense that he took a narrative approach to explain how various detection methods work without considering the different types of fake news and their motives. Contrary we give a state-of-the-art approach by detailing each detective model with a working example and comparing their success rate. Also related is the work of Oshikawa and Wang [13] which focuses on an automatic method to detect fake news using NLP. Their survey is based on one form of detection method i.e., NLP. Contrary to our work, we gave details of different types of detection models including both automatic and manual-facts checking as well as hybrid.

The objective of this study is to get an insight into the various type of fake news as well as the method of detecting them. We opine that fake news have different types with different motives and so one method cannot be used to detect all fake news because of the different goals and objectives of those spreading them. The rest of the paper is arranged as follows: in Sect. 2 we focused on how fake news proliferate on social media, Sect. 3 give details account of the various type of fake news while in Sect. 4 we detailly discussed the various detection models with a working example. Section 5 we discuss the open challenges and made our concluding remark in Sect. 6.

2 How Fake News Proliferate on Social Media

The proliferation of fake news on social media have short-term as well as long-term implications for its consumers which can result in a reluctance to engage in genuine news sharing and posting due to fear of such information being misleading, this is due to the fact that fake news constitute two major ways in which they are proliferated through the social media which are; disinformation and misinformation.

Misinformation refers to those who share fake news without knowing that it is fake mostly simply because they see their friends or others sharing it [14]. The echo chamber effect contribute enormously to this aspect, the social media system is made of an algorithm that recommend certain news or information to a consumer due to the group in which he/she belongs to on the social media, their prior history, circle of friendship such that when a friend view something, another friend is recommended the same thing and it will notify the user that such a content has been viewed or liked by his/her friends which will motivate such an individual also to share or like it. This recommendation algorithm also acts as a motivating factor for the consumer to share content even when they don't know the veracity of such content.

People who have the same belief or are in the same political party will spread and share information that favors their political aspiration without proper verification. Cognitive theories [3] holds that human beings are generally not good at detecting what is real and what is authentic and posit that due to the gullible nature of human being, they are prone to fake news. In [3], the author contends that people usually tend to believe something that conforms with their view (confirmation bias) and will share it without verification because it is in accord with their thinking and will distort those that are not in accordance with their view even if there are factual.

Disinformation refers to those who are aware that such information is fake and continue to spread it either for political or financial gains. This aspect is further exacerbated by the use of social bots and trolls. Social bots and trolls are potential sources of fake news on social media. Social bots here refer to an online algorithm that interacts in human forms. Although social bots were initially created to respond to customers' needs by some companies, some ill-minded individuals have used social bots to spread malicious and misleading information, Social bot easily retweets and follow thousands of account on twitter as well as share a post on facebook within a short time. Dickerson et al. [15] used sentiment to detect bots on twitter and found out that human gives stronger sentiments than bots. While trolls refer to human control account, they are so many accounts that are trolls account control by human beings also meant to spread malicious and distorted information. Figure 1 above shows a social bot account that runs automatically and spreads false and misleading information. Xiao and colleagues [16] build a cluster to detect trolls and malicious accounts on the social media network and were able to detect whether an account is a troll account or legitimate. A psychological study by [17] has proven that attempt to correct fake news has often catalyzed the spread of fake news, especially in cases of ideological differences.

3   Type of Fake News

In this section, we made a classification of the different types of fake news. In detecting fake news, it is important to distinguish the various forms of fake news which include; clickbait, hoax, propaganda, satire and parody, and others, as seen in Fig. 2.

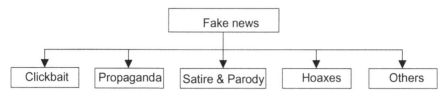

Fig. 2. Type of fake news

3.1 Clickbait

Clickbait is a fake story with eye-catchy headlines aimed at enticing the reader to click on a link. Clicking on the link will generate income to the owner of that link in the form of a pay per click [14, 18]. A study by [18] finds most clickbait headlines to be enticing and more appealing than normal news. They define eight types of clickbait and contend that clickbait articles usually have misleading information in the form of gossip with low quality that is generally not related to the headlines [18]. Clickbait has proven to be a very lucrative business especially to the Macedonia teenagers [14], the Macedonia city of Veles is now termed the fake news city as fake news producers are already preparing for the 2020 US presidential election [14].

3.2 Propaganda

Propaganda is also a form of fake news, although date back during wartime, propaganda was famous in war reporting where journalists often report false information to save the public from panic especially during first and second world wars. According to [9] propaganda refers "to news stories which are created by a political entity to influence public perceptions". States are the main actor of propaganda, and recently it has taken a different turn with politicians and media organs using it to support a certain position or view [14]. Propaganda type of fake news can easily be detected with manual fact-based detection models such as the use of expert-based fact-checkers.

3.3 Satire and Parody

Satire and Parody are a widely accepted type of fake news, this is done with a fabricated story or by exaggerating the truth reported in mainstream media in the form of comedy [8]. According to [9], Satire is a form of fake news which employs humorous style or exaggeration to present audiences with news updates. The difference with a satirical form of fake news is that the authors or the host present themselves as a comedian or as an entertainer rather than a journalist informing the public. However, most of the audience believed the information passed in this satirical form because the comedian usually projects news from mainstream media and frame them to suit their program. Satirical and comic news shows like *The John Stewart Show and The Daily Show with Trevor Noah* has gained prominence in recent years.

Although both satire and parody uses comedy to pass out information in the form of entertainment, satire uses factual information and modified or frame it to mean something else, contrary to parody, the entire story is completely fake such that if someone is not familiar with such site he/she is meant to believe the story. A good example of a parody site is *The Onion* and Daily *Mash*, which has often misinformed people as they often fabricate eye-catching and human interest information.

3.4 Hoaxes

Hoaxes are intentionally fabricated reports in an attempt to deceive the public or audiences [9, 19]. Since they are done deliberately, it is well coined such that at times, the mainstream media report it believing it to be true. Some author refers to this type of fake new as large scale fabrications and alludes that hoaxing has often caused serious material damage to its victim. It is usually aimed at a public figure [19]. Tamman and Colleagues [20] formulated a TextRank algorithm based on the method of the PageRank algorithm to detect hoax news reported in the Indonesian language. Using Cosine Similarity to calculate the document similarity, the author could rank them in order of their similar nature and then apply the TextRank algorithm. The result of the study was quite impressive given the fact that it was done in the Indonesian language.

3.5 Other (Name-Theft, Framing)

Name-theft refers to a fake news source that attempts to steal the identity of a genuine or authentic news provider in order to deceive the audience to believe that such information is coming from a well-known source. This is usually done with the creation of a website that mimics an already existing authentic news website, for instance, a producer of fake news in order to deceive the public may use credible news source websites such as (cnn. com to cnn1.net, foxnews.com to foxnewss.com). This is usually done with the inclusion of the site logo which easily deceives consumers into believing that such information is coming from the site they already recognized as genuine.

    Framing is also one form of fake news, this aspect tries to deceive the reader by employing some aspect of reality while making it more visible meanwhile the truth is being concealed. It is logical that people will understand certain concepts based on the way it is coined, consumers will normally perceive something differently if framed in two different ways although it all meant the same thing. Framing became more popular during the US presidential debate when most media will provide misconceptions about what a political aspirant actually said. For instance, suppose a leader X says "I will neutralize my opponent" simply meaning he will beat his opponent in a given election. Such a statement will be framed such as "leader X threatens to kill Y" such a framed statement has given a total misconception of the original meaning.

4   Fake News Detection Models

Due to its rapid development and the complexity of solving it, some scholars allude that the utilization of artificial intelligence tools and machine learning techniques should be applied [1, 5]. In this section, we vividly explain the various fake news detection models citing working examples (Fig. 3).

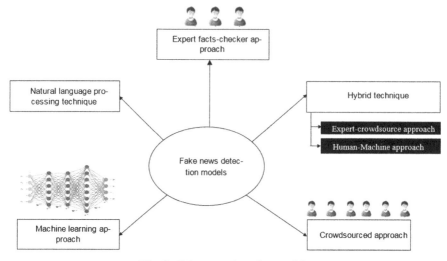

Fig. 3. Fake news detection models

4.1 Experts Facts-Checker Approach

Professional fact-checkers are a small group of experts in various disciplines who are capable of verifying the veracity of certain news items and decide whether such information is fake or authentic. Author in [4] posited that the strength of expert-based fact-checking techniques lies in the fact that they are small in number thus, easy to manage and have a high accuracy rate. A study by [21] explains that an expert-facts checker is a natural approach to verifying fake news which uses "professional fact-checkers to determine which content is false, and then engaging in some combination of issuing corrections, tagging false content with warnings, and directly censoring false content e.g., by demoting its placement in ranking algorithms so that it is less likely to be seen by users". The expert-fact checking technique is slow especially in a situation where they are given a large volume of information to verify due to their small number, also the fact the process is manual. During the 2016 US presidential election as well as the Brexit referendum, most expert fact-checker could not respond to a growing number of fake news that was being proliferated. Some examples of prominent fact-checking sites include; *Snopes, Hoaxslayer, Fullfact, TruthOrFiction, The Washington Post Fact Checker, PolitiFact, FactCheck* mostly focus on American politics. Due to the limitation of the expert-based fact-checkers, the crowdsourced technique is seen as a good alternative.

4.2 Crowdsourced Approach

Crowdsourced or "wisdom of the crowds" approach is based on the premise that no matter how smart someone is, the collective effort of individuals or groups supersedes any single individual intellectual capacity. Brabham [22] see crowdsourcing as, "an online, distributed problem-solving and production model that leverages the collective intelligence of online communities to serve specific organizational goals". Gaining knowledge from different sources such as collective consensus is an important element with the wisdom of the crowd approach [28]. The weaknesses of expert-based fact-checkers have prompted many to seek the "wisdom of the crowds" technique. In [21], the authors used crowdsourced judgments of news source on social media and discovered that the crowd is more effective than professional fact-checker, in judging the news source quality laypeople got a similar rating with professional fact-checkers. In a set of 60 news websites, they classified them into 3 groups, 20 renowned mainstream media websites such as (cnn.com, bbc.com and foxnews.com) and 22 websites that are hyperpartisan in their coverage and reporting of facts i.e. (breitbart.com, dailykos.com) and lastly 18 websites that are well known for spreading fake news such as (thelastlineofdefense.org, now8news.com) Using a set of n = 1,010 recruited from the Amazon Mechanical Turk (AMT), they compare their judgement with those of expert-based facts-checker in a second survey and found their judgment to be accurate. In their study, they could identify the limitation of the "wisdom of the crowds" approach, firstly, because the crowd is made up of laypeople and have little knowledge of some news site, consequently, news sites which they are unfamiliar with are marked as an untrusted site. For instance, Huffington Post, AOL News, NY Post, Daily Mail, Fox News, and NY Daily News were rated as an untrusted site by the crowd as opposed to experts fact-checkers who labeled all the above mentioned as trusted sites. *Fiskkit* is a modeled example of a crowdsourcing site.

4.3 Machine Learning Approach

Early Machine Learning (ML) method in detecting fake news was proposed by [1] because it is assumed that fake news is created intentionally for the political and financial benefit, so they often have an opinionated and enticing headline, at such the extraction of the textual and linguistic feature is necessary for ML. The authors in [1] used Naive Bayes classifier and classified linguistic features such as lexical features, including word count and level, as well as syntactic nature, which involves sentence level characterization. They use datasets from BuzzFeed News aggregator, which contains data from Facebook posts and major political news agencies such as Politico, CNN, and ABC News. They divided the datasets into three sets namely the training, validation, test dataset and got 75% accuracy. Most AI tools for detecting fake news rely heavily on Click-Through Rates (CTR), the position of the stream page increases as the CTR increase and some fake news type such as clickbait articles usually have high CTR due to it enticing and appealing nature. Consequently, such an approach cannot be used to detect fake news types such as clickbait. Biyani and colleagues [18] propose a ML model to detect fake news; using Gradient Boosted Decision Trees (GBDT), their model achieves strong classification performance and saws that *informality* is a crucial factor of the "baity" nature of web-pages. Using datasets from yahoo news aggregator, they collected 1349 (training set) clickbait and 2724 (testing set) non-clickbait web pages. They employ the concept of *Informality* and *Forward Reference*. By comparing clickbait articles, they assert that most clickbait has misleading information such as gossip and most appealing headlines aimed at enticing the reader to click on the link. The landing page is usually of low quality and thus, they contend that because news aggregator site, i.e., yahoo news aim to serve its user with news article via it homepage, the proliferation of clickbait article which usually has low quality increases user's dissatisfaction rate and amplify their abandonment which is bad for business and hence detecting and removing clickbait site become inevitable. This approach is not without limitation, fake news is a broad issue with several types but this study focuses only on one type of fake news, i.e., clickbait which has two ways of detecting it; firstly, it can be easily detected because the content is different from the headline and secondly, based on the fact that the content is of low quality.

4.4   Natural Language Processing Technique

NLP work within automated deception detection technique which involves the application of lexical and semantic analysis, with the use of regression, clustering, as well as classification techniques such as binary classification of text where news are classified as real and not real, in a two-class problem, where it is difficult to detect, a third-class may be added such as partially real or partially fake. Sentiment Score is then calculated using the Text Vectorization algorithm and Natural Language ToolKit. Deception cues are identified in the text which is extracted and clustered [2]. Grammar and style detector and syntactic analyzer such as Standford parser have been reported by [2] which gives accurate results. A study by [23] shows that truth verification with NLP has proven to show greater success when compared with human verification in a sample of n = 90. The basic task is to identify some verbal and lexical cues which will point out linguistic differences when human tell lies as oppose to when they tell the truth. For instance, deceivers produce total words-count and sense-based words such as those that show lower cognitive complexity, the use of more negative emotion words, extreme positive words.

4.5   Hybrid Technique

Hybrid detection techniques emerge as an alternative to several fake news detection methods, due to the complexity and ambiguous nature of fake news, the combination of other method is imperative. According to Mahid and Colleagues [24], the Hybrid-based detection model involves "the fusion of techniques from the content-based model as well as social context-based techniques utilizing auxiliary information from different perspectives". The failure of the single model in detecting fake news prompted scholars to find alternative measures to accurately detect fake news. In this study, we discuss Hybrid Expert-crowdsource and Hybrid Machine-crowdsource detection method.

(a) Expert-Crowdsource Approach
The hybrid expert-crowdsource approach is relatively a new method that emerges as a result of the weaknesses of the previous methods. This approach involves the combination of the two manual fact-checking systems by applying human knowledge as opposed to automatic facts-checking involving the use of the machines. The key idea behind this approach is that where experts failed, the crowdsourced approach can complement and vice versa [24]. Recently, Facebook has announced the combination of an expert-crowdsource approach in fighting the proliferation of fake news on its network. The expert-based has often been accused of being politically biased, not independent, and very slow in detecting fake news [25]. While a study by [21] allude that the crowd is

limited in many areas since they are composed of laypeople and at such, they will give the wrong prediction to content which they are unfamiliar with. Therefore, it is imperative that since the crowd is unbiased and acting independently, larger in number and thus can easily work on a large volume of information, the aggregation of the crowds' decision can be sent to the expert which will yield better results since experts are familiar with many areas.

(b) Human-Machine Approach
Most machine learning algorithms developed to automatically detect fake news has often failed. This is because all news does not have the same writing pattern and also involves several topics with salient features. A study by [26] found out that one of the limitations of automatic fake news detection is low accuracy, those machine algorithms developed to detect fake news through news contend are prone to low accuracy due to the fact that most language use in writing fake news bypass the detection process. While the wisdom of the crowd as seen already is a right approach but slow and time-consuming and lack expert knowledge because usually crowd are compose of laypeople [21], the combination of machine learning algorithms and the collective effort of humans has proven to yield better fruits, especially in the area of detecting fake news automated by social bots. One of the hybrid machine-crowdsource technique was proposed by [26], they propose a model that uses a hybrid machine-crowd approach to detect fake news and satire. They use a dataset from the Fake vs Satire dataset. Crowdsource was use to classify news from Satire and fake news and distinguish them which was difficult to detect by the machine. By applying a combination of ML techniques they got an overall accuracy rate of 87%. The work of Wang [27] achieved a similar result as the author applied a hybrid crowdsource-machine technique in detecting fake news on social media by framing a 6-way multi-class text classification problem, the author design a hybrid CNN to integrate meta-data with text and got higher results [27]. With the application of crowdsourced, they gathered over 12000 manually labeled short statements (LIAR) dataset from politifact.com API of which those datasets are mostly used for fack-checking. By randomly initializing a matrix of embedding vectors to encode the metadata embeddings, the author employs 5baselines which includes LR, SVM a Bi-directional Long Short-Term memory networks model, CNN model as well as majority baseline. The SVM and LR gave a good performance to the classification problem as compare to the other baselines, while the CNN gave an overall high accuracy.

5   Discussion and Challenges

The discourse on fake news detection models reveals that base on the existing models, detecting fake news will still remain a potent challenge. More sophisticated models are required. Manual facts checking, which includes the use of experts, as well as crowd-sourced judgment in checking the veracity of certain news content has yielded some fruits. However, manual fact checking is still faced with a lot of limitations such as labor, and time especially when they are faced with large volumes of information. The automatic fact-checking method is able to deal with large volumes of data within a concise time, however, it has a lot of limitation because most ML algorithm trained to detect fake news is base on particular lexical and textual contents as well as style. The manufacturer of fake news is also improving on new techniques to bypass this algorithm, and hence, manual facts-checking will always be required. The social media networks yield financial benefits not only to it creator but to it users as well and consequently, owner of these social networks are often reluctant to flag and remove some items or information on their site for fear of losing their financial gains, and this is a challenge to many users. Facebook and Youtube have often come under strong criticism for allowing certain fake information on their platforms.

6 Conclusions and Future Works

The proliferation of fake news on social media has often made people reluctant to engage in genuine news and information sharing for fear that such information is false and misleading. The debate on fake news detection has been a challenging one due to the complex and dynamic nature of fake news. In this paper, we did an overview of fake news detection models taking into cognizance the various types of fake news. It is a reality that fake news has caused enormous damage not only to democracy but to the freedom of speech due to its rapid spread on social media and hence detecting them become imperative. We recommend that fake news can be verified based on sources, authors or publishers, and experts can be able to distinguish between those genuine sources and fake sources.

Social bots and trolls account has often acted as a catalyst in generating and spreading fake news, which is a potent challenge. Hence, future work is required in areas of social bots detection, the main problem is not the fake news rather, it is the sharing and spreading of fake news that is causing more harm. The use of social bots in sharing fake news makes it go viral, and it has further exacerbated the proliferation of fake news as these contents are shared and like automatically making it difficult for experts to detect.

Acknowledgment. This research was supported by the Basic Science Research Program through the National Research Foundation of Korea (NRF) funded by the Ministry of Science, ICT & Future Planning (2017R1A2B4009410), and the National Research Foundation of Korea (NRF) grant funded by the BK21PLUS Program (22A20130012009).

References

1. Granik, M., Mesyura, V.: Fake news detection using naive Bayes classifier. In: 2017 IEEE 1st Ukraine Conference on Electrical and Computer Engineering, UKRCON 2017 (2017)
2. Klyuev, V.: Fake news filtering: semantic approaches. In: 2018 7th International Conference on Reliability, Infocom Technologies and Optimization (Trends and Future Directions) (ICRITO), pp. 9–15 (2019)
3. Kai, S., Huan, L.: Detecting Fake News on Social Media. Morgan Publishers, San Rafael (2019)
4. Zhou, X., Zafarani, R.: Fake news: a survey of research, detection methods (2018)
5. Kshetri, N., Voas, J.: The economics of 'fake news'. IT Prof. **19**(6), 9 (2017)

6. Tanikawa, M.: What is news? What is the newspaper? The physical, functional, and stylistic transformation of print newspapers. Int. J. Commun. **11**, 3519–3540 (2017)
7. Gans, H.J.: Deciding What's News: A Study of CBS Evening News. NWU Press, New York (2004)
8. Brummette, J., DiStaso, M., Vafeiadis, M., Messner, M.: Read all about it: the politicization of 'fake news' on Twitter. Journal. Mass Commun. Q. **95**(2), 497 (2018)
9. Tandoc, E.C., Lim, Z.W., Ling, R.: Defining 'fake news': a typology of scholarly definitions. Digit. Journal. **6**(2), 137–153 (2018)
10. Lazer, D.M.J., et al.: The science of fake news. Science **59**(63), 94–106 (2018)
11. Karataş, A., Şahin, S.: A review on social bot detection techniques and research directions. In: ISCTurkey 10th International Information Security and Cryptology Conference, At Ankara, Turkey, no. i, pp. 156–161 (2017)
12. Aniyath, A.: A survey on fake news detection: data mining perspective, vol. 6, no. 1, January 2019
13. Oshikawa, R., Qian, J., Wang, W.: A survey on NLP for fake news detection (2018)
14. Campan, A., Cuzzocrea, A., Truta, T.M.: Fighting fakes news spread in online social networks: actual trends and future research directions. In: IEEE BIGDATA, pp. 4453–4457 (2017)
15. Dickerson, J.P., Kagan, V., Subrahmanian, V.S.: Using sentiment to detect bots on Twitter: are humans more opinionated than bots? In: Proceedings of the ASONAM, pp. 620–627 (2014)
16. Freeman, D., Hwa, T.: Detecting fake accounts in social networks, pp. 91–101 (2015)
17. Roozenbeek, J., van der Linden, S.: Fake news game confers psychological resistance against online misinformation. Palgrave Commun. **5**(65) (2019)
18. Biyani, P., Tsioutsiouliklis, K., Blackmer, J.: 8 amazing secrets for getting more clicks: detecting clickbaits in news streams using article informality. In: AAAI, pp. 94–100 (2016)
19. Rubin, V.L., Chen, Y., Conroy, N.J.: Deception detection for news: three types of fakes. Proc. Assoc. Inf. Sci. Technol. **52**(1), 1–4 (2015)
20. Sucipto, S., Tammam, A.G., Indriati, R.: Hoax detection at social media with text mining clarification system-based. JIPI **3**(2), 94–100 (2018)
21. Pennycook, G., Rand, D.: Fighting misinformation on social media using crowdsourced judgments of news source quality. Proc. Natl. Acad. **116**(7), 2521 (2019)
22. Brabham, D.C.: Crowdsourcing. MIT Press, Massachusetts (1982)
23. Rubin, V.L., Conroy, N.J.: Challenges in automated deception detection in computer-mediated communication. Proc. ASIST Annu. Meet. **48** (2011)
24. Mahid, Z.I., Manickam, S., Karuppayah, S.: Detection techniques. In: ACCA, pp. 1–5 (2018)
25. Della Vedova, M.L., Tacchini, E., Moret, S., Ballarin, G., Dipierro, M.: Automatic online fake news detection combining content and social signals, vol. 79, pp. 273–279 (1957)
26. Shabani, S., Sokhn, M.: Hybrid machine-crowd approach for fake news detection. In: Proceedings of the 4th IEEE International Conference on Collaboration and Internet Computing, CIC 2018, pp. 299–306 (2018)
27. Wang, W.Y.: Liar, liar pants on fire': a new benchmark dataset for fake news detection. In: Proceedings of the 55th Annual Meeting of the Association for Computational Linguistics (Volume 2: Short Papers), pp. 422–426 (2017)
28. Dang, D.T., Nguyen, N.T., Hwang, D.: Multi-step consensus: an effective approach for determining consensus in large collectives. Cybern. Syst. **50**(2), 208–229 (2019)

Design Challenges of Trustworthy Artificial Intelligence Learning Systems

Matthias R. Brust[1](✉), Pascal Bouvry[1,2], Grégoire Danoy[1,2],
and El-Ghazil Talbi[3]

[1] Interdisciplinary Centre for Security Reliability and Trust (SnT),
Luxembourg City, Luxembourg
[2] Faculty of Science, Technology and Medicine (FSTM), University of Luxembourg,
Luxembourg City, Luxembourg
{matthias.brust,pascal.bouvry,gregoire.danoy}@uni.lu
[3] Polytech'Lille, University Lillie - Inria, Lille, France
el-ghazali.talbi@univ-lille.fr

Abstract. In the near future, more than two thirds of the world's population is expected to be living in cities. In this interconnected world, data collection from various sensors is eased up and unavoidable. Handling the right data is an important factor for decision making and improving services. While at the same time keeping the right level of privacy for end users is crucial. This position paper discusses the necessary trade-off between privacy needs and data handling for the improvement of services. Pseudo-anonymization techniques have shown their limits and local computation and aggregation of data seems the way to go. To illustrate the opportunity, the case for a novel generation of clustering algorithms is made that implements a privacy by design approach. Preliminary results of such a clustering algorithm use case show that our approach exhibits a high degree of elasticity.

Keywords: Artificial Intelligence · Trustworthiness · Smart cities · Data-driven economies

1 Introduction

Soon, more than two thirds of the world's population is expected to be living in cities. Governments are pushing forward to implement the smart cities concept to use information and communication technologies (ICT) such as Internet-of-Things (IoT), cloud computing and Artificial Intelligence (AI) systems to improve the life quality in the city by delivering valuable business insights for companies and better services to their citizens. Governments and companies also might be interested to keep control of certain data for prime-services and to provide initiatives for innovative product development by third-parties.

However, with people are each time more connected physically and virtually, data of individuals is not only easier to be collected, but turn out to be unavoidable and natural privacy spheres are shrinking to a size where regulations are more and more emerging to protect the citizen's (virtual) privacy.

© Springer Nature Singapore Pte Ltd. 2020
P. Sitek et al. (Eds.): ACIIDS 2020, CCIS 1178, pp. 574–584, 2020.
https://doi.org/10.1007/978-981-15-3380-8_50

As the smart city depends heavily on data collection, while sensors are getting cheaper and more diverse it is expected that the high rate of generated data will be dramatically potentiated in the near future. For illustration: By 2003, humankind had generated in total five exabytes of data. In 2020, we are generating five exabytes of data every two days [24].

However, the exponentially growing amount of data from increasingly diverse sources and generated in high frequency, requires a novel generation of advanced data analytics and AI techniques to extract useful information and patterns in near real-time. Machine learning algorithms promise to bring valuable insights needed for innovation on the growing volume and complexity of data. A widely used process for unsupervised machine learning is data clustering.

In this paper, we describe (a) the challenges of big data clustering as used in unsupervised machine learning, (b) the challenges of privacy preservation versus the benefit of potential insights, (c) how both challenges could be overcome by developing trustworthy AI systems which are privacy compliant by design.

To this end, we propose to use a network-based clustering algorithm, which (1) is highly adaptive to changes in data and probability distribution, and (2) is based on local policies restricting update operations solely to the relevant data. With preliminary results showing high degree of elasticity, future work will focus on extensive experiments on large-scale networks.

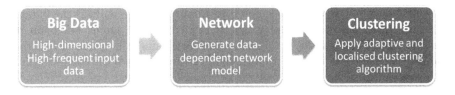

Fig. 1. Illustration of the proposed network-based data clustering process.

The remainder of this paper is as follows: Sect. 2 describes related work. Section 3 discusses the design challenges for a trustworthy AI system. In Sect. 4, we describe a clustering algorithm that fulfills our specifications for a system design approach. Section 5 discusses the status of technical standardization and regulatory aspects for trustworthy AI systems. This paper concludes with Sect. 6.

2   Related Work

This section describes three major privacy and trust problems for AI systems which are actively discussed in the corresponding research communities and dedicated standardization committees: Biased data, data poisoning, and model extraction.

The decisions achieved by AI systems can reinforce discrimination [27] in shortening candidates list for credit approval, recruitment, and criminal legal system [32]. Even though bias is not directly recognized as the privacy and security issue of big data, it is entangled with data and thereby can significantly impact the accuracy and accountability of the results and therefore the trustworthiness of the system. Different types of bias exists: (i) *Sample bias* describing an unbalanced representation of samples in training data, (ii) *Algorithm bias* which refers to the systematic errors in the system, and (iii) *Prejudicial bias* indicates the incorrect attitude upon an individual data. Bias is not a deliberate feature of AI systems, but rather the result of biases presented in the input data used to train the systems [15]. Hence, it targets the training phase and violates the *integrity* of an AI system.

Data poisoning [20] is one of the most widespread attacks developed based on the idea of learning with polluted data. Its disruptive effects in industrial applications have attracted experts of the standard technical committee to investigate on the countermeasures and defence techniques [1]. The attack happens by injecting adversarial training data during the learning to corrupt the model or to force a system towards producing false results [25]. Therefore, the attack works in two ways: (i) a common adversarial type is to alter the boundaries of the classifier such that the model becomes useless. This way the attacker aims the availability of the system. (ii) the other type, however, targets the integrity of the system by generating a *backdoor* such that the attacker can abuse the system in his favor.

The trained model is a valuable intellectual property in ML systems due to (i) the big data source that is been used to train the model, and (ii) the parameters (e.g., weights, coefficients) which generated for the model based on its function (e.g., classification) [1,26]. The adversary's aim from the model extraction is to infer records used to train the model, thus, violates the confidentiality of the system. Based on how sensitive the trained data is (e.g., medical record), the attack can cause a significant privacy breach by disclosing sensitive information [23].

3   Design Challenges for Trustworthy AI Systems

A system that gathers no data will naturally have a high privacy preservation. On the other end of the spectrum, we can have systems where all the sensors are required gathering all possible data and submitting the full unretracted stream of collected data forward. In such a scenario, the need for privacy compliance might be high depending on the regulatory specifications. At the same time, the options on how to limit the sensitivity of the data tremendous. However, there is an important trade-off to make: if the insights the data reveal are yet to be uncovered, any measure to manipulate the data in compliance to privacy regulations or recommendations, is likely to decrease the value of the data – in particular for potential future services.

Besides this trade-off, there is, however, also a tremendous potential to reduce conflict situations: Not all the data which can be sensed will be sensed, and not all the data which was sensed will reach the analytics module. The reason why such a system can still work is due to the fact that many applications exhibit some level of elasticity: the backend can often fill in missing data through interpolation, with some data being more important than others. In this context, it is important to note that missing data aspect is in particular well researched when we deal with data as networks, where the structure of the network reveal evidence on missing links, nodes or even partition. For this reason, we focus on clustering algorithms that receive networks as input data.

Following, we describe the design challenges for a trustworthy AI system that takes into account the performance of the clustering algorithm for a diversity of data characteristics (big data), privacy preservation of sensitive information within the data, and the network-nature of data.

3.1 Clustering Algorithms

Many AI system use clustering as part of the learning of models (Machine Learning (ML)) to group similar data as clusters while increasing the inter-cluster dissimilarity [30]. Therefore, the performance of the system relies heavily on the performance of the clustering algorithm used.

A widely applied traditional clustering algorithm is k-means [29] which uses an iterative approach for center selection and assignment to nearest centers until a steady-state is reached. Methods such as k-means, fuzzy c-means, and hierarchical clustering [30] deliver outstanding cluster quality while showing a low algorithmic complexity [30].

However, as mentioned, today's networked systems such as Internet-of-Things (IoT) have an exponentially higher number of connections, dependencies, sensors and data producing devices, which is changing the nature of the data, thus exposing the limits of traditional clustering algorithms. The age of Big Data where data is often characterized by its volume, variety, velocity, and variability.

At this end, clustering needs to be upgraded to manage all the differentiating factors of Big Data with a reasonable performance. In its core, a AI system described within the context of this papers has to cope with (1) continuous streams of data, arriving at high velocity, (2) tackling high dimensional data, (3) changes in the probability distribution (distribution drift), (4) user interaction during runtime (anytime clustering) [17], (5) dynamic data processing (learning algorithms) [14]. Additionally, centralized clustering algorithms suffer from scale-variance when confronted with massive datasets [2,6].

3.2 Preservation of Privacy

In smart cities with the tremendous number of sensors and data collection apparatus, it is in particularly important to ensure that a citizen's privacy is preserved. Nowadays, governments take more and more an active role to limit the privacy exposure of their citizens. For example, location-based services [19] are extracting location information of mobile users to offer context-aware and personalized services. Location-based services are omni-present in smart cities used in transportation services, lifestyle enhancement systems, and localization applications. These services do not only restrict their on the GPS data, but also include complementary data from others sources such as built-in sensors, user interaction, and social media content. The use of location services carries a high risk of exposure of privacy-sensitive information to undesired parties [28]. This situation presents significant privacy threats to service users and citizens.

With the continuous exchange of location information, it is rather easy for a system to deduce a user's home or office location [19]. Such a problem becomes more thorny due to the recent fast advancement of machine learning and data mining techniques, where activity hotspots and transitions could be revealed through statistics and probabilistic models, and the next place of a user might be inferred. Therefore, privacy preservation for big data analytics is critical for such system to be widely and practically adopted [28].

3.3   Network-Based Analysis

Although inherent in data, networks are often discarded. Network-based analytics plays an increasingly important role machine learning and AI. Growing evidence suggests that data can be better understood through networks rather data points.

There is a wide body of knowledge form network science for analysis, visualization, link prediction, community detection, clustering etc. The network construction from a data set plays an important role and it has been applied in different areas from biology and neuroscience [22] (e.g., brain networks [4]) to modeling and analyzing galaxy distributions [16].

The representation of data as networks offers several advantages. Attractive algorithms can be applied directly on networks such as *Louvain*'s algorithm [5] which is a community detection algorithm and *Page Rank*, that identifies the most influential object within a network. Furthermore, data transformed into network layers can provide evidence for missing or omitted information [18,31] as well as predicting growth of the network in terms of nodes and links [21]. Networks also provide mechanisms for adaptability and to capture dynamicity [7].

4   Use Case: Trustworthy AI by Design

To tackle the challenges of smart city big data analysis and privacy preservation, we propose to enhance existing data analytics techniques with a novel network-based clustering algorithm. Our work focuses on using network structures to design an adaptable and localized clustering algorithm that provides existing machine learning techniques with privacy-preserving mechanisms, which is adaptive and localized.

The proposed design focuses on system integration avoiding modular or component-based approaches. By integrating clustering performance and privacy preservation in one seamless process, and, taking advantage of network properties of the data, the system should deliver a higher degree of trustworthiness as it would be possible with a layered or modular approach (cf. Fig. 2). For example, a system build on these principles would break performance guarantees or fail to work with the networked data, if privacy requirements are violated.

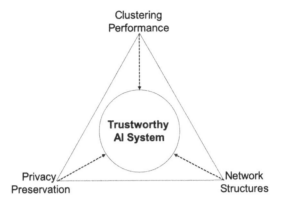

Fig. 2. The proposed design avoids modularity to deliver system integrity that supports trustworthiness.

Our proposed approach uses a network-based approach to transform big data into network structures, which enable to dynamically cluster data while preserving privacy (cf. Fig. 1). First, the transformation of data into network layers occurs by applying a pre-defined linkage threshold as we demonstrated in preliminary research [13]. Second, the method applies a set of rules in order to generate the nodes and connectivity patterns of the network from the source data.

4.1 Clustering

The clustering algorithm under consideration for the use case consists of four rules that describe cluster requirements, which if not fulfilled, triggers one of the transitional rules to reach the *optimal* cluster result [7,8].

The cluster algorithm works on bases of the nodes and is therefor fully distributed and localized. Each node has a weigh w_I which correspondence to the data point. Links to other nodes in the network have been determined by a data-to-network transformation procedure as described earlier.

In the start configuration, a node knows the clusterhead weight, i.e. the weight when a node is assumed to be a clusterhead, and the minimum weight. These weights are named MIN and MAX.

For the execution of the clustering a node v solely needs the information of the direct neighbors $N(v)$ and the corresponding weights $W(N(v))$.

580   M. R. Brust et al.

Following rules describe the state transition for a node v with weight w_v:

1. If there is a neighbor with a highest weight $w_n > w_v$ of all neighbors than node v changes it weight to $w_v \leftarrow w_n - 1$.
2. If weight $w_v = MIN$ and $w_v = w_n$, $w_n \in W(N(v))$, i.e. no neighbor has a higher weight than MIN then node v declares itself as clusterhead, thus $w_v \leftarrow MAX$.
3. If $w_v \neq MAX$ and $w_v \geq w_n$, $w_n \in W(N(v))$, i.e. there is no neighbor with a higher weight then $w_v \leftarrow w_v - 1$.
4. If $w_v = MAX$ and $\exists w_n \in W(N(v))$ with $w_n = MAX$, i.e. two clusterheads appear in transmission range, then choose one clusterhead that weight continues with weight $w \leftarrow w - 1$.

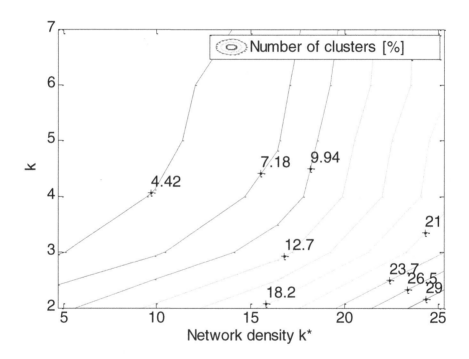

Fig. 3. Analyzing the elasticity degree of the network-based clustering algorithm.

The first rule creates a top-to-down hierarchical structure. The second rule deals with the situation with isolated nodes and their weight assessment. The third rule guarantees clusterheads in each cluster. The fourth rule solves direct clusterhead-to-clusterhead connections. describes the situation where two clusterhead meet in 1-hop neighborhood. Note that the last rule can be more elaborated to address additional disadvantageousness situation.

4.2 Elasticity

Depending on the application and the data, it can be important to tune the number of clusterheads in a highly controllable way, e.g. by extending or reducing the cluster size. For example, the larger the cluster size, the smaller the number of clusters and the number of clusterheads, respectively. For the considered clustering algorithm, a human-in-the-loop or fully automatized procedure can be put in place for cluster(head) tuning.

Besides this attractive possibilities, and since we are dealing with networks as cluster objects, the elasticity of the clustering algorithm is important to be analyzed. For this, we consider in the first step, geometric random graphs with different network densities, which is defined as: $k^* = \frac{1}{l^2} \sum_{v \in N} A\left(SLT\left(v\right)\right)$ that is k^* is the sum of the total area A of all nodes $v \in N$ divided by total area l^2. The spatial linkage threshold (SLT) determines the linkage patterns of the network N.

In Fig. 3, we plotted the network density k^* against the allowed cluster radius starting from 2 to inclusively 7. As result, we retrieved a characteristic profile for the number of clusters within certain network density and how the radius parameter k can influence the number of clusters. Based on this promising results, an extensive set of experiments will be conducted using large-scale networks in future work.

4.3 Privacy Preservation Policies

For instance, location-based and bio-medical data, which is collected continuously from diverse sources (e.g. smart watches) requires data anonymization. Mobile media discovery services tend to be more successful with enhanced privacy settings [3] and online social network users are highly sensitive towards privacy options [10]. In network-based clustering algorithms, k-anonymity techniques can be applied by e.g. generating network to decrease correlations between sensitive data. Using the privacy exposure metric [28], we measure the privacy quality of the proposed scheme. The network structure is beneficial for providing not only privacy preservation but also adaptability of the data clustering process. More specific experiments shall be conducted in future work.

5 Standardization and Regulations

Any innovation can have unintended consequences, and control measures in form of standardization and regulations are often not only desirable, but mostly essential for the growth of a healthy and sustainable innovation-based economy. For example, a primary concern to integrate AI systems in society, there is a great need for auditing and regulations to hold these systems accountable.

Standardization plays an essential role in the adoption of AI within the industry ecosystem [12]. There are different organizations that bring all the stakeholders such as entrepreneurs, governments, industries, and researchers together in various levels, from national standardization organization to European level (e.g., CEN, CENELEC, ETSI) and finally, the international level (e.g., ISO, IEC, ITU-T). All these standardization organizations are engaged on challenges from different aspects of AI, from defining the life-cycle and use cases, to highlighting the issues raised by the topic with respect to the data protection, privacy, and trustworthiness of AI.

IEEE as a leading international standards body has mainly focused on developing standards to address the legal and ethical perspectives of AI rather than the technical aspects regarding privacy and data protection. The organization has recently approved [11] various projects to address ethical aspects of AI in various domains and applications ranging from data privacy and ethical design to threats posed by AI. Moreover, the third international standards developing organization, the ITU, has directed AI activities to communication technologies.

Standardization activities are not only limited to the international level. On the European level, CEN and CELENEC have recently announced [9] the development of "Focus Group Artificial Intelligence" starting from 2019, to focus on developing standards in AI considering the European requirements. ETSI also initiated projects that focus on the use cases, applications and security challenges of AI.

6   Conclusion

To deal with the increasing amount of data in smart cities that needs to be continuously analyzed while preserving the citizen's privacy, we propose a network-based adaptive and localized clustering algorithm. The algorithm promises to be tolerant to probability distribution drifts (adaptivity), exhibit low computational complexity (locality), and support privacy preservation by using network-based clustering. Most importantly, we propose a system-based approach for better addressing multi-interest aspects as expected for trustworthy AI systems.

We expect that our approach will have a transformative impact on the design and management of techniques such as unsupervised data mining and adaptive learning. Additionally, we plan on providing our research results as input for technical standardization efforts in the area of AI and privacy preserving techniques.

Acknowledgment. This work has been partially funded by the joint research programme University of Luxembourg/SnT-ILNAS on Digital Trust for Smart-ICT.

References

1. ISO/IEC PD TR 24028: Information technology - Artificial Intelligence (AI) - Overview of trustworthiness in Artificial Intelligence. Standard, International Organization for Standardization, Geneva, CH
2. Abadi, M., et al.: Tensorflow: a system for large-scale machine learning. In: OSDI, vol. 16, pp. 265–283 (2016)

3. Andronache, A., Brust, M.R., Rothkugel, S.: Hycast-podcast discovery in mobile networks. In: Proceedings of the 3rd ACM Workshop on Wireless Multimedia Networking and Performance Modeling, pp. 27–34. ACM (2007)
4. Bassett, D.S., Zurn, P., Gold, J.I.: On the nature and use of models in network neuroscience. Nat. Rev. Neurosci. **19**, 566–578 (2018)
5. Blondel, V.D., Guillaume, J.L., Lambiotte, R., Lefebvre, E.: Fast unfolding of communities in large networks. J. Stat. Mech. Theory Exp. **2008**(10), P10008 (2008)
6. Brust, M.R., Akbaş, M.I., Turgut, D.: VBCA: a virtual forces clustering algorithm for autonomous aerial drone systems. In: 2016 Annual IEEE Systems Conference (SysCon), pp. 1–6. IEEE (2016)
7. Brust, M.R., Frey, H., Rothkugel, S.: Adaptive multi-hop clustering in mobile networks. In: Proceedings of the 4th International Conference on Mobile Technology, Applications, and Systems and the 1st International Symposium on Computer Human Interaction in Mobile Technology, pp. 132–138. ACM (2007)
8. Brust, M.R., Frey, H., Rothkugel, S.: Dynamic multi-hop clustering for mobile hybrid wireless networks. In: Proceedings of the 2nd International Conference on Ubiquitous Information Management and Communication, pp. 130–135. ACM (2008)
9. CEN-CENELEC: Artificial Intelligence, Blockchain and Distributed Ledger Technologies (2019). https://www.cencenelec.eu/standards/Topics/ArtificialIntelligence
10. Chen, J., Brust, M., Kiremire, A., Phoha, V.: Modeling privacy settings of an online social network from a game-theoretical perspective. In: IEEE CollaborateCom (2013)
11. Cihon, P.: Standards for AI governance: international standards to enable global coordination in AI research & development (2019)
12. Dilmaghani, S., Brust, M.R., Danoy, G., Cassagnes, N., Pecero, J., Bouvry, P.: Privacy and security of big data in AI systems: a research and standards perspective. In: Proceedings of the IEEE International Conference on Big Data (IEEE BigData 2019), International Workshop on Privacy and Security of Big Data (PSBD 2019). IEEE BigData (2019)
13. Dilmaghani, S., Brust, M.R., Piyatumrong, A., Danoy, G., Bouvry, P.: Link definition ameliorating community detection in collaboration networks. Front. Big Data **2**, 22 (2019)
14. Celebi, M.E., Aydin, K. (eds.): Unsupervised Learning Algorithms. Springer, Cham (2016). https://doi.org/10.1007/978-3-319-24211-8
15. Hinnefeld, J.H., Cooman, P., Mammo, N., Deese, R.: Evaluating fairness metrics in the presence of dataset bias. arXiv preprint arXiv:1809.09245 (2018)
16. Hong, S., et al.: Discriminating topology in galaxy distributions using network analysis. Mon. Not. R. Astron. Soc. **459**(3), 2690–2700 (2016)
17. Mai, S.T., He, X., Feng, J., Böhm, C.: Efficient anytime density-based clustering. In: Proceedings of the 2013 SIAM International Conference on Data Mining, pp. 112–120 (2013)
18. Pan, L., Zhou, T., Lü, L., Hu, C.K.: Predicting missing links and identifying spurious links via likelihood analysis. Sci. Rep. **6**, 22955 (2016)
19. Rao, B., Minakakis, L.: Evolution of mobile location-based services. Commun. ACM **46**(12), 61–65 (2003)
20. Rubinstein, B.I., et al.: Antidote: understanding and defending against poisoning of anomaly detectors. In: Proceedings of the 9th ACM SIGCOMM Conference on Internet measurement (2009)

21. Sha, Z., et al.: A network-based approach to modeling and predicting product coconsideration relations. Complexity **2018**, 14 (2018)
22. Shirinivas, S., Vetrivel, S., Elango, N.: Applications of graph theory in computer science an overview. Int. J. Eng. Sci. Technol. **2**(9), 4610–4621 (2010)
23. Shokri, R., Stronati, M., Song, C., Shmatikov, V.: Membership inference attacks against machine learning models. In: IEEE Symposium on Security and Privacy (SP), pp. 3–18 (2017)
24. Siegler, M.G.: Eric schmidt: Every 2 days we create as much information as we did up to 2003, August 2010. http://social.techcrunch.com/2010/08/04/schmidt-data/. Accessed 7 Mar 2018
25. Steinhardt, J., Koh, P.W.W., Liang, P.S.: Certified defenses for data poisoning attacks. In: Advances in Neural Information Processing Systems (2017)
26. Tramèr, F., Zhang, F., Juels, A., Reiter, M.K., Ristenpart, T.: Stealing machine learning models via prediction APIs. In: 25th USENIX Security Symposium (2016)
27. Wall, M.: Biased and wrong? Facial recognition tech in the dock, July 2019. https://www.bbc.com/news/business-48842750
28. Wu, F.J., Brust, M.R., Chen, Y.A., Luo, T.: The privacy exposure problem in mobile location-based services. In: Global Communications Conference (GLOBE-COM), 2016 IEEE, pp. 1–7. IEEE (2016)
29. Wu, J.: Advances in K-means Clustering: A Data Mining Thinking. Springer, Heidelberg (2012). https://doi.org/10.1007/978-3-642-29807-3
30. Xu, R., Wunsch 2nd, D.: Survey of clustering algorithms. IEEE Trans. Neural Netw. **16**(3), 645–678 (2005)
31. Yang, J., Zhang, X.D.: Predicting missing links in complex networks based on common neighbors and distance. Sci. Rep. **6**, 38208 (2016)
32. Zhang, S.X., Roberts, R.E., Farabee, D.: An analysis of prisoner reentry and parole risk using COMPAS and traditional criminal history measures. Crime Delinq. **60**, 167–192 (2014)

Author Index

Printed in the United States
By Bookmasters